International Economics

The globalized world economy is more important than ever before. This book provides a clear and up-to-date look at how the international economy works. Attractively presented, with abundant full-color diagrams and graphs incorporating contemporary trade data, the authors explain the principal concepts in an engaging and accessible manner that is open to students from any discipline. Economic models are discussed in the context of recent international trade issues to ensure students gain a concrete understanding of how various frameworks help us make sense of the real world. Written for undergraduate students taking their first course in international economics, the book includes feature boxes that show how theory can be applied in practice, a featured real-world application for every chapter, and over 240 end-of-chapter questions to help students consolidate their learning. Online resources for instructors include a solutions manual, lecture slides, and the figures and tables from the book as JPEGs.

Menzie D. Chinn is Professor of Public Affairs and Economics at the University of Wisconsin–Madison. He is co-editor of the *Journal of International Money and Finance*, a Research Associate in the International Finance and Macroeconomics Program of the National Bureau of Economic Research, and has been a visiting scholar at the International Monetary Fund, the Congressional Budget Office, the Federal Reserve Board, the European Central Bank, and the Banque de France. In 2000–2001, Professor Chinn served as Senior Staff Economist for International Finance on the President's Council of Economic Advisers. He is coauthor with Jeffry Frieden of *Lost Decades: The Making of America's Debt Crisis and the Long Recovery* (W.W. Norton, 2011), and contributor to Econbrowser, a weblog devoted to current macroeconomic issues.

Douglas A. Irwin is John French Professor of Economics at Dartmouth College. He is a Research Associate of the National Bureau of Economic Research and a non-resident Senior Fellow at the Peterson Institute for International Economics. He has worked on trade policy issues while on the staff of the President's Council of Economic Advisers and later at the International Finance Division at the Board of Governors of the Federal Reserve System in Washington, DC. The author of many books and articles on trade policy, he was named one of Foreign Policy's 100 Global Thinkers of 2019 and the *Financial Times* has called him "one of the world's foremost trade scholars" for his work on past and present trade policy. He is the author of *Clashing over Commerce: A History of US Trade Policy* (University of Chicago Press, 2017), which *The Economist* and *Foreign Affairs* selected as one of their Best Books of the Year.

"At a time when globalization is under threat everywhere, a clear and simple analysis of the effects of international trade and finance – who gains, who loses, what risks are created and reduced, and what policies are best on balance – grounded in good theory, and supported by data relevant to today's world, is essential. Chinn and Irwin provide that in this outstanding new textbook. I wish it was required reading for the general public, not just for classroom use."

Avinash Dixit, *Princeton University*

"Two outstanding international economists have brought us a first-rate new textbook. Written very clearly, it will be highly accessible to the typical student. It is chock-full of historical examples, as recent as the effect of Russia's war in Ukraine on global wheat prices. The historical cases introduce each chapter and then illustrate the theory afterwards."

Jeffrey Frankel, *Harvard University*

"Chinn and Irwin's *International Economics* is definitive but also accessible. Economic theory is brought alive with a combination of practical applications, historical examples, and real-world applications. Students are sure to be engaged."

Barry Eichengreen, *University of California, Berkeley*

International Economics

Menzie D. Chinn
University of Wisconsin, Madison

Douglas A. Irwin
Dartmouth College, New Hampshire

Shaftesbury Road, Cambridge CB2 8EA, United Kingdom

One Liberty Plaza, 20th Floor, New York, NY 10006, USA

477 Williamstown Road, Port Melbourne, VIC 3207, Australia

314–321, 3rd Floor, Plot 3, Splendor Forum, Jasola District Centre, New Delhi – 110025, India

103 Penang Road, #05–06/07, Visioncrest Commercial, Singapore 238467

Cambridge University Press is part of Cambridge University Press & Assessment, a department of the University of Cambridge.

We share the University's mission to contribute to society through the pursuit of education, learning and research at the highest international levels of excellence.

www.cambridge.org
Information on this title: www.cambridge.org/highereducation/isbn/9781009397681

DOI: 10.1017/9781009397698

© Menzie D. Chinn and Douglas A. Irwin 2025

This publication is in copyright. Subject to statutory exception and to the provisions of relevant collective licensing agreements, no reproduction of any part may take place without the written permission of Cambridge University Press & Assessment.

When citing this work, please include a reference to the DOI 10.1017/9781009397698

First published 2025

Printed in Mexico by Litográfica Ingramex, S.A. de C.V

A catalogue record for this publication is available from the British Library.

Library of Congress Cataloging-in-Publication Data
Names: Chinn, Menzie David, author. | Irwin, Douglas A., 1962–, author.
Title: International economics / Menzie D. Chinn, University of Wisconsin, Madison, Douglas A. Irwin, Dartmouth College, New Hampshire.
Description: First edition. | New York, NY : Cambridge University Press, [2025] | Includes bibliographical references and index.
Identifiers: LCCN 2024010454 (print) | LCCN 2024010455 (ebook) | ISBN 9781009397681 (hardback) | ISBN 9781009397704 (paperback) | ISBN 9781009397698 (epub)
Subjects: LCSH: International economic relations. | International trade. | International finance.
Classification: LCC HF1359 .C515 2025 (print) | LCC HF1359 (ebook) | DDC 337–dc23/eng/20240308
LC record available at https://lccn.loc.gov/2024010454
LC ebook record available at https://lccn.loc.gov/2024010455

ISBN 978-1-009-39768-1 Hardback
ISBN 978-1-009-39770-4 Paperback

Additional resources for this publication at www.cambridge.org/international_economics

Cambridge University Press & Assessment has no responsibility for the persistence or accuracy of URLs for external or third-party internet websites referred to in this publication and does not guarantee that any content on such websites is, or will remain, accurate or appropriate.

BRIEF CONTENTS

Preface		page xix
Acknowledgments		xxi

PART 1 — INTERNATIONAL TRADE — 1

CHAPTER 1	Introducing the Global Economy	3
CHAPTER 2	The Gains from Trade	11
CHAPTER 3	Exploring the Gains from Trade	33
CHAPTER 4	Trade and Comparative Advantage	50
CHAPTER 5	Factor Endowments and Trade	73
CHAPTER 6	International Factor Mobility	99
CHAPTER 7	Firms and Trade: Economies of Scale and Product Variety	123
CHAPTER 8	Trade Policy Analysis	149
CHAPTER 9	Arguments for Trade Intervention	178
CHAPTER 10	Trade Politics, Trade Agreements, and Trade Laws	205

PART 2 — INTERNATIONAL FINANCE — 233

CHAPTER 11	Measuring the Economy and Its Interaction with the World	235
CHAPTER 12	Exchange Rates, Interest Rates, and the Foreign Exchange Market	255
CHAPTER 13	Spending and Income Determination in the Short Run	279
CHAPTER 14	Income and Interest Rates under Fixed Exchange Rates	304
CHAPTER 15	Floating Exchange Rates and the International Trilemma	325
CHAPTER 16	Income, Money, and the Price Level in an Open Economy	345
CHAPTER 17	The Determinants of the Exchange Rate	367
CHAPTER 18	Emerging Market Crises: The Boom–Bust Cycle	388
CHAPTER 19	The Global Financial Crisis	413
CHAPTER 20	The Eurozone Crisis	424

References	436
Index	442

DETAILED CONTENTS

Preface | page xix
Acknowledgments | xxi

PART 1 — INTERNATIONAL TRADE — 1

CHAPTER 1 Introducing the Global Economy — 3

Learning Objectives — 3
Introduction — 3
1.1 Thinking about Trade — 4
    Lower Trade Barriers — 6
    Lower Transport Costs — 6
1.2 The Growth of International Finance — 7
    Growing Trade Interconnectedness — 7
    The End of the Fixed Exchange Rate System and the Rise of Financial Openness — 8
Conclusion — 9
Key Concepts — 9
Review Questions — 10
Recommended Resources — 10

CHAPTER 2 The Gains from Trade — 11

Learning Objectives — 11
Introduction — 11
2.1 Autarky — 12
    The Production Possibility Frontier — 12
    Indifference Curves — 14
    The Budget Constraint — 15
2.2 Competitive Equilibrium under Autarky — 16
    Maximizing Consumer Utility — 17
    Competitive Equilibrium — 17
2.3 Competitive Equilibrium with Trade — 19
    Production and Trade — 20
    Consumption and Trade — 20
    The Gains from Trade — 21
    In Practice The Natural Propensity to Trade — 22
2.4 Empirical Evidence on Trade and Income — 23
2.5 Trade in Partial Equilibrium — 23
    Import Demand — 24
    Export Supply — 25
    The Trade Equilibrium — 25
    Producer and Consumer Surpluses — 27
    Application China in World Trade — 27

Conclusion	29
Summary	29
Key Concepts	30
Review Questions	30
Exercises	30
Recommended Resources	32

CHAPTER 3 Exploring the Gains from Trade — 33

Learning Objectives	33
Introduction	33
3.1 Quick Review	**34**
Mercantilism	34
Jobs	35
Balanced Trade	35
3.2 The Terms of Trade	**36**
In Practice The Terms of Trade	37
3.3 Static versus Dynamic Gains from Trade	**39**
Application Shoguns, Embargoes, Canals, and Blockades – What Past Attempts to Stop Trade Have Taught Us	40
3.4 Does Everyone Benefit from Trade?	**43**
The Pareto Test and Compensation	43
The Utility Possibility Frontier under Autarky	44
The Utility Possibility Frontier with Trade	46
Pareto Improvement with Dynamic Gains from Trade	46
Conclusion	47
Summary	47
Key Concepts	48
Review Questions	48
Exercises	48
Recommended Resources	49

CHAPTER 4 Trade and Comparative Advantage — 50

Learning Objectives	50
Introduction	50
4.1 Absolute versus Comparative Advantage	**51**
Comparative Advantage, Illustrated	51
Opportunity Cost	52
Autarky Production	53
4.2 Comparative Advantage and the Gains from Trade	**55**
In Practice Absolute versus Comparative Advantage: United States–Japan	57
4.3 What Determines the Terms of Trade?	**58**
4.4 Wages and Productivity	**59**
Evidence on Productivity and Wages	61
In Practice Are Countries in Competition with One Another?	63
4.5 The Multi-Good Ricardo Model	**64**
Application Nike and Athletic Shoe Production	67
Conclusion	69

Summary	69
Key Concepts	69
Review Questions	69
Exercises	70
Recommended Resources	72

CHAPTER 5 Factor Endowments and Trade — 73

Learning Objectives	73
Introduction	73
5.1 The Specific Factors Model	**74**
Output as a Function of Capital	74
Deriving the Production Possibility Frontier	76
How Factors Affect the Production Possibility Frontier	77
5.2 Income Distribution in the Specific Factor Model	**77**
Income Distribution	79
Impact of Price Change	80
Impact of a Change in Productivity	82
Impact of Changes in Specific Factors	82
Theory Ricardo's Version of the Specific Factor Model	83
5.3 The Mobile Factors Model	**83**
The Allocation of Production Factors	84
Pattern of Trade	85
5.4 Income Distribution in the Mobile Factors Model	**87**
Trade a Pareto Improvement?	88
5.5 Evidence on Trade and Factor Endowments	**88**
5.6 Evidence on Trade and Income Distribution	**90**
Application Does Labor Behave as a Specific or a Mobile Factor?	93
Conclusion	95
Summary	96
Key Concepts	96
Review Questions	96
Exercises	97
Recommended Resources	97

CHAPTER 6 International Factor Mobility — 99

Learning Objectives	99
Introduction	99
6.1 The Gains from International Labor Mobility	**100**
Modeling the Effects of Labor Mobility	101
6.2 The Gains from International Capital and Technology Mobility	**103**
Capital Mobility	103
Technology Mobility	105
6.3 International Labor and Technology Mobility in the Ricardo Model	**106**
Technology Mobility	107
Labor Mobility	108
Theory Mill on Factor Mobility and Comparative Advantage	111

DETAILED CONTENTS

6.4	**International Labor and Capital Mobility in the Specific Factors Model**	111
	Capital Mobility	111
	Labor Mobility	113
6.5	**International Factor Mobility in the Mobile Factors Model**	114
6.6	**Empirical Evidence on Immigration and Wages**	116
	Application The Reunification of Germany	118
Conclusion		120
Summary		120
Key Concepts		120
Review Questions		120
Exercises		121
Recommended Resources		121

CHAPTER 7 Firms and Trade: Economies of Scale and Product Variety 123

Learning Objectives		123
Introduction		123
7.1	**Monopolistic Competition**	124
	Product Differentiation and Economies of Scale	124
	The Model	125
	In Practice Monopolistic Competition in Action	127
7.2	**Monopolistic Competition and Trade**	128
	The Market-Size Effect	128
	The Within-Market Effect	129
	Autarky Equilibrium and Trade	130
	The Shakeout Effect	131
7.3	**Variety Gains from Trade for Consumers**	133
	Empirical Findings	135
7.4	**Firms in International Trade**	135
	Exporting Firms	136
	Import-competing Firms	139
	Empirical Evidence	140
	Application The US Textile Industry	141
Conclusion		142
Summary		143
Key Concepts		143
Review Questions		143
Exercises		144
Recommended Resources		144
Appendix 7.A Monopolistic Competition: An Alternative Approach		146

CHAPTER 8 Trade Policy Analysis 149

Learning Objectives		149
Introduction		149
8.1	**Import Tariffs in Partial Equilibrium**	150
	Impact on Resource Allocation	151
	In Practice Tariff Engineering	152
	Impact on Economic Welfare	152

DETAILED CONTENTS xi

	Equivalency of Trade Policy and Domestic Policies	154
	A Tariff's Impact on Economic Welfare	155
	Effective Rate of Protection	156
	Application The Trump Trade Tariffs	157
8.2	**Import Quotas**	**159**
	The Non-Equivalence of Tariffs and Quotas	161
8.3	**Export Subsidies and Taxes**	**163**
	Export Subsidies	164
	Export Tax	166
8.4	**Import Tariff in General Equilibrium**	**167**
	Production and National Income	168
	Consumption	169
	Export Tax in General Equilibrium	170
8.5	**Empirical Evidence on Trade Barriers**	**172**

Conclusion 175
Summary 175
Key Concepts 175
Review Questions 175
Exercises 176
Recommended Resources 177

CHAPTER 9 Arguments for Trade Intervention 178

Learning Objectives 178
Introduction 178

9.1	**The Terms of Trade Argument for Export Taxes**	**179**
	Export Supply and Import Demand	180
	OPEC Welfare	181
	Theory The Formula for the Optimal Tariff	182
	Rest-of-World Welfare	182
	Terms of Trade and Import Tariffs	183
	Empirical Evidence	184
9.2	**Second-Best Arguments for Protection**	**185**
	Tariffs for Revenue	185
	Tariffs to Increase Employment	186
	Tariffs to Correct Externalities	186
	Non-Economic Objectives	188
9.3	**Infant Industry Protection**	**189**
	In Practice Infant Industry Policies	192
9.4	**Export Subsidies and Strategic Trade Policy**	**193**
	Export Subsidies and the Large Country Case	194
	Strategic Trade Policy	195
	In Practice Mercantilism as Strategic Trade Policy	198
	Application China's Industrial Policies	198

Conclusion 200
Summary 201
Key Concepts 201
Review Questions 201

Exercises 202
Recommended Resources 203

CHAPTER 10 Trade Politics, Trade Agreements, and Trade Laws — 205

Learning Objectives 205
Introduction 205
10.1 Trade Politics — 206
Evolution of US Trade Policy 209
In Practice The Smoot–Hawley Tariff of 1930 212
10.2 Trade Agreements — 213
Types of Trade Agreements 215
Welfare Effects of Tariff Agreements 216
Theory Was NAFTA a Bad Deal? 218
Multilateral Trade Agreements 219
10.3 Trade Laws — 222
Dumping and Antidumping Duties 223
Subsidies and Countervailing Duties 225
Escape Clause 226
In Practice Did Temporary Protection Save Harley-Davidson? 226
National Security 227
Application Protection in Practice: Washing Machines and Steel 228
Conclusion 229
Summary 229
Key Concepts 229
Review Questions 230
Exercises 230
Recommended Resources 231

PART 2 INTERNATIONAL FINANCE — 233

CHAPTER 11 Measuring the Economy and Its Interaction with the World — 235

Learning Objectives 235
Introduction 235
11.1 Income and Production — 235
The Closed Economy 235
Opening Up the Real Economy 237
11.2 Saving, Investment, and the Current Account Balance — 238
11.3 The Balance of Payments — 241
The Overall Accounting 241
Theory Double-Entry Accounting and the Balance of Payments 242
The Current Account, Again 242
11.4 The Financial and Capital Account — 245
Theory The Global Current Account Discrepancy 248
11.5 The Financial Account and the Net International Investment Position — 249
Application China's Balance of Payments 250
Conclusion 251
Summary 252

Key Concepts	252
Review Questions	253
Exercises	253
Recommended Resources	254

CHAPTER 12 Exchange Rates, Interest Rates, and the Foreign Exchange Market — 255

Learning Objectives	255
Introduction	255
12.1 Exchange Rates and Currency Trading	256
Theory Why Is the Dollar the World's International Currency?	258
12.2 Supply, Demand, and Exchange Rates under Fixed and Floating Regimes	259
Currency Supply and Demand in the Foreign Exchange Market	259
Fixed Rate Regimes	261
12.3 Exchange Rate Regimes in the Real World	262
12.4 The Relationship between Exchange Rates and Interest Rates	266
Theory Does Uncovered Interest Parity Hold?	269
12.5 More on Exchange Rates	270
The Value of a Currency	270
Real Exchange Rates for Goods and Services	270
The Real Value of a Currency	272
Application Argentina	273
Conclusion	274
Summary	275
Key Concepts	275
Review Questions	276
Exercises	276
Recommended Resources	278

CHAPTER 13 Spending and Income Determination in the Short Run — 279

Learning Objectives	279
Introduction	279
13.1 Equilibrium Output and Income Determination: The "Keynesian Cross"	280
Aggregate Demand	281
Demand as a Function of Income	281
The Economy in Equilibrium	282
The Keynesian Cross	283
13.2 How Do Government Spending and Taxes Affect Income?	284
The Effects of Government Spending	285
The Impact of Taxes	286
13.3 How Are the Government Budget and Trade Balances Related?	287
13.4 The Role of the Real Exchange Rate	288
Exchange Rate Effects	289
The Exchange Rate and the Trade Balance	290
Theory Exchange Rates and Trade Flows	292
13.5 The Spillover Effects of Fiscal Policy	293
Application Responding to the Global Great Recession	295
Conclusion	298

Summary	298
Key Concepts	299
Review Questions	299
Exercises	299
Recommended Resources	301
Appendix 13.A Solving the Two-Country Model	302

CHAPTER 14 Income and Interest Rates under Fixed Exchange Rates — 304

Learning Objectives	304
Introduction	304
14.1 An Economy with Money and Interest Rates: The *IS–LM* Model	305
Modeling the Financial Sector	307
14.2 Policy Options for Affecting Output	309
Fiscal Policy	309
Monetary Policy	310
Exchange Rate Policy	311
The Relative Magnitudes of Policy Effects	311
14.3 Introducing an External Balance Condition	312
14.4 Policy Options under Fixed Exchange Rates	314
Fiscal Policy	314
Monetary Policy under Fixed Exchange Rates	316
Responding to Balance of Payments Deficits: Devaluation vs. the Interest Rate Defense	317
Application China's Surpluses and Reserve Accumulation	318
Conclusion	321
Summary	321
Key Concepts	321
Review Questions	322
Exercises	322
Recommended Resources	324

CHAPTER 15 Floating Exchange Rates and the International Trilemma — 325

Learning Objectives	325
Introduction	325
15.1 Fiscal and Monetary Policy under Floating Exchange Rates	326
Fiscal Policy	326
Monetary Policy	327
Interest Rate Shocks	328
15.2 Summarizing Effects under Fixed and Floating Exchange Rates	329
Empirical Estimates of Policy Effects	329
Application Monetary and Fiscal Policy at Cross Purposes	331
15.3 The Implications of Perfect Capital Mobility	334
Floating Exchange Rates	334
Fixed Exchange Rates	334
15.4 The International Trilemma	335
Empirical Evidence of the Trilemma	337
15.5 Another Limit to Monetary Policy Effectiveness	338
Theory Negative Interest Rates	340

Conclusion	341
Summary Points	341
Key Concepts	342
Review Questions	342
Exercises	342
Recommended Resources	344

CHAPTER 16 Income, Money, and the Price Level in an Open Economy — 345

Learning Objectives	345
Introduction	345
16.1 Allowing the Price Level to Change	**347**
16.2 The Demand and Supply Sides	**348**
The Demand Side	348
The Supply Side	349
16.3 Putting the Demand and Supply Sides Together	**351**
Fiscal Policy	351
Monetary Policy	352
16.4 Adding in Expectations of Inflation	**353**
An Expectations-Augmented Phillips' Curve	353
The Dynamics of Output and the Price Level	354
16.5 Supply Shocks	**356**
What is a Supply Shock?	356
The Dynamics of a Supply Shock	356
Offsetting the Contractionary Impact of the Supply Shock	357
Application Understanding the Inflation of 2021–2022 in the US	358
In Practice Declining Impact of Oil Prices on Inflation and Output	361
16.6 Adjustment under Fixed Exchange Rates	**362**
Conclusion	363
Summary	364
Key Concepts	365
Review Questions	365
Exercises	365
Recommended Resources	366

CHAPTER 17 The Determinants of the Exchange Rate — 367

Learning Objectives	367
Introduction	367
17.1 The Monetary Approach with Flexible Prices	**369**
The Exchange Rate as a Function of Contemporaneous Factors	369
The Effect in the Present of Expectations about the Future	371
Application Hyperinflation in Zimbabwe	372
17.2 How Well Does the Flexible Price Monetary Model Work in Normal Times?	**374**
Identifying the Problem: Prices Are Not Perfectly Flexible	374
17.3 Exchange Rates and Sticky Prices	**375**
A More Realistic Model	376
17.4 Empirical Evidence for the Sticky Price Model	**378**
In Practice Can We Predict Exchange Rates?	379

17.5 Real Models of the Real Exchange Rate	380
In Practice Tales from the Big Mac	382
Conclusion	383
Summary	384
Key Concepts	384
Review Questions	385
Exercises	385
Recommended Resources	386
Appendix 17.A Derivation of the Sticky Price Monetary Model	387

CHAPTER 18 Emerging Market Crises: The Boom–Bust Cycle — 388

Learning Objectives	388
Introduction	388
18.1 Capital Surges and Reversals	390
18.2 Managing Booms	391
Option 1: Accumulate Foreign Exchange Reserves	392
Option 2: Sterilize the Inflows	393
Option 3: Revalue the Currency	393
Option 4: Capital Controls	394
How Well Do Capital Controls Work?	394
18.3 Understanding How Busts Happen	396
A Rise in Foreign Interest Rates	397
Loss of Confidence in Government Solvency	398
18.4 Why Is Devaluation Contractionary?	400
18.5 Complications: Balance Sheet Effects	402
Theory Can We Predict Emerging Market Crises?	406
Application The Mexican Peso Crisis	407
Conclusion	409
Summary	409
Key Concepts	410
Review Questions	410
Exercises	410
Recommended Resources	411

CHAPTER 19 The Global Financial Crisis — 413

Learning Objectives	413
Introduction	413
19.1 Why Did the Global Crisis Start in America?	414
Interest Rates and Tax Policy	414
Under-regulation and Financial Innovation	415
Theory Leverage, Liquidity, and Financial Crisis	415
The Feedback Loop	417
19.2 The Crisis Goes Global	418
Financial Linkages	419
Linkage Through Trade	419
19.3 The Policy Response	420
Conclusions	421
Summary Points	422

Key Concepts	422
Review Questions	422
Exercises	422
Recommended Resources	423

CHAPTER 20 The Eurozone Crisis — 424

Learning Objectives	424
Introduction	424
20.1 Lead-up to the Euro	**424**
20.2 Economic Motivations for and Challenges of Monetary Union	**425**
Challenges of a Common Currency	425
Disappearance of Risk	428
20.3 The Euro Sovereign Debt Crisis and Adjustment Deferred	**428**
20.4 The Incomplete Recovery	**433**
Conclusions	434
Summary Points	434
Key Concepts	434
Review Questions	435
Exercises	435
Recommended Resources	435
References	436
Index	442

PREFACE

WHY THIS BOOK?

More than ever before, the US economy is influenced by the vicissitudes of the global marketplace. Whether it is new foreign competition affecting US firms and employment, China's aim for technological self-reliance, the effects of the trade war launched by President Trump, fluctuations in the foreign exchange value of the dollar, or the question of China's financing the US budget deficit, news about the international economy is routinely covered in newspapers, on television, and across the internet.

Just as the world has changed, the approach we adopt to teaching international economics is different from that used in the past. Rather than covering all topics, we focus on those of current interest and policy relevance. First, we eschew models that no longer seem relevant to explaining the world today – and where theory dominated in the earlier texts, our exposition is much more empirically oriented, and grounded in current economic developments. Second, our treatment, in contrast with earlier texts, deals with the challenges facing emerging and developing economies as much as it does developed economies.

OUR INTEREST

Both of us have taught international economics for many years. In addition to teaching undergraduate students, we have taught public policy and MBA students who demand focus on questions that are relevant to the real world. Furthermore, we have both worked on the staff of the President's Council of Economic Advisers, where we gained experience in dealing with economic policy issues important to those in government. Chinn maintains a popular blog on international macroeconomic issues, while Irwin is the author of many well-received books on international trade policy, including *Free Trade under Fire* (Princeton University Press, 2020) *and Clashing over Commerce* (University of Chicago Press, 2017). We hope to convey our enthusiasm for the study of international economics to the readers of this book.

OUR APPROACH

Like economics generally, international economics is divided into two subfields: microeconomics and macroeconomics. The first half of the book focuses on microeconomics in order to understand how international trade and trade policies affect economic welfare and the distribution of income. The second half of the book focuses on macroeconomics in order to aid understanding of the impact of exchange rates and capital flows on the domestic economy, as reflected in economic measures such as inflation and unemployment.

Chapters 2 and 3 use two basic microeconomic tools, the production possibility frontier and indifference curves, to analyze the impact of trade and to demonstrate its economic benefits. These chapters also consider historical experience and empirical data related to the effects of opening or closing of trade between countries.

Chapters 4 and 5 consider reasons why trade takes place. Chapter 4 examines differences in technology across countries and introduces the concept of comparative advantage. Chapter 5 examines differences in factor endowments – land, labor, and capital – across countries and how trade affects the income earned by those factors. This will allow us to say something, not just about the drivers of trade, but about the impact of trade on wages and incomes earned by different factors of production. A key lesson will be that, although trade is generally believed to be beneficial, not all segments of society will be better off as a result of trade.

An important feature of the global economy is the movement of people and capital across national borders. Chapter 6 examines this phenomenon, known as international factor mobility, to see how it affects a country's economy. This chapter uses the frameworks developed in Chapters 4 and 5 to understand immigration and foreign investment.

It is often said that countries do not trade with one another, firms do. Chapter 7 looks at the role of firms in international trade. The opening of export opportunities and the competition that comes from imports often has differential effects on domestic firms: some are "winners" and expand production, while others are "losers" and must shut down. This chapter examines how international competition affects firms differently, depending on how they are positioned.

Chapters 8 through 10 then turn to trade policy. Chapter 8 provides a basic analysis of import tariffs and import quotas, as well as export policies such as export taxes and export subsidies. It examines the trade-restricting and trade-expanding effects of these policies, as well as the consequences for producer and consumer welfare. Chapter 9 examines the various rationales given for governments to restrict or promote trade. Chapter 10 provides some institutional detail on the politics of trade policy, trade laws such as antidumping measures, and trade agreements such as those overseen by the World Trade Organization.

Chapter 11 sets the stage for the macroeconomic aspects of international interactions by defining the measures of a country's external and internal flows: Gross Domestic Product (GDP), the balance of trade, and the financial account. The relative price at which currencies, exports, and imports are traded – the exchange rate, in other words – is the topic of Chapter 12: how exchange rates are determined for the over $5 trillion worth of currencies traded each day, and why interest rates and exchange rates are linked.

Chapters 13–15 present a model of how GDP, interest and exchange rates, and trade flows are all jointly determined. To begin with, financial markets are ignored. In Chapter 14, money and external sources of financial capital are added for an economy operating under fixed exchange rates. The workings of an economy under floating exchange rates are explored in Chapter 15. Chapter 16, then, follows up by introducing the supply side of the economy, so that the sources of inflation and deflation can be examined. The workings of exchange rates are closely examined in Chapter 17.

In the final chapters, the analytical tools developed in the preceding chapters are applied to some key questions on macroeconomic policy. Chapter 18 recounts the special challenges facing policymakers in emerging market economies: why is it that the Argentina's and the Turkey's of the world seem to face recurrent financial crises? Chapter 19 reviews the international aspects of the global financial crisis and world recession of 2008–2009. Finally, Chapter 20 details the ongoing challenges facing the economic and monetary union known as the eurozone.

ACKNOWLEDGMENTS

In writing this textbook, we have incurred many debts. We are deeply grateful to our first editor, the late Jack Repcheck. Jack's unbridled enthusiasm for this project not only gave us a start but kept us going. We sorely miss him.

We are grateful to our students at the University of Wisconsin and Dartmouth College for sharing our interest in international economics and for helping us shape and hone our teaching over the years. Many of our students have contributed in direct and indirect ways to our completion of this textbook. In particular, we wish to thank Michael Zhang at Dartmouth for his assistance.

Finally, we are indebted to a great team at Cambridge University Press who shepherded our rough manuscript into the beautiful production you have before you. Thanks to Jane Adams and Rachel Norridge for support and patience as we made our way through the production process. We also appreciate Anne Rix for her skillful editing of the book.

Every work incorporates the insights and knowledge imparted by the authors' teachers. This book is no different. We acknowledge the many lessons we received from Jeffrey Frankel, Jagdish Bhagwati, and Ronald Findlay.

Finally, we thank our families for their support and encouragement over the long gestation of this project.

PART I

International Trade

CHAPTER 1

Introducing the Global Economy

LEARNING OBJECTIVES

In this chapter, we learn about:
- what the term globalization means
- how the global economy involves exchanges between countries around the world
- how these exchanges involve both trade in goods and services and trade in assets (financial instruments)

INTRODUCTION

We live in an era of **globalization**, in which most producers operate internationally on a global scale. We, as consumers, are affected by events taking place on distant shores – to say we live in an age of interconnectedness is a cliché, but it is still true. Just check out the labels on the clothes in your closet. Your shirts, sweaters, jackets, and jeans were probably not produced in the United States. More likely, they were made in China, Bangladesh, Vietnam, India, Sri Lanka, or Mexico. The same is true for your shoes.

Or think about your smart phone. Where was it made? The back of an iPhone will tell you that it was *designed* in California and *assembled* in China. However, in that process, hundreds of individual parts were sourced from all around the world. The flash memory came from Toshiba in Japan, the application processor was supplied by Samsung in South Korea, the camera module was put together by Infineon in Germany, and the Bluetooth hardware came from Broadcom in the United States. The cost of assembling all of these components sourced from around the globe is a small fraction of the total cost of the phone.

Our food supply is globalized, too. We happily eat locally harvested fruits and vegetables when they are in season, but the rest of the year we enjoy asparagus from Peru, grapes from Chile, apples from New Zealand, and avocados from Mexico. We eat sushi wrapped in seaweed grown in China or South Korea. We top our salads, or stuff our pita sandwiches, with chickpeas grown in India or Australia. For dessert, we indulge in a little chocolate made from cocoa beans grown in Côte d'Ivoire or maybe Ecuador. Whatever your favorite meal or snack might be, these days it is likely that some of what is going into your mouth came from a country far away.

Even our finances are globalized. Each year, when the Federal government borrows to finance its budget deficit, billions of dollars' worth of Treasury bonds and bills are bought up by the central banks of other nations, and also by private foreign entities. Of the over $24 trillion of outstanding Treasury debt, about $7.4 trillion is held by foreigners, with $2 trillion held by just two central banks, namely, the Bank of Japan and the People's Bank of China. The speed with which the Chinese accumulate Treasury bonds helps establish the **exchange rate** between the US dollar and the Chinese Yuan, which in turn affects the price of imports from China. The United States also imports Chinese goods – over $500 billion worth in 2022 – including, of course, loads of completed iPhones.

In short, wherever you go, whatever you do, and whatever you buy and sell, the world economy is now involved in some way or another more than ever before. The goal of this book is to explain how the global economy works, and to develop some basic tools with which to understand how the world economy shapes our own, national economy. We will want to know how an economy that is open to the rest of the world – open to trade in goods and services, and open to capital inflows and outflows, i.e., cross-border flows of money – performs differently than a closed economy. Does trade with other countries boost wages or lower them? Do capital flows between countries make inflation and unemployment easier or harder to manage? These represent the questions we will be asking – and hopefully answering!

1.1 THINKING ABOUT TRADE

In 1776, the Scottish philosopher Adam Smith established economics as a distinct field of study with his book *The Wealth of Nations*. At the center of his framework was trade: the exchange of goods between producers and consumers, regardless of their location. Smith observed that human beings have a natural propensity to "truck, barter, and exchange" goods with one another.

Figure 1.1 The Basic Logic of Trade?
Source: Frank & Ernest © Thaves. Used By permission of Andrews Mcmeel Syndication. All rights reserved.

If you seek evidence that human beings have an innate desire to trade with one another, think back to your days in the grade-school cafeteria. Although well-intentioned parents may give their children healthy lunches to take to school, youngsters do not necessarily eat what is packed for them. The school cafeteria sometimes resembles a giant market, with apples being exchanged for bananas, potato chips for cookies, sandwiches for drinks, brownies for homework, all without any money changing hands.

The fundamental reason that individuals engage in trade is that it can make them better off. When children decide to trade part of their school lunch, each does so because they believe they will be better off. Each of them believes that they are exchanging something of lesser value for something of greater value. If undertaken voluntarily, trade is mutually beneficial. (If, however, a bully simply takes someone's cookies under threat of harm, such involuntary "trade" will not be beneficial for both parties.)

Today, we are all part of a complex and sophisticated economic system that is based on specialization and exchange. Working adults specialize in a certain activity and devote most of their day to that activity. Whether they are doctors or lawyers, plumbers or construction workers, teachers or policemen, photographers or web designers, they are essentially selling their labor time to others who are willing to pay for their particular service. In return, they earn an income which they use to buy food and clothes, housing and health care, electronic equipment and vacations – goods and services that have been produced by other people who have specialized in producing them to sell to others.

The economy works by people exporting their labor time to the rest of the economy and importing goods and services produced by others. We engage in trade because it is beneficial for us to do so. You probably did not grow the food you will eat today. It is cheaper to buy it from farmers who spend their whole day focusing on how to grow their crops better. Grocery stores intermediate this trade, and store managers spend their whole day obtaining the best varieties of, and prices for, food for their customers. You probably did not make the shirt you are wearing; it is cheaper to buy it from a firm that hires workers who spend their whole day making shirts, which are sold in retail outlets whose managers spend their whole day getting the best variety and prices of clothing for their customers.

Trade is not a **zero-sum game** in which one side wins and the other side loses. Rather, trade is a **positive-sum game** in which both sides can benefit from the exchange: the farmer benefits from buying clothes from apparel workers, and apparel workers benefit from buying their food from farmers.

Yet when goods and services cross national borders, that "international" trade somehow becomes controversial. People worry that imports take away jobs from domestic workers: why should we import cars or steel from other countries when we could produce them here at home with our own citizens? People worry that trade agreements may be unfair or just serve the interests of elites. Reflecting this concern, many politicians express unease about international trade. President Donald Trump once scribbled the words "Trade is Bad" in an official document, reflecting his view that other countries were taking advantage of the United States through trade. President Joe Biden insists that US construction projects benefit US workers by only using US-made materials, particularly steel, without imports.

One reason for the debate over the impact of **international trade** and *foreign competition* on the economy is that, over the past half-century, trade has become enormously important for the world economy. Figure 1.2 shows the value of world exports (all cross-border trade in goods and services) as a share of the value of world Gross Domestic Product (GDP) from the late 1820s to the present (three different data sources are presented). For most of the nineteenth and twentieth centuries, world exports were about 5–10% of world GDP, i.e., about 5–10% of production was exchanged between countries.

Starting in the 1970s, however, international trade soared. Now exports are about 25–30% of world GDP. Not only are countries that have long engaged in trade, such as the United States, trading more, but countries that were previously relatively isolated from world trade, such as China and India, have become major players in the world economy.

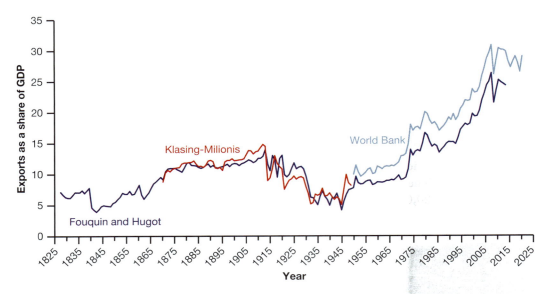

Figure 1.2 World Exports as a Share of World GDP, 1827–2021

What accounts for the phenomenal growth in trade over the past 50 years? The basic reason is the falling costs of engaging in trade across countries, due to two factors: lowering of the trade barriers imposed by national governments, and lower transportation costs because of innovations in shipping technology.

Lower Trade Barriers

As we will see in later chapters, governments often limit trade through taxes and other restrictions on imports known as **trade barriers** (the following chapters will also explain why governments tend to do this). The United States, for example, has long imposed taxes – known as tariffs – on imports. The average tariff on dutiable imports reached almost 60% in the early 1930s, a period when the world economy was sliding into the Great Depression. Not surprisingly, this substantial tax on foreign goods entering the US market significantly limited trade. Since the end of World War II in 1945, however, the United States has reduced its tariffs in negotiated trade agreements with other countries. Some of the negotiations have included many countries (multilateral agreements such as the World Trade Organization), while others have been bilateral or regional (such as the North American Free Trade Agreement, signed in 1993, or its replacement the US–Mexico–Canada agreement in 2019).

As a result of these trade agreements and other factors, the average tariff imposed on dutiable imports is now about 8%, and the average tariff on total imports is 3%.

The United States is not alone in having welcomed more imports. Before 1979, China was essentially closed to foreign trade. As it moved from central planning to a mixed economy where some private enterprise was allowed, China gradually began to reduce its barriers to trade and expand both its exports and imports. The same is true for many other countries around the world.

Lower Transport Costs

The cost of moving goods between markets has fallen not only because of lower trade barriers but also because of improved technology associated with moving goods, that is,

1.2 THE GROWTH OF INTERNATIONAL FINANCE

transportation costs. In the old days, ships were loaded with barrels or bags of commodities and other goods and had to be offloaded manually by teams of dockworkers.

In the 1960s and 1970s, the use of truck-sized shipping containers, carried on specially outfitted containerships, took off. Instead of dockworkers, huge track-mounted cranes now handled the loading and off-loading of cargo. According to one study, between 1965 and 1970, before and after the containership had been introduced, the productivity of dock labor jumped from handling 2 tons per hour to 30 tons per hour. In addition, the average size of ships rose from 8 gross registered tons to 20.

The containerization of international shipping has reduced the cost and increased the efficiency of a primary way in which goods and commodities are traded around the world. The world's largest container ship is currently the *OOCL Hong Kong*, which can carry over 20,000 containers!

(a)  (b)

Figure 1.3 (a) Dockworkers Unloading Cargo by Hand in 1932 in Singapore, (b) The World's Largest Cargo Ship, the OOCL *Hong Kong*
Sources: Bettmann/Getty Images & Ji Haixin/VCG via Getty Images.

1.2 THE GROWTH OF INTERNATIONAL FINANCE

While international trade deals with the composition of the trade in goods and services across borders, **international finance** – sometimes called open economy macroeconomics – deals with the level of cross-border flows of goods, services, and capital, and how these variables affect the level of economic activity. High employment and fast growth now spill over into neighboring countries to an unprecedented extent. Moreover, one of the defining features of the recent period is record levels of cross-border holdings of assets – everything from factories and other real estate to stocks and bonds. This means that someone from Poland might take out a mortgage on her house from a Swiss bank, or an American credit card holder might pay a record low interest rate because of China's eagerness to lend to the rest of the world.

Growing Trade Interconnectedness

As noted earlier, one of the defining features of the post-World War II period is lower trade barriers and rapid growth in the volume of international trade. Greatly increased trade means that a drop in economic activity in one country, associated with a drop in the consumption of goods, including imported ones, is transmitted more strongly to other countries, as they see their export volume go down.

Countries open to international trade, either because their economies were too small to support specialization, or because of geographic proximity to other large economies, have always been susceptible to such economic shocks from outside. However, over time, with increased trade, trade openness has become more and more pervasive, so that even large countries that once would have been fairly self-sufficient now see their fortunes inextricably tied up with the fortunes of their trading partners. The more countries trade with each other, the more the prices, at which goods are traded, matter, which, in turn, depends in the short term on a **currency**'s *exchange rate*.

An exchange rate is the price of one country's currency in terms of another, such as the rate between the US dollar and the Euro, or the price between the British pound and the Swiss franc. The exchange rate is a key factor that links markets around the world, as all trade flows and asset flows between countries usually involve the exchange of money between countries. As such, the exchange rate is a variable that has proven difficult to understand, let alone predict, even as it has become more important in this global economy.

"On the foreign-exchange markets today, the dollar fell against all major currencies and the doughnut."

Figure 1.4 On the Foreign-exchange Markets Today, the Dollar Fell Against all Major Currencies and the Doughnut
Source: www.CartoonStock.com/Bob Mankoff.

The End of the Fixed Exchange Rate System and the Rise of Financial Openness

In the wake of World War II, the Allies – most prominently the United States and the United Kingdom – established a set of international institutions aimed at stabilizing and advancing the world economy. The World Bank provided long-term development financing to developing countries, while the **International Monetary Fund (IMF)** oversaw a system of fixed, yet occasionally adjustable, exchange rates known as the Bretton Woods system. Central banks maintained the official rates by offering to buy and sell currency at those rates. When central banks ran short of currency reserves, the IMF would step in with support, conditional on adjustment of exchange rate values and on changes in monetary and fiscal policy.

This system came under strain during the 1960s, as various countries, most notably the US, failed to maintain macroeconomic policies that would sustain the fixed exchange rate regime. In 1971, US President Nixon took a series of steps that amounted to an abandonment of the fixed-rate system. This move toward free-floating exchange rates liberated countries from having to limit the flow of financial capital between countries, and by the 1990s, countries were dismantling the capital controls they had had in place. These developments are illustrated by the figure of two indices.

Flows of financial capital, in the form of bank loans, bond and equity purchases, and the cross-border acquisition of firms, surged. "Hot capital" – short-term loans and bonds – became a topic of concern for policymakers, as seemingly fickle international investors shifted

KEY CONCEPTS

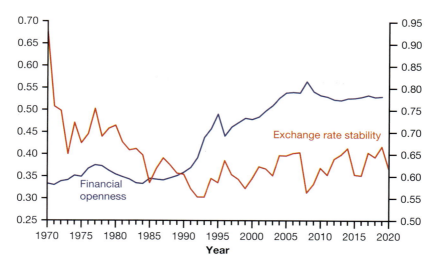

Figure 1.5 Higher Values Denote Greater Openness or Greater Stability
Source: Aizenman, Chinn, and Ito (2010).

their funds back and forth in response to the news of the day, and sometimes based on mere rumors.

The confluence of high capital mobility, the often tight trade interlinkages, and floating exchange rates forced policymakers to confront new choices. Should a nation's central bank focus on managing employment and growth, or should it seek to stabilize the exchange rate with foreign trading partners? Should there be strong controls on capital in- and outflows, or is it a good idea to subject domestic monetary policy to the spillover effects of other nation's monetary policies? Moreover, exchange rates sometimes fluctuated much more than could be explained by observed fundamentals, such as money supply, GDP, interest and inflation rates; this further complicates policymaking.

CONCLUSION

This chapter sets the stage for this book by introducing you to the growth of global interconnection over the past 50 years. International trade has been propelled by lower trade barriers and lower transportation costs. International financial transactions have been propelled by lower financial barriers and improvements in information technology. As a result, the world is more interconnected than ever before in human history. This book will introduce you to the basic framework used by economists to analyze globalization. This framework will help you understand the implications of these historic developments for people around the world.

KEY CONCEPTS

Currency, page 8
Exchange rate, page 4
Globalization, page 3
International finance, page 7
International Monetary Fund, page 8

International trade, page 5
Positive-sum game, page 5
Trade barriers, page 6
Transportation costs, page 7
Zero-sum game, page 5

REVIEW QUESTIONS

1. What are the factors that have made the countries of the world more interconnected and interdependent in recent decades?
2. How do we measure the growth of international trade and assets in recent decades?
3. How might economic disturbances in one country (say, a recession – a downturn in economic activity – or a drought that affects agricultural production) affect the economy of other countries? Is it possible or desirable to limit that interdependence?

RECOMMENDED RESOURCES

Marc Levinson provides a marvelous look at how the container reshaped world trade and with it the global economy in his book *The Box: How the Shipping Container Made the World Smaller and the World Economy Bigger* (Princeton, NJ: Princeton University Press, 2008).

For a panoramic survey of the world economy over the past century and more, see Jeffry Frieden, *Global Capitalism* (New York: W. W. Norton, 2020).

For a truly historic look at the evolution of the world economy, see Ronald Findlay and Kevin H. O'Rourke, *Power and Plenty: Trade, War, and the World Economy in the Second Millennium* (Princeton, NJ: Princeton University Press, 2009).

On the rise of international finance and capital flows, see Barry Eichengreen, *Globalizing Capital: A History of the International Monetary System*, third edition (Princeton, NJ: Princeton University Press, 2019).

CHAPTER 2
The Gains from Trade

LEARNING OBJECTIVES

In this chapter, we will learn about:
- the role of prices in coordinating the behavior of producers and consumers
- the impact of trade on production and consumption decisions
- the role of exports and imports in international exchange
- how trade makes more goods available to an economy

INTRODUCTION

There is a parable about an entrepreneur who invents an amazing machine. Wheat, soybeans, lumber, and oil are fed into one end of the contraption. As if by magic, smartphones, coffee, and tea, and all manner of clothing and apparel come out the other end. The inventor is praised as a genius – until further investigation reveals that the wheat and the other inputs were being secretly shipped to other countries in exchange for the electronics and apparel that later emerged. When this news is made public, the inventor is denounced as an unpatriotic fraud who is destroying jobs.

This instructive parable reminds us that we can think of international trade as a way of transforming one set of goods into another. We sell – or export – some of the goods produced in our country in exchange for things we buy – or import – from other countries.

As individuals, we are all deeply enmeshed in a web of trade and exchange. Look around you and think of all the things you use and consume every day – your smartphone and your laptop; the clothes you are wearing; the meals you eat; the entertainment you have chosen to stream. How many of these things did you make yourself? Most likely, you did not make any of them (preparing food you have bought does not really count). Instead, you probably purchased these things from wholesalers or retailers nearby who have made them available to you via specialized producers far away.

No one is forcing you to engage in such trade, but you can probably consume a lot more food and wear better clothing by buying it from others than by making it yourself. And the only way you are able to pay for all the things you buy is by selling your labor services – doing something you are specialized in, whether that means being a doctor, lawyer, programmer, administrative assistant, or coffee barista – to others. You exchange your labor to earn an income that enables you to buy food, clothing, shelter, and entertainment produced by others.

While domestic trade is the exchange of goods and services between producers and consumers within a country, international trade is simply the exchange of goods and services between different countries. The principles of specialization and exchange apply not just to individuals, but also to countries. The country of Chile in South America, for example, does not produce smartphones or automobiles or machines, and it probably could not do so very efficiently. Yet these goods are still readily available in the country. Chile exports copper, wine, salmon, and fruits and vegetables to earn the dollars with which they import those products.

Some countries specialize in producing electronics, others in automobiles, clothing, petroleum, or other raw materials. Just as voluntary trade is beneficial to the merchants who sell and the individuals who buy, trade between countries is also beneficial to both parties. The country exporting food and importing clothing benefits from trade just as the country exporting clothing and importing food does. Of course, if the trade is not voluntary – if one country simply invades another to take its resources instead of buying them – then the mutual advantage principle does not apply. (In fact, there are three ways you can get goods: you can make it, you can take it, or you can trade for it.)

The purpose of this chapter is to lay out the basic analytical tools needed to understand the gains from international trade. The approach will rely mostly on diagrams, by which we can depict a country's exports and imports graphically and visualize some of the results. Before studying the effects of international trade, however, we will first consider an economy that is *not* engaged in trade. Once we understand how, in that context, producers allocate resources to satisfy the desires of consumers, we can then introduce trade and see how things change.

2.1 AUTARKY

In a state of **autarky**, a country does not exchange goods and services with the rest of the world; the country is *self-sufficient*: everything consumed by the country must be produced by the country. Some historical examples of countries under autarky will be considered in Chapter 3, but today no nation seriously pursues a strategy of economic self-sufficiency. Even the closed pariah state of North Korea, which has elevated the concept of self-sufficiency to a national ideology (called *Juche*), engages in a small amount of international trade.

While autarky is mostly a theoretical possibility rather than a real-world phenomenon, it is still a useful construct for highlighting the potential advantages of trade. We can study a self-contained economy by using two tools you probably learned about in earlier courses: the production possibility frontier and indifference curves. The production possibility frontier tells us about the supply of goods and services coming from producers. Indifference curves tell us about consumers' demand for those same goods and services.

The Production Possibility Frontier

The first step to analyzing an economy under autarky is to determine the quantity of goods it can produce. That amount, you will recall from Chapter 1, depends on the **factors of production** available in a country. These factors of production include **land**, **labor**, and **capital.** Land is the terrain available for cultivation. Labor is the human work force. Capital refers to factories and other production-related equipment and infrastructure. The more

2.1 AUTARKY

land, the larger the labor force; the greater the capital stock, the larger the country's productive output, all else being equal.

The other thing production depends on is **technology**. Technology refers to the collective knowledge and practical skills needed to make the factors of production yield goods and services. It tells us about the efficiency with which inputs (factors of production) are used to produce outputs (production of goods and services). The more advanced the technology, the greater the output from a given set of factors of production.

As you might expect, countries differ markedly in their factors of production and their technology. At about 780 million people, China's labor force is almost five times the size of the US labor force, which is about 170 million. However, the US Gross Domestic Product (GDP) is larger than China's GDP (there is some debate about this) because the United States has more capital per worker and better technology.

At any given time, every economy has only a finite amount of each of the factors of production, meaning that it can only produce a finite quantity of goods. Even the richest economies in the world have resource constraints. Despite having the best, most cutting-edge technology, these constraints prevent the production of as many goods as we might want to have for consumption.

Furthermore, there are tradeoffs. If the United States wants to produce more food, it can do so by devoting more of its labor force and land to agriculture. However, that means fewer workers are left to produce clothing and other goods. Similarly, the United States can produce more steel by devoting more of its labor and capital to steel production, but then fewer workers and less capital will be available for the production of other goods.

We can illustrate these resource constraints and tradeoffs with the **production possibility frontier**. Let us consider two basic consumption goods everyone requires: food and clothing.

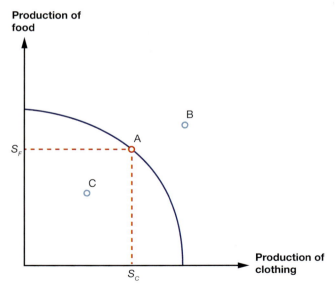

Figure 2.1 The Production Possibility Frontier The production possibility frontier shows the various combinations of food and clothing that can be produced with a country's resources. Point A refers to the production of a specific quantity of food and clothing production, labeled S_F and S_C, respectively.

The production possibility frontier, or PPF, shown in Figure 2.1, represents the different combinations of food and clothing that some unnamed country can produce, given its factors of production and its technology. Every point on the PPF represents a specific combination of food and clothing being produced. For example, at point A, the quantity (or supply) of food produced is denoted S_F and the quantity (or supply) of clothing produced is denoted S_C.

The PPF slopes downward because more of one good can be produced only by producing less of another good. This is because producing more food, for example, requires shifting factors of production, such as labor, away from the production of clothing. The (negative) slope of the PPF at a given point, such as A in Figure 2.1, is called the **marginal rate of transformation** (MRT). The MRT is the rate at which one good can be transformed into another by shifting resources to produce less of the first good and more of the second.

The PPF is commonly drawn with a convex shape, signifying that successive increases in the production of one good can arise only by giving up greater and greater amounts of the production of the other good. This indicates that there is an *increasing opportunity cost of production*. The motivating idea behind a convex PPF is that as production shifts to make more and more of one good, it can become increasingly difficult to maintain increases in output: shortages of supplies, tools, and workspace arise, less-skilled workers are increasingly relied on, and so on.

The PPF is drawn under the assumption that the quantities of the factors of production in the country are fixed, as is the state of the country's technology. However, the PPF can shift outward for one of two reasons: (i) an increase in the quantity of the factors (more land, labor, and/or capital) or (ii) an improvement in the country's technology. Improvement in technology is a particularly important way of increasing production because it represents an improved use of available resources: the same land, labor, and capital generate more output.

All of the points on the production possibility frontier are *feasible*, meaning that they represent goods combinations that are within the producers' ability to produce. All points on the PPF are also *efficient*, meaning that no productive capacity goes unused. Producing beyond the PPF (point B) is not feasible. Production inside the PPF (point C) is feasible but not efficient; either some factors of production are unemployed, or the best available technology is not being used.

Indifference Curves

If all points on the PPF are efficient and feasible, what is the right combination of food and clothing to produce? The answer, from a societal point of view, is the combination that best satisfies the preferences of consumers. Economists typically use a **utility function** to represent consumer preferences for various goods. The utility function is an indicator of the level of satisfaction derived from the consumption of goods and services.

If we focus on just food and clothing, the utility function can be represented as:

$$U = U(D_F, D_C), \tag{2.1}$$

where D_F and D_C stand for the respective amounts of food and clothing consumed (demanded) by consumers. This generic form simply indicates that utility (U) is a function of the quantity of food and clothing consumed, without specifying exactly how utility is calculated. (However, there is no reason why a precise formula cannot be stipulated for a particular case; see Exercises 2.1 and 2.2.) We assume that a person's utility increases the more food or the more clothing he or she consumes. In other words, consumers always want more goods rather than fewer. Put formally: the partial derivative of the utility function with respect to either quantity consumed is positive.

An **indifference curve** represents different combinations of food and clothing that yield the same level of utility. Consumers are said to be "indifferent" between any two points on the same curve. For example, in Figure 2.2, the combination of food and clothing at point A (D_F, D_C) yields the same utility as the combination of food and clothing at point B (D_F', D_C'). Meanwhile, any point on indifference curve U_2, such as C, is preferred to any point on curve U_1. This is implied by the positive partial derivatives of the utility function: any movement either upward or to the right from a point on U_1 produces an increase in utility.

There are an infinite number of indifference curves in Figure 2.2, even though just two are shown. Every combination of food and clothing is associated with a certain level of utility. An indifference curve simply connects all the combinations of food and clothing for which the utility is the same.

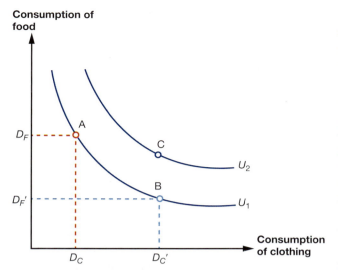

Figure 2.2 Indifference Curves The indifference curve represents different combinations of food and clothing that a consumer has that yield a constant level of utility, or well-being. For example, a consumer at point A has more food and less clothing than at point B, but because the points lie on the same indifference curve (U_1) the consumer's utility is the same. Point C represents a higher level of utility (U_2) because the consumer has access to more food and clothing than the consumer on U_1.

The slope of the indifference curve is called the **marginal rate of substitution**, or MRS. This is the rate at which one good can be substituted for another while keeping utility constant.

The shape of the indifference curves reflects a dependence of the MRS on the proportions in which goods are held or available. The more clothing a person has relative to food, the more units of clothing the person would be willing to give up in exchange for one unit of food. That is why the indifference curves are flat in the lower right area of the graph: the near-zero slope means that a loss of one unit of food must be offset by a gain of many units of clothing to keep utility the same overall.

Conversely, the indifference curves are steep in the upper-left area of the graph. For a person with a lot of food compared to clothing, many more units of food would be required to compensate for the loss of one additional unit of clothing. This should all make intuitive sense. Whether we would be willing to trade a clean shirt for a bowl of cereal would depend on whether we had plenty of cereal on hand but were short on clean shirts, or vice versa.

The Budget Constraint

Because consumers want more goods rather than fewer, they will consume as much as they can afford. (We ignore savings for the moment.) How much consumers can afford to buy is determined by the **budget constraint**. A budget constraint identifies the various combinations of goods an individual is able to consume given a fixed amount of income and market prices. Let us denote a consumer's income as Y, the prices of food and clothing as p_F and p_C, respectively, and the quantities consumed as D_F and D_C. Given a certain amount of income and faced with prices fixed by the market, consumers will choose how much food and clothing to buy. This can be expressed in the following equation:

$$Y = p_F D_F + p_C D_C. \tag{2.2}$$

This equation represents the assumption that, for given prices of food and clothing, the consumer will adjust D_F and D_C to spend the entire amount of income Y. For example, suppose you have $100 to spend, the price of food is $1 per unit, and the price of clothing is $2 per unit. You could then buy 100 units of food and no clothing, or 50 units of clothing and no food, or 25 units of clothing and 50 units of food, and so forth.

By solving for D_F, equation (2.2) can be rewritten in the form

$$D_F = -(p_C/p_F)D_C + Y/p_F \tag{2.3}$$

This is the equation of a line with a slope $-p_C/p_F$, an intercept on the vertical axis of Y/p_F, and an intercept on the horizontal axis of Y/p_C. Figure 2.3 shows the budget constraint line and its intercepts.

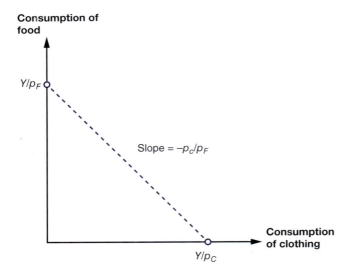

Figure 2.3 The Budget Constraint The budget constraint shows all the combinations of food and clothing that a consumer can purchase with a given amount of income. The slope of the budget constraint is given by the relative price of clothing in terms of food. The endpoints of the budget constraint, which indicate the maximum amount of food or clothing that could be purchased by the consumer, are determined by the total income of the consumer divided by the price per unit of the goods.

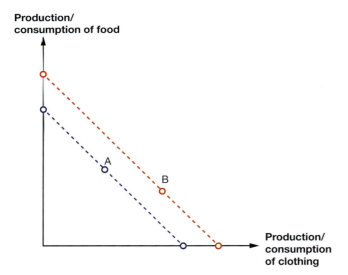

Figure 2.4 Comparing National Income at Two Different Production/Consumption Points This figure compares two production or consumption points, A and B. Both represent different combinations of food and clothing, making them hard to compare alone. If the market prices are those indicated by the downward-sloping dashed line, however, national income is higher at point B than at point A. If the relative price of food was much higher, as would be indicated by a very flat relative price line, the budget constraint at point A would be higher than at point B.

The two intercepts or endpoints are where all the income is being spent on just one of the two goods, either Y/p_F units of food or Y/p_C units of clothing. You should recall from your earlier economics classes that when either price changes, the corresponding endpoint moves and the line pivots. For example, if the price of clothing falls, the individual can consume more clothing but not more food; therefore, the budget constraint remains fixed on the D_F axis but shifts outward along the D_C axis.

The budget line serves several purposes. Sometimes we just focus on the slope of the line, which reflects the **relative price** of the two goods, or the rate at which one good can be exchanged for another. Then we call the budget line a **relative price line**. When the goods are clothing and food, the slope $-p_C/p_F$ indicates that the price of clothing relative to food is $p = p_C/p_F$. Another purpose is to determine the budget constraint, or the level of *real income*, for the nation as a whole. If we pass the relative price line through different production points, that represents the country's real national income.

For an example of the latter application, suppose we have two possible production points or consumption bundles in a country, points A and B in Figure 2.4. If we do not know anything about the production possibility frontier or the indifference curves, how do we know which point is better? One way is to see whether national income, at a given set of prices, is higher or lower at point A or B. If we know what the market prices are, such as those prevailing on the world market, we know the slope of the relative price line and can draw it through both points. The way that we have drawn the price line through the two points in the figure indicates that national income (the country's budget constraint) is higher at B than at A. (Question: if the prices were different, might we come up with a different answer?)

2.2 COMPETITIVE EQUILIBRIUM UNDER AUTARKY

We can now determine the competitive equilibrium for a country under autarky by putting the PPF and the indifference curves together. This equilibrium also determines the position of the budget constraint facing consumers in the country.

Maximizing Consumer Utility

As already noted, every point on the PPF is efficient. The question is which point on the PPF – that is, which combination of food and clothing – best satisfies consumer demand. The answer is the combination of food and clothing that produces the highest level of utility, as represented by the indifference curves.

The production possibility frontier tells us what we can produce. The indifference curves tell us what we want to consume. By putting them together, we can determine the best equilibrium for an economy under autarky. (For simplicity, all consumers are assumed to have the same income and preferences, so we can represent their situation using a single set of indifference curves and a single budget constraint. We will relax these assumptions in Chapter 3.)

In Figure 2.5, point A represents the ideal situation from a social-welfare point of view. There is no point on the production possibility frontier where consumer utility is higher. Note that the indifference curve running through point A is tangent to the PPF, and therefore the marginal rate of transformation in production is equal to the marginal rate of substitution in consumption, i.e., MRT = MRS. Any indifference curve that represents a higher level of utility would not be touching the PPF and therefore would not be feasible.

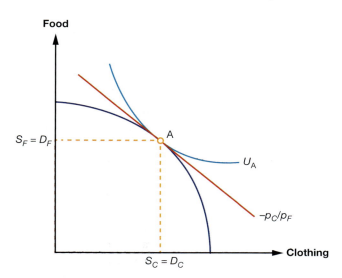

Figure 2.5 Competitive Equilibrium under Autarky The maximum feasible level of consumer utility is where the indifference curve is tangent to the production possibility frontier, at point A. At this point, the marginal rate of substitution in consumption (the slope of the indifference curve) is equal to the marginal rate of transformation in production (the slope of the production possibility frontier). Point A indicates the combination of food and clothing that best suits consumer preferences.

Notice also that point A represents both the production and the consumption point for this economy. Reading the PPF, point A indicates that the production of clothing is S_C and the production of food is S_F. Reading the indifference curve, point A indicates that the consumption of clothing is D_C and the consumption of food is D_F. Since the production of food equals the consumption of food, and the production of clothing equals the consumption of clothing, the economy is self-sufficient and not engaged in any trade.

Competitive Equilibrium

Point A represents the combination of food and clothing that this economy can produce to best satisfy consumer preferences. But how do we know that a competitive market economy will actually *get* to point A?

The answer is that producer and consumer decisions will be guided by *prices* to point A. So long as markets are competitive, prices will adjust to bring producers and consumers into alignment with each other. Producers do not really know the shape of consumers' indifference curves. Consumers do not really know the shape of the production possibility frontier. But producers and consumers both face market prices, and those prices transmit information between the two groups.

On the producers' side, producers seek to maximize profits. In equilibrium, the relative price of clothing in terms of food (the slope of the relative price line) will equal the marginal rate of transformation (the slope of the PPF). If the two were not equal, producers could increase profits by making more of one good and less of another. For example, if the relative price of clothing in terms of food were two while the MRT were one, producers would find it advantageous to shift toward producing more clothing. Why? Because under those conditions, giving up one unit of food (in order to produce an additional unit of clothing) would bring in two units of food (through the sale of the added clothing unit).

Similarly, consumers seek to maximize utility. In equilibrium, the relative price of clothing in terms of food will equal the marginal rate of substitution (the slope of the indifference curve). If the two were unequal, there would be a misalignment between prices and the valuation of the goods as seen by individuals. For example, if the relative price of clothing in terms of food was two but the MRS was one, consumers would find it advantageous to buy more food and less clothing. Why? Because the slope of the indifference curve (the MRS) indicates consumers could exchange one unit of clothing for one unit of food with no change in utility. However, at market prices, the money saved by giving up one unit of clothing could be used to buy not one but two units of food, making consumers better off.

As a result, at equilibrium point A in Figure 2.5, we also have a relative price line that is tangent to both the PPF and the indifference curve. This indicates that MRT = p_C/p_F = MRS, which is the condition for the maximum level of utility on the production possibility frontier.

To visualize the dynamic that drives an economy toward the consumer optimum, equilibrium point A, consider any arbitrary point on the PPF, such as point B in Figure 2.6. The production of this combination of food and clothing is clearly feasible, because point B is on the PPF. However, point B is not optimal, because the marginal rate of transformation in production is not equal to the marginal rate of substitution in consumption (MRT ≠ MRS).

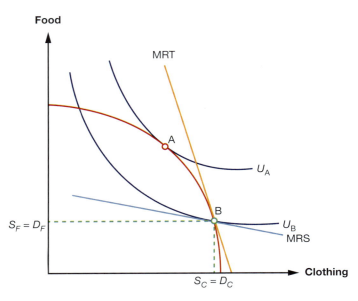

Figure 2.6 Non-Equilibrium Conditions At any point other than A such as point B, the indifference curve U_B and the production possibility frontier are not tangent, i.e., the marginal rate of substitution in consumption is not equal to the marginal rate of transformation in production. Such points are not a competitive equilibrium and are suboptimal from the standpoint of consumer welfare.

If we take B as our initial starting point, and assume that it is an equilibrium production point, then it must be the case that the marginal rate of transformation is equal to the relative market price faced by producers. This means that p_C/p_F = MRT, as shown by the relative price line tangent to the PPF at point B. If this is the case, there is no incentive for producers to alter their production and make more food or more clothing.

However, consumers are not in equilibrium at point B. The marginal rate of substitution (the slope of the indifference curve) is not equal to the relative price p_C/p_F, the slope of the line tangent to the PPF at point B (i.e., MRS ≠ p_C/p_F). The very steep slope of the relative price line indicates that giving up a little clothing will buy someone a lot of food (i.e., food is relatively cheap). The flat slope of the indifference curve indicates that consumers would be willing to give up a lot of clothing to get some food and would be at the same utility level, implying that if they could obtain more food in exchange for a certain amount of clothing, they would willingly do so. As a result, consumers will start buying a lot more food at the existing price. This shift in demand will increase the relative price of food, giving producers an incentive to increase output of food.

As the relative price of food increases, producers will respond by changing their production mix – producing more food and less clothing along the PPF – always with the goal of keeping p_C/p_F = MRT. The economy moves along the PPF until producers and consumers are aligned at point A, where p_C/p_F = MRT = MRS. Thus, market competition and a flexible price system guide producers and consumers to point A. This is an equilibrium point in that producers have no incentive to produce a different mix of food and clothing, and consumers have no incentive to alter their purchases of food or clothing.

That said, there are three situations in which an economy can remain stuck at point B and not allocate its resources to best serve consumers. First, if there is a lack of competition among producers (firms have market power or there is a monopoly), then producers will not be under the competitive pressures required to guide the production point to the consumer optimum.

Second, if there are taxes or subsidies on either the producers' or the consumers' side, then the producers' earnings and consumers' costs will diverge, which affects the allocation of resources. Third, if the economy is centrally planned, then resources will not be allocated on the basis of production costs and consumer demands but by government directive.

2.3 COMPETITIVE EQUILIBRIUM WITH TRADE

What happens when we allow our autarky economy to trade with the rest of the world? Initially, we assume that trade does not change the production possibility frontier, because trade does not immediately change the country's factors of production or technology. (We will relax this assumption in Chapter 3.) We also assume that trade does not change consumer preferences for the two goods; in other words, indifference curves are unaffected by trade.

The only difference trade makes to our economy is that world prices become the new prevailing prices in the domestic market. Here, we will make what is known as the **small country assumption.** Under this assumption, this country takes world prices *as given*. That is, changes in domestic production and domestic consumption are not enough to alter those world prices. Just as when we as consumers go to grocery story, we take the posted prices as given to us; we can buy as much or as little as we want at those prices without affecting them because we are a small part of the market. Of course, market prices do change, but for reasons outside of our control.

To distinguish autarky conditions from trade conditions, we will write the relative price of clothing in terms of food, p_C/p_F, as p_W when referring to the world relative price, and as p_A when referring to the autarky relative price

What happens if, by strange coincidence, $p_W = p_A$? The answer is: nothing! If the slope of the relative price line does not change once trade is allowed, then there is no incentive for producers or consumers to move away from point A in Figure 2.7. Because the relative price has not changed, producers and consumers do not change their position (i.e., MRT = p_W = MRS). There is no change in domestic production or consumption, and therefore there is no international trade or any improvement in consumer welfare.

Of course, it is highly unlikely that the world relative price is the same as the autarky relative price. Therefore, let us assume that the world price of clothing in terms of food is higher than the autarky relative price, i.e., $p_W > p_A$. This is because the rest of the world has a relative shortage of clothing production, or a relative abundance of food production, in comparison to the domestic economy. Thus, we can draw a new world relative price line p_W through our initial equilibrium point A. Immediately, we see that point A is no longer an equilibrium point, because MRT $\neq p_W \neq$ MRS. Therefore, trade will induce a shift in both production and consumption to restore equilibrium. Let us examine each shift in turn.

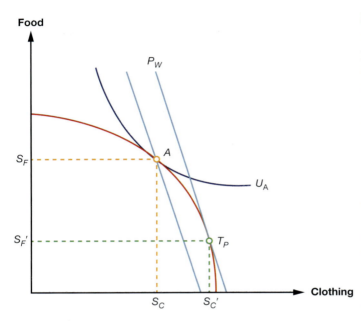

Figure 2.7 Production and Trade This diagram shows the autarky equilibrium (point A) and a trade equilibrium (point T_S). At point A, the indifference curve is tangent to the production possibility frontier and production of food and clothing equals consumption of food and clothing. If the world relative price of food in terms of clothing is higher than the autarky relative price, production will take place at a point such as T_S where more clothing and less food is produced compared to autarky.

Production and Trade

Starting from point A but using the world relative price line, there is now a mismatch between the relative *price* of clothing in terms of food, p_W, and the relative *cost* of producing clothing in terms of food, i.e., the slope of the production possibility frontier, MRT. Clothing producers will respond to the relatively higher price of their product by expanding their production of clothing. They can only expand their production by hiring labor and other factors of production away from the food sector. The expansion of clothing production and contraction of food production will continue until the marginal rate of transformation equals the world relative price.

In Figure 2.8, point T_P is the new equilibrium production point (T for trade, P for production). Production of clothing has increased from S_C to S_C', while production of food has fallen from S_F to S_F', with the result that MRT $= p_W$.

Note that trade does not enable this economy to produce more of both goods. The PPF did not shift outward, because the quantity of land, labor, and capital in the economy has not changed, nor has technology improved. All that happened is a change in prices increased the incentive to produce more clothing. To do so, factors of production must be taken away from the other sector of the economy, food.

Consumption and Trade

Although production of clothing has increased and production of food has decreased as we move along the PPF, it does not follow that consumption of the two goods does the same. While the production and consumption of each good must be equal under autarky (when domestic supply equals domestic demand), they need not be equal with trade. In fact, *trade breaks the link between domestic production and domestic consumption.* For example, the United States consumes more clothing than it produces, which is made possible by importing clothing from other countries. Conversely, the United States produces more food than it consumes by exporting some of it to the rest of the world. Meanwhile, other countries – such as Bangladesh and Vietnam – will export clothing and import food.

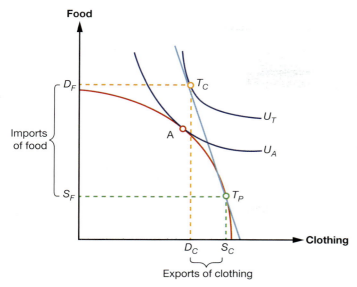

Figure 2.8 Production and Consumption with Trade This diagram shows how moving from autarky to trade shifts the production equilibrium from A to T_P and the consumption equilibrium from A to T_C. Although production takes place at T_P along the production possibility frontier, consumption takes place where the indifference curve is tangent to the world price line that is tangent to the PPF. With trade, the country produces more clothing than it consumes, exporting the difference for imports of food, allowing it to consume more than it produces.

All this means that the new production bundle (S_C, S_F) at point T_P does not have to be consumed domestically. Instead, some of it can be exported to the rest of the world. The income earned by producing the new production bundle can be used to purchase any combination of food and clothing as long as the budget constraint is satisfied.

The budget constraint is the line p_W tangent to the PPF at T_P, our production point with trade. Consumption can take place anywhere on the country's new budget constraint. Consumers can choose to consume any combination of food and clothing along this line to maximize their utility. Hence, in Figure 2.8 they will choose to consume at T_C, the point that lies on the highest indifference curve. Because this is the one point where $p_W =$ MRS, the consumers can be described as striving to make $p_W =$ MRS true.

How does the economy get from producing at point T_P to consuming at point T_C, our consumption point with trade (T for trade and C for consumption)? By exporting some of its clothing in exchange for imports of food. Even though it is only producing S_F of food at point T_P, it can consume D_F of food because it is importing some from the rest of the world. In the diagram, the country exports clothing $(S_C - D_C)$ for imports of food $(D_F - S_F)$. In addition, the points T_P and T_C are in equilibrium because MRT $= p_W =$ MRS.

The Gains from Trade

With the production possibility frontier unchanged, it is not possible to *produce* more of both goods as a result of trade. However, as you might be able to see in Figure 2.8, it is possible to *consume* more of both goods as a result of trade. All that is required is that final consumption point T_C lies northeast of point A. However, even if the shape of the indifference curves causes the final consumption point to be to the northwest of A, or southeast, the country will still be better off. It will still be on a higher indifference curve after trade.

Did these **gains from trade** arise simply because we assumed that $p_W > p_A$? What happens if $p_W < p_A$? If that is the case, then the world relative price of clothing is lower than the autarky relative price of clothing, so the country shifts toward the production of more food, which it then exports in exchange for imports of clothing. The country still gains from trade, but the pattern of trade is different: now the country exports food and imports clothing.

How do we see that there are gains from trade? The gains from trade can be measured either in terms of utility or in terms of income. The gains in utility terms are simply the movement onto a higher indifference curve. Therefore, the gains can be represented as $\Delta U = U_T - U_A$. Since utility is a nebulous concept, we will not spend much time developing this measure of trade gains.

Income is another matter entirely. We can readily quantify the increase in a country's real income, the result of shifting from production point A to production point T_P, by using world relative prices as a reference point. The country can always trade goods with other countries at those world prices, whereas it cannot trade with others at its own domestic prices. Therefore, world prices constitute a true opportunity cost for the country – opportunity cost in the sense that the country is foregoing the buying and selling of goods at those world prices. Just as in Figure 2.4, we can see that real national income is higher at production point T_P, where p_W is tangent to the PPF, than at point A. In other words, trade increases national income. (We will explore this further in Chapter 3.)

IN PRACTICE   The Natural Propensity to Trade

The concept of gains from trade is not new. In 1776, the Scottish moral philosopher Adam Smith published *An Inquiry into the Nature and Causes of the Wealth of Nations*. In this groundbreaking book, one of the first major treatises in economics, Smith made a powerful case for free trade. He argued that voluntary exchanges of goods benefit all parties – be they individuals, households, or nations – by allowing each party to play to its strength, producing and selling the goods it is especially adept at producing and purchasing the others. These others are the goods that, as the quote at the start of the chapter puts it, "cost more to make than to buy."

Smith's arguments were so compelling that almost all subsequent discussions of trade policy have taken his views as a starting point. The gains from trade shown in Figure 2.7 illustrate Smith's point. We will explore this diagram in greater detail in Chapter 3.

"Nobody ever saw a dog make a fair and deliberate exchange of one bone for another with another dog," Smith wrote. By contrast, human beings have a "propensity to truck, barter, and exchange one thing for another."

There are plenty of examples of individuals engaging in barter, which simply means trading one good for another without the use of money. During World War II, prisoners of war used cigarettes as a medium of exchange to facilitate trade. Prisoners were given rations of bread, jam, chocolate, and sugar. Prisoners also had different preferences for the rations, so those were not all priced the same. Some brands of cigarettes were more popular than others and therefore could be used to purchase more rations. There was also trade in services, such as laundry and work (Radford, 1945).

Today, there is an extensive network of trade in the US prison system. Prisoners are not allowed to possess cash or cigarettes (smoking is banned in federal prisons). As a result of that restriction, mackerel – either cans or plastic-and-foil pouches – has become the "coin of the realm." It is not clear why, but prisoners use mackerel to get clothes pressed, shoes shined, beards trimmed, and few even want to eat the fish! (Scheck, 2008).

Trade sometimes involves intermediaries. Intermediaries are sometimes willing to go to great lengths in matching consumers who want to buy things with producers who want to sell things. For example, KFC set up a restaurant in El Arish, Egypt, close to the border with the Gaza strip in Palestine. For a time in 2013, Palestinians in Gaza could call and order KFC, which was then smuggled into Gaza through underground tunnels. The chicken was not cheap: a twelve-piece bucket that sold for $11.50 in Egypt sold for $27 in Gaza.

Figure 2.9 Smuggling KFC into Gaza This picture shows the delivery of KFC from Egypt into Gaza via underground tunnels in 2013. For a short time Palestinians in Gaza were able to order KFC in Egypt and have it smuggled to them.
Source: AFP/Getty <Images.

> Sadly for Gaza's KFC fans, the trade in smuggled chicken did not last long. Israel and Egypt, for security reasons, had already begun taking steps to render the tunnels unusable. Israel used airstrikes, while Egypt mostly relied on more down-to-earth measures, such as flooding the tunnels with sewage. As trade barriers go, forcing intermediaries to wade through sewage is highly effective. The natural propensity to trade has its limits.

2.4 EMPIRICAL EVIDENCE ON TRADE AND INCOME

We have seen that trade leads to higher income, at least in theory. Is there strong empirical evidence that this is the case? Although trade and income are positively correlated across countries, it is difficult to interpret this correlation. One cannot simply assume that more trade is driving the higher incomes because the causality could run the other way: countries with higher incomes might be able to engage in more trade because they have better port facilities to accommodate more trade.

Economists Jeffrey Frankel and David Romer (1999) overcame this problem that had bedeviled previous analysis of the relationship between trade and income. They noted that one of the most important determinants of the extent of trade between two countries is the distance between them. For example, after controlling for other factors, such as the size of their economies, common languages, common currency, and so forth, a country such as Britain would be expected to trade more with Germany than with Indonesia – simply because they are closer to one another. In fact, geographic distance is a key determinant of trade, but one that is unrelated to a country's income (New Zealand is far removed from most of its trading partners but still enjoys a relatively high income).

To determine whether countries that trade more have a higher income than similar countries that trade less, Frankel and Romer used distance to predict how much trade a country would have with other countries and then used that predicted trade (which is independent of income effects) to see if more trade was associated with a country having a higher income. They found that trade was associated with higher income: a $1 increase in trade was associated, on average, with $1 higher income.

One shortcoming of this result is that it was based on data for only one year. In subsequent work, James Feyrer (2019) employed a proxy for trade that focuses on how changing shipping and airfreight costs affects geographic distance over time. This new proxy allows one to control for the impact of country-specific, time-invariant factors, such as distance from the equator, or historically determined institutions that might confound the relationship between trade and income.

Like Frankel and Romer, Feyrer found that trade has a significant effect on income: a $1 increase in trade led to a $0.50 increase in income. Furthermore, differences in predicted trade growth could explain roughly 17% of the variation in cross-country income growth between 1960 and 1995. Thus, a positive relationship between trade and income exists not just because higher-income countries can afford to trade more, but because trade raises income, as theory suggests.

2.5 TRADE IN PARTIAL EQUILIBRIUM

We have just looked at international trade through the lens of the production possibility frontier and indifference curves. What about simple supply and demand curves? We can use those as well, but only to address certain questions.

There are two methods of microeconomic analysis: **general equilibrium** and **partial equilibrium**. General equilibrium looks at two or more markets and shows how they are related to one another; this chapter has focused on the case of two markets, food and clothing, using the production possibility frontier and indifference curves. (In principle, we could look at three or more markets by using a mathematical specification of general equilibrium, including production functions and a utility function.) General equilibrium analysis is very useful in thinking about international trade, which is the exchange of one class of good for another (exports for imports), and therefore necessarily involves more than one good.

Partial equilibrium looks at one market in isolation, using supply and demand curves. A shortcoming of partial equilibrium analysis in studying international trade is that such trade cannot be fully understood by looking at one market in isolation: a country exchanges exports for imports, and usually those exports and imports are different goods. By contrast, general equilibrium allows us to get an overall picture of how trade affects an economy and see how exports and imports interact with one another.

Despite this limitation, partial equilibrium analysis is useful for illustrating how international trade affects the market for a particular good. (We will also be using partial equilibrium extensively when we get to the topic of trade policy in Chapters 8 and 9.) In particular, examining the role of trade in the market for one good illustrates how price differences in different geographical markets lead to international trade and the equalization of prices across markets. To do this, we construct one country's export supply and another country's import demand, both of which are derived from the respective countries' domestic demands for, and domestic supplies of, the good.

Import Demand

As we have seen, a country will import a good when the world price is below its autarky price. If that is the case, the quantity demanded by domestic consumers will exceed the quantity supplied by domestic producers. That extra demand will be satisfied by imports.

The demand for imported goods can be derived as follows. The left side of Figure 2.10 shows domestic supply and domestic demand for a particular good. The autarky price, p_A, is determined by the intersection of domestic demand and domestic supply. At this price, the quantity demanded equals the quantity supplied. The demand for imports is zero.

As the price falls below p_A, however, domestic demand exceeds domestic supply by increasing amounts. The gap between domestic demand and supply is the import demand, shown in the right side of Figure 2.10. The equation for a country's import demand is simply

$$M = Q_D - Q_S, \tag{2.4}$$

where M is import demand, Q_D is domestic demand, and Q_S is domestic supply.

Notice that for any given price, the import demand line's slope is flatter than that of either the domestic demand or the domestic supply curve. Import quantities are very responsive to price changes because both domestic demand and domestic supply adjust to the change in price. In other words, for a given reduction in price, demand increases and supply decreases, and imports are the difference between the two. This implies that the elasticity of import demand will be greater than the absolute value of the elasticity of either demand or supply.

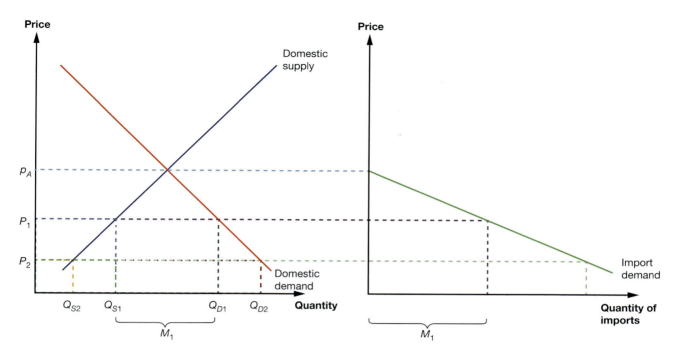

Figure 2.10 The Derivation of Import Demand This figure shows how the import demand schedule (right side) can be derived from the difference between domestic demand and supply (left side) at difference prices below the autarky price.

Export Supply

A country will export a good when the world price is above the autarky price. In that case, the quantity supplied by domestic producers will exceed the quantity demanded by domestic consumers and the extra supply will be sold to foreign consumers at the world price.

Export supply can be derived as follows. The left side of Figure 2.11 shows domestic supply and domestic demand for a particular good. The autarky price, p_A, is determined by the intersection of domestic demand and domestic supply, where the quantity demanded equals the quantity supplied. At that price, the supply of exports is zero.

As the price rises above p_A, domestic supply exceeds domestic demand by increasing amounts. Those amounts constitute the export supply, shown in the right side of Figure 2.11. The equation for a country's export supply is simply

$$E = Q_S - Q_D, \tag{2.5}$$

where E is export supply, Q_S is domestic supply, and Q_D is domestic demand.

As with import demand, the elasticity of export supply is greater than the elasticity of domestic demand or domestic supply. Exports are highly responsive to price changes because domestic demand and domestic supply adjust in opposite directions, and exports are the difference between the two.

The Trade Equilibrium

To simplify matters, let us assume we have only two countries in the world. The world price of a good is determined by the intersection of country A's export supply of a good and

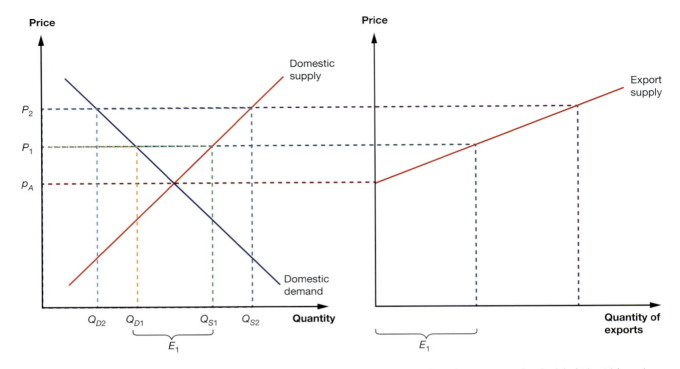

Figure 2.11 The Derivation of Export Supply This figure shows how the export supply schedule (right side) can be derived from the difference between domestic demand and supply (left side) at difference prices above the autarky price.

country B's import demand for the good. This is shown in Figure 2.12. The left panel shows the domestic market for the good in country A, the exporting country. The right panel shows the domestic market in country B, the importing country. The middle panel shows country A's export supply and country B's import demand put together.

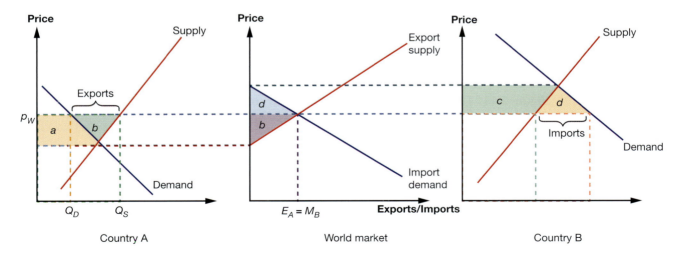

Figure 2.12 Import Demand and Export Supply Determine the World Price This figure shows how supply and demand in country A (left) and supply and demand in country B (right) interact to set the world price and trade through export supply and import demand (middle).

2.5 TRADE IN PARTIAL EQUILIBRIUM

Notice that country A has a lower autarky price of the good than country B; therefore, country A will export to country B. The world price is determined by the intersection of export supply and import demand. This intersection occurs where the quantity of export supply in country A (the difference there between domestic supply and domestic demand) is the same as the quantity of import demand in country B (the difference between its domestic demand and domestic supply).

Producer and Consumer Surpluses

Figure 2.12 can also be used to depict the gains from trade to both countries, using the concepts of producer surplus and consumer surplus. (If you are not familiar with these concepts, you can skip this subsection. The concepts will be revisited, with more explanation, in Chapter 8.) For example, when the price in country A rises from the autarky price to the world price, domestic consumers lose (and cut back their purchases of the good) while domestic producers gain (and start producing more of the good).

In the left panel of Figure 2.12, the loss in consumer surplus is represented by area *a*, the area *under the demand curve* bounded by the old and new prices. The gain in producer surplus is represented by the combined area *a* + *b*, the area *above the supply curve* bounded by the old and new prices. Because the quantity supplied exceeds the quantity demanded, the gain to producer surplus exceeds the loss to consumer surplus, with a net gain to the exporting country represented by area *b*. This is also the area above the export supply curve and below the world price in the middle panel of the figure.

Meanwhile, in country B, the importing country, the price of the good decreases from the autarky price to the world price. Country B's domestic consumers gain (and are able to purchase more of the good) and the domestic producers lose (and start producing less of the good). In the right panel of Figure 2.12, the gain in consumer surplus is represented by area *c* + *d*, while the loss in producer surplus is represented by area *c*, and so the net gain to the importing country is area *d*. Area *d* is also the area below the import demand curve and above the world price, as shown in the middle panel.

This example shows how both the exporting country and the importing country benefit from trade. The partial equilibrium approach also shows how trade in a commodity is really just moving goods to take advantage of a price difference: the country with the high autarky price imports a good from other markets where the price is lower; the country with a low autarky price exports a good to other markets where the price is higher. In equilibrium, this will equalize the prices in the two markets and there will be net gains from trade for both countries.

APPLICATION   China in World Trade

If any nation has had a volatile relationship with international trade over the years, it is China. In the 1200s and 1300s, China was a maritime power with a large fleet of sizeable vessels that engaged in trade throughout Asia and beyond. However, the Hongwu Emperor of the first Ming Dynasty, Zhu Yuanzhang, issued a ban on Chinese ships on the high seas in 1371. Some scholars today believe the threat of piracy was the reason for the ban. Others suggest that maritime trade was abandoned due to the urging of the political elite inside the emperor's civil service, who had become alarmed at the rise of a newly rich merchant class.

Figure 2.13 A Replica of a Large Trading Ship Now in Nanjing
Source: China Photos/Getty Images AsiaPac.

Whatever the case, all foreign trade was to be handled by representatives of the empire on official missions. Private foreign trade was made punishable by death, with the offender's family and neighbors exiled from their homes. Ships, docks, and shipyards were destroyed, and ports sabotaged with rocks and pine stakes.

By 1525, China's large trading ships had been destroyed. The country remained more or less closed to foreign trade over the next 500 years. China, which had been technologically sophisticated, fell behind the Western powers. Its foreign trade was limited to only a handful of local firms in a single port, Canton (Guangzhou).

Some trade continued, however, and in the seventeenth and eighteenth centuries, European demand for Chinese goods (particularly silk, porcelain, and tea) created a trade imbalance between Qing Imperial China and Great Britain. Silver flowed into China to pay for the imports, but the drain on precious metals caused consternation in Britain. To counter this imbalance, the British East India Company began to auction opium grown in India to independent foreign traders in exchange for silver, and in doing so strengthened its trading influence in Asia. This opium was transported to the Chinese coast, where local middlemen made massive profits selling the drug inside China. The influx of narcotics reversed the Chinese trade surplus, drained the economy of silver, and increased the numbers of opium addicts inside the country – outcomes that outraged Chinese officials.

In 1839, the emperor decided to ban the opium trade. When opium was confiscated by officials, Britain dispatched the Royal Navy and by "gunboat diplomacy" forced the Qing Dynasty, in 1842, to sign what became known as the unequal treaties. These treaties gave Britain control of Hong Kong and required China to be open to trade (through so-called treaty ports). These treaties bred deep resentment in China. Another opium war was fought, and lost by China a few years later, leading to widespread social unrest and resentment against Western imperialism.

China closed itself off again to international trade after the Communist Revolution brought Mao Zedong to power in 1949. Trade fell to just 2% of GDP, a very small amount, by the late 1960s. Millions of people died in a famine caused by the Great Leap Forward policies of forced industrialization in 1958–1962. The Cultural Revolution in the late 1960s and early 1970s added to the economic turbulence of that period.

China's new leader, Deng Xioaping, undertook economic reforms that reduced government control of the economy and relaxed restrictions on international trade beginning around 1978. China's trade surged, and with it the country's national income. As Figure 2.14 shows, the expansion of trade is closely tied to China's national income (GDP).

However, since 2013, President Xi Jinping has been moving toward greater government control, reducing the role of foreigners in China's economy and seeking to make the country more self-sufficient. While it is unlikely that China will fully withdraw from trade again, one never knows, given the cycles in China's past.

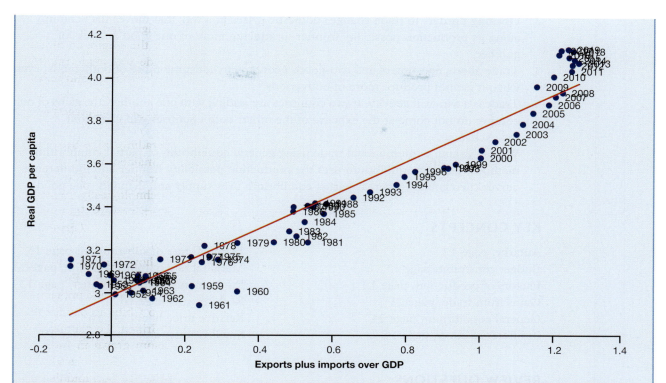

Figure 2.14 The Relationship between China's Trade Openness and GDP, 1952–2019 This shows the tight correlation between China's openness to trade (average of exports and imports as a share of GDP) and its real per capita GDP.
Source: Used with permission of Springer Nature, from Keller, Li, and Shiue, p337, © 2013; permission conveyed through Copyright Clearance Center, Inc.

CONCLUSION

This chapter has developed a set of tools to examine the nature of specialization and trade and the benefits from this arrangement. While we have applied these tools to a country, the principles they help us explore apply to individuals, as well. Individuals benefit by applying their labor to a few tasks, earning an income from their specialized labor, and then spending their income on the goods produced and services offered by others who have specialized in these products and services. Similarly, countries benefit from specialization and trade, as well: small island states and even medium-sized countries do not produce their own automobiles or electronics, instead they allow others to do so while specializing themselves in other activities that earn them an income by which they can purchase automobiles and electronics from other countries. In sum, there are gains from specialization and trade to individuals and countries alike.

SUMMARY

1. Autarky refers to a situation of no trade. Trade consists of exchanging exports for imports.

2. Opening borders to trade changes domestic prices in a way that moves the economy along its production possibility frontier, producing more of one good and less of another.
3. Trade allows consumers in a two-goods economy to consume more of both goods, even when it cannot produce more of both goods.
4. Trade is a win–win activity. If two countries are trading with one another, the gains of one country do not come at the expense of the other: both countries will gain from the exchange.
5. We can examine international trade using general equilibrium or partial equilibrium methods. General equilibrium uses the production possibility frontier and indifference curves (two goods), whereas partial equilibrium uses supply and demand (one good).

KEY CONCEPTS

Autarky, page 12
Budget constraint, page 15
Factors of production, page 12
Gains from trade, page 21
General equilibrium, page 24
Indifference curve, page 14

Marginal rate of substitution, page 15
Marginal rate of transformation, page 13
Production possibility frontier, page 13
Real income, page 16
Relative price line, page 16
Small country assumption, page 19

REVIEW QUESTIONS

1. What does the term *autarky* mean?
2. How are exports and imports related to domestic production and consumption? Is it possible to export without importing, or vice versa?
3. Do the gains from trade consist of higher utility for consumers or higher income for the country as a whole?
4. Is there evidence that trade ensures that a country has higher income than under autarky?
5. How does showing trade in partial equilibrium (supply and demand) differ from general equilibrium (PPFs and indifference curves)?

EXERCISES

1. Naomi has a monthly income (budget constraint) of $200, which she allocates between two goods: meat and potatoes.
    a. Suppose meat costs $4 per pound and potatoes cost $2 per pound. Write down the equation for the budget constraint and draw it graphically.
    b. Suppose that Naomi's utility function is given by the formula $U = 2D_M + D_P$. (The indifference curves are then straight lines.) What combination of meat and potatoes should Naomi buy to maximize her utility? (*Hint*: Meat and potatoes are perfect substitutes.)
    c. An outbreak of potato rot raises the price of potatoes to $4 per pound. What does the budget constraint look like now? What combination of meat and potatoes maximizes Naomi's utility?

EXERCISES

2. The utility Taylor receives by consuming food and clothing in quantities D_F and D_C, respectively, is given by the formula $U = D_F D_C$. (This leads to standard-looking, concave indifference curves.)
   a. Suppose that food costs $1 per unit and clothing costs $3 per unit, and Taylor has $12 to spend. What is the budget constraint?
   b. What is the utility-maximizing choice of food and clothing? (*Hint*: Solve graphically.)
   c. What is the marginal rate of substitution of food for clothing when utility is maximized?
   d. Suppose that Taylor buys three units of food and three units of clothing with his $12. Would Taylor's MRS of food for clothing be greater or less than 1/3? Is this an equilibrium point?
3. Suppose a country opens up to international trade but world relative prices are identical to autarky relative prices in the country. Why are there no gains from trade?
4. Suppose a formerly closed country opens up to trade, and world prices differ from autarky prices, but the country cannot alter its production of food and clothing away from its autarky production. Will the country still gain from trade? (*Hint*: See the diagram below.)

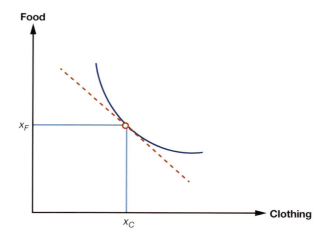

5. Suppose two separate countries have exactly the same factors of production and exactly the same technology (i.e., their production possibility frontiers are exactly the same). However, the preferences of consumers in the two economies differ: in one country people prefer relatively more food, and in the other they prefer relatively more clothing. Draw a diagram to illustrate this situation. Will the autarky prices be the same in the two countries? Can the two countries gain from trade?
6. Draw the diagram for the gains from trade with a curved production possibility frontier. If the PPF shifts out, due to an increase in the labor force or an improvement in technology, but world prices remain the same, what happens to the level of utility attained by the economy? What happens to the quantity of exports and imports and the gains from trade?
7. Suppose US domestic demand for maple sugar is given by the equation $Q_D = 110 - 2P$ and US domestic supply is given by the equation $Q_S = 10 + 2P$.
   a. What is the autarky US price? How much of the good will the United States produce and consume without trade?

b. What is the equation for US import demand? What is the equation for US export supply? Will the United States export or import the good if the world price is 40, and how much will it trade?
c. Continuing with the above question: If Canada's supply of maple sugar is given by the equation $Q_S = 10 + 3P$ and its demand is given by $Q_D = 30 - P$, what is Canada's autarky price? Will the United States and Canada trade maple sugar with one another?
d. What will be the price if the two countries trade and how much will be traded?
e. What are the gains to the United States from trading with Canada?

RECOMMENDED RESOURCES

For a classic discussion of international trade, see Adam Smith, *An Inquiry into the Nature and Causes of the Wealth of Nations, Glasgow Edition of the Works of Adam Smith* (Oxford: Oxford University Press, 1976).

For a more advanced treatment, see Robert C. Feenstra, *Advanced International Trade: Theory and Evidence*, 2nd edition (Princeton, NJ: Princeton University Press 2016), or the older approach of Jagdish Bhagwati, T. N. Srinivasan, and Arvind Panagariya, *Lectures on International Trade*, 2nd edition (Cambridge, MA: MIT Press, 1998).

The origins of the classic "gains from trade" diagram is discussed by Andrea Maneschi and William O. Thweatt, "Barone's 1908 Representation of an Economy's Trade Equilibrium and the Gains from Trade," *Journal of International Economics* 22 (1987): 375–382.

For an analysis of how China opened up to the world economy, see Nicholas Lardy, *Foreign Trade and Economic Reform in China, 1978–1990*, (Cambridge, UK: Cambridge University Press, 1991).

CHAPTER 3

Exploring the Gains from Trade

LEARNING OBJECTIVES

In this chapter, we learn about:
- the static and dynamic gains from trade
- how the terms of trade affect the gains from trade
- historical examples of the gains from trade
- whether everyone in society benefits from trade

INTRODUCTION

Russia's invasion of Ukraine in February 2022 sent shock waves though the world's wheat market. The world price of wheat jumped from about $8 per ton to more than $13 per ton within a few days. The markets feared that wheat supplies from the region – which account for a third of the world's wheat harvest – would be disrupted.

The price spike created particular concern among the wheat-importing nations of the Middle East and sub-Saharan Africa. Social stability in these regions depends upon cheap and available food for consumers, who devote a considerable portion of their budget to bread. (The public protests around the Arab Spring of 2011 were triggered in part by a spike in food prices.) Meanwhile, wheat farmers in Canada, the United States, and other exporting nations enjoyed a temporary windfall even as consumers in those countries suffered with the higher prices.

The price spike gradually subsided after agreements were reached to allow the export of some Ukrainian wheat through the Black Sea. However, the continuing conflict kept alive fears that wheat supplies could be easily disrupted given the precarious nature of the region's stability.

Although short-lived, the rise in the price of wheat affected the terms on which countries bought and sold wheat on the world market, helping wheat exporters and hurting wheat importers. The changing price also affected different groups within these countries: consumers were harmed by the higher price, while producers benefited. Of course, the reverse is true when wheat prices fall.

Clearly, then, there is more to be said about gains from trade. The optimistic picture of the gains from trade, as discussed in Chapter 2, must also allow for a more complex one. In this chapter, we will see that trade is not, automatically and without qualification, a good thing for everyone. We begin by considering how changes in world prices affect the gains from trade.

We go on to distinguish between static and dynamic gains from trade, and finally consider whether everyone in a country is necessarily better off because of trade.

3.1 QUICK REVIEW

In Chapter 2, we used the production possibility frontier, indifference curves, and relative prices to model the competitive equilibrium for a country. We began by studying what happens in autarky and then introduced international trade.

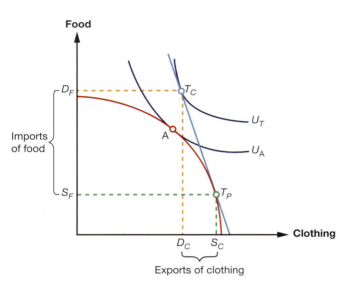

Figure 3.1 Trade Equilibrium This diagram presents the production possibility frontier, the indifference curve, and the world relative price line. The world price line is tangent to the production possibility frontier and shows where production takes place. The world price line is also tangent to an indifference curve and shows where consumption takes place. In this case, international trade consists of exporting clothing and importing food, which link the production and consumption points.

Figure 3.1 considers the role of trade in such an economy. The autarky equilibrium at point A is where indifference curve U_A (corresponding to the highest utility level under autarky) is tangent to the production possibility frontier (PPF). At A, the marginal rate of transformation (the slope of the PPF) is the same as the marginal rate of substitution (the slope of the indifference curve). A line indicating the autarky relative price of clothing in terms of food (p_A) is not drawn, but it would be tangent to both the production possibility frontier and the indifference curve at point A. In addition, at A the country is self-sufficient: the production of food equals the consumption of food, and similarly the production of clothing equals the consumption of clothing.

If world relative prices are different from autarky relative prices, then a country that opens to world trade will produce more of the good whose relative price has increased and produce less of the good whose relative price has decreased. The country will export some portion of the good whose relative price and production have increased. The country will import some of the good whose relative price and production have decreased.

In Figure 3.1, the world relative price of clothing in terms of food is higher than the autarky relative price. As a result, production shifts to point T_P, where there is more production of clothing and less production of food compared to autarky. Trade breaks the link between production and consumption. It is possible for consumption to take place anywhere along the budget constraint line indicated by the world relative price. Of course, consumption actually takes place at one specific point: where the indifference curve U_T (corresponding to the highest utility level with trade) is tangent to that line at point T_C. From its production point, the country will export clothing and import food to reach that consumption point.

The striking thing we learned about trade in Chapter 2 is that while trade does not enable a country to produce more of both goods, it is possible for it to consume more of both goods. There is, however, more to be gleaned from Figure 3.1.

Mercantilism

Before Adam Smith published *The Wealth of Nations* in 1776, the prevailing view of international trade was something called **mercantilism**. Mercantilists believed that exports were good for a country because they increased domestic production and created jobs, and that, conversely, imports were bad because they reduced domestic production and destroyed jobs. Accordingly, mercantilists favored promoting exports and restricting imports.

Figure 3.1 tells a fundamentally different story about trade: imports are the benefit of trade, and exports are its cost. Imports directly increase consumers' utility by making higher utility combinations of goods available than under autarky. Exports, however, do not directly benefit anyone inside the country; they are goods that are produced but given up to other countries. However, the revenue earned from the exports is what pays for the imports that enable consumption to be higher. In other words, the gains from trade arise from imports, and exports are the cost of acquiring the imports.

If this is not intuitive, imagine that the Organization of Petroleum Exporting Countries (OPEC) gave away their oil for free. What would other importing nations, capable of producing some oil but also other goods, do? Clearly they would cut back on oil production ("Why work to produce oil when we have a free supply?") and increase their oil consumption ("Hey, it's free!"). The thought experiment shows how, when it comes down to it, countries import because they want to and export only because they have to. They would happily take a pass on producing oil if they could import it at no cost.

This does not mean, turning mercantilism on its head, that imports are good and exports are bad. Exports are not bad. But they are good mainly as a means of paying for imports. That is why, in criticizing mercantilist policy prescriptions, Adam Smith did not say that exports should be restricted, and imports should be promoted. Rather, he said that trade was an economic activity like other forms of commerce and should, in principle, be neither restricted nor promoted but left free.

Jobs

Figure 3.1 also tells us something about the impact of trade on jobs. At any production point on the PPF, be it A or T_P, the economy is operating at full capacity, which means full employment. Trade, by itself, does not cause unemployment, but trade can shift labor from one sector to another. Compared to autarky, more labor will be employed in sectors of the economy that export, and less labor will be employed in sectors of the economy that face competition from imports. In our example, imports destroyed jobs in the food sector, but exports created jobs in the clothing sector.

There is a caveat: the production possibility frontier implicitly assumes that workers can easily switch sectors. In Chapter 5, we will examine the case where workers may not be able to move between sectors of the economy. Furthermore, as we will see in Chapter 14, macroeconomic policies may be required to keep the economy on the path of full employment.

Balanced Trade

How can a country afford to consume more food than it produces? By producing more clothing than it consumes and exporting the surplus. Exports of clothing pay for the imports of food, and so exports and imports go hand in hand.

Note, however, the phrase "pay for." It appears in Figure 3.1 that the quantity of exports is smaller than the quantity of imports. And indeed, there is no reason why export quantity $S_C - D_C$ must be numerically equal to import quantity $D_F - S_F$. If exports are to pay for imports, what matters is the *monetary value* of clothing exports equals the monetary value of food imports.

In fact, trade is **balanced** in Figure 3.1 in that the value of the country's exports equals the value of its imports. (Trade surpluses and deficits will be discussed in Chapter 11.) Trade is balanced when the production point and the consumption point are on the same relative price line, in this case p_W. Why is this so? Recall from Section 2.2 that income is constant along the budget constraint. All the income earned from production at point T_P can be spent any way consumers want, so long as their consumption bundle lies on or inside the budget constraint. Because both production and consumption lie on the same budget line, the value of production at point T_P is equal to the value of consumption at point T_C.

In symbols, the value of production equals the value of consumption can be represented this way:

$$p_C S_C + p_F S_F = p_C D_C + p_F D_F. \tag{3.1}$$

Simply rearranging this expression yields:

$$p_C(S_C - D_C) = p_F(D_F - S_F), \tag{3.2}$$

which says the value of exports equals the value of imports. Thus, as long as the production and the consumption point are on the same relative price line, trade is balanced.

3.2 THE TERMS OF TRADE

As we have seen, international trade is the exchange of exports for imports. The relative price at which this exchange takes place is called the **terms of trade**. Specifically, a country's terms of trade is defined as the price of its exports divided by the price of its imports, or, in other words, the price of its exports relative to the price of its imports. Since exports are the payment for imports, the terms of trade tell us the ratio at which one is exchanged for the other. Put differently, it represents how many imports a country can buy in exchange for a certain amount of exports.

For the country shown in Figure 3.1, the terms of trade is the world price of clothing in terms of food (p_C/p_F), because the country is exporting clothing and importing food. For a country that is exporting food and importing clothing, the terms of trade would be the relative price of food in terms of clothing (p_F/p_C).

The terms of trade is closely related to the gains from trade and has consequences for a country's economic welfare. In general, a country wants a high price for its exports and a low price for its imports, to maximize the volume of imports that a given quantity of exports will buy. An increase in the price of a country's exports relative to its imports is said to be an *improvement* in the country's terms of trade; a decrease in the relative price of the exports is a *deterioration* in the country's terms of trade. Graphically, the country in Figure 3.1 wants the relative price line to become steeper, not flatter.

Figure 3.2 shows what happens when the terms of trade change. Suppose that the country is originally producing at point T_P with terms of trade p_W. Then the terms of trade improve – either the price of clothing goes up or the price of food goes down (it does not matter which) – and the new price becomes p_W'. This will lead the country to produce more

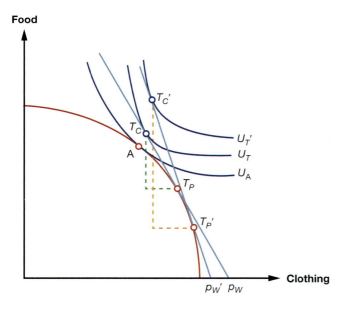

Figure 3.2 Changes in the Terms of Trade This figure shows the impact of an increase in the world relative price of clothing on a country exporting clothing. This terms of trade improvement means that the country will produce more clothing and be able to export it at a more favorable ratio in exchange for imports of food. The terms of trade improvement enables the country to reach a higher level of utility.

clothing and less food, at point T_P'. Because the relative price of clothing has increased, every unit of clothing exported translates into imports of more food. Consequently, the country can reach a higher indifference curve than it could before. Overall, the country is better off.

Note that in a typical scenario, such as the one illustrated above, the country imports more than it did before. This is reflected in the greater vertical distance between the production point and the consumption point. The volume of imports goes up because the relative price of food (the imported good) goes down. However, the volume of exports, as reflected in the *horizontal* distance between the production and consumption points, does not necessarily go up. In fact, export volume may fall, because each unit of export now buys more imports than before.

Conversely, suppose the terms of trade deteriorate from p_W' to p_W. This could happen because the price of clothing falls or because the price of food increases. Either way, the country produces less clothing and more food and moves from point T_P' to point T_P on the PPF. The ratio at which it exchanges its exports for imports is now inferior to what it had been: the exports of clothing buy fewer imported units of food, even though the country may be exporting just as much, or even more, than before. Its consumption point is on a lower indifference curve, and the country is worse off.

We saw in Chapter 2 that when two countries trade, both countries are usually better off than they would be without trade. In other words, trade is a positive-sum activity in which both countries benefit. By contrast, changes in the *terms* of trade are zero-sum: when the terms of trade change, some countries benefit but other countries suffer. In the case of oil, an increase in the world price of oil makes oil-exporting countries better off (their terms of trade have improved) and oil-importing countries worse off (their terms of trade have deteriorated).

Of course, when a country's terms of trade deteriorate, that does not mean that it should stop trading altogether. Eliminating trade would push the country back to autarky and make it even worse off! Still, a deterioration in a country's terms of trade does reduce its overall well-being. Just ask the citizens of a developing country whether they are better off after the price of their major exported good has collapsed on world markets.

The situation is in principle no different with countries than with individuals. Each of us engages in trade with the rest of the economy: we export our labor time to others and import goods and services produced by others. The price of our exports is our wage rate, while the price of our imports is summarized by the consumer price index, a weighted average of the prices of the goods and services we buy. Then each person's terms of trade is that person's wage rate divided by the consumer price index. Economists call this the **real wage**. It is the purchasing power of wages in terms of the goods and services it can buy.

Just like countries, we as individuals want favorable terms of trade. That is, we want to sell our exports (our labor) at high prices (our wage rate) and obtain our imports (goods and services) at low prices (what we pay at the cash register). In short, as workers we want high real wages.

IN PRACTICE   The Terms of Trade

Countries whose exports are dominated by a single commodity often experience wide swings in their terms of trade when the prices of those commodities move up or down on the world market. Examples include Saudi Arabia and oil, Colombia and coffee, Honduras and bananas, and Chile and copper.

The gains from trade for these countries is highly dependent on the price of their exports. If their export earnings fall because of lower world prices of their export products, they will not be able to afford as many imports of food, fuel, and other goods, and their standard of living will suffer. However, for countries that export and import a diversified array of goods, such as the United States, the terms of trade tend to be relatively stable over time. Changes in the world prices of a few goods will not affect the overall price index of exports or imports.

In the past, fluctuations in the price of oil were a key variable in the world economy and in the division of the gains from trade between exporters and importers. Most oil exporters are members of the Organization of Petroleum Exporting Countries. OPEC's terms of trade is the price of oil (the exported good) relative to the price of almost all other goods (their imported goods).

If the world price of oil increases, OPEC's terms of trade improve, because every supertanker of oil that leaves its shores will now bring a bigger flow of Mercedes Benz cars, Apple iPads, bushels of wheat, and foreign holiday makers in return than it did before. By the same token, with an increase in the world price of oil, oil-importing countries' terms of trade deteriorates. Those countries now have to export more of their goods in order to buy the same amount of oil. In general, they will be worse off.

Australia is one country whose terms of trade have substantially improved in recent years. Australia exports iron ore, coal, and other commodities and has benefited from the rapid economic growth in China, which has increased demand for these products and raised their prices. Australia's terms of trade improved dramatically from 2004 to 2011 (Figure 3.3). In 2005, the proceeds from a shipload of iron ore could have bought 2,200 flatscreen TVs; in 2011, the same shipload could buy 22,000 flatscreen TVs (see *The Economist*, March 31, 2011). More recently, however, the slowdown in China's growth has brought with it falling commodity prices. With those falling prices has come a decline in the terms of trade for Australia and other commodity exporting countries.

These changes in the terms of trade are sometimes a matter of life and death. About 70% of Zambia's exports are copper. When copper prices tumbled in 2014, Zambia's economy faced great hardship. The decline in the price of its main export meant that export earnings fell severely, making it harder for the country to import necessary goods such as food and fuel. Electricity shortages and blackouts followed. The mining sector shrank, leading to high unemployment even as the prices of imported consumer goods soared.

One lesson is that there is a gain from having a more diversified export structure. The more diversified a country's exports are, the less it will be subject to wide swings in its terms of trade.

Figure 3.3 Australia's Terms of Trade, 1959–2022 Australia's terms of trade were relatively stable between 1960 and 2005, fluctuating within a narrow margin. With China's enormous demand for imports of raw materials, the prices of Australia's commodity exports soared after 2005, resulting in a huge improvement in the country's terms of trade. This made for a prosperous period in the country's economic history.
Source: Australian Bureau of Statistics, www.rba.gov.au/education/resources/explainers/australia-and-the-global-economy.htm.

3.3 STATIC VERSUS DYNAMIC GAINS FROM TRADE

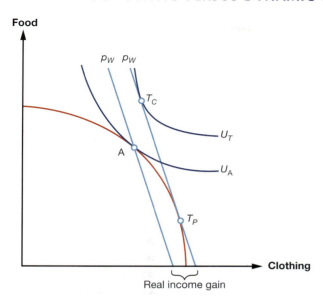

Figure 3.4 Static Gains from Trade The static gains from trade can be measured by applying world relative prices to the autarky production bundle (A) and to the trade production bundle (T_P). This outward shift in the country's budget constraint is one indicator of the gains from trade.

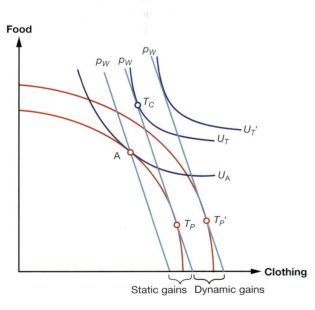

Figure 3.5 Static and Dynamic Gains from Trade The static gains from trade can be seen by applying world relative prices through the autarky and trade production points. If the production possibility frontier shifts out as a result of an improvement in technology and arises because of imports, this is a dynamic gain from trade and will shift the country's budget constraint out further.

We have seen that a country is better off reallocating its production along the PPF and engaging in trade than it is remaining in autarky. This improvement is called the **static gains from trade**. The gains are static because the economy's underlying resources and technology do not change. All the country is doing is reallocating existing resources to take advantage of the opportunity to trade.

To illustrate the higher income that comes from trade, Figure 3.4 shows a world relative price line drawn through the autarky production point A. This line represents the value of producing this combination of goods at world prices. The figure also shows a world relative price line drawn through the production point T_P, with trade. The budget line (the value of income at world prices) is further out when the price line is tangent to the point T_P than when it is drawn through point A. By extending the lines down to the clothing axis (or up to the food axis), we can show the gain in real income as measured in terms of clothing (or food). This outward shift of the budget constraint represents the real income gain that comes from trade.

A more important gain from trade comes from improved technology. When a country opens up to international trade, it usually gets access to better technology. With this better technology, a country can increase its productivity and shift outward its PPF. This shift of the PPF, which is a **dynamic gain from trade**, is illustrated in Figure 3.5. Whereas the static gains from trade refer to the reallocation of existing resources as a result of trade, the dynamic gains from trade refer to the improvement in productive efficiency as a result of trade. Static gains involve improving a country's situation by making less of one good in order to make more of another – the one exported. Dynamic gains involve the ability to make more of both goods.

The dynamic gains from trade are generally much larger than the static ones. This is especially true for developing countries, which are behind the world technological frontier. As we will see later in this chapter and in those that follow, some developing countries have seen higher rates of economic growth after opening up to world trade, because they can import and adopt better production technologies from the rest of the world. The higher growth rates arise from increases in labor productivity, as the state of production technologies in those countries catches up with the rest of the world.

APPLICATION Shoguns, Embargoes, Canals, and Blockades – What Past Attempts to Stop Trade Have Taught Us

We have used an imaginary world to illustrate the gains from trade in theory, but can we actually see these gains in the real world? Can we observe the static gains from trade – the change in real income – that arise in moving from autarky to trade? Or maybe the static losses that arise in moving from trade to autarky?

For better or worse, these kinds of observations are difficult in today's world, where the interconnectedness of national economies is a global fact of life. Going back in history, however, we can find examples of what we are looking for. Before the mid-nineteenth century, Japan's *shōgun* leaders pursued a policy of autarky. They wanted no contact with the barbarians in the rest of the world and would jail or kill merchants or missionaries from other countries who landed on their shores.

In 1854, a US naval expedition led by Commodore Matthew Perry forced Japan to change its policy of economic isolation and open up to trade. As a result, prices in Japan changed dramatically: the price of silk (abundant in Japan, but highly sought elsewhere) rose considerably, while the price of machinery (scarce or nonexistent in Japan, but available elsewhere) plummeted. The static gain from trade has been estimated by Bernhofen and Brown (2005) to have been about 8% or 9% of GDP.

The dynamic gains from trade for Japan are thought to have been orders of magnitude larger than the static gains. Under autarky, Japan was a very backward economy. With trade, the country had the ability to import new equipment (and ideas) from abroad. The economy began growing at double-digit rates, and, by the turn of the century, Japan had become a world power. (In the movie *The Last Samurai*, Tom Cruise plays a disillusioned Civil War veteran who comes to Japan as the country is grappling with the enormous cultural changes that trade was introducing.)

Whereas Japan provides a good historical example of a country going from autarky to trade, the United States provides a good historical example of a country going from trade to autarky, at least briefly. In December 1807, President Thomas Jefferson declared an embargo on all shipping between the US and foreign ports. The purpose of the embargo was to stop Britain from interfering with American shipping during its war with France.

The main consequence of the embargo was that US exports and imports plummeted. As foreign trade ground to a halt, the economy suffered. The domestic prices of imported goods, such as pottery and clothing, increased by 30% within a few months of the embargo taking effect. Meanwhile, the domestic prices of goods the United States exported, such as cotton and flour, fell by 20–40% almost immediately – good in the short term for consumers, no doubt, but a catastrophic development for producers. Irwin (2003) calculates the lost income as 5% of GDP. Needless to say, because of its failure to persuade Britain to end the interception of neutral shipping on the Atlantic and high domestic economic cost, the embargo quickly became unpopular. It was abandoned in early 1809.

Another, more recent historical situation that illustrates the impact of changed trade relationships on a country's income is the closure of the Suez Canal in June 1967 due to the Six Day Arab–Israeli War. The Egyptian authorities did not reopen the canal until 1975. The closure of the canal meant that ships traveling between Europe and Asia had to go around Africa, adding an additional 4,000 nautical miles to the journey between India and Britain. After looking at the countries most affected by the increased distance to trading partners, such as Pakistan and India, Feyrer (2019) estimated that a $1 decrease in trade reduces national income by $0.25.

Figure 3.6 Role of Suez Canal on Trade between Asia and Europe As this map shows, the Suez Canal cuts travel distances between Asia and Europe by at least 4,000 kilometers, saving time and fuel in shipping goods between the regions. The vast majority of China's exports to Europe pass through the canal.

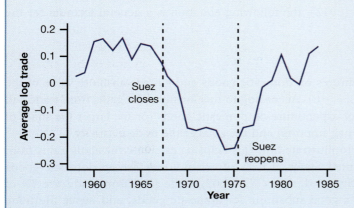

Figure 3.7 Effects of Closing the Suez Canal This figure shows the impact of the closure of the Suez Canal on trade. The trade of affected countries dropped by about 20% during the years of the closure. *Source:* Feyrer (2019).

A final example, of going from trade to no-trade and then back to trade, is the Israeli blockade of the Gaza Strip in 2007–2010. Israel blockaded Gaza for security reasons during this period, but it did not blockade the West Bank, which has a similar economy to Gaza's. The West Bank is a useful "control" that allows us to see what might have happened to Gaza in the absence of the blockade.

Figure 3.8 shows real per capita consumption in Gaza and the West Bank around the time of the blockade. Consumption was similar in the two economies until the blockade, when it fell in Gaza but continued to rise in the West Bank. Etkes and Zimring (2015) found that consumer welfare fell by 27% in Gaza (relative to the West Bank) as a result of the blockade. They also found that productivity in Gaza fell considerably

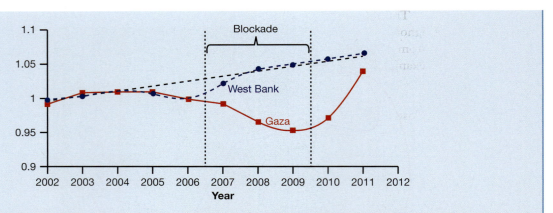

Figure 3.8 Real Consumption (per capita) in the West Bank and Gaza, 2002–2011 During Israel's blockade of Gaza, consumption by residents fell by 5%, creating a 10% gap in comparison with the West Bank.
Source: Etkes and Zimring (2015).

when firms there were unable to import components and intermediate goods needed for production of final goods. This illustrates that being cut off from trade will not only lead to a static loss, but the production possibility frontier will shrink inward as well – a dynamic loss on top of the static one.

In sum, we can conclude that both theory and evidence support the contention that trade increases a country's real income, often by a significant amount.

Up to this point, we have assumed that trade left the PPF unchanged, so that while a country might consume more goods because of trade, it could not produce more goods. However, with the dynamic gains from trade and, more specifically, the new production technologies that trade makes available, it becomes possible for a country to produce more goods.

Can we calculate the static gains from trade? In fact, the gains from trade are closely related to the value of imports in GDP. Across many different trade models, according to Arkolakis, Costinot, and Rodriguez-Clare (2012), the following equation is a general formula for the static gains from trade (GT):

$$GT = 1 - \lambda_D^{1/\varepsilon} \qquad (3.3)$$

where λ_D is the share of expenditures on domestic goods and ε is the absolute value of the elasticity of import demand (i.e., $\varepsilon \geq 0$). According to this formula, the gains from trade will be larger the smaller the share of expenditure on domestic goods (or the larger the share of expenditures on foreign goods, i.e., imports) and the smaller the trade elasticity.

Let us use a simple example to illustrate how this helps us calculate the static gains from trade. For example, for the United States, if 92% of expenditures are on domestic goods ($\lambda_D = 0.92$) and the trade elasticity $\varepsilon = 4$, then $GT = 0.02$, or the gains from trade, are 2% of GDP. If foreign goods are not a good substitute for domestic goods, and hence the trade elasticity is lower, at 2, then the gains from trade will be larger at 4% of GDP. For another country, say, Canada, where the share of spending on foreign goods is much higher, about 30%, the gains from trade will be larger. In this case, if $\lambda_D = 0.7$ and if the trade elasticity $\varepsilon = 4$, then the gains from trade are 8.5% of GDP.

This formula is an extremely short-cut way of calculating the static gains from trade, and it ignores many other sources of gains from trade. These include dynamic gains, as well as gains from product variety and intermediate goods, as will be explored in later chapters. For example, while US gains from trade appear to be low at just 2% of GDP in this formula, a multisector model (one with different industries) has the gains from trade at 4% of GDP. Also including intermediate goods increases the gains from trade to 8% of GDP, according to Costinot and Rodríguez-Clare (2014, 206). Likewise, for Canada, the gains from trade go from 4% of GDP in the simplest model to 17% of GDP with multiple sectors, to 30% of GDP with multiple sectors and intermediate goods.

The take-away is that any calculated estimate of the gains from trade is model-specific and depends largely on what assumptions one is comfortable making. Fortunately, we do have some historical evidence on what happens when trade is disrupted.

3.4 DOES EVERYONE BENEFIT FROM TRADE?

Up to this point, we have represented a country's consumers by a single indifference curve and a single, common budget constraint. In doing so, we implicitly assumed that everyone has the same preferences and the same income. Of course, a country consists of diverse individuals, with different incomes and preferences. Once we suspend our simplistic assumption, we are faced with an awkward truth: the fact that trade makes a larger bundle of goods available to an economy does not mean that the *distribution* of those goods will enable everyone to consume more. Trade that benefits an economy in general does not automatically benefit everyone in that economy.

The Pareto Test and Compensation

A simple example: suppose an economy consists of two individuals instead of a single representative consumer. Suppose, further, that the economy provides ten units of food and ten units of clothing for consumption in autarky, and that after trade the economy provides 14 units of food and 14 units of clothing. If the two individuals receive equal shares of each consumption bundle – five units of food and five units of clothing to each individual before trade and seven units of each good after trade – then both individuals will be better off. In such a case, trade will not be controversial.

However, what if each individual receives five units of each good before trade, and after trade one individual receives 10 units of each good while the other receives only four? Although aggregate consumption is still larger, the distribution of goods has changed. Now we cannot say that everyone is better off as a result of trade. In other words, when a country's overall income is higher as a result of trade, we cannot automatically say that the country's people are better off. In our example, one person is better off but the other is not.

We need a principle for judging whether one allocation of goods is better than another when there is more than one person involved. More than a century ago, the Italian economist Vilfredo Pareto came up with such a criterion: a change that makes at least one person better off and no one worse off is said to be a **Pareto improvement**.

As our example has shown, trade does not always constitute a Pareto improvement over autarky. Fortunately, by making more goods available, trade has the *potential* to make everyone better off, through the redistribution of goods. In our example, if the person who got ten units of each good after trade were to give two units of each to the other person, then trade compared to autarky would mean eight units of each good instead of five for the first person, and six units of each good instead of five for the second person. Now everyone would benefit from trade. This scheme of **compensation** for those who would otherwise be harmed by trade makes trade a Pareto improvement over autarky.

The Utility Possibility Frontier under Autarky

We can deepen our understanding of compensation through redistribution using a diagram of a **utility possibility frontier**. Suppose we have two individuals who must share the goods consumed in an economy. Let us call these individuals Robin (Hood) and Karl (Marx), after two prominent historical figures who each, in their own way, were fans of redistribution.

Now think back to Figure 3.1, showing the gains from trade. First consider the autarky consumption bundle, the combination of food and clothing consumed without trade. These goods could be allocated between Robin and Karl in many different ways. One extreme would be to give all the goods to Karl and none to Robin. In that case, Karl would have some positive utility level and Robin would have zero utility. If, starting from this point, we began to take some of the goods away from Karl and give them to Robin, then Karl's utility would fall and Robin's would rise. At the end of the process, Robin would have all of the goods and some positive utility, and Karl would have no goods and zero utility.

If we graphically map out all the possible combinations of Robin's and Karl's utilities, we obtain something like Figure 3.8. U_R refers to Robin's utility level, and U_K refers to Karl's. The irregular curve is the utility possibility frontier (UPF), with "everything to Karl" at the upper left end and "everything to Robin" at the lower right end.

Points along the UPF represent **Pareto efficient** utility combinations, meaning that there is no way to achieve a Pareto improvement by redistributing the goods. So, for instance, if Robin were allowed to keep all the clothes but all the food were given to Karl, it might well be that both of them would prefer that Karl got some of Robin's clothes while giving Robin some food in return. Then "all clothes to Robin and all food to Karl" would not be Pareto efficient; the resulting U_R, U_K combination would lie somewhere inside the UPF, not on it. By contrast, a goods combination that could not be changed without lowering either Robin's or Karl's utility would be Pareto efficient; the corresponding U_R, U_K combination would lie on the UPF.

When a fixed set of goods can be allocated between two groups, the distribution of those goods affects the utility level that each group can achieve. This figure illustrates the maximum possible utility level for each group depending on how the goods are allocated.

The UPF is a continuous curve, because we assume that goods can be transferred in fractions of a unit. (Actually, the continuous curve implies some additional assumptions, as well, but we will not go into those.) Also, although the curve's exact shape does not matter, the curve slopes downward at every point. (If it ever sloped upward, this would imply that the points along the upward-sloping portion did not fit the definition of Pareto efficiency, since both Robin's and Karl's utility could be increased.)

All points on the UPF are Pareto efficient allocations of the autarky consumption bundle, which is established by the dynamic described in Chapter 2, Section 2.3. But there is only one equilibrium point, which is determined by factors such as the distribution of income. Let us designate point A as representing the equilibrium autarky consumption bundle (with no redistribution), reflecting Robin's and Karl's respective autarky utility levels.

The Utility Possibility Frontier with Trade

With trade, more goods are available for consumption. This allows us to trace out a new utility possibility frontier, for trade, which lies outside the autarky frontier, as shown in

Figure 3.10. What happens, now, in the absence of redistribution? If the trade consumption point lies to the northeast of the autarky consumption point, like point C, then both Robin and Karl are better off – they both have a higher utility – than they did under autarky. In this case trade is a Pareto improvement over autarky. Trade will not be controversial because everyone is better off (or at least no one is worse off).

With trade, there are more goods available for consumption, which shifts out the utility possibility frontier. However, there is no guarantee that the utility level of each group is higher despite the shift in the frontier. While both groups are better off at point C than at point A, one group is worse off at point B than at point A. Redistributing goods from one group to another may be necessary to make both groups better off after trade.

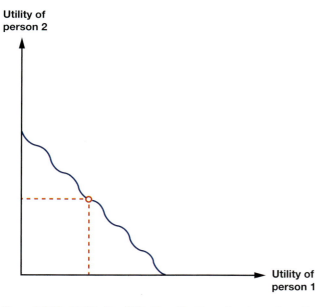

Figure 3.9 The Utility Possibility Frontier The utility shows the utility levels of two individuals or group between whom a fixed amount of goods is divided. At the end points, all of the goods are allocated to one individual or group and none to the other.

Now suppose that the trade consumption point does not lie to the northeast of the autarky consumption point. Suppose it lies to the northwest, like point B. Then trade is not a Pareto improvement over autarky; one individual, Karl, is better off with trade but the other, Robin, is worse off. To ensure that trade is a Pareto improvement, we would need to redistribute enough goods from Karl to Robin to slide down the utility possibility frontier and move from point B to point C, or at least far enough to end up to the right of the vertical line through point A.

Thus, trade is a *potential* Pareto improvement over autarky, because it is possible to redistribute the goods between the two individuals and make both of them better off. Note that the reverse is not true: autarky is *not* a potential Pareto improvement over trade. It is impossible to redistribute an autarky bundle of goods and make both individuals better off than they would have been under trade. (In Figure 3.9, no point on the autarky UPF lies northeast of any point on the trade UPF, simply because the autarky UPF lies entirely inside the trade UPF.)

Many economists think that this analysis explains the different reactions to globalization by blue-collar workers and white-collar workers in the United States. Since the US imports many manufactured goods but exports goods with high intellectual-property content, blue-collar workers in the Rust Belt of America's Midwest and Northeast have been hurt by trade, while white-collar workers in Silicon Valley have benefitted from it. We will explore this issue further in Chapter 5.

The distributional aspects of trade have important implications for the politics of trade. In Figure 3.10, if trade leads to consumption at point B, if Karl controls the political system, then the outcome will be trade, with no compensation paid to Robin. Why? Because Karl is in charge, and he is better off with trade. But if Robin controls the political system, he will prefer point A, under autarky. In that case, however, Karl might be able to use some of his gains at Point B to compensate – or, to put it crudely, bribe – Robin into allowing trade. Thus, depending on who benefits from trade and who is represented in a nation's legislature, some horse trading might be needed in order to get a majority of legislators to enact policies that expand trade.

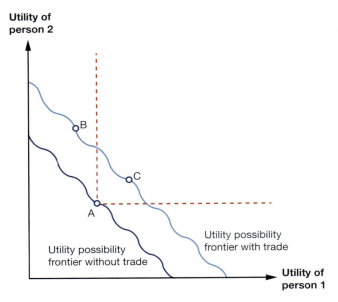

Figure 3.10 Trade and Compensation Because trade leads to more goods being available to an economy, the utility possibility frontier with trade is shifted out from that under autarky. If the starting point under autarky is point A, then if trade leads to a new point B, then person 1 is worse off and person 2 is better off. If some of the gains to person 2 can be redistributed to person 1, we can end up at point C, in which both individuals are better off, and trade is a Pareto improvement.

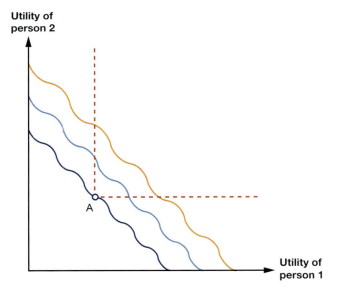

Figure 3.11 The Utility Possibility Frontier with Static and Dynamic Gains from Trade The static gains from trade yield small gains, so the utility possibility frontier shifts out slightly. Given point A as our reference, the chances that the static gains make trade a Pareto improvement is very slight. The dynamic gains are much larger than the static gains, shifting out the utility possibility frontier much more, making it more likely that trade is a Pareto improvement.

Compensation and redistribution policies are debated by economic policy analysts. Some worry that, as a practical matter, those whose income falls are not compensated for their losses, and policies that lead to more trade might also increase inequality (a topic considered in Chapter 5). Others worry that establishing too generous a safety net would be expensive and lead to higher taxes that might reduce the incentive to work. There is no easy way of determining the right balance between these tradeoffs.

Pareto Improvement with Dynamic Gains from Trade

The larger the gains from trade, the more goods are available to those in the economy and the more the UPF is shifted outward. This increases the likelihood that trade will be a Pareto-improvement over autarky. Therefore, large gains from trade diminish the potential need for compensation. Put differently, static gains from trade are less likely to lead to a Pareto improvement than dynamic gains from trade.

To illustrate this point, Figure 3.11 shows the original autarky utility possibility frontier along with two other UPFs, where the one that lies farther out represents bigger gains from trade. The key point is this: the farther the UPF with trade is from the autarky UPF, the larger the range of points on the trade UPF that lie northwest of the autarky equilibrium – and, therefore, the smaller the likelihood that compensation will be needed because someone will be worse off from trade.

The dynamic gains from trade means that more goods are available to a country, and hence the utility possibility frontier shifts out more than with just static gains from trade. This means that it is more likely that all groups are better off with trade than without.

Considering this insight, we might expect that trade agreements promising small, static gains from trade will be fiercely contested. For example, in 1994, the North American Free Trade Agreement (NAFTA) established free trade in goods and services between the United States, Canada, and Mexico. NAFTA involved a relatively minor reduction in US trade barriers, which would be expected to produce a relatively small expansion of trade, and hence a relatively small increase in income. Consequently, there was almost no chance that NAFTA would be a Pareto improvement for the United States. Therefore, it is no surprise that

NAFTA was hotly debated in the United States when it was being considered in 1993, and it continues to be controversial more than a quarter century later.

By contrast, policy changes that bring about large, dynamic gains from trade will face little domestic opposition. For example, China's decision to open up to world markets in 1978 has led to huge gains and breathtaking improvements in Chinese standards of living. Incomes have risen so sharply that there is hardly anyone in China who is worse off (in absolute economic terms) than they would have been under autarky. China's opening may have constituted a Pareto improvement. But, if everyone is better off, why did China not reform earlier? The answer: politics and the ideology of communism under Mao Zedong. As Steve Radelet wrote in his 2016 book *The Great Surge*: "In 1976, Mao single-handedly and dramatically changed the direction of global poverty with one simple act: he died."

Thus, while there are some groups in the United States who would be happy to abolish NAFTA and reduce US trade with Mexico, it would probably be hard to find many people in China who would want to roll back that nation's economic reforms and withdraw from world trade, at least for economic reasons.

CONCLUSION

In this chapter, we further developed our understanding of gains from trade. For a country considered as a whole, trade is better than autarky – but the terms of trade (the price of exports relative to imports) determines the size of the gains from trade. A fall in the price of a country's exports or a rise in the price of a country's imports constitute a deterioration in the country's terms of trade and make it worse off. Although the country will still not be worse off than under autarky, it can be much worse off than before. Countries whose exports consists largely, or entirely, of a single commodity are especially at risk of this happening, since the relative price of their export good tends to fluctuate more than the relative price of a more diverse range of exports.

Gains from trade for a country as a whole do not guarantee that all individuals in the country are better off. Some may be made worse off, and in that case, compensation may need to be made to them before they will support an open-trade economic policy. Ideally, the gains from trade will be so large that this problem does not arise, because large gains are more likely than small ones to make everyone better off. Large gains tend to be dynamic gains, associated with technology-related increases in productive capacity, rather than the static ones inherent to the switchover from autarky to trade.

SUMMARY

1. Terms of trade refers to the ratio at which exports are exchanged for imports, or the price of exports divided by the price of imports.
2. The more favorable the terms of trade (i.e., the higher the price of a country's exports relative to its imports), the greater the gains from trade.
3. Static gains from trade arise from re-allocating existing resources to take advantage of trade. Dynamic gains from trade arise from using existing resources more productively as a result of trade. Both gains increase a country's real income.
4. For countries behind the world's technological frontier, the dynamic gains from trade can be greater than the static gains from trade.

5. Although trade does not necessarily make every individual in an economy better off, there is always the *possibility* of making everyone better off, through compensation/redistribution. By contrast, compensation cannot be used to make autarky preferable to trade.

KEY CONCEPTS

Balanced trade, page 35
Compensation, page 44
Dynamic gains from trade, page 39
Mercantilism, page 34
Pareto efficient, page 44

Pareto improvement, page 43
Real wage, page 37
Static gains from trade, page 39
Terms of trade, page 36
Utility possibility frontier, page 44

REVIEW QUESTIONS

1. How did mercantilists view exports and imports differently from Adam Smith and most economists?
2. What does it mean to say that trade is balanced?
3. What is a country's terms of trade? What does it mean to say that the terms of trade have improved or deteriorated?
4. What is the difference between the static and dynamic gains from trade? What type of country is more likely to experience dynamic gains from trade? Why is the United States unlikely to reap large dynamic gains from trade?
5. "Trade makes everyone better off." Is that statement true, false, or uncertain?
6. "Autarky can dominate a trade equilibrium as long as compensation is paid to the losers from the move." Comment on that statement.

EXERCISES

1. Suppose a country's autarky relative price of clothing in terms of food is 1. If the world relative price of clothing in terms of food is 2, what will the country export and what will it import? Would the country be better off or worse off if the world relative price of clothing went from 2 to 3?
2. Suppose a country can only produce food, but its consumers like to consume food and clothing. Draw a diagram showing the gains from trade as a result of being able to trade food for clothing. Does real income (at world prices) increase with trade? Does utility increase with trade? In the same diagram, suppose the country's terms of trade improve. Work out the result and diagram it. Must exports of food increase? Must imports of clothing increase?
3. The figure below shows two utility possibility frontiers and three consumption points.
   a. Compared to point A, is person 2's utility higher or lower at point B? What about person 1's utility?
   b. Is point C a Pareto improvement over point B?
   c. Is point B a Pareto improvement over point A?
   d. Is point B a *potential* Pareto improvement over point A?
   e. Is point A a *potential* Pareto improvement over point C?

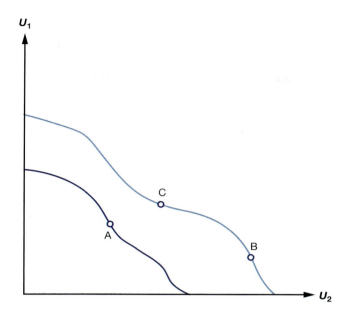

4. Suppose blue-collar workers make up 70% of the labor force and white-collar workers make up the other 30%. What can economists or public policy analysts say about the following scenarios?
   a. Blue-collar workers receive an average income of $40,000; white-collar workers receive an average income of $80,000.
   b. Blue-collar workers receive an average income of $30,000; white-collar workers receive an average income of $90,000.
   c. Blue-collar workers receive an average income of $30,000; white-collar workers receive an average income of $70,000.
   d. Blue-collar workers receive an average income of $50,000; white-collar workers receive an average income of $70,000.

RECOMMENDED RESOURCES

This chapter has used historical examples to illustrate various theoretical points. For a panoramic view of how trade has shaped history, see William J. Bernstein, *A Splendid Exchange: How Trade Shaped the World* (New York: Atlantic Monthly Press, 2008).

Trade has contributed to rapid growth in many parts of the world, particularly Asia in recent decades. For that story, see Michael Shuman, *The Miracle: The Epic Story of Asia's Quest for Wealth* (New York: Harper-Collins, 2009).

Robert Driskill (2012) argues that the distributional aspects of trade are not discussed enough by economists; see Robert Driskill, "Deconstructing the Argument for Free Trade: A Case Study of the Role of Economists in Policy Debates," *Economics and Philosophy* 28(1) (2012): 1–30.

CHAPTER 4

Trade and Comparative Advantage

LEARNING OBJECTIVES

In this chapter, we learn about:
- how productivity differences across countries influence international trade
- why relative, not absolute, productivity differences determine trade patterns
- how labor productivity determines wage rates across countries
- how comparative advantage is determined when many goods are being traded
- recognizing why countries are not in competition with each another for world markets

INTRODUCTION

You may not know it, but the tomato has always been the subject of controversy. Botanists debate whether the tomato is a vegetable or a fruit (it is actually a fruit). Linguists debate whether it is pronounced as to-*may*-toe or to-*mah*-toe (who cares!). Meanwhile, agricultural economists debate where the best place to produce this nutritious and delicious crop might be.

The United States is probably the world's most efficient place to produce tomatoes: a two-row tomato harvester operated by one driver can pick 12–15 acres in one day! Meanwhile, in Mexico, it can take several workers a day to pick just 1–2 acres of tomatoes. And yet, the United States imports tomatoes from Mexico.

If efficiency were the driver behind trade flows, you would not expect this to be the case. Why would a country import a good that it could produce more efficiently itself? The key – and paradoxical – insight on this topic was developed by the nineteenth-century British economist David Ricardo: a country might import a good even if it can produce the good more efficiently than other countries can. Conversely, a country might export a good even if the importing country could produce that good more efficiently themselves. Ricardo's framework also allows us to examine the interaction between wages and technology in determining the pattern of trade.

This chapter seeks to explain Ricardo's surprising conclusion about trade. Countries can have different production possibility frontiers (PPFs) for one of two reasons: different factors of production, or different technology. Differences in factor endowments will be the subject of the next chapter. Here in this chapter, we focus on differences in technology – how they create differences in autarky relative prices and thereby lead to trade.

4.1 ABSOLUTE VERSUS COMPARATIVE ADVANTAGE

The inspiration for Ricardo's work on trade came from Adam Smith. In describing the gains from trade in *The Wealth of Nations*, Smith also discussed the underlying determinants of the patterns of trade. Smith is generally thought to have believed that a country would export whatever goods it produced most efficiently – that is, more efficiently than other countries. Similarly, a country would import goods that other countries could produce more efficiently. And indeed, it seems perfectly reasonable to explain trade in terms of such **absolute advantage**: in any group of trading countries, find the one that can produce a given good most efficiently; it will be the exporter, and the other countries will be the importers.

However, this analysis proved problematic. In 1799, David Ricardo, a London stockbroker, came across the *Wealth of Nations* while on holiday and became so fascinated by it that he began a new life as an economist. In 1817, Ricardo published *On the Principles of Political Economy and Taxation*. It was a breakthrough in bringing logical rigor to economic analysis.

In the chapter he devoted to foreign trade, Ricardo considered the trade in cloth and wine between England and Portugal. He made a key simplifying assumption: there was just one factor of production, labor, used for both goods. If we knew how much labor it took to produce each good in each of the two countries, would it be possible to determine which country would export cloth and which would export wine? Yes, Ricardo said. But then, startlingly, he disagreed with Smith. Ricardo said that between the two countries, the country that was better at producing cloth (i.e., required less labor) would not necessarily be the country that exported it. In other words, trade was not based on a country's absolute **productivity** advantage.

After all, Ricardo pointed out, one country might have an absolute advantage in the production of *both* goods, and yet that country could not export both cloth and wine while importing nothing. Instead, according to Ricardo's analysis, trade would still take place – because countries would specialize in the production of goods in which they had a **comparative advantage**. As this new concept was defined, every country could count on having a comparative advantage at something. Therefore, every country would be able to export and import and so participate in the gains from trade.

Essentially, Ricardo agreed that a country would export the good or goods it was best at producing. But best compared to what? Compared to other countries, was the common answer. Ricardo's rejoinder was that the comparison had to be not only across countries, but across goods, as well: a country would export that good for which the country's *relative* productive efficiency stacked up most favorably – or least unfavorably – against other countries. Efficiency could be measured in terms of labor but could also be measured in terms of goods, using the concept of opportunity cost.

Comparative Advantage, Illustrated

Let us retrace Ricardo's reasoning using the United States and China as our two countries, and food and clothing as the two goods. We will adopt Ricardo's assumption that there is only one factor of production, labor. (This allows us to put off until Chapter 5 the consideration of different factor endowments.) Table 4.1 gives simple, hypothetical figures for the productivity of labor – output per worker – in food and clothing for the United States and China.

In the United States, one worker can produce 18 units of food or 3 units of clothing. In China, one worker can produce two units of food or one unit of clothing. Workers in the United States are more productive, not because of any innate differences between workers in the two countries but simply because US-based workers have access to more capital and

Table 4.1 Absolute Labor Productivity in the United States and China

	Food units per worker	Clothing units per worker
United States	18	3
China	2	1

better technology. In other words, if, say, Chinese farmers were to come to work in the United States, they would also be able to produce 18 units of food, because they would have access to good farmland, modern tractors and other equipment, and the best irrigation and harvesting technology in the world.

In this example, the United States has an absolute advantage over China in producing both goods: it can produce food and clothing more efficiently than China can. Does this productivity advantage mean that the United States should produce its own food and clothing? Should we expect the United States to export both goods to China and import nothing in return? Or consider the situation from China's perspective. In terms of productivity, China is at an absolute disadvantage in producing both goods. Should China leave the production of those goods to the United States and expect to import both, while exporting nothing?

The answer to all these questions is no, because of *comparative* advantage. Notice that the United States produces food nine times more efficiently than China, while it produces clothing only three times more efficiently than China. Because the productivity ratio is greater with food, the United States is said to have a comparative advantage in the production of food. Conversely, China is just 11% (1/9) as efficient as the United States in producing food, but it is 33% (1/3) as efficient in the production of clothing. China does not have an absolute productivity advantage in producing either good. But because its relative productivity is greater in clothing, China is said to have a comparative advantage in clothing.

Opportunity Cost

Differences in comparative advantage translate into differences in **opportunity cost**. A country's opportunity cost of producing food is the amount of clothing it would have to give up producing in order to produce a unit of food. (If this sounds familiar, it should be. This concept is simply the slope of the PPF, or the marginal rate of transformation (MRT), from Chapter 2.) If the United States devotes more of its resources to producing food, it must reduce its production of clothing. If we transfer one worker from clothing production to food production, US output of clothing falls by three units in order for its output of food to go up by 18 units. Therefore, the United States gives up 1/6 of a unit of clothing for every unit of food that it produces.

Similarly, in China, if one worker shifts from producing clothing to producing food, the country's output of clothing will fall by one unit in order for its output of food to go up by two units. Therefore, the country must give up 1/2 a unit of clothing for every unit of food that it produces. The upshot is that China has a higher opportunity cost of producing food: it has to give up 1/2 a unit of clothing to produce one of food, whereas the United States only has to give up 1/6 of a unit of clothing to produce a unit of food. This suggests that we would want the United States to produce food, because it is not giving up as much clothing as China does.

Conversely, if the United States shifts a worker from the food sector to the clothing sector, then the United States gives up six units of food for every unit of clothing added. Meanwhile,

4.1 ABSOLUTE VERSUS COMPARATIVE ADVANTAGE

if China makes the same adjustment in its allocation of labor, that country gives up only two units of food for every unit of clothing added. This suggests that we would want China, and not the United States, to concentrate on clothing production.

Because labor is the only production factor, opportunity costs represent ratios of labor productivities. Table 4.2 summarizes the ratios for each good in each country:

Table 4.2 Relative Labor Productivity in the United States and China

	Food per unit of clothing	Clothing per unit of food
United States	6	1/6
China	2	1/2

Each cell represents the **relative productivity of labor** within a country across the two sectors. For example, the food cell for the United States indicates that the productivity of US workers in the food sector is six times what it is in the clothing sector. In other words, a worker who could produce one unit of clothing can produce six units of food. The food cell for China indicates that the productivity of Chinese workers in the food sector is twice that of Chinese workers in the clothing sector. Looking at the food column in Table 4.2, we see that the United States has a greater relative advantage – a comparative advantage, if you will – in the production of food. Looking at the clothing column, we see that China has a greater relative advantage in producing clothing (because 1/2 is more than 1/6).

Thus, even if the United States can produce both food and clothing more efficiently than China, it still makes sense for the United States to devote its limited resources to producing the good where its relative advantage is greater. As we will see, the United States can export some of its production of that good in exchange for imports from China of the good where the relative advantage lies on China's side.

Autarky Production

We can illustrate the concepts of absolute and comparative advantage by graphing the PPFs of the two countries. To do that, we introduce some notation to set out our assumptions:

- The productivity of a US worker in the food sector is a_F (F for food), and the productivity of a US worker in the clothing sector is a_C. This is the output per worker, or the marginal product of labor, which is taken to be constant (i.e., there are no diminishing returns to labor).
- All US workers earn wage w.
- The economy has a fixed amount of labor that can be used in the production of food or clothing, i.e., $L = L_F + L_C$, where L is the total number of workers in the United States
- All the same variables apply to China, and same fixed-total labor equation holds, but the variables have a $*$ superscript to denote China's status as a foreign country relative to the United States. Thus, workers in China earn wage w^*, and so on.

Table 4.1 presents the absolute productivities of labor for the United States and China in the two sectors: $a_F = 18$, $a_F^* = 2$, $a_C = 3$, and $a_C^* = 1$. The United States has absolute advantage in the production of both goods because $a_F > a_F^*$ and $a_C > a_C^*$.

We can also see, in formal terms, how the relative productivities of labor in Table 4.2 are directly related to opportunity costs, by writing out the production function of each good.

A country's output of food is simply the number of workers in the food sector multiplied by the output per worker in that sector. For the United States, $S_F = a_F L_F$, where S_F is the output (supply) of food, a_F is the (constant) productivity of labor in food production, and L_F is the number of workers in the food sector. Similarly, the production function for clothing is $S_C = a_C L_C$. For China, $S_F^* = a_F^* L_F^*$ and $S_C^* = a_C^* L_C^*$.

The United States' opportunity cost of producing clothing is $\Delta S_F/\Delta S_C$, the change in food produced per unit change in clothing production. Since $\Delta S_F = a_F \Delta L_F$ and $\Delta S_C = a_C \Delta L_C$, it follows that $\Delta S_F/\Delta S_C = (a_F/a_C)(\Delta L_F/\Delta L_C)$. Since we have a fixed amount of labor in the economy that we can allocate either to food or clothing production, $\Delta L = \Delta L_C + \Delta L_F = 0$, which implies that $\Delta L_C = -\Delta L_F$. Therefore, the slope of the PPF is:

$$\Delta S_F/\Delta S_C = -a_F/a_C, \tag{4.1}$$

which corresponds to $a_F/a_C = 6$ in the food cell for the United States in Table 4.2. Thus, except for a difference in sign, the opportunity cost of food equals the productivity of food workers relative to clothing workers.

The one thing we still need, before we can graph either country's production possibility frontier, is a numerical value for the labor force. The United States has approximately 150 million workers; for simplicity let us assume that $L = 150$. If we put all 150 workers in the food sector, we can produce 2,700 units of food ($S_F = a_F L_F = 18 \cdot 150 = 2{,}700$). Similarly, if we put all 150 workers into the clothing sector, we can produce 450 units of clothing ($S_C = a_C L_C = 3 \cdot 150 = 450$). So then, the endpoints of the US production possibility frontier lie at 2,700 units on the food axis and at 450 units on the clothing axis; see Figure 4.1.

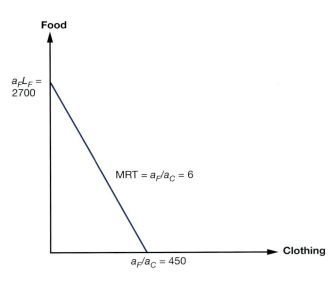

Figure 4.1 The US Production Possibility Frontier The production possibility frontier is the set of all possible production points for the economy, given information on technology and labor supply.

The slope of the PPF at any given point represents the opportunity cost of production, or the marginal rate of transformation (from Chapter 2). When the only factor of production is labor, and the marginal product of labor are constant, the slope of the PPF is constant: $\Delta S_F/\Delta S_C = -a_F/a_C = -18/3 = -6$. The slope also indicates the autarky relative price of clothing in terms of food. Note that this relative price is fixed by production technology and is independent of the indifference curve representing consumer preferences. That is, $p_C/p_F = a_F/a_C = 6$.

We can derive China's PPF, shown in Figure 4.2, in exactly the same way. The labor force of China is approximately 800 million workers. If $L^* = 800$, then China can produce 1,600 units of food and 800 units of clothing. The slope of its PPF will be -2, and the autarky relative price of clothing is $(p_C/p_F)^* = a_F^*/a_C^* = 2$.

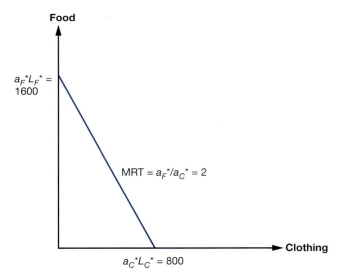

Figure 4.2 China's Production Possibility Frontier The production possibility frontier is the set of all possible production points for the economy, given information on technology and labor supply.

Notice that China is poorer, because its labor is less productive than that of the United States. Despite having a far larger labor force (800 million versus 150 million), China has a production possibility frontier that lies almost entirely inside that of the United States. In practical terms, that means that China's GDP is smaller than that of the United States. Even worse, per capita income in China is much smaller than per capita income in the United States. If both countries just produced food, for example, the United States would have 2,700 units of food using 150 workers, while China would have just 1,600 units of food using 800 workers.

To summarize, there is an important difference between the ratio of productivity (a_F/a_C) and the absolute level of productivity. The ratio of productivity determines the slope of the production possibility frontier, and hence domestic relative prices. The absolute level of productivity determines how far out the production possibility frontier is, and hence how much income a country has.

4.2 COMPARATIVE ADVANTAGE AND THE GAINS FROM TRADE

As the slopes of the two production possibility frontiers (the marginal rate of transformation) indicate, the autarky relative price of clothing is lower in China than in the United States. This price difference will drive trade: we would expect that China will export clothing and the United States will import clothing. Conversely, the relative price of food is higher in China than the United States, so China will import food from the United States.

After trade, the equilibrium price of clothing in terms of food will lie between the two autarky prices, i.e., between 2 and 6. For the sake of convenience, let us assume that the world relative price of clothing in terms of food is 4. (Section 4.3 will discuss where the price comes from.) Then we can sketch the impact on production and consumption and illustrate the gains from trade.

The United States starts at the autarky equilibrium where an indifference curve is tangent to the production possibility frontier. With the opening of trade, the relative price of clothing in the United States falls from 6 to 4, or, conversely, the relative price of food rises from 1/6 to 1/4. The increase in the relative price of food gives US food producers an incentive to increase output and US clothing producers an incentive to decrease output. Consequently, the food sector hires workers away from the clothing sector.

Thus, the United States shifts labor away from producing clothing (whose relative price is now lower than the previous autarky price) to producing food (whose relative price is now higher than the previous autarky price). However, because the production possibility frontier is linear, the cost of producing food in terms of clothing does not increase as more and more food is produced. Therefore, the United States will end up moving all its labor into the food sector and we reach a corner solution. (Because the PPF is linear, there will be no point where MRT $= p_C/p_F$, hence the corner solution.)

Having perfectly specialized in the production of food, and thus producing 2,700 units of food, the United States will export some of this food in exchange for clothing imports along the world price line. Consumption will take place where the slope of the indifference curve (the marginal rate of substitution, or MRS (as discussed in Chapter 2) is equal to the world relative price line. This is shown in Figure 4.3. Consumption will take place at D_C and D_F. Exports will be $S_F - D_F$ and imports will be $D_C - S_C$, which is just D_C, since there is no domestic production of clothing ($S_C = 0$).

In China, the opposite occurs. As a result of trade, the relative price of clothing rises from 2 to 4. There is an incentive for China's producers to expand production of clothing by hiring

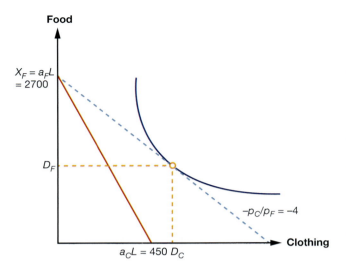

Figure 4.3 US Trade in the Ricardo Model This figure shows the US production possibility frontier and illustrates that when the world relative price of clothing is 4 (as opposed to the slope of the production possibility frontier being 6) the United States will export food and import clothing, enabling it to reach a higher indifference curve with trade.

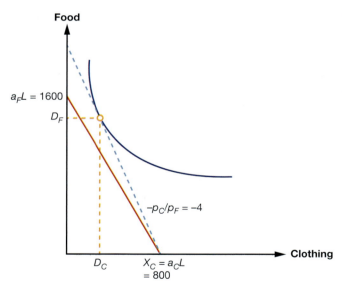

Figure 4.4 China's Trade in the Ricardo Model This figure shows China's production possibility frontier and illustrates that when the world relative price of clothing is 4 (as opposed to the slope of the production possibility frontier being 2) China will export clothing and import food, enabling it to reach a higher indifference curve with trade.

more workers from the food sector, whose output falls as a result. Thus, labor moves into the production of clothing (whose relative price is now higher than the previous autarky price) and away from the production of food (whose relative price is now lower than the previous autarky price). Because the production possibility frontier is linear, China will move all of its labor into the clothing sector.

As Figure 4.4 shows, China perfectly specializes in the production of clothing. China will produce 800 units of clothing and will export some of this clothing in exchange for imports of food along the world price line. Consumption will take place where the slope of the indifference curve (MRS) is equal to the slope of the world relative price line.

These figures illustrate how, in this two-country, two-good example, each country ends up at a consumption point that lies on a higher indifference curve than the country could have reached under autarky. The United States and China both benefit from trade when China produces clothing, even though the United States is more efficient at producing that good, i.e., $a_C > a_C^*$.

Thus, the United States has a comparative advantage in food because it has a lower autarky relative price of food or, conversely, a higher relative price of clothing: $p_C/p_F > (p_C/p_F)^*$. And this arises because the United States has a relative productivity advantage in producing food:

$$a_F/a_C > a_F^*/a_C^* \qquad (4.2)$$

For some in the technologically advanced country, this consequence of comparative advantage can seem unfair. A US shift to producing food and importing clothing drives domestic clothing producers out of business, even though they are more efficient than their Chinese counterparts. What trade makes clear, however, is that US clothing producers are not just competing against Chinese clothing producers. They are also competing against the enormous advantage that US food producers have over Chinese food producers. If US clothing makers wish to remain in business, and to export to China, they do not simply have to exceed the productivity of Chinese clothing producers, rather, they have to exceed the efficiency of Chinese clothing producers by more (by a greater multiple) than US food producers exceed the efficiency of Chinese food producers.

Meanwhile, China has a comparative advantage in producing clothing, because its autarky relative price of clothing is lower than the one in the United States, i.e., $(p_C/p_F)^* < (p_C/p_F)$. Therefore, China will export clothing, even though it is less efficient at producing clothing than the United States, i.e., $a_C^* < a_C$. In fact, you may sometimes read that a poor developing country is unable to benefit from trade because "it does not have a comparative advantage in anything." Such a statement is false: a country always has a comparative advantage in something and can always benefit from trade. And so can its trading partners.

IN PRACTICE   Absolute versus Comparative Advantage: United States–Japan

Our analysis of productivity implies an important difference between comparative and absolute advantage. Comparative advantage – the relative productivity of countries in producing particular goods – determines the pattern of trade: which country exports a given good, and which imports it. However, absolute advantage – the absolute level of productivity, within an industry or across the entire economy – is still very important. Absolute productivity determines how far out a country's production possibility frontier lies, and therefore how high its national income is.

How can we see these concepts in action?

Figure 4.5 shows one measure of productivity – GDP per hour worked – for leading countries. The United States, France, and Germany rank among the highest in the world in this measure. It may come as more of a surprise that GDP per hour worked is relatively low in Japan, only about two-thirds of the level in the United States. Although Japan is known for its prowess in manufacturing production, the bulk of its economy is in the service sector, as is true with most major economies. And low productivity in services can drag down the economy-wide average productivity.

This can be seen in Figure 4.6, which shows labor productivity in Japan for various sectors of the economy. The figure is taken from a 2004 book by former McKinsey executive, William Lewis, *The Power of Productivity*. It compares productivity levels in Japan to those in the United States, which is benchmarked at 100. This allows us to visualize both absolute and comparative productivity advantage across the two countries and the size of the sector in terms of employment. Japan has an absolute advantage in producing steel, automotive parts, metalworking, cars, and consumer electronics. The United States has an absolute advantage in producing computers, soap and detergents, beer, and a large labor productivity advantage in retail, construction, and food processing.

These levels tell us something about the pattern of trade. In this particular case, there may be no conflict between absolute and comparative advantage in the sense that both countries will export goods in which they have an absolute advantage. But in the years prior to this, when Japan did not have an absolute advantage in any product, Japan's exports would be guided by comparative advantage, where its productive disadvantage was the least compared to the United States

Although Japan has an absolute advantage in many manufacturing industries, why is Japan's per capita income only about 65% of that in the United States? The figure gives us a key: the width of the bars indicates the relative amount of labor devoted to each

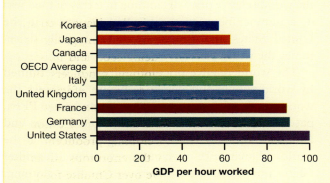

Figure 4.5 Labor Productivity in 2021 in Selected OECD Countries
Source: OECD 2022, Level of GDP per capita and productivity, OECD Annual National Accounts.

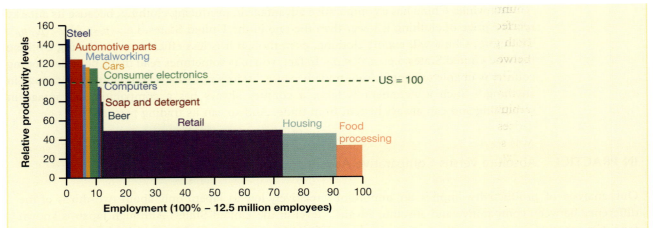

Figure 4.6 Relative Labor Productivity by Industry, United States and Japan
Source: Used with the permission of University of Chicago Press, William W. Lewis, The Power of Productivity: Wealth, Poverty, and the Threat to Global Stability, © 2004; permission conveyed through Copyright Clearance Centre, Inc.

sector of the economy. Japan has relatively poor productivity in very large sectors of the economy, notably retail, construction, and food. While it may have a very large productivity advantage in making steel, that sector of the economy is so small and employs such a small fraction of the labor force that it alone cannot make Japan a rich country.

The policy implication is that Japan, if it should want to increase its standard of living, should focus on improving its productivity in the lagging sectors of retail and house construction. Trying to make its manufacturing producers even more "competitive" on international markets is a diversion from the real factors holding back Japan's economy.

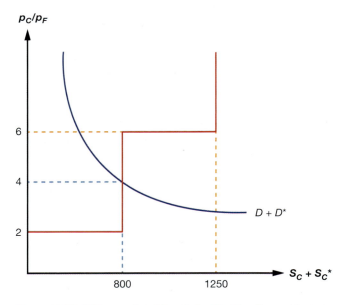

Figure 4.7 World Demand and Supply for Clothing The world price is determined by the intersection of world supply and demand. World supply is a step function based on the linear production possibility frontiers (with the flat portions at the autarky prices of the two countries). World demand is a downward-sloping function based on price.

4.3 WHAT DETERMINES THE TERMS OF TRADE?

In the example we just considered, we assumed that the world relative price of clothing in terms of food was 4, a number between the two autarky prices in the United States and China. But what actually determines the world price?

The world relative price of clothing is determined by world supply and demand. Figure 4.7 shows the world supply of clothing as derived from the two PPFs, based on the assumption that the United States and China are the only two countries in the world. If the world relative price of clothing is below 2, neither China nor the United States will produce clothing. If the world relative price is exactly 2, then China can supply up to 800 units of clothing. If the price is above 2 and below 6, China cannot produce any more clothing, but the price is not high enough for the United States to start producing clothing. At a price of 6, the United States can produce up to 450 units of clothing, bringing the total supply from the two countries potentially up to 1,250. At prices above 6, both China and the United States are perfectly specialized in the production of clothing and cannot produce any more. Thus, if both goods are produced, the world price will end up somewhere between 2 and 6, that is, between the two autarky relative prices.

The world demand curve for clothing slopes downward and, in this example, intersects the world supply curve at a price equal to 4. (The precise location of this demand curve is arbitrary unless we specify an equation for it.) Note that this price is between the two autarky prices of 2 in China and 6 in the United States This is how the world price of 4 in Section 4.3 was set: by the intersection of the demand curve with the supply curve.

We can learn several things from Figure 4.7. First, if world demand for clothing were to increase, the relative price of clothing would increase. Since China is exporting clothing, this would constitute an improvement in China's **terms of trade**. From Figure 4.4, we can see that China would benefit from a higher relative price of clothing because then it would be able to reach a higher indifference curve. With a higher relative price of clothing, a higher amount of food could be imported with the income generated by China's clothing exports. In this case, the world relative price of clothing would be moving further away from China's autarky relative price of clothing. This illustrates a point made in Chapter 3: a greater difference between a country's autarky relative price and the world relative price means greater gains from trade.

Conversely, since the United States is importing clothing, an increase in the price of clothing would constitute a deterioration in the US terms of trade. The gains from trade would shrink for the United States, because the world relative price of clothing would be moving closer to its autarky relative price. If the world price of clothing were to rise to 6, there would be no gains from trade for the United States at all. The world price would equal the US autarky price.

As we learned in Chapter 3, although trade as such is advantageous to both countries, changes in the terms of trade are zero-sum: one country wins, and the other country loses. In this case, the higher price of clothing favors China, which exports clothing, and harms the United States, which imports clothing.

One final point: if the world relative price of clothing happens to lie outside of the two autarky prices of 2 and 6, then there must be some other countries in the mix that we are not accounting for, and hence the demand curve as shown is irrelevant. If so, and the world price lies outside these autarky prices, then the United States and China will trade not with one another. Instead, they will trade with the rest of the world. If the relative price of clothing were less than 2, the United States and China would both import clothing from, and export food to, the rest of the world. If the relative price of clothing were greater than 6, the United States and China would both export clothing to, and import food, from the rest of the world.

4.4 WAGES AND PRODUCTIVITY

This analytical framework also allows us to determine the relative wage between the United States and China. Because labor is the only factor of production, the price of the goods simply reflects the labor costs of producing the goods. For example, in the United States, which is perfectly specialized in the production of food, the price of food is simply the labor cost of producing one unit of food. That cost is the wage rate (the cost per worker) times the number of workers it takes to produce a unit of food, where the latter quantity is simply the reciprocal of productivity, $1/a_F$, or the number of workers per unit of output.

Therefore, we can write: $p_F = w(1/a_F)$, or $p_F = w/a_F$. This means that the wage rate in the United States is the price of food multiplied by the productivity of labor in the food sector, i.e., $w = p_F a_F$. In other words, workers are paid their marginal value product: each worker's wage is equal to the market value of what he or she produces, because each worker produces a_F of output that can be sold at price p_F. The situation is similar in China, which produces clothing. There, the wage is $w^* = p_C a_C^*$.

Because we do not have information on the individual price of either food or clothing, we cannot solve for the wage in the United States or China. However, we do know the *relative* price of the two goods, and therefore we can solve for the *relative* wage across the two countries. By dividing the US wage equation by the Chinese wage equation, we get:

$$\frac{w}{w^*} = \left(\frac{p_F}{p_C}\right)\left(\frac{a_F}{a_C^*}\right) \tag{4.3}$$

What this equation tells us is that the wage rate in the United States relative to that in China depends on two things. First, it depends on the terms of trade from the standpoint of the United States, which is the relative price of food in terms of clothing, because the United States exports food and imports clothing. Second, it depends on the relative productivity of labor in the sectors in which labor is employed. (Notice that here the relative productivity is both a cross-country and a cross-sector comparison: the productivity of US food workers divided by the productivity of China's clothing workers.)

Using equation (4.1), we can calculate the relative wage for our hypothetical numerical example. If $p_F/p_C = 1/4$, $a_F = 18$, and $a_C^* = 1$, then $w/w^* = 18/4 = 4.5$, meaning that wages are four and a half times higher in the United States than they are in China. (In fact, in 2021, the average wage in the United States was about 3.5 times the average wage in China.)

Of course, China's economy has been growing rapidly in recent decades, because of improvements in labor productivity due to the adoption of better technology. In essence, China has been increasing its a_F^* and its a_C^*. What happens to wages? Suppose China is able to double its productivity in both sectors, increasing a_F^* from 2 to 4 and increasing a_C^* from 1 to 2. This improvement in technology shifts China's production possibility frontier outward. Now, with the same amount of labor, China can produce 3,200 units instead of 1,600, or 1,600 units of clothing instead of 800. However, because the slope of the production possibility frontier has not changed, the country's autarky relative price has not changed. Therefore, its comparative advantage with respect to the United States will not change: China will still export clothing and import food, if the world relative price remains between the two autarky price ratios. (However, if the productivity improvement is more rapid in one sector than another, China's autarky relative price will change. A rapid improvement in China's clothing productivity would simply reinforce its comparative advantage in clothing. It would have to increase its food productivity dramatically to acquire a comparative advantage in the production of food.)

Although the pattern of trade does not change, this productivity improvement is unambiguously good for China. Its workforce has become more productive, and therefore its wage rate will rise. We can see that directly because the equation for the wage rate is $w^* = p_C a_C^*$, so when a_C^* increases, so does w^*. When a_C^* is doubled, the wage rate relative to the United States will increase from 22% [$w^*/w = (p_C/p_F)(a_C^*/a_F) = 4 \cdot 1/18 = 2/9$] to 44%. Indeed, increasing the productivity of its labor force is the most direct way for a country to increase its average wage and improve its standard of living.

From the perspective of the United States, its *relative* wage will fall from 4.5 times that in China to 2.25 times that in China. Does this mean that the United States is worse off? Not at all! The actual wage in the United States will remain unchanged. (Recall that the wage in the United States is determined by the marginal value product of labor – $w = p_F a_F$ – so wages do not change unless the price of food changes or the productivity of labor changes.) Wages in China, however, will rise, narrowing the wage gap between the countries. In fact, the impact on the United States might be a positive one: China's growth might increase the supply of clothing, drive down its price, and thereby improve the US terms of trade.

Thus, while a country with an absolute productivity advantage over other countries will not export all goods, it still has an important advantage over other countries. Its workers are more productive than workers in other countries, and therefore labor will command a higher wage. In general, per capita incomes will be higher in countries that have a high level of productivity.

Evidence on Productivity and Wages

This discussion has a striking implication: if the average wage in a country reflects the productivity of its labor force, differences in wages across countries should reflect differences in productivity. Is this true? The answer, by and large, is yes.

Figure 4.8 shows the relationship between labor productivity and the average wage across countries, taking the United States as the benchmark (United States = 100). The United States has the highest productivity and the highest wages of just about any country in the world. Other countries are generally arrayed along the 45-degree line, indicating the close relationship between a country's labor productivity and its wages.

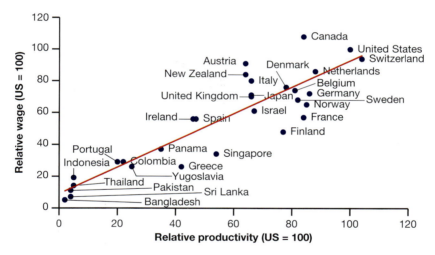

Figure 4.8 Wages and Productivity across Countries

Source: Used with the permission of the University of Chicago Press, Daniel Trefler © 1993; permission conveyed through Copyright Clearance Centre, Inc.

In essence, this figure tells the story behind Adam Smith's *Wealth of Nations*. What determines the average wage earned by workers in a given country? The answer is: the productivity of labor in that country. How can a country become rich? By exploiting raw materials? By receiving more foreign aid? Not really; instead, increasing a country's national income depends on increasing the productivity of its workforce and shifting out its production possibility frontier.

As Paul Krugman (1990, 13) once put it, "Productivity isn't everything, but in the long run it is almost everything." This raises the question of how productivity can be improved. There is no easy answer. Many economists believe that encouraging investment in human and physical capital accumulation (education and machinery) and improving incentives to create and adopt new technology might help.

In our simple Ricardian model developed above, China is a poorer country than the United States with much lower wages. If China wants to become a richer country and see its wages increase, it can either hope for an improvement in its terms of trade (an increase in the relative price of clothing) or it can improve its labor productivity in clothing production (increase a_C^*). In either case, the country can reach a higher indifference curve, but there is a difference between the two. The problem with hoping for an improvement in the terms of trade is that what goes up can go down: the terms of trade might deteriorate in the future, putting the economy back to where it started. Furthermore, there is not much a country can do about its terms of trade.

By contrast, an improvement in technology that increases the productivity of labor is likely to be permanent and therefore irreversible. In fact, China has achieved strong and sustained economic growth by adopting new technology and improving its productivity, allowing its wages to rise rapidly. As Figure 4.9 shows, hourly compensation in manufacturing in China rose from $1 in 2007 to more than $4 in 2014 and has continued to increase significantly since then. By contrast, another emerging market – India – has also modernized, but at a much slower pace. As a result, the growth in wages has been much slower in India than in China. In fact, as late as 2005, wage costs in India were higher than in China, something that is clearly no longer the case.

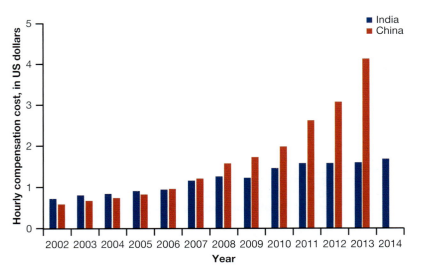

Figure 4.9 Hourly Compensation Costs, Manufacturing, China and India, 2002–2014
Source: The Conference Board, International Labor Comparisons program, February 2018.

Because China's productivity growth has been so impressive over the past few decades, the country's average wage has risen quickly, closing the gap with the United States. As the theory suggested, this means the relative US wage has fallen. According to one set of data, the relative US wage declined from almost 30 times that in China in 2000 to about 6 in 2011 and then to 3.5 in 2023. Of course, the absolute US wage has risen during this period, but at a slower rate in line with US productivity growth.

IN PRACTICE   Are Countries in Competition with One Another?

The analysis in this chapter has suggested that, regardless of whether a country's production technology is superior or inferior to other nations', the country can still benefit from trade. Yet popular discussions of international trade often describe countries as being in fierce competition with one another. These discussions often suggest that countries are pitted against each other, just as individual firms compete against one another for market share.

Firms certainly do compete with one another, sometimes strenuously. Although competition between companies is beneficial for consumers, it tends to be a zero-sum game for the companies themselves. If Coke comes out with a better soft drink than Pepsi, Coke's sales and profits increase, usually at the expense of Pepsi's. Unless demand for all soft drinks increases, what is good for Coke is likely to be bad for Pepsi. Similarly, two countries exporting to the same market – the United States and Australia seeking to sell beef or wheat to Japan – are in competition with one another for sales. Are two countries in competition with one another when they trade with each other? In the case of two-way trade, is what is good for China bad for the United States? As we have seen in this chapter, the answer seems to be no – because both countries benefit from one trading with one another. China can grow rapidly and increase its wages, with no adverse effect on – and possibly even benefit for – the United States.

In a provocative essay, "Competitiveness: A Dangerous Obsession," Paul Krugman (1994a) argued that:

> it is simply not the case that the world's leading nations are to any important degree in economic competition with each other, or that any of their major economic problems can be attributed to failures to compete on world markets. The growing obsession in most advanced nations with international competitiveness should be seen, not as a well-founded concern, but as a view held in the face of overwhelming contrary evidence.

He reaches this conclusion by pointing out that "the growth rate of living standards essentially equals the growth rate of domestic productivity – not productivity relative to competitors, but simply domestic productivity. Even though world trade is larger than ever before, national living standards are overwhelmingly determined by domestic factors rather than by some competition for world markets."

As an example, suppose US productivity growth is 2% per year while China's productivity growth is 4% per year. We would expect that average US wages would increase 2% a year. If China's productivity growth were to fall to 1% per year, we would still expect average US wages would increase 2% per year. In other words, the growth in the US standard of living is determined by domestic factors, not by what is happening in other countries.

In another essay, "Does Third World Growth Hurt First World Prosperity" (1994b), Krugman criticizes the idea that a country can increase its productivity while keeping its wages low, thereby reducing prices and undercutting other countries in world markets. As he writes:

> Economic history offers no example of a country that experienced long-term productivity growth without a roughly equal rise in real wages... The idea that somehow the old rules no longer apply, that new entrants on the world economic stage will always pay low wages even as their productivity rises to advanced-country levels, has no basis in actual experience.

He goes on to add:

> Some economic writers try to refute this proposition by pointing to particular industries in which relative wages don't match relative productivity. For example, shirtmakers in Bangladesh, who are almost half as productive as shirtmakers in the United States, receive far less than half the US wage rate.

Yet this is exactly what standard theory suggests will be the case. To see that, we must consider a model with more than just two goods, as in Section 4.5.

4.5 THE MULTI-GOOD RICARDO MODEL

The two-country, two-good Ricardo model illustrates how comparative advantage determines the patterns of trade: each country has a comparative advantage in exactly one good; it exports that good and imports the other. But what happens, now, when we add a third good, or several more goods? Now the idea of comparative advantage is not so sharply defined.

To illustrate this in concrete terms, let us consider five goods that the United States and China could produce. Once again, we will use a_i to indicate US labor productivity (output per worker) in industry i and a_i^* to denote labor productivity in industry i in China. Assume we have a configuration of labor productivity across five goods as summarized in Table 4.3.

Table 4.3 Productivity in the United States and China

	Aircraft	Machinery	Electronics	Shoes	Clothing
United States (a_i)	15	24	50	40	30
China (a_i^*)	1	2	5	8	10
a_i/a_i^*	15	12	10	5	3

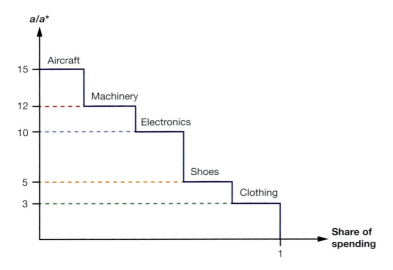

Figure 4.10 United States–China Relative Productivity, by Industry This diagram ranks industries by declining US relative advantage. The US productivity advantage is greatest in aircraft, where US productivity is 15 times greater than China, and least in clothing, where its productivity is 3 times greater than China.

The United States has an absolute productivity advantage with all goods, because $a_i > a_i^*$ in every case. Across these goods, the relative US productivity advantage is as much as 15 and as little as 3. Figure 4.10 displays this graphically and ranks the goods according to declining US relative productivity advantage.

Since each country must produce at least one good, it seems pretty obvious that the United States will produce aircraft (where the relative US advantage is greatest) and China will produce clothing (where the US relative advantage is least). But which country will produce the goods in the middle? For these goods, the idea of comparative advantage is not immediately obvious. It turns out that the country with the lowest costs – and hence the lowest prices – in machinery, electronics, and shoes will produce those goods.

So what determines the cost of production? Since there is only one factor of production (labor) and no profits, the cost of producing a good is the labor cost of production, which – with perfect competition – also equals the price of the good. The labor cost per unit is the wage rate times the number of workers required per unit of output. We have already formalized these relationships as $p_i = w/a_i$, where w is the wage rate and $1/a_i$ is the labor (workers) required per unit of good i produced. (If a_i is output per worker in industry i, then $1/a_i$ is the number of workers per unit of output in industry i.)

So, for example, if the wage is $20 per hour and one worker can produce 5 units of output per hour – meaning that it takes 1/5 of a worker-hour to produce one unit – then the **unit labor cost** is $20(1/5) = $4. Note that all labor is perfectly substitutable and there is one economy-wide wage rate: all workers earn w, regardless of where they happened to be employed (which is why there is no subscript).

Therefore, the United States will produce any good for which it can charge a lower price than China, i.e., $p_i < p_i^*$, which can only happen if it has a lower unit labor cost than China, $w/a_i < w^*/a_i^*$. To continue with the above example, if labor is cheaper in the foreign country, costing only $10 per hour, but it takes 1 full worker-hour to produce one unit of the good, then the home country will have a lower unit labor cost and be able to charge a lower price, $4 < $10. This illustrates how low wages do not always translate into low costs. If one country's wages are low but productivity is even lower compared to another country's wages and productivity, the first country will actually have higher costs of production.

Rewriting $w/a_i < w^*/a_i^*$, we find that the home country will produce a good if $w/w^* < a_i/a_i^*$. In other words, if the US relative wage is less than its relative productivity for the good, the United States will have an overall cost advantage over China.

For example, let us say that the average wage in the United States is 10 times the average wage in China. Then the United States will only export goods for which its productivity is more than 10 times that of China. And the United States will import goods for which its productivity advantage is less than 10 times that in China. To consider the situation from China's perspective: its wages are one-tenth those of the United States. China will only export those goods for which its productivity is more than one tenth that of the United States, and it will import those goods for which its productivity is less than one tenth that of the United States.

Turning to the numbers in Figure 4.10, if China's relative wage is 1/10, then China will produce and export shoes and clothing. Although their workers are only 1/5 or 1/3 as productive as US workers in these sectors, their workers are only paid 1/10 the wage. As a result, the unit costs of producing these goods are lower in China than in the United States. (This is precisely the point made by Paul Krugman in the last paragraph of the second In Practice box)

Electronics are a special case: although US workers are 10 times more productive than their Chinese counterparts, they are paid 10 times the wage rate. When the two countries have the same costs for a good, $w/a = w^*/a^*$, both countries will produce the good. In this example, even though China's wages are lower, it does not have an overall cost advantage. China's lower wages do not allow it to "undercut" the market with lower costs; those low wages simply reflect the lower productivity of its workers. Because the two countries' unit costs are equal, both countries will produce electronics.

This analysis also sets limits on US wages relative to those in China. Wages are bounded by the productivity differences of the extreme goods, aircraft and clothing. American wages can be no more than 15 times higher than wages in China (in which case both countries would produce aircraft, and China would produce all the other goods, as well) and no less than three (in which case both countries would produce clothing, and the United States would produce all the other goods, as well). If US wages were more than 15 times higher than Chinese wages, the United States would not have a unit labor cost advantage in any good. If US wages were less than three times Chinese wages, China would not have a unit labor cost advantage in any good.

If the US wage must be at least three times greater than China's but no more than 15 times China's, what exactly determines the relative wage in this diagram? The relative wage can be determined using the assumption that trade is balanced, i.e., that the value of US exports equals the value of US imports. Since we are assuming there are just two countries, let θ equal the share of income, regardless of where it is earned, spent on US goods and θ^* equal the share of total income spent on Chinese goods, so that $\theta + \theta^* = 1$. (This assumption, that consumer preferences are the same in the two countries so that everyone spends a given fraction of their income on US and Chinese goods, may be implausible but it greatly simplifies the analysis.) US national income is the total wage income of labor, or wL, and China's national income is w^*L^*. The value of US imports is the US income, wL, times the fraction, θ^*, which is spent on Chinese goods, or $wL\theta^*$. The value of US exports is the share of China's income (w^*L^*) that is spent on American goods, or $w^*L^*\theta$. When trade is balanced, $wL\theta^* = w^*L^*\theta$. Rearranging this equation and using $1 - \theta$ for θ^* gives us the following:

$$\frac{w}{w^*} = \left(\frac{L^*}{L}\right)\left(\frac{\theta}{1-\theta}\right) \tag{4.4}$$

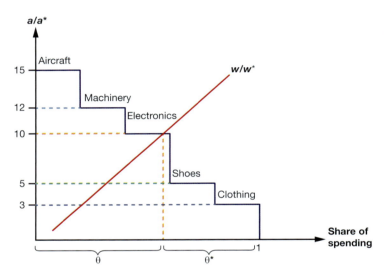

Figure 4.11 Determining Production and Wages in the Multi-good Ricardo Model This diagram combines the relative productivity schedule (from Figure 4.10) with an upward-sloping relative wage line that is based on balanced trade. The intersection of these two schedules determines the equilibrium relative wage between the two countries and the production of goods in one country or another (or possibly both).

This expression gives us a positive relationship between w/w^* and θ. If the right side of the equation increases, because the share of spending on US goods, θ, goes up, then the left side of the equation, w/w^*, must increase as well. In other words, if there is more spending on US goods and US exports go up, then something must push up US imports to keep trade balanced. That something is a higher relative wage for the United States. Therefore, in Figure 4.11, we have an upward-sloping w/w^* schedule that intersects the relative productivity line at some point. In the figure as drawn, the intersection determines the relative wage to be 10, as previously assumed. Both countries produce electronics, the US produces aircraft and machinery, and China produces shoes and clothing.

But now let us say that China improves its productivity by adopting better technology. In this case, all of the a_i^*'s in China increase, as in Table 4.4.

Table 4.4 Productivity in the United States and China

	Aircraft	Machinery	Electronics	Shoes	Clothing
United States	15	24	50	40	30
China in 2010	1	2	5	8	10
China in 2020	1.5	3	10	20	30
Old a/a*	15	12	10	5	3
New a/a*	10	8	5	2	1

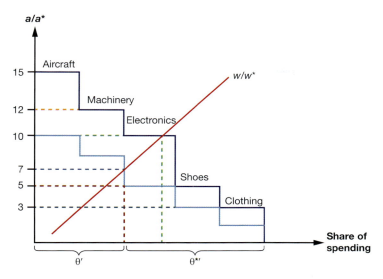

Figure 4.12 Productivity Improvement in China This figure shows how a productivity improvement in China shifts the relative productivity schedule downward. This yields a new equilibrium relative wage rate and more industries can produce in China.

These productivity improvements shift the whole relative productivity schedule downward, as shown in Figure 4.12. This shift leads to a new, lower relative wage rate, perhaps 7. Before the productivity change, the US produced aircraft, machinery, and electronics; after the productivity change, the US produces just aircraft and machinery. Before the productivity change, China produced electronics, shoes, and clothing; after the productivity change they still do, but they are now the sole producers of electronics.

Does this productivity improvement make China better off? We would expect that it would: an increase in productivity would shift out China's production possibility frontier, enabling the country to make more goods with the same labor force and thereby allowing it to reach a higher indifference curve. We can show the improvement in real income using our notation. China's real income is their nominal income divided by the price of goods. In terms of its domestic goods, China's real income is $w^*L^*/(w^*/a_i^*)$, or $L^*a_i^*$. This has unambiguously increased, because the a_i^*s have increased. In terms of US goods, China's real income is $w^*L^*/(w/a_i)$, or $(w^*/w)(L^*a_i)$. This, too, has unambiguously increased, because w^*/w has increased. As expected, China's real income is unambiguously higher because of its improved productivity.

Does this productivity improvement make the United States worse off? We can use the same criteria as for China. US real income in terms of its own domestic goods is $wL/(w/a_i)$, or La_i, which is unchanged (neither the size of the US labor force nor US productivity has changed). US real income in terms of Chinese goods is $wL/(w^*/a_i^*)$, or $(w/w^*)La_i^*$. If $\Delta a_i^* > \Delta w^*$, then the price of goods from China has fallen and US real income has increased. In the example above, US real income in terms of electronics has increased because the unit cost of producing them has fallen ($\Delta a^* = 5 > \Delta w^* = 3$). But if the a^* for clothing did not change, then the US real income in terms of clothing would actually fall because clothing would become more expensive – the wage in China would rise but a^* in clothing did not rise, so the unit cost of clothing in China would increase. So US real income in terms of domestic goods is unaffected by China's growth, while its income in terms of Chinese goods depends on the change in the prices of the individual goods.

> ### APPLICATION   Nike and Athletic Shoe Production
>
> In his memoir *Shoe Dog*, Nike founder Phil Knight recounts how he started the company in the early 1960s. Knight was on a mission to bring inexpensive athletic shoes to American consumers. The athletic shoe business was and is highly competitive, with many competitors (including Adidas, Converse, Asics, New Balance, Reebox, Saucony, and many

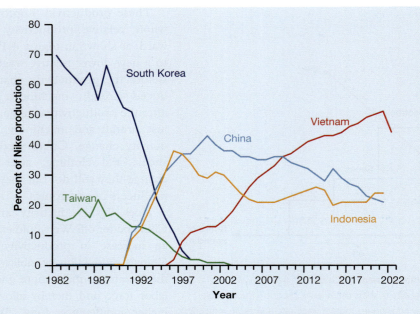

Figure 4.13 Share of Nike Shoe Production (in various countries), 1982–2022
Source: Nike annual reports, available at www.nike.com.

others) vying for sales. Consumers are very price sensitive, the production of shoes is very labor intensive, and so the unit cost for producers is extremely important.

To be competitive in the market, Knight – like everyone else – was trying to keep unit costs low. So where was the best place to undertake low-cost shoe production? We saw in the previous section that unit labor costs could be defined as w/a_i. Therefore, Knight sought to balance labor efficiency (technology) with labor costs (wages) to keep prices low. While the country with the most advanced technology was clearly the United States, the country with the lowest wages was probably somewhere in Africa. Neither was the right place to start production: if a_i was high, then w would be too, and if w was low, so would be a_i.

Operating on a shoestring budget, Knight originally sourced Nike shoes from a then poor, developing country – Japan – which was open to new technology but had relatively low wages. However, by the early 1970s, wages had risen so much in Japan that costs were rising. At that point, Nike began sourcing shoes from new factories that had sprung up in Taiwan. By the early 1980s, wages had risen so much in Taiwan that Nike began sourcing shoes from Korea. By the early 1990s, wages had risen so much in Korea that Nike began sourcing shoes from China. By the early 2000s, wages had risen so much that Nike began sourcing shoes from Vietnam. Figure 4.13 shows this pattern from 1982 onward.

When Nike shut down production in Taiwan and Korea, workers there did not suffer, because productivity (due to new technology) had

Figure 4.14 Nike Shoe Factory in Thailand
Source: Yvan Cohen/LightRocket via Getty Images.

> improved so much that average wages had risen considerably. At some point, wages will become too high in China and shoe production there will migrate to another country. But the Nike case is a reminder that a country that is "most efficient" – the country that has an absolute productivity advantage – in producing something is not necessarily going to be the country that actually produces and exports the product.

CONCLUSION

This chapter introduced the idea of comparative advantage to explain what goods a country will export and import. The simple framework, in which production is based on labor inputs, examines the productivity of labor in producing various goods across countries. The pattern of trade does not depend on a country's absolute productivity level in a particular good, but its relative productivity, or comparative costs of production. The framework also allows us to determine relative wages across countries.

SUMMARY

- The Ricardo model is based on one factor of production (labor) and different levels of technology across goods and countries. In this framework, the pattern of trade is not determined by absolute productive efficiency. Rather, it is based on comparative advantage, or, in other words, the opportunity costs of producing goods.
- Wages are determined by labor productivity. Therefore, a country's absolute productivity level determines the average level of wages in the country. Countries with a lower wages do not have a competitive advantage or a cost advantage over other countries; rather, lower wages reflect lower productivity.
- With many goods, unit labor costs determine where production takes place.

KEY CONCEPTS

Absolute advantage, page 51
Comparative advantage, page 51
Productivity, page 51
Relative productivity of labor, page 53
Terms of trade, page 58
Unit labor cost, page 65

REVIEW QUESTIONS

1. Define the concepts of absolute and comparative advantage. How would you explain the concepts to your parents? What products might the US have an absolute disadvantage in producing?
2. Give some examples of absolute and comparative advantage from your own life. What activities are you especially good at doing? And what activities are you not so good at doing, but you do them anyway because you are better than others around you?
3. Why does comparative advantage determine what products a country will specialize in and export? What does absolute advantage determine for a country?
4. What determines relative wages across countries? What role is played by the terms of trade?
5. How are countries in competition with one another for international markets? How are countries not in competition with one another?
6. How is comparative advantage determined when there are more than two goods involved?

EXERCISES

1. Which of the following are assumptions made in the Ricardian model of comparative advantage?
   a. the law of diminishing returns
   b. constant returns to scale
   c. perfect mobility of labor across industries
   d. perfect mobility of labor across countries
   e. identical technology across industries
   f. identical technology across countries
   g. perfect competition
   h. consumer preferences same across goods
   i. consumer preferences same across countries

2. Assume that Vietnam can produce rice and clothing. Workers can produce 2 units of rice if they are in the countryside, or 4 units of clothing if they are in the city. Workers can move freely between the countryside and the city. Let us also assume that Vietnam has a labor force of 80 million workers.
   a. What is the relative price of clothing in terms of rice in Vietnam under autarky?
   b. What is the maximum amount of clothing and rice that Vietnam can produce? Draw the production possibility frontier. What is the equation that describes the production possibility frontier?
   c. If Vietnamese consumers always wish to consume rice and clothing in equal quantities, regardless of the relative price, what will be the autarky consumption bundle? How much rice and clothing will be produced? (*Hint*: This will not be an even number.)
   d. Suppose Vietnam opens up to world trade and the relative price of clothing in terms of rice is 2. How much rice and clothing will Vietnam produce?
   e. If Vietnamese consumers always wish to consume rice and clothing in equal quantities, how much of each good will be consumed after trade? How much will Vietnam export and how much will it import? (*Hint*: This will not be an even number.)
   f. If the utility function of the average Vietnamese consumer is $U = (D_C + D_R)^{1/2}$, how much does utility increase as a result of trade?

3. Suppose we have the following technology matrix that indicates the productivity of workers in Spain and Portugal in two sectors of the economy:

	Tomato units per worker	Wine units per worker
Spain	16	4
Portugal	6	3

   a. What is the autarky relative price of wine in terms of tomatoes in Spain and Portugal? At what range of world relative prices will the two countries trade with one another? At what range of prices will they not trade with one another? What are the gains from trade for Spain if the relative price of wine is 4?
   b. Does one of the countries have an absolute advantage over the other in the production of one or both of the goods? Which country has a comparative advantage in tomatoes? Which country has a comparative advantage in wine?

EXERCISES

c. Draw the production possibility frontier for each country if Spain has a labor force of 40 and Portugal has a labor force of 10.
d. Suppose the world relative price of wine in terms of tomatoes is 3. Which country has the higher wage? By what% is that country's wage higher than the others'?
e. If Portugal improves its labor productivity in wine production to 6, what is the impact on comparative advantage and the pattern of trade? If the relative price of wine remains at 3, what happens to the relative wage between the two countries?

4. The table below shows the labor productivity per week of workers in China and Taiwan for five goods.

	China	Taiwan	Ratio
Televisions	5	20	
Rice	10	20	
Computers	1	5	
Clothing	20	60	
Automobiles	0.4	4	

a. For each good, calculate the ratio of productivity in Taiwan compared to China and enter it into the last column.
b. In the absence of any trade, the wage in China is $10 per week and the wage in Taiwan is $120 per week. Calculate the autarky price of each good in each country.
c. If the wage in China is fixed at $10 per week, in what direction must the wage change in Taiwan if both countries open up to trade in order for both countries to have something to export to one another? What are the highest and lowest wages that can prevail in Taiwan, given China's wage at $10? For which of the five goods can you correctly predict the pattern of trade without information on wages?
d. If both countries produce televisions, what is the wage in Taiwan? At that wage, in which goods has the real wage of Taiwan's workers increased as a result of trade? (*Hint*: Calculate the autarky price in Taiwan and then the price that the good can be obtained in China.) At that wage, in which goods has the real wage of China's workers increased as a result of trade?

5. Suppose Hong Kong and China can produce these goods. The following table gives the productivity of labor for each good.

	Sporting Goods	Rice	Clothes and Footwear	Electronics	Financial Services
Hong Kong	6	5	8	6	8
China (*)	2	10	2	1	1
Ratio (a^*/a)					

a. In which goods does China have an absolute advantage? In which goods does Hong Kong have an absolute advantage? In which goods does China have a comparative advantage?
b. What is the highest that wages can be in Hong Kong relative to China? What is the lowest they can be?
c. If wages in Hong Kong are three times what they are in China, which goods will Hong Kong produce and which goods will China produce?
d. If wages are four times in Hong Kong as high as in China, which goods will Hong Kong produce?
e. Suppose wages in Hong Kong are four times as high as in China, but China improves its productivity and reduces its labor requirement from 2 to 4 in clothing and from 1 to 2 in electronics. If this pushes up China's wages so that they are now one-third of the wage in Hong Kong, which country now produces which good? Is Hong Kong better off or worse off in terms of the goods it buys from China?

RECOMMENDED RESOURCES

Although Adam Smith is commonly believed to have suggested a theory of absolute advantage, recent research has called this into question. See in particular Reinhardt Schumacher, "Adam Smith's Theory of Absolute Advantage and the Use of Doxography in the History of Economics," *Erasmus Journal for Philosophy and Economics* 5(2) (2012): 54–80.

For an excellent collection of accessible essays on trade, productivity, and competition, see Paul Krugman, *Pop Internationalism* (Cambridge: MIT Press, 1997).

For a nice assessment of Ricardo's contribution to the trade debate, see Daniel M. Bernhofen and John C. Brown, "Retrospectives: On the Genius Behind David Ricardo's 1817 Formulation of Comparative Advantage," *Journal of Economic Perspectives* 32(4) (2018): 227–240.

The multi-good Ricardo model was developed by Rudiger Dornbusch, Stanley Fischer, and Paul A. Samuelson, "Comparative Advantage, Trade, and Payments in a Ricardian Model with a Continuum of Goods," *American Economic Review* 67(5) (1977): 823–839.

On Nike's constant struggle to compete in the athletic shoe market, see Phil Knight, *Shoe Dog* (Scribner, 2016) by the founder of the company.

CHAPTER 5
Factor Endowments and Trade

LEARNING OBJECTIVES

In this chapter, we learn about:
- how a country's factors of production shape the pattern of its trade
- how trade affects income distribution among the different factors of production
- how the mobility of factors between sectors, along with the pattern of trade, influences the economic interests of those factors

INTRODUCTION

The distribution of the world's natural resources is highly unequal. Norway is blessed with an abundance of oil, making it among the richest countries in the world, whereas its equally cold neighbor Finland has to live by its wits without such resources. Much of Algeria and Namibia is arid desert, whereas Brazil and Indonesia are lush and tropical. Chile is loaded with copper and Australia with iron ore and coal, while South Korea and Bangladesh are bereft of any natural resources.

Aside from natural resources, such as minerals or petroleum, a country can have different human resources – skilled and unskilled labor – or other productive factors – arable land and capital equipment. Simply contrast Singapore, Vietnam, and the United States. Singapore is a small city-state with a tiny but well-educated population at the bottom of the Malay Peninsula; Vietnam is a country with a large and poor population of nearly 100 million people; the United States is geographically diverse country with the Great Plains of the Midwest and a high-tech capital stock that can churn out innovative products from aircraft to semiconductor manufacturing equipment to other types of machinery.

These economic attributes shape the pattern of a country's trade. Singapore must import all of its food and energy needs, exporting electronics and financial services to pay for those imports. Bangladesh and Vietnam have enormous quantities of unskilled labor that can be used for simple manufactured goods (such as clothing), which they export in order to import food and automobiles. And it should come as no surprise that, given its vast economic resources, the United States would export food and capital-intensive goods in exchange for all manner of imports, ranging from clothing to coffee to consumer electronics.

As we saw in Chapter 4, countries usually have different production technologies, and this is one basis for international trade. But it is clearly not the end of the story. Another reason for trade is that countries have different resources. Furthermore, to understand such trade, we have to move away from the Ricardo framework in which labor was the only factor of production. We will want to consider how a variety of different factors of production – land, labor, and capital – help shape what a country exports and what it imports.

An additional advantage of considering how different factors of production shape trade is that we can see how trade affects the returns to different factors, i.e., the distribution of income among workers, capital-owners, and landowners. This will enable us to understand why there is often a contentious political fight over trade: some factors of production will see their income go up as a result of trade, while others will see their income fall. This is one reason why there are frequent domestic disputes over trade policy.

5.1 THE SPECIFIC FACTORS MODEL

The Ricardo model of comparative advantage developed in Chapter 4 involved the production of two goods, food and clothing, and one factor of production, labor. Labor is considered a **mobile factor** of production because workers can be used to produce either food or clothing, i.e., labor could move between sectors.

The **specific factors model** keeps the two goods and the one mobile factor, but it adds an additional factor that can only be used in the production of one particular good, i.e., it is specific to it. Such a **specific factor** cannot move between sectors. In addition to his writing on comparative advantage, Ricardo elsewhere stipulated that labor and capital were needed to produce clothing, while labor and land were needed to produce food. In this setting, labor could move between the clothing and food sectors, but capital was specific to clothing and land was specific to food (see the Theory box for how Ricardo's theory was relevant to the controversy over trade in his day).

To update the model for the twenty-first century, we will consider two goods – "tech" goods and "old" goods, instead of food and clothing. Tech goods are products of modern, high-tech industries: software, medical devices, all manner of "smart" gadgets, and so forth. Old goods are well-established manufactured products, such as clothing, automobiles, and appliances. And instead of labor, our mobile factor will be capital that can be shifted between the tech and old goods sectors. Imagine an auto parts warehouse being converted into a robotics research lab, or a shuttered shoe factory being reconfigured into an office park for a data-storage company.

The two specific factors will be two different types of labor: white-collar workers and blue-collar workers. White-collar workers are college-educated professionals, such as engineers, industrial designers, lawyers, managers, and information technology specialists. Blue-collar workers have a high-school education and work on the production line, or provide maintenance, transportation, or logistical services.

White-collar workers are needed to produce tech goods, while blue-collar workers are needed to produce old goods. These factors are *not* mobile across sectors: white-collar workers do not know the first thing about sewing together the pieces to make a shirt or jacket, and blue-collar workers do not know how to troubleshoot somebody else's buggy computer code. (Again, this is the specific factors model. We will alter these assumptions when we consider the mobile factors model later in the chapter.)

Output as a Function of Capital
If two countries have the same technology and factors of production, they will have exactly the same production possibility frontiers. If the two countries also have the same preferences for the two goods, they will have the same autarky relative prices and therefore will not trade

5.1 THE SPECIFIC FACTORS MODEL

with one another. However, if two countries have different factors of production, their production possibility frontiers will differ, naturally leading to different autarky prices. As a result, these countries will trade with one another. We can show this by deriving the production possibility frontier for the specific factor model.

Let us start with the production function for each sector. At any given point in time, the country we are modeling has a fixed number of white-collar and blue-collar workers, which are fully employed in the tech and old goods sectors, respectively. Because these workers cannot move between sectors, production can change only by shifting the mobile factor, capital, between sectors.

For each sector, output is a function of the amount of factors employed in the sector. So, for example, the output of tech goods, S_T, is a function of the amount of capital employed in the sector, K_T and the number of white-collar workers, L_{WC}:

$$S_T = F(K_T, L_{WC}). \tag{5.1}$$

Remember, however, that in the specific factors model, the number of white-collar workers is fixed. Therefore, we can regard L_{WC} as given and take S_T to be a function simply of K_T, as shown in the left-hand panel of Figure 5.1. As the white-collar workers have more and more capital at their disposal, the output of tech goods increases, but at a diminishing rate. Thus, there are diminishing returns to capital, meaning that the marginal product of capital declines as more and more capital is added to the fixed amount of white-collar labor. The declining marginal product of capital, the slope of the production function on the left, is shown in the right-hand panel of Figure 5.1.

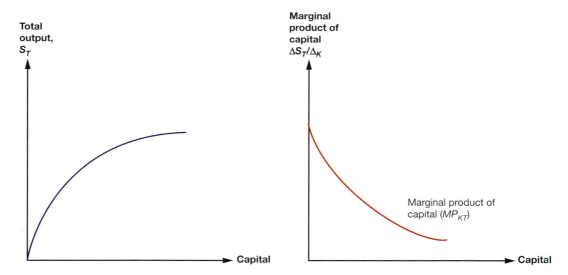

Figure 5.1 The Production Function for Tech Goods The figure on the left presents a production function with diminishing returns: production of tech goods rises as more capital is added to a fixed number of white-collar workers, but at a diminishing rate. The figure on the right indicates the declining marginal product of capital, which is the change in output of tech goods as more capital is added.

If the number of white-collar workers increases, or if there is a technological improvement in production, the entire production function curve climbs more steeply, because more workers or better technology mean that there is more output per unit of capital. Because each unit of capital is now more productive, the marginal product of capital schedule shifts up.

In the old goods sector, the production function is similar: for a given number of blue-collar workers (L_{BC}), output of old goods (S_O) will increase, but at a diminishing rate, as more capital (K_O) is added.

Deriving the Production Possibility Frontier

From the two production functions, we can derive the production possibility frontier. The four-quadrant diagram in Figure 5.2 shows how this is done. The tech sector's production function has been flipped leftward into the second quadrant (upper left), while the old goods sector's production function has been rotated downward into the fourth quadrant (lower right).

The third quadrant (lower left) shows the economy's budget constraint with respect to capital, represented by the equation $K = K_T + K_O$. Here K is the total amount of capital in the economy, an amount assumed to be constant; and K_T is the amount of capital dedicated to the tech sector, while K_O is the amount dedicated to the old goods sector. The country's limited stock of capital can be allocated to the production of either tech or old goods. The slope of this capital-stock budget constraint is −1, because increasing the amount of capital allocated to the tech sector by one unit means decreasing the amount of capital allocated to the old sector by one unit.

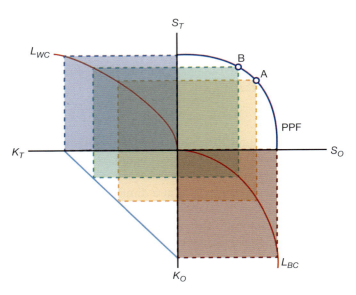

Figure 5.2 The Production Possibility Frontier for the Specific Factors Model This figure shows how to derive the production possibility frontier (in the first quadrant) based on the production functions for each sector (quadrants II and IV) and the supply of capital (quadrant III).

If we take any particular allocation of capital between the two sectors in quadrant III, we can draw a line to each of the production functions (in quadrants II and IV) to determine the output of each sector. Those two outputs can then be mapped into quadrant I (upper right) to determine a point on the production possibility frontier. As we plot the different output combinations for all the possible allocations of capital, we trace out the entire production possibility frontier. The curved shape of the PPF reflects the diminishing returns to capital in each sector.

Recall what we learned in Chapter 2. The equilibrium production point on the production possibility frontier will be the point where the tangent line to the PPF has a slope equal to the negative of the relative price of old goods in terms of tech goods, $-p_O/p_T$. That unique production point determines a unique allocation of capital between the two sectors.

As the relative price of the two goods changes, the production point moves along the production possibility frontier, corresponding to a reallocation of capital between the tech and old goods sectors. For example, suppose we are initially producing the combination of old goods and tech goods indicated by point A in Figure 5.2. If the price of old goods falls, output of old goods will fall and output of tech goods will rise. This movement along the production possibility frontier is accomplished by shifting capital from the production of old goods to the production of new goods.

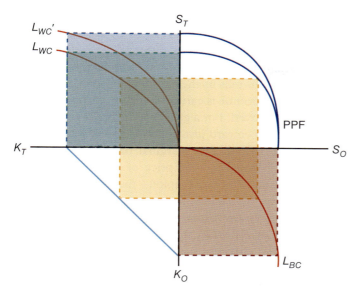

Figure 5.3 An Increase in the Number of White-collar Workers in the Specific Factors Model This figure shows that an increase in the number of white-collar workers will shift up the production function for tech goods. This, in turn, produces an asymmetric shift in the country's production possibility frontier as it can now produce more tech goods without being able to produce more old goods.

How Factors Affect the Production Possibility Frontier

Figure 5.2 can also be used to show how changes in the factors of production affect the shape of the production possibility frontier and influence the pattern of trade. To start, suppose two economies are initially identical. If the countries have the same factors of production and the same technology, and if the countries' consumers have the same preferences, then the autarky relative prices will be identical. In this case, the two countries will not trade with one another.

Now suppose that one of the countries increases its number of white-collar workers, perhaps through more schooling or through increased immigration. As Figure 5.3 shows, an increase in the number of white-collar workers shifts up the production function for tech goods, so that every unit of capital becomes more productive. This leads to an asymmetric shift in the production possibility frontier: the country can now produce more tech goods, although it can still only produce the same amount of old goods as before.

If we assume that old and tech goods continue to be consumed in the same proportion, then the slope of the PPF at the autarky production point also becomes steeper. This indicates that countries with a relative abundance of white-collar workers will have a lower autarky price of tech goods relative to old goods. This lower relative price means that a country with an abundance of white-collar workers would tend to export tech goods and import old goods. Thus, we have a prediction about patterns of trade: all other things being equal, a country with a greater proportion of one specific factor will tend to export the good that uses that specific factor and import the good that uses the other specific factor.

Later in this chapter, we will review empirical evidence for this prediction. However, it would be surprising if we did *not* find evidence in its favor. We would expect a country with an abundance of skilled workers to export goods that use a lot of skilled labor, just as we would expect a country with an abundance of raw materials to export those raw materials.

5.2 INCOME DISTRIBUTION IN THE SPECIFIC FACTOR MODEL

In the Ricardo model of comparative advantage, labor was the only factor of production. This model could not be used to examine the impact of trade on the distribution of income. (With only one factor of production, all income goes to that factor.) By contrast, the specific factors model can give us insight into the distribution of income among the three factors, which in this case are white-collar workers, blue-collar workers, and capital. The workers earn wages and the income that accrues to capital goes to the capital's owners.

Recall that the production function exhibits diminishing returns to capital. Thus, the marginal (physical) product of capital in the tech sector, MP_{KT}, which is the slope of the

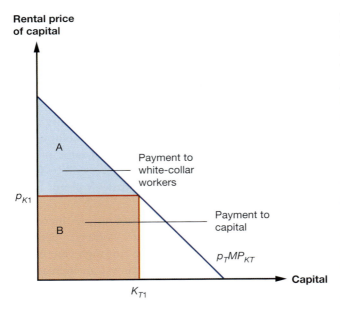

Figure 5.4 Income Distribution in the Tech Sector This figure uses the declining marginal value product of capital line to show the distribution of income. A given rate of return to capital, shown on the horizontal axis on the left, determines how much capital will be employed in the sector. The area below the marginal value product line but above the return on capital is the area of income distributed to white-collar workers. The rate of return to capital times the amount of capital employed is the total payment to capital in the tech sector.

production function, decreases as the quantity of capital increases. If we multiply MP_{KT} by the price of tech goods, p_T, which we take as given, we get the **marginal value product** of capital in the tech sector, or $p_T MP_{KT}$. This tells us the marginal revenue of capital – how much revenue is earned for each additional unit of capital employed. For a given p_T, the $p_T MP_{KT}$ schedule will slope downward just as the MP_{KT} schedule does.

In equilibrium, that marginal revenue from added capital will equal p_K, the price of capital, sometimes called the rental price of capital – the amount it costs to hire a unit of capital for a given period of time. Therefore, the downward-sloping marginal value product of capital schedule, shown in Figure 5.4, represents the demand curve for capital in the tech sector. For a given rental price of capital, p_{K1}, reading horizontally across to the curve ($p_{K1} = p_T MP_{KT}$) and then down will give the quantity of capital, K_{T1}, allotted to the tech sector at that price. Any less capital would leave potential profits unrealized ($p_T MP_T > p_{K1}$), while any additional capital would begin to incur losses ($p_T MP_{KT} < p_{K1}$).

Figure 5.4 also shows the distribution of income between capital and workers in the tech sector. The total amount of revenue generated by the tech sector is the entire area under the marginal value product of capital schedule, up to the amount of capital employed. Of that total revenue, the part that goes to capital owners is the rental price of capital multiplied by the amount of capital employed, $p_{K1} K_{T1}$, corresponding to area B.

The remainder of the revenue, area A, is available to pay the specific factor of production in the tech sector, namely the white-collar workers. Thus, each white-collar worker's wage is equal to what he or she is worth to the sector. Conceptually, this is the marginal value product of labor, i.e., the marginal product of labor times the price of tech goods: $W_{WC} = p_T MP_{LT}$. Graphically, W_{WC} is area A divided by the number of workers.

What happens if the rental price of capital falls? This will not only increase the amount of capital employed in the tech sector but also increase the revenue available to pay workers (area A becomes larger). Intuitively, because the same number of white-collar workers will now be working with more capital, the workers are more productive and hence will earn a higher wage. More formally, as more capital is added to the tech sector, the marginal product of labor in the tech sector (MP_{LT}) increases, and hence the wage received by white-collar workers (W_{WC}) must also increase, given the price of tech goods (p_T).

Finally, three changes can shift the marginal value product of capital schedule to the right.

- *A change in the price of goods*: if the price of tech goods, p_T, increases, the marginal value product of capital, $p_T MP_{KT}$, will increase and the schedule will shift out.
- *A change in the number of white-collar workers*: if there is an increase in the number of white-collar workers, the marginal product of capital, MP_{KT}, will increase because every unit of capital now has more labor to work with. The $p_T MP_{KT}$ schedule will shift out.

5.2 INCOME DISTRIBUTION IN THE SPECIFIC FACTOR MODEL

- *An improvement in technology*: if technology improves in the tech sector, the marginal product of capital, MP_{KT}, will increase and the $p_T MP_{KT}$ schedule will shift out.

For a given rental price of capital, the outward shift in the marginal value product of capital schedule will increase area A, because the curve has moved, and increase area B, because additional capital will be acquired and put to use. Where the shift is due to a change in the price of goods or to technological improvement, the increase in area A means an increase in workers' wages. However, where the shift of the schedule is due to an increase in the number of workers, the increase in the size of triangle A is offset by the need to pay more workers.

A diagram such as Figure 5.4 can be constructed for the old goods sector. In this case, the horizontal axis is the amount of capital in the old goods sector (K_O), and the curve describes the marginal value product of capital in the old goods sector. The triangle above the rental price of capital line (area A) indicates the revenue available to pay the wages of blue-collar workers.

Income Distribution

How can we determine the distribution of income between capital-owners, white-collar workers, and blue-collar workers all at the same time? By combining diagrams. If we flip the tech sector diagram over and join it to the old goods sector diagram, the result is Figure 5.5. Now the horizontal axis, with its finite length, represents the total amount of capital in the economy, K, and a point along that axis divides the capital into allocation K_T to the production of tech goods and K_O to that of old goods. Starting from the left and moving right, we are adding capital to the old goods sector, just as in Figure 5.4. Starting from the right and moving left, capital is being added to the tech goods sector.

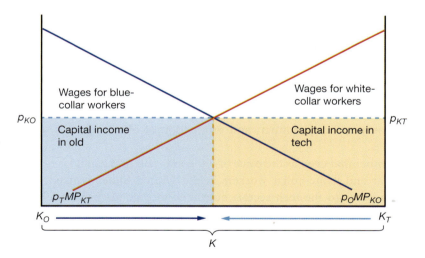

Figure 5.5 Capital Allocation and Income Distribution in the Specific Factors Model This figure presents the two downward-sloping marginal value of product schedules, the intersection of which determines the rental price of capital (vertical axes) and the allocation of capital in the tech and old goods sectors (horizontal axes).

The intersection of the two schedules determines where the marginal value product of capital is equal in the two sectors. At this intersection, the rental price of capital will be the same in the two sectors ($p_{KO} = p_{KT}$). This equilibrium determines the rental price of capital and the allocation of capital to the two sectors. The rate of return to capital will be the same in the old sector and the tech sector because capital is mobile and will move where its reward is the highest. (If the rental prices were not equal, there would be an incentive to move capital from the low-rental price activity to the higher-rental price activity.)

This equilibrium also determines the funds available to pay the wages of the specific factors. Those funds are represented by the triangles above the rental price of capital. Thus, Figure 5.5 summarizes the distribution of income across all three production factors: the triangular area above the capital-price line on the left represents total wages paid to blue-collar workers, the corresponding triangular area on the right represents total wages paid to white-collar workers, and the rectangular area below the capital price line, spanning the full width of the diagram, represents the rent paid to the owners of capital.

Impact of Price Change

The real usefulness of a diagram like Figure 5.5 comes from seeing how the distribution of income changes when we subject it to some shocks. The most important change we will consider is what international trade does: it changes prices.

The specific factor model can be used to tell a story about trade and the US economy over the past few decades. Suppose the United States is exporting tech goods and importing old goods when China emerges as a major player in the world economy, as it began to do in the 1990s. With its enormous abundance of unskilled labor, China starts producing old goods – clothing, shoes, auto parts, plastic housewares – in such huge quantities that the world price of old goods is driven down by 10%. For simplicity, we assume that the price of tech goods remains the same.

Because the United States imports old goods, the decline in the price of old goods is an improvement in the US terms of trade. As we saw in Section 3.3, this improvement in the terms of trade should be beneficial for the United States and increase the overall gains from trade. But does everyone in the United States benefit from the improvement? The answer is no.

The 10% fall in the price of old goods is represented by a downward shift in the marginal value product of capital schedule in the old goods sector ($p_O MP_{KO}$), as shown in Figure 5.6. The equilibrium rental price of capital falls from p_K to p_K'. Capital is reallocated from the production of old goods to the production of tech goods; in other words, auto parts plants close and new high-tech offices open. As capital is reallocated, the economy moves along the production possibility frontier, and production of old goods falls while production of tech goods rises.

Remember that even as the price of old goods falls and capital is reallocated, the number of blue-collar and white-collar workers in the United States is fixed. As noted earlier, when capital moves into the tech sector, output of tech goods per white-collar worker increases. As the workers become more productive, the increase in MP_{LT} causes the workers' wage, $W_{WC} = p_T MP_{LT}$, to increase. In Figure 5.6, you can see that the triangle representing the wage pool for white-collar workers increases when the price of old goods falls.

However, the wage increase is an increase in white-collar workers' *nominal* wage. What about their *real* wage? The real wage, representing the purchasing power of the nominal wages in terms of goods, is calculated by dividing the nominal wage by the prices of the goods workers consume. In this case, the real wage of white-collar workers goes up in terms of both goods. It goes up in terms of tech goods because the nominal wage increases and the price of tech goods does not change. And the real wage goes up in terms of old goods because the nominal wage increases and the price of old goods is 10% less than before. Thus, white-collar workers are unambiguously better off as a result of the fall in the price of old goods.

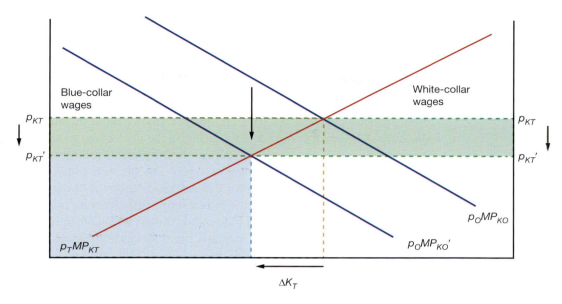

Figure 5.6 A Fall in the Price of Old Goods A fall in the price of old goods shifts the marginal value product of capital schedule in the old goods sector. This reduces the rental price of capital and shifts capital out of the old goods sector into the production of new goods.

What about blue-collar workers? Because capital moves out of the old goods sector and into the tech sector, blue-collar workers now have less capital to work with. Output of old goods per blue-collar worker falls, so the wages received by blue-collar worker fall. (The triangle representing the wage pool for blue-collar workers decreases in size.) Here again, the wage of blue-collar workers (W_{BC}) is their marginal value product, the price of old goods multiplied by the marginal product of labor in the old goods sector: $W_{BC} = p_O MP_{LT}$. Not only does p_O fall by 10%, but MP_{LT} falls as well, so the combined impact means that blue-collar wages fall by *more* than 10%.

Not only does the nominal wage of blue-collar workers fall, but their real wage falls, as well. The real wage of blue-collar workers falls in terms of tech goods because the nominal wage falls while the price of tech goods does not change. The real wage also falls in terms of old goods because the nominal wage declines by more than 10%, and the 10% decline in the price of old goods only partly makes up for that. Thus, blue-collar workers are unambiguously worse off as a result of the fall in the price of old goods.

In sum, the two specific factors of production are affected differently by trade with China: white-collar workers are better off, and blue-collar workers are worse off. This finding suggests that trade will never be a Pareto improvement because, when prices change, one of the specific factors will be worse off. Therefore, it is not surprising that trade with China generates controversy.

What about the owners of capital? Capital is much less affected by the price drop than workers are because capital is a mobile factor of production, i.e., it can move from the old goods sector to the tech sector. Because the price of old goods falls, the nominal rate of return to capital falls. But does the real return to capital fall? The real return falls in terms of tech goods because the price of tech goods does not change. However, the real return to capital in terms of old goods increases. As Figure 5.6 shows, the rental price of capital falls by less than

10%, the amount of the drop in the price of old goods, i.e., $\Delta p_O > \Delta p_K$, and therefore the real return to capital increases in terms of old goods. Thus, the impact on capital-owners of a decline in the price of old goods is ambiguous: the real return to capital is higher in terms of old goods and lower in terms of tech goods. We would need to know more about whether those earning income from capital consume more old goods (in which case they would be better off) or tech goods (in which case they would be worse off).

In previous chapters, we have emphasized that changes in *relative* prices affect resource allocation. We have just considered a decline in the price of old goods, but the impact is exactly the same if we had considered an increase in the price of tech goods. In that case, we would shift up the marginal value product of capital line for tech goods by the extent of the price increase. Capital would move from the old goods sector into the tech sector. The wage of white-collar workers would increase in real terms (they increase more than the increase in the price of tech goods). The wage of blue-collar workers would fall in real terms; and although the nominal return to capital would increase, the real return to capital would rise in terms of old goods and fall in terms of tech goods, just as before. Thus, the impact of the price change on the income of capital owners would be ambiguous and depend on their consumption pattern.

For the specific factor model, our findings on the impact of a price change on income distribution come down to this: The specific factor used to produce the good, whose relative price has increased, will be better off because of the price change. The specific factor used to produce the good, whose relative price has fallen, will be worse off. The impact of a price change on the mobile factor is ambiguous and depends on the spending patterns of the mobile factor owner.

Impact of a Change in Productivity

Another experiment we can try is a productivity increase in the tech sector. This would shift up the marginal value product of capital schedule in the tech sector. For every allocation of capital, the rental price of capital – that is, the value of capital – is now higher (try drawing that for yourself). Such a shift would increase the rental price of capital and capital would shift from the production of old goods to the production of tech goods.

What would be the impact on income distribution? Capital owners are obviously better off with the higher rental price of capital. White-collar workers in the tech sector are better off because they have more capital to work with and they become more productive. Blue-collar workers in the old sector are worse off because they have less capital to work with and they become less productive. So once again there are clear winners and losers from a tech boom. Because we assumed that the prices of tech goods and old goods did not change, i.e., remained fixed on the world market, we do not have to worry about the impact of prices on the distribution of income.

Impact of Changes in Specific Factors

The specific factors framework can also be used to analyze the impact on income distribution of changes in the factors of production. Suppose the United States issued more special immigration visas (H1-B, as they are known) to increase the number of college-educated, white-collar workers in the country. Alternatively, suppose the United States were to see greater immigration from Central America, increasing the number of blue-collar workers. Finally, what would happen if the United States received foreign investment that increased the amount of capital in the country? All of these scenarios will be discussed in Chapter 6, which examines the movement of factors of production across national borders.

THEORY   Ricardo's Version of the Specific Factor Model

David Ricardo did not just come up with the theory of comparative advantage, as discussed in Chapter 4. In 1815, he also developed the specific factors model. His aim was to address a major policy question facing Britain after the Napoleonic Wars: whether to allow cheap food to be imported from abroad, or to protect domestic agriculture from foreign competition using high tariffs.

The specific factors model is a useful way of thinking about the British economy in the early nineteenth century. Aristocrats – landlords – owned large estates and enormous tracts of land that produced agricultural crops. New-money investors – capitalists – set up textile mills in places such as Lancashire. And workers – laborers – were just trying to feed and clothe themselves by getting whatever employment they could, in a factory or field. (Think of Oliver Twist at the workhouse, picking old ropes apart by hand so the fibers could be re-used.)

With capital and land as the specific factors and labor as the (impoverished) mobile factor, what should the policy be regarding free trade in grain? Ricardo took up these questions in his 1815 pamphlet *The Influence of a Low Price of Corn upon the Profits of Stock*. In Ricardo's view, free trade in corn (the British term for wheat) would lower its price, reducing agricultural output and land rents, thereby harming aristocrats but helping workers and capital owners. Real wages would go up, as would the profits earned by capital.

What policy would the government be expected to adopt? It depends on which factor of production holds political power. Perhaps not surprisingly, given that it was composed of land-holding aristocrats, Parliament voted for high tariffs to keep out imported grain in 1815. The outcome would have been different if the British parliament reflected the interests of the capital owners and the working class. In fact, the Corn Laws that limited grain imports were repealed in 1846, after the reform bill of 1832 allowed for more democratic voting, and after Ireland's Great Potato Famine (1845–1849) began putting pressures on food supplies.

Figure 5.7 Oliver Twist, Mobile but Hungry Factor of Production
Source: Chris Ware/Hulton Harchive/Getty Images.

Figure 5.8 Some Aristocratic Landlords: Would They Want Free Trade in Food?
Source: English Heritage/Heritage Images/Getty Images.

5.3 THE MOBILE FACTORS MODEL

Similar to the specific factor model, the **mobile factors model** is a modification of the basic Ricardo model. The mobile factor model is also called the **Heckscher–Ohlin model**, after the two Swedish economists who developed it in the early twentieth century. Whereas the specific factor model has two sector-specific factors and just one mobile factor, the mobile factor model has two **mobile factors**, and no specific factors at all. Imagine that goods are produced using capital and labor, or skilled and unskilled labor, or land and labor, whichever two factors you thought were important. In each scenario, the production of each good requires the use of the two factors, each of which is mobile and can be employed in either sector. We also assume that the two goods differ in the *intensities* with which they use these two factors of production.

To develop this idea, we again consider tech goods and old goods, as in the specific factor model. For simplicity, we ignore capital and suppose that the production of tech goods and old goods each require both white-collar workers and blue-collar workers: a textile mill has managers and production workers, as does a semiconductor plant. Only, tech goods require relatively *more* white-collar workers, whereas old goods require relatively more blue-collar workers. That is what is meant by different intensities in the use of production factors. As with the specific factor model, the mobile factor model gives us two predictions, one about the pattern of trade and another about income distribution. The model's prediction about the pattern of trade is often called the *Heckscher–Ohlin theorem*. This theorem states:

A country will *export* those goods that use *intensively* those factors found in *relative abundance*.

Just as the theory of comparative advantage tells us that a country will export the goods where its *relative* productivity advantage is greatest, the idea here is that a country will export the goods whose production relies on factors of production the country has in *relative* abundance. Conversely, the country will import the goods whose production relies mainly on factors that are *relatively* scarce, just as a country will import goods in which it has a *relative* productivity disadvantage.

The distinction between *absolute* abundance and *relative* abundance is important. Between two countries, one country may have a greater abundance of factors across the board in absolute terms; nonetheless, there will be a factor where the other country has a *relative* advantage. Between India and Singapore, for instance, India has both more white-collar and more blue-collar labor, but Singapore has a *relative* abundance of white-collar labor, meaning that its ratio of white-collar to blue-collar labor is higher. Therefore, we would expect, by the Heckscher–Ohlin theorem, that of our two example goods, Singapore would export the tech good and import the old good.

The Allocation of Production Factors

Figure 5.9 gives a graphic representation of the mobile factors model, using our chosen goods and factors. The number of blue-collar workers, L_{BC}, is on the horizontal axis, and the number of white-collar workers, L_{WC}, is on the vertical axis. The two curved lines are **unit-value isoquants**. Each isoquant shows the different combinations of blue- and white-collar workers required to produce one dollar's worth of either tech goods or old goods, so that $p_T S_T = 1$ along one isoquant and

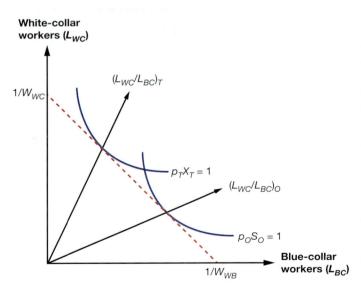

Figure 5.9 The Mobile Factors Model This figure depicts two isoquants, combinations of white-collar and blue-collar workers needed to produce a certain amount of old goods and tech goods. Production of old goods is intensive in the use of blue-collar workers and production of tech goods is intensive in the use of white-collar workers, as indicated by the rays from the origin. The downward-sloping iso-cost line indicates the relative wages of blue-collar and white-collar workers.

$p_O S_O = 1$ along the other. The isoquant for the tech good lies generally closer to the white-collar axis, because production of tech goods tends to use white-collar workers more intensively. The isoquant for the old good is closer to the blue-collar axis, because production of old goods tends to use blue-collar workers more intensively.

The slanted dashed line is a **unit iso-cost line**. Along this line, blue- and white-collar labor are used in combinations that each represent one dollar's worth of labor costs:

$$W_{BC}L_{BC} + W_{WC}L_{WC} = 1, \tag{5.2}$$

where W_{BC} and W_{WC} are the wages of blue-collar and white-collar workers, respectively. The line hits the L_{WC} axis where $W_{WC}L_{WC} = 1$, and therefore $L_{WC} = 1/W_{WC}$. Similarly, the iso-cost line hits the L_{BC} axis where $W_{BC}L_{BC} = 1$, and therefore $L_{BC} = 1/W_{BC}$. As a result, the slope of the unit iso-cost line constraint indicates the ratio of blue-collar wages to white-collar wages, or $\Delta L_{WC}/\Delta L_{BC} = -W_{BC}/W_{WC}$. The unit iso-cost line, then, is also a relative-wage line.

The tech and old goods industries are both assumed to be perfectly competitive. This means that, in each sector, blue- and white-collar labor is allocated so as to minimize production costs. In the resulting equilibrium of prices, wages, and production methods, one dollar's worth of labor can be used to produce either one dollar's worth of tech goods or one dollar's worth of old goods, and there is no way to make production cheaper in either sector by fine-tuning the factor mix. Hence the iso-cost line lies tangent to both the unit-value isoquants, as shown. The two points of tangency represent optimal cost-efficiency, in that movement along either isoquant will cause production of one dollar's worth of that good to cost more than a dollar on labor.

We can also draw two rays from the origin through the points of tangency. The slopes of these rays indicate the **factor intensity** of production in each sector, that is, the ratio of white-collar to blue-collar workers employed in the two industries. These have been labeled $(L_{WC}/L_{BC})_T$ for the tech sector and $(L_{WC}/L_{BC})_O$ for the old sector. The factor-intensity ray is steeper for tech goods than for old goods, because tech goods use white-collar workers more intensively.

Pattern of Trade

To help us determine the pattern of trade, we need to know the number of white-collar and blue-collar workers in the economy. In Figure 5.10, let factor endowment point E, with coordinates (L_{BC}, L_{WC}), represent the amounts the country has of labor factors L_{BC} and L_{WC}. From the total number of workers of each type (point E) and the factor proportions in each sector (the two rays), we can deduce the number of blue- and white-collar workers employed in each sector. This is done by forming a parallelogram, using the two rays and point E as shown.

The points of intersection on the factor-intensity rays show the number of white- and blue-collar

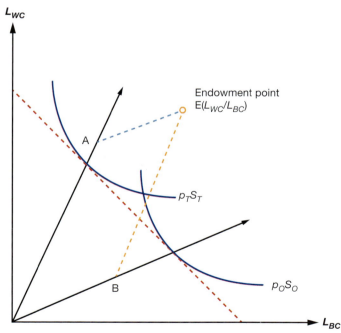

Figure 5.10 Allocation of Labor and Production in Mobile Factors Model The endowment point E indicates how many blue- and white-collar workers the economy has. The trapezoid formed by the two rays and the endowment point indicate the allocation of blue- and white-collar workers to the production of the two goods.

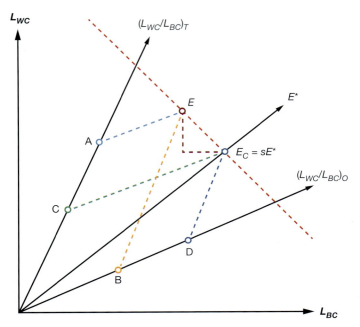

Figure 5.11 Production, Consumption, and Trade in the Mobile Factors Model While the endowment point E indicates the total supply of white- and blue-collar workers in the economy, how that matters for international trade depends upon whether the economy is relatively abundant or scarce for those types of labor. The world endowment of the two types of workers is given by the ray E^* and suggests this economy is relatively abundant in white-collar workers. This diagram can be used to show trade in factor services, that the country will be an exporter of white-collar worker-intensive goods, and an importer of blue-collar worker-intensive goods.

workers in the tech goods sector (point A) and the old goods sector (point B). This determines the output in each sector and, thereby, a specific point on the production possibility frontier.

We know that trade is simply the difference between production and consumption. Having determined production in each sector, through the allocation of labor, how can we determine consumption? First, let us add the country's budget constraint to the diagram. We do this by drawing a line parallel to our relative wage line through the factor endowment point E, as in Figure 5.11. This line represents the country's total national income, given the amount of labor in the country and the wage rate for each type of labor. The country's consumption point must lie on this budget constraint.

Where will the consumption point be, with trade? We know that world production of a good has to equal world consumption of a good. The world production point depends upon the world factor endowment of white- and blue-collar labor, denoted by point E^* – far up and to the right. Note that since the endowment ray E^* lies below E, it implies that the world has a higher ratio of blue-collar workers to white-collar workers than our hypothetical country does. The world factor endowment point implies a world production mix of old and tech goods, and thus also a world consumption mix.

To keep things simple, let us assume that consumption patterns around the world are identical. This means that our country will consume the two goods in proportion to the country's share of the world's factor endowment. In other words, the economy's consumption will be as if it were an autarky with labor endowment $E_C = sE^*$, where s is the home country's share of world income and E^* is the world factor endowment of white- and blue-collar labor. In Figure 5.11, consumption point E_C is where that ray intersects the home country's budget constraint. The figure reflects an assumption that our home country is relatively abundant in white-collar workers, $(L_{WC}/L_{BC}) > (L_{WC}{}^*/L_{BC}{}^*)$; that is why the ray through point E^* runs below the ray through point E.

If we form a parallelogram from consumption point E_C back to the factor intensity rays, we determine the "factor intensity" of consumption of tech and old goods. In other words, these points indicate the implicit amounts of white-collar and blue-collar labor that would be needed to produce domestically what the country will consume.

Along the factor intensity ray for tech goods, we see that production (point A) is greater than consumption (point C): more workers are used to produce tech goods than are needed to meet the domestic consumption demand for tech goods. Therefore, the country will export tech goods – or, more precisely, the country will export white-collar worker-intensive goods. Along the factor intensity ray for old goods, we see that consumption (point D) is greater than production (point B). Fewer workers are used in the production of old goods than are needed to meet the consumption demand for old goods. Therefore, the country will import old goods, which are intensive in the use of blue-collar workers.

Our analysis confirms the Heckscher–Ohlin theorem: a country with a relative abundance of white-collar workers, compared to the rest of the world, will export white-collar worker-intensive goods (tech goods) and import blue-collar worker-intensive goods (old goods). Of course, we cannot see the physical levels of output in the diagram, only the allocation of factors involved in the production and consumption of the two goods. Therefore, it would be more accurate to say that Figure 5.11 indicates that the home country will be a net exporter of white-collar labor services and a net importer of blue-collar labor services. These net service exports and imports are represented, respectively, by the vertical and horizontal legs of the right triangle linking E and E_C.

What happens to this country's trade if other countries begin to educate more workers, thereby increasing their endowment of white-collar workers? The E^* ray swings up closer to E. This also means an adjustment in the country's consumption point E_C. Because the world's relative factor endowment has become more similar to the country's endowment, there is less reason to trade. As a result, the country will export fewer white-collar labor-intensive goods and import fewer blue-collar labor-intensive goods.

5.4 INCOME DISTRIBUTION IN THE MOBILE FACTORS MODEL

The mobile factors model also gives us a prediction about how a change in the relative price of tech goods and old goods affects the distribution of income between the two factors of production. This prediction is called the **Stolper–Samuelson theorem**, named for Wolfgang Stolper and Paul Samuelson who came up with this idea in a famous paper (1941). The theorem states that:

> An increase in the relative price of a good will increase the return to the factors used intensively in its production and decrease the real return to other factors.

Specifically, in our two-good, two-factor example, an increase in the relative price of the tech good will increase the real wage of white-collar workers and decrease the real wage of blue-collar workers.

To state this in terms of the Heckscher–Ohlin theorem: an increase in the relative price of the good that intensively uses the factor found in relative abundance will increase the real return to the abundant factor and decrease the real return to the scarce factor. In short, trade benefits the abundant factor and harms the scarce factor in a particular country. (Recall, however, that abundance is a *relative* concept. A country may have more blue-collar workers than white-collar workers in absolute number, but the proportion of white-collar workers could be higher relative to other countries. In this case, the country is said to have a *relative* abundance of white-collar workers.)

Intuitively, the Stolper–Samuelson theorem reflects the fact that when the price of old goods falls, production responds by shifting away from old goods and toward tech goods. This shift involves moving workers from the old goods sector into the tech goods sector. Now, because there is no unemployment in our model, every worker released by the old goods sector has to be hired by the tech goods sector. However, because blue-collar workers are less in demand in the tech sector, the tech sector will only hire all those laid-off blue-collar workers if the blue-collar wage falls. Meanwhile, the expanding tech sector wants to hire more white-collar workers than are made

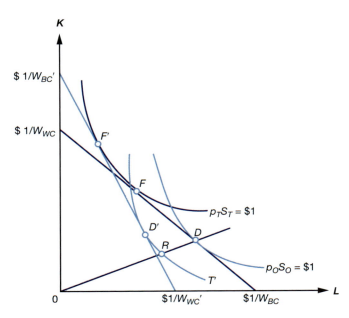

Figure 5.12 The Stolper–Samuelson Theorem This diagram shows a decrease in the price of old goods as represented by the outward shift in the old goods isoquant. The decrease in the price of old goods, which are blue-collar worker intensive, reduces the wage of blue-collar workers and increases the wage of white-collar workers.

available by the shrinking old goods sector, so the wage of white-collar workers is bid up. Thus, when the relative price of tech goods goes up, the wage of white-collar workers rises and the wage of blue-collar workers falls.

A change in relative prices can be modeled by a shift in isoquants. Figure 5.12 considers instead a rise in the price of old goods. A higher price means that more white- and blue-collar workers are needed to produce a unit value of output. Or in other words, if the old-goods isoquant is characterized by $p_O S_O = 1$, then if p_O increases to a new value, p_O', then S_O must fall from $1/p_O$ to $1\ p_O'$. The higher price means that producing a dollar's worth of old goods requires fewer workers, and so the isoquant shifts in.

By the assumption of perfect competition, the unit iso-cost line must still run tangent to the two unit-value isoquants. To maintain the tangency, the iso-cost line becomes steeper than before: its slope $-W_{BC}/W_{WC}$ increases. This implies that the relative wage of blue-collar workers has increased. Looking at the points where the iso-cost line meets the two axes, we see that the blue-collar wage has risen, and the white-collar wage has fallen. This is the Stolper–Samuelson theorem in graphical terms.

One other implication from Figure 5.12 is worth noting. Because the wage of blue-collar workers has increased, producers have an incentive to economize on their use; because the wage of white-collar workers has decreased, producers have an incentive to use more of them in production. As a result, production in both industries becomes more intensive in the use of white-collar workers. The increase in rotation of both factor-intensity rays reflects the shift toward using more white-collar intensive production techniques, as a result of the higher relative price of blue-collar workers, as seen in the rotation from F to F' in new goods and D to D' in old goods.

Trade a Pareto Improvement?

As with the specific factors model, we also find with the mobile factors model that when trade changes the relative price of two goods, one production factor gains while the other factor loses. In Chapter 3, we saw that trade had the *potential* to be a Pareto improvement over autarky. It now appears that this will always require redistribution, at least where static gains are concerned. Without redistribution, trade will *never* be a Pareto improvement over autarky: one factor will inevitably lose, namely the factor that is domestically scarce relative to the rest of the world.

The Stolper–Samuelson result helps explain political conflict over trade policy. If blue-collar workers outnumber white-collar workers in a certain region, they may put pressure on their elected representatives to restrict trade. In fact, representatives from states with a large number of blue-collar workers, such as Ohio, Michigan, and Pennsylvania, have been the most critical of open US trade policies in recent years.

5.5 EVIDENCE ON TRADE AND FACTOR ENDOWMENTS

Both the specific factors model and the mobile factors model suggest a link between a country's factors of production and its international trade, namely, that countries will export goods that use the factors of production found in relative abundance at home and will import goods that use factors of production found in relative abundance in other countries. This is common sense – we would expect a country with a lot of a certain kind of resource to export goods whose production consumes a lot of that resource. But do scholarly studies confirm this view?

Most empirical tests of the relationship between a country's trade and its factor endowments – land, natural resources, capital, skilled and unskilled labor – have historically focused on the mobile factor model. The Heckscher–Ohlin theorem implies that a country's net exports of factor services will be the difference between a country's endowment of factors and the world's endowment of factors (scaled to the country's relative size). Unfortunately, in early tests, this hypothesis failed miserably (Baldwin, 2008). The relationship between a country's trade and its relative factor endowments was so weak that a coin toss could do just as good a job as the mobile factor model at predicting a country's exports or imports – not a good outcome for a major economic theory!

Figure 5.13a Wheat Production Requires Suitable Land and Clime
Source: Daniel Acker/Bloomberg via Getty Images.

Figure 5.13b China has an Abundance of Semi-skilled Workers
Source: Kevin Frayer/Getty Images.

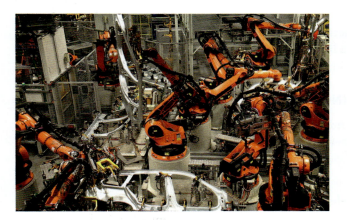

Figure 5.13c Germany is the Home to Advanced Technology, as the BMW Factory Illustrates
Source: Johannes Simon/Getty Images.

Figure 5.13d Bangladesh has an Abundance of Workers Available for Producing Garments
Source: Zabed Hasnain Chowdhury/SOPA Images/LightRocket via Getty Images.

However, the empirical tests did not relax the very strict assumptions used in the theory. For example, the empirical tests were based on the simplifying assumption that technology is the same across countries, something that is clearly not the case. Economists Donald Davis and David Weinstein (2001) showed that three adjustments were needed to make the model more realistic.

First, technological differences across countries must be considered. In this chapter, for simplicity, technology was assumed to be the same across countries so that we could focus on differences in factor endowments; in reality, of course, technology does differ across countries, as the Ricardo model of comparative advantage (Chapter 4) suggests. Second, the model had to account for the existence of non-traded goods, such as services – countries differ considerably in the size of their service sector, which tends to be more insulated from trade than agriculture or manufacturing. Third, the model had to incorporate frictions that inhibit trade. Countries trade much less than economic models predict, either because tariffs, transportation expenses, and such like make trade costly, or because consumers are used to domestically produced goods and prefer them (think of France and its cheese, Vietnam and its rice, or Japan and its fish).

Having made these adjustments, Davis and Weinstein compared the trade patterns predicted by the adjusted Heckscher–Ohlin theory with actual data on trade and production for the major OECD economies. Although capital and labor were the only factors of production considered, the adjustments resulted in the model's predictions matching the data on trade flows reasonably well. As expected, capital-intensive goods tended to be exported by countries with a relative abundance of capital and imported by countries with a relative abundance of labor. And the model corresponded with the data: measured factor trade was over 80% of predicted factor trade, and the direction of trade was correct in 90% of the cases.

John Romalis (2004) provided even firmer support for a modified Heckscher–Ohlin model. He found that countries that use the countries' abundant factors more intensively have larger shares of world production and trade of goods. In addition, countries that rapidly accumulate more of a particular factor of production see their production and export structures systematically shift toward industries that intensively use that factor. Thus, the composition of a country's trade can change if its underlying accumulation of capital, educated workers, and natural resources changes over time.

In sum, empirical evidence generally supports the view that international differences in factor endowments, appropriately adjusted for technology and other factors, explain at least part of the observed pattern of world trade.

5.6 EVIDENCE ON TRADE AND INCOME DISTRIBUTION

The specific factor model and the mobile factor model both suggest that when a high-wage country increases its trade with low-wage countries, this would tend to depress the wage of blue-collar workers and raise the wage of white-collar workers. This was Paul Krugman's (2007) conclusion:

> For the world economy as a whole – and especially for poorer nations – growing trade between high-wage and low-wage countries is a very good thing. Above all, it offers backward economies their best hope of moving up the income ladder. But for American workers the story is much less positive. In fact, it's hard to avoid the conclusion that growing US trade with third world countries reduces the real wages of many and perhaps most workers in this country.

How much has wage inequality really increased in recent decades? And is trade responsible for whatever trend exists? To glean answers from the data, we have to put workers into different categories. There is no precise way to distinguish between blue- and white-collar workers, but economists often do so based on educational attainment. Figure 5.14 shows the premium earned by college-educated workers relative to high-school-educated workers between 1965 and 2013. The premium increased significantly in the 1980s and early 1990s, and it continued to grow at a slower pace after that.

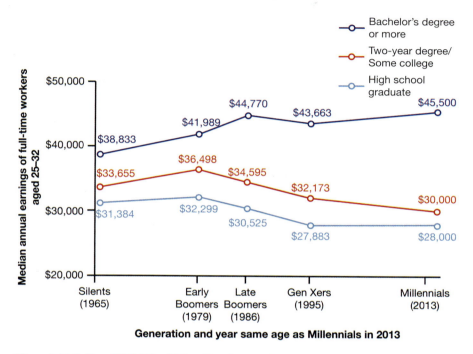

Figure 5.14 College–High School Wage Premium, 1965–2013
Source: "The Rising Cost of Not Going to College", Pew Research Center, February 10, 2014.

Another imperfect way to distinguish blue- and white-collar workers is by income level. Figure 5.15 shows that workers earning the median wage (at the 50th percentile) have seen little growth in real wages since 2000. By contrast, higher-wage workers, those at the 90th percentile and above in the wage distribution, have seen larger wage increases. (Since the COVID pandemic of 2020-21, however, these trends have reversed.)

Here, then, we do see declining real wages for those at the bottom of the wage distribution (blue-collar workers) and rising real wages for those at the top (white-collar workers). But has trade contributed to this rise in wage inequality?

One way of assessing the impact of trade on wages is to look at the "factor content" of traded goods and see how much more the United States is importing of blue-collar worker-intensive goods than it used to. This is actually hard to do, because many US imports from low-wage countries do not embody much "blue-collar content" from those countries. For example, the US imports from China include computers, smart phones, office equipment, and other electronics that are assembled in China but contain a lot of sophisticated technology that comes from elsewhere.

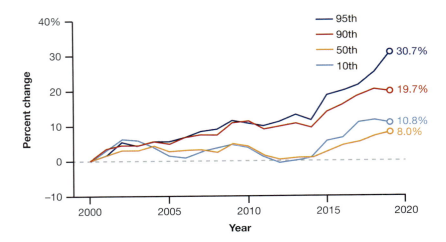

Figure 5.15 Cumulative Change in Real Hourly Wages of Men, by Wage Percentile, 2000–2019
Source: Elise Gould (2020), State of Working America Wages 2019: A Story of Slow, Uneven, and Unequal Wage Growth over the Last 40 Years. Economic Policy Institute, February 2020.

That said, most studies that examine the factor content of trade do not find large wage effects. As Krugman (2008) noted, "although the aggregate picture suggests that the distributional effects of trade should have gotten substantially larger, detailed calculations of the factor content of trade ... do not seem to support that conclusion." For example, the college-non-college wage premium rose 65% between 1979 and 2005, but calculations based on the factor content of trade indicate that only 6.9 percentage points of that 65% were due to increased trade with developing countries.

Indeed, economists have generally concluded that trade is only responsible for a small part of the increased wage inequality in the United States. Why is the apparent impact of trade not that large?

There are in fact two pieces of evidence arguing against the Stolper–Samuelson theorem as an explanation for the observed changes in wages. First, if trade were the driving factor, then declining relative wages for blue-collar workers in advanced countries, such as the United States, ought to be matched by declining relative wages for white-collar workers in developing countries, such as China, where the Stolper–Samuelson theorem should be operating in reverse. In fact, however, a rising relative wage for more-educated workers is a world wide phenomenon. This finding is hard to reconcile with the theorem.

Second, as noted in the discussion of Figure 5.12, a corollary of the Stolper–Samuelson theorem is that as the blue-collar wage falls, both the tech and old goods sector will substitute cheaper blue-collar workers for more expensive white-collar workers. This would lead to the production of tech and old goods becoming more intensive in the use of blue-collar workers. In fact, however, American producers are substituting more skilled workers (and capital equipment) for unskilled workers.

What explains the worldwide increase in the relative wage of white-collar workers, and the shift toward more sophisticated production methods? One factor has been technological change that has increased the demand for white-collar workers and decreased the demand for blue-collar workers. For example, the assembly lines that turned out automobiles used to keep many workers busy; now much of the work is done by robots, which the remaining workers must be able to supervise. In the 1980s, it took ten worker hours to produce a ton of steel; now it takes only about one worker hour to produce a ton of steel: the substitution of machinery for manual labor means that fewer steel workers are needed to produce the same output as before. Other technological innovations, such as smartphones and the internet, have decreased the demand for bank tellers, secretaries, and travel agents, all of whom are not blue-collar workers but occupations for which a college degree is often unnecessary. This phenomenon is sometimes called "skilled-biased technical change" – technical change that is biased in favor of employing white-collar workers and capital rather than blue-collar workers.

And even though the wages of blue-collar workers have not risen (or have even declined, until recently) in the United States, the price of capital has fallen even faster in recent decades. This is a worldwide phenomenon and has led producers – even in low-wage countries – to substitute technology and capital for labor. For example, the shoe manufacturer Nike is investing in advanced technology that will enable machines to manufacture shoes, even though shoe production has traditionally been a very labor-intensive activity that relied on cheap labor in China and other Southeast Asian countries.

Both the worldwide rise in the wage premium for educated workers and the substitution in production of white-collar workers for blue-collar workers are consistent with an increase in demand for white-collar workers. These trends are consistent with skill-biased technical change, but not with the simple version of the Stolper–Samuelson theorem.

Looking beyond the United States, it is difficult to find strong links between globalization in inequality. As Bourguignon (2016, 108) points out, "it is simply not true that inequality is on a three-decade rising trend everywhere." Instead, he points out that there are many diverse experiences with inequality around the world. Furthermore, he continues, the "evidence that the main cause of increased inequality is globalization and technical change is not compelling." Clearly there are many causes of economic change that have an influence on wages and incomes across countries and a debate about which factors are involved.

APPLICATION   Does Labor Behave as a Specific or a Mobile Factor?

We have considered two different models of the economy, and in particular of labor as a factor of production. Is one model better than the other? Are workers better viewed as specific factors, essentially tied to their industry of employment? Or are workers mobile factors, able to work in various different industries?

Either outcome seems possible, and it may be that one answer applies to blue-collar workers but another to white-collar workers. A 50-year-old steel worker laid off from a steel plant is unlikely to have an easy time finding other work. Decades of experience in the steel mill does not prepare one for many other jobs other than working in the steel industry. In contrast, a software programmer for a bank has readily transferable skills. Even if the bank has to downsize, the programmer has skills that can be used in industries other than financial services.

One way to differentiate between the specific factors model and the mobile factors model is to determine whether workers identify with their industry of employment or with their factor type (or economic class). To the extent that workers are specific factors, their trade policy preferences will be based on their industry of employment: in export-oriented industries, US blue- and white-collar workers alike will favor low trade barriers, while their counterparts in import-competing industries will favor high trade barriers. To the extent that workers are mobile factors, their trade policy preferences will be based on their factor type: across sectors, in the United States, high-skill workers (represented by years of education) will favor low trade barriers, because trade pushes white-collar wages upward; and blue-collar workers in all lines of work will favor high trade barriers, because trade exerts downward pressure on blue-collar wages.

By using detailed survey evidence, economists can determine which factors are most closely related to an individual's trade policy preferences. The American National Election Studies regularly asks the following question:

> Some people have suggested placing new limits on foreign imports in order to protect American jobs. Others say that such limits would raise consumer prices and hurt American exports. Do you favor or oppose placing new limits on imports, or haven't you thought much about this?

One interesting finding is that a substantial number of people surveyed (almost 30%) said that they were not well informed enough to express an opinion. In general, people with less education were more likely to feel "uninformed" about the issue of trade protection.

Blonigen (2011) finds that education is the only variable that regularly explains the variation in the individual answers. The more years of education respondents have, the more likely they are to favor open trade and oppose imposing new limits on imports. Other variables, such as wage rate or sectors of employment, are less significant. From all this, it appears that the mobile factor model may be better than the specific factor model at explaining the individuals' views on trade policy issues. For related work on other countries, see Mayda and Rodrik (2005).

Magee (1980) has another clever take on whether the specific or the mobile factors model is more appropriate. He looks at the positions of unions (representing labor) and management (representing capital owners) on a particular trade issue. If labor and capital took the same position in supporting or opposing the legislation, that would be evidence in favor of specific factors. If labor and capital took opposing positions over the legislation, that would be evidence in favor of mobile factors.

In looking at Congressional testimony regarding a trade bill in 1974, Magee came up with the following table. The figure in each cell indicates the number of industries in each cell:

	Position of Industry's Labor Representatives	
Position of Industry's Management	Protectionist	Free Trade
Protectionist	14	1
Free Trade	1	22

In other words, in most instances, an industry's labor and management representatives spoke with the same voice – either in favor of reducing tariffs (the free trade position, in 22 instances) or against reducing tariffs (the protectionist position, in 14 instances). In only two cases did labor and management take the opposite position to one another. Magee's evidence suggests that capital and labor employed in a specific industry view their economic interests as the same, consistent with the specific factors model. In later research, Eugene Beaulieu (2002) studied Congressional votes on the North American Free Trade

Agreement (NAFTA) and other trade initiatives. Like Magee, he also found support for the specific factors model.

More recent evidence on how labor responds to trade come from what is known as the "China Shock." Figure 5.16 shows US imports from Japan, Mexico, and China as a share of US GDP over the past 50 years. Imports from Japan surged in the 1980s and then retreated, and imports from Mexico rose after the passage of NAFTA in 1993. But imports from China really surged in the 1990s and 2000s. This import surge had many benefits for consumers in terms of inexpensive clothing and electronics, but it also harmed domestic workers in such sectors as furniture and apparel. Research by David Autor, David Dorn, and Gordon Hanson (2013) has shown that workers in manufacturing sectors affected adversely by imports from China had a difficult time finding new employment in other sectors of the economy.

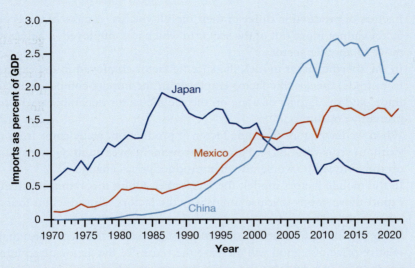

Figure 5.16 The China Shock: US Imports from Japan, Mexico, and China as a Share of GDP, 1970–2021
Source: Top Trading Partners, Foreign Trade, US Census Bureau.

The local labor market effect of the China shock in certain regions of the country was profound. Imagine working in a furniture factory in a small town in southwestern Virginia, far from other urban centers. If the local plant closed down, you would have to uproot from your community to find work elsewhere because there would be few other employment opportunities close by. Unfortunately, research has suggested that these workers did not easily move either geographically (to other regions) or economically (to other industries) after being displaced from their jobs. This finding is consistent with labor being a specific factor of production and old manufacturing industries losing jobs as a result of trade. It should come as no surprise that trade with China is viewed negatively in many parts of the United States.

CONCLUSION

Countries differ widely not just in the technology they have at their disposal, but in the relative amounts of different factors of production. Two different models point to the same conclusion about patterns of trade: if between two trading countries, one country has a greater relative abundance of one production factor than the other country, then that country will tend to export the good whose production intensively uses that factor. The same country will tend to import the good associated with the relatively scarce factor.

The two models also point to the same conclusion about how trade affects income: once different production factors are distinguished, and associated with different goods, trade with only static gains will increase the real income of the factor associated with the export good but will decrease the income of the factor associated with the import good. These findings help explain why trade is so politically controversial: it always hurts someone. The compensation through redistribution that Chapter 3 stated might be necessary to gain broad support for pro-trade policy will, it turns out, always be required if all sectors are to see trade as a benefit.

SUMMARY

1. Factors of production differ in their mobility across sectors of the economy. A specific factor cannot move out of the sector in which it is employed, whereas a mobile factor can move to another sector.
2. In the specific factor model, the specific factor employed in the export sector benefits from trade, the specific factor employed in the import-competing sector is harmed by trade, and the impact of trade on the mobile factor depends on which good it primarily consumes.
3. When we have more than one factor of production, static gains from trade are never (without redistribution) a Pareto improvement over autarky: at least one factor of production will be worse off when product prices change.
4. In the mobile factors model, the Heckscher–Ohlin theorem states that a country will export those goods that use intensively the factors of production found in relative abundance.
5. In the mobile factors model, the Stolper–Samuelson theorem states that an increase in the relative price of a good will increase the return to the factors used intensively in its production and decrease the real return to other factors.
6. Wage inequality has increased in recent decades in the United States, but studies suggest that this is being driven more by technological change (increasing demand for white-collar workers) than by international trade.

KEY CONCEPTS

Factor intensity, page 85
Heckscher–Ohlin theorem, page 85
Mobile factor, page 74
Mobile factors model, page 83
Specific factor, page 74

Specific factors model, page 74
Stolper-Samuelson theorem, page 87
Unit iso-cost line, page 85
Unit-value isoquant, page 84

REVIEW QUESTIONS

1. Think of countries that have a great abundance or scarcity of the following factors of production: unskilled labor, skilled labor, capital equipment, arable land. Can a country have an abundance of all these factors of production?

2. Think of a country whose factor endowments have changed dramatically over the past few decades. What has been the impact of that change on their foreign trade?
3. Give a few examples of "specific" factors and "mobile" factors of production. What programs or policies might encourage a specific factor to be transformed into a mobile factor?
4. What does the specific factors model and the mobile factors model tell you about trade politics in any given country? Which factors will be in favor of trade and which will be opposed to trade?

EXERCISES

1. In the context of the specific factors model, what difference does it make to the production possibility frontier if the mobile factor were to increase, compared to a scenario where one of the specific factors increases?
2. In the context of the specific factors model, illustrate graphically and analyze the impact of a decrease in the price of tech goods.
3. What is the impact of an increase in the productivity of the tech sector in the specific factors model?
4. In the context of the specific factors model, assume that capital is the mobile factor of production, and the economy can produce old goods (steel, coal, automobiles) and tech goods (semiconductor technology, software). Old goods use capital and blue-collar workers (a specific factor) and tech goods use capital and white-collar workers (the other specific factor).
   a. Set up a diagram to show the return to capital and the wages to blue- and white-collar workers.
   b. What happens if China and other developing countries start exporting more old goods and thereby reduce the US price of those goods? Who is better off, and who is worse off?
5. Under the Heckscher–Ohlin theorem, why wouldn't China export labor-intensive goods and capital-intensive goods, since it has more labor and capital than any other country?
6. Use a diagram like Figure 5.10 to show that the Stolper–Samuelson theorem has the same implications whether the price of old goods falls or the price of tech goods increases.
7. What are the two major reasons that the Stolper–Samuelson theorem does not provide a good explanation for rising wage inequality today?

RECOMMENDED RESOURCES

It is always fun to study the classics. You can read Heckscher and Ohlin in the original here: *Heckscher–Ohlin Trade Theory,* edited by Harry Flam and M. June Flanders (Cambridge: MIT Press, 1991).

The Heckscher–Ohlin theory of trade has long been a workhorse model of international trade economists. For an excellent overview of the model's importance, see Edward E. Leamer, *The Craft of Economics: Lessons from the Heckscher-Ohlin Framework* (Cambridge, MA: MIT Press, 2012).

The specific and the mobile factor models can be linked, as done elegantly here: J. Peter Neary, "Short-Run Capital Specificity and the Pure Theory of International Trade," *Economic Journal* 88(351) (1978): 488–510.

Another short classic worth reading is Wolfgang F. Stolper and Paul A. Samuelson. "Protection and Real Wages," *Review of Economic Studies* 9(1) (1941): 58–73.

On the trade and inequality debate, see Pinelopi Koujianou Goldberg, *The Unequal Effects of Globalization* (Cambridge, MA: MIT Press, 2023).

Finally, for an overview of research on the China Shock: see Autor, David H., David Dorn, and Gordon H. Hanson. "The China Shock: Learning from Labor-Market Adjustment to Large Changes in Trade," *Annual Review of Economics* 8 (2016): 205–240.

CHAPTER 6

International Factor Mobility

LEARNING OBJECTIVES

In this chapter, we learn about:
- the incentives for labor, capital, and technology to move between countries
- how the international movement of factors of production affects economies
- whether immigrants take the jobs and reduce the wages of native-born workers
- the difference between absolute and comparative advantage with international factor mobility
- what past examples of mass immigration and emigration reveal about the impact on wages

INTRODUCTION

For as long as people have roamed the earth, there has been a fear of strangers. The term xenophobia comes from Ancient Greek and combines *xeno* (meaning foreign or alien) and *phobia* (meaning fear). In particular, it is common for natives of a country – whether today or in the distant past – to worry about **immigration**, especially illegal immigration.

While the United States has a long history of immigration, there has been a great deal of concern in recent years as to whether the border with Mexico is insecure, allowing too many undocumented migrants from Central America to enter the United States. The European Union has been engaged in a similar debate about the influx of workers from Eastern Europe and political refugees from the Middle East. Britain's decision to leave the EU in the 2016 Brexit vote is often seen as an indication that the immigration policy is fraught with political sensitivities.

Much of the controversy over immigration has to do with cultural matters, such as assimilation. Yet economic issues are never far behind: does immigration pose a threat to the jobs of domestic workers, or drive down their **wages**? It seems that admitting a larger number of foreign workers would increase the supply of labor and hence reduce the local wage rate. Yet, as the National Academies of Sciences recently reported, there is not much evidence that local wage rates are affected by immigration or **emigration** of workers. How can that be?

To understand the issue, we have to consider the broader question of what happens when factors of production can move between countries. In previous chapters, we assumed that goods can move between countries but factors of production cannot. This assumption allowed us to draw a country's production possibility frontier, which depends on a fixed amount of land, labor, and capital and technology. But what happens when these factors of production and technology can move across countries? If countries were to allow factors of production and technology to move between them, would that equalize wages and the return to capital around the world? And would there be an economic gain like we saw with international trade in goods?

This question is most controversial when it comes to the immigration of low-skilled workers into high-wage countries. Does such immigration reduce the wages and take away the jobs of native workers? That has been the fear in the United States, with large-scale immigration from Mexico and Central America, and in Western Europe, with large-scale immigration from Eastern Europe and the Middle East.

This chapter explores the impact of allowing labor, capital, and technology to move across national borders. The first step is to document how much factor mobility takes place and whether it is enough to equalize wages and the return to capital. Then we will consider the implications of labor and capital mobility in the models that we studied in previous chapters, particularly the Ricardo model of Chapter 4 and the specific factor and mobile factor models of Chapter 5. Finally, we will briefly review the empirical evidence on the impact of labor and capital mobility to see how it conforms to the implications from the theory.

6.1 THE GAINS FROM INTERNATIONAL LABOR MOBILITY

Within a country, labor can, in principle, move pretty freely across regions. You can graduate from college in New England and get a job on the West Coast, thousands of miles away, without many formal barriers blocking your way. When post-Cold War cuts in defense spending sent California's economy spiraling downward in the early 1990s, millions of Californians moved to other states to get jobs. The outbreak of the COVID-19 pandemic in early 2020 led many people to leave cities and work remotely in rural areas.

To be sure, people do not always relocate to where the jobs are. In late 2013, the unemployment rate in North Dakota was just 2.7%, due to the economic boom driven by shale oil discoveries, while the unemployment rate in Nevada, which was suffering from the housing bust, was 9.7%. Yet not many people moved from Nevada to North Dakota. One reason for a decline in inter-regional mobility has been the aging of the population; the elderly are less mobile than the young. Still, broadly speaking, the United States has a national labor market in which people are free to move from one region to another.

Movement between countries is a different matter. A US citizen who earns a college degree in New England cannot easily get a job in Canada, even though Boston is closer to Montreal than to Los Angeles. There are formal barriers to American citizens getting jobs in Canada, and to Canadians getting jobs in the United States. Even in the European Union, which formally has a unified labor market, labor is much less mobile than goods. Spain's produce, such as its delicious oranges and tomatoes, can easily be shipped to France and Germany. However, even though Spaniards face few official obstacles to getting a job in France or Germany, not many seize the opportunity. Most are deterred by differences of language and culture.

The lack of international **labor mobility** across borders is one reason why wage rates are not equalized across countries. Figure 6.1 shows average wages across several countries for 2021 from the Organization for Economic Cooperation and Development (OECD). The gap between wages in Germany and Mexico, let alone China, is enormous. If workers could migrate from China to Norway, these wage differences might be narrowed.

6.1 THE GAINS FROM INTERNATIONAL LABOR MOBILITY

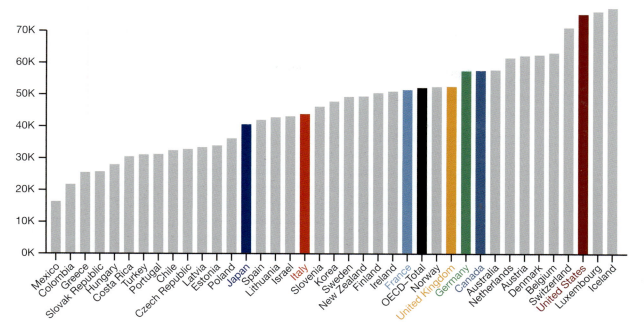

Figure 6.1 Average Annual Wages across Countries In 2022 USD using 2022 USD purchasing power exchange rate
Source: OECD (2023), *"Average annual wages,"* OECD Employment and Labour Market Statistics.

Of course, international labor mobility is not zero. In 2022, 29 million individuals in the US labor force – more than one in seven – were foreign born, according to the Bureau of Labor Statistics. In particular, there is substantial migration of people from low-wage to high-wage countries.

Higher-skill workers tend to go through the legal process to get permanent residency permits ("green cards") and H1-B work visas. On the other hand, in past decades, many Mexican workers and refugees from Central America have crossed the long US–Mexican border illegally. In part, this movement is simply a response to economic incentives: wages are higher and working conditions are better in the United States than in Mexico and Central America. When the wage gap between the two countries shrinks, so does illegal immigration. For a time, the Great Recession of 2009 in the United States, together with improvements in the Mexican economy, reduced migration from Mexico to the United States almost to zero.

However, large and persistent differences in wages across countries – sometimes by a factor of ten – imply that there are significant barriers to international labor migration. Official restrictions on immigration to high-wage countries are the most obvious barrier. The United States has an annual Diversity Immigrant Visa lottery, which allocates immigration slots to individuals from developing countries. In 2021, only 1% of the 11.8 million applicants were selected to receive a green card.

Modeling the Effects of Labor Mobility

The large differences in wages across countries imply that there would be large economic gains if labor could be made internationally more mobile. Economist Michael Clemens (2011) proposes this interesting thought experiment:

Divide the world into a "rich" region, where one billion people earn $30,000 per year, and a "poor" region, where six billion earn $5,000 per year. Suppose emigrants from the poor region have lower productivity, so each gains just 60% of the simple earnings gap upon emigrating – that is, $15,000 per year. This marginal gain shrinks as emigration proceeds, so suppose that the *average* gain is just $7,500 per year. If half the population of the poor region emigrates, migrants would gain $23 trillion – which is 38% of global GDP.

Figure 6.2 translates Clemens's thought experiment into a modified specific factors-type diagram. The vertical axis on the left gives the wage for a hypothetical low-wage country, while the vertical axis on the right is for a hypothetical high-wage country's wage rate. The two sloping lines describe the two countries' marginal products of labor. The horizontal axis represents the world's total labor supply, where the allocation of labor to each country is denoted by L. All labor from O^* to L resides in the low-wage country, where wages are W^*. All labor from O to L resides in the high-wage country, where wages are W.

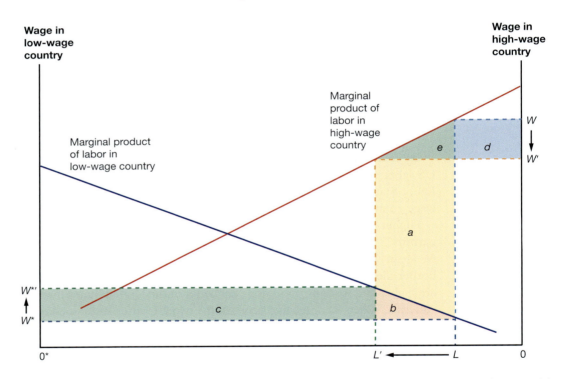

Figure 6.2 The Impact of International Labor Movement This figure uses the graph from the specific factors model in Chapter 5 to see what happens to wages when workers move from a low-wage country to a high-wage country. The total labor supply is on the horizontal axis and the wage rate is on the vertical axis. Labor shifts from L to L', reducing wages in the high-wage country and increasing wages in the low-wage country.

If labor were perfectly mobile, the wage rates would equalize across the two countries, with L beneath the intersection of the two marginal product of labor lines. Of course, labor is not mobile, and therefore wages in the two countries are not equal. However, suppose that we allow *some* migration from the low-wage country to the high-wage country, so that the allocation of labor shifts from L to L'. This is not enough to equalize the two wages, but it increases wages in the low-wage country from W^* to $W^{*\prime}$, and it decreases wages in the high-wage country from W to W'.

How does this reallocation of labor affect the world's distribution of income? The workers who migrate from the low-wage country to the high-wage country see their wages increase from W^* to W'. They clearly benefit from the move and gain areas $a + b$ in the diagram. Workers who remain in the low-wage country also see their wages increase, but only from W^* to $W^{*\prime}$; they gain area c in the diagram. However, other factors of production in the low-wage country – capital, land, or other factors that benefitted from the low wages paid to workers – lose area $c + b$ as a result of the higher wages. Total national income falls by b, because of the loss of income to those other factors. However, if the migrants send back some portion of their higher earnings as remittances, the labor-losing country could see its national income rise.

Meanwhile, in the high-wage country, native workers see their wages decline from W to W', so they lose area d in the diagram. However, other factors of production (perhaps land and capital owners) in the high-wage country gain area $d + e$ from the fall in wages. As a result, national income rises by area e.

Taking into account all the gains and losses in the two countries, the net gain to the world from labor migration is area $a + e$. In algebraic terms, the low-wage country loses b, the high-wage country gains e, and the migrants themselves capture $a + b : -b + e + (a + b) = a + e$. Graphically, the net gain is the area between the two marginal product of labor schedules in the two countries and between L and L'. The gain of this wedge, by shifting workers with a low marginal product in one country to another country where they will have a high marginal product, represents a gain to global productivity and income. Most of the gain is captured by the migrants themselves, in the form of higher wages. The opponents to migration are native workers in the high-wage country and other (non-labor) factors of production in the low-wage country.

Because the wage and productivity gaps are so large between countries, the gains from closing these gaps can be sizeable. Clemens cites studies that point to gains as much as 50% or 100% of world GDP. He concludes that "the emigration of less than 5% of the population of poor regions would bring global gains exceeding the gains from total elimination of all policy barriers to merchandise trade and all barriers to capital flows."

6.2 THE GAINS FROM INTERNATIONAL CAPITAL AND TECHNOLOGY MOBILITY

While the barriers to international labor mobility are obvious, the barriers to the movement of capital and technology are less so. This section considers some empirical evidence on the mobility of capital and technology between countries.

Capital Mobility

Financial capital is much freer to move between countries than labor. Every day, trillions of dollars in stocks, bonds, and other financial instruments are traded on foreign exchange markets, as investors buy assets denominated in one currency and sell assets denominated in another currency. This is considered in detail in Chapters 12 and 17 of this book.

Productive capital, on the other hand, is harder to relocate than financial capital or even labor. Here we are talking about buildings and machinery ("plant and equipment," in accounting parlance) that contribute to a country's capital stock. A transfer of *ownership* is a

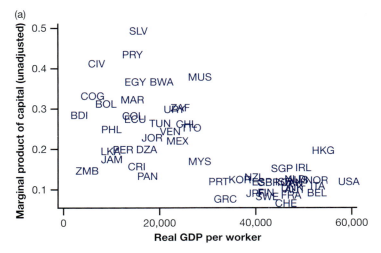

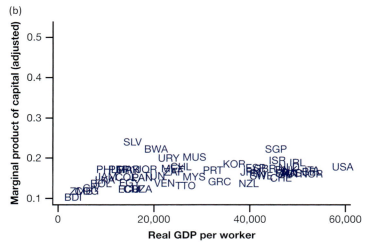

Figure 6.3 Marginal Product of Capital across Countries, Unadjusted and Adjusted, 1996 Economists have long wondered why more capital did not flow from developed countries, where capital is relatively abundant and the rate of return is presumably low, to developing countries, where capital is relatively scarce and the rate of return is presumably high. The presumption is that there must be a large misallocation of the world's capital stock. However, after accounting for differences in the price of capital, the marginal product of capital appears to be similar around the world. Of course, developed countries may have substantially more capital than developing countries because they have additional factors that are complementary to capital, such as high levels of education and better technology.

Source: Used with the permission of Oxford University Press, Francesco Caselli and James Feyrer "The Marginal Product of Capital," Quarterly Journal of Economics 122 (2007): 535–568, © 2007; permission conveyed through Copyright Clearance Centre, Inc.

movement of financial capital but not of productive capital. For example, if a US firm buys an existing Mexican firm, that does nothing to increase Mexico's stock of productive capital. On the other hand, if a US firm sets up a new production facility in Mexico, that investment adds to Mexico's capital stock.

The movement of financial capital between countries tends to equalize asset prices and interest rates, depending on risk, inflation, and many other factors. The movement of productive capital tends to equalize the marginal product of capital. Therefore, one indicator of the mobility of capital – or the potential gains from allowing greater mobility of capital – is the rate of return on capital. If the rates of return on capital are not very different across countries, the implied barriers to international **capital mobility** would seem to be relatively small (unless they are roughly equal for other reasons). And if that is true, the additional gains from reducing those barriers would not be significant.

The upper chart in Figure 6.3 shows a standard measure of the marginal product of capital plotted for countries ranked in terms of GDP per worker. The downward slope of the distribution seems to indicate that poorer countries have a higher marginal product of capital than richer countries. This implies that the allocation of capital across countries is inefficient, due to some market frictions that prevent capital from moving to countries where it is most valuable.

However, developing countries have a higher price of capital than industrialized ones, and this necessitates an adjustment. The lower chart in Figure 6.3 adjusts the marginal product of capital for differences in the price of capital. For various reasons, lower income countries tend to have a higher price of capital goods, which reduces the return on investment. Once the adjustment for the price of capital goods is made, the real marginal product of capital is roughly comparable in developed and developing countries.

The bottom line is that capital may be sufficiently mobile internationally to ensure that the real marginal product of capital is roughly comparable across countries

Technology Mobility

Technology is the knowledge used to transform labor and capital into final goods. It may consist of general ideas or techniques that can be passed from one person to another, such as the use of fracking to extract oil from the ground, or the use of digital motion-capture filming in motion picture production. Or it may be a specific advance in design that is embodied in new capital equipment, such as GPS-controlled harvesting machines or high-capacity batteries for commercial electric vehicles. In either case, it would appear that technology should be readily moveable between countries.

Because there is no well-defined "price" of technology, we cannot compare prices across countries to see if the countries' technology markets are integrated. We can, however, try some other approaches. First, we can infer technological differences between countries from productivity differences between their respective industries. And, second, we can look at the speed with which specific new technologies have spread around to the rest of the world. Both lines of evidence strongly suggest that technology is not perfectly mobile across countries.

When it comes to productivity, there are significant differences across countries, both in the aggregate and in particular industries. For example, automobile production is vastly more efficient in South Korea and Japan than in Malaysia and Indonesia. In fact, even within a single country, firms within the same industry sometimes differ widely in their productivity, as we will see in Chapter 7.

When to comes to the international spread of specific technologies, the pace at which these are adopted has varied significantly from country to country. Consider the telephone, for example. As shown in Figure 6.4, Japan started out far behind Germany and Argentina in 1900, but it surpassed Argentina in the 1960s and caught up with Germany in the 1970s.

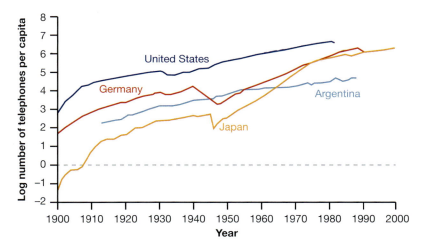

Figure 6.4 The Diffusion of the Telephone, 1900–2000
Source: Used with the permission of the University of Chicago Press, Diego A. Comin and Bart Hobijn (2011), "Technology Diffusion and Postwar Growth," NBER Macroeconomics Annual *25: 209–259.*

The speed with which a country adopts a new technology depends on a variety of factors, such as the size of the market and consumers' real income (GDP per person). Structural barriers also play a role; these can include political instability, a lack of property rights, or government restrictions on the use of new technology. (China bans Google, Facebook, and other foreign websites, and North Korea has yet to allow people free access to the internet as such.) These barriers to the spread of technology are quantitatively important. One study finds that cross-country variation in the adoption of technologies accounts for at least 25% of per capita income differences.

However, technologies spread more quickly around the globe today than they did a generation ago. As Figure 6.5 shows, steam ships and railways were adopted much more slowly around the world than cell phones and the personal computer have. In particular, cell phones have proliferated very quickly. In 2001 India had 4 million cell phone users; a decade later, that number had reached 750 million, and in 2015 the figure topped 1 billion.

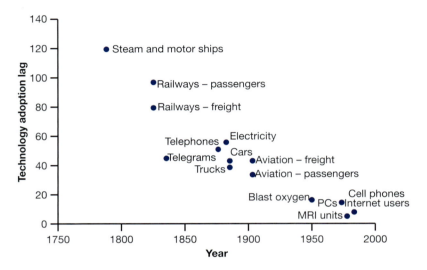

Figure 6.5 The Diffusion of Technology
Source: Diego Comin and Bart Hobijn (2010), "An Exploration of Technology Diffusion," American Economic Review *100: 2031–2059; reproduced with permission of the* American Economic Review.

6.3 INTERNATIONAL LABOR AND TECHNOLOGY MOBILITY IN THE RICARDO MODEL

Broadly speaking, evidence suggests that labor is not very mobile across countries, capital is quite mobile, and technology is becoming more mobile over time. What do our models have to say about the impact of such mobility on national economies?

In Chapter 4, we developed a simple two-country model with two goods – food and clothing – and one factor of production, labor. Labor is mobile between sectors; that is, workers can produce either food or clothing. While goods can move freely between countries, labor is assumed to be immobile across countries. As a result, each good can be priced the same in the two countries, but wages may differ because of productivity differences. This gives workers an incentive to move from the low-wage country to the high-wage country. Since wages are tied to productivity, labor would have an incentive to move from countries where technology is poor and productivity is low to countries where technology is better and productivity is higher.

In this framework, what happens if we allowed labor to move between countries? In Chapter 4, we used the example of the United States and China, but now let us use the United States and Mexico. These two countries share a long border that, despite legal restrictions and physical barriers, makes it relatively easy for Mexican workers to migrate to the United States in search of higher wages, at least in comparison to people in Africa or Asia.

In Chapter 4, we used a_C and a_F for the productivity of labor – units of output per worker – in the clothing and food sectors, respectively. The top panel of Table 6.1 gives some hypothetical numbers for the two countries. In this case, the United States has the absolute advantage in the production of both goods: it can produce food more efficiently than Mexico ($a_F > a_F^*$, with * denoting Mexico) and it can produce clothing more efficiently than Mexico ($a_C > a_C^*$). Because labor is more productive in the United States, American wages will be higher than Mexican wages.

Table 6.1 Absolute and Comparative Advantage

Absolute Advantage

	Food units per worker	Clothing units per worker
United States	20	10
Mexico	8	8

Comparative Advantage

	Food per unit of clothing	Clothing per unit of food
United States	2	1/2
Mexico	1	1

However, as you will recall, what determines the pattern of production and trade is not absolute advantage but, rather, comparative advantage. In the lower panel of Table 6.1, the two countries' ratios of productivity indicate that the United States has a comparative advantage in producing food ($a_F/a_C > a_F^*/a_C^*$) and, conversely, Mexico has a comparative advantage in producing clothing ($a_C^*/a_F^* > a_C/a_F$). This table also gives us the autarky relative prices of food and clothing in each country. In the United States, the relative price of clothing in terms of food (a_F/a_C) is 2 and in Mexico the relative price of clothing (a_F^*/a_C^*) is 1.

Although Mexico has a comparative advantage in clothing, it would be better to have Mexico's labor producing clothing with the superior US technology. This can be accomplished in one of two ways: either Mexican labor can move to the United States, so that it produces clothing with $a_C = 10$ instead of $a_C^* = 8$, or US clothing technology can be moved to Mexico, so that a_C^* rises from 8 to 10. In other words, labor can move to where the best technology is (through labor migration), or technology can move to where the labor is (through foreign investment). The mobility of labor and technology are substitutes for one another, but let us consider each in turn.

Technology Mobility

Let us begin by allowing technology to move to labor. If US technology can quickly and easily be adopted by Mexico, then a_F^* will rise from 8 to 20 and a_C^* will rise from 8 to 10. Mexico's production possibility frontier will shift out as its workers become more productive. Wages in

Mexico will increase because of the productivity improvement, rising to the same level as in the United States.

Once the two countries have the same technology for producing food and clothing, however, and the same wages, the two countries will have the same autarky relative prices. This means the slopes of the two countries' production possibility frontiers will be identical, and so there will be no incentive for the countries to trade with one another. Mexico will be better off, even without trade, because its production possibility frontier will have shifted out. The United States, however, will be worse off, because it will no longer engage in trade with Mexico and so will no longer be able to obtain clothing at a lower relative price than before.

This scenario became the topic of controversy when Paul Samuelson, one of the most distinguished economists of the twentieth century and Nobel Prize winner, wrote (2004) that the United States might suffer a permanent, measurable loss of real income if China were to improve its productivity in goods exported by the United States. China's increased efficiency at producing those goods would increase their supply and reduce China's import demand for them, thus deteriorating the US terms of trade. In the worst-case scenario, as we have just seen in the example above, China would gain (because its productivity had improved) but the United States would lose, because it would be reduced to autarky, and there would be no gains from trade.

Some non-economists took this finding to imply the United States would lose from free trade and therefore would gain from a protectionist trade policy. Not so, responded Avinash Dixit and Gene Grossman, two leading international economists. As they wrote (2005): "Professor Samuelson's theoretical proposition remains valid as a logical possibility. But what are its policy implications? Alas, none." The United States could only choose whether to continue trading or to retreat into a protectionist "Fortress America." There is not much the country could do to prevent the terms of trade from deteriorating and trade from declining. Adding tariffs to reduce trade even more would not improve the situation.

The one policy measure that might make sense for advanced countries is to try to prevent their technology from leaking out to other countries in the first place. During the Industrial Revolution of the nineteenth century, Britain tried to ban machinery exports and to prevent skilled artisans from leaving the country with technical knowledge. The United States is trying that with export controls on semiconductor technology. In the long run, however, it is almost impossible to prevent the international diffusion of technology.

Labor Mobility

Instead of having technology move to labor, as we have just done, let us assume that labor moves from Mexico to the United States in search of the better technology. Suppose that the labor force in each country initially numbers 200 workers. Figure 6.6 shows the production possibility frontiers for the two countries. The United States (on the left) can produce a maximum of 4,000 units of food or 2,000 units of clothing, and its relative price of clothing is 2. Mexico (on the right) can produce a maximum of 1,600 units of food or 1,600 units of clothing; its relative price of clothing is 1.

Without international labor mobility, we find the world production possibility frontier (PPF) by combining the individual United States and Mexican PPFs, as in Figure 6.7. When both countries produce just food, the maximum amount of food that can be produced is 5,600 units: 4,000 units in the United States and 1,600 units in Mexico. As we begin to produce some clothing, we initially do so in Mexico, the country with the lowest opportunity

6.3 INTERNATIONAL LABOR AND TECHNOLOGY MOBILITY IN THE RICARDO MODEL

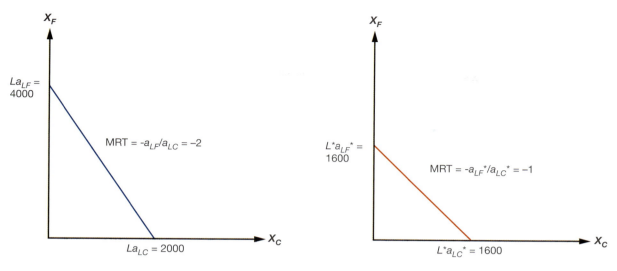

Figure 6.6 The United States' and Mexico's Production Possibility Frontiers This figure shows the production possibility frontiers of the United States and Mexico in isolation, without any labor mobility between them.

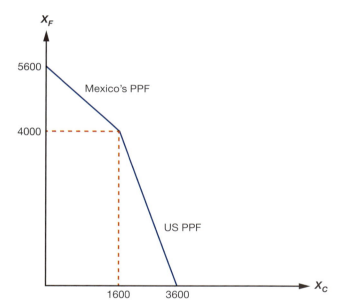

Figure 6.7 The Combined Production Possibility Frontier without Labor Mobility The world production possibility frontier, which is the combined production of the United States and Mexico without labor mobility between them, simply puts the two individual production possibility frontiers together. The joint PPF has two slopes based on the slopes of the individual country PPFs.

cost of producing clothing; i.e., the country with the comparative advantage in clothing. That is because less food production is sacrificed in making clothing in Mexico than in the United States. Therefore, the slope of the world PPF is initially that of Mexico.

However, Mexico can only produce a maximum of 1,600 units of clothing. If we wish to produce more clothing than that, we must do so in the United States, with a more costly marginal rate of transformation. Hence, we shift to a steeper slope that is equivalent to the US production possibility frontier. The United States can produce a maximum of 2,000 units of clothing, so if both countries only produce clothing, the maximum amount is 3,600 units. Thus, the combined PPF is "kinked" where the Mexican and the US PPFs meet.

Allowing international labor mobility changes the world production possibility frontier. Now a good will be produced only in the country with an absolute advantage in that good. Since the United States has an absolute advantage in both food and clothing, both goods will be produced only in the United States. Because wages are tied to productivity, US wages will exceed Mexican wages. All workers in Mexico will move to the United States, to avail themselves of the higher wages there.

What happens to the combined production possibility frontier? The total labor force of the two countries together is $L + L^* = 400$, and all workers are using US technology. The

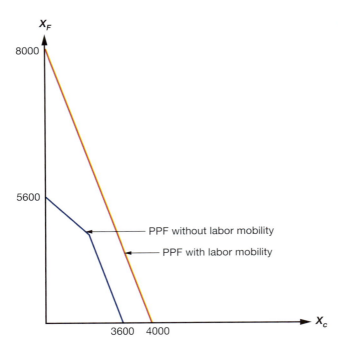

Figure 6.8 Joint United States–Mexico Production Possibility Frontier with and without Labor (or Technology) Mobility If labor is mobile between the United States and Mexico, workers will move to the country and produce the good where productivity is the greatest. The sectors with the highest productivity will attract workers because they can pay the highest wages. If technology is mobile between the two countries, Mexico will adopt US technology. In either case, workers become more productive and the world PPF shifts out compared to that without any mobility in workers or technology.

maximum amount of food that can be produced is 8,000 units, since $(L + L^*)a_F = 400 \cdot 20 = 8,000$. Note that this production level exceeds the level without labor mobility, where half of the world's labor force is using a less efficient technology: $La_F + L^*a_F^* = 200 \cdot 20 + 200 \cdot 8 = 5,600$. Similarly, with labor mobility, the maximum amount of clothing the two countries can produce is $(L + L^*)a_C = 400 \cdot 10 = 4,000$, which is larger than the maximum world production without labor mobility, $La_F + L^*a_F^* = 200 \cdot 10 + 200 \cdot 8 = 3,600$.

Figure 6.8 shows the two combined production possibility frontiers, with and without labor mobility. The world PPF with labor mobility looks like the left half of Figure 6.6, with the same slope, because all labor uses US technology; but the world frontier with labor mobility lies further out, because the size of the labor force using US technology has doubled. The combined PPF with labor mobility in fact lies entirely *outside* of the one without it. This implies that international labor mobility yields an economic gain beyond the standard gains from trade in goods.

This is the exact same combined production possibility frontier as the one we would have obtained by allowing cross-border movement of technology: either way, 400 workers end up producing food with productivity 20 and clothing with productivity 10. In our present Ricardian framework, labor mobility and **technology mobility** are substitutes for one another. Instead of having all Mexican workers move to the United States, US technology could move to Mexico and the result would be exactly the same. The free flow of technology, by foreign direct investment or other means, is a substitute for the movement of labor across countries.

How does the international mobility of labor or technology affect wages in the two countries? In either case, wages will be equalized. This does not mean, however, that US wages fall and Mexican wages rise, meeting somewhere in the middle. Instead, Mexican wages rise to the US level, while US wages are unaffected. (Because the productivity of American workers is unaffected, US wages do not change.) Wages of Mexican workers increase because they are now use a better technology and become more productive.

In fact, wages will be equal in the two countries because workers use the same technology. Recall from Chapter 4 that the wage paid in the food sector is $W_F = p_F a_F$ and the wage paid in the clothing sector is $W_C = p_C a_C$. So if the prices of the goods are the same in both countries because of trade, and if a_C and a_F are the same for US workers and Mexican workers, then their wages will be the same.

The finding that US wages are unaffected by immigration from Mexico, or the movement of US technology to Mexico, is based on the assumptions in the analysis. Later in this chapter, we will discuss empirical evidence about the impact of immigration on wages, to see if that outcome is plausible.

THEORY: Mill on Factor Mobility and Comparative Advantage

In his *Principles of Political Economy* (1848), John Stuart Mill, the great British economist and philosopher, explained how factor mobility was the basis for the distinction between absolute and comparative advantage. If there was free trade in goods, but labor and capital could also move across locations, then the goods would be produced only where it was absolutely the most efficient place to produce them. Comparative advantage would cease to exist as a separate concept.

To make the point, Mill contrasted productivity differences between nations with a hypothetical productivity difference between two neighboring parts of London:

> England might import corn from Poland and pay for it in cloth, even though England had a decided advantage over Poland in the production of both the one and the other. England might send cottons to Portugal in exchange for wine, although Portugal might be able to produce cottons with a less amount of labour and capital than England could.
>
> This could not happen between adjacent places. If the north bank of the Thames possessed an advantage over the south bank in the production of shoes, no shoes would be produced on the south side; the shoemakers would remove themselves and their capitals to the north bank, or would have established themselves there originally; for, being competitors in the same market with those on the north side ... they would not long content themselves with a smaller profit, when, by simply crossing a river, they could increase it. But between distant places, and especially between different countries, profits may continue different; because persons do not usually remove themselves or their capitals to a distant place without a very strong motive. If capital removed to remote parts of the world as readily, and for as small an inducement [in profits], as it moves to another quarter of the same town ... profits would be alike (or equivalent) all over the world, and all things would be produced in the places where the same labor and capital would produce them in greatest quantity and of best quality.

Mill went on to note that mobility of labor and capital seemed to be increasing as cultural differences between nations diminished. Even so, he doubted whether there could be enough international capital and labor mobility to ensure the equality of factor prices across countries. Today, as we saw in the previous section, capital is mobile enough to ensure that the marginal product of capital in different countries is roughly equivalent. But neither labor, nor even technology, is mobile enough to ensure that wages and productivity are equal across countries.

6.4 INTERNATIONAL LABOR AND CAPITAL MOBILITY IN THE SPECIFIC FACTORS MODEL

The Ricardo model has just one factor of production. What happens with international factor mobility in the other models? Chapter 5 set out the specific factors model, in which there are two goods, old and tech, and three factors of production: capital, which can be used in the production of either good; blue-collar workers, which can only be used to produce old goods; and white-collar workers, which can only be used to produce tech goods.

When we extend this model to consider the possibility of international factor mobility, we can study the movement of the mobile factor (capital) or of one of the two sector-specific factors (blue-collar workers or white-collar workers).

Capital Mobility

Let us first consider the international mobility of capital. We would expect capital to move from countries where the rate of return on capital is low to countries where the rate of return is high.

Suppose our country is relatively scarce in capital. Each unit of capital will then be used especially intensively, due to a relative surplus of workers, and therefore the return to capital in our country is higher than in the rest of the world. With international capital mobility, our country would receive an *inflow* of capital from the rest of the world. This inflow would give the country a larger capital stock than it had before, more capital for its specific factors (blue- and white-collar workers) to work with. The additional capital would increase the productivity of both types of labor, so the wages received by blue-collar and white-collar workers would increase. In other words, both specific factors benefit from having more of the mobile factor around. However, owners of existing capital would not welcome the inflow of capital. The additional capital would reduce the marginal value product of capital and therefore reduce the rate of return on capital in the country.

We can see this graphically in Figure 6.9. The horizontal axis represents the total amount of capital in the economy. An increase in the capital stock due to foreign investment means that the base of the diagram is extended, as shown on the right. (It does not matter whether the left axis or the right axis is moved, so long as the length of the horizontal axis increases.) The two marginal value product of capital curves are attached to the vertical axes and are pulled apart as the width of the diagram increases. (The marginal value product of capital schedules themselves do not shift, because the prices of old goods and tech goods do not change.) The increase in the amount of capital reduces the rental price of capital from p_K to p_K', and therefore the return on capital falls. Because the marginal value product of capital curves do not shift, the fall in the price of capital means that the area representing the wages of blue-collar and white-collar workers increases.

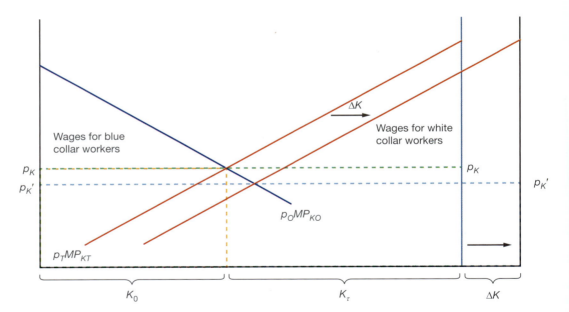

Figure 6.9 The Specific Factors Model with an Increase in Capital In the specific factors model, the mobile factor is represented on the horizontal axis. An increase in the amount of capital expands the base of the diagram, and the return to capital falls. The returns to the specific factors (blue-collar and white-collar workers) increases because each has more capital to work with.

Thus, an increase in the amount of capital means that existing capital owners (the mobile factor) are worse off, while blue- and white-collar workers (the specific factors) are better off.

Thus, both specific factors would welcome more of the mobile factor (foreign capital inflows) while existing capital owners would resist those inflows.

If instead of attracting capital, the country was to export capital to other countries, the local effects would be reversed. Capital-owners would welcome the chance to earn a higher rate of return on capital in other countries. Blue- and white-collar workers would suffer harm by having less capital to work with, leading to lower productivity and lower wages.

Labor Mobility

What about international mobility of one of the specific factors? Consider an influx of blue-collar workers, with no change in the number of white-collar workers or the amount of capital. An increase in the number of blue-collar workers would shift the marginal value product of capital curve in the old goods sector. As illustrated in Figure 6.10, this amounts to an increase in the demand for capital in the old goods sector. This raises the return to capital and attracts capital from the tech goods sector into the old good one. Owners of capital would benefit from this development.

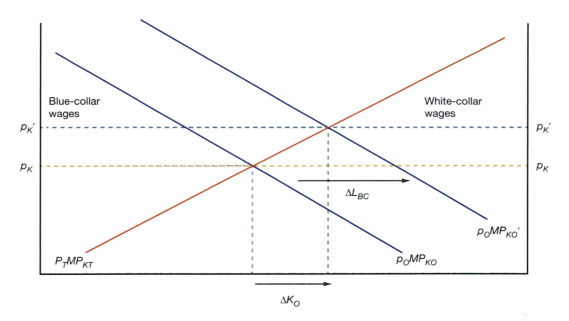

Figure 6.10 The Specific Factors Model with an Increase in Blue-Collar Workers An increase in the number of blue-collar workers is represented in the diagram by a shift in the marginal value product of capital in the old goods sector. This shift increases the return to capital, as it is shifted into the old goods sector, and reduces the wages of both blue-collar and white-collar workers.

What about wages? Wages of white-collar workers would fall because capital is reallocated away from the tech goods sector. Since white-collar workers would have less capital to work with, they would be less productive and hence earn a lower wage.

The impact on blue-collar wages at first seems ambiguous: there is more capital in the old goods sector, but there are also more blue-collar workers. The impact on wages depends on which increased more. If the overall amount of capital per worker increases, workers are more productive, and wages increase. If capital per worker falls, workers are less productive, and wages decrease. But which is it?

The answer can be seen in Figure 6.10. The marginal value product of capital curve in the old goods sector is shifted to the right, and note that the price of capital increases, as the old goods sector tries to attract capital from the tech goods sector. The implied increase in the marginal productivity of capital in the old goods sector points to a drop in the amount of capital per blue-collar worker. As a result, the wages of those workers fall, because their productivity falls.

Consequently, an increase in *one* of the specific factors reduces the returns to *both* specific factors. In this case, an increase in the number of blue-collar workers depresses the wages of both blue- and white-collar workers. However, an increase in one of the specific factors increases the return to the mobile factor, in this case capital. Therefore, both blue- and white-collar workers would oppose blue-collar immigration, while owners of capital would favor it.

A similar result occurs with the immigration of white-collar workers in the tech sector. Suppose there was an expansion of the H1-B visa program, which allowed skilled foreign labor to work in the United States. This would shift capital from the old goods sector to the tech sector and would increase the output of tech goods while decreasing the output of old goods. The return to capital would increase, while the wages received by white- and blue-collar workers would fall. Again, both kinds of workers would be against immigration, while owners of capital would welcome it.

Thus, immigration has different implications in the specific factors model than in the Ricardo model. In the Ricardo model, immigration has no impact on domestic wages, because wages are determined by labor productivity (technology), which does not change as a result of immigration or emigration. In the specific factors model, if labor is the specific factor, immigration reduces domestic wages, because they are determined by the marginal product of labor, given a fixed amount of capital in the economy. With more workers and the same amount of capital, wages fall.

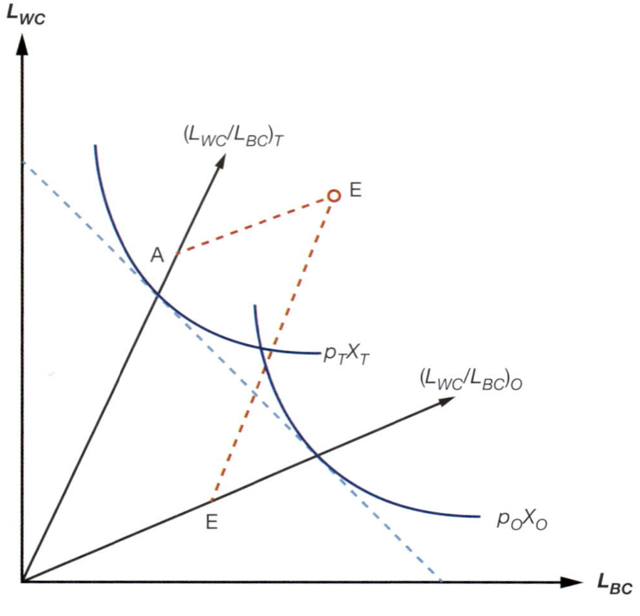

6.5 INTERNATIONAL FACTOR MOBILITY IN THE MOBILE FACTORS MODEL

Chapter 5 also presented the mobile factors model, in which tech and old goods are each produced by a mix of blue-collar and white-collar workers, but in different proportions: tech goods are white-collar worker intensive, and old goods are blue-collar worker intensive. How does adding international factor mobility to the mobile factors model play out?

Figure 6.11 recaps the mobile factors model. Each unit-value isoquant represents a range of combinations of white-collar and blue-collar workers that can be used to produce a dollar's worth of one of the two goods. The different locations of the isoquants reflect the difference in how intensively each type of worker is relied on. The dashed line tangent to the isoquants indicates the equilibrium wage of blue-collar workers relative to white-collar workers. The slopes of the rays running

Figure 6.11 The Mobile Factors Model This diagram, used in Chapter 5, shows the isoquants related to the production of old goods and tech goods, both of which use blue-collar workers and white-collar workers. The production of old goods uses blue-collar workers intensively and the production of tech goods uses white-collar workers intensively.

6.5 INTERNATIONAL FACTOR MOBILITY IN THE MOBILE FACTORS MODEL

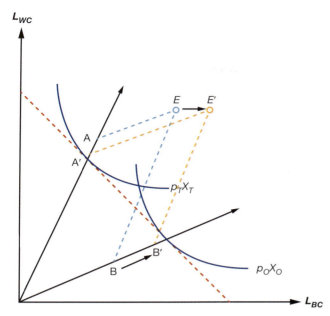

Figure 6.12 An Increase in the Number of Blue-Collar Workers in the Mobile Factors Model An increase in the number of blue-collar workers shifts the factor endowment point from E to E', leading to a shift in production. More blue- and white-collar workers are employed in the old goods sector, where production increases as the economy moves from B to B'. Fewer blue- and white-collar workers are employed in the tech sector, where production decreases as the economy moves from A to A'.

from the origin through the two points of tangency indicate the equilibrium proportions of white- to blue-collar workers used in the production of each goods. The rays clearly show that tech goods are white-collar intensive and old goods are blue-collar intensive, i.e., $(L_{WC}/L_{BC})_T > (L_{WC}/L_{BC})_O$.

The economy's endowment of white-collar and blue-collar workers is represented by point E. Using the factor proportion rays and the factor endowment point, we can draw a parallelogram that gives the number of white- and blue-collar workers employed in each sector. Point A represents the workers in the tech sector, producing (the parallelogram reveals) more than a dollar's worth of tech goods. At point B, a greater mix of blue-collar workers are producing old goods – less than a dollar's worth.

Now we are set to consider the impact of immigration on production and relative wages. Suppose blue-collar workers immigrate to the country. As shown in Figure 6.12, this shifts the economy's endowment point E horizontally rightward, to E'. Now the economy has the same number of white-collar workers as before, but more blue-collar workers. How does this affect the country?

First, we assume that the prices of goods are set on the world market – the small country assumption first mentioned in Chapter 2 – and do not change as a result of immigration. (In essence, we are assuming that the country is not big enough for changes in its output to affect world prices.) Since prices do not change, the unit value isoquants do not change, and therefore neither does the relative wage line tangent to them, or the factor proportion rays. Thus, because we assumed no change in the prices of the two goods, immigration does not change the relative wages of white- and blue-collar workers.

What has changed? Production. In Figure 6.12, when the endowment point changes from E to E', the parallelogram changes, too. The movement from A to A' along the tech sector factor proportion ray means that less labor (both white- and blue-collar) is devoted to the tech goods sector, and the shift from B to B' means that more labor (both white- and blue-collar) is devoted to the old goods sector. With this shift in the allocation of labor, production of tech goods falls and production of old goods increases. Thus, the economy absorbs the inflow of blue-collar workers through a change in the production mix: output of the blue-collar worker intensive good increases, and output of the white-collar worker intensive good decreases.

The result would be similar in the case of immigration of white-collar workers. Then the country's endowment point would shift up, not rightward, from point E. Forming the parallelogram from this new point would increase the labor force in the tech goods sector and reduce the labor force in the old goods sector.

All along, the relative wage line has remained static, indicating that changes in factor endowments have no impact on factor rewards. However, this result comes with a caveat: it only holds if the new endowment point remains within the region bounded by the two factor intensity rays, a region sometimes called the **cone of diversification**. Inside the cone, both goods will be produced, and wages remain unchanged when factor endowments change. But if the endowment point ends up outside the cone, then the country will no longer produce both goods, and factor prices will have to adjust. In such a scenario, which we will not go into in detail, the parallelogram no longer applies. Instead, relative wages are given by a line passing through the endowment point, tangent to an isoquant for the good that remains in production.

One last implication from this diagram is worth noting. Suppose we have two countries with identical production technologies, identical prices on goods, and free trade between them. If the endowments of the two countries both lie within the cone of diversification, then both countries will have the same factor prices. This is known as **factor price equalization**. In this case, trade in goods is enough to equalize product prices and therefore factor prices, even if factor endowments are different.

Of course, we have already seen that wage rates are not equalized across countries. Because production technology is not the same in all countries, we would not expect to see factor price equalization. However, as technology spreads around the world and labor productivity in developing countries catches up to that in the developed countries, we might expect to see a gradual **convergence** in factor prices.

6.6 EMPIRICAL EVIDENCE ON IMMIGRATION AND WAGES

According to polls, most people believe that more immigration means fewer jobs and lower wages for domestic residents. Such sentiments are thought to have contributed to the "Brexit" movement in the United Kingdom and the election of Donald Trump in 2016. Yet the surprising conclusion from our simplified models is that the international movement of labor may not have a big impact on wages. In the Ricardo model and the mobile factors model, immigration does not reduce domestic wages (provided the economy remains in the cone of diversification). Only in the specific factors model does immigration reduce domestic wages.

What does the available empirical evidence say about the impact of immigration on wages? The best way of studying the relationship is to look at examples where the migration is driven by some large, sudden, and unexpected political event (in economic terms, is exogenous) rather than by existing wage differentials.

In a famous paper, David Card (1990) looked at the Mariel boatlift of 1980. Over a span of six and a half months, Cuba allowed roughly 125,000 of its citizens to leave the country for Miami, Florida. This amounted to a 7% increase in Miami's labor supply in a very short period of time. Many observers would expect such a large influx of workers into one city to depress local wages. But Card found otherwise. He examined the wages, employment rates, and unemployment rates for unskilled whites and blacks, for non-Cuban Hispanics, and for Cubans. While the wages of Cubans already in the United States were adversely affected, there was no discernible impact on the other groups. This suggests that the immigrant Cubans were a good substitute for native Cuban Americans but not a good substitute for other workers.

Another example comes from the 1960s. During World War II, when the United States had massive labor shortages, the government let farmers hire Mexican workers on seasonal permits, under a policy called the Bracero program. Over the program's 22-year life, more than 4.5 million Mexicans were permitted to work in the United States. In time, the program became politically untenable. "It is adversely affecting the wages, working conditions, and employment opportunities of our own agricultural workers," President John F. Kennedy declared in 1962. The program was terminated in 1964.

Very recently, however, Michael Clemens, Ethan Lewis, and Hannah Postel (2018) reviewed the data on American agricultural jobs and wages in the 1960s. They found that after the Bracero program was ended, farm wages rose in states where there had been many migrant workers, states where there had been few migrant workers, and states where there had been almost none. As shown in Figure 6.13, the preexisting trends seemed to continue, without being affected by the termination of the program. What *was* affected was the availability of cheap labor to pick crops. Producers responded by substituting capital for labor. In 1964, 97% of California tomatoes were picked by hand. By 1966, 90% of California tomatoes were picked by machine.

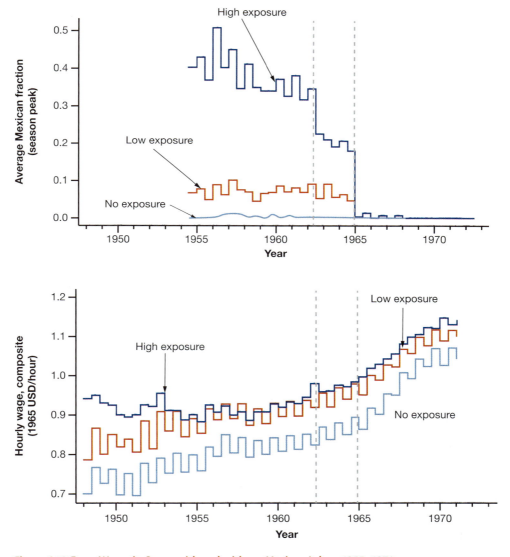

Figure 6.13 Farm Wages in States with and without Mexican Labor, 1955–1971

Source: Michael A. Clemens, Ethan G. Lewis, and Hannah M. Postel. 2018. "Immigration Restrictions as Active Labor Market Policy: Evidence from the Mexican Bracero Exclusion." American Economic Review, *108(6): 1468–1487; reproduced with permission of the* American Economic Review.

Another example comes from the massive immigration of Soviet Jews into Israel after the collapse of the Soviet Union in 1991. Between 1989 and 1996, 670,000 Russian Jews emigrated to Israel, increasing the country's population by 11% and its labor force by 14%. Most of the immigrants were highly skilled, with an education level greater than that of the existing Israeli population. Yet Neil Gandal, Gordon Hanson, and Matthew Slaughter (2004) found that the relative wage of skilled workers *increased* during this period. The explanation is not so much that the composition of industrial output changed to accommodate the increase in labor, as suggested by the mobile factors model, but that skilled-biased technical change increased the demand for skilled workers more than the increased supply.

Finally, Jennifer Hunt (1992) studied the repatriation of nearly a million people from Algeria into France in 1962. The immigrants settled in regions culturally and climatically similar to Algeria; in 1968, they represented 1.6% of the total French labor force. Hunt found that repatriates increased the 1968 unemployment rate of non-repatriates by 0.3 percentage points at most. Average annual salaries were reduced by 1.3%, at most, in 1967 due to their arrival.

As a result of studies such as those just described, economists have generally concluded that immigration has very little impact on domestic wages. In reviewing what economists know about the issue, Rachel Friedberg and Jennifer Hunt (1995) concluded: "Most empirical analysis ... finds that a 10% increase in the fraction of immigrants in the population reduces native wages by at most 1%. Even those natives who should be the closest substitutes with immigrant labor have not been found to suffer significantly as a result of increased immigration."

APPLICATION   The Reunification of Germany

After World War II, Germany was split into two countries. West Germany was a market-oriented democracy and East Germany was a communist country with a planned economy. Over time, standards of living became much higher in West Germany than in East Germany. In 1961, the East German government erected a wall in Berlin to keep its citizens from fleeing to the West. In 1989, in an amazing turn of events, East Germany opened its border to the West and citizens on both sides began taking down the wall. Soon, the two Germanys were reunified, although in truth West Germany simply absorbed East Germany.

What happened when the economies were joined together? Compared to the West, East Germany had lower wages and inferior technology. Unification meant that capital and technology could flow from the West to the East, and that workers could move from the East to the West. As expected, capital investment and new technology flowed from west to east and people moved from east to west. Between 1989 and 2001, nearly 8% of the population of East Germany migrated to West Germany. As shown in Figure 6.15, per capita GDP in

Figure 6.14 The Fall of the Berlin Wall in 1989
Source: Jacques Langevin/Sygma/Sygma via Getty Images.

6.6 EMPIRICAL EVIDENCE ON IMMIGRATION AND WAGES

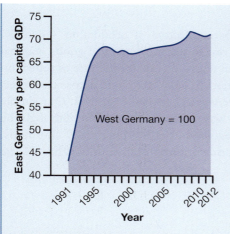

Figure 6.15 GDP per Capita in East Germany, Relative to West Germany, in %
Source: GDP per Capita: East Germany incl Berlin (2020) CEIC.

East Germany rose very quickly from about 40% to about 70% of West German levels, all within about five years after unification.

After this initial jump, however, wage and per capita GDP convergence slowed considerably. Significant differences in labor productivity between East and West Germany explain the persistent gap in wages and GDP per capita, which time has not eroded. Economists are still trying to understand why there has not been full convergence between the two regions (Burda and Weder, 2017).

The unification of Germany is an instructive experiment in market integration. Did the standard of living of West Germans suffer because of unification? Did competition from East Germany drive down West German wages? To the contrary, the main impact – consistent with the models developed in this chapter – was that East German living standards rose to approach West German levels, rather than West German standards falling to East German levels. (Of course, taxpayers in the West had to bear the burden of paying for many of the budgetary costs associated with unification.)

There was another important consequence of unification: 25 years after the fall of the Berlin Wall, which enabled East Germans to enjoy freedom and a higher standard of living, their reported happiness level rose almost to that prevailing in the West.

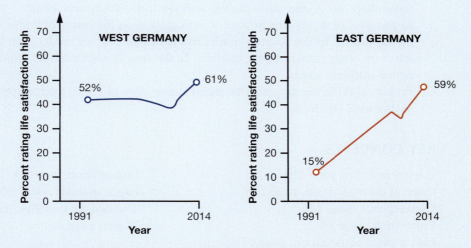

Figure 6.16 Life Satisfaction in West and East Germany, 1991 and 2014 Response to question: On the ladder of life 0 to 10, on which step do you stand at the present time? Percent answering 7, 8, 9, or 10
Source: "East Germans now as satisfied with life as West Germans," Pew Research Center, Washington, DC, November 6, 2014.

Are there other parts of the world that are ripe for such dramatic changes? Perhaps at some point, rich South Korea can peacefully absorb poor North Korea. Or perhaps Cuba will open up its economy to trade and investment from the rest of the world. There are many other parts of the world that could benefit from greater openness to capital and technology from other countries.

CONCLUSION

This chapter has examined the implications of different factors of production – namely, capital and labor – moving across countries, in contrast to the movement of goods. Capital appears to be highly mobile between countries, which tends to equalize the rate of return on capital across countries. Because there are more barriers to labor migration across countries, there is less evidence on whether it tends to equalize wages between countries. Our simple models do not give a common prediction about the wage effects of migration, although the gains to those who move from low-wage to high-wage countries are potentially enormous. Existing empirical evidence does not suggest that immigration in such countries has a large effect on local wages.

SUMMARY

1. Free trade in goods does not necessarily lead to the equalization of factor prices across countries, and hence there may be an incentive for labor or capital to move internationally.
2. Large differences in wages across countries suggest that labor mobility is low, and that the gains from international labor mobility are potentially quite large.
3. Capital is much more internationally mobile than labor. This is reflected in the low international differences in the rate of return on capital.
4. The mobility of technology lies between that of labor and that of capital. However, technology has gotten more mobile over the last century and a half.
5. At the level of theory, the impact of immigration on the wages of native workers depends on the model. In the Ricardo model and the mobile factor model, immigration does not affect the wage rates of native workers. In the specific factor model, immigration reduces native workers' wages.
6. Empirical evidence suggests that immigration does not have a large impact on the wages of domestic residents.

KEY CONCEPTS

Capital mobility, page 104
Cone of diversification, page 116
Convergence, page 116
Emigration, page 99
Factor price equalization, page 116

Immigration, page 99
Labor mobility, page 100
Technology mobility, page 110
Wages, page 99

REVIEW QUESTIONS

1. Why is labor less mobile internationally than capital or technology?
2. It is commonly believed that immigration reduces the wages of native workers. Why do the predictions from the Ricardo model, the specific factor model, and the mobile factor model differ so much in this prediction? What accounts for this difference?
3. What are the similarities and differences between technology moving between countries and labor moving between countries? How does it depend on the specific model being used?

4. What does the evidence of large, sudden migrations of people between countries suggest about the impact on wages in the receiving country?

EXERCISES

1. In 1989, the Berlin Wall fell and East Germany merged with West Germany. The level of technology in the West exceeded that in the East. Suppose that in each region there were the same two industries, with the labor productivities shown:

	Automobiles per worker	Sausages per worker
West	10	8
East	2	4

   a. Prior to unification, if there was trade between East and West Germany, which would specialize in which good?
   b. Where would wages be higher, and what would be the range of the wage rates (the wage in one country relative to the wage in another)?
   c. If there were 100 workers in West Germany and 100 workers in East Germany, draw the production possibility frontiers for both countries.
   d. Draw the combined production possibility frontiers for the two countries with and without labor mobility. Which way would labor move? How would things differ if technology could move just as easily? Who is better off under either scenario?

2. Consider the British economy using the specific factor model, in which white-collar workers are a specific factor in the finance sector, blue-collar workers are specific to manufacturing, and capital is mobile between the two sectors. When Britain left the European Union, suppose some white-collar workers in finance relocated to Frankfurt or Zurich, and the country lost capital as well. Which groups benefit and which groups lose as a result of Brexit?

3. In the mobile factor model, a change in the amount of capital or labor does not change the factor prices (return to capital, wages of labor) if the country remains in the cone of diversification. Does domestic consumption adjust to the change? Does domestic production adjust to the change?

4. In the mobile factor model, with capital and labor as the factors of production, what happens if a country receives more capital and labor in the same proportion as those factors are already found in the country?

RECOMMENDED RESOURCES

On general thinking about labor mobility over the past decades, see Michael Clemens, "Migration on the Rise, a Paradigm in Decline: The Last Half-Century of Global Mobility," *AEA Papers & Proceedings*, 112: 257–261.

A superb, recent book in immigration in the United States is Ran Abramitzky and Leah Boustan, *Streets of Gold: America's Untold Story of Immigrant Success* (Princeton, NJ: Princeton University Press, 2022).

The impact of immigration on labor markets is always a controversial subject. For some recent surveys, see Giovanni Peri, "Immigrants, Productivity, and Labor Markets,"

Journal of Economic Perspectives 30(4) (2016): 3–29. On the different findings of different studies, see Christian Dustmann, Uta Schönberg, and Jan Stuhler. "The Impact of Immigration: Why Do Studies Reach Such Different Results?" *Journal of Economic Perspectives* 30(4) (2016): 31–56.

On the barriers affecting labor migration, see Michael A. Clemens and Lant Pritchett. "Income per Natural: Measuring Development for People Rather than Places," *Population and Development Review* 34(3) (2008): 395–434.

On technology diffusion, see Diego Comin and Bart Hobijn, "An Exploration of Technology Diffusion," *American Economic Review* 100 (2010), 2031–2059, and Diego A. Comin and Bart Hobijn, "Technology Diffusion and Postwar Growth," *NBER Macroeconomics Annual* 25 (2011): 209–259.

CHAPTER 7

Firms and Trade: Economies of Scale and Product Variety

LEARNING OBJECTIVES

In this chapter, we learn about:
- "intra-industry trade," that is, two-way trade in similar but differentiated products
- how economies of scale give rise to specialization and trade
- how product variety is another source of gains from trade for consumers
- how increased global competition leads to larger firms and more varieties for consumers
- how individual firms respond to competition from imports and the opportunity to export

INTRODUCTION

The automobile industry has long captured America's imagination. Not only are cars an iconic part of national culture, but they are also essential for moving around – unless you happen to live in New York City.

The auto industry is dominated by a handful of large firms. Toyota, Volkswagen, Daimler, General Motors (GM), Ford, Honda, Fiat Chrysler, Nissan, and BMW are the global sales leaders. Each firm produces a wide array of vehicles: small and large sedans, minivans, SUVs, and pickups. And then there are specialty producers such as Tesla and Lamborghini.

International trade is also an important feature of the industry. The United States imports cars assembled in Canada, Mexico, Japan, Korea, and Germany. But it also exports cars – not just the cars turned out by GM and Ford, but also those produced by Toyota and Honda, BMW and Daimler – to other markets, most notably Canada, China, and Germany.

In some ways, this trade is puzzling. In previous chapters, we learned that international trade is based on differences in technology (Chapter 4) or factor endowments (Chapter 5). And trade consists of exports of one type of good (clothing) for imports of another, a wholly different type of good (food). Yet neither technology nor factor differences explain why the United States trades so many cars with Canada (whose technology and factors are similar to those in the United States), nor why the United States both exports *and* imports cars.

This suggests that our previous models of international trade were missing something. That something might be economies of scale and product differentiation, two features of the automobile market. One car plant will typically produce just one type of vehicle, in large quantities, to recoup the high fixed costs of production incurred each time an assembly line is reconfigured for a new vehicle type. On the consumption side, consumers value product variety, so that one family is liable to have a minivan or SUV for transporting kids and pets, or a sedan for long work commutes, or possibly a pickup for hauling loads.

This chapter examines why similar countries trade differentiated products with one another and why large firms play a major role in world trade. First, we want to explore the impact of trade on consumers and producers when firms are producing differentiated products with economies of scale. This situation is known as **monopolistic competition**. Second, we want to see how firms in an industry are affected by international competition, both in foreign markets, where the industry's export goods must compete with goods from other countries, and in the domestic market, where the industry's locally produced goods must compete with goods imported by foreign sellers. Although the framework in this chapter will be different from what we have seen before, the conclusion will be similar: countries can reap gains from trade. The nature of these gains, however, will be different from what we have seen before.

7.1 MONOPOLISTIC COMPETITION

Previous chapters focused on the reasons why countries would export one type of good and import another type, something known as **inter-industry trade**. In Chapter 3, the main example was the United States exporting food to China, in exchange for imports of clothing. Yet countries often export and import *similar* goods as well, as we have seen in the case of automobiles. This is called **intra-industry** trade, because it consists of two-way trade of goods in the same product category. To analyze this, we will need a different framework, called monopolistic competition, that incorporates product differentiation and economies of scale.

Product Differentiation and Economies of Scale

The reason for intra-industry trade, of course, is that goods can be quite different even within a product category. A luxury sedan differs from a sport utility vehicle or a pickup truck. Thus, intra-industry trade usually involves **differentiated products**, such as cars or consumer electronics, rather than homogeneous products, such as wheat, cotton, and coal. With the latter, one batch of a good is just like another batch of the same good, regardless of the producer; in other words, one bushel of wheat is pretty much a **perfect substitute** for another. However, when firms differentiate their products, one product is an **imperfect substitute** for another.

Of course, from the perspective of consumers there is a spectrum of substitutability. For many smartphone users, an Android phone is an imperfect substitute for an Apple iPhone, even though they perform similar functions. For most drivers, a Toyota Camry is a reasonably close substitute for a Honda Accord, but a Chevy pickup is a very imperfect substitute for a minivan.

Such differentiated products are often produced by large firms that enjoy **economies of scale**. When firms have to pay a fixed cost to produce a good, for instance to set up an assembly line, a large production volume makes each unit of output cheaper to produce. For example, if it takes $100 million to set up an automobile production facility, the auto maker will not want to produce just 100 or even just 1,000 cars. That low level of output would make the production cost per car prohibitively high. Instead, the firm will want to spread the $100 million fixed cost across tens of thousands of cars per year, for multiple years.

Unfortunately, differences in technology and factor endowments do not appear to explain intra-industry trade in differentiated products very well. In the case of automobiles, the technology and factors of production required to produce different vehicle types are very similar, and, in general, intra-industry trade often takes place between countries with similar technology and factor endowments, such as the United States, Japan, and European Union. Also, the technology and factor endowment explanations of trade that have assumed perfect competition tell us nothing about individual firms that might, by offering differentiated products, acquire some market power – that is, some ability to set their prices rather than just accept the market price as given.

The Model

To explain intra-industry trade, we need a framework that incorporates both product differentiation and economies of scale. This framework is known as **monopolistic competition**, because it is a hybrid of monopoly and competition. The monopoly element comes from the assumption that each firm produces a unique product that is an imperfect substitute for other products on the market. As a result, firms are not price-takers who face an infinitely elastic demand curve for their products (as they would if they were producing a homogeneous good). Rather, each firm faces a downward-sloping demand curve and can set its own price, somewhat like a monopolist.

At the same time, an individual firm is not a pure monopolist: the firm does face competition from other substitute products. This competition drives profits down to the normal industry level, which we assume for convenience to be zero.

Let us now see how monopolistic competition works. Figure 7.1 is the standard monopoly diagram, with downward-sloping demand (D), which is equivalent to average revenue (AR) for the firm, and marginal revenue (MR) curves. Although the marginal cost line, MC, is upward-sloping, the firm's average cost (AC) takes a U-shape, reflecting the economies of scale that come with fixed costs of production. So average costs fall over some range of output as those fixed costs are spread over a larger production volume.

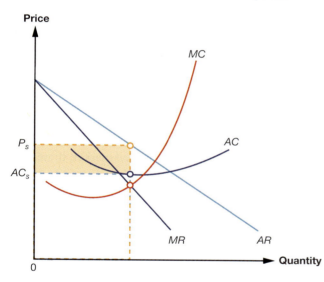

Figure 7.1 Monopoly Equilibrium In a situation of monopoly, the firm produces where marginal revenue equals marginal cost. The resulting price is above the firm's average cost and it earns profits.

As you will recall from your introductory economics class, the requirement for profit maximization is that marginal revenue equals marginal cost. Therefore, the profit-maximizing level of output is determined by the intersection of the MR and MC curves (where $MR = MC$). The firm earns profits, since the price, on the demand curve, exceeds the average cost of production ($P > AC$) at the profit-maximizing quantity. Compared to the outcome in a competitive market, where the price would equal the marginal cost, the monopolist firm restricts its output to increase the price and thereby increase its profits (represented by the shaded area). In other words, the monopolist is "under-producing" relative to the total industry output in a perfectly competitive market.

This monopoly might persist if barriers prevented other firms from entering the market. But if there are no barriers to entry, other firms will take note of the monopolist's success and start producing similar products. The entry of new firms increases competition in the market, even if those new firms are producing differentiated products that are only imperfect substitutes for the good produced by the monopolist.

Increased competition does two things to the demand curve facing the incumbent monopolist: it *shifts* the demand curve, and it also *rotates* it. First, when consumers have a greater number of substitute products to choose from, their demand for the former monopolist's product declines, which shifts the demand curve left (or down). In other words, the market is now being divided among two or more firms, so demand is being pulled away from the former monopolist. Second, the demand that remains is more price-sensitive, and hence the demand curve also becomes flatter (more elastic). With perfect competition, the demand curve would become a horizontal line and the firm would have no control over price at all. However, because the competitor's goods are imperfect substitutes for the monopolist, the demand curve remains non-horizontal (because it is still producing a unique variety) but acquires a shallower slope.

How should we think about this shift and rotation of the demand curve? Imagine competition between restaurants. If there is only one restaurant in town, it can charge a relatively high price. If there are two restaurants in the town, by contrast, then even if the two dining experiences are not quite the same, any price difference will steer some patrons toward the cheaper establishment. The more restaurants there are, the greater this price-sensitivity will be, and hence the flatter the demand curve.

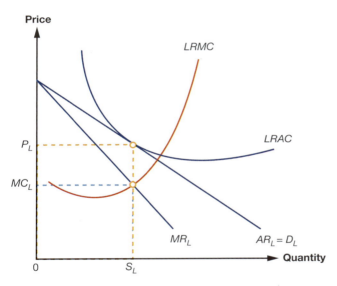

Figure 7.2 Monopolistic Competition Equilibrium In a situation of monopolistic competition, a firm produces where marginal revenue equals marginal cost. However, competition ensures that there are no extra profits to be made and the price equals the firm's average cost.

The shifting and rotating of the demand curve also reduces market prices. The entry of new firms into the market continues until the monopolistically competitive equilibrium, shown in Figure 7.2, is reached. We still have $MR = MC$, the condition for profit maximization, but now competition has lowered prices and has completely eliminated firms' profits. The market, therefore, no longer looks attractive to would-be entrants. At the profit-maximizing output quantity, price will just equal average cost, and the demand curve will be tangent to the average cost curve. Remember that the introduction of more competition did not change the shape or position of the average cost curve, but it did change the position of the demand curve. Therefore, the price fell to meet the average cost curve.

Starting from the monopolistic competition equilibrium in Figure 7.2, we can imagine yet another increase in competition, driven by the entry of yet more firms. Once again, these new firms produce close substitutes to existing products on the market. Once again, the demand curve facing each firm shifts and rotates. Once again, the tangency between the demand curve and the average cost curve must be maintained. However, the flatter demand curve will be tangent to the average cost curve at a higher level of output.

Because more competition means lower prices, firms respond by increasing output to reduce average costs (taking advantage of economies of scale) so that they can survive with the lower prices. Not all firms will be able to do this. The intensification of competition does not mean that all firms will be able to survive in the market. Not every firm may be able to have enough demand so that they can achieve economies of scale and become profitable. Those firms unable to produce enough to reduce average costs will be forced to drop out of the market. A firm in this situation may try to adjust its production processes so as to lower the AC curve. But if it cannot achieve profitability or at least break even, the firm will be forced to drop out of the market.

The bottom line is that, starting in a monopolistic competition equilibrium, a further intensification of competition will force firms to take advantage of economies of scale – increasing the scale of their output – to reduce average costs. In such markets characterized by economies of scale and product differentiation, we would expect a relatively small number of large firms, not the many small firms in the idealized world of perfect competition.

IN PRACTICE Monopolistic Competition in Action

Do monopolistically competitive markets actually work in the way described in this chapter? Often, yes. In 1984, Chrysler introduced a strange new kind of vehicle, the minivan. Designed for families, the minivan was larger than a sedan and more comfortable than a station wagon, but smaller than a truck. Although the minivan was dubbed "uncool at any speed," US consumers loved the concept, and Chrysler made a bundle of money. For a brief period, it had the minivan market to itself. Other automobile companies, however, quickly set about producing minivans of their own: the Honda Odyssey, the Toyota Sienna, the Ford Aerostar, the Chevy Astro, the Mazda MPV, and a host of other vehicles that were similar, but not identical, to Chrysler's Dodge Caravan and Plymouth Voyager. The new competitors gave consumers an increasing range of choices. They began to erode Chrysler's market share and reduce its profits in the minivan market.

More recently, the market in tablet computers has undergone a similar evolution. Soon after the tremendous success of the Apple iPad, other firms began selling competing tablets, such as the Samsung Galaxy Tab and the Amazon Kindle Fire. This competition eroded Apple's domination of the market and provided consumers with a wider array of products, at lower prices. Apple cannot prevent its competition from entering the market, so it tries to maintain its dominant position by staying one step ahead of the competition and out innovating its rivals.

Figure 7.3 Lee Iacocca Introduces the Chrysler Minivan in 1983
Source: Bettmann/Getty Images.

Figure 7.4 Steve Jobs Introduces the iPhone in 2007
Source: David Paul Morris/Getty Images.

7.2 MONOPOLISTIC COMPETITION AND TRADE

In many ways, a monopolistically competitive market with trade works just like a domestic monopolistically competitive market. As more firms enter the market, the market power of existing firms is reduced, i.e., every firm's demand curve flattens (demand becomes more elastic), and it becomes important for firms to reduce average costs if they want to stay in business. Those firms that cannot keep the average cost in contact with the demand curve will be forced to drop out of the market.

The key difference that trade makes to the picture is the expansion of the market. The appearance of new competitors flattens the demand curve and tends to shift it leftward, and it does the same to the marginal revenue curve. But making a firm's goods accessible to a much larger pool of potential consumers tends to shift the demand and marginal revenue curves to the right. This makes it possible for the intersection of the marginal revenue and marginal cost curves to end up to the right of where they started, instead of the left. What this means is that, with trade, there is a new way for firms to minimize average cost, to increase output, to take advantage of economies of scale. This is something that does not readily happen with domestic monopolistic competition, where the market size is much less variable.

For firms struggling to stay in the market, then, trade can present a stark choice: grow or fail. Consider what happened to the US automobile industry when it faced serious foreign competition for the first time in the 1970s. At the time, there were four US automobile manufacturers: General Motors, Ford, and Chrysler – the Big Three – and American Motors Corporation (AMC). But Japanese producers (Toyota, Datsun – later renamed Nissan – and Honda) began increasing their share of the US market in the 1970s and 1980s. They put AMC out of business and forced the Big Three producers to cut their costs and become more efficient. Consumers gained by having more varieties to choose from and from having greater price competition in the market.

How can we incorporate international trade into our monopolistic competition framework? We will begin by constructing a diagram that shows the relationship between the *number of varieties* consumers can choose from and the *average size* of firms. Our proxy for the number of varieties will be the number of firms in the market, under the assumption that each firm is producing a distinct variety. Our proxy for the average size of firms will be average output volume. Since there are economies of scale, larger-output firms will have lower average costs and therefore will be able to charge consumers a lower price. (An appendix to this chapter presents an alternative, algebraic version of the monopolistic competition model.)

We can now create a model based on relationships between our two variables: firm size and number of firms. The two relationships we will describe are the market-size effect and the within-market effect.

The Market-Size Effect

The **market-size effect** describes a positive relationship between the number of firms (varieties) and the average firm size (output) as the market size increases. Larger markets – meaning those with more consumers or higher incomes – have more firms in competition with one another. In addition, those firms will, on average, be larger, meaning that they will have lower average costs than smaller firms. Thus, large markets will have large firms with many varieties to choose from, while small markets will have small firms with fewer varieties to choose from.

To picture this effect in action, think about a small, rural town, with only one store for each type of service: one hardware store, one drug store, one grocery store, one diner. Each of those stores is small, and the goods are on the pricey side. And now contrast that with a major

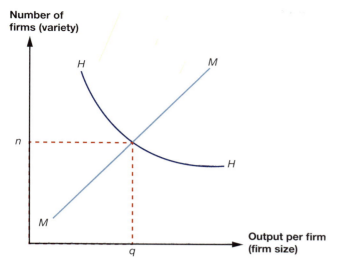

Figure 7.5 Monopolistic Competition Equilibrium The *HH* line represents the tradeoff within a country between having many small firms producing many varieties or having a few large firms producing a few varieties. The *MM* line represents the market-size effect and shows that larger markets have more and larger firms. The intersection of the two schedules shows the equilibrium number of firms and the average firm size for a particular country.

metropolitan area, where there are many competing stores, and each store is pretty large. There are big-box hardware stores like Lowe's and The Home Depot; drug stores such as Rite Aid, Walgreens, and CVS; supermarkets like Kroger and Albertson's; and restaurants such as Applebee's, Olive Garden, and Red Lobster. These large firms all keep their costs down through large sales volume.

Thus, as a market grows larger, we would expect to see more firms (greater varieties) and larger firms (lower costs and hence lower prices). In Figure 7.5, the upward-sloping *MM* line represents the market size effect, with a positive relationship between number of firms and average firm size: as one moves outward along the *MM* line, we are considering a larger market in which both the number of firms and the firms' average size increases. This relationship comes out of our earlier discussion of monopolistic competition: with more firms operating in a market, the demand curve facing each firm will be more elastic (flatter) and firms will have to become larger to lower their costs, which is done through economies of scale.

The Within-Market Effect

The **within-market effect** considers the tradeoff (a *negative* relationship) between the number of firms (variety) and the size of firms (output per firm) in a market of fixed size, meaning one where the number of consumers and their purchasing power are held constant.

Within a market of fixed size, there is a range of ways to organize production. At one extreme, we could have many small firms each producing a small amount and charging relatively high prices, because economies of scale are not fully utilized. This market would be rich in variety, but consumers would have to pay for that variety via higher prices. At the other extreme, we could have few firms each producing a large amount and charging relatively low prices, because economies of scale had reduced their production costs. This market would lack variety, but consumers would pay lower prices. Thus, there are costs and benefits to consumers at each extreme. (We are less interested in the effect on producers because, in any case, competition is sufficient to ensure zero profits.)

Thus, in a market of a fixed size, consumers face a tradeoff: they can have many varieties produced by many small, high-cost firms, or a few varieties produced by a few, low-cost firms. This tradeoff between variety and size is reflected in the downward-sloping *HH* curve in Figure 7.5.

By way of example, consider the beer industry. One way of organizing the industry would be to have dozens of microbreweries, each producing a unique and distinctive brew. Their cost, and hence the sale price, would be high, but consumers would have many beers to choose from. Another, very different way to organize the industry would be to have one massive factory churning out just one type of beer (Keystone Light, perhaps). The beer would be cheap because of the extreme economies of scale, but consumers would have to content themselves with one type of beer.

Or consider the automobile industry. If there were unlimited economies of scale, one might minimize costs and prices with one enormous production facility that produced just one model of car. Henry Ford, who revolutionized the auto industry by introducing the assembly line, would have approved of this approach. When he introduced the Model T in 1908, he famously said that you could have the car in any color you wanted "as long as it was black." Ford was focused on churning out identical black Model T's at the lowest possible cost, to make them affordable to the general public.

A very different way of organizing the automobile industry would be to have many different firms producing many different varieties of automobile, each customized to cater to the tastes of a narrow consumer niche. Some firms would specialize in two-seater sports cars, others in luxury sedans, still others in off-road capable SUVs. There would be firms that made only gasoline-powered cars and firms that made only electric cars (like Tesla). There might be a firm that turned out stainless steel DeLoreans (as featured in the 1985 film *Back to the Future*), and another firm that sold amphibious cars, like the WaterCar Panther (Figure 7.6). This abundant variety would satisfy consumers' desires for different types of cars, but each specialized vehicle would be very expensive to produce, because firms would not be able to take full advantage of economies of scale.

Figure 7.6 Product Differentiation in Auto Production: Amphibious Cars
Source: Kevin Sullivan/Digital First Media/Orange County Register via Getty Images.

Autarky Equilibrium and Trade

In Figure 7.5, the intersection of the market-size schedule MM and the within-market schedule HH determines the equilibrium number of firms, n, and the average size of those firms, q. Obviously the location of the equilibrium depends on the locations of the curves. If the market were larger, the HH schedule would lie further out. The equilibrium in this larger market would involve more firms, and they would be larger and thus have lower costs. For consumers, that equilibrium would mean more varieties and lower prices. However, if consumers' tastes were different, so that they preferred more variety, even at a higher price, the MM schedule would lie higher. The equilibrium would have more varieties but smaller firms, and therefore higher prices for consumers, which they would be willing to pay in order to enjoy the greater number of varieties.

We are now ready to examine the effects of international trade. Consider two countries of unequal size, the United States and Canada, represented by two HH schedules in Figure 7.7. We assume identical consumer preferences in the two countries, and therefore we have just one MM schedule. The United States is the larger

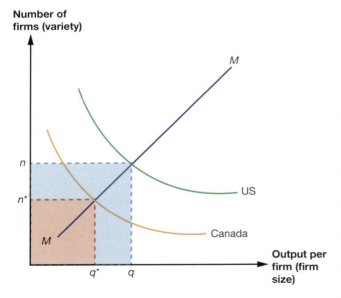

Figure 7.7 Monopolistic Competition: United States and Canada in Isolation This diagram shows that the United States has a larger market than Canada, as indicated by the HH line being drawn further out than the market size line. As a result, the United States has more firms and larger firms, in equilibrium, than Canada does.

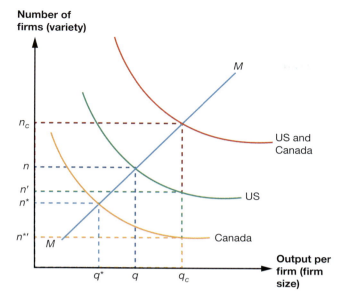

Figure 7.8 Monopolistic Competition: United States and Canada in Single Market When the United States and Canada integrate their two separate markets, there is a larger single market that is a combination of the two of them. Together, the single market has more firms and larger firms than either market had in isolation. Firms in the United States and Canada must become larger to reduce average costs and compete against more rivals, but the number of firms in each market separately declines. This is more the case in Canada than in the United States because Canada is a smaller market.

country and, in the autarky equilibrium, has more and larger firms than Canada does. The autarky number of firms is n in the United States and n^* in Canada, while the average firm size is q in the United States and q^* in Canada. This implies that American consumers enjoy a greater variety of products (since there are more firms in the US market) and lower prices (since firms are larger and have lower average costs) than Canadian consumers do.

Now suppose the United States and Canada reach an agreement to integrate their two economies, which in fact they agreed to do in 1988. What happens when the two markets are put together? In essence, the individual US and Canadian markets become a single North American market. This means vertically adding together the US and Canada HH schedules, as shown in Figure 7.8. To see why we add vertically, suppose instead the two markets were initially of identical size. Then the initial average firm size would be $q = q^*$, and that would also be the initial q for the combined market, prior to re-equilibration. The new number of firms, however, would be $n + n^*$ (i.e., $2n = 2n^*$ for $n = n^*$). The new US and Canada schedule now represents the within-market effect for the integrated North American market.

The new equilibrium is where the joint US and Canada HH schedule intersects the MM line. In the combined market, there will be more firms competing with one another than there were in each country in isolation. In addition, each firm has to become larger than before, because the market is larger, competition has intensified, and the demand curve facing each particular firm has become more elastic. In becoming larger, each firm will be able to reduce their costs due to the economies of scale.

The Shakeout Effect

We can trace what happens in the individual US and Canadian markets by drawing lines from our new equilibrium point back to the original US and Canada schedules. The new single market equilibrium consists of n_C firms producing q_C output, more and larger firms producing in the larger market. However, because competition has intensified, some domestic firms – those with higher costs or producing specialty products for which there is limited demand – will be driven out of business. Small firms with high fixed costs will not be able to survive in the market where competition has pushed prices down. Therefore, the number of producing firms in each country declines: in the United States, n falls to n', and in Canada n^* falls to $n^{*\prime}$. The firms that ultimately survive will take advantage of the larger integrated market by expanding and reducing their costs: the average size of US firms increases from q in the United States and q^* in Canada to q_C in the combined market.

The decline in the number of domestic firms is called the **shakeout effect**, in which smaller, high-cost firms will go out of business or be absorbed by larger firms in an industry consolidation. In fact, around the time that two markets become integrated, there is usually a wave of firm mergers. This is because firms seek to position themselves to take advantage of the larger market and to prepare themselves for new competition.

Notice, however, that the severity of the shakeout effect is different in the two countries. Because the United States is much larger than Canada, adding the Canadian market onto the US market is a minor event for US firms. The fraction of US firms that drop out of the market, because of the new Canadian competition, is relatively small, and the required percentage change in firm size also is fairly small. For Canadian firms, by contrast, it is a shock, because they must now compete in the much larger North American market. A relatively small number of Canadian firms, modest in size, are exposed to competition from the larger and more numerous American firms. Some Canadian firms will go bankrupt or be absorbed by their competitors, and the survivors must become much larger to service the entire North American market.

In other words, firms that survive in the smaller country have to adjust more than firms in the larger country when the two markets are integrated. In algebraic terms, $(n^* - n^{*\prime})/n^*$ is larger than $(n - n')/n$, and $(q_C - q^*)/q^*$ is larger than $(q_C - q)/q$. To illustrate with specific numbers: suppose there are 20 firms in the United States producing 100 units of output each, and ten firms in Canada each producing 60 units of output. When the two markets are integrated, there are initially 30 firms competing with one another, but not all of them can survive. After the shakeout effect, perhaps 25 firms can survive – say, 18 from the United States and seven from Canada. The surviving firms will produce more output – perhaps 110 units on average, a huge increase for the surviving Canadian firms but a much smaller increase for the US firms. Note that the number of US firms has fallen by two and the number of Canadian firms has fallen by three. These firms either go out of business or merge with competitors.

Do producers gain from market integration? In a sense, no: firms earn zero profits in the monopolistic competition equilibrium in autarky, and they earn zero profits in the monopolistic competition equilibrium with trade. However, some firms will be winners in the sense that they will expand and take advantage of the larger market, while other firms will lose and go out of business or be taken over by their rivals. These firm-level effects will be examined in more detail later in the chapter.

What about consumers? Consumers in both countries unambiguously benefit from the market integration. With our hypothetical numbers, Canadian consumers used to be able to choose from ten domestic varieties (because there were only ten domestic firms), but after integration they get to choose from 25 varieties. And American consumers, with the addition of Canada to the overall market, see their options increase from 20 varieties to 25. In addition, consumers in both markets will see lower prices because of market integration. Because of economies of scale, the larger average firm size translates into lower average costs and hence lower prices. In sum, for consumers, there is no tradeoff: they will enjoy more variety *and* lower prices as a result of market integration.

While Canadian firms have more of an adjustment to make than their American counterparts, Canadian consumers get more of the benefit from market integration: prices fall more for Canadian consumers than for American consumers because there is a greater proportional increase in firm size on the Canadian size and therefore a greater reduction in firms' costs. As we saw in Chapter 2, smaller countries tend to gain more from increased trade than larger countries.

7.3 VARIETY GAINS FROM TRADE FOR CONSUMERS

The preceding analysis suggests that having access to a wider variety of goods is associated with a monetary gain for consumers, in the form of lower prices. But there is also a more direct benefit: people like variety because it gives them a wide range of options that will increase their utility level. If everyone were content to buy the same phone, firms would not bother producing such a wide array of different phones, each with slightly different characteristics and features. Evidently, consumers value the different features of the phones differently. (Of course, there are diminishing returns – or increasing costs – to variety. We do not have an infinite variety of smartphones, breakfast cereals, or automobiles.)

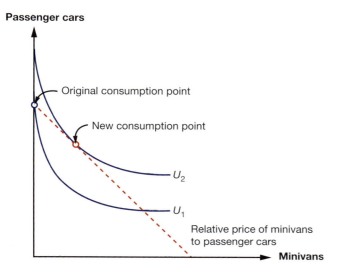

Figure 7.9 Welfare Impact of New Goods When there is only one type of vehicle on the market, the passenger car, consumer utility is measured solely on the vertical axis. When a new good (the minivan) is introduced onto the market, consumers now have a choice to buy either product. Consumer utility will rise with the newly available option.

Indifference curves provide us with one way of understanding the issue. Figure 7.9 shows the indifference curves for the consumption of an original good, namely a passenger car, and a new good, the minivan. Before the introduction of the minivan, consumers could only buy the passenger car. Utility increases along the vertical axis, and the original consumption point is on this axis. The indifference curve associated with this consumption point gives us a utility level U_1, but there is no possibility of substituting a non-existent minivan for a passenger vehicle. The budget constraint is effectively vertical, indicating that the price of the new good is essentially infinite – in fact, it does not even exist – and that only the original good will be consumed.

When a new good, the minivan, is introduced onto the market, consumers are now able to purchase it at some price. To maximize utility and get onto the highest indifference curve possible, consumers will reallocate some of their consumption expenditure to include purchases of minivans in addition to passenger cars. Note that the budget constraint (indicated by the dashed line) of the individual has not changed, because the individual's total spending has not changed; the same quantity of original goods could have been purchased as before. Now, however, the consumer is spending less on passenger cars and some nonzero amount on minivans. Consequently, the utility level is higher, because a new and different good is available for purchase.

How do we treat the value of variety in formal terms? We can try to specify this through a particular utility function that indicates how much consumers value variety. A family that wishes to have two cars can purchase two units of the very same car, or they can purchase cars designed for two different purposes – a pickup truck for hauling things and a minivan for hauling kids and dogs. The number of cars is the same, but the family with two – a pickup and a minivan – gets some extra measure of utility from having two *different* cars. Can we model this increase in utility?

One way of illustrating the potential gains from variety is to modify our standard utility function. The standard utility function expresses utility simply as a linear function of the quantity of a good consumed: if c_A stands for the number of automobiles consumed, then a simple utility function could be written as

$$u(c_A) = c_A, \tag{7.1}$$

where c_A is the number of automobiles consumed. In this case, if $c_A = 2$, then the utility level is 2; if $c_A = 3$, then the utility level is 3. In this case, the type of car does not matter: a BMW counts the same, and is viewed as being identical to, a Subaru. Every car is viewed as a perfect substitute for any other car and adds the same amount to a person's utility.

We can modify this utility function to incorporate the effects of variety by introducing the **elasticity of substitution**, usually denoted σ. The elasticity of substitution tells us how "substitutable" one good is for another. The elasticity of substitution is formally defined as the percentage change in the relative quantities of two goods consumed divided by the percentage change in the relative price of two goods. For example, the elasticity of substitution between good q_1 and good q_2 is the percentage change in the relative consumption of the two goods $(\Delta q_1/\Delta q_2)(q_2/q_1)$ divided by the percentage change in the relative price of the two goods $(\Delta p_1/\Delta p_2)(p_2/p_1)$. (The elasticity of substitution is negative, because an increase in the relative price of good 1 will decrease the relative consumption of good 1, but we sometimes refer to the absolute value of the elasticity.)

The elasticity of substitution is very high if a small change in the relative price of the two goods leads to a large change in the relative quantities of the two goods being consumed. If two goods are viewed as being essentially the same – that is, they are close to perfect substitutes for one another – then the elasticity of substitution will be very large, even infinite in the case of perfect substitutes. If two goods are viewed as being very different from one another – that is, they are imperfect substitutes for one another – then the elasticity of substitution is very low.

For example, the elasticity of substitution of sweaters from JCPenney and Kohl's is relatively high, because those two chains tend to carry merchandise of similar cost, quality, and style. We might imagine that the elasticity of substitution is something on the order of 10, indicating that a small change in the relative price produces a big switch between buying from one store and buying from another. The elasticity of substitution of sweaters from Walmart and Neiman Marcus is much lower, because the price and quality are very different, and there are probably differences of style, as well. In this case, the elasticity of substitution might be relatively low, taking a value of, say, 1. (To put the point another way: JCPenney and Target compete for the same segment of the sweater market; Walmart and Neiman Marcus do not.)

Let's take the utility function in equation (7.1) and modify it by writing

$$u(c_A) = c_A^{(\sigma-1)/\sigma}, \tag{7.2}$$

where σ is the elasticity of substitution between different types of cars. If a consumer views any one car as a perfect substitute for any another car, and thus has no appreciation for product differences, the elasticity of substitution will be infinite (in absolute value, because the elasticity is negative). In this case, $(\sigma - 1)/\sigma$ will be close to 1 as σ approaches infinity. So if the household consumes two cars (so $c_A = 2$) and the cars are viewed as perfect substitutes, then $u(c_A) = 2^1 = 2$.

However, if the household values variety, then different cars are viewed as serving different functions. In this case, the elasticity of substitution is less than infinite: a BMW is not the same as a Subaru. For example, if $\sigma = -5$, then $(\sigma - 1)/\sigma = 1.2$, and two different cars will yield a higher level of utility than two identical cars: $u(c_A) = c_A^{(\sigma - 1)/\sigma} = 2^{1.2} = 2.3$. In this case, an increase in the absolute value of the elasticity of substitution from negative infinity – meaning that $(\sigma - 1)/\sigma$ is close to one and the goods are perfect substitutes – to negative 5 – meaning that the goods are imperfect substitutes and $(\sigma - 1)/\sigma$ is 1.2 – implies a 15% increase in utility! (This is because $2.3/2.0 = 1.15$.) This has a big implication for assessing consumer utility: instead of simply having *more* goods, utility could have increased significantly by having *different* goods.

Figure 7.10 Variety in a Fruit and Vegetable Market
Source: Roberto Machado Noa/LightRocket via Getty Images.

Any utility function is, of course, an abstraction. But combined with empirical estimates of the elasticity of substitution of various goods, economists have used this particular functional form when trying to say something about the benefits of increased variety as a result of trade.

Empirical Findings

Although the consumer is spending as much at the original consumption point as at the new consumption point in Figure 7.9, because both points are on the same budget line, consumers would be *willing* to pay a little more to get more variety. How much would they be willing to pay? One study by Christian Broda and David Weinstein (2006) looked at the increase in variety of particular goods imported into the United States from 1972 to 2001. They concluded that consumers were willing to pay 2.6% of their income to have access to the expanded set of varieties available in 2001 rather than the set in 1972. However, the researchers measure the increase in variety not by specific products, but by the number of countries the United States imported from in a particular product category. Therefore, their number is bound to be an underestimate, because different varieties can come from the same country (see Feenstra 2010, 2018).

It is not just consumers that benefit from variety. Domestic producers also benefit from having access to a wide variety of intermediate inputs to production. (We can think of the utility function as a production function and see how total output increases more than total inputs due to the increasing specialization of the intermediate goods used in production.) This allows them to expand their range of product offerings. Having access to more and different intermediate goods, such as more efficient and specialized capital equipment, also allows domestic firms to increase their output. For example, when India embarked on an ambitious program to reduce trade barriers in 1991, Topalova and Khandelwal (2011) found that productivity at the firm level increased as result of the greater variety of imported intermediate goods allowed into the market.

The intensification of import competition does give rise to adjustment costs, but that does not mean that higher productivity is not worth the cost. Prior to its economic reforms in 1991, India had an autarkic domestic market populated by a multitude of small, inefficient firms that served domestic consumers poorly. The increase in import competition eliminated the least productive firms and forced the survivors to improve their productivity and serve their customers better, according to Goldberg, Khandelwal, Pavcnik, and Topalova (2010). As a result, Indian consumers were much better off.

In sum, the availability of a greater variety of goods to both consumers and to producers is an important, but underrated, gain from trade.

7.4 FIRMS IN INTERNATIONAL TRADE

One often hears that *countries* trade with one another. In fact, it is more accurate to say that *firms* engage in trade, buying and selling goods and services across international boundaries in the hope of selling goods to consumers. Previous chapters have not really discussed "firms," only "sectors" of the economy, or "industries," composed of many firms. Yet clearly, big, multinational firms play a key role in international trade. We cannot discuss the automobile industry without thinking of Toyota and General Motors, or the global electronics industry without thinking of Apple and Samsung, or the footwear industry without thinking of Nike and Adidas.

How do domestic firms respond to increased export opportunities? And how do firms that compete against imports respond to intensified competition? In previous chapters, we focused on how trade shifted resources – capital and labor – between different sectors of the economy, causing movement along the production possibility frontier. Here we will see how trade shifts resources between different firms within an industry: by intensifying competition, an increase in trade prompts a reallocation of resources from less-productive firms to more-productive ones. The less-productive firms lose market share and sometimes go out of business.

The resource shift, which affects both those industries that export their products and those that compete against imports, raises average productivity within an industry. Thus, an overall increase in productivity is another gain from trade, as Melitz and Trefler (2012) show. It comes, however, at the expense of the businesses that could not survive in the more-competitive environment – an illustration of the concept of "creative destruction."

Exporting Firms

In fact, while most countries import a diversified mix of goods, a country's exports are usually more narrowly concentrated, both in the range of goods and the number of firms producing them. In almost every country, a relatively small number of firms export their products to other markets.

For example, in the case of the United States, only 4% of the nation's 5.5 million firms engaged in exports. In the manufacturing sector, only about 15% of American firms export to foreign markets. Not only do a small *fraction* of firms export, those exports are highly concentrated in a small *number* of firms. In the United States, the top 1% of all exporting firms (such as Boeing and General Electric) account for 80% of the total value of exports (Bernard, Jensen, and Schott, 2009). In fact, the top eight exporting companies in the United States account for 10% of total US exports. This list includes companies such as Boeing and General Electric, and perhaps others such as Weyerhaeuser and Arthur Daniels Midland.

The same is true in developing countries. Across an average of thirty-two developing countries, Freund and Pierola (2012) find that the top five exporters account for one third of the country's total exports, on average. Exporting superstars, such as Samsung in Korea and Vietnam, Foxconn in China, and Intel in Costa Rica, shape a country's patterns of exports. The top ten exporting firms in Ecuador account for 64% of the country's exports, and the top ten exporting firms account for 90% of Mali's exports, according to World Bank economists.

These facts suggest that exporters are systematically different from other firms in the economy. Exporters tend to have more employees and larger sales volumes than other domestic firms. They also tend to be more efficient. One potential reason for this is that in highly competitive markets, small differences in prices and costs can mean a large difference in sales volume. A firm that can cut production costs increases its ability to attract foreign buyers for its products.

As we saw earlier in this chapter, increased economic integration results in two outcomes: a larger market (since domestic firms now have access to foreign consumers) and intensified competition (since foreign firms now have access to domestic consumers). Different firms are

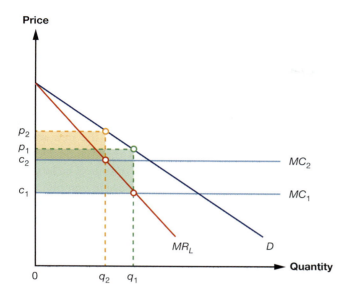

Figure 7.11 Two Firms with Different Costs This figure shows two firms with different marginal costs facing the same demand. The high-cost firm produces less and charges a higher price than the low-cost firm, which produces more and charges a lower price. The low-cost firm also earns higher profits than the high-cost firm.

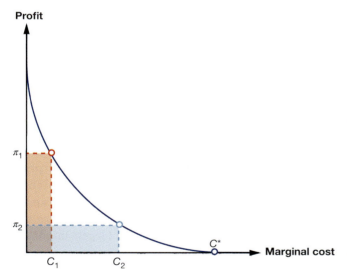

Figure 7.12 Relationship between Profit and Marginal Cost This figure shows the negative relationship between profits and marginal cost: the higher are costs, the lower are profits.

affected differently by these two effects. Low-cost firms may be able to grow and expand, because for them the benefits of the increase in market size exceed the costs of increased competition. High-cost firms, on the other hand, may be forced to shrink or go out of business, because the increased competition is too intense, and they cannot take sufficient advantage of the larger market.

To illustrate the effects of greater competition within an industry, Figure 7.11 depicts two firms producing similar goods that are imperfect substitutes for one another. The two firms, let us suppose, face the same residual demand curve – that is, the demand facing each individual firm, or its share of total demand – and marginal revenue curve. They both equate marginal revenue to marginal cost in order to maximize profits. However, firm 1's marginal costs (MC_1) are lower than firm 2's (MC_2). Because of this difference, firm 1 will produce more (q_1) and charge a lower price (p_1) than firm 2 (with output q_2 and price p_2). In addition, firm 1 has a higher markup of price above costs than firm 2. Consequently, firm 1 earns much greater profits than firm 2, as can be seen by the relative sizes of the shaded areas. Think of Toyota as firm 1 and Chrysler as firm 2 to get a feel for what these differences mean in concrete terms.

Figure 7.12 illustrates how a firm's profit (denoted by π) varies with its marginal cost. Of course, profit is a decreasing function of marginal cost. (C^* is the marginal cost that hits the intercept of the demand curve on the vertical axis in Figure 7.6; a firm with a higher marginal cost than this would not earn profits.) Thus, the figure shows which firms will survive and produce in the market (where $c_i < C^*$) in a market of a given size.

What happens when competition intensifies through the enlargement of the market via trade? A larger market can support a larger number of firms than a smaller market, which implies more competition in the larger market. As discussed earlier, this competition causes the residual demand curve facing each firm to shift down and rotate (flatten). The same combination of effects also acts on each firm's marginal revenue curve. Figure 7.13 shows the impact of greater competition on the two firms. As in the previous figure, MC_1 and MC_2 represent the respective marginal costs of the low-cost and high-cost firms. MR is the initial marginal revenue schedule facing each firm, but with additional competition in the market it flattens to become MR'.

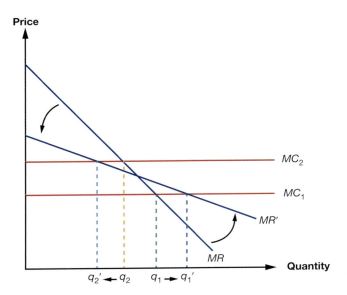

Figure 7.13 Rotating Marginal Revenue and Firm Production This figure shows that an intensification of competition can be depicted as a flattening of the marginal revenue schedule for each firm, as each firm has less of an ability to set prices. The intensification of competition has an asymmetric effect on high-cost and low-cost firms: the output of low-cost firms goes up while the output of high-cost firms goes down.

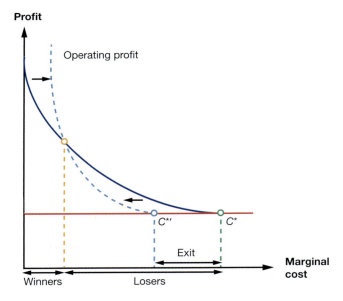

Figure 7.14 Relationship between Profits and Marginal Cost with Rotating Demand This figure shows how an intensification of competition affects firms with various costs. Low-cost firms increase output and increase profits; high-cost firms see reduced profits and some even lose money and are forced out of the market.

This rotation of the marginal revenue curve affects the two firms differently. The new marginal revenue schedule intersects the marginal cost curve of firm 1 at a lower level of output. This smaller, high-cost firm is harmed by the increase in competition, which squeezes its profits and forces it to contract output. (A very high-cost firm might even be forced out of business, as we will see.) Conversely, the new marginal revenue schedule intersects the marginal cost curve of firm 2 at a higher level of output. The larger, low-cost firm responds to the increase in competition by expanding output. This example shows how some firms (with high costs and low productivity) reduce their output after competition increases, while other firms (those with low costs and high productivity) increase their output.

The effects of increased competition are represented by the clockwise rotation of the profit schedule. Figure 7.14 illustrates three potential outcomes. First, the winners are low-cost firms that see higher profits and sales. Second, the losers are high-cost firms that see lower profits and sales. Third, the firms that exit are high-cost producers that are forced out of business. This is because greater competition reduces prices and therefore the marginal cost required to earn a profit. The marginal cost cutoff falls from C^* to $C^{*\prime}$ in Figure 7.14. All firms are forced to reduce their prices and reduce their markup (price–cost margin). But the low-cost firms with the highest markups are able to do so most easily and even take advantage of the larger market by increasing their market share. The high-cost firms have a lower initial markup, so the reduced price puts a squeeze on their profitability; because of their high costs, they cannot take advantage of the expansion in demand and they lose market share to the low-cost firms. And, of course, the biggest losers are the highest-cost firms, who cannot compete and are driven out of business.

In some sense, international competition is just like domestic competition: it benefits low-cost, high-productivity firms but hurts high-cost, low-productivity firms. However, it is different in that trade expands the size of the market, creating new competition but also new opportunities for sales elsewhere. Firms with above-average productivity are the ones that export, and an increase in export opportunities favors the expansion of high-productivity firms. Therefore, an increase in trade increases productivity within an industry.

Import-competing Firms

What is the impact of trade on domestic firms that compete against foreign imports? The effect is similar to the opening of an export market (competition becomes more intense), but dissimilar to the export case because there is no expansion in the size of the market. Consequently, the impact is more painful: an intensification of import competition forces less-productive domestic firms to leave the market. Domestic firms that are more productive do not increase their production, because the market does not expand in size. Still, imports increase average productivity in domestic import-competing industries because low-cost, high-productivity firms survive while high-cost, low-productivity firms shut down.

The impact of import competition on firm exit and industry productivity is illustrated in Figure 7.15. The diagram shows domestic supply and demand, along with the world price, which we take as given. The domestic supply curve consists of a series of steps, each representing a different firm with different (constant) marginal costs. The firms in this market are ranked in terms of their productivity, i.e., firm 1 has the lowest costs of production, firm 2 has the second lowest costs of production, and so forth. There are initially some large, high-productivity, low-cost firms, but as one moves to the right along the supply curve there also exist some smaller, low-productivity, high-cost firms. (Note: something must be preventing low-cost firms from expanding output and driving all the other higher-cost firms out of business.) At world price p_W, domestic production is S_1 and domestic demand is D_1, with imports being $D_1 - S_1$.

We can represent an intensification of import competition as a fall in the world price to p_W'. If that happens, then domestic production falls to S_2 and domestic demand increases to D_2. Imports also increase, to $D_2 - S_2$. Just because domestic supply falls from S_1 to S_2, however, does not mean that all firms reduce their output by the same amount. Each flat portion of the supply curve represents the costs of a different firm. While the lower price reduces the profits of all firms, the biggest impact is on firms operating at the margin. In this case, two high-cost, low-productivity firms – firms 4 and 5 – are forced to go out of business as a result of the increased competition.

This is the painful part of import competition for domestic firms: plant closings and worker layoffs. These firms might be able to survive by adjusting their product mix or moving to different segments of the market where the competition is not so intense. For US firms, this often means improving product quality, if the imports are lower-quality, cheaper goods.

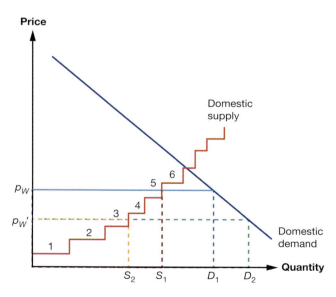

Figure 7.15 Import Competition and Firm Production This figure shows how supply is made up of different capacity-constrained firms with different costs. If the world price falls, and imports go up, some firms (numbers 5 and 6) can no longer survive and are forced out of business.

On the bright side, however, the firms that drop out of the market are the high-cost, low-productivity ones. The remaining firms are the low-cost, high-productivity firms. Those survivors may even have a greater incentive to reduce costs and increase productivity still further to survive in the market. Consequently, the average productivity of firms in the industry increases. These more productive and lower-cost firms will produce goods at lower prices, benefiting consumers. Unfortunately, this result does not usually arise without the pain of driving smaller, high-cost firms out of business.

Empirical Evidence

Is there evidence that increased foreign competition leads to productivity gains? In recent years, many economists have studied this question, and the answer appears to be a solid yes.

Daniel Trefler (2004) examined how the US–Canadian Free Trade Agreement of 1988 affected Canada's labor productivity. The study found that labor productivity of export-oriented plants rose 14% after the agreement. In import-competing industries, labor productivity rose 15%, with at least half of this coming from the exit and/or contraction of low-productivity plants. Canadian firms competing against imports surely had a difficult time restructuring in response to the greater foreign competition. No doubt there were more than a few workers laid off. But productivity did ultimately improve.

In another example, James Schmitz (2005) looked at the US iron ore industry. In the mid-1980s, there was a large shock to the domestic industry as cheaper imports surged in from Canada. As can be seen in Figure 7.16, domestic production quickly fell, but the productivity of labor went up, and in fact doubled within a decade and a half. This improvement in productivity reflected the exit of high-cost firms, the consolidation of existing firms, and the improvement in productivity among the survivor firms.

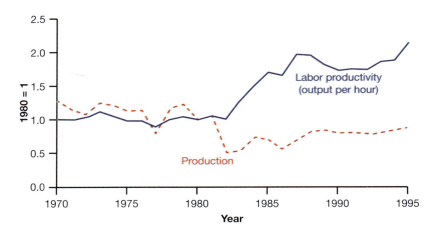

Figure 7.16 Production and Labor Productivity in the US Iron Ore Industry

Source: Used with the permission of the University of Chicago Press, James A. Schmitz Jr., "What Determines Productivity? Lessons from the Dramatic Recovery of the US and Canadian Iron Ore Industries Following Their Early 1980s Crisis," Journal of Political Economy 113(3) (2005): 582–625; © 2005; permission conveyed through Copyright Clearance Centre, Inc.

These productivity effects are observed in other countries as well. One influential study by Nina Pavcnik (2002) examined the productivity of manufacturing firms in Chile, when that country unilaterally lowered its tariffs on imports in the 1980s. Allowing more imports into the market increased the level of competition for domestic firms and thereby affected the entry and exit decisions of Chile's producers. The productivity of firms competing against imports improved on average by 3–10% more than the productivity of firms in the non-traded goods sector. In addition, the productivity of plants that shut down was 8% lower than the productivity of plants that continued to operate.

All in all, there is a body of evidence suggesting that increased trade competition leads to an improvement in productivity for both export-oriented and import-competing industries.

APPLICATION   The US Textile Industry

Over the past few decades, the American textile industry has been beset by enormous structural change, driven by changing technology and intense foreign competition, notably from China and other low-wage developing countries. (See the discussion of the China Shock in Chapter 5.) The textile industry is regionally concentrated in North and South Carolina, which has borne the brunt of these shifts. As Figure 7.17 shows, industrial production of textiles and textile mill products fell by 50% between 2000 and 2009. (The shaded bars indicate recessions, with the Great Recession of 2009 standing out.) Since then, production has stabilized but not rebounded. Similarly, the number of workers in the textile industry fell by nearly 500,000 between 1995 and 2010 but has since stabilized.

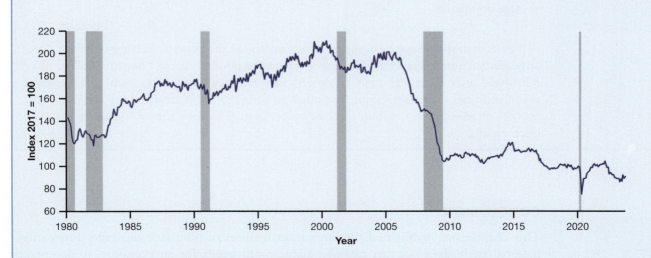

Figure 7.17 Industrial Production, Textile Mills Products, 1980–2022
Source: Industrial Production: Manufacturing: Non-Durable Goods: Textiles and Products, Board of Governors of the Federal Reserve System.

> The adjustment of the textile industry to increased competition illustrates many of the principles noted in this chapter. Smaller, less-efficient firms – unfortunately the ones that were still relatively labor intensive and slow to adopt modern technology – were driven out of business. The surviving firms adopted state-of-the-art production techniques and were much more efficient or served market niches in which they faced less competition. (Using terms introduced in this chapter, the elasticity of substitution between their goods and those of their competitors was very low.)
>
> In a report written in 2017, journalist Debbie M. Price writes the following: "Catawba County, North Carolina – a former textile production powerhouse decimated by offshoring – is enjoying a renaissance fueled by innovation, high-tech materials, automation, and custom work. Textiles are coming back here, but not the old jobs. 'The state-of-the art plant in 1990 had line shafts with a leather belt running the knitting machines. Now we have robots closing the toes and that eliminates half the plant,' says Dan St. Louis, executive director of the nonprofit Manufacturing Solutions Center, a division of the Catawba Valley Community College."
>
> The report continues:
>
> Today, mills today are hiring computer designers, software engineers, and people trained to program and operate the increasingly complex knitting machines – an in-demand job that can command a salary upwards of $80,000. The Manufacturing Solutions Center specializes in applied research and development, prototyping, testing, domestic sourcing, and of course, training for 21st-century textile jobs. "Our whole purpose and mission is to help create jobs here in the US – bottom line," says St. Louis.
>
> In many ways, this is the story of manufacturing across the South, where automation is giving American companies, large and small, the edge needed to compete with cheap labor overseas. Made-in-America sentiment, along with rising wages in China, shipping charges, and tariffs are added incentives to do business at home for some large companies.
>
> (Price, 2017)
>
> The economist Joseph Schumpeter once described the process of competition as "creative destruction." The Southern economy has responded to the "destruction" of older industries such as textiles with "creation" in other new industries, such as automotive manufacturing, financial services, and other growing sectors of the economy. That said, the process of adjustment – within a sector or between firms in a sector – is never easy and often painful.

CONCLUSION

This chapter has highlighted two important features of international trade. First, international trade does not just make available more goods for an economy, it also makes available a wider array of different goods than can be produced domestically. Since consumers value having the ability to choose from a variety of goods, the gains from international trade should include the benefits from increased choice given to households and businesses. Second, exports and imports are made possible by firms, sometimes domestic ones, sometimes multinational ones. This chapter has shown how trade affects which firms will be able export – usually due to their higher productivity – and how trade competition affects the domestic market. Trade increases competition and contributes to the process of "creative destruction" in which more productive firms survive, if not export, and less-productive firms are forced out of the market.

SUMMARY

1. In monopolistic competition, firms produce differentiated products under economies of scale. This situation combines elements of monopoly (each firm produces its own distinct variety of a good and has market power) and competition (ability of new firms to enter the market reduces prices until profits are zero).
2. When two countries allow trade in a monopolistically competitive sector, the result will be a single, larger market with more competition. That will entail larger firms, lower average costs, and lower prices for consumers. There will be a shakeout effect in which some smaller, high-cost firms will not be able to survive the new competition.
3. Consumers benefit from having access to a wider variety of goods when there is trade in a monopolistically competitive sector.
4. An expansion of export opportunities means exposure to greater competition and the opportunity to sell in a larger market: great competition means lower markups (of price over cost), but the larger market gives low-cost, high-productivity firms an opportunity to expand while forcing high-cost, low-productivity firms to contract.
5. An increase in import competition forces low-productivity domestic firms to exit the market.
6. In both exporting and importing sectors, trade promotes the allocation of resources from high-cost firms to low-cost firms and thereby increases average productivity in the industry.

KEY CONCEPTS

Differentiated products, page 124
Economies of scale, page 124
Elasticity of substitution, page 134
Imperfect substitute, page 124
Inter-industry trade, page 124
Intra-industry trade, page 124

Market-size effect, page 128
Monopolistic competition, page 125
Perfect substitute, page 124
Shakeout effect, page 132
Within-market effect, page 129

REVIEW QUESTIONS

1. Define and give a practical example of the within-market effect and the market-size effect.
2. How are the variety gains from trade different from the standard gains from trade analyzed in Chapter 2?
3. Why does the marginal revenue curve rotate with greater competition?
4. Based on this chapter, which domestic groups (producers or consumers) would view free trade in a favorable light or in an unfavorable light?

EXERCISES

1. Using the diagram for monopolistic competition, such as Figure 7.2, examine how the integration of two different sized countries (one large and one small) differ from two similarly sized countries in monopolistic competition?
2. In the same diagram, what happens if consumers decide they prefer more variety relative to lower prices? (Hint: the MM curve will shift.)
3. Using the utility function that allows for differentiated products, that is, $u(c_A) = c_A^{(\sigma - 1)/\sigma}$, will the gains from trade be greater the larger is the elasticity of substitution (σ) or the smaller it is? To be specific, suppose the elasticity of substitution between varieties of wheat is 10 and the elasticity of substitution between automobiles is 2. How different, quantitatively, will the gains from variety be in these two markets?
4. Using Figures 7.13 and 7.14, what happens to the two firms if demand falls but the demand curve does not rotate? What happens if the marginal costs of the two firms increase?
5. This question is based on the numerical model developed in the appendix. Using the CC and PP schedules, solve for the equilibrium number of firms in the market. What happens to the equilibrium number of firms when the market size increases, fixed costs increase, or the elasticity of demand (b) increases?
6. This question is based on the numerical model developed in the appendix. Suppose two countries produce automobiles in a monopolistically competitive market. Assume the following: $b = 1/30,000$, $F = \$750,000,000$, and c is $\$5,000$. Suppose 900,000 units are sold in the home country and 1,600,000 in the foreign country. Calculate the following for the two markets:

	Home market (pre-trade)	Foreign market (pre-trade)	Integrated market (after trade)
Total auto sales			
Number of firms			
Sales per firm			
Average cost			
Price			

Which firms, home or foreign, face the greater adjustment?

RECOMMENDED RESOURCES

A classic text on monopolistic competition and trade is Elhanan Helpman and Paul Krugman, *Market Structure and Foreign Trade* (Cambridge, MA: MIT Press, 1985). Paul Krugman won the Nobel prize for economics for his contributions to this area; see J. Peter Neary, "Putting the 'New' into New Trade Theory: Paul Krugman's Nobel Memorial Prize in Economics," *Scandinavian Journal of Economics*, 111 (2009): 217–250.

For a survey of how product variety affects the gains from trade, see Robert C. Feenstra, "New Evidence on the Gains from Trade." *Review of World Economics / Weltwirtschaftliches Archiv* 142(4) (2006): 617–641, as well as Robert C. Feenstra, "Measuring the Gains from Trade under Monopolistic Competition," *Canadian Journal of Economics* 43(1) (2010): 1–28.

For a related, classic paper, see Paul Romer, "New Goods, Old Theory, and the Welfare Costs of Trade Restrictions," *Journal of Development Economics* 43(1) (1994): 5–38,

On restructuring and the labor market effects of the US Canada free trade agreement, see Brian Kovak and Peter Morrow, "The Long-Run Labor Market Effects of the Canada-US Free Trade Agreement," NBER working paper no. 29793, February 2022.

APPENDIX 7.A

Monopolistic Competition: An Alternative Approach

The model of monopolistic competition outlined in the preceding chapter was presented mainly in intuitive terms, but one can also formulate it using simple algebra. Once again, we will have a situation in which each firm produces a differentiated product under economies of scale.

The production costs faced by domestic firms are usually broken out as a fixed cost (such as the one-time cost of setting up a new factory) and the marginal cost of production (including variables labor and materials costs). We can express total cost (TC) as:

$$TC = F + cQ,$$

where TC is total cost, F is the fixed cost, c is the marginal cost, and Q is the quantity produced. Average cost (AC) is simply total costs divided by the quantity produced:

$$AC = F/Q + c.$$

We can see the economies of scale in this equation, since an increase in Q leads to a decrease in AC. The greater the output quantity over which the fixed cost can be spread, the lower the average cost.

The demand curve facing a firm depends on the size of the market (total industry sales), the number of competitors, and the price the firm charges relative to the average price charged by other firms. We can express demand as

$$Q = S[1/n - b(p - \dot{p})],$$

where Q is the quantity produced by the firm, S is total industry sales, n is the number of firms in the industry, b is the responsiveness of demand to the firm's price, p is the price that the firm charges, and $\dot{p}$ is the average price charged by other firms. As this equation indicates, the demand for a firm's products increases in S, decreases in n, decreases in p, and increases in $\dot{p}$.

If all firms charge the same price, then $p = \dot{p}$ across the board and all firms have an equal share of the market ($Q = S/n$). But if different firms price their goods differently, then a firm charging more than the average price ($p > \dot{p}$) will have a smaller-than-average market share and a firm charging less than the average price ($p < \dot{p}$) will have a larger-then-average market share. (A simplifying assumption is that total industry sales, S, is unaffected by price. This means that price competition simply rearranges market share without changing the total.)

APPENDIX 7.A

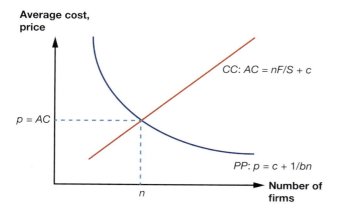

Figure A7.1 Equilibrium in Alternative Model of Monopolistic Competition This figure determines the price (average cost) and number of firms in an industry. The upward-sloping *CC* schedule shows that average costs rise as more firms enter a market of a given size. The downward sloping *PP* schedule indicates that prices will be lower as more firms are competing in the market.

From these two equations, we can determine the equilibrium prices/costs and the equilibrium number of firms in the industry.

The first step is to determine the relationship between the costs of production in a market and the number of firms in the market. (Recall that under monopolistic competition, price equals average cost so if we know average cost, we will know the average price.) This will give us a supply curve coming from the average cost function. To simplify matters, we assume that $p = \bar{p}$, so that demand is $Q = S/n$. We can put this into our average cost function and get:

$$AC = nF/S + c.$$

In Figure A7.1, this is the upward-sloping CC schedule because the average cost of each producer increases with the number of firms (n) in the market. This is because more firms fighting over a given market size gives each firm a small level of output, and average costs rise because each cannot spread its fixed costs across a larger output.

The other schedule reflects the relationship between prices and the number of firms in the market. As one might expect, the more firms in the market means that competition is greater in the market, forcing firms to become more efficient (increase their size to reduce their costs), which will be reflected in lower prices. Working with the demand curve, we can solve for a pricing rule of marginal revenue equals marginal cost. We know marginal cost is c, so we have to find marginal revenue, which turns out to be:

$$p - 1/bn = c,$$

where marginal revenue is $p - 1/bn$ and marginal cost is c.

Where does marginal revenue come from? Let us assume that we have a linear demand function of the form

$$Q = A - BP,$$

This form is similar to our firm demand equation where $A = s/n + sb\bar{p}$ and $B = sb$. Rearranging this equation for P we have $P = A/B - Q/B$. Total revenue is PQ or $(A/B - Q/B)Q$. This means that marginal revenue is simply the derivative of this, or how this changes with Q. Marginal revenue of the firm is $MR = (A/B - Q/B) - Q/B$, or $p - Q/B$. Since $B = sb$, we have $p - Q/sb$, or (since $s = Q/n$) $p - 1/bn$.

Therefore, setting marginal revenue equal to marginal cost is $p - 1/bn = c$, or

$$p = c + 1/bn.$$

This tells us that as the number of firms increases, the price charged by each firm must fall due to the additional competition. This gives us the downward-sloping *PP* relationship in Figure 7.14.

The intersection of the *CC* and the *PP* schedules in Figure 7.18 determines the equilibrium price and average cost in the industry and the equilibrium number of firms.

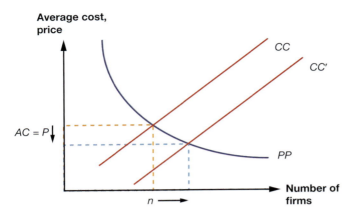

Figure A7.2 Monopolistic Competition: An Increase in Market Size If the size of the market increases, the CC schedule shifts to the right, indicating that more firms can exist at the existing price. This results in a new equilibrium in which there are more firms and lower prices for consumers.

We can consider three comparative static exercises. Let us first consider international trade, in which we have market integration whereby two individual country markets are put together. (This could be something like European integration, or the North American integration through NAFTA, or some other policy change to reduce trade barriers. Or we could consider the opposite, taking a single market and breaking them up into two parts, such as Brexit, the United Kingdom leaving the European Union.)

If we put two markets together, that is an increase in the total size of the market, exposing firms to more competition. This is the same as an increase in S. An increase in S will shift the CC curve down, as shown in Figure A7.2.

An increase in S, therefore, brings about an increase in the number of firms and a decrease in the prices charged by firms (along with a decrease in the average costs of firms, since the output of the surviving firms will go up). This is all consistent with the framework developed earlier in the chapter. Consumers will benefit from more variety and lower prices, while some firms will increase their output, reducing their costs and their prices as the elasticity of substitution has increased with the availability of more substitute goods.

Another exercise is to consider an increase in fixed costs F. This shifts the CC schedule up, implying higher average costs and higher prices, and fewer firms in the market. This is shown in Figure A7.3. Another exercise to consider is an increase in marginal costs, which will shift both the CC and PP schedules up.

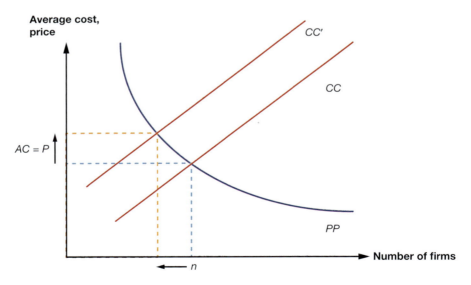

Figure A7.3 An Increase in Fixed Costs If there is an increase in fixed costs, the CC schedule shifts up, resulting in higher prices and fewer firms in the industry.

CHAPTER 8
Trade Policy Analysis

LEARNING OBJECTIVES

In this chapter, we learn about:
- how import tariffs and export subsidies affect production and consumption
- how import tariffs and export subsidies affect a nation's welfare
- the similarities and differences between import tariffs and import quotas
- the contrast between partial equilibrium and general equilibrium analyses of trade policy
- the surprising equivalence of import tariffs and export taxes

INTRODUCTION

Americans are big consumers of sugar, eating and drinking some 66 pounds each of it per year, on average. This is not just a dietary issue; it is also a big trade issue. The United States imports sugar from the tropical climes of the Caribbean, which has the natural conditions suited for growing sugar cane. But sugar imports are much less now than they once were – not because Americans have cut back on sugar consumption but because low-cost imports were hurting domestic cane producers in Florida and Louisiana. To help them out, the federal government began restricting imports decades ago. (Just ask any representative or senator from those states whether they believe free trade in sugar would be a good idea.)

These import barriers increased the domestic price of sugar – it is now about twice the world price – which had all sorts of ripple effects. The high price helped kill the US candy manufacturing industry, forcing Brachs and other makers of sweets to move production to other countries without sugar import restrictions. Coca Cola and Pepsi kept stateside production going but substituted high-fructose corn syrup for sugar in their soft drinks. At the same time, sugar's high price spurred growing production of sugar beets – an alternative source of sugar besides sugar cane – in Minnesota and Idaho; and so on.

As a result, US sugar policy is highly contested. Owners of sugar plantations in Florida reap large benefits from existing import limits, a policy supported by sugar beet farmers and also by corn farmers, from whose product high-fructose syrup is made. They formed the Sugar Alliance to maintain the existing policy. Meanwhile, sugar refiners and the food manufacturing industry, particularly the candy and confectionary industry, have formed the Alliance for Fair Sugar Policy to fight for an end to Big Sugar's stranglehold on import policy.

In the end, of course, consumers end up paying higher prices for sugar-based goods than they otherwise would.

Although previous chapters explained how countries gain from engaging in international trade, we have also seen that some groups may not benefit from trade. The example of US sugar policy is just a microcosm of how some groups win and others lose when it comes to trade, and to trade barriers. Consequently, it should come as no surprise that most countries have an ongoing, robust debate about the degree to which they should be open to world commerce.

In analyzing the gains from trade, previous chapters compared two opposite situations: autarky and free trade. The reality, though, is that few countries completely embrace one or the other. While North Korea is pretty close to autarky (although it has some trade with China) and Singapore pursues a policy of almost completely free trade, most countries fall somewhere between those extremes, using government policies to selectively limit trade without cutting it off completely.

This chapter provides a basic economic analysis of government intervention in trade and considers its impact on economic welfare and resource allocation. We will use both partial equilibrium analysis (supply and demand) and general equilibrium analysis (indifference curves and the production possibility frontier) to understand the economic impact of trade policies. The most important policy to consider is the import tax, also called the import tariff. Once the impact of tariffs is understood, the analysis of export subsidies and taxes will be relatively straightforward.

8.1 IMPORT TARIFFS IN PARTIAL EQUILIBRIUM

As we have seen, trade consists of imports and exports. Either can be encouraged by the government, through subsidies, or discouraged by it, through taxes. Recall, however, the Chapter 2 discussion of mercantilism, the view that exports are good, and imports are bad. Because this view is still widely held, governments typically intervene in trade by subsidizing exports and taxing imports. (Governments occasionally tax exports, but not as often; and they almost never subsidize imports.) We will examine these policies, starting with the most basic of them, an import tariff.

An **import tariff** is a tax on foreign goods as they are brought into a country. The tax may be **ad valorem**, calculated as a percentage of the good's value, or it may be **specific**, a fixed amount per imported quantity. Coffee, for instance, might be taxed ad valorem at 14%, or it might be subject to a specific tax of $1.35 per pound. In this discussion, we will mainly assume that all rates are ad valorem.

Governments impose import tariffs for two main reasons: to raise revenue and to protect domestic industries from foreign competition. (Trade policy is also used to achieve reciprocity with trade partners, something that will be considered in Chapter 10.) Historically, revenue has been an important motive. In the United States, import duties accounted for about 90% of the federal government's revenue prior to the Civil War. Once income taxes became feasible, however, they quickly displaced import duties as the largest source of government revenue.

Today, the share of the federal government's revenue derived from import tariffs is tiny. The same is true in most other developed nations. Many developing countries still rely on import tariffs for a significant fraction of government revenue. But industrialized nations use import tariffs primarily to protect domestic industries from foreign competition. The goal of limiting imports is to shore up domestic output in import-competing industries, and thereby to save domestic jobs in those sectors.

President Donald Trump was a big fan of tariffs, calling them "the greatest!" In 2018, his administration imposed a 25% tariff on steel imports, a 10% tariff on aluminum imports, a 25% tariff on billions of dollars of imports from China, as well as special import duties on imports of washing machines and solar panels – and planned for more to come. In various tweets, he justified such tariffs on the grounds that they will protect domestic producers from foreign competition, will raise revenue that will help reduce the budget deficit, and will bring other countries to the bargaining table to reach better trade deals.

Impact on Resource Allocation

We begin by considering a tariff on a particular imported product, such as clothing. By virtue of the small country assumption introduced in Chapter 2, we will assume that the importing country takes the world price as given. Thus, the importing country can buy as much clothing as it wants at the world market price. (We will relax this assumption in Chapter 9.) In addition, we assume that imports of clothing and domestically produced clothing are perfect substitutes for one another, not differentiated products such as automobiles or computers.

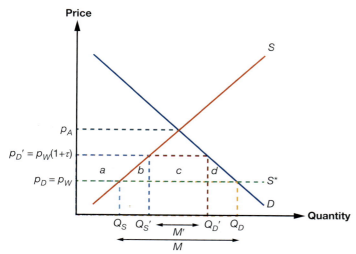

Figure 8.1 Import Tariff in Partial Equilibrium This figure shows domestic supply and demand along with the world price (p_W), which determines the quantity supplied and demanded and hence imports. An import tariff raises the domestic price above the world price and increases the quantity supplied by domestic producers, decreases the quantity demanded by domestic consumers, and reduces imports.

Figure 8.1 uses a partial equilibrium (supply and demand) diagram to show the impact of an import tariff on the clothing market. In the absence of any trade barriers, the domestic price (p_D) is determined by the price on the world market (p_W). Because the country is importing clothing, the world price is lower than the domestic autarky price (p_A). The small country assumption means that the foreign supply curve is perfectly elastic at the world price. The foreign supply curve (S^*) is perfectly elastic and intersects the domestic supply curve at quantity Q_S and the domestic demand curve at quantity Q_D. Imports (denoted M) are simply the difference between domestic consumption and domestic production, so that $M = Q_D - Q_S$.

If we now impose an (ad valorem) tariff of rate τ, the domestic price rises by the full extent of the tariff, so that the new domestic price, p_D', is $p_W(1 + \tau)$. For example, if the world price of an article of clothing is $20, and the tariff rate is 25%, then the domestic price after the imposition of the tariff is $20·(1 + 0.25) = $25. The tariff drives a wedge between the domestic price, which is now $25, and the world price, which remains unchanged at $20.

As a result of the higher domestic price, domestic producers increase their supply from Q_S to Q_S'. The same higher price also prompts domestic consumers to reduce their purchases from Q_D to Q_D'. As a result of the tariff, then, imports fall from M to M'. The more the tariff increases, the more imports fall because domestic production increases and domestic consumption decreases. A **prohibitive tariff** eliminates imports completely by increasing the domestic price up to the autarky price, so that $Q_D = Q_S$ and imports are zero. Thus, compared with free trade, a tariff increases domestic production, decreases domestic consumption, and reduces imports.

Because consumers generally want to pay the lower world price for the goods they buy, import tariffs give rise to incentives to avoid the tax. In colonial America, merchants would sometimes smuggle goods into the country to avoid paying import duties. Even today, the United States bans imports of illegal drugs, such as cocaine, but that does not mean these products are not imported from abroad.

IN PRACTICE   Tariff Engineering

One legal way to avoid paying an import tariff is to change the characteristics of the imported good so that it falls under a different tariff classification – a practice known as **tariff engineering**, legal in principle but sometimes challenged in particular cases. A lot of money is at stake when it comes to tariffs, and many of these cases end up in the US Court of International Trade, a specialized court designed to adjudicate tariff disputes.

For example, the United States maintains a 2.5% tariff on imported passenger cars and a 25% tariff on imported light trucks. (The higher tariff on trucks dates back to the "chicken war" of the 1960s, when the United States imposed the higher tariff on trucks to retaliate against a European Union tariff on imports of US chicken. The EU never lifted its chicken tariff, and hence the truck tariff has remained in place.) Ford takes advantage of the tariff system when it imports the Transit Connect cargo vehicle from its factory in Turkey. To avoid paying the higher truck tariff, the Transit arrives in an American port with carpet and back seats, so that it qualifies as a passenger vehicle and is only subject to the 2.5% tariff. Once the vehicles have cleared US customs, Ford rips out the carpet, unbolts the back seats, and sells the vehicles as small cargo vans for businesses. When the Customs Service (part of the US Treasury Department) classified the imports as trucks and not passenger vehicles, Ford took the government to court and, in 2017, won the right to continue its now-you-see-them, now-you-don't maneuver with the carpet and seats.

Figure 8.2 Ford Transit Connect: Truck or Passenger Vehicle?
Source: Smith Collection/Gado/Getty Images.

Another case of a product that is altered to fit into a different, lower-tariff product category is the Converse All-Stars athletic shoe. More than half the sole consists of fuzzy material, sometimes justified on the grounds that it increases the shoe's "traction." Actually, the fuzz has more to do with avoiding the tariff on shoes, which can run as high as 37.5%. By adding the fuzz, the "shoe" can be classified as a "slipper" on which the tariff is just 3%. Given the volume of shoes imported by Converse, the cost savings are enormous.

Impact on Economic Welfare

By raising the domestic price of imported goods, import tariffs set up a conflict between domestic producers and domestic consumers. Producers benefit from the higher price, while consumers are harmed. How can we assess the welfare implications of the tariff more systematically? By looking at changes in producer surplus and consumer surplus as a result

8.1 IMPORT TARIFFS IN PARTIAL EQUILIBRIUM

of the tax. You might recall these concepts from your earlier economics classes, but we will provide a brief refresher here.

Producer surplus is a measure of the benefit producers receive from selling a product. For an individual transaction, it is the difference between the price the producer receives and the minimum amount the producer would accept for the good. For example, suppose a farmer brings some tomatoes to market and is willing to sell them for $2 per pound, but the market price that day turns out to be $2.50 per pound. Then the farmer's producer surplus is 50 cents (= $2.50 − $2).

The *total* producer surplus is the sum of the surpluses on all the individual transactions. Graphically, it is the area above the supply curve but below the market price. What we are interested in, however, is the *change* in producer surplus as a result of a new tariff. In Figure 8.1, the tariff increases the domestic price from p_D to p_D'. The amount by which domestic producers are better off is represented by trapezoidal area a in the figure, representing the increase in the producer surplus.

Consumer surplus is a measure of the benefit consumers receive from buying a product. For a single transaction, it is the difference between the price the consumer pays and the maximum amount the consumer would be willing to pay. Suppose your smartphone costs $600, along with a monthly fee of $75; if you keep it for three years, that is a cost of less than $100 a month. And as you know, the device does an astounding array of things: you can use it to check your email, read newspapers from around the world, listen to your favorite music, navigate while driving, and call or text friends to coordinate dinner plans. Most consumers would be willing to pay quite a bit more than they actually spend to have such a small device with such amazing capabilities; in 2013, McKinsey estimated that consumer surplus for wireless internet access was about $350 billion.

The total consumer surplus is the area below the demand curve but above the price. In Figure 8.1, the tariff raises the domestic price from p_D to p_D', and so domestic consumers are worse off. This means a decrease in consumer surplus, corresponding to trapezoidal area $a + b + c + d$.

The tariff also affects a third actor, namely the government, for which the tariff is a source of revenue. In general, tax revenue is calculated as the tax rate multiplied by the tax base. Here, the tax rate is the tariff rate τ, and the tax base is the market value of imported goods. Thus, the revenue will be $\tau p_w M'$, where p_w is the price of imports and M' is the volume (number of units) of imports. In Figure 8.1, tariff revenue is represented by the rectangle area c.

In sum, the import tariff redistributes income from consumers to producers and the government. If we want to consider the overall, or net, impact of the tariff on welfare, we can take the gains to producers and the government and deduct the losses to consumers. In Figure 8.1, we then find that the losses to consumers, $a + b + c + d$, exceed the gains to producers, a, and the government, c, so there is an overall net loss in welfare of the amount $b + d$. The triangles b and d are known as **deadweight losses**. The deadweight loss arises because the import tariff distorts the behavior of producers and consumers in ways that lead to economic inefficiency.

The **production deadweight loss**, area b, represents the extra production costs incurred in increasing domestic production from Q_S to Q_S' along the supply curve. Note that the marginal cost of domestic production over that range of output, indicated by the slope of the supply curve, is above the country's opportunity cost, which is the world price p_W, the price at which it could have purchased imports in the absence of tariffs. In other words, at the margin, it may cost domestic producers $55 to produce a pair of pants at point Q_S', when the pants are only worth $45 on the world market. Producing something at a cost of $55 when it could be bought for $45 and then re-sold is inefficient from a production perspective. Another way to think of this deadweight loss is that consumers are paying for area *b* in terms of higher prices, but producers are not capturing it as surplus because it is part of their costs of production.

On the other side of Figure 8.1, area *d*, the **consumption deadweight loss**, represents the consumer surplus lost as a result of consumers being forced to reduce their purchases from Q_D to Q_D' as a result of the tariff. To put the point another way: area $a + b + c + d$, which represents the total loss in consumer surplus, can be broken down into area $a + b + c$, which is lost income for consumers who *continue* to buy the product at the higher price; and area *d*, which represents the loss for consumers who *no longer* buy the product. The higher price has forced the latter consumers out of the market, and the benefit that they used to receive from consuming the product has disappeared. For example, when the price of pants goes up from $45 to $55, a consumer who was willing to pay up to $50 but no more will stop buying the pants and thus loses $5 worth of benefit. That is the difference between what the pants were worth to that buyer ($50) and what the buyer was previously paying ($45).

The net loss due to tariffs should not be surprising. If there are gains from trade in moving from autarky to free trade, then imposing a barrier to trade, which moves the country back toward autarky, should reduce those gains. If the purpose of the tariff is to help out domestic producers, it seems to be an inefficient way of doing so. Consumers pay much more than producers receive, and deadweight losses are incurred as a result.

Equivalency of Trade Policy and Domestic Policies

Because a country's imports of a good are the difference between production and consumption, any policy that affects domestic production or consumption of a good has an impact on imports. This suggests that domestic policies that alter supply or demand can *replicate* the effects of a trade policy. For example, notice in Figure 8.1 that the import tariff increased domestic production and decreased domestic consumption. Another means of increasing domestic production is a production subsidy, and another way of decreasing domestic consumption is a consumption tax. In fact, in its welfare impact an import tariff is equivalent to a production subsidy and a consumption tax put together.

To see how this works, suppose the government enacts a production subsidy; that is, it pays domestic producers an extra amount to supply their output. If the subsidy raises the total price received by producers by the same amount as the tariff shown in Figure 8.1, then $p_W(1 + s)$ is the same as $p_W(1 + \tau)$, where *s* is the subsidy rate. This is an ad valorem subsidy, based on a percentage of the price. For example, if the subsidy rate is 20%, then $s = 0.20$ and the effective price received by domestic producers is $1.2 \cdot p_W$ per unit.

As a result of the higher price received by domestic firms, domestic production will increase from Q_S to Q_S'. The cost to the government of the subsidy is the per unit subsidy ($s \cdot p_W$) times the subsidy base (Q_S', or production under the subsidy), or area $a + b$. Producer surplus increases by area *a* as a result of the production subsidy. Therefore, the net welfare impact of the production subsidy is the gain in producer surplus minus the cost of the subsidy, which is −*b*.

Meanwhile, if the government enacts a consumption tax at the same rate as the import tariff, the domestic price facing consumers increases from p_D to p_D'. As a result, domestic consumption falls from Q_D to Q_D'. The consumption tax reduces consumer surplus by the area $a + b + c + d$ and generates revenue of the amount of area $a + b + c$ (the per unit tax revenue − $\tau \cdot p_W$) rate multiplied by the tax base, consumption, or Q_D'). Therefore, the net welfare impact of the consumption tax is −*d*.

Thus, the production subsidy and the consumption tax put together would have the same impact as a tariff: domestic production would increase, domestic consumption would decrease, imports would fall, and the net welfare impact would be $-(b + d)$. Domestic production increases because producers receive a higher price; it does not matter to them whether that price comes about because the market price rises due to imports being squeezed out of the market by the tariff, or because of a government subsidy. Domestic consumption decreases because consumers pay a higher price; it does not matter to them whether that price comes about because the market price rises due to imports being squeezed out of the market by the tariff, or because of an equivalent government tax on all consumption.

This means that the outcome of any trade policy can be replicated using domestic policies. Therefore, trade negotiators must be careful that they are not snookered by their foreign counterparts. For example, suppose the president asks you to negotiate with China about a tariff that adversely affects US chicken exports. You manage to persuade the Chinese authorities to reduce the country's tariff, but they argue that they need to provide a temporary subsidy to Chinese chicken producers to cushion the blow from American competition, and to impose a tax on chicken consumption to make up for the lost tariff revenue. If you, as the president's negotiator, agree to this deal, you will not achieve your goal of increasing US exports. Although the Chinese tariff will be abolished, the production subsidy and consumption tax will merely reproduce its effects and China's imports of American chicken will not increase.

A Tariff's Impact on Economic Welfare

Economists sometimes make a rough calculation of welfare costs of a tariff by measuring the area of the two deadweight loss triangles in Figure 8.1 (areas b and d). Another way of calculating the deadweight loss relies on the import demand curve and yields a useful little formula. You might recall from Chapter 2 that a country's import demand is simply its demand schedule minus its supply schedule. Import demand is more elastic than either domestic supply or demand, because when prices change, both supply and demand change.

Figure 8.3 shows an import demand schedule in which, without any tariffs, a country would import amount M of a good at the world price (p_W). If the country imposes a tariff of rate τ_1, the domestic price will rise to $p_W(1 + \tau_1)$ and imports will fall to M'. The government collects tariff revenue equal to the rectangle $c + c'$ (equivalent to area c in Figure 8.1) and the deadweight loss triangle is $b + d$ (the combined $b + d$ from Figure 8.1).

The area of this single deadweight loss triangle, $b + d$, can be approximated as one-half the base times the height. (We use the term approximated because the area is, strictly speaking, only a triangle in the case of linear demand.) In this case, the base is the change in quantity of imports demanded, ΔM, or $M - M'$, and the height is the change in the domestic price, Δp_D, i.e., the change from $p_D = p_W$ to a new value of $p_W(1 + \tau)$. Therefore, we can express the deadweight loss as:

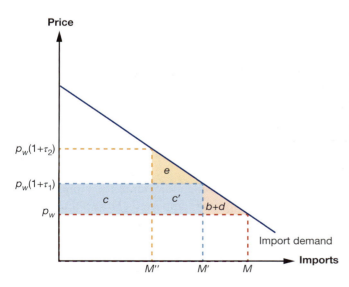

Figure 8.3 Tariffs and Import Demand This figure shows the demand for imports as a function of the price. As an import tariff raises the domestic price, the quantity of imports demanded falls. The areas under the demand schedule are government revenue and a deadweight loss.

$$\text{DWL} = \tfrac{1}{2}(\Delta M)(\Delta P_D) \tag{8.1}$$

To make this formula useful, we can make some substitutions for the change in imports and the change in price. The change in the domestic price of imports as a result of the tariff is $\Delta P_D = P_W(1 + \tau) - P_W = \tau \cdot P_W$. The change in import demand (ΔM) can be derived from the elasticity of import demand (η), which is the percentage change in imports demanded over the percentage change in price, or $\eta = (\Delta M/M)/(\Delta P_D/P_D)$. Solving that elasticity formula for ΔM, and making the appropriate substitutions ΔM and then for Δp_D in equation (8.1), we arrive at the following expression for the deadweight loss:

$$\text{DWL} = \tfrac{1}{2}(\eta)(P_W M)\tau^2 \tag{8.2}$$

Thus, the deadweight loss is one-half times the elasticity of import demand times the post-tariff value of imports, $P_W M$, times the square of the tax rate. If we divide both sides of the equation by GDP, then we have

$$\text{DWL}/\text{GDP} = \tfrac{1}{2}\eta m \tau^2 \tag{8.3}$$

where m is the ratio of imports to GDP, or the share of imports in GDP.

In the real world, of course, there are many goods, many prices, many tariff rates, and many import elasticities. But in greatly simplified terms, equation (8.3) gives an approximation for the aggregate deadweight loss caused by a tariff. For example, suppose we have the hypothetical country of Agraria where imports are 40% of GDP, the average tariff is 25%, and the elasticity of import demand is -2. Then the deadweight loss of the tariff would be roughly $\tfrac{1}{2}(-2)(0.4)(0.25^2) = -0.025$, or -2.5% of GDP.

One implication of equation (8.3) is that the welfare cost of a tariff increases by the square of the tariff rate. So if Agraria's tariff rate doubles, from 25% to 50%, then the deadweight loss quadruples, from 2.5% of GDP to 10% of GDP. Figure 8.2 shows the point graphically. Suppose we start with an import tariff of rate τ_1 and an associated deadweight loss $b + d$. If the tariff then increases to τ_2, the deadweight loss triangle gets not only taller but also wider, as imports are reduced from M' to M''. The additional deadweight loss is not merely an additional triangle e, but also the rectangle c', for a total loss of $e + c' + b + d$. The rectangle c' arises because the additional tariff magnifies the distortion caused by the initial tariff.

Effective Rate of Protection

The ad valorem tariff on imports is known as the **nominal rate of protection**. For domestic firms competing against imports, a 10% tariff on imports is just like a 10% production subsidy: in both cases, the price they receive goes up by 10%, under the assumption that the country is "small" and takes world prices as given.

However, the nominal rate of protection can be a misleading indicator of the support given to domestic producers when some of the production inputs are imported. The **effective rate of protection** takes into account tariffs on inputs, as well as on output, to determine how the structure of tariffs affects an industry. The effective rate of protection may be greater or less than the nominal rate of protection, depending on the configuration of the tariffs.

The effective rate of protection can even be negative, meaning that tariffs are hurting rather than helping the domestic industry. For example, suppose there is a 20% duty on imported candy. That is the nominal rate of protection, and one might conclude that the domestic candy industry is receiving a 20% subsidy, because the domestic price of candy is 20% above the world price. But this does not consider any tariff on sugar, a major input into the production of candy. A tariff on sugar raises the costs of candy production and diminishes the benefit of the candy tariff for candy producers. If that is the case, the nominal rate of protection does not indicate the degree to which the tariff code protects candy producers from foreign competition.

The derivation of the formula for the effective rate of protection is complicated, so let us just present it and examine its implications. Suppose we have an intermediate good, i, and a final good, j. The tariff on the intermediate good is τ_i, the tariff on the final good is τ_j, and a_{ij} represents the share of the intermediate good in the costs of producing the final good. Then the formula for the effective rate of protection, e_j, is:

$$e_j = \frac{\tau_j - a_{ij}\tau_i}{1 - a_{ij}} \tag{8.4}$$

Let us work through an example. Suppose that a country has a 50% duty on imported sugar and a 20% tariff on imported candy. And suppose that sugar accounts for half the cost of candy production, so that $a_{ij} = 0.5$. We can now calculate the effective rate of protection given to candy producers as a result of these tariffs: $(0.2 - 0.5 \cdot 0.5)/(1 - 0.5) = -0.05/0.5 = -0.1$, or -10%. The nominal rate of protection for candy producers is 20%, but the effective rate of protection is -10%. Instead of being subsidized as a result of tariffs, the candy industry is actually being taxed. The condition for effective protection to be negative is $\tau_j < a_{ij}\tau_i$, i.e., the tariff on the final good is less than the tariff on the intermediate good weighted by the cost share of the intermediate good.

Negative effective protection is a real-world phenomenon. Life Savers, the iconic US candy, are no longer produced in the United States because of the high cost of sugar due to import restrictions. The last Life Saver's production facility in Michigan closed in 2002, laying off about 800 workers. Life Savers are 95% sugar, and production required 113 tons of sugar every day. At the time the plant closed, the domestic price of bulk sugar was 21 cents per pound, compared to 6 cents a pound on the world market. Life Savers production was moved to Canada to take advantage of the lower sugar costs there.

The lesson is that high tariffs on intermediate goods harm downstream industries. This happens all the time: tariffs on imported steel hurt domestic car producers, tariffs on imported cotton hurt domestic clothing producers, tariffs on imported semiconductors hurt domestic computer producers, and so forth.

Of course, there are other outcomes as well. If the nominal final good tariff exceeds the nominal intermediate good tariff, then the effective rate of protection is greater than the nominal rate; i.e., if $\tau_j > \tau_i$, then $e_j > \tau_j$. In that case, the nominal rate of protection *under*states the degree to which the domestic industry is being helped by tariffs. And if there is a uniform tariff, the same rate on all intermediate and final goods, then the nominal rate of protection equals the effective rate of protection, i.e., $e_j = \tau_j = \tau_i$.

APPLICATION   The Trump Trade Tariffs

In his January 2017 inaugural address, President Donald Trump stated: "We must protect our borders from the ravages of other countries making our products, stealing our companies and destroying our jobs. Protection will lead to great prosperity and strength." He firmly believed that trade was a bad deal for the United States and that imports hurt

American industries and workers and made the country weaker. In 2018, his administration imposed stiff tariffs on about half of US imports from China. The United States also imposed 25% duties on imported steel and 10% duties on imported aluminum.

These tariffs give us an opportunity to see what happens when a country imposes a tariff. Economists try to assess the impact of tariffs on producers, consumers, and the government (revenue) using a diagram such as Figure 8.1. Amiti, Redding, and Weinstein (2019) found that US prices rose to the full extent of the tariff, as assumed in the figure. That study found that the cumulative deadweight welfare cost (that is, the reduction in real income, or areas $b + d$ in Figure 8.1) from the tariffs were about $8.2 billion during 2018. The cost to domestic consumers was about $14 billion, far exceeding the gains to domestic producers.

Fajgelbaum, Goldberg, Kennedy, and Khandelwal (2020) took a slightly different approach to calculating the impact of the tariffs. This study found that resulting real income loss to US consumers and firms was $51 billion, or 0.27% of GDP. The producer gains amounted to $9.4 billion, or 0.05% of GDP. Adding up these gains, tariffs revenue, and the losses from higher import costs yields a short-run loss of the 2018 tariffs on aggregate real income of $7.2 billion, or 0.04% of GDP.

Figure 8.4 President Trump Speaking about His Trade Polices
Source: Bill Pugliano/Getty Images.

This study also considered the impact of foreign retaliation against US exports as a result of the tariffs. These countermeasures increased tariffs from 7% to 20% on 8,073 export products covering $127 billion (8.2%) of annual US exports. The retaliatory tariffs reduced US exports by 10% within those product categories.

The 2018 steel tariffs also illustrate the concept of negative effective protection. Although these steel tariffs may have increased domestic steel employment, some estimates saying by about 1,000 workers, they also raised the cost of production in steel-using industries, such as automobiles and machinery. These higher costs translated into lower production and lower employment in steel-using industries, with as many as 75,000 workers in steel-using industries losing their jobs. The steel industry benefited from protection at the cost of downstream industries.

Of course, just about every president has found occasion to impose import restrictions in some case. In September 2009, President Barak Obama imposed new duties on car and truck tires imported from China. The tariffs were set to last three years, and the existing tariff of 3 to 4% was augmented by an additional 35% in the first year, 30% in the second year, and 25% in the third year. US importers shifted their source of supply away from China to other, more expensive countries, such as Indonesia, and domestic tire producers were able to increase their prices, as consumers shifted their purchases from imported tires to domestic tires. Gary Hufbauer and Sean Lowry (2012) estimated that annually, consumers paid $817 million more as a result of the higher cost of imported tires and $295 million more due to the higher cost of domestically produced tires. Thus, the total net cost to consumers was $1,112 million per year.

> The same study also estimated that a maximum of 1,200 jobs were saved because of the tire tariff (at a cost to consumers of over $900,000 per job saved). Average worker compensation in the tire industry is $40,000 per year. Thus, $1,112 million was extracted from consumers to give $48 million to potentially unemployed tire workers (until they found another job). At the same time, the study continues, consumer spending on other goods would have been $1,064 million lower as a result of higher spending on tires, costing an estimated 3,731 jobs in other sectors of the economy.
>
> In other words, President Trump was not the first to impose trade barriers, and he will not be the last.

8.2 IMPORT QUOTAS

Instead of imposing a tax on imports, governments sometimes impose a quantitative limit on the amount of imports that can enter the country. Under an **import quota**, the volume of imports is capped at a fixed amount.

For example, the United States maintains a quota on sugar imports that is much more restrictive than the tariff on imported sugar. The US import quota allows 1,117,195 tons of raw sugar and 22,000 tons of refined sugar into the country, although this number can be increased if a shortage is expected. The quota is allocated among 40 countries based on the market share in US sugar imports from 1975 to 1981, but the shares have not been updated to reflect the changing location of foreign production. These quotas restrict the supply of sugar in the domestic market and push the US price of sugar significantly above the world price.

Many other countries use quotas to restrict imports. The European Union once imposed a quota on imported "non-human" dolls, presumably to help out its beleaguered toy industry. The quota set an absolute limit on the number of such dolls that could be imported. Human dolls, such as Barbie and GI Joe, could be imported without limit, but non-human dolls, such as teddy bears and bunny rabbits, were strictly limited. A question arose about whether the quota applied to action figures from the *Star Trek* film and TV franchise. An unlimited number of Captain Kirks could be imported because Kirk is a human, but what about Spock? Spock is human-like but technically a Vulcan – meaning he is super-logical, without any emotion, and has big, pointed, elf-like ears, as well as green, copper-based blood.

EU bureaucrats actually had to decide whether Spock was a human character or not to determine if the quota applied to him. They eventually ruled that Spock was not human: "we've never seen a human with ears that size," the press was told (Milbank, 1994). Actually, the issue is more complicated than that. As devoted Trekkies know, Spock is half human: his mother is human, and his father is Vulcan.

Figure 8.5 Dr. Spock and Captain Kirk from *Star Trek* Spock, being used to human irrationality, is not upset about the unequal quotas.
Source: CBS via Getty Images.

Like an import tariff, an import quota will lead in Figure 8.1 to an increase in domestic production from Q_S to Q_S', and a decrease in domestic consumption from Q_D to Q_D'. With imports restricted to $Q_D' - Q_S'$, the domestic price will increase to the same amount as it would with the tariff. Therefore, a tariff and a quota that result in the same volume of imports have similar effects on supply and demand. (What would happen to the domestic price if the import quota were set at zero? That would be a situation of autarky, and the domestic price would rise to the autarky price, just as with a prohibitive tariff.)

The welfare effects of a quota are also similar to those of a tariff. Because the quota increases the domestic price by the same amount as the tariff, the impact on producer and consumer surplus is the same: domestic producers receive area a as additional producer surplus, and domestic consumers suffer loss $a + b + c + d$ of consumer surplus.

However, there is one big difference between a tariff and a quota: a quota is not a tax and does not raise revenue for the government. Instead, with a quota, area c is known as the **quota rent**. The quota rent is the total markup on the imported good, i.e., the quantity imported times the difference between the world price and the domestic price in the protected market.

Who collects the quota rent depends on how the quota is administered – that is, how the restriction on import quantities is enforced. One way is for the importing country to create a system of import licenses: only someone who possesses a license has the right to import the good in question, and only in a specified amount. The license is valuable because it allows whoever has it to gain the quota rent, i.e., the ability to buy goods at the world price and sell them at the higher domestic price. Who gets the licenses and therefore the quota rent? That depends on how the quota is allocated. The government could auction licenses off to the highest bidder. The auction should raise nearly the same amount of revenue that could have been collected with a tariff. In this case, the government collects area c as revenue and the quota ends up being very similar to a tariff in its revenue impact.

The United States, however, does not auction off quota rights, but instead simply tells foreign countries how much of a given good they each can export to the US market. The government of each exporting country then turns around and parcels out its allotted share of US imports to its domestic firms. The exporting government may do this by auctioning off licenses to export to the US, thereby capturing the quota rent as revenue for itself. The US will not capture any of the quota rent, and for the US the welfare cost of the quota is $b + c + d$. In this arrangement, the quota rent, c, is usually much larger than the combined deadweight loss, $b + d$, and so the welfare cost of a quota is usually much greater than the welfare cost of a tariff.

Some governments simply give import licenses to domestic firms, who enjoy the ability to buy low on the world market and sell high on the domestic market. If the licenses are awarded based on some vague criterion ("merit"), as is sometimes done in developing countries, this almost inevitably leads to corruption. Government bureaucrats responsible for the administration of import licenses can be bribed by well-connected firms to give them the valuable licenses. This is known as **rent seeking**, because the firms are offering bribes to get the quota rents (Krueger, 1974).

A **voluntary export restraint**, or VER, is very similar to an import quota – really, just a variant form of it. Here, an exporting country "voluntarily" decides to limit its exports to a particular market, usually to keep the importing country from imposing an even more burdensome import quota. The other benefit of a VER is that while the country's exports fall, it or its exporting firms (depending on how the VER is administered) will receive the quota rent on exported goods. In 1981, famously, the United States pressured Japan into agreeing to limit the number of automobiles it exported, to help out US auto producers. The VER froze Japan's auto exports at 1.68 million cars per year, and the price of a Japanese car in the United States jumped by about $1,000 (Feenstra, 1988). This implies that the approximate value of the quota rent was nearly $1.7 billion!

The Non-Equivalence of Tariffs and Quotas

While tariffs and quotas have very similar effects on production and consumption in a static partial equilibrium model of perfect competition, the effects of tariffs and quotas diverge when there is a demand shift or if competition is imperfect.

If demand increases when a tariff is in place, there is no limit on how many imports can come into the country. Therefore, when domestic demand increases, imports simply expand one-for-one with the increase in demand. Domestic production does not change because the domestic price does not change. When a quota is in place, by contrast, imports are fixed in quantity and so cannot expand with the increase in demand. If consumers want to buy more of the good, they must get it from domestic producers. But domestic producers will not supply more unless the price goes up. Therefore, as demand shifts, the domestic price will increase and domestic producers will fill the additional demand, while the quantity of imports remains fixed. Foreign sellers, for their part, will be pleased even though their sales volume is limited, because they get the higher price, as well. In other words, the quota rent goes up.

These two situations are illustrated in Figure 8.6. The left-hand panel depicts an increase in demand when a tariff is in place. The perfectly elastic foreign supply is $S^{*\prime}$, where the '

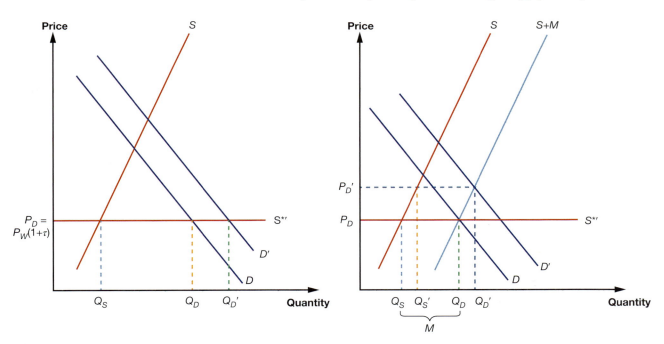

Figure 8.6 Shifting Demand with a Tariff and Quota A shift in demand has quite different implications when a tariff or a quota is in place. A tariff on imports places no restriction on the volume of imports, whereas a quota does. With a tariff, a shift in the demand schedule (from D to D' in the left panel) increases the quantity of imports with no change in the domestic price or in domestic production. But with a quota in place and the same shift in demand (right panel), imports cannot increase, and the greater demand must be satisfied by more domestic supply, which requires an increase in the domestic price.

indicates that the foreign supply curve has been shifted up by the tariff. With the domestic supply curve S and the domestic demand curve D, imports under the tariff are $Q_D - Q_S$. When demand shifts from D to D', the consumption equilibrium moves along the foreign supply curve and imports increase by the amount $Q_D - Q_D'$, the full extent of the increase in demand. Because the domestic price did not increase, domestic supply does not increase. Similarly, if demand were to fall from D' to D, imports would decline but the domestic price would not change.

The impact of an increase in demand when a quota is in place is shown in the right-hand panel of Figure 8.6. In this case, the domestic price is initially p_D and imports are again $Q_D - Q_S$, but this time an import quota keeps that difference fixed. The total supply to the market is the $S + M$ schedule, representing the sum of domestic supply, S, and the fixed volume of imports, M. The initial domestic price, p_D, is set by the intersection of the domestic demand curve and the total supply curve. Now, when demand shifts from D to D', the consumption equilibrium moves along the total supply curve. The domestic price goes up to p_D', the quantity demanded goes up to Q_D', and the quantity supplied by domestic producers goes up to Q_S', while imports remain unchanged.

The second scenario in which a tariff and a quota are not equivalent is imperfect competition in the domestic market. Suppose the domestic market is represented by a single producer, one that would have a monopoly position in the market were it not for imports. With free trade, this firm has no market power: the ability of domestic consumers to buy imports prevents the firm from charging any price higher than the world price. (Without foreign competition, the domestic firm would set marginal revenue equal to marginal cost and charge a high price off the demand curve.)

If an import tariff is now imposed, the domestic price goes up by the extent of the tariff and the domestic firm increases its output. But the firm still does not have any market power; it cannot charge any price higher than $p_W(1 + \tau)$, because consumers could always look to imports to buy the good at that price in any quantity they wanted. The analysis changes dramatically if instead an import quota is imposed. An import quota limits the threat of foreign competition, because domestic consumers cannot buy more than the quota amount of imports. This restores some of the market power of the firm; it can reduce its output and raise its price without fearing that consumers will simply buy more imports.

Figure 8.7 illustrates this situation. In this diagram, MC is the marginal cost curve of the monopolist (and therefore the firm's supply curve), D is the demand curve, and imports can come in at the world price. The quantity demanded is Q_D, the quantity supplied domestically is Q_S, imports are the difference between the two, and the monopolist has no power. Now suppose the government does an odd thing: it imposes a quota that restricts the volume of imports to an amount equal to that under free trade. In other words, this is a non-binding quota in that there is no reduction in imports. Because imports are simply frozen at the free-trade level, one would think that the quota would have no effect on the market.

Yet the quota changes everything, because now the single domestic firm knows that imports cannot increase beyond the quota amount. Therefore, the firm no longer fears losing consumers to foreign suppliers, and it is free to maximize its profits off the "residual" demand curve it faces. This is the total demand curve minus the fixed volume, M, of imports allowed under the quota. In the right panel of Figure 8.7, the residual demand curve is labeled $D - M$. Associated with this residual demand curve is a downward-sloping marginal revenue curve below it.

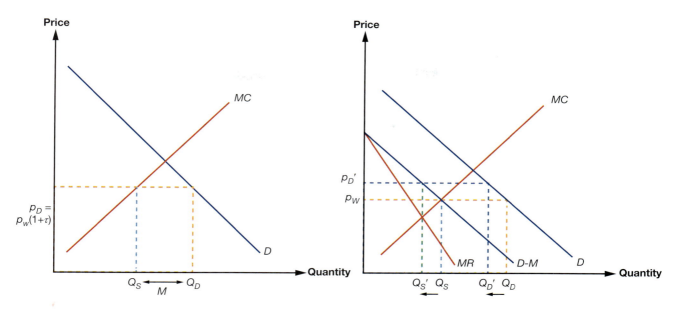

Figure 8.7 Import Quota with a Domestic Monopoly When an import quota is in place, a domestic monopolist can charge a higher price because consumers cannot buy more imports when it does so. It therefore reduces supply (produces where marginal revenue equals marginal cost) and raises prices.

The domestic firm maximizes profits by setting marginal revenue equal to marginal cost. This profit maximization entails a reduction in its output from Q_S to Q_S'. With no change in imports, the fall in domestic production leads to an increase in the domestic price from p_W to p_D'. Domestic consumption must fall one-for-one with the reduction in domestic output. The foreign sellers shipping their goods under the quota are delighted that the domestic monopolist has chosen to reduce its output, because the foreign sellers also get to charge the higher domestic price for their goods; in other words, they are able to earn a quota rent.

Thus, tariffs and quotas are not similar in their effects when there is imperfect competition. A tariff reduces imports and raises the domestic price, but a domestic firm still faces competitive pressure from imports and has an incentive to increase output. A quota also reduces imports and raises the domestic price, but the firm no longer faces competitive pressure from imports. It has an incentive to reduce output so that the domestic price and its profits go up.

For this reason, import quotas may be especially detrimental when the domestic industry is not perfectly competitive. Policymakers who impose import quotas to protect the domestic industry from foreign competition usually expect it to increase output and hire more workers. Yet the domestic industry might do exactly the opposite. Some economists believe that highly concentrated American industries – that is, those with few domestic firms, such as the automobile industry and the steel industry, that would have market power in the absence of foreign competition – have used import quotas in the past to increase profits rather than to expand output and employment (Blonigen, Liebman, Pierce, and Wilson, 2013).

8.3 EXPORT SUBSIDIES AND TAXES

We have just explored import tariffs and quotas in a partial equilibrium framework. Now export subsidies and export taxes should be relatively straightforward to analyze. The effects

Export Subsidies

While governments tend to restrict imports with tariffs, they tend to promote exports with subsidies. An **export subsidy** is a government payment to domestic firms on the output they sell to foreign consumers. The main goal of an export subsidy is to increase exports.

Figure 8.8 illustrates the effects of an export subsidy. Because the country is exporting, the world price of the good is above the country's autarky price, i.e., $P_W > P_A$. The small country assumption, in which the country takes the world price as given, implies that the country can export as much as it wants at the world price. In other words, foreign demand (D^*) for the country's exports is perfectly elastic at the world price.

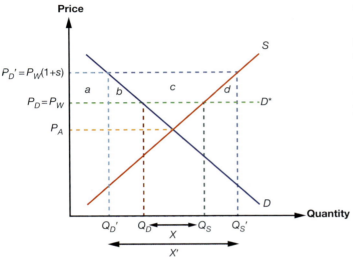

Figure 8.8 Export Subsidy This figure shows the impact of an export subsidy on domestic supply and demand. The subsidy increases the domestic price above the world price, leading to a greater quantity supplied and a lower quantity demanded, and hence more exports. The subsidy also costs the government money (areas $b + c + d$), while increasing producer surplus ($a + b + c$) and reducing consumer surplus ($a + b$), resulting in a deadweight loss of $b + d$.

With free trade, the domestic price of the good is simply the world price, since domestic producers will export their entire output unless domestic consumers are willing to pay the world price. So domestic production is Q_S and domestic consumption is Q_D. Exports, which are denoted X, are the difference between domestic production and consumption, so $X = Q_S - Q_D$.

An export subsidy means that the government is paying producers to export. Domestic producers now receive a price of $P_W(1 + s)$, where s is the rate of subsidy on their exports. For example, if the world price of wheat is $5 per bushel and the government introduces a 20% export subsidy, domestic farmers will receive $6 per exported bushel – $5 from foreign consumers and $1 from the government subsidy.

The small country assumption means that the world price does not change as a result of the subsidy; the country is a small part of the world market, and so its decisions do not affect the world price. Foreign consumers, therefore, do not notice the subsidy and continue to buy the good at the world price. However, since the exporters do not get a subsidy for goods sold domestically, they will only sell to domestic consumers if they get the new, higher price of $P_W(1 + s)$. Thus, if domestic consumers can only get the product good from domestic producers – we will revisit that caveat momentarily – then the price domestic consumers pay is higher than the world price.

By increasing the price received by domestic producers from $5 to $6, the export subsidy leads to an increase in domestic supply from Q_S to Q_S'. The higher domestic price also leads domestic consumers to decrease their consumption from Q_D to Q_D'. Therefore, the export subsidy expands exports both by increasing domestic production and by decreasing domestic consumption.

8.3 EXPORT SUBSIDIES AND TAXES

Wait a minute! If domestic producers are charging domestic consumers a price above the world price, won't the consumers seek to buy the same good as an import instead, at the world price? And won't there be importers happy to meet that demand?

Unfortunately for the consumers, buying at the world price will not normally be an option. The reason is illustrated by the story of an export subsidy for live cattle introduced by Colombia many years ago when its ranchers were suffering from depressed prices. The government thought that an export subsidy would help eliminate surplus cattle on the market that was thought to be keeping prices low. On the day the subsidy took effect, ranchers showed up at Colombia's borders and took their cattle across the border for sale in Ecuador, Venezuela, and Peru, and in so doing collected their subsidy from customs officials. The next day, the ranchers showed up with even more cattle, and so it went on for days. Government officials were ecstatic that cattle exports were surging, day after day, making the subsidy even more successful than they had anticipated.

The officials' enthusiasm was dampened, however, when they realized that the subsidy was going to cost the government a lot more money than originally planned. Furthermore, they discovered the real reason for the surge in cattle exports: ranchers were simply smuggling their cattle back into the country at night, crossing the border at unguarded spots, only to march them across the border again in the morning to collect the subsidy. No wonder ranchers loved the subsidy!

Customs agents tried to put a stop to the ranchers' subterfuge by branding cattle, insisting that each head of cattle could be exported only once, not multiple times with a subsidy each time. The ranchers got around that rule by buying cattle in neighboring countries at the world price, importing them into Colombia, and then "exporting" them for the higher, subsidized price. If you buy a good at P_W and sell it at $P_W(1 + s)$, it is very easy to make money off the government. The Colombian authorities finally responded by banning all cattle imports as long as the export subsidy was in place.

The lesson is that a country with an export subsidy for a particular good must also restrict imports of that good. Otherwise, the government sets up an arbitrage opportunity that taxpayers have to finance: savvy entrepreneurs simply import goods at the world price and then export them to collect the subsidy. But if there is a ban on imports, then domestic consumers will not have access to the good at the world price. Instead, they will be forced to buy from domestic firms, who insist on receiving price $P_W(1 + s)$ because, as noted earlier, that is the price they can get on the export market for however much they are able to produce.

What about the welfare impact of the export subsidy? Because the domestic price increases, consumers are worse off; their consumer surplus falls by area $a + b$ in Figure 8.8. Domestic producers benefit from the higher price they receive for both domestic and foreign sales; their producer surplus increases by area $a + b + c$. The government does not collect revenue with a subsidy; instead, it makes a payment. The cost of the subsidy to the government is the per unit subsidy payment ($s \cdot p_W$) times the subsidy base (exports, $Q_S' - Q_D'$), which corresponds to area $b + c + d$.

Like an import tariff, an export subsidy redistributes domestic income among producers, consumers, and the government. In this case, income is transferred from consumers and the government to producers. The net impact of the export subsidy on the country's economic welfare is $-(b + d)$. Like a tariff, the export subsidy introduces a deadweight loss distortion both to production and consumption. The distortion to production, d, is similar to that under a tariff, wherein the cost of the additional production is greater than the value of the good at the world price. The distortion to consumption, *b*, is lost consumer surplus, because consumers enjoy less of the good than before the subsidy was imposed.

Like an import tariff, the export subsidy can be decomposed into two domestic policy instruments. The export subsidy increases domestic supply (just like a production subsidy) and decreases domestic demand (just like a consumption tax). Therefore, an export subsidy is equivalent to a production subsidy and a consumption tax.

Export Tax

Governments occasionally impose **export taxes**, either to raise revenue or to reduce the domestic price of a good. For example, Argentina has sometimes imposed an export tax on raw soybeans, to drive the domestic price down. This makes it less profitable to export raw, unprocessed soybeans, but makes it a cheaper input for Argentina's exporters of processed soybeans and soybean products, who thereby enjoy a competitive advantage on world markets. Until recently, the United States banned the export of crude oil to try to keep the price low for domestic consumers, i.e., refineries. China has also taxed exports of rare-earth metals such as cerium and neodymium, which are essential for the manufacture of modern electronics, to keep the price low for its domestic producers of smartphones, televisions, and so on.

As these cases make clear, the goal of the export tax is to help domestic consumers (households and other industries) of the exported good, not the exporters themselves. Taxing exports takes money away from exporters, thereby discouraging them from selling their goods abroad. The domestic price falls from P_W to $P_W(1 - \tau)$, where τ is the tax rate on exports, because that is the price domestic producers collect on exports and therefore the price they will settle for the domestic market. (Once again, the small country assumption means that the world price is unaffected and remains the same.)

For example, if the world price of soybeans is $10 per bushel and the government imposes a 20% export tax, then the government takes away $2 from the price received by exporters, leaving them with $8. (In other words, the price that producers receive will be $1 - \tau$ times the world price. If the tax is 20%, exporters only get to keep $1 - 0.2 = 0.8$, or 80%, of the world price.) The exporter cannot make foreign consumers pay the tax; they cannot charge even $11 for their soybeans, let alone $12. The world price is $10 per bushel, and producers have no choice but to sell exported soybeans at that price. (If they tried to charge a higher price, foreign consumers would simply buy their soybeans from other suppliers.)

Figure 8.9 shows the impact of an export tax. The price received by exporters falls from P_W to $P_W(1 - \tau)$ after the tax. This reduces domestic production from Q_S to Q_S'. Because

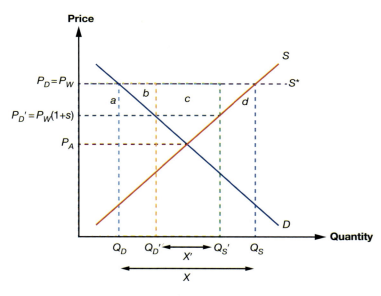

Figure 8.9 An Export Tax This figure shows the impact of an export tax on domestic supply and demand. The tax reduces the domestic price below the world price, leading to a smaller greater quantity supplied and a greater quantity demanded, and hence fewer exports. The tax also raises money for the government (area c), while decreasing producer surplus (a + b + c + d) and increasing consumer surplus (a), resulting in a deadweight loss of b + d.

the domestic price falls to $P_W(1 - \tau)$, as well, domestic consumption increases from Q_D to Q_D'. Therefore, an export tax reduces exports two ways: domestic production decreases and domestic consumption increases, and exports are simply the difference between the two.

Why does the domestic price facing consumers drop to $P_W(1 - \tau)$? If the world price of soybeans is $10, could producers earning $8 per bushel on exports hope to get a price of at least, say, $9 on the domestic market? The problem with that scenario is that so long as the domestic price is above $8, producers will shift their output from the export market to the domestic market. In the end, the shift of goods to the domestic market will drive down the domestic price, until it hits $8.

If that is not clear, consider an extreme case: a **prohibitive export tax**. A prohibitive export tax is so high that it eliminates all exports and drives the domestic price down to the autarky level. If Argentina imposed a prohibitive export tax on soybeans, the country would be so awash with soybeans that the domestic price would fall to the autarky level. If Honduras imposed a prohibitive export tax on bananas, the country would be so awash with bananas that the domestic price would fall to the autarky level. If Saudi Arabia imposed a prohibitive export tax on oil, the country would be so awash with oil that the domestic price would fall to the autarky level. A non-prohibitive export tax works the same way, though with less extreme effect. It pushes the domestic price closer to the lower autarky price, a rare tax that reduces the price.

What is the welfare impact of an export tax? In Figure 8.9, domestic producers receive a lower price and therefore lose producer surplus equivalent to area $a + b + c + d$. Domestic consumers pay a lower domestic price and therefore gain consumer surplus equivalent to area a. The government collects revenue equivalent to the tax rate times the tax base, or area c. (The per unit tax is $\tau \cdot p_W$ and the tax base is exports, or $Q_S' - Q_D'$.)

Thus, the overall welfare impact of the export tax is $-(b + d)$. We have seen these deadweight loss triangles before, but here they have a slightly different interpretation. The production deadweight loss, d, comes from depriving producers of some extra producer surplus that they would have received if they had not reduced their output from Q_S to Q_S' because of the tax. The consumption deadweight loss, b, comes from encouraging overconsumption. By reducing the domestic price below the value of the goods as indicated by the world price, consumers buy goods that they value less than their true worth on the market. This is a loss because the very last (marginal) consumers who buy at Q_D' value their purchase at P_D' when the true (opportunity) cost of the good is P_W. In the Argentine soybean case, it means that consumers are purchasing and using soybeans as if they were worth $8 per bushel, when in fact their market value is $10 per bushel.

And just as we saw with an import tariff, an export tax can be decomposed into two domestic policy instruments. An export tax decreases domestic supply and increases domestic demand. Therefore, an export tax is equivalent to a production tax and a consumption subsidy.

8.4 IMPORT TARIFF IN GENERAL EQUILIBRIUM

The partial equilibrium analysis of supply and demand is a useful way of spelling out the impact of a tariff in a particular market. However, general equilibrium analysis allows us to focus on the economy-wide impact of a tariff on different sectors of the economy. In particular, we can see the impact of an import tariff on a country's exports, something that we cannot capture by looking at partial equilibrium.

The diagram depicting an import tariff in general equilibrium is tricky. We will take it in two steps, first showing the impact on production and then the impact on consumption.

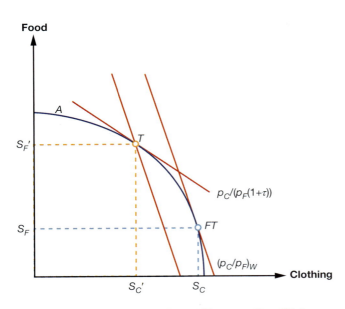

Figure 8.10 Production Effect of a Tariff in General Equilibrium In this diagram, a tariff increases the domestic relative price of food (the imported good). This leads to a shift along the production possibility frontier toward more food output and less clothing output.

Production and National Income

Let us start with the production possibility frontier for food and clothing, just as we did in Chapters 2 and 3. The country depicted in Figure 8.10 is initially open to trade with the rest of the world and takes the world relative price of clothing (p_C/p_F) as given, under the small country assumption. The production point is where the world relative price p_W is equal to the marginal rate of transformation (the slope of the production possibility frontier). The free-trade equilibrium is at point FT, where production of clothing is S_C and production of food is S_F. As before, the country exports clothing and imports food, although to keep the diagram simple, we do not show the consumption point.

Now suppose the country imposes a tariff on imported food. This raises the domestic price of food, and so the domestic relative price of clothing falls. The higher domestic price of food means that food production is more profitable. With the tariff, then, the production point, T, moves along the production possibility frontier by shifting factors of production from the clothing sector to the food sector, so that more food and less clothing is produced. This shift continues until the marginal rate of transformation equals the new domestic relative price, i.e., $MRT = p_C/(p_F(1+\tau))$. If the tariff is prohibitive – leading to zero trade – the new production point will be the autarky equilibrium, at point A. In general, however, T will land somewhere between FT and A.

We already saw in the partial equilibrium analysis that the tariff increases the production of food. But now we see something that was hidden before: the increase in food production has an opportunity cost: there is a decrease in clothing production. In other words, the extra food output does not come out of thin air; rather, labor and capital are diverted away from the clothing sector in order to produce the additional food.

We can measure national income under the tariff by drawing the world relative price line through our new equilibrium production point, T, in Figure 8.11. (Recall that we did this at the end of Section 2.2.) Real national income is lower in the tariff equilibrium than in the free trade equilibrium. This is because the furthest out the relative price line can be is when it is tangent to the production possibility frontier; in other words, when the world relative price is equal to the marginal rate of transformation, or $p_W = MRT$. In the tariff equilibrium, the world relative price line, which represents the budget constraint of the country, is no longer tangent to the production possibility frontier.

If you understand the idea of opportunity cost and understand that a change in the relative price of two goods that increases the production of one must decrease the production of the other, then you know more about trade policy than most politicians. Many politicians believe that resources are free – that food and clothing production, for instance, are independent from each other. They believe that simply by changing prices, a country can increase its food production without sacrificing any clothing production. (If you believe that, then you should be able to increase the amount of time devoted to your studies without sacrificing any sleep or leisure time – good luck!) The simple fact that a tariff may help some sectors of the economy but will hurt others is a subtle point that escapes many observers.

Consumption

Now that we are producing at point T, our tariff equilibrium on the production possibility frontier, where will *consumption* take place? Our new consumption point is, of course, determined by indifference curves. And our new consumption must satisfy two conditions.

First, our consumption point must be on the world relative price line. With the tariff, the country will still be exporting clothing and importing food. Because of the small country assumption, we know that the world price of clothing in terms of food – the terms of trade – does not change. Therefore, we know this country will still be exchanging food for clothing along a line with slope p_W – only, we must draw the terms of trade line extending out from our new production point. (Recall that the country's terms of trade show how much clothing must be given up to acquire food from the rest of the world.)

Second, on the line we just drew we must be at a point where the slope of the indifference curve – the marginal rate of substitution, or MRS – is equal to the relative price faced by consumers, which includes the tariff. This is where things get tricky. The indifference curve must be on the world relative price line (p_W), but it will not be tangent to the world relative price line ($MRS \neq p_W$). This is because domestic consumers do not face the world price of food, but rather the higher, tariff-inclusive price of food. Because of the higher domestic price of food, consumers substitute away from food and toward clothing, which is now relatively cheaper. (This is exactly what is seen in Figure 8.1, where consumers reduce their purchases of food.) Notice that the indifference curves that intersect the world price line are flatter as we move down along the line and consume less food and more clothing.

The final equilibrium is depicted on Figure 8.12. The indifference curve U_T is the indifference curve tangent to the world relative price line, but that tangent point is not our equilibrium. The indifference curve U_T is still on the world price line but has moved down somewhat as consumers substitute food for clothing. Notice that the slope of this indifference curve is the same as the slope of the domestic price line that includes the tariff, i.e., $MRS = p_C/p_F(1 + \tau)$, the tariff-inclusive domestic price. The gap between the domestic price line tangent to the production possibility frontier and the parallel domestic price line tangent to the

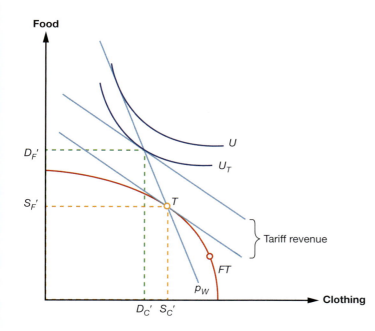

Figure 8.11 Consumption Effect of an Import Tariff in General Equilibrium From the production point T, consumption with a tariff will take place along the terms of trade line (p_W) where the indifference curve is tangent to the domestic relative price of the two goods.

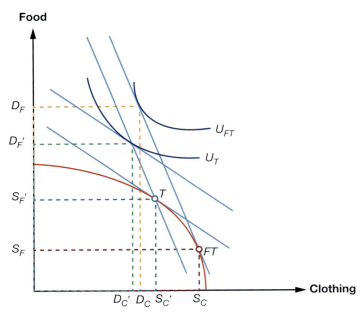

Figure 8.12 An Import Tariff in General Equilibrium This diagram puts together the production effect of a tariff (from Figure 8.10) and the consumption effect of a tariff (from Figure 8.11). A tariff reduces imports and the exports needed to pay for them, shrinking the trade triangle and resulting in a lower level of utility.

indifference curve U_T is the tariff revenue. We assume that this tariff revenue has been rebated to domestic consumers, in one way or another, for spending on the two goods.

Figure 8.12 puts the production and consumption effects of an import tariff on food together. With the tariff, the country produces more food but less clothing than it did under free trade. The country still exchanges exports of clothing for imports of food. However, the trade triangle – which depicts how many exports are exchanged for how many imports along the world price line – is smaller than it was under free trade: the volume of imports of food is smaller, and the volume of exports of clothing is also smaller. The tariff has succeeded in reducing imports, but it has also reduced exports.

This diagram is consistent with the partial equilibrium analysis of the tariff: imposing a tariff on imported food increases domestic food production and decreases domestic food consumption, leading to a reduction in food imports. However, we also see what is going on elsewhere in the economy: clothing production is lower, while clothing consumption is probably higher (although it is ambiguous due to the offsetting income and substitution effects, which you will recall from your earlier classes in economics). As a result, exports of clothing are, in general, reduced.

This finding has important implications. When policymakers impose a tariff on imported food, they have no intention of reducing production of the exported good (clothing), nor of reducing exports at all. Yet that was the actual outcome. Furthermore, policymakers had no intention of reducing the country's real national income. Yet that was the outcome. There is sometimes a difference between the intentions of a policy and the consequences of a policy.

Export Tax in General Equilibrium

We just saw that a country imposing an import tariff would see its exports fall. What happens if the country were to impose an export tax? The diagram for an export tax in general equilibrium is identical to Figure 8.12, because in a two-good economy, an import tariff on one good is equivalent to an export tax on the other. More generally, tariffs applied to imported goods have the same overall effect as export taxes applied to exported goods. This proposition is called the Lerner Symmetry Theorem, named after Abba Lerner (1936).

Why are tariffs and export taxes functionally equivalent? Think about the production side first. An import tariff on food increases the domestic price of food. An export tax on clothing reduces the domestic price of clothing. Since resource allocation depends upon the price of clothing relative to the price of food, it does not matter whether the price of clothing falls (as with an export tax) or the price of food increases (as with an import tariff). The impact will be the same on production along the production possibility frontier, as illustrated in Figure 8.7.

8.4 IMPORT TARIFF IN GENERAL EQUILIBRIUM

The two policies are also similar with respect to consumption. Once again, since relative prices are guiding consumer decisions, it does not matter if the price of clothing falls (as with an export tax) or the price of food increases (as with an import tariff). The impact on consumption will be the same as illustrated in Figure 8.11. (In this case, the parallel lines will represent the rebate of export tax revenue to consumers, instead of import tariff revenue.)

Regardless of whether the tax is imposed on exports or imports, the trade triangle is squeezed and both exports and imports fall. To take an extreme example, a prohibitive import tariff is the same as a prohibitive export tax – both put a country back to autarky. Since the function of exports is to pay for imports, if a country eliminates its imports, there will be no need for its exports, and conversely if it eliminates its exports, there will be no means of paying for imports.

What is the intuition behind this result? One way to think about it is to consider how the foreign exchange market helps keep exports and imports in balance with one another. Suppose the United States suddenly imposes a large, across-the-board import tariff. This makes foreign goods more expensive to American consumers, so they will no longer want to buy as many imports as they did before. This means that Americans will be putting fewer dollars on the foreign exchange market to buy the foreign currency necessary to purchase imports. As a result, the dollar will rise in value (appreciate) against other currencies. As the dollar appreciates in value, foreign consumers will find that US goods become more expensive to them, leading to a decline in the demand for US exports.

Is there evidence in favor of the symmetry between export taxes and import tariffs? Chile provides an example of how exports and imports are linked, and how exchange rate policy is important in maintaining a balance between the two. From the 1950s until the early 1970s, Chile maintained high import tariffs and an uncompetitive (overvalued) exchange rate that suppressed exports and led to strict foreign exchange controls and import licenses (Edwards and Leiderman, 2002). In 1973, for example, Chile's average tariff was 105%. Figure 8.13 shows that exports were only about 5% of GDP in the 1950s and 1960s, while imports were running at about 10% of GDP.

Economic policy changed radically in late 1973, when the socialist government of Salvador Allende was overthrown in a military coup. The new government devalued the Chilean peso, began cutting tariffs, and abolished import licenses. By 1979, the average tariff had fallen to just 10%. However, the country suffered a financial crisis in 1982 after the peso had been allowed to become overvalued again. The government devalued the peso once again, and temporarily increased tariffs. Once macroeconomic stability had been restored, trade liberalization resumed, and the average tariff was reduced to 10% by the end of the 1980s.

As Figure 8.13 shows, Chile's imports soared from 10% of GDP to nearly 30% by the late 2000s. And yet during the period when import tariffs were dramatically reduced, exports also surged to more than 30% of GDP. If exports and imports were not linked, the reduction in Chile's import barriers should have increased imports without bringing about any change in exports. But the country's exports and imports were linked, not only by the reallocation of resources along Chile's production possibility frontier, but by changes in the real value of the peso relative to other currencies. By maintaining such high barriers to imports and an uncompetitive exchange rate, Chile implicitly maintained high barriers on its exports.

The Lerner Symmetry Theorem – that an import tariff is equivalent to an export tax – carries a powerful message: a country that tries to protect import competing industries from foreign competition may be able to help those industries expand, but it will also force other industries to contract. High trade barriers will harm export-oriented industries, erase some of

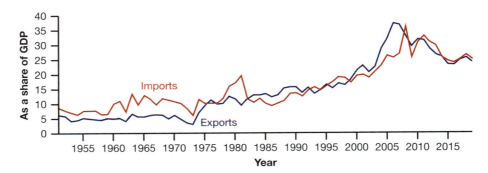

Figure 8.13 Chile's Exports and Imports as a Share of GDP, 1951–2019
Source: Data from Penn World Table 10.01.

the gains from trade, and reduce national income. And yet, under certain circumstances, government trade interventions might have some benefits that offset the disadvantages. These benefits will be explored in Chapter 9.

8.5 EMPIRICAL EVIDENCE ON TRADE BARRIERS

Because import barriers take many forms – tariffs, quotas, and various regulations and product requirements – it is very difficult to measure the combined impact of policy in reducing imports. (For example, one reason that the United States does not import many automobiles from China is because they do not yet meet US safety standards.) One way of tackling the problem is to collapse the various barriers into a single "average" percent tax on imports, called the Trade Restrictiveness Index (TRI). The TRI summarizes the trade policy stance of a country by calculating the uniform tariff that would keep overall imports at the same level as the current results from different tariffs for different goods (Kee, Nicita, and Olarreaga, 2009; Coughlin, 2010).

Table 8.1 presents estimates of the TRI by country and commodity type – agriculture or manufacturing – for 2009. For example, the overall TRI for Australia is 11%, indicating that the country would reduce its imports just as much as it now does, with all of its various existing tariffs on different goods, if instead it had an across-the-board 11% tariff on imports.

Developed countries have very low trade restrictions on manufactured goods and much higher restrictions on agricultural goods. However, developing country tariffs and non-tariff barriers on labor-intensive goods (such as apparel and leather goods) tends to be much higher than on capital-intensive goods (such as electronics and machinery). Developing countries, which are more likely to export agricultural goods and labor-intensive manufactured goods, also have high restrictions on agricultural imports, but restrict imports of manufactured goods as well.

How large are the deadweight losses from these import restrictions? Kee, Nicita, and Olarreaga (2008) have calculated that, as well, but just for import tariffs and not for all the other non-tariff import barriers. The deadweight losses from import tariffs range from a high of about 3% of GDP in the case of Egypt and Ghana, to 2% of GDP for Tunisia, 1% of GDP for Morocco and Mauritania, to less than 1% of GDP in most other cases. For most developed countries, the estimates are less than 1%; for the United States, the estimate 0.09% of GDP, a very small fraction. The welfare losses are relatively small for developed countries because trade barriers are relatively low and also because the ratio of imports to GDP is modest.

Table 8.1 Trade Restrictiveness Index, 2009

Country	Total imports	Agricultural imports	Manufactured imports
Developed countries			
Australia	11	30	10
Canada	5	19	3
European Union	6	34	3
Korea	9	50	5
Japan	9	38	5
United States	6	17	5
Middle income countries			
Argentina	9	10	9
Brazil	22	25	22
Chile	7	22	6
Mexico	15	28	14
Malaysia	27	66	25
Russia	15	22	14
Developing countries			
China	10	14	9
Egypt	33	44	32
India	15	70	13
Philippines	21	44	18
Tanzania	53	39	55
South Africa	5	13	5

Source: The Overall Trade Restrictiveness Index (OTRI).

Although an import quota may be converted, for TRI purposes, into a tariff that restricts imports to a comparable extent, the welfare costs of the import quota likely exceeds that of the tariff, as noted earlier in the chapter. One reason for this is that import quotas give rise to quota rents. These valuable rents give rise to rent seeking, such as lobbying, whether legal or illegal, by domestic firms for the acquisition of the right to import under the quota. Whenever government officials are responsible for determining who gets to import foreign goods and who does not, the process is likely to be corrupt to some degree.

Developing countries tend to have many more quantitative restrictions on imports than developed countries, which makes rent-seeking a greater problem there. In the mid-1960s, when India had its "license raj," in which almost all imports needed some form of government permission, economist Anne Krueger (1974) estimated that the costs of rent seeking amounted to 7% of GDP. A subsequent estimate for India in 1980 put the cost of rent seeking for import license and export incentives at 3% of GDP, but much higher when capital- and labor-market controls were included (Mohammad and Whalley, 1984).

Since the mid 1980s, developing countries have reduced trade barriers and opened up their economies to world trade. Figure 8.14 shows the steady decline in the average tariff for developing countries from the late 1980s through the early 2000s.

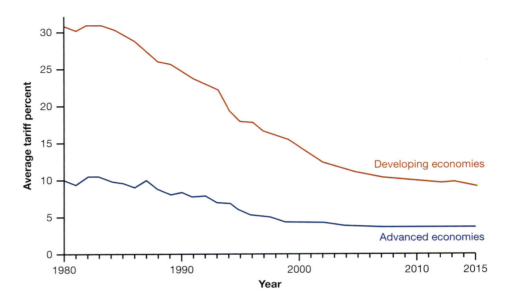

Figure 8.14 Average Tariff in Developing Countries, 1988–2015
Source: Tariff rate, applied, simple mean, all products (%) – Low income, High income, Low & middle income (1988–2017) World Bank Open Data.

What has been the consequence of this trade liberalization on the part of developing countries? Has the reduction in trade barriers helped increase national income? Economists have generally found that it has.

Romain Wacziarg and Karen Welch (2008) examined countries that liberalized their trade regime between 1950 and 1998 and found that liberalizing countries experienced average annual growth rates that were about 1.5 percentage points higher than before liberalization. Trade reforms raised investment rates by 1.5–2.0 percentage points, indicating that lower tariffs helped promote growth through increased capital accumulation. Liberalization raised the average trade to GDP ratio by roughly 5 percentage points, suggesting that trade policy liberalization did indeed raise the actual level of openness of liberalizers. However, these average effects mask large differences in outcomes across countries.

Antonio Estevadeordal and Alan Taylor (2013) found a significant correlation between tariff reductions and the acceleration of economic growth, an effect that was much stronger for reductions in tariffs on capital goods and intermediate goods than for tariffs on final consumer goods. In other words, reducing tariffs on machinery and electronics for producers is more important in increasing national income than reducing tariffs on clothing for consumers. The estimated effect was about 1 percentage point per year, which adds up to a significant amount of income over time.

Thus, both in theory and in practice, it appears that high trade barriers are detrimental to a country's economic performance. However, Chapter 9 will consider whether there are any important exceptions to these findings.

CONCLUSION

Governments often intervene in international trade by using taxes and subsidies: tariffs (taxes) restrict trade, while subsidies expand it. Import tariffs are a commonly used trade policy tool. Tariffs restrict imports and lead to a deadweight loss. An import quota also restricts imports but can have different effects than a tariff. Both result in losses because they unwind some of the gains from trade; a prohibitive tariff, for example, eliminates trade and pushes a country back to autarky. And because of the interdependence of imports and exports, a tax on imports is equivalent to a tax on exports, in the sense that reducing imports systematically reduces exports as well.

SUMMARY

1. An import tariff is a tax on imports. By raising the domestic price of the imported good, a tariff helps domestic producers and hurts domestic consumers.
2. An import tariff redistributes income and leads to a deadweight loss associated with too much production and too little consumption.
3. Because any trade intervention affects production and consumption, a trade policy can be replicated by domestic policies. For example, an import tariff is equivalent to a production subsidy and a consumption tax. An export tax is equivalent to a production tax and a consumption subsidy. An export subsidy is equivalent to a production subsidy and a consumption tax.
4. An import quota is a quantitative restriction on imports. A quota generates a valuable quota rent which is captured by whatever entity has the right to import at the world price and to sell at the higher domestic price.
5. In general equilibrium, an import tariff is equivalent to an export tax.

KEY CONCEPTS

Ad valorem tax, page 150
Consumer surplus, page 153
Consumption deadweight loss, page 154
Deadweight loss, page 153
Effective rate of protection, page 156
Export subsidy, page 164
Export tax, page 166
Import quota, page 159
Import tariff, page 150
Nominal rate of protection, page 156

Producer surplus, page 153
Production deadweight loss, page 153
Prohibitive export tax, page 167
Prohibitive tariff, page 151
Quota rent, page 160
Rent seeking, page 160
Specific tax, page 150
Tariff engineering, page 152
Voluntary export restraint, page 160

REVIEW QUESTIONS

1. Explain intuitively why an import tariff is equivalent to a production subsidy plus a consumption tax.

2. Diagram the impact of an import subsidy on production, consumption, and imports, using the small country assumption. What two domestic policy instruments is an import subsidy equivalent to?
3. What is the economic impact of an import quota that is larger than the existing amount of imports?
4. Discuss four different ways in which the quota rent from an import quota can be allocated, depending on the rule for determining who is able to import.
5. In general equilibrium, how does an export subsidy affect where an economy produces on its production possibility frontier?

EXERCISES

1. Suppose that for an unspecified good, domestic supply and demand are given, respectively, by $Q_S = 5 + 2P$ and $Q_D = 65 - 4P$.
   a. Determine the autarky equilibrium price and quantity.
   b. If the world price is 5 and the country is small, determine domestic demand, domestic supply, and imports with free trade.
   c. If a 40% import duty is imposed, what will be the new domestic price, quantity supplied and demanded, and imports.
   d. What is the equation for import demand?
   e. Determine tariff revenue, and the change in producer and consumer surplus as a result of the tariff.
   f. What is the consumer and producer deadweight loss associated with the tariff?
2. Suppose that for an unspecified good, domestic supply and demand are given, respectively, by $Q_S = 10 + 2P$ and $Q_D = 50 - 2P$.
   a. Determine the autarky equilibrium price and quantity.
   b. If the world price is 5 and the country is small, determine domestic demand, domestic supply, and imports with free trade.
   c. If an import quota of eight units is imposed, what will be the new domestic price, supply, and demand?
   d. What is the quota rent? What is the change in producer and consumer surplus as a result of the quota, and what are the resulting deadweight losses?
   e. With the quota in place, suppose demand increases to $Q_D = 54 - 2P$. What is the new equilibrium domestic price and quota rent? What happens to domestic supply and demand?
3. If steel constitutes 30% of the manufacturing cost of farm equipment, and the tariff on steel is 20% and the tariff on farm equipment is 30%, what are the nominal and effective rates of protection given to domestic farm equipment producers?
4. Show in a diagram the impact of an increase in demand when the domestic industry is protected by a tariff.
5. Sketch out a diagram of a prohibitive export tax. Where are the deadweight losses? How much revenue does the government collect?
6. Sketch out a diagram of an import subsidy.
7. If, in general equilibrium, an import tariff is equivalent to an export tax, what is an export subsidy equivalent to?
8. The supply of wine in France is giving by the equation $S = -20 + 3P$. The demand for wine in France is $D = 100 - P$.

a. What are the autarky price of wine in France, the quantity produced, and the quantity consumed?
b. If the world price of wine is €40 per unit, then on the small country assumption with free trade, how much wine will France produce, how much will it consume, and how much will it export?
c. Draw a diagram that illustrates France's production, consumption, and trade, as well as the price.
d. If France enacts a €10 export subsidy for wine, what is the new domestic price of wine ? How many units will France produce, how many will it consume, and how many will it export? Justify the answers using the diagram from part c.
e. How much does the export subsidy in part d cost the French government?
f. What is the value of the change in producer surplus due to the subsidy in part d? The change in the consumer surplus?
g. What is the overall effect of the subsidy in part d on France's welfare? Why would France enact such a policy?

RECOMMENDED RESOURCES

An old but still informative introduction to trade policy is W. Max Corden, *Trade Policy and Economic Welfare* (Oxford: Oxford University Press, 1974).

The most recent work in economics is covered comprehensively in Kyle Bagwell and Robert W. Staiger (eds), *The Handbook of Commercial Policy*, 2 volumes (Amsterdam: Elsevier, 2016).

On whether trade reform in developing countries has improved their economic prospects, see Douglas Irwin, "Does Trade Reform Promote Economic Growth? A Review of Recent Evidence," *World Bank Research Observer*, August 2024.

The US–China trade conflict has been prominent in recent years. For surveys of economic work on the issue, see Lorenzo Caliendo and Fernando Parro, "Lessons from US–China Trade Relations," *Annual Review of Economics* 15(1) (2023): 513–547; and Pablo D. Fajgelbaum and Amit K. Khandelwal, "The Economic Impacts of the US–China Trade War," *Annual Review of Economics* 14(1) (2022): 205–228.

CHAPTER 9

Arguments for Trade Intervention

LEARNING OBJECTIVES

In this chapter, we learn about:
- some limitations to the case for free trade
- why countries with market power in exports or imports could benefit from restricting trade
- how tariffs can be used, as a second-best policy, to raise revenue and correct market failures
- whether tariff protection for infant industries is a good idea
- under what conditions an export subsidy might be beneficial

INTRODUCTION

When you switch on your smartphone, you are probably not aware of all the minerals that have been dug up around the world to make the electronics work. An iPhone screen has been polished with lanthanum and cerium, a magnet inside is made with neodymium and praseodymium, the circuitry in semiconductors uses arsenic metals, rechargeable batteries depend on cadmium, and light bulbs and heating elements rely on tungsten. It turns out that these so-called "rare earth" minerals are essential for modern life and are used in products ranging from smartphones to MRI machines to advanced defense technology to hair dryers.

One country – China – dominates the market for rare earth minerals. China accounts for about 60% of the world's mining of rare earth minerals and about 85% of the processing of those metals. In 2010, China imposed a 5–20% tax on its exports of rare earth minerals. The United States challenged this tax at the World Trade Organization and won its case, forcing China to rescind it. But, if free trade is such a good idea, why would a country ever tax its exports in the first place? The answer is that China was not interested in free trade because it dominated the market. By restricting its exports, China thought that it could use its market power to shift the burden of the tax on to foreign consumers, while also reducing the domestic price of such metals for its own consuming industries. And in fact, prices of rare earths rose around the world, and fell in China, as a result of the tax. "These duties are China's attempt to game the system so that raw materials are cheaper for their manufacturers and more expensive for ours," the US Trade Representative charged at the time.

This is not an entirely unusual situation. The Organization of Petroleum Exporting Countries (OPEC) was formed in 1960 to coordinate production decisions and increase the world price of oil. At times, OPEC controlled as much as 80% of the oil sold on world markets and it succeeded, particularly in the 1970s, in significantly increasing world oil prices. Oil exporting countries boosted their terms of trade and earned hundreds of billions of dollars in extra revenue. Other developing countries that controlled other natural resources, such as copper and zinc, have tried to emulate OPEC, but with less success.

Should rare earth or oil exporters have followed a policy of free trade? The question almost answers itself. Yet every single trade intervention considered in Chapter 8 – import tariffs, export taxes, and export subsidies – resulted in deadweight losses and diminished gains from trade. This does not mean that free trade is always best, because the policy conclusion depends on the assumptions made in the analysis. The conclusion that tariffs and subsidies always reduce welfare was based on the small country assumption, by which a country takes the world price of its exports and imports as given. If a country accounts for a large share of world production of a particular good, that country may have significant market power, so that by restricting its exports – as OPEC did – it can increase the price it receives for those exports, and thereby improve its terms of trade and its economic welfare.

This chapter examines this case, along with several others in which it is argued that government intervention in trade can improve a country's welfare. These cases include using import tariffs to raise revenue, increase employment, or correct for market externalities (Section 9.2). Other cases include protecting infant industries from foreign competition (Section 9.3) and using export subsidies to give a strategic advantage to certain industries (Section 9.4). In each case, we hope to have a simple framework for determining whether government intervention might be justified or not.

9.1 THE TERMS OF TRADE ARGUMENT FOR EXPORT TAXES

Under the small country assumption, an idea first introduced in Chapter 2, a country takes as given the prices it receives for its exports and pays for its imports. Thus, for example, Canada and Russia count as small countries in the clothing and smartphone markets, because these countries constitute only a small part of global supply of, or demand for, clothing and smartphones. Therefore, whatever goods they bring to the markets or buy from others, their actions do not affect their prices on the world market.

The small country assumption is a useful simplification in many instances, but it is not always appropriate. For example, Saudi Arabia and Kuwait are small countries in terms of their share of world population and income, but they are not small countries in the world oil market. They do not take the world price of oil as given because the world price of oil depends in part upon how much they decide to produce. Through its decisions about production, OPEC helps determine the world price of oil. They can drive down the world price of oil if they produce more, or they can increase the world price if they produce less.

The same is true of other countries. The United States produces about 80% of the world's almond crop. Mediterranean countries (Spain, Italy, and Greece) account for 90% of the world's olive oil production. Although their positions are less dominant, Chile is the world's largest copper producer, China is the world's largest tobacco producer, Brazil is the world's largest coffee producer, Iran is the world's largest pistachio producer, and Turkey and the Czech Republic are the world's largest producers of poppy seeds. Through their decisions about production, all of these countries influence, to some degree, the world prices of these commodities.

Notice that this list consists mainly of raw materials and natural resources, not manufactured goods. The big difference between the two is that almost any country can produce manufactured goods, importing the raw input materials as needed, so a large market share does not necessarily translate into market power. For example, in the early 2000s, the city of Datang in China, all by itself, accounted for about a third of the world's sock production. (In fact, it is known as "sock city," and at one point it produced about 8 *billion* socks per year.) But that does not mean that China can influence world sock prices the way OPEC can influence world oil prices. If China reduces its sock production, the price of socks would initially increase, but then other countries in Asia and elsewhere would have an incentive to build sock factories and ramp up production. There are, in other words, many *potential* producers of socks, and they would happily produce the socks that China declined to make. That would push the market price back down. In the case of raw materials, such as oil, other countries cannot simply start production when the world price goes up – either a country has the natural resources, or it does not.

Export Supply and Import Demand

Under the small country assumption, a country faces a perfectly elastic demand for its exports: it can export as much as it wants without affecting the world price. A large country, by contrast, faces downward-sloping demand for its exports: if it exports more, the additional supply will reduce the world price. In this case, we cannot use our partial equilibrium diagram to show what will happen when there is an export tax: our diagram will have one supply curve and two downward-sloping demand curves (one domestic and one foreign), which makes things complicated. Instead, we can examine the world market by looking at a country's export supply and the rest of the world's import demand, concepts introduced in Chapter 2.

Let us use the example of OPEC and oil. In Figure 9.1, the world price of oil is determined by the intersection of OPEC's export supply curve (X_S) and the rest of the world's import demand curve (M_D). (The import demand curve of the rest of the world is the same as the export demand curve facing OPEC.) As the diagram shows, OPEC exports (and the rest of the world imports) quantity X at world price p_W.

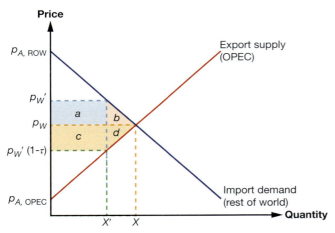

Figure 9.1 Large Country Export Tax This figure shows export supply and import demand. The downward-sloping demand schedule facing the exporter means that if it restricts exports, from X to X', it will improve its terms of trade by increasing the world price.

Now suppose that OPEC enacts an export tax of rate τ to reduce its exports of oil, then the price world consumers pay for oil does not go entirely to OPEC producers, because the producers must turn over some of their earnings to OPEC governments. As we saw in Chapter 8, with an export tax, domestic producers receive $1 - \tau$ times the world price. In Figure 9.1, the export tax reduces the price that producers receive from p_W to $p_W'(1 - \tau)$, and the lower price leads producers to reduce their exports from X to X'.

If OPEC were a small country, the export tax would have no impact on the world price, and the burden of the tax would fall entirely on domestic producers. However, in this case OPEC faces a downward-sloping export demand curve, and therefore the reduction in exports increases the world price of oil. In Figure 9.1, the reduction in exports increases the world price from p_W to p_W' along the rest-of-the-world's import demand curve (OPEC's export demand).

In this large country case, the burden of the export tax is shared by domestic producers and foreign consumers. The price of oil within OPEC, obtained by producers, does not fall by the full extent of the tax, as in the small country case, but neither does the world price of oil rise by the full extent of the tax.

A numerical example: suppose the world price of oil is initially $100 per barrel, and OPEC imposes a 25% export tax. If OPEC were a small country, the world price would remain $100 and the price received by OPEC producers would fall to $75. Because OPEC is a large country, however, the world price of oil increases as its exports decline. One possible outcome is that, as a result of the tax, the world price rises to $120 per barrel, of which OPEC exporters collect $90. In that case, OPEC producers pay $10 of the tax and rest-of-the-world consumers pay $20. (Then the OPEC price is 0.75 times the new world price of $120, or $90.) The exact incidence of the tax depends on the elasticities (slopes) of the export supply and import demand curves.

OPEC Welfare

Unlike a small country, a large country that restricts its exports can increase the world price of its exports. This constitutes an improvement in the exporter's terms of trade, which might also improve the country's welfare.

Let us look at Figure 9.1 from OPEC's standpoint. The price of oil in OPEC falls from p_W to $p_W'(1-\tau)$. This brings a *net* loss of producers' surplus of $c + d$ along the export supply curve. This loss is the net of an even greater total loss in producer surplus that is partly offset by an increase in OPEC's consumer surplus. The net loss shows up in the figure as a loss in producer surplus because OPEC is a net exporter, i.e., producer, of oil. The government collects revenue from the export tax equal to the tax per unit, $\tau p_W'$, times the tax base (exports of X'), which appears as the area $a + c$.

In terms of OPEC's overall welfare, area c is simply a transfer from producers to the government and therefore cancels out. Thus, the net welfare effect of the export tax for OPEC is $a - d$. Area d is the standard deadweight loss that arises because the tax distorts domestic production and consumption; this occurs in the small country and large country cases alike. Area a represents the terms of trade gain to the country, due to the increase in the world price from p_W to p_W' for its exports X'. This is tax revenue received by OPEC that is paid for by foreign consumers.

The welfare effect $a - d$ will be positive if the rectangle gain a is greater than the triangle loss d. In that case, the terms-of-trade gain exceeds the deadweight loss and the export tax improves the country's welfare.

Not just any export tax will make the country better off. A prohibitive export tax would not increase welfare: the world price would rise to p_A, but exports would be zero, so there would be no area a, while area d would be the entire triangle above the export supply curve and below p_W. To see this point, go back to Figure 9.1 and start at the original equilibrium without the export tax. As a small export tax is imposed and gradually increased, exports fall. As the tax is increased, the deadweight loss d always becomes larger in size, while the terms of trade area a increases for a while but at some point begins to shrink again. So if the export tax is set too high, area d will exceed area a, and the welfare effect of the tax will be negative.

This implies that there is an **optimal tariff** on exports, which maximizes the area $a - d$. The formula for the optimal export tax is $\tau^* = 1/\eta$, where η is the absolute value of the elasticity of foreign demand for the country's exports. The more inelastic the export demand curve is, the easier it is to make foreign consumers pay a higher world price, which makes area *a* larger. Using this formula, if $\eta = 2$, the optimal export tax is 50%; if $\eta = 4$, then the optimal export tax is 25%, if $\eta = 10$, the optimal export tax is 10%, etc.

As the elasticity increases, the export demand curve becomes flatter and there is less area *a* to be captured by an export tax. In the limit, as η approaches infinity, the export demand curve becomes perfectly elastic at the world price, in which case we have a small country. In this case, there is no area *a* from an export tax and the optimal export tax is zero, because any such tax leads to deadweight loses that reduces welfare. (Recall our discussion of this in Chapter 8.)

THEORY The Formula for the Optimal Tariff

The text states that the formula for the optimal export tax is $\tau^* = 1/\eta$, where η is the absolute value of the elasticity of foreign demand for the country's exports. Where does this formula come from? The goal of the optimal tax is to maximize the area $(a - d)$ in Figure 9.1. Area *a* can be represented as $\Delta P_W X'$ and area *d* can be represented as $(1/2)[P_W - P_W'(1 - \tau)] \cdot \Delta X$. The optimal export tax is such that the marginal gain to area *a* equals the marginal cost in area *d*. As a rough approximation, this means $\Delta P_W X' = P_W' \tau \cdot \Delta X$. Solving this yields $\tau = \Delta P_W X / P_W \Delta X$, which is the reciprocal of the elasticity of export demand, in absolute value, defined as $\eta = (\Delta X/X)/(\Delta P_W/P_W)$.

An alternative derivation is based on the fact that the government wants to set the export tax such that the marginal revenue from exporting equals the marginal cost of exporting (just as a monopolist sets marginal revenue equal to marginal cost). Revenue from exporting is $P_W X$, and so marginal revenue is $(\Delta P_W/\Delta X) \cdot X + P_W$. This can be rearranged to be $P_W(1 - 1/\eta)$, where η is again the absolute value of the elasticity. This should be set equal to marginal cost, which is simply the domestic price along the export supply curve, or $P_W(1 - \tau)$. Equating marginal revenue and marginal cost means that $(1 - \tau) = (1 - 1/\eta)$, or $\tau = 1/\eta$.

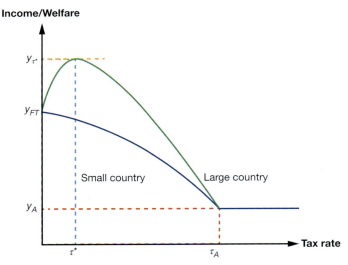

Figure 9.2 Income and Export Taxes: Small and Large Country Cases
This figure shows the relationship between a country's welfare (utility level, or national income) and the tax it levies on exports. For a small country, the optimal export tax is zero – free trade – and welfare decline with a higher tax. Welfare levels off when the tax becomes prohibitive, when the economy is at autarky. For a large country, welfare rises until reaching the optimal export tax (τ^*) and then falls until autarky is reached.

Figure 9.2 shows the welfare effects of an export tax for a small and a large country as a function of the export tax rate. For a small country, the maximum level of national income (y) is under free trade (y_{FT}) and therefore the optimal export tax is zero. As the export tax is increased, income falls until the country reaches autarky. The autarky level of income (y_A) is reached with a prohibitive export tax (τ_A), after which further increases in the tax does not affect income. For a large country, by contrast, income is higher under the optimal export tax ($y_{\tau*}$) than under free trade. Further increases beyond the optimal export tax reduce income until autarky is reached. Thus, only export taxes within a certain range dominate free trade in terms of their ability to raise income.

Rest-of-World Welfare

In the small country case, an export tax has no impact on the rest of the world because the world price does not change. (If Mongolia stopped exporting beer, would anyone outside of

Mongolia notice?) In the large country case, an export tax does affect the world price, so the tax does affect the rest of the world. A higher price of oil may be good for OPEC, but it is bad for the rest of the world that imports oil. As we learned in Chapter 3, a terms of trade improvement for exporting countries constitutes a terms of trade loss for importing countries.

In Figure 9.1, the increase in world price as a result of the export tax means that the rest of the world loses $a + b$ of consumer surplus. (Here again, the loss is the net of an even greater loss in consumer surplus that is partly offset by an increase in the rest of the world's producer surplus.) And note that the rest of the world's loss, $a + b$, is greater than OPEC's gain, $a - d$.

In terms of aggregate world welfare, area a is simply a transfer payment from the rest of the world to OPEC, leaving the world with a deadweight loss of $b + d$. So, the export tax succeeds in transferring income from the rest of the world to OPEC, but from a global perspective it is inefficient. OPEC's gains from the export tax come at the expense of the rest of the world, which is why it is sometimes called a **beggar-thy-neighbor policy.**

Terms of Trade and Import Tariffs

Just as large countries can have market power in the goods they export, large countries can have market power in terms of the goods that they *import*. This is called **monopsony** power; it refers to large purchasers of goods whose purchase volume can affect the prices for the goods they buy. For example, the United States is a huge consumer of petroleum and may not take the world price as given: an increase in US demand may drive up the world price of oil, and a slackening of US demand may reduce it. Such countries can use import tariffs to reduce their demand for imported products, reducing the price of their imports on world markets and thereby improving their terms of trade.

Notice in Figure 9.1 that the rest of the world has monopsony power in the oil market: it is not a price taker and does not face a perfectly elastic export supply curve from OPEC. Instead, it faces an upward-sloping export supply from OPEC, indicating that if demand in the rest of the world increases, so will the world price.

To show how the rest of the world could gain by imposing an import tariff, Figure 9.3 reproduces Figure 9.1, but from the perspective of the importing country. Let us start out at our original equilibrium with world price p_W and the rest of the world importing (and OPEC exporting) quantity M. The rest of the world imposes a tariff on imported oil. That would increase the price in the rest-of-the-world market from p_W to $p_W'(1 + \tau)$ and reduce the rest-of-the-world's imports (and OPEC's exports) from M to M'. The decrease in demand for OPEC's exports would reduce the world price from p_W to p_W'. This constitutes a terms of trade deterioration for OPEC and a terms of trade improvement for the rest of the world. The rest of the world collects $a + c$ as tariff revenue but loses $a + b$ as net consumer surplus, leaving it with $c - b$. If c is greater than b, then the rest of the world is better off. The optimal import tariff would maximize $c - b$.

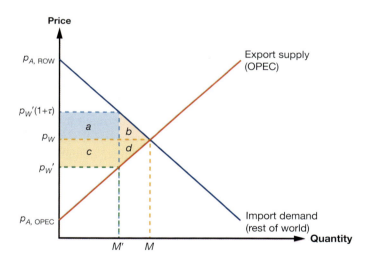

Figure 9.3 Large Country Import Tariff When a large importing country faces an upward sloping supply from the rest of the world, it has the market power to improve its terms of trade (reducing its import price) by imposing an import tariff. The tariff drives up the domestic price but lowers the world price when its imports fall from M to M'.

Meanwhile, the OPEC exporting countries would be worse off by area $c + d$ as lost net producer surplus. This loss arises because of the deterioration in OPEC's terms of trade, from p_W to p_W'. Just as when OPEC imposed the export tax, the losses of the country facing the tax (now OPEC) are greater than the gains to the country imposing the tax (now the rest of the world). Therefore, from a world wide perspective, the world is worse off by deadweight loss $b + d$. This import tariff is also a beggar-thy-neighbor policy, one that benefits the rest of the world at the expense of OPEC.

Empirical Evidence

Are there examples of large countries benefiting from export taxes and possibly even import tariffs? The example of OPEC has been used to motivate this analysis, because it is one of the world's most prominent cartels. In 1982, OPEC established production quotas to limit the supply of oil. The price elasticity of demand for crude oil is thought to be very inelastic: empirical estimates put it at around 0.05 in the short run and 0.30 in the long run. OPEC member countries account for about 40% of world crude oil production and about 60% of globally traded crude oil. While OPEC is far from having a perfect monopoly, it does have tremendous market power (see Smith, 2009).

Yet OPEC is a very imperfect cartel, and compliance with the quotas has been lax. OPEC lacks an effective mechanism to monitor, detect, and punish members who exceed their quotas: since the start of the quota system, total OPEC production of crude oil has exceeded the ceiling by 4% on average, but sometimes as much as 15% or more. Petroleum producers who are not members of the cartel also limit OPEC's ability to control the price of oil, as do the rise of substitutes, such as natural gas. In fact, most of the large increases in oil prices have been due, not to cartel behavior, but to military conflicts causing sharp, unexpected falls in production.

At the same time, some OPEC countries have become incredibly rich. OPEC is divided between countries with a large volume of low-cost reserves that are concentrated in certain countries with small populations and therefore enjoy relatively high incomes (such as Kuwait, Saudi Arabia, and the United Arab Emirates) and others with smaller volumes of higher-cost reserves in populous and therefore relatively poor countries (such as Nigeria, Ecuador, and Venezuela). The large-volume, low-cost reserve countries in the Middle East have reaped trillions of dollars in producer surplus, but the low-volume, high-cost reserve countries are not nearly as wealthy.

The spike in oil prices after the Arab–Israeli war in 1973 transferred billions of dollars from oil-consuming countries to oil-producing countries. This led other developing-country exporters of raw materials to believe that they, too, could become rich by forming a cartel to raise world commodity prices. For example, major copper producers started taxing their exports in an effort to raise revenue and the world price. Unfortunately for them, there are many substitutes for copper on the world market, such as aluminum in power lines and plastic in plumbing, and so the price elasticity of demand is not nearly as inelastic for copper as for oil. The copper producers succeeded in reducing their exports, but they did not enjoy higher prices. As a result, their export revenues fell. In Figure 9.3, they suffered area d but did not enjoy much area a.

Looking further into the past, the United States had significant market power in the world cotton trade prior to the Civil War. From 1820 to 1860, the US produced about 80% of the world's cotton. This cotton was largely exported to Britain, where it was used to produce cotton textiles in the mills of Manchester. Irwin (2003) estimates that the elasticity of export demand for cotton facing the US was about −1.7. This implies that the optimal export tax was about 60%. However, the US could not exploit this market power, because the US Constitution prohibits export taxes. Furthermore, cotton-producing states in the South, such as South Carolina, would have violently opposed any such tax at the federal level. In any event, the estimated gains from such an export tax would have been very small, only about 0.3% of GDP, so the US was not foregoing huge gains.

In sum, free trade is not always the best policy. Countries with significant market power in the goods they export can improve their terms of trade by restricting exports. However, they risk overplaying their hand if the demand for their goods is more elastic than they had anticipated. Then the countries will not enjoy higher export prices, and the export restrictions will simply make them worse off.

9.2 SECOND-BEST ARGUMENTS FOR PROTECTION

If a country has world market power in its export markets, then the **first-best policy** is to impose an export tax at the optimal rate to improve the country's welfare. A first-best policy is one that is most efficient at achieving the desired goal of increasing national income. Of course, a country having market power does not mean that *any* export tax dominates free trade, but an optimal tariff can increase national income, compared to free trade.

This is not the only argument in favor of restricting trade in order to increase national income, or to achieve some other objective. However, in most instances, using tariffs or other trade policies to achieve a stated objective is a **second-best**, or even third-best, policy. This means that, while a trade policy intervention can help to achieve the objective in question, it is not the most efficient way to do so. In such cases, there are other *domestic* policies, not trade policies, that are first-best.

We can illustrate this proposition with three examples: revenue, employment, and externalities.

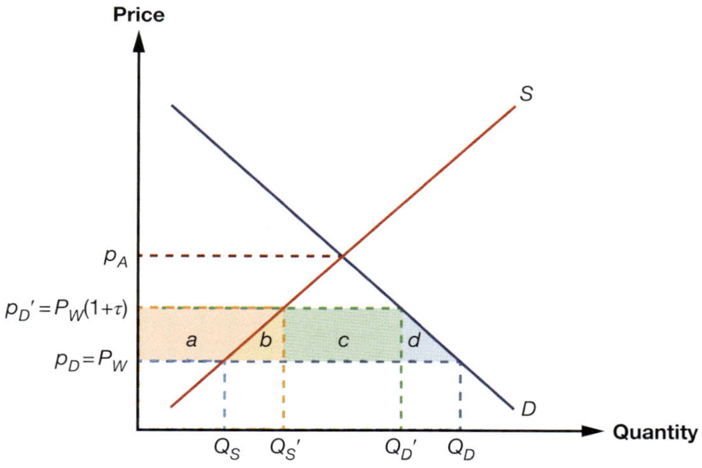

Tariffs for Revenue

Suppose the government wants to raise revenue. As an economic advisor, you are asked the following question: what is the best way – meaning the most efficient or least costly way – of achieving that objective? Your job is not to question the desirability of the objective, but simply to figure out the best way of meeting the objective.

One possible answer is an import tariff. But while a tariff can raise revenue, it is a second-best policy, because there are other, better ways of doing that, such as a consumption tax. Figure 9.4 presents our basic partial equilibrium tariff diagram. As we know, if we impose an import tariff, the government will collect area c in revenue at the cost of deadweight losses $b + d$, while area a is transferred from domestic consumers to domestic producers.

Now consider instead a consumption tax, which also raises the price paid by domestic

Figure 9.4 Comparing an Import Tariff and Consumption Tax An import tariff and a consumption tax of the same rate have the same impact on domestic prices and domestic consumption. However, a tariff on imports increases domestic production and the government collects area c as revenue. With a consumption tax, the domestic price does not rise for domestic producers, who continue to produce at S, and the government collects areas $a + b + c$ as revenue. The deadweight loss from a tariff is area $b + d$, whereas the deadweight loss from a consumption tax is area d.

consumers. Domestic consumption would still fall from Q_D to Q_D'. But with a tax on consumption, not imports, the domestic price does not increase for domestic producers, and so production remains at Q_S. The government would collect area $a + b + c$ as revenue, and the deadweight loss would be area d. Therefore, a consumption tax raises more revenue than a tariff does, with less deadweight loss. (Of course, this calculation ignores the cost of tax administration and alternative tax policies, such as an income tax.)

In a head-to-head comparison then, a consumption tax comes out as a first-best policy to raise revenue, and a tariff is second best. Unless there is some political reason why a consumption tax should be ruled out, governments should prefer it to import tariffs as a means of raising revenue.

Tariffs to Increase Employment

Suppose a government's objective is to increase the number of workers in a particular industry, which is competing against imports. (This is a very different objective than increasing overall employment in the economy, which would require macroeconomic policies.) As an economic advisor, you do not necessarily question the merits of this goal, if that is what your political bosses wish to do. Your goal is to determine the most efficient way of achieving this objective.

Given the objective of increasing employment in an import-competing industry, an import tariff might be a reasonable policy to consider. Such a tariff would increase the industry's output and thereby tend to add to the number of workers employed. Thus, the tariff helps achieve the stated objective. However, the tariff brings about a deadweight loss to both production and consumption. By contrast, a production subsidy also increases output and employment, but with a deadweight loss only to production. This is a reason to prefer a production subsidy to an import tariff as a way of increasing employment.

Yet even a production subsidy is not the first-best policy, because paying firms to produce more is not guaranteed to increase employment. With a production subsidy, domestic firms might purchase more machinery or equipment, not hire more workers, to generate the additional output. The first-best policy to increase employment is to subsidize employment directly, through wage subsidies or corporate tax breaks for hiring workers. A production subsidy would be a second-best policy, and an import tariff would be a third-best policy. Those policies simply increase production in a sector of the economy, which is only indirectly related to the goal of increasing employment.

Tariffs to Correct Externalities

For a given market behavior, be it production or consumption, an externality is a cost imposed on, or a benefit received by, others who are not involved in the behavior. Because the externality does not affect the producers and consumers directly, they do not take it into account when deciding how much to produce or consume. In such cases, competitive markets will not allocate resources efficiently, because prices will not reflect the true costs and benefits of different activities.

A **negative externality** is a cost imposed on others. Pollution is the classic example. If polluters do not have to pay for the air or water resources they spoil, the harm done to the environment is not a part of a firm's production costs. From society's point of view, then, firms will produce too much output, because their private costs of production will be lower than the social costs of production that take into account the costs of pollution. For example, the horrible air pollution in China arises because state-owned, coal-fired electric power plants do not take pollution into account in their production decisions.

The ideal amount of domestic production can be achieved by aligning the private costs of production with the social costs. This could be accomplished by using the price system in one of two ways. The government could tax polluters' output to raise the private costs of production up to the social costs. Or the government could create a "price" for pollution by requiring polluters to acquire the permits needed to pollute a certain amount. These permits would cap the amount of permissible pollution each year but could be traded on the open market so they would be allocated efficiently. In any event, an import tariff would be an inappropriate way to correct a negative externality, because it would encourage domestic firms to produce more output, which is the opposite of what is desirable. (If the negative externality were in an exporting industry, an export tax would restrict output, but only based on foreign sales, not domestic production, and therefore would be inefficient at fully correcting the externality.)

A **positive externality** is a benefit for others that does not show up in the economic incentives considered by producers or consumers. Think of the social benefits of new biomedical technology – benefits that go far beyond the financial rewards for the firm that bore the R&D costs. For example, pharmaceutical firms would have to invest millions of dollars to come up with a new antibiotic that could kill a new and deadly drug-resistant strain of bacteria. However, if the drug ends up being effective in preventing a major outbreak – a huge social benefit – relatively few people will be infected and require treatment. Then the revenue stream from selling the drug will not compensate the firm for its R&D investment. This will make private firms reluctant to sink a lot of money into coming up with new antibiotics.

The problem with positive externalities is that firms will under-produce relative to the socially desired level, because costs are concentrated among the firms rather than distributed across the society that benefits. The government can correct this misalignment between private and social costs through a production subsidy. Since an import tariff can also encourage domestic production, import protection is sometimes proposed to assist industries thought to have positive externalities, assuming that those industries can be identified.

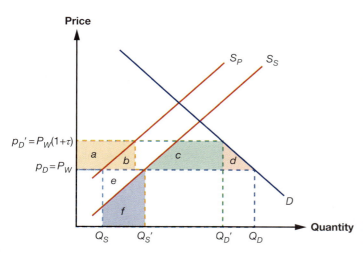

Figure 9.5 A Positive Externality in Production A positive externality means that the private costs of production are higher than the social costs of production, leading to suboptimal output (S < S′). A production subsidy will increase output to where the world price equals the social cost of production and lead to a net gain of e. A tariff will do the same but will also raise the price to consumers, reduce consumption, and result in deadweight loss d.

Figure 9.5 illustrates the potential benefits of a production subsidy in an industry with a positive externality. For a given production quantity Q, the triangular area under the supply curve S_P represents the private costs of production. The triangular area under S_S represents the **social costs of production**, which are calculated as the private costs minus the social benefit of domestic production. (We could also say that S_S is what the producers' supply curve would look like if their costs were reduced in proportion to the social benefit they were providing, so that the externality was "internalized.") Without the subsidy, domestic producers will produce at Q_S, where the world price is equal to the private costs of production.

Ideally, a production subsidy that raises the price received by domestic producers to P_D' will increase domestic production from Q_S to the socially desirable level of production, Q_S^*.

The cost of the subsidy to the government is area $a + b$, while the benefit to producers is an increased produce surplus, area a. If there were no externality, the subsidy would result in a deadweight loss of area b. But the gap between S_P and S_S represents the benefit of domestic production, so there is also the social gain of area $b + e$ from expanding domestic output. In the end, the subsidy brings a gain of area e, a positive benefit from government action, presuming they are able to impose the optimal subsidy that increases output to exactly Q_S^* and does not overshoot or undershoot that target.

Here is another interpretation of this diagram. The private cost of increasing domestic output from Q_S to Q_S^* is area $b + e + f$, the cost of importing those goods is $e + f$, and the social cost is area f. The country will import these goods because the cost of imports $(e + f)$ is less than the private domestic costs $(b + e + f)$. But those goods should be produced at home because the social costs (f) are less than the cost of importing $(e + f)$. Therefore, if that extra output is acquired through domestic production, the economy saves resources e.

As we know, a tariff amounts to a production subsidy and a consumption tax. While the production subsidy part of the tariff helps capture area e, the consumption tax part of the tariff raises prices for domestic consumers, reduces domestic consumption, and results in a deadweight economic loss of area d. It could be that the loss of area d completely offsets the gain of area e, resulting in no improvement in welfare. Using a tariff to correct the production distortion (too little output) has created a new consumption distortion (too little consumption). For this reason, the use of a tariff to correct production externalities has been called "acupuncture with a fork" – it remedies the problem of insufficient production but also creates a distortion that results in insufficient consumption.

It is unrealistic to expect that a government tax or subsidy policy can be used to correct externalities very precisely. This is even more of a challenge when the policy instrument being used is a second-best one, as is the case with import tariffs or export subsidies. As the economist Harry Johnson (1970) once quipped, "The fundamental problem is that, as with all second-best arguments, ... improvement in social welfare requires detailed theoretical and empirical investigation by a first-best economist. Unfortunately, policy is generally formulated by fourth best-economists and administered by third-best economists."

However, the analysis of a second-best trade policy is important. What this analysis suggests is that there is no connection between "free trade" and a policy of "laissez faire." Before these findings were recognized, the case for free trade was often equated with the case for laissez faire (meaning no government intervention). However, if the case for laissez faire depended on markets working well, then the case for free trade would be compromised if markets did not always work well. This analysis shows that markets may be imperfect due to externalities, but free trade would still remain a desirable policy. That is because the market imperfections should be addressed with domestic policies that directly target the "market failures," not with trade policies that create new distortions even as they correct others.

To sum up: governments have many different objectives. Although import tariffs can sometimes help achieve those objectives, it does not follow that tariffs should be imposed. Other policy instruments are often better solutions for the problem at hand.

Non-Economic Objectives

A non-economic objective is one where the goal is not to increase overall economic welfare but to achieve some other worthwhile goal. The achievement of such goals requires economic resources. For example, national defense is an objective that requires the diversion of resources from civilian to military use. Economists usually leave it to others to determine the desirability of a proposed goal but might have something to say about how that goal is achieved. For example, Adam Smith argued that some domestic industries might deserve protection from foreign competition for national security reasons because, as he put it, "defense is more important than opulence." However, trade policy is usually a second-best means of achieving non-economic objectives. For example, a production subsidy may be a more efficient way of promoting defense industries, rather than an import tariff, for reasons like those set out above.

Of course, there is a limit to how much a government might be willing to spend on non-economic objectives. For example, Saudi Arabia has long sought to be self-sufficient in food, particularly wheat production, in case it was cut off from world trade for an extended period and could not import foreign supplies. Growing wheat in the desert is a challenge, but Saudi Arabian producers were up to the task. The government paid farmers nearly $1,000 per ton of wheat at a time when the world price of wheat averaged about $100 per ton. The domestic price of wheat was so high that in some years it led to large surplus production, which Saudi Arabia exported (with further subsidies) to other countries. From 1980 to 2005, the Saudi government spent almost $100 billion, nearly 20% of the total oil revenue accumulated during this period, on subsidies for wheat farmers. The real cost of the subsidy was the diversion of precious water resources from urban use to irrigation in the desert. The financial and resource cost, as well as the unlikelihood that the country would ever be unable to import food from the rest of the world, led Saudi Arabia in 2008 to begin cutting back the price offered to wheat farmers with the plan being to be entirely reliant on imports again by 2016.

9.3 INFANT INDUSTRY PROTECTION

A common rationale for import restrictions in developing countries is the desire to promote infant industries. An **infant industry** is one that is just starting out and cannot compete with the more-established competitors in other advanced countries: without import restrictions, the developing country industry would be wiped out by foreign competition. Therefore, temporary import tariff barriers are needed to give an infant industry the time and space to mature. Once the nascent industry has grown up, the restrictions on imports can be removed, and the industry, it is hoped, will be able to stand on its own and survive without protection.

The infant industry argument has always been controversial. Adam Smith thought that government protection would most likely just lead an infant industry to become dependent on government support. By contrast, John Stuart Mill ([1848] 1909) argued that the temporary protection of infant industries was a valid exception to free trade:

> The only case in which, on mere principles of political economy, protecting duties can be defensible, is when they are imposed temporarily (especially in a young and rising nation) in hopes of naturalizing a foreign industry, in itself perfectly suitable to the circumstances of the country... [I]t cannot be expected that individuals should, at their own risk, or rather to their certain loss, introduce a new manufacture, and bear the burthen of carrying it on until the producers have been educated up to the level of those with whom the processes are traditional. A protecting duty, continued for a reasonable time, might sometimes be the least inconvenient mode in which the nation can tax itself for the support of such an experiment.

Many countries have industries that currently cannot compete in the world market. With government support, they might be able to mature and become competitive. However, the point of an infant industry policy is not to protect an industry from foreign competition forever, but to give it *temporary* assistance so that it can reduce its costs and eventually compete in the world market without aid. For example, the United Nations Conference on Trade and Development (UNCTAD, 2003) has argued that "technical efficiency requires access to new technologies from across the world, but simply exposing local industries to international trade, investment, and information is not enough ... Without any strategic support from the government, [countries] find it difficult to bridge the gap between their skills, technologies, and capabilities and those needed for international competitiveness."

The logic of the infant industry argument is that the short-term costs of temporary protection could be offset by long-run gains from domestic producers. This is a *dynamic* argument for protection, because the industry is evolving over time, perhaps through "learning by doing." Learning by doing means that a firm's production costs fall as a result of production experience. This is different from the static notion of economies of scale in which costs fall with more production because fixed costs can be spread out over more units of output. Learning by doing means that today's production costs are lower because of production in the past.

This principle certainly applies to us as individuals: the first time we do something, we usually do not do it very well; but the more we try, the better we get – at least up to a point. The same goes for firms: the more they produce, by refining their production processes, the better they get. (Of course, there is a limit to this. Ford and General Motors have been producing cars for more than a century, but that does not mean that they have the lowest costs or the best technology of any auto maker.)

Figure 9.6 illustrates the case for infant industry protection. In the left panel, we have the domestic supply curve of the infant industry, as well as the demand curve. The world price is

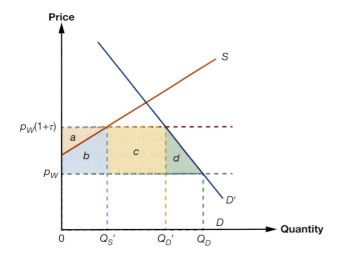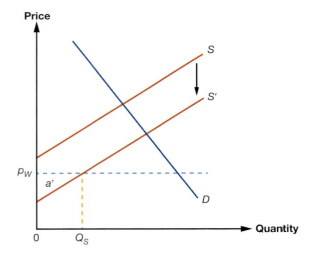

Figure 9.6 Infant Industry Protection With infant industry protection, the aim is to have domestic producers reduce their costs once they start producing output. In the left panel, domestic costs are so high that there is no domestic production at world prices. A tariff can make such production profitable, but at large deadweight losses indicated by areas *b* and *d*. If that situation continues, there is no economic gain from promoting the infant industry, which never grows up. In the right panel, a reduction in costs because of production experience makes domestic production profitable even at world prices, leading to a gain of area *a*.

taken as given. At this stage, domestic producers are not competitive at the world price: if there was free trade, domestic supply would be zero and all domestic consumption (Q_D) would be provided by imports. (This is not unusual: most countries do not produce their own citrus fruit, laptops, smartphones, or automobiles, and are therefore entirely dependent on importing those goods.)

Suppose, now, that this industry is thought to have the potential to be a competitive industry, needing only some production experience to reduce its costs and survive in the world market. The government could help start domestic production of this good by imposing an import tariff. If the tariff raises the domestic price to $p_W(1 + \tau)$, then domestic production will be profitable and output will be Q_S'. Of course, the tariff also raises the price to domestic consumers and reduces their consumption to Q_D'. Consumer surplus falls by area $a + b + c + d$ while domestic producer surplus increases by area a, and the government collects area c as revenue. Notice that the production deadweight loss, area b, is larger than the usual triangle because there would be no domestic production without the tariff. In other words, because the industry is not economically viable at the world price, domestic production is very inefficient, and the deadweight loss is larger than when there is some domestic production even without a tariff.

If this were the end of the story, one might ask: why would a government do this? If the domestic supply curve remains fixed, the industry will never become competitive at the world price. Of course, Argentina could produce smart phones if it raised the domestic price high enough, just as Saudi Arabia could produce wheat and New Zealand could manufacture automobiles. Would it be worthwhile to have domestic production in the industry? On purely economic grounds, the answer would be no.

In the case of infant industries, the hope of policymakers is that temporary protection will stimulate costs reductions so that the industry's supply curve shifts down. If its costs fall far enough, the industry can survive without tariff protection. The right panel of Figure 9.6 shows a shift down in the domestic supply curve from S to S'. This is assumed to be the result of the industry's costs having fallen once it began production. If this happens, the tariff can be removed, and the industry can survive without protection. (Note that the country is still importing the good and is not self-sufficient, but at least the domestic industry is viable and can survive on its own.)

What would be the benefit from having established domestic production in this industry? The gain is that domestic production yields producer surplus of area a', the area above the supply curve S' but below the world price. (Note that this is not the same as area a, which is producer surplus *above* the world price, and accrues only because of the tariff.) This constitutes the income that the industry generates for the economy; it arises because the industry has costs that are below the world price. This producer surplus comes without the side effects of the tariff intervention, such as the deadweight loss, $b + d$, and producer surplus a and tax revenue c.

Would temporary infant-industry protection be worthwhile in this case? To make this determination, we need to make a cost–benefit calculation over time. In the short run, protecting the industry requires that net costs $b + d$ must be incurred for some period. If the policy works, the country will reap producer surpluses a' for some future period. The cost–benefit test is whether the present discounted value of the benefits is greater than the present discounted value of the costs.

For example, if a country must pay a cost of $1 billion annually for 20 years in order to reap a gain of $2 million annually for ten years, those benefits will never exceed the high initial costs. On the other hand, if a $1 million annual cost must be incurred for five years to reap an annual benefit of $2 million for 50 years, then the project would pass a cost–benefit test. Whether tariff protection passes the cost–benefit test depends upon several factors: the size of the deadweight losses, the length of time that they must be incurred, the size of the producer surplus gains, and the discount rate that is applied to the costs and the future benefits.

Critics of infant industry protection, such as economist Robert Baldwin (1969), argue that a tariff is an inappropriate way of helping such industries. By raising the domestic price, a protective tariff makes existing production techniques profitable and provides no guarantee that entrepreneurs will undertake greater investments in acquiring new technological knowledge. Furthermore, if there is a positive externality because learning from domestic production creates knowledge that can become available to other potential competitors, there will be underinvestment in learning, but the tariff will not directly correct that externality. As Baldwin argues, "What is required to handle the special problems of infant industries is a much more direct and selective policy measure than non-discriminatory import duties."

How do we know whether a particular industry warrants protection as an "infant industry"? And what is the actual experience with infant industry protection? Unfortunately, we do not have good answers to either of these questions. It is virtually impossible to know ahead of time whether an industry will flourish or flounder if it is protected from foreign competition. As for experience, Ann Harrison and Andrés Rodríguez-Clare (2010) conclude: "Given the varied experiences across countries and time periods, the different interpretations possible, and the difficulties in conducting clean empirical analyses, it is not easy to arrive at strong conclusions regarding the role of industrial, trade, and FDI [foreign direct investment] policy in development."

IN PRACTICE Infant Industry Policies

Infant industry policies continue to generate controversy. Some observers point to the East Asian economic miracle and argue that government policies were responsible for the economic successes of those countries. Other observers point to the wasteful failures of government support for industries elsewhere.

In South Korea and China, the government has played a role in allocating credit toward favored industries (private firms in the case of Korea, state-owned enterprises in the case of China), and sometimes protecting them from foreign competition. Some economists have pointed to South Korea's steel industry as an example of infant industry protection that worked out well (Westphal, 1990). In the Korean case, the country relied not just on import protection but on export promotion; that is, protection from foreign competition was tied to success in exporting to world markets. There was a strong political commitment to withholding support from industries that did not successfully export to foreign markets or improve their technologies. This "tough love" policy seems to have worked.

However, many governments are incapable of taking this approach: they are happy to shower their industries with love but afraid to get tough when the industries do not perform well. In many instances, government support for particular industries has not worked out particularly well. Government support for selected firms can sometimes breed corruption, not efficiency.

The initial export success of East Asian and Southeast Asian countries was based on developing labor-intensive manufacturing industries. The efforts by governments to develop industries that were more advanced have been less successful. Korea's heavy and chemical industry drive in the 1970s is widely viewed as having distorted the economy, promoting capital-intensive industries before the labor-intensive industries had fully developed, depriving them of the capital they needed to grow. As Dwight Perkins (2013), an expert on the East Asian economies, has noted, "Malaysia and Thailand have also made some progress in moving up to more sophisticated industries, many of them foreign owned, but government initiatives have had little to do with these developments. The major government initiatives to promote heavy industries in Indonesia and Malaysia were largely failures" (p. 119). As the Indonesian economic adviser Widjojo Nitisastro used to say, "governments are bad at picking winners, but losers are very good at picking governments."

There are many more examples of failed infant industries that either never grew up or never were able to give up government support. For example, Nigeria has long wanted to establish a domestic steel industry to promote the country's industrialization and to end its dependence on imported steel. In 1981, the government took the lead in establishing the Ajaokuta steel project. This enormous plant was set on 60,000 acres and was expected to take six years and cost $1.4 billion to construct. More than 30 years later, the Nigerian government has sunk nearly $7 billion into the project, which has been fraught with cost overruns and delays. The project has yet to produce any steel. Yet Nigerian officials have refused to give up on the project. In February 2012, the chairman of the House Committee on Steel Development, Sadiq Asema Mohammed, rejected calls to privatize the project and said that government should invest $513 million more to complete the Ajaokuta steel plant, arguing that no private investor would want to invest such a huge amount in the project. If the Nigerian steel industry was an infant industry, it has never been born, let alone left the cradle.

One problem with infant industry protection is that policymakers can never be certain that the domestic supply curve will shift enough to make the industry viable at world prices. Even potentially promising projects can become unprofitable for unanticipated reasons. World prices may shift and change the calculation. For example, in the late 1960s France and the United Kingdom spent $1.3 billion to build 20 supersonic passenger aircraft, called the Concorde, which were designed to compete with the Boeing 747. The Concorde first flew in 1969, and the authorities hoped it would be profitable, but in 1973 the world price of oil unexpectedly quadrupled. Unfortunately, the Concorde was a gas-guzzler, virtually a flying fuel tank, because of the afterburners needed to reach Mach 2 speed. Higher fuel costs pushed ticket prices way up, but consumers did not want to pay those prices simply to save a few hours on trans-Atlantic travel. The Concorde was not a commercial success, and it was finally retired from service in 2003.

Figure 9.7 The Concorde
Source: Alain Jocard/AFP via Getty Images.

9.4 EXPORT SUBSIDIES AND STRATEGIC TRADE POLICY

Chapter 8 examined export subsidies in the case of a small country. Like import tariffs, export subsidies redistributed income but resulted in deadweight losses that left the country with lower income. This chapter has shown that import tariffs could be beneficial in the case of a large country by improving its terms of trade. Is it similarly possible for export subsidies to be beneficial in the case of a large country? The answer is no, because such subsidies will deteriorate, not improve, the terms of trade. However, there is a possibility that export subsidies will prove beneficial if it shifts profits to domestic firms when there is *imperfect competition* in world markets. This section briefly reviews these cases.

Export Subsidies and the Large Country Case

Let us think back to our OPEC example developed earlier in this chapter but consider what would happen if OPEC ministers got mixed up and decided to implement an export subsidy for oil instead of an export tax. Figure 9.8 shows OPEC's export supply and the rest of the world's import demand. As before, the intersection of the two lines determines the world price of oil and the quantity exported by OPEC (imported by the rest of the world).

Now OPEC imposes an export subsidy that raises the domestic price of oil in OPEC to the world price times $1 + s$, where s is the rate of subsidy. This higher, subsidized price encourages OPEC to produce and export more oil. In Figure 9.8, exports increase from X to X'. Because OPEC faces a downward-sloping demand for its exports, the increase in exports drives down the world price of oil from p_W to p_W'. Therefore, the price received by OPEC exporters is $p_W'(1 + s)$. For example, suppose the world price of oil is $100 per barrel. If OPEC were to institute a 20% export subsidy, and OPEC were a small country, whose terms of trade were unchanged as a result of the subsidy, then OPEC exporters would receive $120 per barrel. However, in the large country case, the increase in exports that comes from the subsidy decreases the world price from $100 per barrel to (say) $90 per barrel. The 20% subsidy would then increase the price received by exporters to $108 per barrel (adding 20% of $90 means adding $18). In any case, the export subsidy reduces the world price of the large country's exports and thus deteriorates its terms of trade.

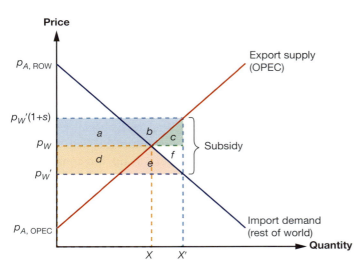

Figure 9.8 Export Subsidy in a Large Country When a large country subsidizes its exports, the increased exports reduce the world price, deteriorating its terms of trade. Unlike an export tax that improves the terms of trade, the export subsidy makes the country worse off.

How does the terms-of-trade deterioration make the country worse off? Let us look at the welfare effects of the export subsidy in Figure 9.8. OPEC producers benefit from the export subsidy, and their net producer surplus increases by area $a + b$. But the government is paying out the subsidy, the cost of which is the subsidy rate times the subsidy base. The subsidy rate is the difference between p_W' and $p_W'(1 + s)$, and the subsidy base is exports after the subsidy, or X'. Therefore, the cost of the subsidy is area $a + b + c + d + e + f$.

So, what is the net effect of the subsidy? Taking the producer gains and subtracting the government subsidy cost gives us a loss of income of $c + d + e + f$. We can divide this loss into two parts. First, the triangle c is the standard deadweight loss from distorting production and consumption decisions by the subsidy (too much domestic production, too little domestic consumption). This deadweight loss would occur in the small country case as well. Second, the rectangle $d + e + f$ is the terms of trade loss from the decline in export prices. The size of this loss depends on the slope of the export demand curve facing OPEC (the rest of the world's import demand curve), which determines how much the price of oil falls with the increase in exports.

Thus, a large country might want to tax its exports because the terms of trade gain would exceed the deadweight loss. A large country, however, would never want to subsidize its exports, because the terms of trade loss would simply add to the deadweight loss. It would be crazy for OPEC to subsidize its oil exports, but the rest of the world would like OPEC to do so. The terms of trade loss for OPEC is a terms of trade gain for the rest of the world. The rest of the world would gain areas $d + e$ in net consumer surplus from the export subsidy. Therefore, the net effect on the world's welfare would be a loss of $c + f$. Thus, OPEC loses more than the rest of the world gains and the policy is inefficient from a worldwide standpoint. The OPEC export tax was also inefficient from a worldwide standpoint but was a "beggar-thy-neighbor" policy. Perhaps we should call the OPEC export subsidy a "beggar-thy-self" policy!

Strategic Trade Policy

Another occasional purpose of an export subsidy is to shift profits from foreign rivals to domestic firms when there is imperfect competition in international markets. This is known as strategic trade policy.

A strategic situation is one in which the actions of one firm affect the payoffs to another firm. In such an interdependent situation, government support for one firm can give it a strategic advantage. In an international context, if a market is exceptionally profitable, perhaps because there are only a few firms in it, then strategic trade policy can help shift profits toward a domestic firm and therefore may be able to benefit the domestic economy at the expense of one or more other economies. The simplest setting in which to examine strategic interactions among firms is a **duopoly,** which simply means that two firms are competing with one another (more competition than a monopoly, but less than an oligopoly!).

The leading duopoly of today is the rivalry between Boeing and Airbus in the market for long-distance, wide-bodied aircraft. For decades, Boeing dominated this market with its 747. In 2005, Airbus started producing the A380 super jumbo jet to challenge Boeing's monopoly in this market segment. The A380 is an enormous aircraft, capable of carrying over 500 passengers and having a cruising range of about 8,500 miles (Figure 9.9). One reason few firms produce for this market is that the fixed costs of production are huge. Airbus spent about $12 billion in developing the A380 – those are up-front costs that were incurred even before a single jet was produced or sold. This means that the economies of scale are simply enormous. This astronomical fixed cost must be spread over as many A380s as possible, otherwise the cost per aircraft will be exorbitantly high and Airbus will be unable to make any money.

Given these enormous fixed costs and the limited demand for such wide-bodied aircraft, it is possible that only one firm could survive in the market. The entry of a new firm to challenge an incumbent monopoly could drive down prices and drive-up costs (since both firms have to incur fixed costs but would divide the market between them) so that neither firm would be profitable.

Figure 9.9 The Airbus A-380 with a Boeing 747 in the Foreground

Source: aviation-images.com/Universal Images Group via Getty Images.

In such a market, where the decisions of one firm clearly affect the decisions of another, government policy could be used to shift the profits toward the domestic firm. Some analysts, including at Boeing, believe that is exactly what has happened. About a third of Airbus's start-up costs for the A380 came from loans from European governments, and it is thought that these loans were in effect subsidies. That is, it is believed that the European subsidies were designed to guarantee that Airbus would enter the market and take profits away from Boeing.

Simple game theory can illustrate the possible outcomes when two firms compete with one another. Each firm faces the decision whether to produce its wide-bodied aircraft or not. Table 9.1 shows the payoffs (profits) to Boeing and Airbus given their respective decisions. In the upper right-hand box, Boeing has chosen to produce and Airbus not to produce. That gives Boeing a monopoly, and it earns profits of $100, while Airbus earns zero profits. In the lower left-hand panel, Airbus produces aircraft and Boeing does not, in which case Airbus has the monopoly and earns $100 while Boeing earns nothing. If neither firm produces, then both firms earn zero profits. But if both firms produce, then they each lose $5. This is because we assume that the market cannot support two firms: competition drives down the price of aircraft, and each firm produces fewer aircraft, resulting in higher average costs, both of which undermine industry profitability.

Table 9.1 Boeing's First Mover Advantage

Boeing \ Airbus	Produce	Don't produce
Produce	−5 / −5	0 / 100
Don't produce	100 / 0	0 / 0

Because Boeing entered the market first with the 747 in 1969, it has a "first mover advantage." Given that Boeing is already in the market, Airbus must make the best decision for itself. And looking at the payoffs in Table 9.1, Airbus has a choice between earning −$5 if it chooses to produce and earning $0 if it chooses not to produce. With Boeing as an established producer, there is no incentive for Airbus to enter the market, and so it leaves Boeing to earn the $100 profit.

However, suppose the European Union wants to help Airbus, and so it provides a subsidy of $25 for production of the A380. This government subsidy changes the payoffs, as shown in Table 9.2, in a way that makes it profitable for Airbus to enter the market, regardless of what Boeing does. If Airbus produces, it earns $20 if Boeing produces or $125 if Boeing does not produce. The European subsidy has erased Boeing's first-mover advantage: regardless of what Boeing decides to do, Airbus will enter the market, because it will always earn profits.

Table 9.2 Airbus Receives Subsidy of $25

Boeing \ Airbus	Produce	Don't produce
Produce	20 / −5	0 / 100
Don't produce	125 / 0	0 / 0

With the EU subsidy in place, Boeing has a choice between producing and losing $5 or not producing and earning $0. Therefore, its best response is to not produce, either by abandoning production of the 747 or by not producing the next generation of aircraft. As a result of the subsidy, Boeing concedes the market to Airbus and Airbus gets the $100 profit. The $25 subsidy succeeded in shifting the $100 from the United States to Europe, and therefore the subsidy improved Europe's economic welfare. In this case, the subsidy is beneficial from Europe's perspective.

This result seems to indicate that governments should support domestic firms in international competition when there are extra profits to be had. But this result is also subject to some important qualifications.

First, if both governments subsidize their firms, then neither country will be better off. In that case, both countries spend $25 and each firm earns $20, resulting in a net loss to each country of $5. The only beneficiaries would be airline companies and their customers. Hence, if the United States retaliates against Europe for its subsidy, both countries lose. (It still might want to retaliate to bring Europe to the negotiating table.)

Second, the European subsidy also does not work if Boeing is not driven out of the market (Table 9.3). Suppose that Boeing's long production experience means that it has lower costs (by $10) than Airbus, so that it can earn a profit even if Airbus enters the market. If the subsidy does not push Boeing out of the market, the subsidy simply induces Airbus to enter and earn $20 at the cost of a $25 subsidy, a net loss for Europe.

Table 9.3 Airbus Receives Subsidy but Boeing Has Lower Costs

Boeing \ Airbus	Produce	Don't produce
Produce	20 / 5	0 / 110
Don't produce	100 / 0	0 / 0

In sum, the strategic use of subsidies hinges crucially on the underlying payoffs under different scenarios. In the real world, there is usually a great deal of uncertainty about the exact payoffs and whether firms respond as anticipated.

The United States and the European Union have fought over the Airbus subsidies in the World Trade Organization (WTO). (As will be discussed in Chapter 10, the WTO has a dispute settlement system for resolving conflicts between its member countries.) The United States argues that the Airbus subsidies are illegal under world trade rules and have harmed Boeing's sales. The European Union argues that it has only made commercial loans to Airbus and that Boeing also receives implicit subsidies from military contracts. WTO panels have ruled against the subsidies on both sides in various cases that stretch back decades. Because the WTO has no way of enforcing its judgement and both governments insisted that the other should stop its subsidies, the US and EU have retaliated against one another, imposing higher tariffs on each other's goods. Finally, in 2021, after 17 years of wrangling, the EU and US agreed to a truce in the aircraft trade war, and removed the retaliatory duties against each other.

IN PRACTICE Mercantilism as Strategic Trade Policy

As discussed in Chapter 3, mercantilism refers to the idea, developed in seventeenth- and eighteenth-century Europe, that exports are good and imports are bad. If true, the policy implication would seem to be that imports should be restricted, and exports should be promoted. Yet economic analysis indicates that "large" countries should not promote exports but restrict them (this chapter) and small countries should neither promote nor restrict exports (Chapter 8).

Yet the mercantilist implication that exports should be promoted may find support in the case of strategic trade policy, which may have been relevant at the time. In the seventeenth century, the English East India Company and the Dutch East India Company vied with one another over the lucrative trade of the Spice Islands of Southeast Asia. These were the only two firms in the world competing over this highly profitable trade route, so that the market was a duopoly. The Dutch government helped the Dutch firm take aggressive actions to deter the English company, including the confiscation of cargoes and the sinking of ships. (This sometimes happens today when small bands of pirates off the coast of Somalia attack enormous cargo freighters and attempt a hijacking. See the 2013 movie *Captain Phillips*, starring Tom Hanks.) This scared off the English firm, and the Dutch company was able to move in, dominate the trade (in what is now Indonesia), and earn most of the profits.

According to Irwin (1991), these profits might have more than compensated the government for its efforts and thus improved national welfare. In the long run, however, the spice and pepper trade became more competitive, squeezing profit margins, and erasing any particular benefit from special government efforts to promote a national trading firm.

Figure 9.10 Dutch and English Ships Fighting in 1653
Source: The Print Collector/Getty Images.

APPLICATION China's Industrial Policies

Many countries encourage domestic producers with what are called *industrial policies*. These policies are designed to promote greater domestic production in targeted industries, sometimes through protection from foreign competition but more often promotion through subsidies and tax breaks.

There may be a sound economic rationale for such subsidies when domestic firms operate under **external economies of scale**. These external economies are a form of externality in which the private costs of domestic production are higher than the social costs, and therefore a subsidy might improve welfare. In this particular case, an increase in the production by one firm lowers the cost of production for other firms in the industry. This effect is called external economies of scale because it is external to each firm (i.e., firms do not recognize the benefits that their production has for the industry as a whole) and it is an economy of scale (i.e., production costs go down for other firms in the industry).

External economies of scale are hard to detect, but they are revealed in industrial agglomerations. There are many examples of firms in an industry that cluster together. For much of the twentieth century, US auto production was clustered around Detroit, Michigan. Many automobile firms and their suppliers benefited from being close to each other and having specialized suppliers, knowledgeable labor force, technological spillovers, and other cost-reducing factors that were close by. High-tech firms cluster around Palo Alto, California, near Stanford University because of the talent, capital, and infrastructure that is readily available for firms to take advantage of. The area was originally referred to as Silicon Valley because of the semiconductor firms that grew up there in the late twentieth century, a growth originally fueled by government contracts (a form of subsidy).

How large are the potential gains from **industrial policy**? According to Bartelme, Costinot, Donaldson, and Rodriguez-Clare (2021), even under optimistic assumptions that governments maximize welfare and have full knowledge of the underlying economy, the gains from optimal industrial policy are relatively small, ranging from 1% of GDP in a baseline case to 3% in a general environment with physical capital and input–output linkages across firms.

Of course, it is one thing to observe industrial clusters and say that external economies of scale exist, it is another to say that governments can know which sectors of the economy deserve subsidies and which do not. If governments pick losers instead of winners, promotion schemes may simply lead to expensive subsidies, deadweight losses, and corruption. A major source of skepticism about industrial policy is that governments simply do not know which sectors should be subsidized at the expense of others.

Nonetheless, many countries have industrial policies to promote certain sectors. None are more controversial than China's. In its "Made in China 2025" plan, issued in 2015, China's government highlighted ten key industries for special treatment in the hope that the country would become the technological leader. In reality, Chinese industrial policy lavishes billions of dollars rather indiscriminately on dozens of sectors, with the hope that something will pay off. DiPippo, Mazzocco, and Kennedy (2022) found that China spent 1.7% of GDP in fiscal outlays, tax breaks, below-market credit, and other kinds of industrial subsidies in 2019. This was much more than other countries such as South Korea (0.7% of GDP) and the United States (0.4% of GDP). This study also found that industrial spending in China is heavily affected by political loyalties, not rational economic analysis. As a result, a disproportionate amount of industrial policy spending goes to inefficient state-owned enterprises (SOEs) and cronies, resulting in widespread corruption.

Because of its economic size, when China decides to subsidize a particular industry the effects ripple through the world economy. Critics argue that China is seeking to give local firms an unfair advantage over foreign companies in the race to dominate the technological frontier of the future. The subsidies are controversial even within China. While supporters argue that subsidies are necessary for China to upgrade its industries, critics say that the government's strong preference for large state-owned enterprises and national champions has put private companies and small and mid-sized enterprises in a disadvantaged position.

Subsidies encourage domestic firms to increase production, but is there a special benefit from having more domestic production? One study finds little evidence to support the view that China's government picks winners. Instead, subsidies tend to flow to less productive firms and the receipt of government subsidies was negatively correlated with subsequent firm productivity growth. Furthermore, neither subsidies promoting R&D and innovation promotion nor subsidies promoting industrial and equipment upgrading are positively associated with firms' subsequent productivity growth, although the subsidies do boost employment (Branstetter, Li, and Ren 2022).

For example, China has lavished massive subsidies on the shipbuilding industry. China accounted for less than 10% of world production of ships in the late 1990s, but with subsidies a decade later its share was more than 50%, most of it at the expense of other producers rather than an expansion in the overall market. Barwick, Kalouptsidi, and Zahur (2021) found that the policy boosted China's domestic investment and entry by more than 200%, but the policy created sizable welfare distortions and generated little net profit gains to domestic producers. Many of the subsidies led to the entry and expansion of unproductive and inefficient producers, which exacerbated excess capacity and kept industry profits low. The study also found little evidence that the shipbuilding industry generated significant spillovers to the rest of the domestic economy (e.g., steel production, ship owning, and the labor market). No evidence of industry-wide learning-by-doing (where production costs decline as industry output increases) or support for strategic trade considerations was found.

Figure 9.11 Shipbuilding in Yichang, Hubei Province, China in 2023 In 2022, for the first time, Chinese shipyards surpassed their Japanese and South Korean counterparts in order intake, completion, and hand orders, according to the International Shipping network.

Alternatively, China's massive subsidies for solar panel producers has resulted in an enormous expansion of production and a sharp reduction in prices. This has harmed panel producers in other countries, leading to trade friction and trade disputes, but it has made solar power available to consumers at a much more affordable price.

Taking a page from China's playbook, the Biden administration has also supported the use of industrial policies to promote domestic production of semiconductors and electric vehicles. The CHIPS act pledged more than $50 billion to revive domestic production of semiconductors in the United States. Likewise, the Inflation Reduction Act provides for tax breaks and other subsidies to incentivize consumers to purchase electric vehicles produced in the United States. It is too soon to say whether these efforts will be successful or not.

CONCLUSION

This chapter has considered whether government interventions in trade might sometimes make economic sense under certain conditions. For countries that have the ability to influence their terms of trade (the prices of their exports and imports), taxes on trade can improve economic welfare despite losing some of the gains from trade. However, while such taxes may help some countries, their gains will come at the expense of other countries. In other instances, trade intervention is a second-best policy, one that is dominated by other government actions. Finally, the chapter considers infant industry policy and strategic trade policy, and other cases for government intervention in trade, finding that such policies may be beneficial under certain circumstances.

SUMMARY

1. If a country can influence its terms of trade, i.e., the prices of its exports and imports, it could benefit by restricting trade through an optimal tariff to exploit this market power. For a large country (one with market power), free trade is not necessarily the best policy.
2. A country imposing an optimal tariff is pursuing a beggar-thy-neighbor policy in which it is better off at the expense of its trading partners. From a global standpoint, the policy is inefficient and leads to a deadweight loss.
3. There are various circumstances in which trade policy can be used to correct market failures (externalities) or achieve various objectives (revenue, employment, etc.), but trade policies are a second-best method of addressing these problems. The case for free trade is *not* the same as the case for laissez-faire (no government intervention).
4. Infant industries in developing countries are often thought to warrant protection from foreign competition. However, whether a country can benefit from protecting infant industries hinges on a difficult cost–benefit calculation over time: whether the short-run costs of tariffs are exceeded by the long-run benefits of the industry. For an infant industry policy to be beneficial, the industry must become efficient and reduce its costs, and it is not clear whether a tariff promotes or retards that outcome.
5. Subsidies can be used to give domestic firms a strategic advantage in international competition over exceptionally profitable markets. However, this is also a beggar-thy-neighbor policy that can depend on the nature of the particular markets involved and can be stymied by the subsidies of other countries.
6. While there are many qualifications to the case for free trade, there are also many qualifications in using interventionist trade policies.

KEY CONCEPTS

Beggar-thy-neighbor policy, page 183
Duopoly, page 195
External economies of scale, page 198
First-best policy, page 185
Industrial policy, page 199
Infant industry, page 189

Monopsony, page 183
Negative externality, page 186
Optimal tariff, page 181
Positive externality, page 187
Second-best policy, page 185
Social costs of production, page 187

REVIEW QUESTIONS

1. What defines a "large country"? Why is "free trade" not necessarily the best policy for a "large" country?
2. What determines the "optimal" export tax in the large country case? Does any export tax dominate free trade in terms of overall welfare?
3. What is a "second-best" argument for a trade intervention?
4. What is the "infant industry" case for protection? What are some of the factors that determine whether such protection would improve economic welfare? Can governments determine whether an industry is an infant deserving of protection or not?
5. Under what conditions might an export subsidy be a useful policy to consider?

EXERCISES

1. What are the pros and cons of imposing an export tax to improve the terms of trade?
2. Suppose the US import demand for oil is 400 − 4P while OPEC's export supply is 80 + 4P.
   a. What is the autarky price of oil in the United States?
   b. If there is free trade, what will be the price and quantity of US oil imports from OPEC?
   c. Suppose OPEC fixes its exports at a quantity of 200 units. Calculate the effects of this tax, i.e., the new US price, the new price in OPEC, and any tariff revenue. What is the implicit export tax that would have to be imposed to restrict the quantity of exports to 200 units?
   d. How much do the US and OPEC each gain or lose through such a tax?
   e. What is the overall effect of the export tax on world welfare?
   f. Suppose OPEC sets the export quota at 160 units. What happens to the price in the US? And is OPEC better off or worse off, relative to the export quota of 200 units?
3. The equation for South Africa's domestic demand for diamonds is $Q = 20 - P$ and South Africa's domestic supply is $Q = 10 + P$.
   a. What is the autarky price of diamonds in South Africa? How much is produced, consumed, and exported at that price?
   b. The equation for South Africa's export demand is $Q = 110 - 2P$. What is the autarky price in the rest of the world? Under free trade, what is the world price and what quantity will South Africa export? Provide a diagram (below) of world export supply and import demand and show the autarky and free trade prices and quantities.
   c. Suppose South Africa restricts its exports by ten units through an export tax. What is the resulting impact on prices? Show the impact in the diagram.
   d. Calculate the amount by which South Africa is better off or worse off as a result of this reduction in exports.
   e. Calculate the impact on the welfare of the rest of the world.
4. The EU's export supply of sugar is $Q = -10 + 2P$. The rest of the world's import demand for sugar is $Q = 90 - 2P$.
   a. Draw a diagram that shows the autarky price of sugar in the EU and the rest of the world (ROW), and that shows the world price and quantity of trade when trade is allowed. Also show the autarky prices in the EU and the ROW.
   b. The EU implements an export subsidy that increases exports by 10 units. What is the new price of sugar in the EU and the rest of the world? Provide a diagram. What is the subsidy rate?
   c. Label the various areas of the diagram in part b with a letter or number. Which letters/numbers illustrate the impact on the EU overall and the rest of the world overall? Calculate the welfare effects.
   d. What is the impact of the export subsidy on these groups? Circle the right answer in each case?
      EU consumers: better off / worse off
      EU producers: better off / worse off
      Rest-of-World consumers: better off / worse off
      Rest-of-World producers: better off / worse off

5. Suppose that the supply curve reflecting private costs of production is $S_P = -20 + P$, and the supply curve reflecting social costs of production is $S_S = -10 + P$. Does this mean that there is a positive externality or a negative externality?
   a. If the world price is 30, how much will private firms produce? How much is the socially desired level of domestic output?
   b. What price has to be offered to domestic producers to get them to produce at the socially desired level? What rate of production subsidy has to be offered to achieve this?
   c. How much does the optimal subsidy cost the government? How much is captured by domestic producers as additional producer surplus? What is the gain from correcting the externality? How much is added to social welfare as a result of the optimal subsidy?
   d. If domestic demand for this good is $D = 150 - P$, how much are imports with and without the subsidy?
   e. Given the demand curve in part d, suppose a tariff is imposed that raises the domestic price to the same level as that under the optimal subsidy. What happens to imports? How does the tariff rank relative to a production subsidy in terms of its welfare effects? Is the tariff welfare improving?
6. What are the pros and cons of an "infant industry" policy? Under what conditions is such a policy likely to achieve its purpose?
7. Suppose the domestic supply curve for a certain good is given by $S = -100 + 2P$.
   a. If the world price is $40, how much will domestic production be? What is the break-even price at which producers might be willing to produce some output?
   b. Suppose domestic demand for the good is represented by $D = 200 - P$. With free trade, how much will be imported?
   c. Now suppose a tariff of 100% is imposed to get domestic production going in this infant industry. What is the new domestic price? What are the new levels of production, consumption, and imports? Calculate the impact of the tariff on producer and consumer surplus, as well as government revenue. What is the net economic impact on welfare?
   d. As a result of learning by doing, domestic producers are able to reduce their production costs such that the supply curve shifts down to $S = -50 + 2P$. What is the new break-even price required of domestic producers? If the 100% tariff remains in place, what is the new level of production, consumption, and imports? What is the impact of the tariff in terms of the production and consumption deadweight losses, as well as government revenue? What happens to the net welfare cost compared to the previous supply curve?
   e. Now suppose the infant industry tariff is removed. What is the level of production, consumption, and imports under free trade with the new supply curve? What is the total level of producer surplus that is gained by having domestic production at free trade?
   f. How would you assess the intertemporal tradeoff between the initial costs of the tariff and the long-run benefit of having domestic production?

RECOMMENDED RESOURCES

For a historical review of the many arguments made against free trade, see Douglas Irwin, *Against the Tide: An Intellectual History of Free Trade* (Princeton, NJ: Princeton University Press, 1996).

Sometimes tariffs are justified on the basis of taxing externalities, such as the so-called carbon border adjustment; see Lionel Fontagné and Katheline Schubert, "The Economics of Border Carbon Adjustment: Rationale and Impacts of Compensating for Carbon at the Border," *Annual Review of Economics* 15(1) (2023): 389–424.

Many developing countries have distorted markets that shape how trade – and trade policy - affects their economy; see David Atkin and Amit K. Khandelwal, "How Distortions Alter the Impacts of International Trade in Developing Countries," *Annual Review of Economics* 12(1) (2020): 213–238.

An old but still useful set of essays on strategic trade policy can be found in Paul Krugman (ed.), *Strategic Trade Policy and the New International Economics* (Cambridge, MA: MIT Press, 1986).

CHAPTER 10

Trade Politics, Trade Agreements, and Trade Laws

LEARNING OBJECTIVES

In this chapter, we learn about:
- some factors behind the political support for, and opposition to, various trade policies
- the types of trade agreements that countries negotiate with one another
- the role the World Trade Organization plays in international trade policy
- various trade laws dealing with "dumping" and "unfair" competition

INTRODUCTION

In January 2017, just three days after taking office, President Donald Trump withdrew the United States from the Trans-Pacific Partnership, or TPP. This trade agreement involving about a dozen Pacific Rim countries would have reduced trade barriers and established rules governing trade in the region. "We're going to stop the ridiculous trade deals that have taken . . . companies out of our country," he stated. Trump had consistently argued that trade agreements such as the North American Free Trade Agreement (NAFTA) with Canada and Mexico were "a bad deal" for US workers and unfair to American business, allowing other countries "to take advantage of us."

Yet many Republicans, including the former governor of Indiana, Mike Pence, who served as Trump's Vice President, supported the TPP. Senator John McCain described the president's decision as a "serious mistake" that will "forfeit the opportunity to promote American exports, reduce trade barriers, open new markets, and protect American invention and innovation." Members of Congress also objected to President Trump's decision to impose tariffs on imported steel, as did the many steel-using firms. The motorcycle maker Harley-Davidson, for example, was not pleased at being hit with higher steel costs as a result of the president's decision. Nor was the firm happy about facing higher tariffs on its sales in Europe and elsewhere, after other countries retaliated in response to the tariff on US steel imports.

So which is it: are trade agreements such as the TPP a good idea or not? Were the tariffs that the United States imposed on imported steel a smart decision or one that hurt the American economy? What is clear is that such debates are not new, and many different constituencies are involved. Because dollars and jobs are at stake, trade policy has always been the subject of intense political debate in every country throughout history. Previous chapters of this book have analyzed the economic impact of various trade policies. However, this analysis does not tell us how governments *actually behave*. Officials in government are subject to political pressures regarding trade policy: some groups want to close markets and impose trade barriers, and other groups want to open markets and reduce trade barriers. What factors and forces are behind the trade policy that a country decides to adopt?

This chapter examines how a nation's political system interacts with economic interest groups in determining trade policy. Of course, government policymakers are inevitably, and perhaps to an extent quite properly, responsive to interest-group lobbying. At the same time, they may want to use trade agreements to further economic or foreign policy goals. Indeed, over the past half-century, most countries have sought to reduce trade barriers, both their own import restrictions and the barriers to their exports in other countries. Trade liberalization has taken place through regional agreements such as NAFTA, and multilateral agreements have been reached through institutions such as the **World Trade Organization** (WTO). These agreements have been controversial, as the contrasting views of Donald Trump and Mike Pence (before they were in office) suggest.

At the same time, as trade barriers have been reduced, governments want to have the option of temporarily increasing import barriers if a domestic industry is injured as a result of those imports. This has given rise to trade laws that permit the government to impose antidumping and countervailing duties to prevent dumped and subsidized imports from harming import-competing producers.

10.1 TRADE POLITICS

Policymakers – including elected representatives and administration officials – serve multiple constituencies and are usually trying to achieve multiple objectives. They must perform a delicate balancing act when different economic interests conflict over trade policy. For example, should a government raise import tariffs to protect import-competing producers, or should it reduce import duties to expand trade and help exporters? How should policymakers balance the interests of workers who will be displaced because of imports against the interests of workers who will have jobs in export industries?

Economists make different assumptions about a government's trade policy objectives. One assumption is that a government designs its trade policies to maximize national income or economic welfare. This view takes the government as an impartial arbiter of the national interest. Another assumption is that the government is simply a clearinghouse for special interest groups that lobby for favors, such as tariffs or subsidies. This view takes the government as offering up policy to the highest bidder, i.e., the most generous campaign contributors. Of course, one could assume that governments do both: they want the economy to benefit from trade, but they are also sensitive to trade-related interest groups. In this case, it could be that government officials want freer trade, but they also seek to minimize the adjustment costs borne by labor and capital due to any market disruption caused by imports.

One can find situations in which any one of these assumptions seems to explain policy outcomes. Sometimes governments are quite open about protecting politically powerful domestic groups from foreign competition, such as the United States with its restrictions on imported sugar and Japan with its restrictions on imported rice. However, sometimes governments get new leaders who have a broad conception of the national interest, defy domestic opposition, and move quickly and decisively toward more open trade, as when China began opening to the world in 1979 or when a new government in India addressed an economic crisis in 1991 by dismantling controls on trade. In general, however, governments usually act conservatively and reserve the option to block any import surges that might threaten domestic industries. In 2018, for example, the United States imposed import duties ranging from 60% to 86% on bio-diesel fuel from Argentina, after domestic producers complained they were losing sales to their Argentine rivals.

The process by which trade policy is made and the speed with which it can change depend on the country's political system. In a dictatorship or authoritarian regime, policies are determined by a single ruler or a ruling elite; those policies can change quickly if there is a change in leadership. For example, from the time he seized power in 1949 until his death in 1976, the Chinese communist leader Mao Zedong imposed a system of central planning that kept his country isolated from world markets. In 1978, Deng Xiaoping took over as leader. Believing that Mao's policies had been disastrous, Deng began opening up the economy to trade and foreign investment. Similarly, General Park Chung-hee, the military leader of South Korea from 1961 until 1979, decided to open up the Korean economy to the world in mid-1960s, a move that brought enormous change to the country. In 2011, Thein Sein, the new president of Myanmar (Burma) and a former military commander, decided to end the country's isolation and begin trading with the rest of the world, although a military coup in 2021 put an end to that process as the country's leaders worried about subversion coming from foreign actors.

In a democracy, by contrast, economic policy is usually based on a broad political consensus that tends to prevent any abrupt change. Elections can shift control of government from one party to another, but often policies do not change very much. This is because power is distributed across different governmental institutions. In the United States, a bill must survive an arduous committee process and then win a floor vote in both the House of Representatives and the Senate, and must finally be approved by the president before it becomes law. This means there is a **status-quo bias** to policy, so that it takes a big disruption to bring about any large change. The trade policies of the United States, the European Union, Japan, and other advanced countries have been very consistent since World War II. These countries have generally supported the gradual elimination of trade barriers, a trend that – until recently - has continued regardless of which political party has been in office.

In the case of the United States, until recently, both Democratic and Republican administrations have tried to push Congress to approve agreements that liberalize trade. The negotiation of NAFTA began under President George Bush (a Republican) but was concluded and enacted under President Bill Clinton (a Democrat). The negotiation of the US–South Korea Free Trade Agreement began under President George Bush but was concluded and enacted under President Barak Obama (a Democrat). However, President Donald Trump has viewed free trade much more skeptically, declaring that other countries have taken advantage of the United States with bad trade deals. He has tried to change the direction of US trade policy, but the American political system – particularly limits on his legal authority – has made this more difficult than he would like. President Joe Biden continued many of the Trump policies, by maintaining tariffs on imported steel and on products from China.

As a hypothetical benchmark, one might ask what trade policy could be expected to be adopted in a pure democracy. In theory, if a country's trade policy were decided by a majority-rule popular vote, the **median voter** would decide the outcome. This is an application of what in political science is called the median voter theorem: if voters are arrayed along a spectrum according to their opinion on a particular policy, ranging from strong support to strong opposition, then in any simple majority yes–no vote on the policy, the views of the median person in the distribution will be decisive in determining the outcome.

For example, researchers often find that the more education a person has, the more likely they are to favor free trade. How much education does the median United States voter have?

In 2021, according to the Census Bureau, 9% of Americans age 25 or older did not have a high school degree, 29% had a high school degree, 14% had some college experience but no degree, 10% had an associate's degree, 24% had a college degree, and 14% had an advanced degree. So if trade policy were determined by referendum and everyone age of 25 and up voted, the median voter in the United States would have some college experience but no degree. Their views would be decisive in choosing policy.

Now recall the mobile factors model we developed in Chapter 5, with two factors of production, blue-collar workers and white-collar workers. Suppose that only those with a college education or an advanced degree will be white-collar workers – about 30% of the population, per the previous paragraph. Then the median voter will be a blue-collar worker with some college experience.

In the mobile factors model, we saw that the two factors of production had diametrically opposed interests: the abundant factor would favor free trade and the scarce factor would favor protection. For purposes of determining the direction of trade flows, a factor's abundance or scarcity is judged relative to the rest of the world, not in comparison to the amount of the other factor at home. Therefore, if, in comparison with other countries, the United States has a relative abundance of college-educated workers, the United States will export white-collar intensive goods and import blue-collar intensive goods. But the median voter, the blue-collar worker with some college, is the scarce production factor and would therefore vote for high tariffs on imports. There is no guarantee that a democratic vote would always have free trade as the outcome.

In reality, the US public is quite divided on whether trade with China is a "good thing" for the United States or a "bad thing." As Figure 10.1 reports, a 2017 poll found that Americans generally believe that free trade agreements have been good for the country, by a 52-to-40% margin. Younger people and the more educated are especially likely to believe that to be the case.

There are just a few historical examples of countries deciding their trade policy by a democratic referendum. In 1906, Britain held a general election in which the major campaign issue was the country's trade policy. Because the median voter was a working-class laborer who spent a sizeable portion of his income on imported food, the Liberal party that favored free trade won the election against the Conservative party favoring higher tariffs. In 2007, Costa Rica held a referendum on whether the country should join the Central American Free Trade Agreement (CAFTA) with the United States and other countries. The voters narrowly approved CAFTA, with 51.6% in favor. Urban voters generally supported the agreement, while rural voters and unionized workers were generally against it.

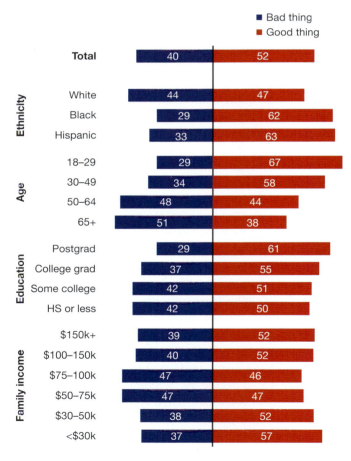

Figure 10.1 American Public Opinion on Trade in 2017
Source: Support for free trade agreements rebounds modestly, but wide partisan differences remain, Pew Research Center, April 25, 2017.

Another reason why it may be hard for democracies to reduce trade barriers, even if that would increase national income, is voters' uncertainty about whether they personally will gain or lose. Suppose there are 100 voters in an economy, and a trade reform will increase the incomes of 51 individuals by \$5 while reducing the income of the other 49 by \$1. The reform would increase national income by $(5 \times 51) - (1 \times 49) = \$206$, and the median voter would gain \$5. If all this is known by all voters, then a majority will support the reform. But now suppose that only 49 individuals know for certain that they will gain, while the remaining 51 individuals do not know if they will be among the remaining 2 who gain or the 49 who lose. These 51 individuals each have an expected gain of $(5 \times 2/51) - (1 \times 49/51) = -\$0.76$. In short, they expect to lose and therefore will vote against the proposal. Even though a majority of individuals will gain from the change, uncertainty creates a status quo bias against it (Fernandez and Rodrik, 1991).

Evolution of US Trade Policy

Rather than holding a popular referendum, most democracies give the legislative branch of government responsibility for trade policy. For example, the US Constitution gives Congress the authority to impose tariffs and regulate trade with foreign countries. In fact, the second law passed by Congress under the new constitution in 1789 was a tariff act to raise revenue for the federal government. From that time until the passage of the Smoot–Hawley tariff of 1930 (see box below), Congress debated and enacted a new tariff schedule every decade or so. (Since then, presidents have become more important, as will be discussed below.) Depending on the configuration of political forces in Congress, the new tariffs would be pushed slightly higher or lower than the ones previously enacted.

Economic interests get represented in Congress through political parties, as the country's founding fathers recognized would happen. In his famous Federalist Paper No. 10, James Madison wrote, "A landed interest, a manufacturing interest, a mercantile interest, a moneyed interest, with many lesser interests, grow up of necessity in civilized nations, and divide them into different classes, actuated by different sentiments and views. The regulation of these various and interfering interests forms the principal task of modern legislation and involves the spirit of party and faction in the necessary and ordinary operations of the government. These different interests often have conflicting views on questions of policy."

For example, Madison continued, "Shall domestic manufactures be encouraged, and in what degree, by restrictions on foreign manufactures? are questions which would be differently decided by the landed and the manufacturing classes, and probably by neither with a sole regard to justice and the public good." In Madison's view, "justice ought to hold the balance between them. Yet the parties are, and must be, themselves the judges; and the most numerous party, or, in other words, the most powerful faction must be expected to prevail."

For much of US history, average tariff levels were fairly high, around 40%. Figure 10.2 shows the average tariff on dutiable imports (those imports subject to a tariff duty) and on total imports (including goods for which no duty is collected, such as tea, coffee, bananas since the 1860s, and imports from countries with which the United States has a free trade agreement). The average tariffs on dutiable imports, which is one way of thinking about the duties protecting US manufacturers, were often in the 40–50% range. During this period, Congress was in charge of setting tariff rates. Starting in the 1940s, particularly after World War II, presidents took a leading role in trade policy, and multilateral agreements to reduce tariffs were signed. As a result, the average tariff on dutiable imports fell dramatically, to about 5% in the early 2000s.

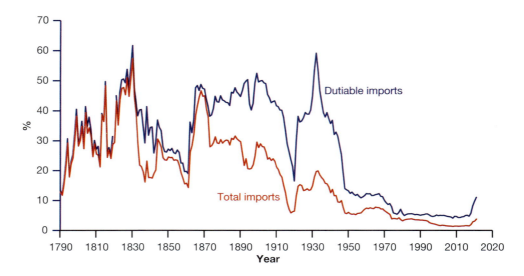

Figure 10.2 Average US Tariff on Dutiable and Total Imports, 1790–2021
Source: Used with permission of University of Chicago Press, from Clashing over Commerce: A History of US Trade Policy, *Irwin, Douglas A., © 2017, permission conveyed through Copyright Clearance Center, Inc.*

Regardless of which political party was in control, Congress as an institution tends to be biased in favor of high tariffs. This bias arises because the political influence of those favoring import restrictions tends to be greater than that of those that favor the removal of the restrictions. As a general pattern, domestic producers facing foreign competition are very politically active in advocating restrictions on imports, whereas consumers and exporters who are harmed directly or indirectly by import restrictions tend to be politically inactive. This asymmetry in political activism reflects a simple cost–benefit calculation. The benefits of a tariff are highly concentrated on a few producers, who are therefore strongly motivated to organize and defend that policy. Conversely, the costs of tariffs are spread widely among many consumers, for whom it does not pay to organize any serious opposition. As for the costs imposed on exporters, they are indirect and less certain in their impact, again a reason for less investment in anti-tariff lobbying.

The US sugar program illustrates this principle of concentrated benefits and dispersed costs. Over the past few decades, import restrictions have kept domestic sugar prices at roughly twice the world price. Domestic sugar producers – sugarcane and sugar beet growers – are estimated to gain about $1 billion per year from these policies. However, 42% of the total benefits to sugarcane and sugar beet growers went to just 1% of all producers. In fact, just 17 sugarcane farms collected over half of all the cane growers' benefits, according to government estimates. Because the benefits of the policy are so highly concentrated, the owners of these few farms have an enormous incentive to persuade the government to maintain the import restrictions. Although the sugar policy imposes far larger costs on consumers of sweeteners (about $1.9 billion) than are transferred to producers, these costs are spread widely among the far more numerous consumers (Irwin, 2020).

This combination of concentrated benefits and dispersed costs leads to an enormous imbalance in the political forces opposing and favoring any change in the sugar policy. The incentive for household consumers to oppose the sugar policy is virtually non-existent: the cost to each individual consumer is only about seven dollars per person per year. However,

10.1 TRADE POLITICS

the policy delivers millions of dollars in benefits to just a few growers, who, therefore have an enormous incentive to ensure that the policy is maintained.

Why is the sugar lobby so politically powerful when sugar is only produced in a few states? Sugar cane is only produced in Florida, Louisiana, Texas, and Hawaii, and sugar beets are grown mostly in the upper Midwest and West, as Figure 10.3 shows. One reason is that it only takes one representative from Florida to serve on the House or Senate agriculture committee to block any potential legislation that would reduce the benefits of the sugar program.

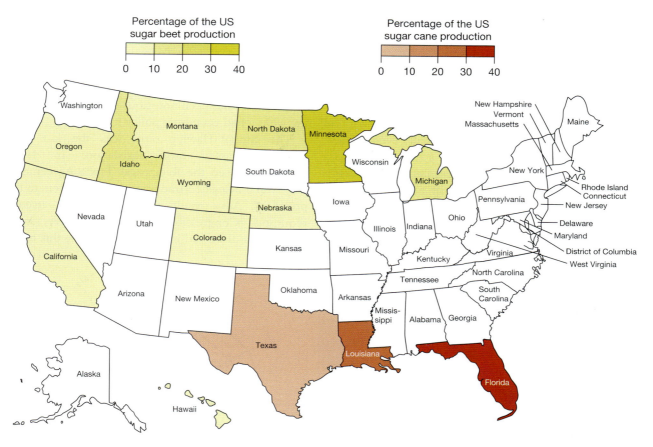

Figure 10.3 Location of US Sugar Production, Cane and Beets

In addition, members of Congress engage in *logrolling* as a way of maintaining high tariffs. Logrolling is vote trading. For example, a representative from North Carolina, whose constituents wanted to stop imports of cheap cotton textiles, might agree to vote for a higher tariff on steel to benefit workers in Pennsylvania and a higher tariff on sugar to benefit producers in Florida if their representatives also vote in favor of a higher tariff on textiles. The benefits to the North Carolina textile producers from the textile tariff are much greater than the costs of higher priced steel and sugar are to consumers in the state. Because this kind of vote trading is a common practice in the halls of Congress, members whose constituents would benefit from lower tariffs find it hard to overcome the entrenched support for those tariffs.

IN PRACTICE   The Smoot–Hawley Tariff of 1930

The ultimate example of the protectionist bias of legislatures due to logrolling and the imbalance between import-competing producers and consumers and exporters is the Smoot–Hawley tariff of 1930. Named after Reed Smoot and Willis Hawley (pictured in Figure 10.4), the chairmen of the Senate Finance Committee and the House Ways and Means Committee, respectively, the tariff was passed just as the United States was entering the Great Depression. Even though imports were not causing very much harm to domestic producers, in part because tariffs were already high and trade was a very small part of the economy, members of Congress were anxious to raise tariffs even further. This is because the benefits of a higher tariff to a particular producer are concentrated and apparent, whereas the costs of that tariff are diffused and obscure. Because producer interests were considered paramount, consumer interests got short shrift in the legislative process.

The Smoot–Hawley tariff was greeted with outrage around the world. Other countries resented the higher duties imposed on their goods. Several countries retaliated by increasing their duties on imports from the United States, and the reduction in US exports contributed to a downward spiral of world trade. This downward spiral is vividly captured in Figure 10.5, which shows how world trade fell month after month in the early 1930s. All of this contributed to the Great Depression of the 1930s, in which trade and output slumped around the world. The Smoot–Hawley tariff has been notorious ever since for showing what a bad economic policy looks like.

The Smoot–Hawley tariff was the last time Congress passed tariff legislation. In 1934, Congress passed the Reciprocal Trade Agreements Act, which delegated trade negotiating powers to the president. As a result, trade agreements, usually requiring Congressional approval, have been reached, as discussed in the text following this box.

Figure 10.4 Hawley (left) and Smoot Congratulate Each Other on the Passage of their Tariff Bills
Source: Library of Congress, Prints & Photographs Division.

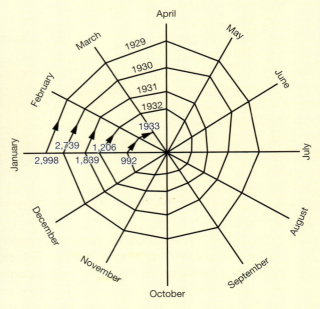

Figure 10.5 Declining Spiral of World Trade, 1929–1933
Source: League of Nations, World Economic Survey, 1933–1934.

Given the importance of the legislature in a democracy, and the bias in favor of import-competing as opposed to export-oriented industries, how is it ever possible for democracies to reduce trade barriers? One answer is executive leadership. While legislatures tend to be dominated by parochial, local interests, the president tends to be more concerned about the national interest. Every member of Congress is accountable to the particular interests in his or her district and would, for instance, have to vote to restrict steel imports if there were a steel plant in the district. However, the president, having a national constituency, can afford to take a broader view of trade policy and consider the interests of consumers, exporters, and others such as the workers who might lose their job as a result of imports.

In the United States, the president only began to have a large trade-policy role in 1934 when a Democratic Congress passed the Reciprocal Trade Agreements Act (RTAA), just four years after a Republican Congress had passed the Smoot–Hawley tariff. The RTAA allowed the president to reach trade agreements with countries in which lower US tariffs would be exchanged for lower tariffs on US goods in foreign markets. This legislative change took Congress out of the business of routinely passing tariff legislation and put that policy in the hands of the president. The shifting of power from Congress to the president has tilted the political balance of US trade policy significantly in favor of trade liberalization. Since that time, most presidents have wanted to reach trade agreements with other countries, to open up foreign markets for US exports in exchange for a reduction in US tariffs on foreign goods.

10.2 TRADE AGREEMENTS

The past few decades have been an era of globalization. Most countries have moved to reduce trade barriers and take advantage of growing world trade. How have they done so? One way a country can reduce its tariff and non-tariff barriers is simply to act unilaterally. A unilateral tariff reduction occurs when a government decides to reduce its import duties on its own, independently of other countries. In recent years, many developing countries have chosen this path. When China, India, Vietnam, and other Asian countries opened up to world markets, they did so based on domestic political changes in favor of economic reforms, including a more open trade policy.

One problem with unilateral tariff reductions is that they require strong domestic political leadership to overcome entrenched interests that defend the status quo. As a result, sometimes trade reform only happens during a period of economic crisis. In 1846, as mentioned in Chapter 4, the Irish Potato Famine helped persuade the British prime minister Robert Peel to go against his landlord constituents in the Conservative party and to propose abolishing the Corn Laws, which restricted grain imports. Peel succeeded in getting the support of enough Conservative members of Parliament to usher in an era of free trade for Britain. In 1985, Mexico's foreign exchange crisis led to unilateral liberalization of very tight import restrictions, and the country began opening up to the world. In 1991, India's balance of payments crisis led to the dismantling of the license *raj*, a massive regulatory scheme in which almost every import required multiple official permissions and permits.

Sometimes domestic political obstacles to unilateral trade liberalization make it beneficial for countries to sign agreements to reduce trade barriers with one another. There are economic and political advantages to trade agreements that can avoid the imbalance between the direct pain inflicted on import-competing producers and the indirect benefits for exporters. A trade agreement helps stimulate the interest of exporters because they benefit directly from greater market access in other countries that have lowered their import barriers.

In addition, any deterioration in a large country's terms of trade that would result from a unilateral tariff reduction will be mitigated in a trade agreement that increases the country's exports. Therefore, it may be easier to liberalize trade for one's own economy in agreements with other countries, because the harm to domestic import-competing interests is directly offset by the help given to export-oriented interests. Thus, the support from exporters in getting access to a foreign market helps neutralize the opposition from import-competing producers to lower domestic tariffs.

Another argument in favor of trade agreements, and against unilateral trade policy changes, is the need to ensure **reciprocity**. To be sure, in our discussion of the gains from trade, we have made no reference to the trade policies of other countries. Regardless of other countries' trade posture, a country can still benefit from trade. If Jamaica were to keep its market closed while it waited for the United States and other countries to treat its exports the way it might wish, Jamaica would be waiting a very long time and would forgo huge gains from trade. As economist Joan Robinson once quipped, the fact that other countries have rocks in their harbors does not give you a good reason to throw rocks in your own. The gains from trade do not depend on reciprocity.

Still, there may be a case for the *strategic* use of retaliatory threats to pressure trading partners to open their markets. One country could say to another: "open up your market for our commodities, or else we will impose punitive tariffs on the goods you export to us." The success of this strategy depends on the credibility of the threat (will the threat be carried out?) and the potential costs to the nation on the receiving end of the threat (what happens if the threat is carried out?). If Jamaica threatens sanctions unless the United States opens up its market for sugar, that threat is likely to be ignored. And if Jamaica follows through by imposing duties on US goods, it is unlikely to change US policy and therefore it would only be shooting itself in the foot. Small countries usually do not have much leverage over big countries.

However, when the United States threatens other countries with trade sanctions unless they open up their markets, the strategy sometimes works. This is because the US market is large enough for it to be able to damage the trade of any country that does not give in to US demands. Such threats can sometimes have the desired effect of changing the foreign country's trade policy – benefiting both the United States and often the country being threatened (helping to overcome domestic interest groups opposed to open trade). But sometimes the threats can backfire and stoke nationalist resentment in other countries. For example, when the Trump administration imposed high tariffs on Chinese imports, China made no serious concessions and simply retaliated by imposing its own duties on imports from the United States. The outcome was a trade war that reduced overall trade rather than an opening of China's market for US goods.

There is little to be said analytically about the use of reciprocity or retaliatory threats to change another country's trade policy, because everything depends on how the other country reacts. In the *Wealth of Nations*, Adam Smith gave some characteristically sound advice about reciprocity:

> The case in which it may sometimes be a matter of deliberation how far it is proper to continue the free importation of certain foreign goods is, when some foreign nation restrains by high duties or prohibitions the importation of some of our manufactures into their country... There may be good policy in retaliations of this kind, when there is a probability that they will procure the repeal of the high duties or prohibitions

complained of. The recovery of a great foreign market will generally more than compensate the transitory inconveniency of paying dearer during a short time for some sorts of goods ... When there is no probability that any such repeal can be procured, it seems a bad method of compensating the injury done to certain classes of our people to do another injury ourselves, not only to those classes, but to almost all the other classes of them.

Types of Trade Agreements

A country may negotiate a bilateral trade agreement with a single partner country, a **regional trade agreement** with several neighboring countries, or a **multilateral trade agreement** with a large group of countries. The United States has done all three: the United States–South Korea Free Trade Agreement is a bilateral trade agreement, the NAFTA), and its successor the United States–Mexico–Canada (USMCA) agreement, is a regional trade agreement; and the **General Agreement on Tariffs and Trade** (GATT) is a multilateral trade agreement.

When two or more countries decide to reduce tariffs on one another's' exports, different degrees of integration are possible. A **free trade agreement** (FTA) abolishes tariffs on bilateral trade, but each country continues to tax imports from non-partner countries. For example, under the terms of USMCA, the United States, Canada, and Mexico have phased out tariffs on one another's goods but continue to impose their preexisting tariffs on imports arriving from non-partner countries.

The fact that United States, Canada, and Mexico have *different* tariffs on goods from other countries can give rise to *transshipment*. This is a form of tariff evasion in which a firm does an end-run around a high tariff by first shipping its good to a low-tariff country that the high-tariff country has a free trade agreement with, and then from there shipping the good to the high-tariff country. For example, if the Canadian tariff on trucks is 10% and the US tariff on trucks is 25%, a firm might bring a truck into Canada and then try to ship it (duty free) into the United States so that the lower Canadian tariff is paid, instead of the higher US tariff.

Free trade agreements use regulations called **rules of origin** to prevent transshipment. In the case of automobiles, for example, NAFTA requires that for a car assembled in Canada or Mexico to qualify for duty-free shipment into the United States, 62.5% of the car's manufacturing costs must be of North American origin. The USMCA, which replaced NAFTA in 2018, bumped this share up to 75%. This provision prevents Asian and European car makers from sending their automobiles to (say) Mexico and then getting tariff-free access to the US market by passing the car off as a Mexican product. The rule of origin is designed to give the United States and Mexico open access to each other's markets, not to give overseas countries low-tariff access.

However, rules of origin are incredibly detailed and complex. Rather than create a labyrinth of rules to prevent transshipment, countries could simply agree to form a **customs union**. In a customs union, countries agree to eliminate tariffs on trade within the partnership and impose a common external tariff on trade with other countries. Then transshipment is not an issue, because all the partner countries impose the same tariff on goods coming from non-partner countries. When the European Economic Community (EEC) was formed in 1958, a precursor to today's European Union, the member countries created a customs union. That is, Germany, France, Italy, and the other participating countries all applied the same uniform tariff to goods coming from outside the union. However, this kind of arrangement is not entirely free of complications. One issue that arises is how the tariff revenue is split up among the participating countries, particularly if some countries are landlocked and imports must come through a partner country.

Countries can also take a step beyond a customs union and form a common market. In a common market, the countries not only eliminate tariffs on each other's goods, but they also allow factor mobility – the free movement of capital and labor – between each country. An **economic union** goes beyond a common market and occurs when countries harmonize their economic policies (such as tax and regulatory policy) and even adopt a single currency. The United States has been an economic union for more than 200 years, with internal free trade and free labor and capital mobility between the states. The European Union has been moving in this direction for some time, although labor mobility is limited due to language and cultural differences across the member states.

Welfare Effects of Tariff Agreements

Unilateral and multilateral tariff reductions usually take the form of across-the-board cuts that apply in a non-discriminatory way to all imports. The welfare analysis of such reductions is discussed in Chapter 7. By contrast, in bilateral and regional trade agreements tariffs are usually eliminated on the partner's goods while maintaining the existing tariffs on non-partner countries. Thus, these agreements give preferential market access to partner countries and discriminate against non-partner countries. For example, NAFTA eliminated all tariffs on trade between the United States, Canada, and Mexico, but each country continues to impose import duties on other countries (unless it also has a free trade agreement with them). Because participating nations gain a tax advantage, the welfare effects of such a **preferential**, or **discriminatory**, **tariff reduction** can be different from those of a non-discriminatory tariff reduction.

One way of assessing the two types of tariff reductions is in terms of trade creation and trade diversion. **Trade creation** is the expansion of trade because of a lower tax imposed on imports. Both preferential and non-discriminatory tariff reductions can lead to trade creation because, in both cases, at least some tariff rates are falling. However, the preferential tariff reduction in a free trade agreement can also result in **trade diversion**: because imports from the partner country no longer face any tariffs while imports from other countries do, the source of imports can be "diverted" from the latter to the former.

For example, suppose the United States can import bicycles from China for $100 and from Mexico for $120. If the United States levies a $50 import tariff on bicycles, the US price of Chinese bicycles will be $150, and the US price of Mexican bicycles will be $170. If the bicycles are essentially the same, the United States will only import them from China.

Now suppose that the United States and Mexico sign a free trade agreement that abolishes tariffs on each other's goods. The US price of Chinese bicycles will remain at $150, but the US price of Mexican bicycles will fall from $170 to $120. The United States will begin to import the bicycles from Mexico instead of China – not because Mexico is a more efficient producer, but because it has been given a tax advantage in the US market.

In this case, the free trade agreement with Mexico will produce both trade creation and trade diversion. The trade creation comes from the fact that the US price of bicycles will fall from $150 to $120: because bicycles cost less, US consumers will buy more of them. Trade diversion comes from the fact that the trade agreement makes Mexican bicycles cheaper than Chinese ones: the United States will shift its source of supply from China to Mexico.

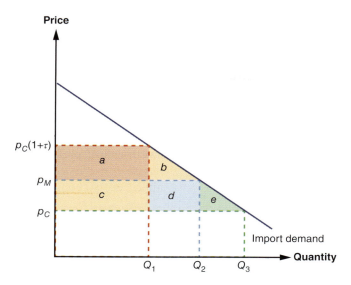

Figure 10.6 Preferential Tariff Reduction If the United States can import a good from China at price p_C or Mexico at price p_M, it will choose to import from China since $p_C < p_M$. However, if it eliminates the tariff on goods from Mexico, the United States will start importing from Mexico if $p_C(1 + \tau) < p_M$. This tariff reduction may not improve US welfare because it diverts trade from China to higher-cost Mexico, thereby deteriorating the terms of trade.

However, this diversion is not necessarily a good thing. Originally, the United States paid $100 for bicycles from China, whereas with the discriminatory tariff regime in place, it pays $120 for bicycles from Mexico. This is a deterioration in the US terms of trade. Put differently, the United States used to collect $50 in tax revenue for every imported bicycle; now that revenue has disappeared (imports of Mexican bikes do not generate revenue), but consumers save $30. So on every bike, consumers gain $30, but the government loses $50.

Figure 10.6 illustrates the difference between a discriminatory and a non-discriminatory tariff reduction. The United States, the importing country, can buy as many imports as it wants from China at a price of p_C and from Mexico at a price of p_M. A tariff of rate τ is applied to imports from both countries. Because the tariff-inclusive price from China is lower than that from Mexico, the United States will import the quantity Q_1 from China. In the figure, the import price is p_C, the price paid by consumers is $p_C(1 + \tau)$, and the government collects from area $a + c$ as tariff revenue.

Now suppose that the United States and Mexico sign a free trade agreement that abolishes the tariff on imports from Mexico. Then consumers will compare the China price plus the tariff with the Mexican price without the tariff. Because $p_M < p_C(1 + \tau)$, they will now opt to buy their goods from Mexico. Consumers will benefit from the lower price and imports will expand to Q_2. Consumer surplus will increase by area $a + b$, but the government will lose the tariff revenue of area $a + c$. Area a is simply a transfer from the government to consumers. Thus, the net effect on overall welfare will be $b - c$. We can think of area b as the gains from trade creation (additional consumer surplus) and area c as the loss from trade diversion (the deterioration in the terms of trade, which is the increase in the price of imports from p_C to p_M).

As this example suggests, area c may be larger than area b and therefore $b - c$ may be negative. If that is the case, the loss from trade diversion (the terms of trade effect) is greater than the gains from trade creation (the net addition to consumer surplus) and the country is hurt by the tariff reduction. Of course, this result is not guaranteed; area b may instead be greater than area c and so the welfare effect may be positive. This is more likely to be the case under two conditions: first, if the prices of goods from Mexico and China are close to one another (making area c smaller), so that the terms of trade loss is smaller; and second, if import demand is more elastic, making area b larger.

This finding can be contrasted with a non-discriminatory tariff reduction. If the import tariff were simply abolished, there would be trade creation but no trade diversion. There would be no trade diversion because China would be the most efficient supplier both before and after the tariff change. The price to consumers would fall from $p_C(1 + \tau)$ to p_C, and imports would increase from Q_1 to Q_3. Consumer surplus would increase by area $a + b + c + d + e$, while the government's tariff revenue would fall by $a + c$, leaving a net effect of $b + d + e$. This is always positive, and so the tariff reduction is sure to be welfare improving.

(Note that the United States could also have chosen to sign a free trade agreement with China instead of Mexico, in which case there would have been no trade diversion, despite the discriminatory tariff reduction.)

In sum, a discriminatory and a non-discriminatory tariff reduction are potentially quite different in their effects. A non-discriminatory tariff will result in trade creation but no trade diversion, and there is a presumption that welfare will improve. A discriminatory tariff reduction will result in trade creation and could result in trade diversion. If so, the welfare effect is ambiguous. For this reason, many economists, such as Jagdish Bhagwati (2008), have a preference for non-discriminatory tariff reductions and have argued against preferential tariff reductions.

THEORY   Was NAFTA a Bad Deal?

Before, during, and after he was US president, Donald Trump stated that NAFTA was "a disaster," complaining in a tweet that it was "the worst trade deal maybe ever signed anywhere, but certainly ever signed in this country." If that was not enough, he added that NAFTA "has destroyed our country."

Under NAFTA, the United States, Canada, and Mexico virtually eliminated tariffs on cross-border trade in North America starting in 1994. Although trade in some small, politically sensitive sectors is still restricted, such as US imports of sugar and Canadian imports of dairy products, by and large the countries charge no tariffs on each other's goods. So, in what sense is NAFTA a "bad deal"?

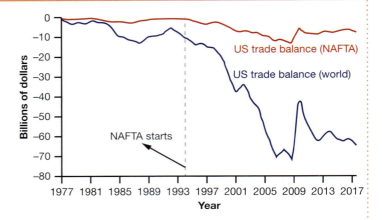

Figure 10.7 Overall US Trade Balance and with NAFTA Countries
Source: US Census Bureau.

Trump pointed to a loss of manufacturing jobs since NAFTA took effect in 1994. While imports of labor-intensive manufactured goods from Mexico have undoubtedly reduced the number of jobs in some sectors of the US economy, the United States has also created some jobs as a result of increased exports to Mexico. As pointed out in Chapter 5, most of the job loss in manufacturing is the result of technological change and the substitution of capital for labor, not imports.

Trump also pointed to the trade deficit, sometimes saying that the United States is "losing" because it imports more than it exports. While the underlying causes of trade imbalances will be covered in Chapter 11, a trade deficit is not necessarily a bad thing. This is especially true on a bilateral basis; one might be concerned with the overall balance of trade, but that does not mean trade should be balanced with every country. (You might care if you are spending more than you are earning, that is, running a trade deficit with the economy overall, but that does not mean you should seek balanced trade with your grocery store, with whom you presumably run a large deficit.) In any event, as Figure 10.7 shows, the trade deficit with NAFTA countries is small in comparison to the overall trade deficit.

Even prior to NAFTA, US tariffs on Mexican products were relatively low. At the time NAFTA was debated, in the early 1990s, Krugman (1993) summarized the way most economists thought about NAFTA in terms of four simple principles. He maintained that NAFTA would:

1. Have no effect on number of US jobs
2. Not hurt the environment, and might help it
3. Result in a small overall gain in US real income
4. Slightly reduce the real wages of unskilled US workers

Why did Krugman think this? He reasoned that macroeconomic policy would help keep the United States on its production possibility frontier (point 1), that the higher incomes coming from greater gains from trade (point 3) would allow both countries to afford the policies needed to improve the environment (point 2), and that the Stolper–Samuelson effect discussed in Chapter 5 would lead to harm for unskilled US workers (point 4).

In sum, most economists believe that NAFTA would be a modest plus for the US economy, not a disaster. A detailed study by Caliendo and Parro (2015) concluded that Mexico's welfare had increased by 1.31% and the US's welfare had increased by 0.08% because of NAFTA. At the same time, Hakobyan and McLaren (2016) found that NAFTA did reduce wages of US workers in industries directly affected by imports from Mexico.

In the end, President Trump decided not to scrap NAFTA but renegotiate it. Despite the vitriol directed at NAFTA, the renegotiation preserved the same basic framework, with some tighter rules on automobile imports. The agreement was blandly titled US–Canada–Mexico agreement, or USMCA.

Figure 10.8 Mexican President Enrique Pena Nieto (L), US President Donald Trump (C), and Canadian Prime Minister Justin Trudeau Sign a New Agreement Replacing NAFTA in November 2018
Source: SAUL LOEB/AFP via Getty Images.

Multilateral Trade Agreements

Until the mid-twentieth century, there was very little multilateral cooperation on trade policy. Governments determined their own trade policies based largely on their own domestic economic interests. In the 1920s, after World War I, the League of Nations (a precursor to the United Nations) tried to promote trade liberalization among European countries, but nothing came of the effort. Trade was then, as it is today, a very sensitive domestic political issue. Countries were very reluctant to reduce their tariffs and expose their industries to foreign competition, even if that meant gaining greater market access for export industries.

The Great Depression of the 1930s marked a turning point in world trade relations. Declining production and employment led to a tremendous increase in protectionist pressures around the world. Many countries thought that if they could reduce their imports, domestic production would increase and would help revive their economy. But this beggar-thy-neighbor approach failed miserably. Because one country's imports are another country's exports, the attempt by every country to restrict its imports led to a general collapse in exports, so that the increase in import barriers not only failed to spur any domestic economic revival but actually made things worse. In the United States, the Smoot–Hawley tariff of 1930, which increased import duties and triggered foreign retaliation against US exports, epitomizes this development. Furthermore, once imposed, the import restrictions proved very difficult to remove because vested interests grew up behind them and had a stake in maintaining them.

The United States, which up to this point had been fairly isolationist in its foreign policy, became concerned about the impact of foreign trade barriers on US exports. In 1934, Congress passed the RTAA, which delegated trade-negotiating powers to the president. This legislation authorized the president to reach trade agreements that would reduce US import duties if other countries agreed to open up their markets to US goods. The United States concluded some bilateral trade agreements during the 1930s, but they had little effect on trade barriers or overall trade.

During World War II, the United States became convinced that multilateral cooperation to expand international trade was needed to promote economic growth around the world and to reduce the chances of another world war. As a result, the United States led the world in creating the GATT in 1947. The GATT was designed to be both an international agreement on rules about trade policy and a forum in which countries could negotiate the reduction in trade barriers.

As an agreement, the GATT set out the basic framework for trade policy today. The major articles of the GATT are listed in Table 10.1. Many of the GATT provisions seek to ensure non-discrimination. For example, Article 1 requires each participating country to extend unconditional **most-favored nation** (MFN) treatment to other participating countries. What this means is that all countries that sign the GATT must extend to other GATT signatories the tariff treatment given to the countries that are "most favored" in their tariff code. In essence, GATT participants cannot discriminate against one another in the tariff treatment of imported goods. However, there is a big exception to this rule: Article 24 of the GATT allows countries to establish customs unions and free trade areas, which inherently violate the MFN rule. This provision permits agreements such as NAFTA, in which the United States can impose zero tariffs on goods from Canada and Mexico and higher "MFN" tariffs on imports from other GATT countries.

Table 10.1 Major Provisions of the General Agreement on Tariffs and Trade

Provision	Description
Article 1	General Most Favored Nation Treatment
Article 2	Schedule of Tariff Concessions
Article 3	National Treatment on Internal Taxes and Regulation
Article 6	Antidumping and Countervailing Duties
Article 10	Transparency of Trade Regulations
Article 11	General Elimination of Quantitative Restrictions
Article 12	Restrictions to Safeguard the Balance of Payments
Article 14	Exceptions to Rule of Non-Discrimination
Article 16	Subsidies
Article 17	State Trading Enterprises
Article 19	Emergency Action on Imports of Particular Products (Safeguards)
Article 20	General Exceptions
Article 21	Security Exceptions
Article 23	Nullification and Impairment
Article 24	Customs Unions and Free Trade Areas

The GATT has many other provisions. Article 3 sets out the principle of "national treatment" for foreign firms in terms of domestic taxation and regulation; i.e., a country cannot have one set of taxes and regulations for domestic firms and stiffer taxes and tougher regulations for foreign firms. The GATT also allows countries to impose **antidumping** and **countervailing** duties; these will be discussed shortly. The GATT also tries to replace all

10.2 TRADE AGREEMENTS

import quotas with import tariffs and allows countries to impose trade restrictions to assist infant industries (economic development) and to deal with balance of payments problems.

One of the most important provisions is Article 20, on "general exceptions." This article allows countries to impose or maintain trade barriers in certain instances. It reads:

> Subject to the requirement that such measures are not applied in a manner which would constitute a means of arbitrary or unjustifiable discrimination between countries where the same conditions prevail, or a disguised restriction on international trade, nothing in this Agreement shall be construed to prevent the adoption or enforcement by any contracting party of measures:
>
> (a) necessary to protect public morals;
> (b) necessary to protect human, animal or plant life or health;
> ...
> (f) imposed for the protection of national treasures of artistic, historic or archaeological value;
> (g) relating to the conservation of exhaustible natural resources if such measures are made effective in conjunction with restrictions on domestic production or consumption;

In other words, Article 20 allows countries to restrict trade to protect the environment and natural resources.

As a forum for trade negotiations, the GATT enabled the countries participating in the original 1947 conference to reduce tariffs on each other's goods. Subsequent trade negotiating "rounds," as they are called, further reduced tariffs on manufactured goods. For example, the Kennedy Round in the 1960s reduced the average tariff on industrial products by one-third, and the Tokyo Round in the 1970s and the Uruguay Round in the late 1980s and early 1990s continued the process.

While the reduction in trade barriers contributed to a rapid expansion of world trade after World War II, there were two major gaps in the GATT system. First, agricultural goods were largely exempt from the negotiated tariff reductions and GATT rules. As a result, trade in agricultural products is still plagued by subsidies and government import restrictions. Second, although developing countries were signatories to the GATT, they were exempt from many of its provisions and did not participate in the multilateral agreements to reduce tariffs. Because they did not participate in the negotiations, tariffs were not always reduced on products of interest to them, particularly labor-intensive goods, such as textiles and apparel.

These shortcomings of the GATT were partially addressed in the Uruguay Round negotiations, which concluded in 1994. Developing countries participated in this round, which took up the issue of agricultural trade policies. Furthermore, in recognition that global commerce involved more than just trade in goods, the negotiators concluded other agreements: the General Agreement on Trade in Services (GATS), and the agreements on Trade-Related Aspects of Intellectual Property Rights (TRIPs) and Trade-Related Investment Measures (TRIMs).

Furthermore, the Uruguay Round established the World Trade Organization (WTO) to oversee the GATT and the new trade agreements. The WTO is a formal international economic institution, like the World Bank and the International Monetary Fund. (The GATT itself was never formally such an institution.) However, unlike the World Bank and the IMF, the WTO has almost no formal powers and almost no financial resources. It is known as a member-driven institution, because the organization itself does not have the power to compel its members to do anything; its actions are in fact just the actions of its membership.

For this reason, the WTO is run by consensus, meaning that no formal agreement is ever reached unless all the members agree to its provisions. With more than 160 member countries, the WTO has had difficulty concluding any new trade agreements. Indeed, the Doha Round of trade negotiations, launched in 2001, collapsed in 2008 and was formally abandoned by the membership a few years later. The WTO membership has never concluded a major multilateral trade agreement.

The difficulty in reaching consensus at the WTO has led countries to consider making unilateral policy changes, or to conclude bilateral or regional trade agreements among like-minded countries, to speed up the process of global economic integration.

Until recently, dispute settlement had been one area in which the WTO was much stronger than its standalone GATT predecessor. The GATT by itself lacked a formal system to resolve disputes among its participants about how its rules might apply in any given case. The WTO's dispute settlement system involves the creation of an independent Panel to hear both sides of a dispute and issue a judgment. (If there is a dispute about the Panel's decision, a country can appeal to an Appellate Body.) If a country has been found in violation of a WTO agreement, it is obligated to change its policy. However, the WTO has no power to force sovereign countries to comply with a Panel decision. Of course, if a country chooses not to comply with the WTO decision, other countries may have the right to retaliate against it for non-compliance with an international agreement.

Most countries that bring a dispute to the WTO win their case, because it is only worthwhile to bring strong cases to the resolution process. For example, in 2002, President George W. Bush imposed tariffs on imported steel under the safeguard provision in the GATT, a provision that will be discussed below. The European Union and other members objected and filed a complaint with the WTO. The Panel ruled against the United States on the grounds that the safeguard provision had been improperly applied in the steel case. The United States appealed the decision to the Appellate Body, which upheld the Panel's decision. In 2005, the United States decided to comply with the ruling, and it removed the steel tariffs.

However, adherence to WTO rules and dispute settlements have been crumbling in recent years. Upset with some of the WTO's rulings, the United States began blocking the appointment of new jurists in the system, leaving the WTO dispute settlement system in limbo. In 2018, President Donald Trump imposed tariffs on imported steel under a provision regarding trade and national security. The European Union and other members filed a complaint with the WTO. The Panel ruled against the United States on the grounds that the national security provision had been improperly applied. The Trump administration ignored the ruling, and other countries retaliated by imposing tariffs on US exports. The Biden administration has also rejected the authority of the WTO to rule on cases involving national security and the tariffs remained in place. The rules-based system of world trade appears to be eroding and the WTO seems to be a bystander to the major trade developments of today.

10.3 TRADE LAWS

While sometimes signing agreements to reduce trade barriers with other countries, most governments want the flexibility to impose temporary import restrictions when foreign goods suddenly disrupt domestic producers. The GATT permits new trade barriers to be imposed in certain carefully defined circumstances. The so-called fair-trade laws allow for temporary tariffs in two cases where imports are deemed to be unfair: when foreign goods are "dumped" in the domestic market, and when the foreign goods benefit from government subsidies. The remedies are antidumping duties to prevent the dumping and countervailing duties to offset the subsidies. In addition, governments may invoke an escape clause in the GATT that allows tariffs to be temporarily imposed when an unexpected import surge harms a domestic industry. These exceptions – antidumping duties, countervailing duties, and escape-clause tariffs – are usually initiated by private firms that file petitions with the government, asking for relief from foreign competition.

Dumping and Antidumping Duties

The term **dumping** conjures up the image of foreign firms unloading an unusually large volume of goods onto the domestic market and driving the domestic price down to unreasonable low levels. One specific definition of dumping is predatory pricing, in which an exporter reduces its price below cost in an effort to drive other producers out of business. The fear about predatory pricing is that, if the perpetrator succeeds, it will have a monopoly in the market and can then raise its price and earn high profits by exploiting consumers. Governments may want to prevent predatory pricing if it threatens to harm competition. Yet predatory pricing is rare: firms engaging in the practice must be prepared to incur substantial losses in the hope that those losses will be recouped through the future exercise of monopoly power. It is almost impossible for a firm to drive all of its competitors out of the market. And even if it temporarily succeeded, other firms would probably try to reenter the market as soon as the predatory firm raised its prices to levels yielding high profits. In other words, predatory pricing is almost always a bad business strategy. It is hard to drive all of one's rivals out of the market; colluding to raise prices with them is more profitable, but illegal.

However, under international trade law, dumping is *not* defined as predatory pricing, but rather as price discrimination. A firm is guilty of dumping if it charges a lower price in its export market than in its domestic market. The problem many economists have with this definition is that price discrimination does not necessarily harm consumers and therefore does not necessarily require a government remedy. Indeed, price discrimination, which is simply charging different prices in different markets, is a normal business practice and an accepted feature of domestic competition. One reason firms engage in dumping is that exporters often find competition more intense in the international market than in their home market, where they have a more secure position with domestic consumers (perhaps because of trade barriers). Stronger competition in foreign markets forces the exporters to charge a lower price there.

Figure 10.9 illustrates how a profit-maximizing firm can be technically guilty of dumping (price discrimination) without harming consumers in any market. Suppose the Korean firm Samsung is exporting microwave ovens from Korea to the United States. Samsung has one marginal cost curve for producing microwave ovens, but faces two separate demand curves for microwave ovens, one in Korea and one in the United States. As the dominant firm in Korea, it faces a downward-sloping domestic demand curve on its home market sales. In the US market, by contrast, the competition is more intense, and Samsung is just one of many brands. Therefore, Samsung is a price-taker in the US market; it has no market power in the United States, and it faces a perfectly elastic export demand at price P_{US}.

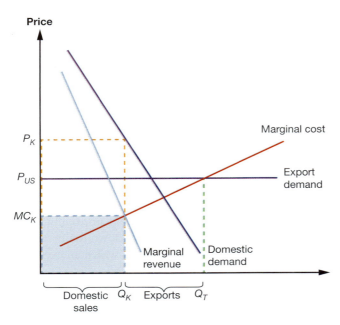

Figure 10.9 Dumping as Price Discrimination This figure shows how a firm may charge two different prices when it sells in two different markets. The export faces a downward-sloping demand schedule in its domestic market and a perfectly elastic demand schedule in the US market. While a profit-maximizing firm always sets marginal revenue equal to marginal cost, the price will be higher in its home market because it has greater market power there.

To maximize profits, Samsung sets marginal revenue equal to marginal cost in each market. In the Korean market, this means producing Q_K units, where marginal cost equals marginal revenue from the Korean demand curve. For those units, Samsung will charge price P_K off of the demand curve and will earn profits equal to its price-marginal cost margin, $P_K - MC_K$, times the quantity produced, Q_K. Samsung will earn further profits by selling additional units on the US market at price P_{US}, until it reaches the point where the marginal cost equals the US price. Samsung's total output will be Q_T, where it produces Q_K for the Korean market and $Q_T - Q_K$ for the US (export) market.

In this scenario, Samsung is "guilty" of dumping in the US market, even though it has no choice over what price to charge on its exports and is not harming competition or consumers in the United States. Samsung's behavior counts as dumping simply because the firm is charging a lower price on its exports than on its home market sales. Under the antidumping law, the United States is permitted to impose import duties equivalent to $P_{US} - P_K$ as a remedy. Because Samsung cannot charge a higher price in the United States than the prevailing one, it would either have to absorb such duties in its profit margin (cutting back on its export sales to reduce its marginal costs by the extent of the antidumping duties), or stop exporting to the United States altogether, or else reduce the price in Korea to the same level as the US price, thereby ending the dumping.

Of course, a country imposing antidumping duties is doing so to protect its producers from foreign competition, not its consumers. Domestic consumers would presumably benefit from cheaper imported goods, as would the country as a whole because of improved terms of trade. For example, in 1999 a group, the Texas oil producers, filed an antidumping case against Saudi Arabia, Mexico, Venezuela, and Iraq on the grounds that they were selling their oil at prices that were too low. Although the US government rejected the petition on legal grounds, consumers would presumably welcome the dumping of cheap oil onto the US market.

How does the process of imposing antidumping duties work? In the United States, the antidumping process begins when a domestic industry files a petition with the Department of Commerce and the International Trade Commission (ITC), alleging that dumping is occurring. The Commerce Department determines whether dumping has occurred and, if so, calculates the "dumping margin." The dumping margin is simply the difference between the price the exporter charges in its home market and the price it charges in the United States. For example, if a foreign firm charges $100 for a good in its own market and exports it to the United States for $80, then the dumping margin is ($100 − $80)/$80, or 25%. These margins can be large. For example, Commerce once determined that natural bristle paintbrushes from China were sold at less than their fair value with a dumping margin of 351.9%, and imposed tariffs of the same amount. When the data are available, Commerce sometime issues company-specific dumping duties. In December 2023, Commerce made a preliminary determination in the case of paper shopping bags from Cambodia, China, Colombia, India, Malaysia, Portugal, Taiwan, Turkey, and Vietnam. It issued the following company-specific margins: for China, Dongzhen Paperbag Factory at 59.41% and Fujian Eco Packaging Co. at 40.55%, for India, Asha Overseas 57.87%, for Turkey, Babet Kagitsilik at 47.56%, and so forth.

However, before duties can be imposed, the ITC must determine if the domestic industry has suffered or is threatened with material injury as a result of the less-than-fair-value imports. The legal definition of material injury is "harm which is not inconsequential, immaterial, or unimportant" – in other words, harm that presumably is consequential, material, and important! Only the harm to the competing industry is considered, not the harm or injury to consumers or other domestic industries that result from the imposition of import duties. The injury determination is a more difficult hurdle for the domestic petitioner to clear, because of the injury standard itself and because the ITC is a quasi-independent agency (as opposed to Commerce, which is typically an advocate of the domestic industry in the process). Still, the ITC rules affirmatively in a majority of cases.

If dumping is found to exist and the domestic industry is deemed to have suffered material injury, then antidumping duties are imposed. The United States has imposed antidumping duties on such narrowly defined goods as frozen concentrated orange juice from Brazil, cotton shop towels from Bangladesh and China, oil country tubular goods from Canada, fresh salmon from Chile and Norway, paper clips from China, large newspaper printing presses from Germany, stainless steel wire rod from France and elsewhere, fresh kiwi fruit from New Zealand, pasta from Italy and Turkey, aspirin from Turkey, and a host of other products.

When antidumping duties are imposed, trade diversion is often the result. In most cases, imports subject to antidumping duties fall by more than 50%. To a large extent, however, imports from countries not subject to the antidumping duties fill the void left by those hit by the duties. This is because antidumping duties are only imposed on imports from countries named in the petition, leaving the market open to others who can produce similar products.

One famous antidumping story involves a now-ancient product, the typewriter. In the early 1990s, before personal computers became ubiquitous, the typewriter market was dominated by an American firm, Smith–Corona, and a Japanese firm, Brother. Brother was exporting typewriters to the United States and capturing market share from Smith–Corona. Smith–Corona responded by seeking antidumping duties against Brother's imported typewriters, but also began shifting some of its production to Asia to reduce its costs and become more competitive. Brother tried to avoid the antidumping duties by moving some of its typewriter production to the United States. Soon Brother, producing in the United States, was facing competition from Smith–Corona imports, produced in Southeast Asia. So Brother decided to file an antidumping petition against Smith–Corona! However, the Commerce Department rejected the petition on the grounds that Brother was a Japanese company, not an American one, and only American companies (regardless of where they produce) could file such petitions (Reich, 1991).

Subsidies and Countervailing Duties

Just as foreign dumping that harms a domestic industry is considered an unfair trade practice that can be remedied with antidumping duties, foreign subsidies that harm a domestic industry are also considered unfair and can be remedied with countervailing duties.

Countervailing duties are tariffs imposed on imports that have been found to benefit from foreign government subsidies.

The sanctions process for subsidy cases is very similar to the one for dumping cases. A domestic producer files a petition with the Commerce Department and the ITC. The Commerce Department determines whether there is a subsidy and, if so, the subsidy margin. The ITC determines whether the domestic industry has been harmed by such imports by applying the material injury standard. If the two agencies make an affirmative ruling, that both a subsidy and material injury are found to exist, a tariff to countervail the subsidy will be imposed on those imports.

Domestic firms tend to file antidumping petitions rather than countervailing duty petitions because proving the existence of a subsidy is tricky, while proving the existence of dumping is easy. One famous countervailing duty case involved imports of solar panels from China. In 2012, US producers filed a case alleging that the importers had benefited from Chinese government subsidies. The Commerce Department ruled that this allegation was true, and the ITC found that the domestic industry had been materially injured as a result of the imports. However, the Commerce Department disappointed the domestic industry by setting very low preliminary countervailing duties for subsidized Chinese firms, at about 15%.

Escape Clause

International trade law also has a provision for protecting domestic firms adversely affected by imports even when those imports are not judged unfair because of dumping or subsidies. This provision is known as a safeguard or escape clause, because it releases a government from its obligation under trade agreements to keep tariffs at existing levels if it needs to safeguard the interests of a particular industry. If imports result in serious injury to some domestic producers, those producers are entitled to temporary relief from foreign competition, to help them adjust to the new conditions. That is, the escape clause provides a mechanism for domestic industries to get a temporary exception to any negotiated tariff reduction. The imports do not have to be unfair in the sense of being dumped or subsidized.

Under the escape clause, domestic firms can file a petition with the ITC for temporary relief from import competition but must include a specific plan that details how protection will be used to help the industry adjust. The ITC determines if the imports are "a substantial cause of serious injury," where a substantial cause is defined as "a cause which is important and not less than any other cause." This legalistic language is nontrivial: The ITC rejected a petition from the automobile industry in 1980 on the grounds that the most important source of the industry's difficulty was not imports, but rather the recession of that year.

If the ITC reaches an affirmative injury finding, it then recommends an appropriate remedy to the president. This remedy can include limits on imports, such as higher tariffs, or other policies that would help facilitate the adjustment efforts of the domestic industry. The president then has complete discretion to accept, reject, or modify the ITC recommendation. If the president decides that import relief is warranted, import tariffs are usually imposed over five years, declining every year after the first year. The tariffs must apply to imports from all sources, unlike antidumping and countervailing duties, which are applied selectively.

IN PRACTICE Did Temporary Protection Save Harley-Davidson?

A famous safeguards case from the early 1980s involved the motorcycle producer Harley-Davidson, which was on the verge of bankruptcy. At the time, Harley-Davidson only produced "heavyweight" motorcycles, with piston displacements of over 1000 cc, while Japanese producers mainly exported medium-weight bikes (700 cc to 850 cc) to the United States.

The ITC ruled that imports of medium-weight bikes were adversely affecting sales of the heavyweight bikes and recommended a tariff of 45% on imports of motorcycles over 700 cc. (The tariff was set to decline over five years.) President Ronald Reagan accepted this advice, and the tariffs took effect. However, Suzuki and Yamaha were able to evade the tariff by updating their product line. Seeing that the new imported bikes were still medium weight in appearance and performance, Harley-Davidson thought that the Japanese producers were cheating. But after buying and tearing down some of the new bikes, Harley-Davidson's engineers found that the piston displacement had been changed to exactly 699 cc!

The main reason the tariffs did not help Harley-Davidson, however, was that Japan was already producing motorcycles in the United States, and imports from Japan were poor substitutes for the US-made motorcycles. The main reason Harley-Davidson survived is that it became more efficient in its production methods. Furthermore, the economic recovery from the deep recession in the early 1980s helped boost consumer demand for its products. Kitano and Ohashi (2009) found that "the safeguard provided by the US government until 1987 explains merely 6% of Harley-Davidson's sales recovery."

Figure 10.10 Harley-Davidson Motorcycles for Sale
Source: Scott Olson/Getty Images.

National Security

Aside from the escape clause, and antidumping and countervailing duties, there are very few ways for US officials to increase tariffs without violating commitments made under the WTO or various free trade agreements. There is, however, one obscure provision of US trade law, Section 232 of the Trade Expansion Act of 1962, that empowers the president to restrict imports if, after an investigation by the Department of Commerce, they are imported "in such quantities or under such circumstances as to threaten or impair the national security." The president has full authority to restrict such imports after the Commerce Department's report is issued. And there is no statutory definition of what constitutes a threat to national security. Restricting imports on grounds of national security is also permitted under the WTO.

The Trump administration discovered this legal provision and began using it to protect the steel industry (see Chapter 8 for more analysis). In 2018, President Trump imposed a 25% tariff on imported steel and a 10% tariff on imported aluminum, both on grounds of national security. The tariffs were applied to imports from Canada and Mexico, despite NAFTA, and from the European Union, despite the NATO military alliance, as well as on most other countries. The tariffs were controversial, because many observers (including the Department of Defense) did not see any national security threat when imports accounted for about 27% of domestic consumption, and most of those imports came from neighboring countries and military allies.

The steel tariffs caused widespread controversy and had widespread consequences. Steel-using firms, such as beer keg manufacturers, argued that they could not pass on their higher costs to consumers and still compete against imports. These industries petitioned the Commerce Department for exemptions from the tariffs on the specialty items they imported. Meanwhile, many countries affected by the duties complained that the national security case for restricting imports was bogus and imposed retaliatory duties against US exports. They targeted politically sensitive US industries, such as blue jeans, Florida orange juice, Kentucky bourbon, and Wisconsin-made Harley Davidson motorcycles. The latter action forced Harley to shift production abroad to avoid the higher duties.

In 2022, the United States lost a WTO case regarding the steel tariffs, but the Biden administration rejected the ruling and refused to eliminate the tariffs. Now other countries may begin to use national security as a justification for protectionist measures.

In sum, although governments have negotiated trade agreements that have pushed average tariffs to very low levels, several legal provisions sanctioned in the GATT and elsewhere allow governments to impose higher, temporary duties on imports. Domestic firms competing against imports most often seek antidumping duties, rather than countervailing duties or safeguards, because the procedure for obtaining tariffs on competing imports are the easiest to satisfy.

APPLICATION   Protection in Practice: Washing Machines and Steel

Figure 10.11 Washing Machines: A Pair of Maytag Washers Displayed in a Store
Source: Spencer Platt/Getty Images.

The US washing machine industry, led by Maytag, has long sought to limit foreign competition by using trade laws. It first succeeded in getting antidumping duties imposed on washing machines from Mexico and South Korea in 2012. After Samsung and LG shifted their production to China, antidumping duties were imposed against that country in 2016. Then foreign investment allowed Thailand and Vietnam to become became new sources of supply. In 2018, Maytag succeeded in filing a Section 201 safeguard (escape clause) case in which a uniform tariff was imposed on washing machine imports from all countries.

Flaaen, Hortaşçu, and Tintelnot (2020) found that the country-specific antidumping tariffs did not have a significant effect on US washer prices. This is because those tariffs were easily evaded when Korean firms shifted production to different countries. However, the tariffs imposed as a result of the safeguard tariffs were completely passed through to consumer prices and raised the median price of washing machines and clothes dryers by about 12%, or $86 per unit, on average. Moreover, prices of a complementary good – clothes dryers – also jumped at the same time by a similar magnitude, even though these products were not subject to any new tariffs during this period. The study also found that tariffs resulted in increased consumer costs of just over $1.5 billion annually and tariff revenue amounted to about $82 million. The action saved the jobs of about 1,800 workers at an average annual cost to consumers of over US$815,000 per job created (after netting out tariff revenues).

CONCLUSION

This chapter has considered a variety of topics related to trade policy in the real world. First, we briefly considered the politics of trade policy and how economic interests interact with the political system to determine trade policy. We then turned to trade agreements and how preferential tariff reductions may or may not increase economic welfare, depending on the circumstances. The World Trade Organization sets broad rules for trade policy but has become increasingly ignored by leading countries. Finally, most governments have trade laws that allow them to impose tariffs on foreign goods that have been dumped or subsidized in the domestic market. This process of ensuring so-called fair trade is a leading way that governments today restrict imports.

SUMMARY

1. If a country used a referendum to determine its trade policy, the preferences of the median voter would be critical. If the median voter benefits from trade, we would expect the country to be relatively open to trade; if the median voter is harmed by trade, we would expect the country to have relatively high trade barriers.
2. In the context of the mobile factor model, the "abundant" factor of production is not necessarily in the majority in a country, because abundance is relative to other countries, not to other domestic factors.
3. The principle of concentrated benefits and diffused costs might explain the persistence of import restrictions.
4. Sovereign countries can set their own policy unilaterally or join other countries in signing trade agreements. A free trade agreement abolishes tariffs on the goods of the participating countries. A customs union is a free trade agreement in which countries agree on a common external tariff (goods from non-partner countries) and share the tariff revenue.
5. Free trade agreements are preferential, favoring partner countries over non-partner countries. These agreements can produce trade creation (more trade due to lower tariffs) and trade diversion (a shifting of trade from non-partner to partner countries).
6. Not all tariff reductions are welfare improving: a trade-diverting trade agreement could deteriorate a country's terms of trade and make it worse off.
7. The World Trade Organization is a multilateral institution that oversees trade rules (such as the provisions of the GATT), provides a forum for trade negotiations, and tries to settle trade disputes.
8. Governments have trade laws that allow tariffs to be increased, at least temporarily, under specially defined circumstances. Tariffs can be imposed to counteract dumping (price discrimination) and subsidies given to imports.

KEY CONCEPTS

Antidumping duties, page 220
Countervailing duties, page 220
Customs union, page 215
Dumping, page 223
Economic union, page 216

Free trade agreement, page 215
General Agreement on Tariffs and Trade (GATT), page 215
Median voter, page 207
Most-favored nation, page 220

Multilateral trade agreement, page 215
Preferential/discriminatory tariff
  reduction, page 216
Reciprocity, page 214
Regional trade agreement, page 215

Status-quo bias, page 207
Trade creation, page 216
Trade diversion, page 216
World Trade Organization (WTO),
  page 206

REVIEW QUESTIONS

1. Why is trade policy inherently political? In what way does the political system help determine the trade policy outcome?
2. In what direction has the average US tariff moved over the past century?
3. What factors influence Congress's consideration of the tariff?
4. What is the principle of reciprocity in trade agreements?
5. What are some of the differences between bilateral and multilateral trade agreements?
6. What are the three different legal methods by which a country can increase tariffs that have been otherwise capped by trade agreements?

EXERCISES

1. Under what circumstances will a majority of voters in a country vote for freer trade? When will they vote for higher tariffs?
2. When will a government attempt to reduce tariffs unilateral as opposed to doing so in the context of a trade agreement with other countries? Why might a trade agreement be a better way to open trade? How would a trade agreement affect the politics of trade policy, as well as the economic calculation of the benefits of trade?
3. What are three different views of the "objective function" of governments with respect to trade policy? Which is most realistic?
4. The US demand for tyke bikes is 70 − 2P. (Assume that the United States does not produce tike bikes.) Bikes can be imported from China at a price of $10 and from Mexico at a price of $12. (The supply curves from each country are perfectly elastic.) The United States imposes a non-discriminatory tariff of $5 on all imported tyke bikes.
   a. How many bikes will the United States import, and from which country?
   b. Suppose the United States gives duty-free treatment to goods coming from Mexico. What happens to the sourcing of imports and to the quantity consumed?
   c. Is giving duty-free access to Mexico welfare improving for the United States? Diagram the impact and show/calculate the gains to consumers and the tariff revenue that the government loses.
   d. What happens to its welfare if the United States then abolishes the tariff entirely?
   e. How is this entire scenario different if the price of Mexican tyke bikes is $16?
5. What would be gained or lost if the WTO were to be abolished?
6. Why do most countries win cases that they bring to the WTO dispute settlement process?
7. Will temporary trade restrictions help a domestic firm adjust to foreign competition? Or will it slow the adjustment process?

RECOMMENDED RESOURCES

The political economy of trade policy is covered in Dani Rodrik, "The Political Economy of Trade Policy," in *Handbook of International Economics,* edited by Gene Grossman and Kenneth Rogoff, volume 3, 1995, pages 1457–1494, and John McLaren, "The Political Economy of Commercial Policy," in *Handbook of Commercial Policy*, edited by Kyle Bagwell and Robert W. Staiger, volume 1, Part A, 2016, pages 109–159.

On the evolution of US trade policy, see Douglas A. Irwin, *Clashing over Commerce: A History of US Trade Policy* (Chicago, IL: University of Chicago Press, 2017), available at www.nber.org/books-and-chapters/clashing-over-commerce-history-us-trade-policy

For a short version, see Douglas Irwin, "Trade Policy in American Economic History," *Annual Review of Economics* 12(1) (2020): 23–44.

For a history of the Smoot-Hawley tariff, see Douglas A. Irwin, *Peddling Protectionism: Smoot-Hawley and the Great Depression* (Princeton, NJ: Princeton University Press, 2011).

On the history of the World Trade Organization see Craig Van Grasstek, *The History and Future of the World Trade Organization* (Geneva: WTO, 2013), www.wto.org/english/res_e/booksp_e/historywto_e.pdf

For many illuminating articles on trade policy and institutions, see *Handbook of Commercial Policy*, edited by Kyle Bagwell and Robert W. Staiger, 2 volumes (Amsterdam: Elsevier, 2016).

On trade laws and institutions, see Bernard Hoekman and Michel Kostecki, *The Political Economy of the World Trading System*, 3rd edition (New York: Oxford University Press, 2010). For an old but fun view of antidumping laws, see James Bovard, *The Fair Trade Fraud* (New York: St. Martin's, 1991).

For a skeptical view of trade agreements, see Dani Rodrik, "What Do Trade Agreements Really Do?" *Journal of Economic Perspectives* 32(2) (2018): 73–90.

PART II

International Finance

CHAPTER 11

Measuring the Economy and Its Interaction with the World

LEARNING OBJECTIVES

In this chapter, we learn about:
- how economic output, income, and spending are measured
- how trade with the rest of the world is measured
- how the balance of payments is measured
- how national saving, government saving, and investment are linked to the current account
- how foreign exchange reserves are accumulated
- how a country's net asset position changes with the current account

INTRODUCTION

In the first part of this chapter, we examine how to measure the size and composition of the overall economy. We use these methods to see how saving and investment levels imply how much will be loaned to or borrowed from the rest of the world. Then we define in greater detail the nature of the trade and financial links between the economy and the rest of the world economy. At the end, we discuss how borrowing from the rest of the world affects the status of a country as a net debtor or creditor.

11.1 INCOME AND PRODUCTION

We first examine how to measure the economy, and track the flows of production, spending, and income when the economy stands isolated from the rest of the world. While unrealistic, this allows us to more clearly define the terms we are going to use. After that, we show how we have to add more terms to account for interactions with the rest of the world.

The Closed Economy

We measure the size and composition of the economy using **national income accounting**. The objective is to measure total spending, income, and production. In principle, all three of these concepts should be equal. It is easiest to show why this is the case by first examining a closed economy, completely cut off from the rest of the world.

$$GNI \equiv GDP \equiv GNE \equiv C + I + G \qquad (11.1)$$

The "≡" symbol means that this expression is true by definition, so the equation is termed an **identity**. *GDP* (**Gross Domestic Product**) is the sum of the value of all final production created within the borders of the country. In this case, GDP is the same Gross National Product, the sum of total value of final production made with factors of production owned by residents of the country, since this is an economy closed off from the rest of the world. The circularity of the flow of income and spending and production is illustrated in Figure 11.1. Starting at the top of the figure is GDP and moving clockwise, *GDP* is by definition equal to *GNI* (**Gross National Income**), since the production of any good entails use of factors of production – land, labor, and capital – and their use must be compensated for. Continuing clockwise, GNI equals *GNE* (**Gross National Expenditure**) because the income that is received has to be spent. Ending the circle, that amount of expenditure must equal *GDP* because all expenditures fall upon goods and services that are produced.

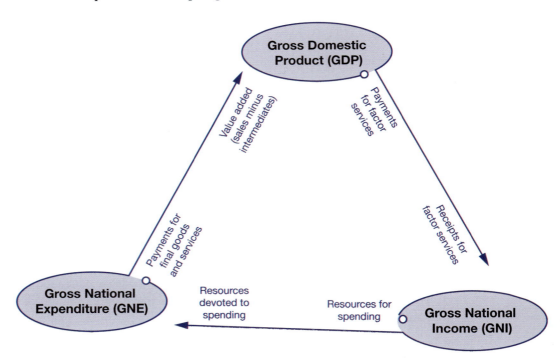

Figure 11.1 Income, Production, and Spending This figure shows the circular flow of income in a closed economy. The factors of production that are used in the production of goods must be paid, and is the source of income that is used for purchases of goods produced.

Because of the equality of all these measures by accounting, we do not need to calculate all three numbers. In practice, GDP is most commonly measured using the expenditure concept because it is easier to measure spending than it is to measure the total amount of production, or to measure total income. To understand why, recall that GDP, as measured by the expenditure approach, refers to *final* goods. **Final goods and services** are those purchased for an end use. That means intermediate goods – for instance a block of steel produced but then incorporated into the assembly of an automobile – is not counted, except insofar as it is incorporated into the total value of the auto when finally purchased by a consumer.

To measure GDP directly using the production approach would be a much more complicated exercise. It would entail tallying up all the amount of value that is added at each stage of the production process for *all* the goods and services produced in the economy. In the automobile example, one would have to calculate the value added in digging up the iron ore. Add to that the value associated with refining the iron ore into steel. Then add to that the value that comes from converting the steel block into an automobile. Conceptually, the **value added** from each of the production steps should equal the total spent on purchasing the automobile – but it is a daunting task to collect all the data required by the value-added approach. The income approach would also be challenging, albeit slightly less so. It would require tracking down and adding up all the income received by all the households and firms in the economy. The United States calculates GDP using all three approaches, but relies primarily on the expenditure approach for construction of the quarterly data. The income approach is a secondary approach, and is calculated with something of a lag relative to that generated using the expenditure approach. Finally, due to the heavy data requirements, the value added measure is reported with a substantial lag. Other countries, particularly with less well-funded statistical agencies, rely even more heavily on the expenditure approach.

Expenditures fall into three categories, depending on what types of entities do the spending. C, I, and G are, respectively, spending on final **consumption**, **investment**, and **government** goods and services. Consumption goods are by definition those purchased by households, while investment goods are by firms. That means that expenditure on a truck can fall into either the consumption category or the investment category, depending on whether a the expenditure has been undertaken by a household or a firm.

The fact that the expenditures are categorized by end-user is another reason why it is convenient to use the expenditure approach. Having data categorized by consumption, investment, and government corresponds nicely with modeling the economy's aggregate behavior by modeling the behavior of consumers, firms and the government. In the remainder of the book, we will discuss GDP with the understanding that it is measured using the *expenditure approach*.

Now that we have established the circular flow of income, production, and spending for a closed economy, we can move to opening up the economy to the rest of the world. To begin with, we introduce international trade. GDP is now defined as:

$$GDP \equiv C + I + G + (X - IM) \equiv C + I + G + NX \tag{11.2}$$

where X, **exports**, is spending by foreigners on domestically produced goods, while IM, **imports**, is spending by home residents on goods produced by foreigners. Imports are subtracted from the total because GDP is the sum of domestic production, and some consumption, investment, and government expenditures fall upon imported goods, which are produced abroad. Hence, not subtracting imports would result in double-counting some of the final goods and services in GDP that were not produced within the borders of the country. In a closed economy, GNP (**Gross National Product**), the sum of the value of all final goods and services produced by resident factors of production, is the same as GDP.

Opening Up the Real Economy

In the open economy, GNP now differs from GDP because the latter pertains to location of production, while the former pertains to the location of the owners of the factors of production. When all domestic residents own all the factors of production within the borders of the country, and do not own any factors abroad, and, moreover, no one makes cross-border transfers of income, then *GNP* and *GDP* will be quantitatively and conceptually the same. However, in an open economy that will no longer be the case.

$$GNP \equiv GDP + F + V \equiv C + I + G + CA \tag{11.3}$$

GNP is the sum of *GDP* and **net factor income** from abroad and **net unilateral transfers** from abroad (*F* and *V*, respectively). Net factor income is the difference between income received from assets owned by residents that are abroad (bonds, equity, direct investment) and income paid to foreign residents on the assets they own in the home country. For instance, interest paid on a German government bond held by an American would count as a positive item in *F*. Net transfers, *V*, are primarily **remittances**; for instance, the income a Philippine resident working in the United States sends back to his family in the Philippines would count as a negative item in unilateral transfers.

The circular flow of income and spending, modified to account for the interactions with the rest of the world, is shown in Figure 11.2. Notice that the interactions come in several places. Net exports (equivalently, the trade balance) results in a possible gap between *GNE* and *GDP* – that is, expenditures can exceed, or fall short of, domestic production, with the difference showing up in trade. Net factor income and net unilateral transfers augment (or deduct) from the resources available for spending (in *GNI* + *F*, what is sometimes termed Gross National Disposable Income). The current account comprises net exports, net income, and net transfers, and these linkages are shown in orange in the figure.

Just as an individual can get resources by borrowing, an economy can borrow from the rest of the world. We add two components, which we return to discuss in detail in Section 11.3: the **total financial account**, the sum of the **private financial account** and **official reserves transactions** (*FA* + *ORT*) and the **capital account** (*KA*). The capital account is a small category (for the United States) and pertains to items such as debt forgiveness (shown in purple). The **financial account** refers to borrowing (purchases of assets from abroad) or lending (sales of assets to abroad). Obviously borrowing adds to the resources available for spending in the current period, while lending does the reverse. The total financial account links are shown in green in Figure 11.2.

Figure 11.2 is read in the same fashion as Figure 11.1. As one moves clockwise, the flows between the *GDP*, *GNI* plus unilateral transfers (this sum is called Gross Disposable National Income), and *GNE* are shown, with each of the components of the **balance of payments** introducing differences at the indicated points.

The evolution of *GNE*, *GDP*, and *GNP* over time are shown in Figure 11.3.

Notice that *GDP* is less than *GNE*; the two series differ by net exports (equivalently the trade balance), so when *GDP* is less than *GNE*, the United States is importing more than it is exporting. *GNP* in turn differs from *GDP* by net factor income and transfers. Since *GNP* exceeds *GDP*, then the US is receiving more income and transfers from abroad than the US is sending abroad.

11.2 SAVING, INVESTMENT, AND THE CURRENT ACCOUNT BALANCE

Thus far, we have been defining terms and accounting. This means we cannot say anything about what factor causes one aspect or the other to change. However, accounting is useful for telling us what must be true. One of the implications of working through the accounting for an open economy is that any excess of spending in an economy must manifest itself in a deficit on the current account, and vice versa.

11.2 SAVING, INVESTMENT, AND THE CURRENT ACCOUNT BALANCE

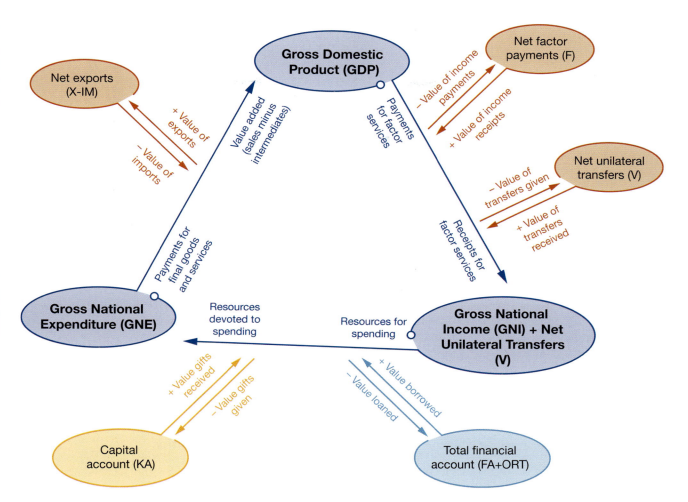

Figure 11.2 Income, Production and Spending in an Open Economy This figure shows the circular flow of income in an open economy. The factors of production that are used in the production of goods must be paid for, which is augmented by net income from production undertaken abroad by factors of production abroad, to equal Gross National Income. That GNI, augmented by net borrowing and gifts from abroad, is the amount that is spent on goods and services produced by factors of production. Adding in net foreign demand for goods and services equals gross domestic production.

As previously described, all spending on final goods and services must be categorized into consumption, investment, government, exports, and imports, which in turn must sum to *GDP*. *GNP* adds to *GDP* the net income and net transfers. Income must equal production, so we repeat equation (11.3), substituting Y (income) for *GNP*:

$$Y \equiv C + I + G + CA \qquad (11.4)$$

Because spending on domestically produced goods must be met by domestic production, then the spending must equal income. That income must then be either taxed (T), consumed (C), or saved (S). Government transfers (such as social security payments, for instance) aredefined as negative values of T.

$$C + S + T \equiv Y \qquad (11.5)$$

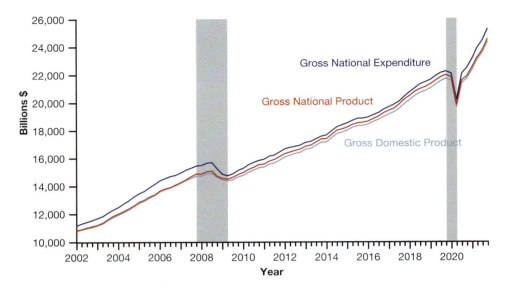

Figure 11.3 Spending and Production Measures This graph shows Gross National Expenditures, Gross Domestic Product, and Gross National Product, in billions of dollars, SAAR. Recession dates are shaded gray.
Source: BEA.

Combining the two definitions of Y leads to the following expression:

$$C + S + T \equiv C + I + G + (X - IM) + F + V \qquad (11.6)$$

Rearranging equation (11.5) leads to the **National Saving Identity**:

$$(S - I) + (T - G) \equiv (X - IM) + F + V \equiv CA \qquad (11.7)$$

where $(T - G)$ is the government budget balance, and $(S-I)$ is private saving net of private investment. In words, the sum of public saving and private saving minus investment must equal the current account balance. This relationship is shown in Figure 11.4.

One way to interpret this identity is to observe that the current account balance is positive when net private saving and public saving (the budget balance) sum to a positive number. A positive current account balance means that the country is spending less than it is producing and receiving in income from the rest of the world.

When the current account is in surplus, then the country is on net saving, and hence lending, to the rest of the world. The reverse is also true; if the sum of net private saving and public saving is negative, then the current account balance must by definition be negative, and the country is borrowing from the rest of the world. As of 2023, with the country running a current account deficit, the United States is on net borrowing from the rest of the world.

Two episodes in government policies illustrate the power and the limitations of accounting. The first is the US experience after the election of Ronald Reagan in 1980, in which the country embarked upon a program of large tax cuts and massive increases in defense spending. The Federal government budget balance moved decisively toward a deficit in the mid-1980s. The private saving–investment balance moved toward zero. By accounting, the current account had to be in deficit. The near simultaneous onset of these two imbalances led observers to term this phenomenon "**the Twin Deficits**." Then, as the budget balance

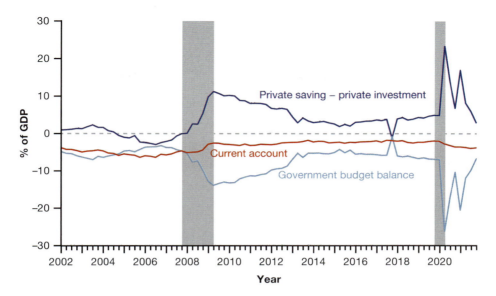

Figure 11.4 The National Saving Identity This graph shows the private saving – investment balance, net government saving, and the current account balance, all expressed as a percent of GDP. Recession dates are shaded gray. *Source: BEA.*

moved back toward zero at the end of the 1980s, so too did the current account. The second, more recent episode, is associated with tax cuts of the George W. Bush administration, starting in 2001, and the subsequent increases in defense spending associated with the war in Iraq. Because the correlation is less pronounced, sometimes the 2000s deficits are referred to as "siblings," rather than twins.

Because equation (11.6) is an accounting identity, one cannot always say the budget deficit caused the trade deficit. For example, in the 1990s, under the Clinton Administration, the *opposite* relationship was observed: the budget balance improved as the current account deteriorated. In order to explain what causes what in these different situations, we need a model. That is reserved for Chapter 13.

11.3 THE BALANCE OF PAYMENTS

We now turn to detailing the linkages between the domestic economy and the rest of the world. We record these international transactions in what is called the balance of payments.

The Overall Accounting

The balance of payments accounting identity requires that the current account and private financial account plus official reserves transactions must sum to zero. Technically, the capital account should also be included, but it is quantitatively small for the United States, so we will suppress this term. The capital account records transfers of capital, such as debt forgiveness.

$$CA + FA + ORT \equiv 0 \qquad (11.8)$$

This identity can be interpreted to mean that any surplus (deficit) on current transactions must be balanced by financial transactions by agents (firms, households, governments) on the private financial account (*FA*) and by central banks on the public financial account, known as official reserves transactions (*ORT*). The key difference between the current account and the financial account (including both the private and public financial account) is that the former involves trade in goods and services – essentially things used currently – while the latter involves trade in assets – claims on future resources. How these transactions are recorded in the real world, using double-entry accounting, is detailed in the Theory box below.

THEORY   Double-Entry Accounting and the Balance of Payments

The balance of payments accounts keep track of payment receipts using double-entry accounting. This means each transaction is recorded in two places on a balance sheet – hence the term double-entry bookkeeping. Receipts from foreigners are counted as credits, while payments to foreigners are recorded as debits. Total credits and debits must then equal each other exactly because each transaction is paired.

To illustrate how this accounting works, it will be useful to consider three examples, which involve the three accounts of the balance of payments – trade, financial, and capital accounts. In all the examples below, the perspective is from the United States.

First, consider the case where an American purchases a Japanese auto for $30,000, and uses a US bank check to pay for the auto. The auto purchase then enters the balance of payments as a debit of $30,000 (under the current account as a US import). There is a corresponding sale of a bank deposit by the US bank, which is counted as a credit of $30,000 (under the financial account as a US asset sale).

Second, let us shift to the financial account. An American buys a share of a German company for $1,000. She purchases it and pays using an American bank check. Then a $1,000 credit shows up as a stock purchase (under the financial account, US asset purchase), and a $1,000 debit shows up as a claim on a bank account at the American bank (under the financial account as a US asset sale).

Third, suppose the United States government forgoes the debt of a foreign country by $1 million. This shows up as a $1 million debt (under the capital account as a US transfer payment). This is a reduction in US government claims on the foreign country of $1 million (under the financial account as a US asset sale).

There are many other conceivable combinations of credits and debits. It is unclear where the offsetting debit for any credit will show up, but by double-entry accounting it will show up somewhere.

While this description seems removed from the previous discussion about the balance of payments, the link is actually quite close. Recall that in the aggregate, the sum of the *CA* and *FA* is equal to the negative of the financial account. In other words, any negative sum of *CA* and *FA* has to be met by a reduction in net asset holdings, i.e., net sales of assets.

In principle, $CA \equiv -(FA + ORT)$. However, due to the fact that not all transactions are recorded, equality does not hold exactly. The difference is made up by the statistical discrepancy. Figure 11.6 presents data for the US current account and total financial account (*FA* plus *ORT*). It highlights the fact that the US current account deficit has to be financed by net borrowing from the rest-of-the-world, or decumulation of **foreign exchange reserves**.

The two series are mirror images of each other, more or less. The difference is accounted for by a statistical discrepancy that reflects gaps in the reporting of transactions.

The Current Account, Again

The current account records trades on goods, services, and other current transactions. This is further broken down into subcategories. The key subcomponents of the current account are net exports, income receipts and payments, and net unilateral transfers.

$$CA \equiv (X - IM) + F + V \tag{11.9}$$

11.3 THE BALANCE OF PAYMENTS

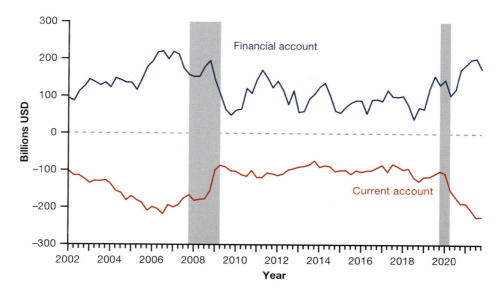

Figure 11.5 Components of the Balance of Payments This graph shows the current account, the private financial account plus official reserves transactions in billions of dollars, quarterly, 2002Q1–2021Q4. Recession dates are shaded gray.
Source: BEA, International Transactions.

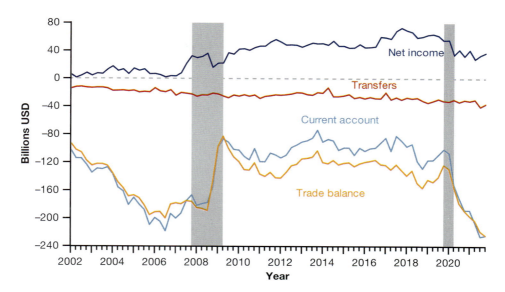

Figure 11.6 Components of the Current Account Trade balance, net income, net transfers, and current account in millions of dollars, quarterly, 2002Q1–2021Q4. Recession dates are shaded gray.
Source: BEA, International Transactions.

Table 11.1 displays the current account data for the US over the 2012–2021 period. The column under "Balance on goods and services" corresponds to data on $(X-IM)$, the column under "Balance on **primary income**" corresponds to F, the column under "Balance on **secondary income**" corresponds to V, and "Balance on *current account*" corresponds to CA.

A graphical breakdown of the current account data over time is displayed in Figure 11.6.

Table 11.1 The US Current Account, 2012–21

	Current account 1											
	Goods			Services				Primary income receipts and payments				
Period	Exports	Imports	Balance on goods	Exports	Imports	Balance on services	Balance on goods and services	Receipts	Payments	Balance on primary income	Balance on secondary Income	Balance on current account	Current account balance as a percentage of GDP
2012	1,562,630	2,303,749	−741,119	684,823	469,610	215,213	−525,906	791,613	593,754	197,859	−90,134	−418,181	−2.6
2013	1,593,708	2,294,247	−700,539	719,413	465,736	253,678	−446,861	811,501	616,041	195,460	−88,115	−339,516	−2.0
2014	1,635,563	2,385,480	−749,917	757,051	491,086	265,965	−483,952	845,858	645,623	200,235	−86,339	−370,056	−2.1
2015	1,511,381	2,273,249	−761,868	769,397	498,305	271,092	−490,776	824,929	639,724	185,205	−102,882	−408,453	−2.2
2016	1,457,393	2,207,195	−749,801	783,431	513,088	270,343	−479,458	857,240	660,798	196,442	−113,199	−396,216	−2.1
2017	1,557,003	2,356,345	−799,343	837,474	548,475	288,999	−510,344	995,442	737,501	257,942	−108,618	−361,021	−1.9
2018	1,676,913	2,555,662	−878,749	865,549	565,395	300,155	−578,594	1,102,964	847,689	255,275	−116,530	−439,850	−2.1
2019	1,655,098	2,512,358	−857,260	891,177	593,594	297,584	−559,676	1,136,799	893,244	243,555	−129,836	−445,957	−2.1
2020	1,432,218	2,346,103	−913,885	726,433	466,537	259,896	−653,989	936,236	773,146	163,090	−128,799	−619,698	−3.0
2021	1,761,364	2,851,660	−1,090,296	795,273	550,025	245,248	−845,047	1,052,080	912,587	139,493	−140,800	−846,354	−3.7

Note: Millions of dollars; quarterly data seasonally adjusted.
Source: CEA and JEC, *Economic Indicators*, August 2022.

The trade balance (or net exports) is the difference between total exports (X) and imports (IM). Sometimes reference is made to the merchandise trade balance, which equals *goods* exports minus *goods* imports, so, when reading, be careful about the adjectives.

Services include transportation, tourism, and business and professional services. Transportation includes expenditures incurred moving both passengers and freight. Notice that tourism expenditures by a country's citizens abroad constitute a service import, while foreign citizens' expenditures in the country are service exports. Business services are provided by engineers, architects, management consultants, lawyers, and so forth. Also included are royalty payments and license fees.

In 2021, the US balance of trade on goods was –$1,090.3 billion. Net services (including military transactions) amounted to $245.2 billion, so that the balance on goods and services, also known as net exports, was –$845.0 billion.

Income receipts were $1,052.1 billion, while income payments were $912.6 billion. The balance on income was then $139.5 billion. Unilateral current transfers (foreign assistance and private remittances) amounted to –$140.8 billion. Summing up the balance of trade, net income receipts, and unilateral transfers yields a 2021 current account balance of –$846.4 billion.

Several aspects about the US current account are notable. The first is that the trade balance and the current account are close to the same size. This is the case for the US because the surplus in net income is roughly offset by a deficit in net transfers. However, this is a specific case, and the near equality does not hold in general for other countries. In fact, for some countries, the current account could be much smaller than the trade balance – as it is in countries that have lots of foreign ownership of domestic assets. Ireland is a case in point; in 2019, the Irish trade balance was 3.5% in surplus, while the current account was in deficit to the tune of 19.8%.

Second, while the US runs a large merchandise trade deficit, it runs a substantial surplus on trade in services. The US is a net exporter of travel services (air travel, for instance), but an increasingly important category in recent years is US exports of business services.

11.4 THE FINANCIAL AND CAPITAL ACCOUNT

Table 11.2 displays financial and capital account data for the United States, over the 2002–2021 period.

The net private financial account (FA) is the difference between transactions on US private assets and on other foreign assets. Private financial outflows were $1977.3 billion, private inflows were $1164.6 billion in 2021. Hence, FA equaled $812.7 billion, so that foreigners accumulated more US assets than US residents accumulated foreign assets.

Total private flows can be further broken down into foreign direct investment, long-term and short-term capital flows.

Foreign direct investment occurs when the residents of one country acquire control over an enterprise in another country. This acquisition can occur either by virtue of a purchase of the firm, purchase of sufficient amounts of equity to have a controlling influence (defined as 10%), or by building a new factory or factories from the ground up (which are called greenfield plants).

Long-term portfolio investment involves the acquisition of securities, including equities – or shares of stock – and bonds with an original maturity of more than a year. **Short-term financial capital flows** involve assets with an original term of maturity of a

Table 11.2 The US Capital and Financial Account, 2012–2021

Period	Balance on capital account 1	Net US acquisition of financial assets excluding financial derivatives [net increase in assets / financial outflow (+)]					Net US incurrence of liabilities excluding financial derivatives [net increase in liabilities / financial inflow (+)]				Financial derivatives other than reserves, net transactions	Net lending (+) or net borrowing (−) from financial account transactions	Statistical discrepancy	US official reserve assets, net (unadjusted, end of period)
		Total	Direct investment assets	Portfolio investment assets	Other investment assets	Reserve assets	Total	Direct investment liabilities	Portfolio investment liabilities	Other investment liabilities				
2012	931	171,359	377,239	243,182	−453,522	4,460	632,034	250,343	747,017	−365,327	7,064	−453,611	−36,361	150,175
2013	−6,559	626,189	392,796	457,734	−221,242	−3,099	1,052,068	288,131	511,987	251,949	2,222	−423,657	−77,582	144,575
2014	−6,535	865,694	387,528	581,668	−99,920	−3,583	1,109,443	251,857	697,607	159,979	−54,335	−298,084	78,506	130,090
2015	−7,940	144,104	302,072	107,154	−258,831	−6,292	503,468	511,434	213,910	−221,876	−27,035	−386,400	29,993	117,581
2016	−6,606	336,438	299,814	37,489	−2,955	2,090	706,693	474,388	231,265	1,040	7,827	−362,427	40,394	117,332
2017	12,394	1,161,984	409,413	540,728	213,533	−1,690	1,559,219	380,823	790,810	387,586	23,998	−373,237	−24,610	123,313
2018	−4,261	429,710	−130,720	381,863	173,578	4,989	712,178	214,716	303,075	194,387	−20,404	−302,872	141,238	125,798
2019	−6,456	307,192	105,677	−11,453	208,310	4,659	831,045	314,743	233,469	282,834	−41,670	−565,524	−113,111	129,479
2020	−5,532	943,091	271,798	406,364	255,956	8,974	1,634,965	148,914	946,560	539,490	−5,107	−696,980	−71,751	144,890
2021	−2,474	1,278,599	421,749	719,095	23,763	113,993	1,977,294	448,325	676,112	852,857	−41,902	−740,597	108,231	251,238

Note: Millions of dollars; quarterly data seasonally adjusted
Source: CEA and JEC, *Economic Indicators*, August 2022.

11.4 THE FINANCIAL AND CAPITAL ACCOUNT

year. These include securities such as Treasury bills, commercial paper, certificates of deposit. Also included are liquid assets, such as bank deposits.

Official reserves transactions, which involve trade in gold, IMF credits and Special Drawing Rights, and – most importantly – foreign exchange, equaled $114 billion.

Figure 11.7 displays the private financial account (FA) and official reserves transactions (ORT) for the United States.

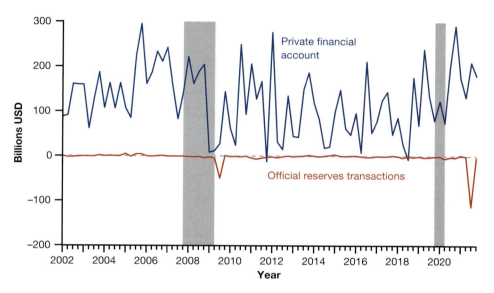

Figure 11.7 Components of the Financial Account This figure shows the private financial account and official reserves transactions in billions of dollars, quarterly, 2002Q1–2021Q4. Recession dates are shaded gray.
Source: BEA, International Transactions.

The term **overall balance of payments** is often used to refer to the sum of the current account, capital account, and private financial account. When the overall balance of payments is in deficit, then, ORT must be positive – that is the stock of foreign exchange held by the central bank is declining. When ORT is negative, the foreign exchange reserves are increasing.

Foreign exchange reserves are often a critical variable, particularly when a country is running an overall balance of payments deficit. By accounting, reserves must then be declining, which, if sustained for a long enough period, means that reserves hit zero. At that juncture, either the current account deficit must shrink, the private financial account surplus must increase, or foreign exchange reserves are replenished by a loan. This is where the International Monetary Fund (IMF) comes in. Of course, the IMF does not lend foreign exchange without some strings attached. These situations in which countries run out of foreign exchange reserves – called balance of payments crises – are discussed (along with the IMF's role) at greater length in Chapter 16.

For the United States, the current account balance has been in deficit for many decades, with only a couple of exceptions. Over that time period, the private financial account has been in surplus, thereby financing the excess of US spending over US production. In other words, the United States as a whole has been borrowing in order to finance its trade deficit.

The capital account includes some select unilateral transfers. The largest single category is that of debt forgiveness. The capital account for the United States is relatively small, in comparison to the other components of the balance of payments. In 2016, it amounted to a mere −$0.06 billion.

A cautionary note: Before 1997, the term "capital account" referred to what is now called the financial account, and it is still common to find the term capital account used to refer to what we call the financial account. The terminology was changed to allow greater precision. In addition, some current treatments still refer to what we term the financial account, the capital account.

One category we have not discussed is statistical discrepancy. In some years, the number can be quite large; for instance, in 2021, the discrepancy was $108.1 billion. This discrepancy arose because of the gaps in the reporting of cross-border transactions. Such gaps can arise because reporting requirements are not comprehensive, or because of the intentional desire to avoid government scrutiny. Consequently, this is not a large issue in understanding how the international economy works. It is a large issue in practical terms, since it signifies the amount to which we mis-measure international transactions. This issue is discussed in the box below.

THEORY The Global Current Account Discrepancy

Since a debit in trade for one country is a credit for another country, the entire world's trade balance should … balance, and balance to zero. And because one country's income receipt is another's income payment, income flows should all net to zero. Taken together, this means that the global current account balance should be zero. Figure 11.8 indicates that this is far from the case.

From 1980 through 2003, the current account balance typically summed to less than zero. As a share of world GDP, the discrepancy was large, up to −0.9% of world GDP in 1982. Since shifting to the positive side, the discrepancy's size has increased in both dollar terms and proportionately. By 2021, it was three quarters of a trillion dollars, or nearly 0.8 percentage points of world GDP.

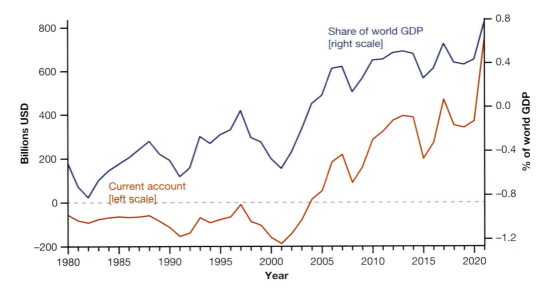

Figure 11.8 **The World Current Account Balance** This figure shows the sum of current account balances for all countries, in trillions of US dollars (red, left scale), and as a percent of world GDP (blue, right scale).
Source: IMF, *World Economic Outlook*, April 2022, database.

A 2009 IMF study attributes the early negative values to under-reporting of interest income during the early 1980s when interest rates were fairly high. Transportation services were also responsible for some portion of the negative discrepancy. The shift toward a positive discrepancy in the early 2000s is driven mainly by the large increase in the discrepancy associated with the category of "other services," which includes financial and legal services, insurance, and consultancies.

With global trade including ever more of these types of services, there is no reason to believe that the problems measuring the current account balances will disappear, and in fact it might become even more difficult to tabulate countries' current account balances (let alone their financial accounts).

11.5 THE FINANCIAL ACCOUNT AND THE NET INTERNATIONAL INVESTMENT POSITION

When the total financial account is in surplus (the private financial account and official reserves transactions), then it must be true that the current account must be in deficit. And when the current account is in deficit, the country is consuming more than it is producing, and receiving income from abroad. This means the country is borrowing from abroad.

The flow of borrowing implies that the country's residents will increasingly own less assets (factories, bonds, stocks, land) abroad, and/or foreigners will own more assets in the country. Often people will characterize this process as increasing "net indebtedness," even though the assets involved in the calculation are not restricted to debt. For the United States, the difference between what US residents own abroad minus what foreigners own in the US is termed the **Net International Investment Position** (NIIP). Figure 11.9 depicts the cumulated current account balance and the NIIP for the US.

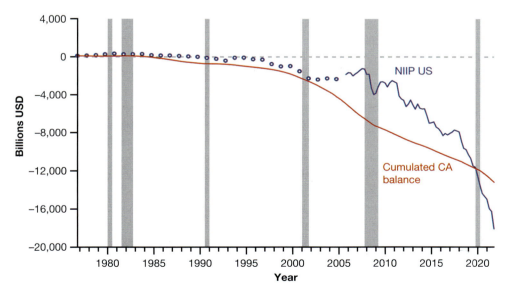

Figure 11.9 The Net International Investment Position This figure shows the difference between the assets and liabilities of the United States at year-end (blue line), and the cumulated current account balance (red line), both in billions of US dollars. Recession dates are shaded gray.
Source: Bureau of Economic Analysis, and author's calculations.

Clearly, the United States has moved from a position of net creditor (in 1976) to net debtor in 2016: foreign residents now own more US assets (securities such as stocks and bonds, factories, real estate) than US residents own of foreign assets, to the tune of approximately $18.0 trillion. This amount is large, and it amounts to about 74.4% of end-2021 US GDP.

Note that a current account deficit (and hence a financial account surplus) implies corresponding increasing foreign claims on the United States. However, the cumulation of these current account deficits, shown as the red line in Figure 11.9 (starting off at the same value as the recorded NIIP in 1976) does not move in exactly the same manner as the actual estimates. In fact, the red line implies a much larger negative position.

The reason these two lines do not match more closely is a source of considerable debate. At least part of the reason is that some assets change value over time. For instance, Japanese investors might purchase real estate in the US at a high price, and that property then loses value over time. That change shows up in the NIIP, but not in the flows (as they are currently recorded). Another reason is that exchange rate fluctuations will change valuations – for the US, the NIIP is expressed in dollar terms. Hence, a dollar depreciation – such as that which has occurred between 2002 and 2007 – will tend to push upward the dollar value of US holdings of foreign assets.

If we inspect the NIIP in Figure 11.10 and the net income flow in Figure 11.7, we see a seeming inconsistency: while the US is a net debtor, the US records a net positive income! How can this be? One way in which the two facts can be reconciled is to consider the possibility that the US earns a higher rate of return on the assets it owns abroad than foreigners earn on the assets they own in the US.

US assets abroad equaled $35.0 trillion at the end of 2021, while liabilities to foreigners amounted to $53.2 trillion. The composition of assets and liabilities differs dramatically. US assets are more heavily weighted toward foreign direct investment, while foreign-owned US assets tend to be heavily weighted toward US government securities, which tend to have lower returns, particularly between 2009 and 2016.

APPLICATION China's Balance of Payments

The evolution of China's external balances – in particular the increase in trade surpluses during the middle of the last decade – has been a chronic source of political friction. The massive accumulation of foreign exchange is a natural by-product of these trade surpluses. We examine the mechanics of this outcome in this box.

In 2013, China's current account was $148.2 billion. The capital account was $51.3 billion. The financial account was $343.0 so that private foreigners' claims on Chinese assets were rising over time.

The overall balance of payments was $494.3 billion, so that foreign exchange reserves increased by that amount. This is demonstrated by the fact that from 2012 to 2013, international reserves (which includes other items) rose from $508.4 billion, to $3,331.1 billion, and then to $3,839.5 billion. Each year that the overall balance is positive (and the official reserves transactions are negative) is a year that reserves rise.

This point – that a positive overall balance leads to increments to official foreign exchange reserves – is highlighted by the evolution of China's reserves. As of the end of 2021, these reserves exceeded $3.3 trillion (Figure 11.10).

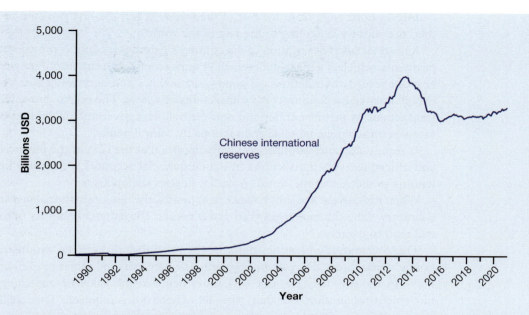

Figure 11.10 Chinese International Reserves This figure shows China's international reserves which mostly comprise foreign exchange, excluding gold, in billions of US dollars.
Source: IMF, International Financial Statistics.

Notice that in 2014, China's foreign exchange reserves experienced a dramatic change in trajectory. In a mechanical sense, this was the outcome of a negative balance of payments surplus arising from a notably smaller current account balance and financial outflows.

CONCLUSION

Measuring the size of the economy – in terms of spending, production, and income – and how the economy interacts with the rest of the world is critical for understanding how the economy behaves. The first step in that understanding involves the measurement of economic activity. For a closed economy, separated from the rest of the world, spending equals production which equals income. The easiest way in which to tabulate production is to count up the value of all final goods and services purchased by households, firms, the government, and foreigners. In theory, spending should equal production, which in turn equals income. In practice, tabulations using the expenditure approach will not equal that obtained using the production approach or the income approach.

Gross Domestic Product, the sum of the value of all goods and services produced within the borders of the country, differs from Gross National Product. The latter is the sum of the value of all goods and services produced by factors of production owned by the residents of the country. The difference between the two concepts is net factor income and net unilateral transfers, which are included in GNP, but not GDP.

The National Saving Identity provides a link between domestic spending, production and the external balance of the economy. The sum of government saving, plus the excess of private saving over investment, equals the current account. When the first two sum to a negative value, then by accounting the current account balance must be negative, and the country is borrowing from the rest of the world. When the first two sum to a positive value, then the country is lending to the rest of the world.

A more detailed description of the country's external account is provided by the balance of payments, which is a means of recording transactions with the rest of the world. The current account records transactions on goods and services and current income and transfers. The overall financial account records transactions on assets. The private financial account records transactions by private entities and non-central bank governmental entities on assets. Official reserves transactions tabulate transactions by central banks.

A current account surplus necessarily implies that the sum of the private financial account and official reserves transactions (the total financial account) is negative, i.e., the country is lending to the rest of the world. A deficit implies the opposite.

When the current account balance is in deficit, the net international investment position of a country – the difference between assets owned abroad and liabilities owed to foreigners – will tend to decrease.

These accounting identities describe the relationships between various categories of economic transactions. They do not explain, however, why the values of each of these categories move in the way they do, nor why movements in the value of one category might affect movements in another. For that, a model of behavior is required. That challenge is taken up beginning in Chapter 11.

SUMMARY

1. Gross Domestic Product differs from Gross National Expenditures by net exports. Gross National Product differs from Gross Domestic Product by net income and transfers.
2. The sum of government saving, and the excess of private saving over investment, equals the current account.
3. The balance of payments is a means of recording transactions with the rest of the world.
4. The current account records transactions on goods and services and current income and transfers.
5. The private financial account records transactions on assets. Official reserves transactions tabulates transactions by central banks.
6. A current account surplus necessarily implies that the sum of the private financial account and official reserves transactions (the total financial account) is negative, i.e., the country is lending to the rest of the world. A deficit implies the opposite.
7. When the current account balance is in deficit, the net international investment position of a country – the difference between assets owned abroad and liabilities owed to foreigners – will tend to decrease.

KEY CONCEPTS

Balance of payments, page 238
Capital account, page 238
Consumption spending, page 237
Exports, page 237
Final goods and services, page 236
Financial account, page 238
Foreign exchange reserves, page 242

Government spending, page 237
Gross National Expenditure, page 236
Gross Domestic Product, page 236
Gross National Income, page 236
Gross National Product, page 237
Identity, page 236
Imports, page 237

Investment spending, page 237
National income accounting, page 235
National Saving Identity, page 240
Net factor income, page 238
Net International Investment Position, page 249
Net unilateral transfers, page 238
Official reserves transactions, page 238
Overall balance of payments, page 247
Primary income, page 243
Private financial account, page 238
Remittances, page 238
Secondary income, page 243
Total financial account, page 238
Twin Deficits, page 240
Value added, page 237

REVIEW QUESTIONS

1. In a closed economy, does the income earned from producing goods and services equal the amount produced?
2. If one adds up the "value added" at all the steps of producing all the goods and services, will this equal the value of GDP?
3. Can one use an identity to show if a change in one variable causes a change in another?
4. Can a country import more than it exports without borrowing from the rest of the world?

EXERCISES

1. Consider a closed economy; would Gross Domestic Product and Gross National Product be the same? Why?
2. Consider an open economy.
   2.1 Calculate GDP given $C = 1{,}000$, $I = 800$, $G = 400$, and $NX = -200$.
   2.2 Does the calculation change if government taxes are 30?
3. Consider an open economy.
   3.1 Calculate GDP given $C = 1{,}200$, $I = 600$, $G = 300$, and $NX = +100$, while net factor income is 50 and net unilateral transfers are -30.
   3.2 Calculate GNP.
4. Suppose no income or unilateral transfers flow across borders. Show what the trade balance (net exports) must equal by the national income accounting identity.
5. Balance of payments identities. Recalling the balance of payments identity, $CA + FA + ORT \equiv 0$, answer the following questions.
   5.1 If a country maintains a pegged exchange rate and runs a balance of payments deficit, then what must be true about ORT? Explain what this means in words.
   5.2 If foreigners are purchasing more US securities (T-bills, corporate bonds, and stocks) than US residents are purchasing of foreign securities, then what is the value of KA, assuming the US is on a pure float? (Ignore direct investment for purposes of this question.)
   5.3 If $CA < 0$ and the central bank is neither accumulating nor decumulating foreign exchange reserves, what must be true about private capital inflows?
6. Balance of payments calculations. Download the most recent issue of *Economic Indicators*, compiled by the Council of Economic Advisers and published by the Joint Economic Committee. Go to the "publications" link. http://www.gpo.gov/economicindicators
   6.1 Calculate FA for 2016, using the data in *Economic Indicators*, "US International Transactions".

6.2 Show the ORT for 2016.

6.3 Given what ORT is, what is happening to US foreign exchange reserves.

RECOMMENDED RESOURCES

Ricardo Hausmann and Federico Sturzenegger, "Global Imbalances or Bad Accounting? The Missing Dark Matter in *The Wealth of Nations* and Its Implications for Global Imbalances," *Economic Policy* 22 (2007): 469–518.

Philip R. Lane and Gian Maria Milesi-Ferretti, "Where Did All the Borrowing Go? A Forensic Analysis of the US External Position," *Journal of the Japanese and International Economies* 23(2) (2009): 177–199.

CHAPTER 12

Exchange Rates, Interest Rates, and the Foreign Exchange Market

LEARNING OBJECTIVES

In this chapter, we learn about:
- what an exchange rate is
- how an exchange rate of currencies is determined
- how currencies are traded in practice
- how fixed and floating exchange rate regimes differ
- how interest rates and exchange rates are related
- how nominal and real exchange rates differ

INTRODUCTION

The *exchange rate* is the key relative price for an economy open to international trade and finance. The price Americans pay for Japanese automobiles imported into the United States depends on how many dollars it takes to buy 100 yen, i.e., the dollar/yen exchange rate. The stronger the dollar, the more yen it will buy, and therefore the cheaper the imported cars will be. At the same time, a strong dollar makes it harder for US firms to profitably sell heavy earth-moving equipment like bulldozers (say those made by Caterpillar) to the rest of the world. The strength of the dollar against other currencies also affects other sectors, besides trade in manufactured goods. A strong dollar is good for a US tourist visiting Madrid, but places in the United States that cater to foreign tourists, such as Las Vegas, do better business when the dollar is weak. And whether one decides to purchase stocks and bonds **denominated** in dollars, as opposed to, say, German securities denominated in euros, has a great deal to do with how one expects the dollar to move against the euro over time.

For instance, as the dollar rose in strength in 2014–2015, Caterpillar's chief executive noted "We're still very much focused on market share but … the competition for every deal has got greater as we've seen the dollar strengthen." At the same time, the strengthened dollar meant cheaper imported inputs used in manufacturing tractors, most of which are produced in the American Midwest. US prices for benchmark steel products dropped by 25% over the same period, largely due to the stronger dollar. In other words, movements in the currency have a large, and sometimes complicated, effect.

In this chapter, we will take the first steps to understanding what the exchange rate is, and how its numerical value is determined. We start this process by first defining some terms, then describing the marketplace for currencies, and finally discussing the linkage between exchange rates and other asset prices.

12.1 EXCHANGE RATES AND CURRENCY TRADING

An **exchange rate** is the rate of exchange between two currencies. Because this involves the purchase of one paper asset with another paper asset, it is a nominal price. Other meanings include the rate of an exchange of goods (which would be a real exchange rate), or between a currency and a bundle of other currencies. Mostly, we will first focus on the first definition, and relate it to trading in currencies. At the end of the chapter, we will discuss exchange rates between goods and services, and how those relate to exchange rates between currencies.

In the most familiar case, the exchange rate is the number of home currency units required to purchase one unit of foreign currency. In other words, the exchange rate is the price of foreign currency. In Figure 12.1, three exchange rates against the US dollar are shown. In each case, the values refer to the number of US dollars necessary to purchase a single unit of the foreign currency at a given time (sometimes known as a spot exchange rate). Notice that the German mark disappears in 1999, because it is subsumed into a new currency, the euro.

Figure 12.1 Nominal US Dollar Exchange Rates This figure shows the US exchange rates against the Deutsche mark, British pound, and euro. Higher values denote a weaker dollar against the foreign currency (a depreciation of the dollar).

An exchange rate can be thought of as a relative price of two assets, in this case two currencies. From the perspective of an American, it is how many US dollars it takes to buy (for instance) one British pound. (We are accustomed to thinking about how many US dollars it takes to buy a single apple, but that is a different kind of exchange rate, one of a paper asset for a real good; and when the price goes up, the purchasing power of the dollar declines.)

The exchange rate reflects the respective valuations of these assets, which in turn depend on a variety of factors, both those in the present and those expected in the future. Since those expectations change over time, so too does the exchange rate – as illustrated in Figure 12.1 by the wide swings in each of the series over the past 50 years.

The relationship between exchange rates and expectations is explored further in Chapter 17. However, for now, we make a first attempt to explain how these prices of foreign exchange are determined. At the basic level, it is simple – prices are determined in a marketplace.

The marketplace, however, is very special. First, the market is an "**over the counter**" market; hence, there is no centralized exchange, as in the New York Stock Exchange. Rather, trading takes place between a set of actors – dealers, non-dealer financial institutions, corporations, and governments. The latter are "end-users" – that is, they demand currencies for use in their activities. In contrast, dealers trade on behalf of their clients, or they trade in order to make profits for their own financial institution, where those institutions are largely located in major financial capitals.

For instance, if a trader wanted to buy some euros from another trader, using dollars, the trader would directly call a set of other traders at different major banks, and ask for the price at which they would be willing to trade. After receiving several quotes, the trader would, within a few minutes, decide which one to choose. The trader has the choice of who to call, and who to trade with. In a centralized market, any seller could be matched with a buyer, as long as the price matched.

The market is dominated by just a few players. Approximately three-quarters of global foreign exchange trading is accounted for by the top ten banks, of which the top three are Citi, JP Morgan, and Union Bank Switzerland (UBS).

Trading is extensive – daily turnover in April 2022 was valued at 5.7 *trillion* US dollars per day. It is global in nature, with trading taking place almost around the clock. Most of the trading volume is between dealers, followed by financial institutions, and then non-financial firms. This pattern highlights the fact that demand for currency is mostly fueled by the trade in financial assets, not by any trade in goods and services. This trade is in turn driven in part by speculative motives – the desire to profit from anticipated changes in asset prices – and in part by the need to move financial capital across national borders.

The pattern of trading in currencies illustrates the relative importance of the two motivations. The US dollar, the euro, Japanese yen, and British pound lead in terms of currency trading turnover. The Australian dollar recently moved into fifth place, ahead of the Canadian dollar and the Swiss franc. The US dollar is the outsized leader, and yet this cannot be because the US is the biggest exporter or importer of goods and services. Rather, it is the importance of US financial assets – Treasury bills and corporate stocks and bonds – that drives the dollar's importance.

The Australian dollar's recent climb in importance reflects its economic role in a part of the world that has grown in prominence on the world economic scene. Interestingly, despite their economic mass, the currencies of the BRICs – Brazil, Russia, India, China, and South Africa – account for only 10.7% of total turnover (out of 200%). Despite its substantially larger economy, China's renminbi accounted for 7.0%.

These turnover figures do not fully reflect the central role of the dollar. Not only is dollar turnover high, the dollar is involved in 88% of all currency trades. The US dollar/euro pair alone account for 24% of total turnover. The dollar/yen pair is next in importance. The high-volume pairs all involve the US dollar, highlighting the dollar's role as the key global currency. The euro/pound and euro/yen pairs together account for a mere 3.7% of total trading turnover.

The popularity of the dollar in currency trading is self-reinforcing. Because dollars are widely traded, traders are in the habit of holding them, and therefore tend to charge lower transaction fees when dollars are involved. Lower transaction fees, in turn, encourage people to trade in dollars. When the objective is to exchange – for instance, Swedish krona for Thai baht – it turns out to be less expensive to exchange krona for dollars, and then dollars for baht, than to exchange krona for baht directly.

These trading patterns do not change much over time. The dollar/euro pair remained the most important trading pair from 1999 onward. Before 2001, the dollar/German mark had held that position consistently for the preceding two decades. The dollar/yen pair has been the second most important pair over the period the surveys were conducted (about 25 years).

Why is the dollar so dominant in all these foreign exchange transactions – far out of proportion to the US's share of global GDP? This is a complicated question, but a sort of answer is that the dollar enjoys unique status as an **international currency**. See the Theory box below for more on this topic.

THEORY   Why Is the Dollar the World's International Currency?

An international currency is one that fulfills the roles of money – unit of account, medium of exchange, and store of value – globally, for both private actors and governments conducting international transactions. Private actors use certain currencies primarily because of patterns in trade and finance, but also because of the ease with which those currencies can be traded. Governments hold foreign currencies in order to make purchases in the foreign exchange market, and to ensure the ability to import goods.

and trade, the configuration of financial markets, global confidence in various currencies' values, and also the inertia associated with "network externalities" – the tendency for a currency to be used because others use it.

Patterns of Production and Trade. The currency of the country with the biggest share of international trade has an immediate advantage over other contenders for the status of **world reserve currency**. The US economy remains the world's largest in terms of output and second largest in trade,

Table 12.1 Functions of an International Currency

Function of money	Governments	Private actors
Store of value	International reserve holdings	Currency substitution (private dollarization)
Medium of exchange	Vehicle currency for foreign exchange intervention	Invoicing trade and financial transactions
Unit of account	Anchor for pegging local currency	Denominating trade and financial transactions

Source: Kenen (1983).

The dollar has been the dominant currency in the holdings of central banks since the end of World War II and, as shown in Figure 12.2, has retained that lead even as the US share of world GDP has shrunk to about a quarter. The only other currency that really registers on the graph is the euro. The Japanese yen and the British pound vie for third place. Notable by its absence is the Chinese currency, the yuan.

Statistical analyses suggest that the compositions of governments' reserve holdings depend on patterns of production

so it is no surprise it is the world's reserve currency. However, the euro should be a close (rather than a distant) number two, given the eurozone's trading volume. Furthermore, Japan barely registered as a reserve currency even before the advent of the euro, when Japan was the second largest economy.

Financial markets. To attain international currency status, capital and money markets in the home country must be not only be open and free of controls, but also highly liquid and well developed. Nobody wants to hold large sums of a

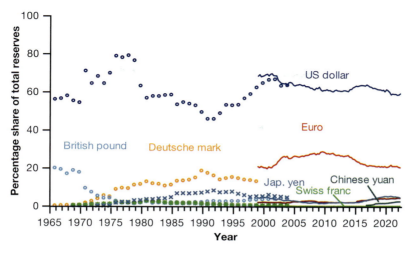

Figure 12.2 Central Bank Holdings of Foreign Currency This figure shows the shares of each currency in central bank foreign exchange holdings, in percent.
Source: IMF, Annual Reports, *Chinn and Frankel (2008), and IMF, Currency Composition of Official Exchange Reserves (COFER), September 30, 2022. Data for USD and EUR since 2000 are estimated.*

currency that are difficult to trade. Hence, the large financial marketplaces of New York and London clearly benefit the dollar and pound relative to the euro, as Frankfurt is still less well developed. The Tokyo and Frankfurt financial markets have changed a lot since the 1990s, but they still lag far behind New York and London. Meanwhile, Singapore and Hong Kong have gained ground, as well.

Confidence. The more it is believed a currency will retain its value, the more likely that currency is to be held as a reserve currency. With the decline in inflation in the United States in the 1980s, the dollar's share of central-bank holdings has rebounded from the lows recorded in the early 1990s.

Inertia. Finally, the dollar benefits because everybody is already using it, by the accident of the United States being the dominant economic force right after World War II. Once the global market has settled on a reserve currency, it is hard to switch, unless that currency becomes sufficiently unattractive on the three other counts as described above.

Chinn and Frankel (2007) conducted a statistical analysis of the determinants of the composition of central bank reserve holdings. They used foreign exchange turnover, and low inflation and currency appreciation as proxies for financial development, and for confidence, respectively. They found that financial development was the key determinant (along with inertia). This finding suggests that – even with China's rapid economic growth – as long as its *financial system* remains underdeveloped and largely closed to the rest of the world, the Chinese yuan will not become a major reserve currency in the near future.

12.2 SUPPLY, DEMAND, AND EXCHANGE RATES UNDER FIXED AND FLOATING REGIMES

Thus far we have discussed some features of the markets wherein the various actors – traders, corporations, central banks – buy and sell currencies. However, we have not explained how market forces interact to determine the price of a particular foreign currency.

Currency Supply and Demand in the Foreign Exchange Market

It turns out that we can use the standard supply and demand framework as a means of thinking about how the exchange rate – the price of foreign currency – is determined. Let the

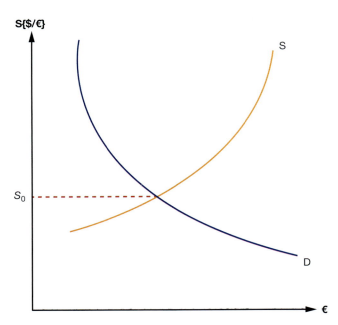

Figure 12.3 Supply and Demand under Floating Exchange Rates
This diagram shows the supply and demand for euros (€) in the market for foreign exchange.

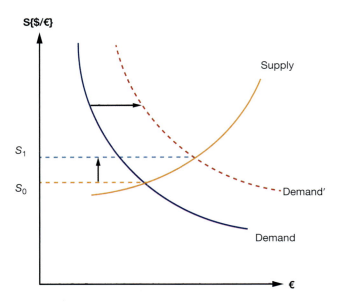

Figure 12.4 An Increase in Demand for Foreign Currency This shows how the increase in demand for euros (€) shifts out the demand curve for euros, and an associated rise in its price ($/€).

proceeds from exports of goods and sales of assets constitute the supply of foreign currency. Spending on imports and purchases of assets are the sources of demand for foreign exchange. If someone holding dollars wants to buy a good invoiced in euros, at some point someone, either the buyer or the seller, is going to want to unload dollars (supply) and acquire euros (demand).

Now consider a diagram where the price of the foreign currency is on the vertical axis, and the quantity of foreign currency is on the horizontal. S is the **spot exchange rate**, the price for an exchange conducted immediately ("on the spot"). A rate written into a contract to exchange currencies in the future (normally in 1, 3, 6, 9, or 12 months), is called a **forward exchange rate**, F for short. In the example shown in Figure 12.3, the market for euros is examined from the perspective of a US resident. The demand for euros is essentially derived from the underlying demand for goods and assets denominated in euros. Similarly, the supply of euros is derived from the underlying demand for supply of goods and assets that eurozone residents purchase.

The demand curve is downward sloping because as euros become cheaper, the quantity demanded rises. (Goods priced in euros attract more foreign buyers.) As euros become more expensive, the quantity supplied increases, and the supply curve is upward sloping. (Holders of euros start buying more foreign goods.) The equilibrium exchange rate – when the market is allowed to determine the price, in what is called a **floating exchange rate regime** – is S_0. At this point, the quantity supplied equals the quantity demanded.

When supply or demand changes, the exchange rate responds. Consider for instance what happens if the demand for euros increases – because, let us say, the demand for European food exports, such as wine, cheese, and olive oil, has increased. Then the demand curve shifts outward, and the exchange rate rises from S_0 to S_1 (Figure 12.4).

Notice that when the exchange rate rises, the foreign currency becomes more expensive. On the flip side, the home country currency, which in this case is the dollar, loses value. Hence, the rise in S represents a dollar **depreciation**.

Next we consider what happens if the supply of foreign currency rises, as shown in Figure 12.5. This could happen if foreign demand for US-made bulldozers increases.

12.2 SUPPLY, DEMAND, AND EXCHANGE RATES UNDER FIXED AND FLOATING REGIMES

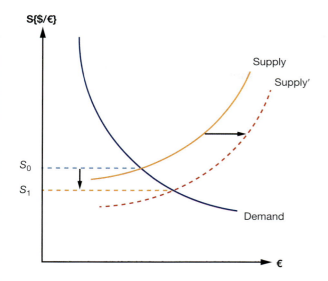

Figure 12.5 An Increase in the Supply of Foreign Currency This diagram shows an increase in supply of euros and an associated drop in their price.

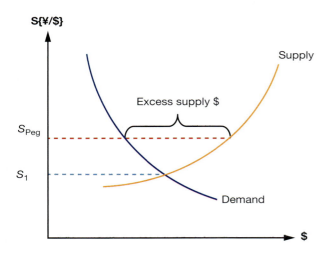

Figure 12.6 Supply and Demand under Fixed Exchange Rates This diagram shows the Chinese supply and demand for dollars under a fixed exchange rate regime.

The equilibrium exchange rate falls from S_0 to S_1. This represents a decrease in the price of euros in terms of dollars, so the dollar is becoming more valuable. Hence, this is an **appreciation** of the dollar.

Fixed Rate Regimes

In the two preceding examples, we have analyzed the repercussions of shifts in supply and demand in a system where the exchange rate is free to adjust to equilibrate the quantities supplied and demanded. This type of regime is called a **freely floating exchange rate regime**. In many cases, however, the exchange rate is not allowed to freely move; sometimes the exchange rate is fixed – or "pegged" – to a specific value against another currency. In fact, the extreme stability of the dollar/German mark and the dollar/pound exchange rates in the late 1960s to early 1970s shown in Figure 12.1 hinted at this possibility. Under a **fixed exchange rate regime**, somebody has to step in to maintain that price. In foreign exchange markets, that somebody is the central bank of the nation issuing the currency.

The central bank's role is easiest to explain by resorting to the same type of supply–demand graph used above. This time, instead of taking the perspective of a US resident, we will take the perspective of a Chinese resident prior to 2005, the year China began allowing their currency, the Chinese yuan, to float against the US dollar. Figure 12.6 depicts the market for US dollars, which are now the foreign currency. The exchange rate is set to S_{Peg}, the number of Chinese yuan (CNY) necessary to purchase one US dollar. In this case, the **exchange rate peg** is above the equilibrium exchange rate, so that there is excess supply of dollars in the foreign exchange market.

In the absence of any other forces, the exchange rate would gravitate downward to S_1; that is, the Chinese yuan would appreciate. Under a fixed exchange rate regime, however, the central bank commits itself to maintaining the currency at the official exchange rate. Hence, the central bank, in this case the People's Bank of China, absorbs the excess supply of dollars by purchasing those dollars in the foreign exchange market. In essence, the central bank artificially creates the added demand necessary to set the exchange rate at the pegged level.

Figure 12.6 depicts a situation where the peg is set above the equilibrium rate. We can consider the opposite case, where the peg is set below the equilibrium rate. Then there is excess demand for dollars, which the central bank must satisfy by selling dollars

In sum, if policymakers aim to keep the exchange rate at a depreciated level relative to the equilibrium determined by private supply and demand, then the central bank must purchase foreign currency; if the policy is to keep the exchange rate at an appreciated level, then the central bank must sell foreign currency.

12.3 EXCHANGE RATE REGIMES IN THE REAL WORLD

The preceding discussion has depicted a sharp distinction between floating and fixed exchange rate regimes. In practice, countries are seldom purists regarding the exchange rate regime they pursue. Rather, countries – particularly emerging-market and less-developed countries – will often allow exchange rates to float in a managed fashion, for instance intervening to smooth movements in rates, or a country might alternate between a floating and a fixed-rate regime, or something in-between. China, for example, left the dollar peg in 2005, but has not let it float freely since then, as shown in Figure 12.7.

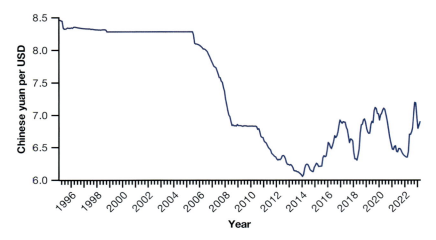

Figure 12.7 The Price of Foreign Exchange over Time This figure shows the Chinese yuan/US dollar exchange rate from the Chinese perspective.

Why might a country's policymakers seek to fix the exchange rate? One reason is that eliminating variations in the exchange rate makes planning by exporters, importers, and those wishing to borrow and lend in foreign currencies, a lot easier. For instance, if a Chinese exporter were considering whether to build a new factory to sell steel to the United States, but the factory would take a couple years to complete, the decision whether to proceed or not would be much easier if one knew what the yuan/dollar exchange rate would be in two years. However, keeping the exchange rate fixed imposes, if not certain costs, at least certain trade-offs in terms of what the policymakers can do with respect to monetary policy and the free flow of capital across the border. Those trade-offs are discussed in Chapter 15.

The IMF tabulates in the *Annual Report on Exchange Arrangements and Exchange Restrictions (AREAER)* the exchange rate policies associated with each country that is a member. From 1950 to 2008, the IMF reported what policies the countries declared themselves as pursuing (what are termed *de jure* regimes). Since 2009, the IMF has instead reported what their staff has assessed as the actual, or *de facto*, regime. The 2021 tabulation (reported in 2022) is reported in Table 12.2. At the top are the most

Table 12.2 De Facto Classification of Exchange Rate Arrangements and Monetary Policy Frameworks, July 2023

Exchange rate arrangement (Number of countries)	Exchange rate anchor			Monetary policy framework			
	US dollar (37)	Euro (26)		Composite (8)	Other (10)	Monetary aggregate target (25)	Inflation-targeting framework (45)	Other (43)

Exchange rate arrangement	US dollar (37)	Euro (26)		Composite (8)	Other (10)	Monetary aggregate target (25)
No separate legal tender (14)	Ecuador El Salvador Marshall Islands Micronesia Palau Panama Timor-Leste	Andorra Kosovo San Marino Montenegro			Kiribati Nauru Tuvalu	
Currency board (12)	Djibouti Hong Kong SAR **ECCU** Antigua and Barbuda Dominica Grenada St. Kitts and Nevis St. Lucia St. Vincent and the Grenadines	Bosnia and Herzegovina Bulgaria			Brunei Darussalam Macao SAR	
Conventional peg (40)	Aruba The Bahamas Bahrain Barbados Belize Curaçao and Sint Maarten Eritrea Iraq Jordan Oman Qatar Saudi Arabia Turkmenistan United Arab Emirates	Cabo Verde Comoros Denmark São Tomé and Príncipe **WAEMU** Benin Burkina Faso Côte d'Ivoire Guinea-Bissau Mali Niger	**CEMAC** Cameroon Central African Rep. Chad Congo Rep. of Equatorial Guinea Gabon	Fiji Libya	Bhutan Eswatini Lesotho Namibia Nepal	Samoa

Table 12.2 (cont.)

Exchange rate arrangement (Number of countries)	Exchange rate anchor			Monetary policy framework				
	US dollar (37)	Euro (26)	Composite (8)	Other (10)	Monetary aggregate target (25)	Inflation-targeting framework (45)		Other (43)
		Senegal Togo						
Stabilized arrangement (23)	Cambodia Guyana Iran Lebanon	Croatia North Macedonia	Singapore		Bolivia Nigeria Papua New Guinea Tanzania Tajikistan	Guatemala Serbia		Azerbaijan Egypt Kyrgyz Rep (1/21) Malawi (9/21) Mongolia Mozambique (6/21) Sudan (7/21)
	Maldives Trinidad and Tobago							
Crawling peg (3)	Honduras Nicaragua		Botswana					
Crawl-like arrangement (24)			Vietnam		Afghanistan (7/21) Algeria (12/20) Bangladesh (8/21) Burundi China Democratic Rep. of the Congo Ethiopia The Gambia (5/21) Guinea Rwanda	Dominican Republic Ghana Kenya (5/21) Romania Sri Lanka (4/21) Uzbekistan		Argentina Lao P.D.R. Mauritania Mauritius (12/20) Switzerland Solomon Islands Tunisia

Pegged exchange rate within horizontal bands (1)		Morocco		
Other managed arrangement (11)		Kuwait Syria	Liberia (10/21) Myanmar Sierra Leone Zimbabwe (8/21)	Haiti South Sudan (3/21) Tonga Zambia
Floating (35)			Angola Belarus Madagascar Suriname (6/21) Yemen	Albania Armenia Brazil Colombia Costa Rica (10/21) Czech Republic (1/22) Georgia Hungary Iceland India Indonesia Israel Jamaica Kazakhstan Korea Moldova New Zealand Paraguay Peru Philippines (6/21) Seychelles South Africa Thailand Türkiye Uganda Ukraine Uruguay	Malaysia Pakistan Zambia (7/21)

Source: IMF, Annual Report on Exchange Rate Arrangements and Exchange Restrictions, 2022.

rigid, or fixed, exchange rate regimes. As one reads down the table, the exchange rate regimes become more flexible. Reading across the table, one can identify the currency which is used as the anchor – most currencies are linked to the dollar or the euro, with some others to a basket of currencies ("composite").

It is interesting that there are quite a few countries that peg their exchange rate (40), as well as free floating (32). But even more numerous are those that claim to follow some version of an intermediate regime (61)! Another 40 claim to be floating, but not free floating, which could also be interpreted as an intermediate regime.

Figure 12.8 illustrates the fact that a few countries manage their currencies in such a way as to fit our characterization of prototypical exchange rate regimes. Most countries allow some flexibility, limiting day-to-day changes in currency value. The countries that allow their currencies to float still manage their rates either by use of occasional foreign intervention (buying and selling currencies in the foreign exchange market), or by changing interest rates in order to influence currency values. The relationship between interest rates and currency exchange rates is the subject of the next section.

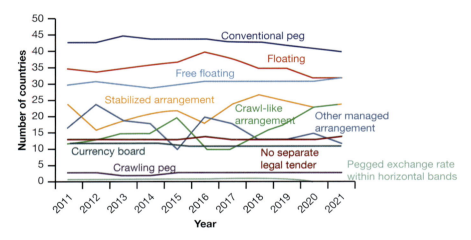

Figure 12.8 Number of Countries by Exchange Rate Arrangements This graph shows the number of IMF member countries adhering to given de facto currency arrangements of IMF members.
Source: Annual Report on Exchange Arrangements and Exchange Rates, 2022.

The correlation between the *de jure* and *de facto* measures is surprisingly low. In 2022 for instance, China states its currency is on a managed float, while the IMF categorizes it as a "crawl-like arrangement," and previously as "other managed float." Sri Lanka says it maintains a free-floating regime, but the IMF views the regime as a crawl-like peg.

12.4 THE RELATIONSHIP BETWEEN EXCHANGE RATES AND INTEREST RATES

Why do households and firms trade currencies? One reason is their need for foreign currencies to conduct cross-border transactions – for instance, buying goods from another country. That was the motivation for the shifts in the supply and demand curves in Section 12.3. However, that is not the only motivation. Firms, in particular, often have funds that they wish to save while earning the highest possible rate of return. How can we analyze the decision-making process facing a firm in that position?

First, consider the two basic options facing the firm's manager: save domestically or save overseas. The firm could save $1 in a risk-free US Treasury bond and earn i^{US} in interest at the end of a year. The firm could convert that same dollar into euros at the rate of $1/S$ euros per dollar, buy a euro-denominated security, and receive i^{Euro} in interest at the end of the year. Thus the firm has the following two possible returns of principal with interest:

Save in US	Save in Euro Area
$(1 + i^{US})$ in \$	$(1/S) \times (1 + i^{Euro})$ in €

Here we assume away transactions costs. For financial institutions making large transactions, such costs are relatively small. Presumably, if you are an American, you do not really care how many euros you expect to have. Rather, you care how many dollars you expect to have, so your decision must also depend upon what you think the exchange rate will be at the end of the year (call this is S^e_{+1}). Hence, the relevant comparison is between these two outcomes:

Save in US	Save in Euro Area
$(1 + i^{US})$ in \$	$(1 + i^{Euro})S^e_{+1}/S$ in \$

The comparison is a little difficult using those formulas. Using approximations that assume i^{Euro} and the change from S to S^e_{+1} to be small, the comparison can be recast as follows:

Save in US	Save in Euro Area
i^{US}	$i^{Euro} + (S^e_{+1} - S)/S$
interest return on US Treasury bond	interest return on euro area bond *plus* depreciation of dollar against euro

If all the saver cares about is the expected return, then if the left-hand side is greater than the right-hand side, put the savings in the United States. If the reverse is true, then put them in the euro area.

If everybody thought the same thing about what the exchange rate would be in a year, all financial capital would migrate in the same direction, driving interest rates up in the "from" location and down in the "to" location until the two returns were equal, and similarly affecting present and expected exchange rates. The resulting identity can be rewritten as:

$$i^{US} - i^{Euro} = \frac{S^e_{+1} - S}{S} \equiv \Delta s^e \qquad (12.1)$$

That is, the interest differential equals the expected depreciation. If, for example, the US interest rate is 5% and the euro area interest rate is 3%, then in equilibrium the expected depreciation of the dollar should equal 2%. This is a type of "**no-arbitrage condition**," meaning that there is no profit to be made by exploiting pricing differences among two more or more assets. The particular condition described here is called *interest rate parity*, more specifically **uncovered interest parity**, or UIP for short. (The "uncovered" will be explained in a moment.)

In the real world, it is precisely because not everybody has the same expectations about future exchange rates such that a large proportion of the trade in foreign currencies involves the financial sector. In the example just given, people who think the dollar will lose more than

2% of its value over the year will convert dollars into euros in order to invest in euro area bonds. Meanwhile, holders of euros who think the dollar will lose less than 2% will be moving their money to the United States

Uncovered interest rate parity is more a convenient theoretical reference point than an empirical reality, as far as can be determined. The following Theory box examines the evidence for and against UIP holding in the real world.

Since we do not ever actually see the market's expectations, the uncovered interest parity condition cannot be directly verified. However, market participants can enter into agreements to trade in the future. These contracts are called forward exchange contracts, or 'forwards' for short. In this case, the relevant equation, in which case one cannot make higher *certain* returns savings in the United States or in the euro area, is:

$$i^{US} - i^{Euro} = (F - S)/S \qquad (12.2)$$

F is a forward exchange rate; then the interest differential equals what is called the forward discount. This is another no-arbitrage condition, called **covered interest parity** (CIP for short). Suppose, for example, that the US interest rate is 10% and the euro area interest rate is 7%. Then, in order for one to not be able to get a higher dollar return in one location versus another, the forward exchange rate for a trade one year hence must be 3% higher than the exchange rate today. Then, one obtains 10% returns whether one saves in the United States (10% interest) or in the euro area (7% in interest plus 3% in the gain of the euro against the dollar).

As this kind of transaction locks in the returns (F and S are both written into the contract), it will be appealing if one does not like taking chances – that is one is "risk averse." But in avoiding unexpected losses, one also foregoes unexpected gains. If the dollar loses 5% of its value instead of 3%, then one still only obtains a 10% return, instead of the 12% return one would have received via the uncovered route.

Interest rate parity, uncovered or covered, will only hold if governments do not put up any barriers to the movement of financial capital. The historical reality is that almost all governments have put up barriers, such as restrictions on how much cash one can move in or out of the country at any one time. Such barriers are termed **capital controls** and are discussed at greater length in Chapter 13. Currently, the extent of such barriers is very modest for developed countries such as the United States, Germany, the UK, and Japan. Hence, covered interest parity holds between such countries. One will often hear discussions about the eurodollar and eurobond markets. These are offshore markets, not necessarily in Europe (the terms arose because the first such markets were in Europe). These markets arose because they enable trade outside the control of regulatory institutions in the various countries. For instance, a UK bank can take deposits in dollars and pay in dollars. Because the bank is in London, it is not subject to the control of the US authorities. These markets originally arose in response to the aforementioned capital controls. They still exist, because they circumvent all sorts of national banking regulations.

For developing nations, however, such as India and China, and most African countries, and some Latin American countries, significant capital controls are likely to be in place, and enforced. Moreover, there is always the threat of the government imposing new restrictions on the movement of capital in and out of the country, or even of seizing it outright. In such cases, it would be highly unlikely that you would find covered interest parity conditions holding.

THEORY   Does Uncovered Interest Parity Hold?

It is hard to test for uncovered interest parity, since expected depreciation is part of the calculation, and expectations cannot be directly observed. All we observe are actual exchange rate depreciations. However, assuming the expected depreciations are reasonably close to the actual ones, we would expect to see a positive correlation between the interest differential $i^{US} - i^{Euro}$ and the rate changes. In fact, we see something much different, as in Figure 12.9.

participants. Statistical tests confirm that their expectations are biased – expectations of exchange rate changes are on average wrong, so much so that for the dollar/euro exchange rate, the dollar appreciates when it is expected to depreciate.

Plotting *expected* depreciation against the interest differential leads to a substantially different picture (Figure 12.10). Then the observations line up much more in line with what is expected.

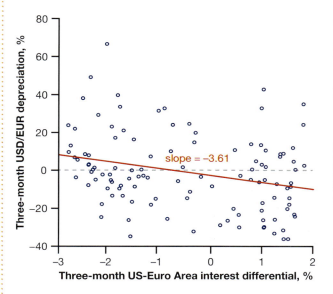

Figure 12.9 Depreciation vs. Interest Differential This graph shows the annualized 3-month depreciation of US dollar/euro exchange rate plotted against US/euro area 3-month interest rate differential, 1999M01–2008M06, in %.

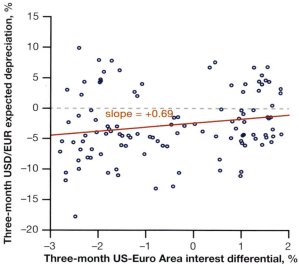

Figure 12.10 Expected Depreciation vs. Interest Differential This graph shows the annualized 3-month expected depreciation of US dollar/euro exchange rate plotted against US/euro area 3-month forward discount, in %.

The slope of the trend line is negative, rather than positive. This is not a finding specific to the dollar/euro exchange rate. It is also holds true for other currencies, and remains one of the most robust stylized facts in the literature until the global financial crisis.

There are several possible explanations for this surprising finding. First, it might be that the participants in the foreign exchange market have systematically wrong expectations about future exchange rate changes. This hypothesis is difficult to test, again because we do not directly observe expectations. However, several organizations survey individuals at major financial institutions involved in foreign exchange trading. Presumably these people's views are representative of the relevant market

The regression slope of 0.69, which statistically is indistinguishable from 1, is consistent with the view that investors do equalize expected returns – it is just that investors are not very good in making accurate forecasts. This finding also holds for other exchange rates, such as the Swiss franc and Norwegian krone.

An alternative explanation for the finding that interest rates wrongly predict the direction of exchange rate changes is that an **exchange risk premium** drives a wedge between exchange rate depreciation and interest rate differentials. This explanation is an alternative to the first one, but not incompatible with it. The idea here is that some currencies are more abundantly supplied than households and firms want to hold.

$$i - i^* - \Delta s^e_{+1} \equiv rp \qquad (12.3)$$

The "risk premium" is the excess return on securities denominated in a given currency, taking into account expected changes in currency values. When uncovered interest parity holds, the risk premium is 0. But there is no reason that this needs be true in the real world. It might be that each household and firm around the world holds a portfolio of assets that includes, for instance, US government bonds, Japanese government bonds, and German government bonds. If households and firms think of these bonds as imperfect substitutes, so that for instance they have a preference for Japanese bonds, then when the expected dollar return on German bonds exceeds that of Japanese bonds, not everyone will dump the Japanese bonds in favor of the German bonds. They might try to increase their holdings of those German bonds, but still retain a few of the Japanese bonds.

In a world where government bonds are not perfect substitutes, the expected excess return on, say, US bonds might be there to compensate for the fact that the US government has issued more bonds than households and firms around the world desire (how many are desired could depend on how the currency and interest rates move together, or on consumption), as well as the extent to which those actors are risk averse. If agents are risk neutral, then the risk premium should be zero, and uncovered interest parity holds.

12.5 MORE ON EXCHANGE RATES

An exchange rate, as the phrase is usually understood, is the price of one currency in terms of a single other currency. This is sometimes called a *bilateral* exchange rate. There are, however, other ways the concept of an exchange rate can be developed. Here we consider two.

The Value of a Currency

It would be nice to have a summary measure of the value of a specific currency, not in terms of any one other currency but generically, as it were. In Figure 12.1 we saw that in mid-2016, the dollar remained stable against the euro, even as it appreciated against the pound. Can we say anything about how the dollar was performing *on average* in 2016?

The natural move is to calculate the value of a currency against the value of a basket of currencies, to obtain what is called an **effective exchange rate index**. However, taking a simple average would not make sense. In constructing an index to track the dollar, should the currency of the Czech Republic, which has very little economic interaction with the United States, be weighted the same as the currency of Canada, the United States' largest trading partner? Clearly not. A typical practice is to weight the currencies in the basket by the amount of trade conducted between the home and foreign countries. For instance, if the US conducted 3/5 of its trade with the euro area, 2/5 with China, and 1/5 with the rest of the world, the weights would be 3/5 for the euro, 2/5 for the yuan, and 1/5 for all the other currencies combined. This is an example of a **trade weighted exchange rate index**, which is the most common version of an effective exchange rate index. Perhaps confusingly, these indices are usually expressed in value terms, i.e., the higher the value, the stronger the home currency. That is the reverse of the convention used for bilateral exchange rates.

Figure 12.11 presents the values of the currencies examined in Figure 12.1. Note that, in this case, the rise in each series is interpreted as an increase in the value of the indicated currency (i.e., German mark, euro, and Japanese yen).

Real Exchange Rates for Goods and Services

So far we have been discussing what are called nominal exchange rates, as they pertain to the tradeoff between paper assets (currencies). However, for economic transactions, we are often

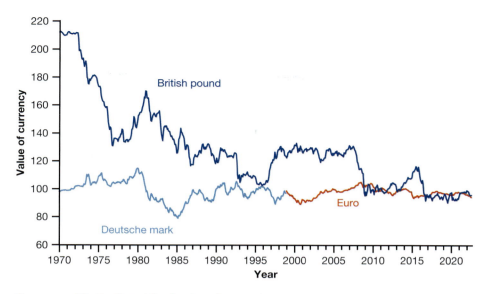

Figure 12.11 The Trade Weighted Value of Currencies This graph shows the exchange rates for the German mark (blue), the British pound (dark blue), and the euro (red) against a basket of currencies, weighted by trade flows and scaled so that all currencies are at 100 in 2010. Higher values indicate a stronger currency.

concerned with real magnitudes; is there a real counterpart to these nominal exchange rates? In fact, there is, conceptually. This is most easily understood by explicitly considering the units. Let us examine for instance the nominal exchange rate between the United States and the euro area, from the perspective of a US resident.

$$S\{USD/EUR\}$$

which is the number of dollars required to obtain a single euro. The **real exchange rate** measures the rate of exchange of real goods, rather than paper assets. Define the prices of widgets in the United States and euro area as:

$$P\{USD/US\ widget\}$$

$$P^*\{EUR/Euro\ area\ widget\}$$

The real exchange rate is thus given by:

$$q\{US\ widgets/Euro\ area\ widgets\} \equiv \left| \frac{S\{USD/EUR\} \times P^*\{EUR/Euro\ area\ widget\}}{P\{USD/US\ widget\}} \right| \quad (12.4)$$

In other words, the real exchange rate is the number of US widgets one has to give up to obtain a single foreign widget.

If US widgets traded off one for one with euro area widgets, then $q = 1$, and the price of a US widget in US dollars should equal the price of a euro area widget in US dollar terms.

$$P\{USD/US\ widget\} = S\{USD/EUR\} \times P^*\{EUR/Euro\ area\ widget\} \quad (12.5)$$

In a world where US and euro area widgets were exactly the same, and there were no impediments to trading those widgets across borders and prices could be easily adjusted, a reasonable value for *q would* be 1. However, in the real world there are barriers to trade and firms do not seem to adjust prices moment by moment; as a consequence, *q* might not always equal 1, although it would seem reasonable that, over time, *q* would gravitate toward that value.

In general, we do not care about widgets, but rather bundles of goods and services that are either produced or consumed. One measure of prices of bundles of goods purchased by consumers is the **consumer price index** (CPI). Figure 12.12 shows the bilateral real exchange rates corresponding to the nominal rates in Figure 12.1, deflated using CPIs. That means that this real exchange rate measures the number of American consumer bundles of goods and services that has to be given up in order to get – for instance in the dark blue line in the figure below – one British consumer bundle of goods.

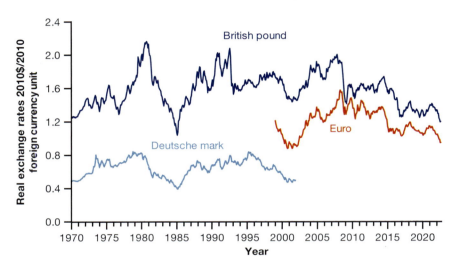

Figure 12.12 The Real Exchange Rate This graph shows the real exchange rates for Deutsche mark (blue), British pound (dark blue) and euro (red) against US dollar. The exchange rates are deflated using consumer price indices (2010=100). Higher values denote a weaker dollar against the foreign currency (a depreciation).

Each of these series can be interpreted as the number of bundles of US consumer goods and services required to purchase a single bundle of foreign consumer goods and services.

One interesting aspect of these series is that they exhibit less-pronounced trends than the corresponding series displayed in Figure 12.1. This contrast makes sense, given our discussion of *q*. Figure 12.1 pertains to the relative price of pieces of paper, namely currencies. Those can drift far apart as demand and supply of pieces of paper vary. Figure 12.12 depicts the relative price of bundles of goods and services. If an American bundle of goods and services is similar to a bundle of European goods and services, then they would seem to be far away from a one for one tradeoff.

The Real Value of a Currency

Finally, it is of interest to consider how the bilateral real exchange rates against the US dollar compare against the real trade weighted US dollar exchange rate. Figure 12.13 illustrates that the trade weighted real exchange rate (with up defined as depreciation) is a useful way to summarize overall movements in a currency.

12.5 MORE ON EXCHANGE RATES

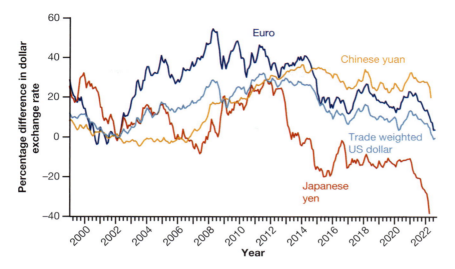

Figure 12.13 The Real Value of a Currency This graph shows the difference in dollar exchange rate for euro (dark blue), Japanese yen (red) and Chinese yuan (tan), and for basket of currencies (light blue), from March 2002, in %. The exchange rates are deflated using consumer price indices. Higher values denote a weaker dollar (a dollar depreciation).

When the US dollar/EUR real exchange rate depreciates, the trade weighted real exchange rate tends to depreciate as the United States has a large amount of trade with the euro area. However, the two series do not move in step because the Japanese yen (as well as the Chinese yuan) is moving in a different direction at various points in time.

APPLICATION   Argentina

Argentina has implemented a series of different exchange rate regimes in the past. In 1991, after experiencing bouts of high inflation, the country implemented what was called "the Convertibility Plan" which entailed a "hard peg" – each peso issued would have to be backed up by a dollar's worth of foreign exchange holdings, and the central bank committed to convert pesos into dollars and vice versa at a one-to-one rate.

The fact is that the peso exchange rate against the dollar did not ensure that the peso stayed at a constant value against other currencies. This is shown in Figure 12.14, where the peso/dollar exchange rate and the trade weighted peso exchange rate are shown.

Notice at that up until the end of 2001, the bilateral exchange rate is essentially constant, even as the peso gained value on average against other currencies.

Toward the end of 2001, as the economy weakened and withdrawals of pesos accelerated, Finance Minister Domingo Cavallo imposed restrictions on withdrawals. The unpopularity of this measure led to the fall of the government. The new government first devalued the peso by 29%, and then subsequently allowed the peso to freely float. By June of 2002, the peso had depreciated by 268% from the previous hard peg.

In the wake of the convertibility plan's end, inflation rose quickly. As a consequence, the real and nominal peso/dollar exchange rates diverged. This is shown in Figure 12.15.

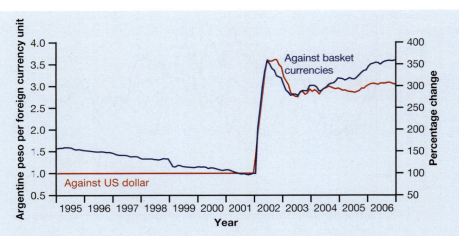

Figure 12.14 The Bilateral and Trade Weighted Argentine Exchange Rate This graph shows the Argentine peso/US dollar exchange rate (blue), and Argentine peso against a basket of currencies (red), normalized to value of 1 in 2001M12, and plotted on a log scale. A rise is a depreciation of the peso.

Notice that in a period of high inflation differentials – Argentine annual inflation was about 25% over the 2007–2017 period, as compared to less than 2% in the United States – the two exchange rate measures will diverge sharply. In this case, even as the nominal value of the peso was declining, the real value was increasing.

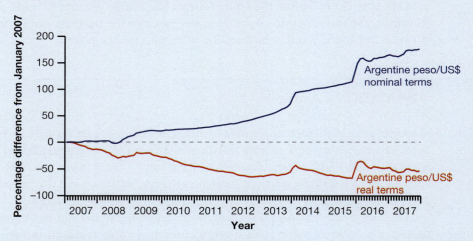

Figure 12.15 The Nominal vs. Real Exchange Rate This figure shows the difference from January 2007 of the Argentine peso/US dollar nominal exchange rate (blue), and real exchange rate (red). A rise is a depreciation of the peso.

CONCLUSION

There are many different exchange rates pertaining to different relative prices. The nominal bilateral exchange rate is the relative price of two currencies, specifically how many units of the home currency necessary to acquire one unit of the foreign one. The real bilateral exchange rate is the relative price of two bundles of goods and, analogously to the nominal rate, the number of bundles of home goods necessary to obtain one of the foreign bundles.

The nominal effective exchange rate is usually expressed as the value of a home currency against several other currencies; the real effective exchange rate is the inflation-adjusted version of the nominal one. The weights for effective exchange rates are typically based on the importance in terms of trade. The greater the extent of the trade with a given country, the heavier the weight ascribed to that country's currency.

Institutionally, nominal exchange rates are determined in a market in foreign exchange, where a limited number of large international banks bid for and offer to sell currencies. Each day, something around $5.7 trillion in foreign currencies are traded. The most-often traded currency pair is the US dollar–euro, with the second being the US dollar–yen.

SUMMARY

1. The nominal exchange rate is the price of foreign currency, in terms of home currency.
2. Under a floating exchange rate regime, supply and demand determine the price. Under a fixed exchange rate regime, the central bank must buy and sell the currency in order keep its relative price at the official exchange rate.
3. Under a floating (fixed) rate regime, a rise in the price is called a depreciation (devaluation), while a fall is an appreciation (revaluation).
4. Most exchange rate regimes in existence incorporate intermediate degrees of flexibility.
5. The forward exchange rate is the rate one can contract in the present for a trade of currencies in the future.
6. The forward and the current (or spot) exchange rate are linked to interest rates by covered interest parity, when there are no barriers to financial capital flows.
7. In theory, if traders did not care about risk, and there were no barriers to financial capital flows, expected returns in one country would equal those in another country.
8. The real exchange rate is the relative price of a bundle of foreign goods, in terms of bundles of home goods.
9. The effective exchange rate index is the value of a currency relative to a bundle of foreign currencies, where the weights are typically based on trade flows.

KEY CONCEPTS

Appreciation, page 261
Capital controls, page 268
Covered interest parity, page 268
Depreciation, page 260
Effective exchange rate index, page 270
Exchange rate, page 256
Exchange rate peg, page 261
Exchange risk premium, page 269
Fixed exchange rate regime, page 261
Floating exchange rate regime, page 260

Forward exchange rate, page 260
International currency, page 258
No arbitrage profits condition, page 267
Over the counter, page 257
Real exchange rate, page 271
Spot exchange rate, page 260
Trade weighted exchange rate index, page 270
Uncovered interest parity, page 267

REVIEW QUESTIONS

1. What is the spot exchange rate?
2. Who trades in foreign currency?
3. How large is the foreign exchange market?
4. What is the most commonly used currency in foreign exchange trading?
5. What currencies do central banks hold as foreign currency?
6. What determines the value of a currency?
7. Is a depreciation of a currency a gain or loss in value?
8. When a currency is devalued, is the currency value lower or higher?
9. What does the central bank have to commit to in order to peg an exchange rate at a certain value?
10. What is a forward exchange rate?
11. What is covered interest parity?
12. What is uncovered interest parity?
13. What is a real exchange rate?
14. What is an effective exchange rate, and is it different from a trade weighted exchange rate?

EXERCISES

1. *The foreign exchange market.* Using a supply and demand diagram, and defining the United States as the home country and either the Philippines or Japan as the foreign, show what happens in the following situations (assuming a floating exchange rate regime).
    a. United States demand for Japanese autos increases.
    b. Japanese demand for American real estate decreases.
    c. Remittances from Filipino citizens in the United States back to the Philippines increase (use a graph of the US dollar/Philippine Peso market).
2. *An exchange rate peg in operation.*
    a. Draw a diagram of the foreign exchange market from the perspective of Jordan. Assume the relevant foreign currency is the US dollar. Show the floating market equilibrium.
    b. Assume the Jordanian monetary authorities peg their currency at a value stronger than the floating market equilibrium. Show the excess supply or demand for foreign currency.
    c. What does the central bank have to do in order to sustain the peg? Show that action in the graph.
    d. Suppose Jordan's central bank runs out of US dollars. What can the central bank do?
3. *Tracking exchange rates.* Using the St. Louis Fed FRED utility (https://fred.stlouisfed.org), answer the following questions.
    a. Calculate the percentage change (depreciation) of the US dollar against the euro over the prior year.
    b. From the perspective of a resident of the euro area, calculate the percentage change (depreciation) of the euro against the US dollar. Is this number the exact opposite of your answer to part a?

EXERCISES

c. How many US dollars does it take to buy a single Canadian dollar now? How many did it take a year ago? Has the US dollar appreciated or depreciated against the Canadian dollar?
d. What is the exchange rate of euros for Canadian dollars, i.e., how many euros does it take to purchase a single Canadian dollar?

4. *Nominal vs. real exchange rates.* Consider the following data on the dollar/pound exchange rate, and the consumer price indexes (CPI's) in the United States and the United Kingdom. The CPIs are normalized to equal 1.00 in 1985.

Year	USD/GBP	CPI US	CPI UK
1983	1.5159	0.926	0.914
1984	1.3368	0.966	0.953
1985	1.2974	1.000	1.000
1986	1.4677	1.019	1.033
1987	1.6398	1.056	1.066
1988	1.7813	1.099	1.107
1989	1.6382	1.152	1.165
1990	1.7841	1.215	1.246
1991	1.7674	1.266	1.340
1992	1.7663	1.304	1.397
1993	1.5016	1.343	1.432

a. Calculate the nominal rate of depreciation of the US dollar against the pound between 1989 and 1992.
b. Calculate the real exchange rate for 1989 and 1992, using the CPI's for the United States and the UK.
c. Calculate the real rate of depreciation of the US dollar against the pound between 1982 and 1992.

5. *Interest parity conditions.* Using the data at https://www.reuters.com/markets/rates-bonds/ answer the following questions (use Germany for euro area).
a. Using the 3-month interest rates, and assuming uncovered interest parity holds, calculate the expected change in the dollar/euro exchange rate over the next three months. Be sure to state what the rate will be, in annualized terms.
b. Considering the actual experience over the 1999–2010 period, what is actual depreciation you actually expect for the dollar/euro exchange rate, on an annualized basis?
c. Assume covered interest parity holds. What is the forward rate today for a trade three months hence?
d. Using ten-year bonds, calculate the implied annual change in the dollar/pound exchange rate, over the next ten years.

6. *Effective exchange rate index.* Suppose country X conducts a quarter of its trade with country Y and three quarters with country Z.
   a. Suppose X's currency holds steady against Y's currency but appreciates by 10% against Z's. What is the change in the trade weighted exchange rate index?
   b. Suppose X's currency depreciates by 10% against Y's currency but appreciates by 10% against Z's. What is the change in the trade weighted exchange rate index?
   c. Suppose that in part b, the inflation rate is 10% higher in X than in either Y or Z. What is the change in the real trade weighted exchange rate index?

RECOMMENDED RESOURCES

Menzie Chinn, "A Primer on Real Effective Exchange Rates: Determinants, Overvaluation, Trade Flows and Competitive Devaluations," *Open Economies Review* 17(1) (2006): 115–143.

Menzie Chinn and Jeffrey Frankel, "Will the Euro Eventually Surpass the Dollar as Leading International Reserve Currency?" in R. Clarida (ed.), *G7 Current Account Imbalances: Sustainability and Adjustment* (Chicago, IL: University of Chicago Press, 2007): 285–322.

Jeffrey Frankel and Kenneth Froot, "Using Survey Data to Test Standard Propositions Regarding Exchange Rate Expectations," *American Economic Review* 7(1) (1987): 133–153.

Carmen M. Reinhart and Kenneth S. Rogoff, "The Modern History of Exchange Rate Arrangements: A Reinterpretation," *The Quarterly Journal of Economics* 119, 1 (2004): 1–48.

CHAPTER 13

Spending and Income Determination in the Short Run

LEARNING OBJECTIVES

In this chapter, we learn about:
- how to model desired spending
- how spending attains equilibrium in the short run
- how changes in government spending and taxes affect income
- how the trade deficit responds to changes in desired spending
- how a change in one country's output affects the output levels of trading partner countries

INTRODUCTION

In a 2008 interview on 'Meet the Press' on US television, then President-elect Barack Obama, while discussing his intention to implement a **stimulus** plan to get the economy moving, qualified that 'things are going to get worse before they get better.' Things did indeed get worse. By the last quarter of 2008, the US economy was shrinking at an annual rate of 8%, as it sank into its deepest and longest recession since the Great Depression. In Figure 13.1, the blue line shows the drastic decline in the growth rate. Household consumption was trending downward at a rate of nearly 5% per year, business investment in factories and equipment was falling at a rate of 21% per year, and new-home construction was plummeting by a disastrous annual rate of 33%. Clearly, if something could be done, it should be, and swiftly.

In January 2009, at the urging of President-elect Obama, the US Congress passed legislation that provided for tax cuts and government spending equal to about 2% of GDP in 2009 (the red line in Figure 13.1). Boosted by the stimulus package, economic growth picked up in the latter half of 2009, rising into positive territory in the second quarter. According to the Congressional Budget Office, the stimulus package raised GDP between 0.7% and 4.1%, above what it would have been in 2010 in the absence of the stimulus, and unemployment was 0.4–1.8 percentage points lower.

This episode highlights several important questions. First, why do large drops in the demand for goods and services occur in the first place? Second, how and why do such declines result in corresponding declines in the production of goods and services, as well as the income received by workers and the owners of firms? Third, why does a given decline in spending on building and equipping new factories and constructing new houses get

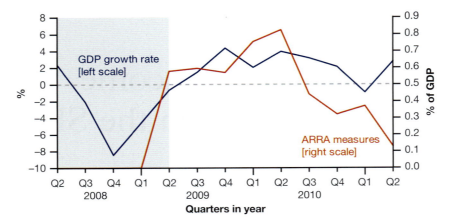

Figure 13.1 Growth and Stimulus This figure shows the quarter-on-quarter growth rate of real GDP annualized as a percentage (blue, left scale), and US Recovery and Reinvestment Act (ARRA) measures expressed as a percentage share of GDP (red, right scale). Recession dates are shaded gray.
Source: Bureau of Economic Analysis.

magnified into a correspondingly larger drop in overall production? And, finally, why would government spending and tax cuts be a means of counteracting economic downturns?

In order to answer these questions, we develop a framework to show how all these parts – demand, production, and income – fit together, with other factors such as the money supply, interest rates, and inflation. The process of building this framework proceeds in a series of steps.

To begin with, we examine the real side of the economy and focus on how the demand side acts as a driver of output. We set the financial sector aside for now; that is, we do not model explicitly the relationship between saving and borrowing as mediated by the market in bonds and other securities. However, our model will provide for the role of government policy in setting exchange rates. Building on this framework, we bring the financial sector into the picture in Chapters 14 and 15, to develop a more realistic depiction of the economy. In Chapter 16, we will further relax the assumption that only demand determines output, by modeling the role of the supply side of the economy – its productive capacity, represented by the available labor force, capital stock, and technology.

As we have done in earlier chapters, in this chapter we start with the analysis of a single economy, describing in detail how consumption and imports depend on income. We discuss what **equilibrium** looks like in such an economy. Then we examine the channels by which changes in government spending and tax policy affect the level of output. We will also introduce a role for exchange rates, which were explained in Chapter 12. Finally, we allow for interactions between two countries in order to highlight how economic effects can spill over borders, and how those effects can also "spill back." In this way, we illustrate one aspect of economic interdependence in the global economy.

13.1 EQUILIBRIUM OUTPUT AND INCOME DETERMINATION: THE "KEYNESIAN CROSS"

We begin with a simple model in which output is determined only by demand, the Keynesian cross model. This model is sufficient to illustrate several concepts: behavioral relationships,

Aggregate Demand

The identity $Y \equiv C + I + G + CA$, introduced in Chapter 11, expresses the fact that on the side of the economy where supply arises, namely the production side, Y represents output and is defined as the sum $C + I + G + CA$. But Y also represents household income, which is earned mostly by providing the factors of production (labor, etc.), and on the demand side in that income determines how much households are willing to spend on goods and services. Since their spending is where C, consumption expenditures, comes from and also determines the imports component of CA, on the demand side the sum $C + I + G + CA$ is a function of Y.

To investigate how the supply- and demand-side relationships lead to equilibrium, we break the identity $Y \equiv C + I + G + CA$ apart and introduce a new variable, AD, meaning **aggregate demand**:

$$AD = C + I + G + \underbrace{X - IM}_{\substack{\text{trade balance} \\ \text{or} \\ \text{net exports}}} \tag{13.1}$$

This equation defines total demand as the sum of planned or desired consumption, investment, government spending, and exports minus imports. For simplicity, we have assumed that in the definition $CA = X - IM + F + V$, the last two terms, net foreign income and transfers, are zero.

For the supply side, we now write the equation that describes what happens when production output matches aggregate demand:

$$Y = AD \tag{13.2}$$

Unlike equation (13.1), this equation is not an identity, because it is possible for production to get out of synch with demand. The key assumption we rely on to explain equilibrium is that the total amount of goods and services demanded determines the amount of goods and services produced: factories ramp up production to meet higher demand, and they cut production when demand falls. Equation (13.2) specifies the equilibrium condition under which production matches demand.

While this model is not completely realistic, particularly in describing the behavior of the economy over the longer term, it serves as a useful starting point. Moreover, in the short run – over the course of a few months or a year – the assumption that firms respond to changes in demand for their goods and services mostly by changing production, rather than by changing prices, is not too far from reality. This approach, involving fixed prices, is sometimes termed 'Keynesian,' after the British economist John Maynard Keynes, who stressed, among other factors, the rigidity of wages and prices. The assumption of fixed prices contrasts strongly with the classical model, wherein wages and prices were modeled as perfectly flexible, so that aggregate demand only fluctuated when production capacity changed, rather than demand.

Demand as a Function of Income

Let us now describe the behavior of each of the components of aggregate demand. Several of these, namely I, G, and initially X, we will represent as **exogenous variables**, meaning that any change in their value is due to influences that lie outside the model. A change in government spending, for instance, is assumed to be driven by policy decisions (e.g., military spending) that are not predictably related to other macroeconomic variables. When we need to identify a variable as *given* in this manner, though not *fixed*, we will place an bar above it. So, the amount of investment (I) in business plant and equipment, residential structures, and inventories of goods is $\overline{I}$; government spending on goods and services is $\overline{G}$; and exports to the rest of the world is (for now) $\overline{X}$.

That leaves C and IM. These variables are called **endogenous**, meaning that they depend on other variables in the model. First, consider the **consumption function**, which describes the behavioral relationship between households' income and their consumption of goods and services:

$$C = \underbrace{\overline{C}}_{\text{autonomous consumption}} + c(Y - \overline{T}) \tag{13.3}$$

On the right side, $\overline{C}$ is a constant term representing a baseline consumption level that does not vary with income. Think of winter heating costs and other unavoidable expenses for which households will, if necessary, dip into their savings. Spending that occurs regardless of other factors is sometimes called **autonomous spending**, so here $\overline{C}$ is called autonomous consumption.

A **parameter** quantifies how strongly one variable affects another. In equation (13.3), the quantity $Y - \overline{T}$ models disposable income very simply as total income minus a **lump-sum tax**. The parameter c, called the **marginal propensity to consume**, indicates the extent to which disposable income affects consumption, C. Consumers increase their spending by c units for every unit of increase in disposable income.

While equation (13.3) appears to express a complicated process in an overly simple equation, it is a surprisingly good approximation to the real world behavior of consumers. Economic models typically assume that the marginal propensity to consume is greater than zero but less than 1. A reasonable value would be $c = 0.80$, meaning that when disposable income rises by 1 dollar, consumption rises by 80 cents.

Finally, consider imports. Again keeping things simple, we assume that exchange rates remain constant, so that imports only depend on domestic income:

$$IM = \underbrace{\overline{IM}}_{\text{autonomous imports}} + mY \tag{13.4}$$

Imports, IM, rise because as income Y rises, consumption also rises, and some of that consumption falls upon imported goods. The parameter m is the **marginal propensity to import**; it describes the change in imports for a one-unit change in income. The standard assumption is that m is greater than zero but less than c. We might suppose that $m = 0.20$; then when income rises by 1 dollar, imports rise by 20 cents.

The Economy in Equilibrium

Pulling together everything else we have established thus far, we obtain the following description of an economy in equilibrium:

13.1 EQUILIBRIUM OUTPUT AND INCOME DETERMINATION: THE "KEYNESIAN CROSS"

$$\underbrace{Y = AD}_{\text{equilibrium condition}} \equiv \underbrace{\overline{C} + c(Y - \overline{T})}_{\text{consumption}} + \underbrace{\overline{I}}_{\text{investment}} + \underbrace{\overline{G}}_{\text{government}} + \underbrace{\overline{X}}_{\text{exports}} - \underbrace{(\overline{IM} + mY)}_{\text{imports}} \quad (13.5)$$

Expanding the right side and collecting terms, we obtain

$$\underbrace{Y = AD}_{\text{equilibrium condition}} \equiv (\overline{C} - c\overline{T} + \overline{I} + \overline{G} + \overline{X} - \overline{IM}) + (c - m)Y \quad (13.6)$$

The equilibrium condition on the left side of equation (13.6) and the identity on the right side are both linear equations relating Y and AD, and therefore it is possible to describe equilibrium graphically as the intersection point of two lines. We will do that in a moment. Meanwhile, however, notice that setting Y on the left equal to the sum on the right produces a third equation, with Y as its only endogenous variable. We can therefore solve that third equation for Y_0, the equilibrium value of income Y:

$$Y_0 = \underbrace{\left(\frac{1}{1 - c + m}\right)}_{\substack{\text{multiplier} \\ \equiv \overline{\alpha}}} \underbrace{[\overline{C} - c\overline{T} + \overline{I} + \overline{G} + \overline{X} - \overline{IM}]}_{\substack{\text{autonomous} \\ \text{domestic} \\ \text{spending} \\ \equiv \overline{A}}} \quad (13.7)$$

$\overline{A}$ is the total amount of autonomous spending by domestic residents (on all final goods and services, including imports). $\overline{A} + \overline{X} - \overline{IM}$ incorporates accounting for that part of autonomous domestic spending associated with trade with the rest of the world. Equation (13.7) states that equilibrium income is a multiple of the adjusted amount.

The fraction denoted by $\overline{\alpha}$ is **the multiplier** that determines how strongly the equilibrium level of income goes up in response to an increase in autonomous spending. From the assumptions $0 < c < 1$ and $0 < m < c$, it follows that $\overline{\alpha} > 1$. Also notice that **lump-sum taxes** contribute in a negative fashion: the higher lump-sum taxes go, the lower equilibrium income goes, all else being equal.

The Keynesian Cross

Now to the graphical depiction of equation (13.6). In Figure 13.2, aggregate demand is on the vertical axis, and income (equal to GDP) is on the horizontal axis. The 45-degree line represents equation (13.2), while the flatter line represents the right side of equation (13.5). Together, the two lines form what is called the **Keynesian Cross**; their intersection point marks the equilibrium income level.

Expanding the right side of equation (13.5) produces the Y-terms cY and $-mY$, which means that the slope of the aggregate demand curve is $c - m$. Because $m < c$, the slope is positive, and so the equilibrium income Y_0 is greater than the AD-axis

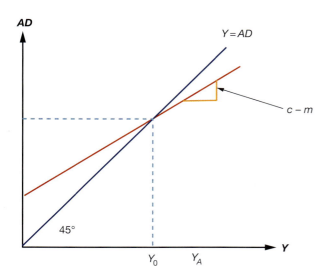

Figure 13.2 The Keynesian Cross This diagram shows the aggregate demand curve and equilibrium.

intercept, $\overline{A} + \overline{X} - \overline{IM}$. Each dollar of autonomous spending results in more than a dollar's worth of income in equilibrium. This effect can be viewed as a consequence of resources circulating through the economy, not once but repeatedly, from consumers to producers in the form of spending, then back to consumers in the form of income, and so on.

We can model this cycle using equation (13.6). Set Y to zero on the right side, use non-zero $\overline{A} + \overline{X} - \overline{IM}$ to evaluate Y on the left side, feed the resulting value back in as Y on the right side, and repeat *ad infinitum*. Each iteration adds another term to this infinite sum:

$$Y = (\overline{A} + \overline{X} - \overline{IM}) + (c - m)(\overline{A} + \overline{X} - \overline{IM}) + (c - m)^2(\overline{A} + \overline{X} - \overline{IM}) \cdots \quad (13.8)$$

You may recognize this as an infinite geometric series. Because our assumptions about c and m imply that $0 < c - m < 1$, the series converges to the expression on the right side of equation (13.7). The multiplying effect of circulation and re-circulation of autonomous spending can have fairly dramatic consequences. Using our earlier rough estimates of $c = 0.80$ and $m = 0.20$, we find that \$1,000 of autonomous spending leads, re equation (13.7), to \$2,500 worth of economic output. It is no wonder that some economists like government policies aimed at increasing autonomous spending. We will consider the consequences of such policy moves in the next section.

Compared to equation (13.7), the graphical, Keynesian Cross analysis has the advantage that it facilitates investigation of what happens if the economy drifts out of equilibrium. Suppose production exceeds aggregate demand, $Y_A > AD$, as shown in Figure 13.3. Then goods enter the inventory from production faster than they exit through consumption, and inventories grow above desired levels. The excess production is shown by the large blue arrow.

Since storage costs money and ties up funds in the form of purchased materials, firms will seek to reduce inventory by cutting back on production (the large red arrow). As production falls, income falls. However, production remains higher than aggregate demand, so unintended inventory accumulation (again denoted by a blue arrow) continues. Hence, firms decrease production again (another red arrow).

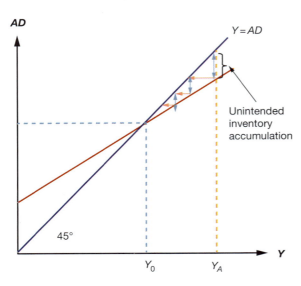

Figure 13.3 Adjustment to Equilibrium This diagram shows the adjustment to equilibrium when output is higher than aggregate demand. Starting at output and income Y_A, production exceeds demand, so inventories build up. Firms cut back production, so income falls and demand falls further. Inventories keep on accumulating but at a slower pace, until output and income fall to match demand.

This process continues, in smaller and smaller increments. Only when income equals aggregate demand ($Y = AD$) will there be no more unintended inventory accumulation. A similar process on the left side has producers ramping up production in response to inventories that are too low, putting stocks at risk of running out, leading to lost sales.

13.2 HOW DO GOVERNMENT SPENDING AND TAXES AFFECT INCOME?

With our model in hand, we are now able to describe how a change in one (exogenous) variable affects another variable. In particular, we can see how income responds to changes in the variables the government controls. It also allows one to examine the behavior of endogenous variables in pairs – when they move in the same direction and when they move in opposite directions.

The Effects of Government Spending

To understand how a change in autonomous spending affects equilibrium income, think about a change of income (ΔY) as being attributable to changes in each of those autonomous spending components. From equation (13.7),

$$\Delta Y = \bar{\alpha}[\Delta A + \Delta X - \Delta IM] \tag{13.9}$$

This is a 'total differential,' holding $\bar{\alpha}$ constant. This indicates that any change in GDP has to be attributable to a change in one or more of the autonomous components of spending. If the only spending component that changes is government spending, then ΔA becomes ΔG, and ΔX and ΔIM zero out

$$\Delta Y = \bar{\alpha}\Delta G \tag{13.10}$$

A change in government spending by 1 dollar leads to an $\bar{\alpha}$-dollar increase in income. This result can be interpreted graphically. In Figure 13.4, the increase in government spending shifts the aggregate demand curve upward by an amount ΔG. The new equilibrium level of income is Y_1.

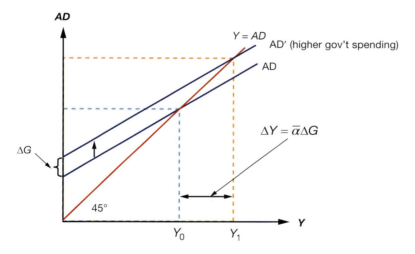

Figure 13.4 The Response to a Government Spending Increase This diagram shows the change in autonomous spending which shifts up the aggregate demand curve, and resulting in an increase in Y.

As the graph illustrates, the increase in GDP, $\Delta Y = Y_1 - Y_0$, is larger than the increase in government spending, because $\bar{\alpha} > 1$. To restate the point in different form,

$$\frac{\Delta Y}{\Delta G} = \bar{\alpha} \equiv \frac{1}{1 - c + m} > 1 \tag{13.11}$$

In other words, the change in GDP for a dollar change in government spending on goods and services is greater than 1. For this reason, $\bar{\alpha}$ is often called the **multiplier for government spending.**

Notice that c and m represent opposing influences on ΔY, because a larger c increases $\bar{\alpha}$, while a larger m decreases it. Consider an increase in government spending of 1 dollar. That

1 dollar adds to GDP immediately, by increasing the G component. From there, the dollar circulates back to those providing labor and other factors of production, and now the dollar is ready to be spent again, this time by the private sector. Whatever part of that dollar is spent on domestically produced final goods contributes to C, further boosting GDP. By contrast, whatever part of the dollar is spent on foreign imports is in effect taken out of circulation, since only a small fraction of it is likely to return via foreign purchases of exports. In that sense, spending on imported goods 'leaks out' of the economy.

The Impact of Taxes

Compared to government spending, taxes have the reverse effect: they reduce output. But in contrast to government spending, which directly increases GDP, taxes increase consumption only indirectly. The direct effect is on disposable income, which *then* causes changes in consumption.

To see the impact of an increase in taxes, ΔT, consider Figure 13.5. As in our discussion of government spending, income starts out at Y_0 and the change ΔY is obtained from equation (13.9). This time, however, from equation (13.7) the nonzero component of autonomous spending, $\Delta A \equiv \Delta C - c\Delta T + \Delta I + \Delta G$, is $-c\Delta T$, and instead of equations (13.10) and (13.11), we get

$$\Delta Y = \overline{\alpha}(-c\Delta T) \tag{13.12}$$

Because the rise in taxes decreases disposable income, $Y - \overline{T}$, consumption falls, and so the aggregate demand curve shifts down. As the aggregate demand curve shifts down, equilibrium income declines to Y_1.

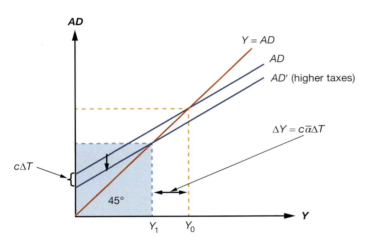

Figure 13.5 The Response to an Increase in Taxes This diagram shows the decrease in autonomous spending as a consequence of the increase in lump sum taxes. The shift down in aggregate demand then results in a change in income.

The tax-hike counterpart to equation (13.11) is

$$\frac{\Delta Y}{\Delta T} = -c\overline{\alpha} \equiv -\frac{c}{1 - c + m} \tag{13.13}$$

Again the total impact on output is a result of the recirculation, only this time it is negative. The higher taxes reduce disposable income, causing a reduction in consumption (part of aggregate demand). That reduction in consumption causes further reductions in production and hence income, leading to more reductions in consumption.

Given that an increase in government spending boosts income, Y, it is no big surprise that an increase in lump-sum taxes reduces income. Accordingly, a lump-sum tax cut will increase income. However, the c in the numerator of equation (13.13) indicates that a dollar's decrease in taxes yields a *smaller impact* than a dollar's increase in government spending.

The reason the magnitudes are not the same is related to how each policy affects income. A dollar's worth of government spending immediately boosts GDP, to the tune of one full dollar (of G). A dollar's worth of tax cuts increases disposable income – but that is not the same as GDP. The rise in disposable income only induces a c dollar increase in GDP

(c dollars of C). In short, a dollar's worth of increased government spending on goods and services has a bigger impact on GDP than a dollar's worth of tax cuts.

Even more interestingly, once the leakage effect of spending on imports is accounted for, it is not necessarily the case that a dollar's worth of tax cuts produces even a full dollar's worth of increase in income. Suppose that in equation (13.13), c equals 0.60 instead of 0.80, and m equals 0.40 instead of 0.20. Then $-c\bar{a} = 0.75$, which means that a dollar's worth of tax cuts, only boosts economic output by 75 cents.

It follows from our admittedly highly simplified analysis that if the government is prepared to let its **budget balance**, $\overline{T} - \overline{G}$, go negative for a while in order to jump-start the economy, the government will get more benefit from the same-size deficit by increasing spending $\overline{G}$ than by a cutting taxes $\overline{T}$ by the same amount. The result that one can increase economic activity even while keeping the budget deficit constant is called the balanced budget multiplier.

13.3 HOW ARE THE GOVERNMENT BUDGET AND TRADE BALANCES RELATED?

Returning to our earlier discussion in Chapter 11 of the twin deficits, we can now examine the link between government spending and tax policies on the one hand and developments in the external accounts on the other. In particular, one sometimes hears the argument that running a budget deficit causes a trade deficit. This certainly seems to have been the case during the mid-1980s, and – to a lesser extent – during the 2000s, as shown in Figure 13.6.

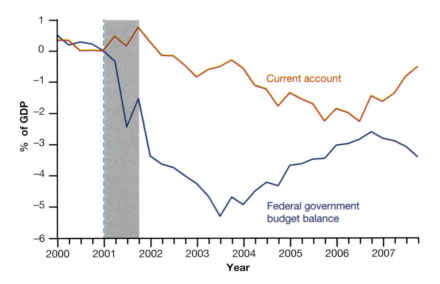

Figure 13.6 Budget and Current Account Deficits This figure shows the change in the percentage point current account to GDP share (red) from the first quarter of 2001, and the change in the percentage point Federal government budget balance to GDP share (blue) from the first quarter of 2001.
Source: BEA.

The blue line drops at the start of the George W. Bush Administration. A year later, the current account also declines, and continues to decline, even after the budget balance starts to improve. Only in 2006, with a lag, does the current account start improving.

To examine why this pattern makes sense, let us show algebraically what happens to the **trade balance** and the government budget balance in response to changes in government spending. Take the trade balance, also known as net exports, the difference between exports and imports:

$$TB = \overline{X} - IM = \overline{X} - (\overline{IM} + mY) \tag{13.14}$$

When income rises then, holding all else constant, the trade balance worsens. (Obviously, changes in foreign consumption of home goods, $\overline{X}$, and in autonomous spending on foreign goods, $\overline{IM}$, also have an impact, but we will hold those constant.) As we showed in the last section, income is positively influenced by government spending. Hence, an increase in government spending causes a deterioration in the trade balance, holding everything else constant, because the resulting higher income brings with it higher imports:

$$\Delta TB = -m\underbrace{\overline{\alpha}\Delta G}_{=\Delta Y} < 0 \tag{13.15}$$

What about the budget balance? We defined this in the last section as government tax revenue minus government expenditures:

$$BuS = \overline{T} - \overline{G} \tag{13.16}$$

Clearly an increase in government spending reduces the budget balance or increases the budget deficit:

$$\Delta BuS = -\Delta G < 0 \tag{13.17}$$

To summarize the impact on the two balances from changes in government spending: an increase in government spending causes a deterioration in both the trade and budget balances. This is the "causal" interpretation of the twin deficits hypothesis.

Notice that if taxes depended on income (perhaps because there was an income tax) and were modeled as $T = \overline{T} + tY$, then if *investment*, rather than government spending, were to increase exogenously, this would send the two balances in opposite directions: the positive (ΔI) would produce a positive ΔY, and then $\Delta TB = -m\Delta Y$ would still be negative but $\Delta Bus = t\Delta Y$ would be positive. Thus, the twin deficits phenomenon is not an iron law. The correlations between these two deficits depends on which variables are changing exogenously. Economists call these exogenous changes to variables "**shocks**."

During the 1990s, the budget balance went into surplus, while the current account balance went very negative. From the accounting perspective discussed in Chapter 11, the only way this could happen is if the private saving–investment balance went very negative. However, that is not a causal explanation. In fact, there *was* a boom in investment, while at the same time personal saving declined. In the context of the model developed in this chapter, there was a positive shock to investment (an increase in $\overline{I}$) and, for good measure, a positive shock to consumption (an increase in $\overline{C}$) that had similar effects.

13.4 THE ROLE OF THE REAL EXCHANGE RATE

In Chapter 12, we introduced the concepts of a real exchange rate – the nominal exchange rate between two countries, adjusted by the respective price levels. The real exchange rate can also be described as the relative price of a bundle of goods produced in the foreign country, in terms of the same bundle produced in the home country. From the perspective of the United

13.4 THE ROLE OF THE REAL EXCHANGE RATE

States, the real exchange rate is the number of US bundles required to purchase one foreign bundle. As this number rises, US goods become relatively cheaper, thus affecting the desirability of US exports and imports.

Exchange Rate Effects

Consider the following example: US tractors start out trading one-for-one for Chinese tractors. Then the US dollar depreciates against the Chinese yuan by 50%, meaning that a yuan costs 50% more dollars than before. However, the dollar price of US tractors remains the same, and the yuan price of Chinese tractors remains the same. At this point, the same amount of money, exchanged as needed, will buy either two-thirds of a Chinese tractor or a whole US tractor. With this new tradeoff, both US and Chinese buyers will tend to buy more US tractors and fewer Chinese ones. US tractor exports to China will increase, and US imports of Chinese tractors will decrease.

We can incorporate this important factor into our model by making exports and imports depend on the real exchange rate. For imports:

$$IM = \overline{IM} + mY - nq \tag{13.18}$$

The parameter n is the sensitivity of imports to the real exchange rate, q. As q rises, it takes more units of the home good to buy a single unit of the foreign good. When home goods become relatively cheaper in this way, the quantity of imports declines.

Exports, instead of being a fixed amount, are now dependent on the real exchange rate just as imports are.

$$X = \overline{X} + vq \tag{13.19}$$

Here v is the sensitivity of exports to the real exchange rate. When q rises, foreign goods become more expensive. The home country's exports thus become more attractive to foreigners, and the quantity of exports rises.

We will treat q as a variable whose value is set by government policy and can be changed by the government when it decides to do so. The government can "peg" the exchange rate, as is described in Chapter 12, by intervening in the foreign exchange market. This is discussed further in Chapter 14. In other words, we treat the real exchange rate as an exogenous variable. We denote this fact with an overbar, $\bar{q}$.

Solving for the equilibrium income, as we did to obtain equation (13.7) but now using the new expressions for imports and exports, leads to the following result:

$$Y_0 = \bar{\alpha}[\overline{A} + \overline{X} - \overline{IM} + (n+v)\bar{q}] \tag{13.20}$$

Now the equilibrium income is a multiple of total autonomous spending *plus* a constant times the real exchange rate. The autonomous-spending component is familiar; the higher its level, the higher the equilibrium level of income. The second component is new to this model. Changes in real exchange rates (which equal changes in the nominal rates when the price levels are fixed) affect the international components of aggregate demand, namely exports and imports.

To analyze the effect of changes in autonomous spending or exchange rates on equilibrium income, we once again consider our equation for Y_0 and relate a change on the left side to changes on the right side:

$$\Delta Y = \bar{\alpha}[\Delta A + \Delta X - \Delta IM + (n+v)\Delta q] \tag{13.21}$$

If, now, the real exchange rate is the only variable allowed to change, then all the other Δ terms drop out and we can relate the change in Y to the change in q that caused it:

$$\frac{\Delta Y}{\Delta q} = \bar{a}(n+v) > 0 \qquad (13.22)$$

A devaluation of the domestic currency causes an increase in GDP. The size depends on the parameters; when the currency is devalued by one unit, imports decrease by n dollars and exports increase by v dollars. The combined increase in net exports is scaled by multiplier $\bar{a}$.

If, as we are assuming, the government controls the exchange rate, then the government can boost the economy by lowering the currency's real value, as shown in Figure 13.7.

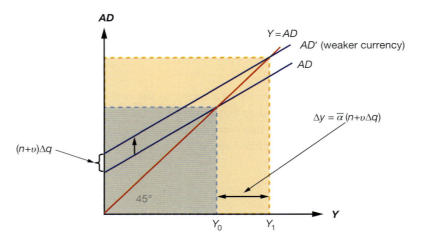

Figure 13.7 The Response to Devaluation This diagram shows the change in autonomous net exports resulting from a devaluation, and the consequent a change in income.

As the example of Chinese-made and US-made tractors illustrated, a rise in q makes for increased purchases of domestically produced goods. The additional goods have to be produced, and the domestic factors of production (labor, capital) have to be paid for. The higher income results in higher consumption, and now the multiplying cycle kicks in.

The Exchange Rate and the Trade Balance

Now that we have introduced a role for the real exchange rate, we can talk fruitfully about different ways of affecting the trade balance. In brief, one can improve the trade balance either by reducing income (and hence reducing imports) or by letting the currency lose value – and hence increasing exports and reducing imports. These two ways of reducing a trade deficit (or improving a trade surplus) are called the **expenditure reduction** and **expenditure switching** approaches.

To show the workings of the expenditure reduction versus expenditure switching approaches, consider again the formal definition of the trade balance, using the revised formulas for exports and imports:

13.4 THE ROLE OF THE REAL EXCHANGE RATE

$$TB = (\overline{X} + v\overline{q}) - (\overline{IM} + mY - n\overline{q}) \tag{13.23}$$

Suppose policymakers face a trade deficit they consider too large. How could they respond? We know from Section 13.3 that they could cut government spending, which would reduce income Y, which would reduce imports and thus reduce the trade deficit. This is the expenditure reduction route. However, on the other hand, the government could hold spending constant and instead devalue the currency. The effect of raising the value of $\overline{q}$ ($\Delta q > 0$), see equation (13.23), is an improvement in the trade balance. Foreigners buy more of the now-cheaper exported goods, home residents buy fewer of the now more-expensive imports – and with exports up and imports down, the trade deficit goes down. This is the expenditure switching channel.

Figure 13.8 illustrates the fact that when the dollar exchange rate appreciates (q falls), the non-oil trade balance deteriorates, with a lag of about two years. Since oil prices are largely denominated in US dollars, oil imports are excluded so as to focus on that part of the trade balance that is affected by the exchange rate. That pattern is consistent with the expenditure switching effect of exchange rate depreciations. (The two-year lag accounts for the fact that it takes some time for exchange rate changes to affect the behavior of firms and households.)

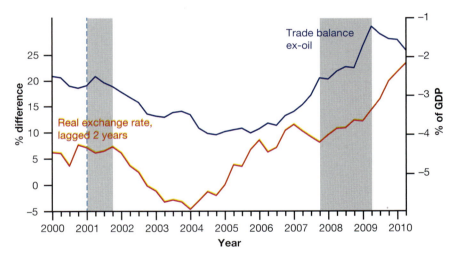

Figure 13.8 Depreciation and the Trade Balance This figure shows the percentage change in the US dollar real exchange rate relative to the first quarter of 2003, lagged two years (blue, left scale), and non-oil net exports as percentage point share of GDP (red, right scale). Gray shading are recession dates.
Source: Bureau of Economic Analysis, Federal Reserve Board.

Figure 13.8 also illustrates the expenditure reduction effect, albeit more subtly. The shaded area denotes **recessions** – periods when the US economy contracts. Notice that as the economy enters recessions, in all but one case the trade balance is rising. When income declines, consumption declines, and because some of the goods and services consumed are imported, imports decline. Since imports are a negative entry in the trade balance, declining imports result in an improved trade balance.

THEORY   Exchange Rates and Trade Flows

According to the model described in this chapter, real exchange rate devaluation straightforwardly raises exports and decreases imports. Although reality is more complex and the pattern does not always hold, it does seem to hold as a general rule.

To see how a devaluation works, consider the following partial equilibrium analysis, where income Y is held constant in order to isolate the impact of exchange rates. Prices at home and abroad are also held constant, so that changes in the nominal exchange rate translate directly into changes in the real exchange rate.

First, consider imports – specifically, widgets imported from China in quantity $\widetilde{IM}$. In Figure 13.9, the downward-sloping demand curves indicate that at any given exchange rate S, import quantity $\widetilde{IM}$ depends negatively on the widgets' price in yuan, $P^*\{¥\}$. The perfectly flat supply curve reflects our assumption that the widgets ship at a fixed price in yuan, $\bar{P}^*_{IM}\{¥\}$. We justify this assumption by supposing that exports are much smaller than China's domestic market, so that changes in export quantities have a negligible impact on producers and therefore do not affect the price. In short, we are assuming infinite price elasticity of the foreign supply.

Now we turn to the export market, depicted in Figure 13.10. As with the widgets made in China, so with those exported from the United States, we assume infinite price elasticity of domestic supply and therefore a fixed price; this time in dollars. When the price is converted to yuan, however, the *level* of the flat export supply curve depends on the exchange rate. At initial rate S_0, US exports will be X_0. Devaluing the dollar (S rises to S_1) decreases the price Chinese buyers face, reflected in a downward shift of the supply curve. As Chinese buyers take advantage of the lowered yuan price, exports rise from X_0 to X_1.

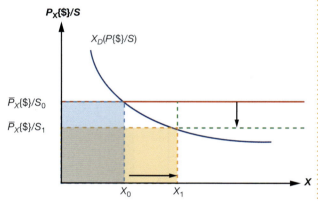

Figure 13.10 Devaluation and Exports This diagram shows the downward shift in export supply due to currency devaluation.

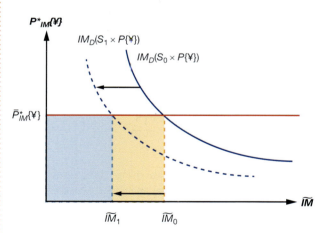

Figure 13.9 Devaluation and Imports This diagram shows the inward shift in import demand due to a currency devaluation.

Initial imports are $\widetilde{IM}_0$ when the exchange rate is S_0. Since US demand for Chinese goods depends on the *dollar* prices, a dollar depreciation ($S_1 > S_0$) will shift the demand curve, resulting in a reduction of imports to $\widetilde{IM}_1$.

Notice that in Figure 13.9, foreign exchange expenditures on imports decline, from $\bar{P}^*_{IM} \times \widetilde{IM}_0$ to $\bar{P}^*_{IM} \times \widetilde{IM}_1$. In Figure 13.10, by contrast, foreign exchange earnings from exports are ambiguously affected. Earnings change from $(\bar{P}_X\{\$\}/S_0) \times X_0$ to $(\bar{P}_X\{\$\}/S_1) \times X_1$. The net effect on earnings of foreign exchange is uncertain, as it depends on the shapes of the demand curves.

The difference between foreign exchange earnings and foreign exchange expenditures on imports is the US trade balance, denominated in yuan:

$$TB\{¥\} = \left(\frac{\bar{P}}{S}\right) \times X - \bar{P}^*\{¥\} \times \widetilde{IM}$$

Given that the dollar's value undergoes change, we may wish to measure the devaluation's overall impact on the trade balance in real terms – widgets instead of dollars. To convert to real terms, we multiply both sides by S (measured in $/¥) and divide by the US price in dollars, $\bar{P}$, to obtain:

$$TB = X - \left(\frac{S\bar{P}^*}{\bar{P}}\right) \times \widetilde{IM} = X - qX^*$$

TB is the trade balance in real terms, i.e., in US widgets, defined as the difference between exports, *X*, and imports ($\widetilde{IM}$) converted into US widgets by the real exchange rate, $q \equiv (S\bar{P}^*/\bar{P})$.

To see how a devaluation shifts the balance of trade when trade is initially balanced, $X = qX^*$, we take the partial derivative of the trade balance with respect the real exchange rate.

$$\frac{\partial TB}{\partial q} = \frac{\partial X}{\partial q} - q\frac{\partial X^*}{\partial q} - X^* \quad (13.24)$$

For a devaluation to improve the trade balance, $\frac{\partial TB}{\partial q}$ must be greater than 0:

$$0 < \frac{\partial X}{\partial q} - q\frac{\partial X^*}{\partial q} - X^* \quad (13.25)$$

We move the X^* to the left side and divide both sides by X^*:

$$1 < \frac{\partial X/X^*}{\partial q} - q\frac{\partial X^*/X^*}{\partial q} \quad (13.26)$$

Our assumption that $X = qX^*$ enables a substitution of X/q for X^* in the first term, followed by rearranging of the q in both terms:

$$1 < \frac{\partial X/X}{\partial q/q} - \frac{\partial X^*/X^*}{\partial q/q} \quad (13.27)$$

The first term on the right is positive, because as we have seen, an increase in the exchange rate leads to increased exports. Including the subtraction as part of the imports term makes that term positive, as well. The two terms can be interpreted as the respective (positive) elasticities of exports and imports with respect to the real exchange rate:

$$1 < \varepsilon_X + \varepsilon_{IM} \quad (13.28)$$

This is the **Marshall–Lerner–Robinson condition**: when the sum of the export and import elasticities is greater than 1, the real trade balance improves in response to a devaluation.

Remember, this derivation assumes:

- Export and import supply price elasticities are infinite.
- Prices of exports are fixed in domestic currency terms, and prices of imports are fixed in foreign currency terms.
- Trade is initially balanced.

The failure of any of these conditions to hold would limit the efficacy of devaluation. The last one is perhaps the most important assumption. Countries seldom devalue their currency when trade is balanced. Usually, devaluations occur when imports exceed exports. In such cases, the elasticities would have to sum to more than 1 in order for the devaluation to improve the trade balance.

It is likely that the elasticities are very small, particularly in the very short term. If the elasticities are smaller in the shorter term than in the longer term, then the response of the trade balance will probably vary over the time horizon. In response to a devaluation, the trade balance may initially deteriorate, and only improve over time. This pattern of response is called "the J-curve," since the trade balance plotted over time looks like a tilted letter J.

13.5 THE SPILLOVER EFFECTS OF FISCAL POLICY

Up to this point, we have assumed that the rest of the world is unaffected by domestic events. While this is a useful simplification, often one wants to examine how large economies interact with other, equally large economies. To model such interactions, we imagine two countries, named Home and Foreign, that trade with, and only with, each other. In addition, to simplify the analysis, we hold the real exchange rate constant, and subsume that effect into the constants of the export and import functions. The algebraic details for what follows are given in the Appendix at the end of the chapter; here we focus on the results and on the graphic representation.

Suppose Home's export function is modified to account for the fact that when Foreign's income (Y^*) rises, Home's exports increase. The intuition is straightforward: Home's exports are Foreign's imports, and their imports depend on their income, just as Home's imports depend on Home's income. Replacing $\bar{X}$ with $\bar{X} + m^*Y^*$ in equation (13.5) makes Home's income depend on Foreign's, with $m^*/(1-c+m)$ being the parameter describing the influence of Y^* on Y – the amount by which Home's income rises in response to a unit increase in Foreign's.

By the same reasoning, Foreign's income depends on Home's income, rising by $m/(1 - c^* + m^*)$ for every unit rise in Home's income. If, now, we consider the effect of income-boosting government policy moves, such as tax cuts and government spending, then it turns out that the impact of such moves is larger in this model than in the single-country model.

The reason for this result is that an increase in, say, government spending induces higher consumption and, as in the single-country model, higher imports. But in contrast to what happens in the single-country model, here part of the spending that leaks out of Home's economy in the form of imports is returned back to Home in the form of higher exports. This is because when Home's imports rise, Foreign's exports rise and, hence, so does its GDP. That higher GDP induces more imports into Foreign. But in this two-country world, Foreign's imports are Home's exports, and so some of the leaked-away spending comes back to Home.

To be sure, not all of the leaked spending comes back. Rather, the end result depends on the sensitivity of each country's imports to its own GDP, i.e. on the marginal propensity to import. For a given m, the larger m^* is, the more of Home's spending circulates back as export demand.

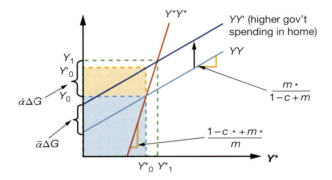

Figure 13.11 The Response to Government Spending When There Are Two Large Countries This diagram shows the home country aggregate demand curve and the foreign country area aggregate demand curve, both as a function of home income. The home aggregate demand function is relatively flat because home exports are a function of euro income. The impact of increased government spending in the home country raises the income level through the standard closed-country multiplier process. However, higher home income raises home imports (which are foreign exports), thereby raising foreign income and to a lesser extent home income again. Hence, in a two-country model, the output change in the home country is larger than in a small open economy model.

Figure 13.11 represents the interaction of the two economies graphically, with Home income on the vertical axis and Foreign income on the horizontal. The flatter line, YY, describes how Home's income depends on Foreign's, where the parameter $m^*/(1 - c + m)$ becomes the slope of the line. The vertical intercept is $\alpha[A + X - IM]$ (See equation (A13.2) in the Appendix.) The steeper line, Y^*Y^*, similarly describes how Foreign's income depends on Home's; that line has a slope of $(1 - c^* + m^*)/m$. Equilibrium, $Y = Y_0$ and $Y^* = Y^*_0$, is given by the intersection of the two lines.

Suppose, now, that Home's government decides on an economic stimulus in the form of an increase in spending, ΔG; this is shown as an upward shift in the YY curve. The shift distance $Y'_0 - Y_0$ is equal to $\alpha \Delta G$ the answer we obtained as $Y_1 - Y_0$ for the single-country model (Figure 13.4). However, a rise in Home's income leads to a rise in Home's imports and therefore a spillover rise in Foreign's income from Y^*_0 to Y^*_1. Consequently, Foreign's demand for Home's exports rises, giving an extra boost to Home income's – a spill*back* effect. Hence, the total change in Home's income is given not by $Y'_0 - Y_0$ but by the longer distance $Y_1 - Y_0$. In short, in the **two-country model** $\Delta Y/\Delta G$ is not $\bar{\alpha}$ but a larger multiple, $\check{\alpha}$, The expression for α is derived in the Appendix to this chapter.

APPLICATION Responding to the Global Great Recession

How relevant are these spillover and spillback effects? Apparently, policymakers believe they are important. During the worldwide economic crisis that began in 2008, policymakers from the G-20 countries – the twenty largest developed and developing economies – agreed that their countries should all simultaneously increase government spending and cut taxes. The idea was that for any given country, the bang for the buck would be greater if all countries stimulated their economies simultaneously.

Figure 13.12 Cooperation on Stimulus Leaders of the G-20 meet in Washington, in November 2008, promising to use fiscal policy to stabilize the world economy.
Source: Michael Gottschalk/AFP via Getty Images.

Figure 13.13 depicts this effect using a modified two-country model, with the US and the euro area as the two countries. If government spending in the US increases, the flatter, $Y^{US}Y^{US}$ curve, describing how Y^{US} depends on Y^{EU}, shifts up. By itself, that shift will cause Y^{US} to increase in to Y_1, as greater US income spurs greater euro area income and

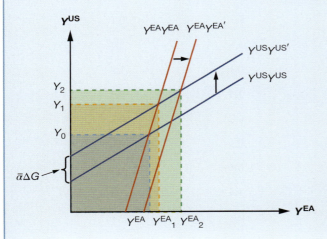

Figure 13.13 The Response to Coordinated Fiscal Stimulus This diagram shows that if both US and euro area countries raise government spending, both aggregate demand curves are shifted out, resulting in a large increase in income in both regions.

hence greater US exports that boost US income. With a coordinated stimulus, the $Y^{EU}Y^{EU}$ curve shifts, as well, so that US income rises all the way to Y_2, higher even than Y_1. The output increase in the home country is larger with a simultaneous stimulus than if the stimulus occurs only in the home country.

Simulations conducted by the IMF in order to provide guidance to the policymakers of the G-20 countries reflect the spillover and spillback effects in the two-country model. While the IMF's model is substantially more complicated than that described above – in particular, its model incorporates a financial side and considerations about expectations about the future – our model confirms the significance of interdependencies.

Table 13.1 records the commitments to discretionary fiscal stimuli that were agreed to by the respective G-20 governments.

Table 13.1 Fiscal Stimulus Packages, as a Percentage of GDP in region. Announced for 2009–10 as of January 17, 2009

	2009	2010
United States	**1.9**	**2.9**
Tax cuts	0.9	1.2
Infrastructure	0.3	0.8
Other	0.6	1.0
Euro area	**0.9**	**0.8**
Tax cuts	0.3	0.3
Infrastructure	0.4	0.0
Other	0.2	0.4
Japan	**1.4**	**0.4**
Tax cuts	0.1	0.1
Infrastructure	0.3	0.1
Other	1.0	0.2
Asia excluding Japan	**1.5**	**1.3**
Tax cuts	0.1	0.1
Infrastructure	1.1	0.0
Other	0.3	1.2
Rest of G-20	**1.1**	**0.3**
Tax cuts	0.5	0.1
Infrastructure	0.2	0.1
Other	0.4	−0.1
Total (PPP-weighted)	**1.4**	**1.3**
Tax cuts	0.4	0.4

Table 13.1 (*cont.*)

	2009	2010
Infrastructure	0.5	0.3
Other	0.5	0.7

Source: Freedman, Kumhof, Laxton, and Lee (2009).

Table 13.2 compares the effects, in the IMF's simulations, of the agreed-on global stimulus package (the first column) to the effects of a stimulus in just one nation or group of nations at a time (the remaining columns). So, for example, for 2010 the impact of a US-only stimulus on US output was a 2.7% boost relative to what would have occurred in the absence of the stimulus. With the planned worldwide stimulus, on the other hand, US output was 3.1% higher. This difference comes from other countries' higher economic activity spilling over onto the US

Table 13.2 Level Effects of Fiscal Stimulus in 2009 and 2010

	All	US	Euro	Japan	Em. Asia	RoW
Effects on GDP in 2009						
World	1.4	0.5	0.2	0.1	0.4	0.2
United States	1.5	1.3	0.0	0.0	0.1	0.1
Euro area	0.9	0.2	0.5	0.0	0.1	0.1
Japan	1.1	0.2	0.0	0.7	0.1	0.0
Emerging Asia	2.1	0.6	0.1	0.1	1.3	0.1
Remaining countries	1.0	0.3	0.1	0.0	0.2	0.4
Effects on GDP in 2010						
World	2.0	1.4	0.1	0.1	0.2	0.2
United States	3.1	2.7	0.1	0.1	0.1	0.1
Euro area	1.2	0.6	0.3	0.1	0.1	0.1
Japan	1.5	0.7	0.1	0.5	0.1	0.1
Emerging Asia	2.3	1.6	0.1	0.1	0.4	0.1
Remaining countries	1.7	1.0	0.1	0.1	0.2	0.3

(*percent deviation from baseline in percent*)
Source: Freedman, Kumhof, Laxton, and Lee (2009).

The spillover effect is even more pronounced for the other regions. A 2010 stimulus in just the euro area improved the projected output there by 0.3%. On the assumption that the entire world undertook the coordinated stimulus, the euro area output was 1.2% higher. The reason for the dramatic difference is that the euro area stimulus itself was quite modest (less than 1/3 the size of the US stimulus); most of the euro area's boost with a global stimulus was due to spillover.

CONCLUSION

This chapter has begun the construction of an economic model that will continue in later chapters. In its present form, the model applies mainly to the short run, where prices are assumed to remain constant. Changes in the amount of desired spending by households, firms, the government, or foreigners can increase or decrease output. To the extent that the spending recirculates as increased income that is spent again, the effect of increased autonomous spending is amplified. Nevertheless, the extent to which spending leaks out of the economy as spending on imports, the amplification effect is reduced.

When it comes to policy, increased government spending is a somewhat more effective means of raising output than cutting taxes is. However, any boost in overall income tends to increase the consumption of exports and thereby tends to worsen the balance of trade. An alternate way to raise income is currency devaluation, as an expanded version of the economic model demonstrates. However, closer analysis reveals that devaluation can only be expected to work when the elasticities of supply on the two sides of the trading relationship are together sufficiently large. This is a sounder assumption in the longer term.

The cross-border leakage of spending due to imports is not an entirely bad thing. Some of the benefits of one country's fiscal policy moves spill over to trading partners, but as the partners' economy is boosted, some of benefits spill back to the home country. Even more powerful is coordinated action, where countries agree to simultaneous policy moves for mutual increased benefit. A two-country version of our economic model demonstrates this result.

SUMMARY

1. In a model where the demand side determines output (sometimes called a Keynesian model), changes in government spending and taxes can affect output.
2. When government spending is increased, output rises by more than the increase in government spending. This is also true for increases in other types of spending, such as autonomous consumption, investment, and exports.
3. When taxes are reduced, output also rises, but to a smaller extent than for a government spending increase of equal magnitude.
4. An increase in government spending will tend to increase the trade deficit.
5. The budget balance and the trade balance need not move in the same direction. Whether they do depends on the types of shocks that hit the economy.
6. When prices are held constant, a devaluation of the home currency will lead to a weaker real exchange rate, which will typically lead to a larger trade balance, all else held constant.
7. There is no guarantee that a currency devaluation will improve the trade balance. The Marshall–Lerner–Robinson condition states that the trade balance will improve if, starting from balanced trade, the price elasticities sum to greater than 1. Typically, it is assumed that the trade elasticities are sufficiently large to meet these conditions, particularly over the longer term, when there is sufficient time for firms and households to adjust.
8. In a two-country model, increases in government spending will have an even larger impact on output because of spillover and spillback effects.

9. In the two-country model, a coordinated increase in government spending will lead to even larger increases in output for a given dollar increase in spending, and a smaller deterioration in the trade balance.

KEY CONCEPTS

Aggregate demand, page 281
Autonomous, page 282
Equilibrium, page 280
Endogenous, page 282
Exogenous, page 281
Expenditure reduction, page 290
Expenditure switching, page 290
Lump-sum taxes, page 282
Marginal propensity to consume, page 282
Marginal propensity to import, page 282
Marshall–Lerner–Robinson condition, page 293
Recession, page 291
Shocks, page 288
Stimulus, page 279
Trade balance, page 288
Two-country model, page 294

REVIEW QUESTIONS

1. How do endogenous variables differ from exogenous variables?
2. What constitutes equilibrium in the model?
3. Do prices adjust to restore equilibrium in the model?
4. How are the government budget deficit and trade deficit related?
5. Does a devaluation always result in an improvement in the trade balance (net exports)?
6. In what ways can the government reduce a trade deficit?
7. When consumers consume a large share of each additional dollar's worth of after-tax income, will the government spending multiplier be relatively large or relatively small?
8. When there are two large countries exporting to each other, will the government spending multiplier be larger than or smaller than in the single country case?

EXERCISES

1. In the Keynesian model, after each round of spending, some proportion of the resulting income is consumed by the recipients. Does this mean the multiplier is infinite?
2. When the marginal propensity to consume is large, is the multiplier is larger or smaller?
3. Is the multiplier larger or smaller in countries that import a lot of goods and services?
4. Suppose we are using the Keynesian model with constant real exchange rates, and there is an income tax.
    a. Consider an increase in government spending. What happens to the budget balance and the trade balance?
    b. Consider an increase in autonomous investment. What happens to the budget balance and the trade balance?
    c. Why do the budget and trade balances move in different directions in the two cases?
5. In the Keynesian model, if autonomous consumption declines, what happens to the trade balance and the budget balance? Does the national saving identity still hold? What happens to CA, $S - I$, and $T - G$?

6. Using the model in Section 13.5, suppose autonomous exports increase by $1 billion. What happens to output? What happens to the trade balance? (Does it also increase by $1 billion?)
7. Over time, Americans have shown an increased preference for foreign goods, even when holding constant the exchange rate and income. How do you interpret this in the context of the Keynesian model?
8. Consider the Marshall–Lerner–Robinson condition, holding output constant.
    a. Suppose that each 1% depreciation in the US dollar induces a 0.75% increase in exports and a 0.25% decrease in imports. If initially exports equal imports, what will be the impact on the trade balance?
    b. Suppose the US experiences the exchange rate depreciation in part (a) while running a large trade deficit. What will happen to the trade balance?
    c. Suppose that instead of the elasticities being constant, they are smaller in the short run and larger in the long run. What happens to the trade balance over time, assuming it starts at zero?
9. Consider the Keynesian model, where exports and imports are partly determined by real exchange rates.
    a. Using the solution for income, show algebraically what the impact of an increase in lump-sum taxes on the trade balance.
    b. Using the solution for income, show algebraically what is the impact of a devaluation of the real exchange rate on the trade balance.
    c. Can one say which policy would have the effect of shrinking a trade deficit? Is it possible to say which policy has a bigger impact (in absolute value) than the other?
    d. Suppose the level of output is already deemed 'too low'. Which policy would you recommend, if either, in order to shrink the trade deficit.
10. In the Keynesian model used in Problem 9, how does the increasing ability of other countries to make goods similar to those made in the United States show up in the parameters in the model?
11. In the Keynesian model used in Problem 9:
    a. If the marginal propensity to import rises, then what is true about the relative effectiveness of expenditure switching versus expenditure reducing as a means of reducing a trade deficit?
    b. If the sensitivity of trade flows to the real exchange rate increases, then what is true about the relative effectiveness of expenditure switching versus expenditure reducing as a means of reducing a trade deficit?
12. Consider a world with only two economies, of equal size, called Home and Foreign. Explain why a dollar's increase in government spending results in a larger increase in GDP than it would in an economy much smaller than the world economy.
13. Again consider a world with only two economies, of equal size, called Home and Foreign.
    a. If Home increases government spending, what happens to output in Foreign? Why? What happens to the Home trade balance?
    b. If Home keeps government spending constant, but Foreign increases its government spending, what happens to Home output? Why? What happens to the *Home* trade balance?
    c. Suppose Home and Foreign are the same size, and behave in the same way (i.e., the marginal propensity to consume, the marginal propensity to import, and the tax

rate are all the same across both countries). Then when both economies increase government spending by the same, amount, what happens to each economy's trade balance?

RECOMMENDED RESOURCES

Alan J. Auerbach and Yuriy Gorodnichenko, "Fiscal Multipliers in Recession and Expansion,"in *Fiscal Policy after the Financial Crisis* (Chicago, IL: University of Chicago Press, 2012).

Charles J. Whalen and Felix Reichling, "The Fiscal Multiplier and Economic Policy Analysis in the United States," *Contemporary Economic Policy* 33(4) (2015): 735–746.

APPENDIX 13.A
Solving the Two-Country Model

In Section 13.5, the workings of the two-country model were described generally. However, we did not show how equilibrium was determined algebraically, nor did we formally demonstrate that the multipliers for government spending are larger in this setting. Here we work through the math.

Let the exports of Home include an autonomous term, as in Section 13.1, but add a term that is dependent on Foreign's income:

$$X = \overline{X} + m^* Y^* \tag{A13.1}$$

Then the equation for Home's income becomes:

$$Y = \left(\frac{1}{1 - c + m}\right)\left[\overline{A} + \overline{X} - \overline{IM} + m^* Y^*\right] \tag{A13.2}$$

For convenience, let $1 - c = s$:

$$Y = \left(\frac{1}{s + m}\right)\left[\overline{A} + \overline{X} - \overline{IM} + m^* Y^*\right] \tag{A13.3}$$

Foreign's economy works just like Home's:

$$Y^* = \left(\frac{1}{s^* + m^*}\right)\left[\overline{A}^* + \overline{X}^* - \overline{IM}^* + mY\right] \tag{A13.4}$$

In this two-country setup, each country's exports are the other country's imports, so $\overline{X}^* = \overline{IM}$ and $\overline{IM}^* = \overline{X}$.

$$Y^* = \left(\frac{1}{s^* + m^*}\right)\left[\overline{A}^* + \overline{IM} - \overline{X} + mY\right] \tag{A13.5}$$

Equilibrium income is found by substituting (A13.5) into (A13.3):

$$Y = \left(\frac{1}{s + m}\right)\left[\overline{A} + \overline{X} - \overline{IM} + m^*\left(\frac{1}{s^* + m^*}\right)(\overline{A}^* + \overline{IM} - \overline{X} + mY)\right] \tag{A13.6}$$

Rearranging:

$$Y(s + m) = \left[\breve{A} + \left(\frac{m^* m}{s^* + m^*}\right)Y\right], \tag{A13.7}$$

APPENDIX 13.A

where $\breve{A} \equiv \left[\overline{A} + \overline{X} - \overline{IM} + \left(\frac{m^*}{s^*+m^*}\right)(\overline{A}^* + \overline{IM} - \overline{X})\right]$

Solving for Home's income:

$$Y\left[s + m - \left(\frac{m^*m}{s^* + m^*}\right)\right] = \breve{A} \qquad (A13.8)$$

$$Y_0 = \breve{\alpha}\breve{A}_0, \text{ where } \breve{\alpha} \equiv \frac{1}{s + m - \left(\frac{m^*m}{s^*+m^*}\right)} \geq \overline{\alpha} = \frac{1}{s+m} \qquad (A13.9)$$

Notice that setting m^* to zero leads to $A = A + X - IM$ and $\alpha = a$. If Foreign's imports from Home are entirely autonomous, the two-country model reduces to the one-country model as far as Home is concerned.

CHAPTER 14

Income and Interest Rates under Fixed Exchange Rates

LEARNING OBJECTIVES

In this chapter, we learn about:
- how interest rates determine investment spending
- what money is, and how the supply and demand for money are determined
- how equilibria on the real and the financial sides of the economy are established
- how fiscal and monetary policies affect output and interest rates
- how external equilibrium is defined, and what determines it
- what fixed exchange rates imply for monetary policy
- how fiscal, monetary, and exchange rate policies affect output and exchange and interest rates

INTRODUCTION

In times of turmoil, one would think that a stable, or relatively stable, exchange rate would be a boon to policymakers, soothing the anxieties of international investors. However, keeping the value of the currency stable against a foreign currency such as the US dollar, when buffeted by shocks, entails sometimes painful tradeoffs.

Consider the case of Russia. In February 2014, the country faced financial capital outflows and a weakening currency; in response, the Russian central bank began using their holdings of US dollars to buy up rubles on the foreign exchange market in order to support the value of the currency. They also raised interest rates, with rates peaking in early 2015 (see Figure 14.1).

The crisis was sparked by a confluence of events – lower prices for the primary export of Russia – oil – and financial sanctions in the wake of Russia's 2014 intervention in Ukraine and seizure of Crimea. Financial capital outflows meant that less foreign saving was available to households, firms, and the Russian government. A weakening currency meant that all imported goods were becoming increasingly expensive to Russians, denting the popularity of the government. Moreover, debts to foreigners, denominated in US dollars – as was much of Russia's debt – became more burdensome.

Purchasing foreign currency, such as dollars, did help prop up the ruble's value. But why did Russia's policymakers think raising interest rates would work to stem the flow of capital out of the country? What were the downsides of these measures? We cannot answer that

14.1 AN ECONOMY WITH MONEY AND INTEREST RATES

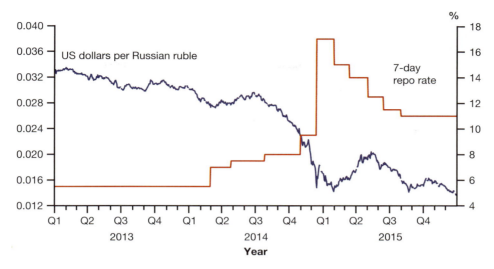

Figure 14.1 Russia's Interest Rate Defense of the Ruble This figure shows the US dollar/Russian ruble exchange rate in rubles per US dollar (blue, down is a depreciation of the ruble), and the Russian overnight seven-day interest rate (red). *Source: Federal Reserve Board and Central Bank of the Russian Federation.*

question without a model of why and how interest rates are determined, and how higher interest rates affect capital flows, and help sustain the value of a currency

In this chapter and the next, we develop an integrated model of how the economy interacts with the rest of the world – a model in which savings can move across borders and the value of the currency can change. To begin with, we examine how the economy behaves when the central bank commits to keeping the exchange rate with a foreign currency pegged at a certain value (or close to a certain value).

14.1 AN ECONOMY WITH MONEY AND INTEREST RATES: THE *IS–LM* MODEL

In order to analyze the role of the financial sector, we modify the model discussed in Chapter 13. This requires that at least one component of aggregate demand depends on a financial sector variable. What we will do is let investment in physical capital (factories and equipment) depend on the interest rate. Hence, on the real side of the economy, everything remains the same as in Chapter 13, except for the investment function:

$$I = \bar{I} - bi \tag{14.1}$$

The $\bar{I}$ term is the hypothetical amount firms would invest if the interest rate, i, were zero. This amount $\bar{I}$ is not necessarily fixed, but it changes in ways determined by factors outside the model. For instance, a sudden increase in optimism regarding future sales by firm owners might, in anticipation of the greater sales, spur greater purchases of plant and equipment.

The variable i represents the interest rate on paper assets. In the real world, there are many such assets and many available rates of return, but for simplicity we will treat i as a single number, the percent of interest paid on **bonds**. Bonds represent an alternative way for firms to allocate their resources. Besides investing in physical capital, they can buy bonds and thereby lend money to other firms or to the government, with the knowledge that at a future date the resources will come back with a predetermined amount of interest added. We will say more about bonds shortly; for now, the important thing to know is that they are (ideally) completely predictable. (In real life, there is always some risk of default, but (particularly with junk bonds and other low-investment grade bonds) it is relatively small.)

The parameter *b* represents the sensitivity of investment: it indicates the change in capital investment due to a one-point change in the interest rate. The minus sign indicates that the higher the interest rate on bonds, the lower the rate of capital investment. Why this relationship between *I* and *i*? Because the higher the interest rate, the higher the *opportunity cost* of investment spending.

To see how this works, imagine a firm, *k*, and consider all the capital investment projects it could conceivably undertake. In Figure 14.2, these projects are ranked from left to right by their rate of return (*RoR*), highest to lowest. The width of each bar corresponds to the cost of the project. The higher the rate of return, the more generously an investment will pay off, and therefore the more attractive the project.

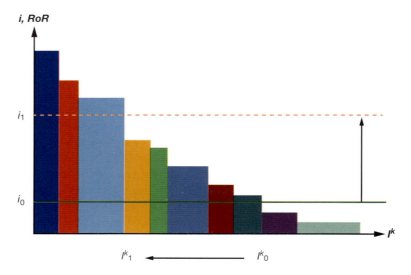

Figure 14.2 Investment and the Interest Rate This diagram shows investment projects (bars), ranked from highest rate of return to lowest, facing firm *k*, and interest rates (horizontal lines). The width of the bars is the size of the investment project. An increase in the interest rate facing the firm is shown as an upward shift in the horizontal line from i_0 to i_1.

When the firm decides which projects to undertake, obviously the most attractive projects are first in line. But how far down the line will the firm go? It depends on the interest rate paid by bonds. When the rate is i_0, then the first eight projects, representing a total investment of $I^k{}_0$, provide a rate of return in excess of the interest rate – the return the firm would gain from buying bonds instead. The firm will therefore find it to its advantage to invest in projects up to amount $I^k{}_0$.

If, now, the interest rate rises to i_1 (the black arrow), then only the top three projects' returns exceed the new rate. The firm will now proceed only on these projects, representing a total cost of $I^k{}_1$, which is less than the original amount of $I^k{}_0$. Investment spending by the firm declines (the thin arrow).

To summarize, at the firm level there is a negative relationship between the interest rate and investment spending in plant and equipment. The same holds true when one aggregates

14.1 AN ECONOMY WITH MONEY AND INTEREST RATES

up to the economy level, since all the firms face a similar decision, and so we have the relationship between i and I described by equation (14.1). If we now modify our analysis in Chapter 13 to incorporate our revised model of investment, then by replacing $\bar{I}$ with $\bar{I} - bi$, we obtain the following revised version of equation (13.7):

$$Y = \bar{\alpha}\left[\bar{A} + \bar{X} - \overline{IM} + (n+v)\bar{q} - bi\right] \qquad <IS\text{ curve}> \qquad (14.2)$$

Recall that in Chapter 13, component C of aggregate demand was a function of Y, $C = \bar{C} + c(Y - \bar{T})$. Therefore, equation (13.7) ended up containing just one endogenous variable, Y. Here, by contrast, I is a function of a new endogenous variable, i, so that equation (14.2) contains not one endogenous variable but two. If we set up a coordinate system with a horizontal Y-axis and a vertical i-axis – which we will do very shortly – then equation (14.2) represents a line, rather than a point with a specific value for Y. (That is why there is no longer a 0 subscript on the Y.)

The line is called the **IS curve**, because it represents the balance firms strike between investment (I) in physical capital and savings (S), understood as resources that households do not consume but rather save. The downward slope of the line expresses a significant fact about the relationship between interest rates and national productivity: as the interest rate goes up, firms are more inclined to save and less inclined to invest, which causes productivity to decline.

Modeling the Financial Sector

Equation (14.2) described the relationship between Y and i in the real sector of the economy, where goods and services are produced. That was the focus of Chapter 13 and has been the focus of this chapter so far. Now we turn to the financial sector, and to the role of **money**.

We often use the term money interchangeably with income. In our model, money is an asset, which we picture concretely as pieces of paper (mostly green, in the US), whose function is to facilitate transactions and, secondarily, to store wealth. Bonds earn returns but cannot easily be used in transactions. Money yields no returns, but since firms and households must conduct transactions, they will want to hold a certain portion of their total wealth in the form of money.

In the economy's real sector, firms' choices lead to equilibrium between investment and saving. We will now model the financial sector as a market where bonds and money change hands. It would be reasonable to represent the financial sector as a market in bonds, graphically depicted with the bonds on the horizontal axis and their price on the vertical axis. However, for our purposes it will instead be convenient to represent the financial sector as a market in *money*, which is the flip side of the same coin.

Equilibrium in the money market is described by the standard condition that quantity demanded equals quantity supplied. Dividing by the price level, P, gives the condition in real (inflation-adjusted) terms:

$$\frac{M^d}{P} = \frac{M^s}{P} \qquad (14.3)$$

Money supply (M^s) is assumed to be given exogenously, set by the central bank. This means that the number of pieces of paper called money circulating through the economy is a number the central bank decides on and has the ability to change at will. This is why we put an overbar over the M. We hold the price level constant and therefore place an overbar over the P, as well.

$$\frac{M^s}{P} = \frac{\overline{M}}{P} \qquad (14.4)$$

Money demand is a positive function of income and a negative function of the interest rate.

$$\frac{M^d}{P} = kY - hi \qquad (14.5)$$

Money demand rises with income, because it is assumed that greater income goes hand in hand with a greater number of transactions and therefore a greater need for money to conduct them. The parameter k is the **income sensitivity of money demand**, the change in dollars of money demanded for a one-unit change in real income.

The parameter h is the **interest sensitivity of money demand**, that is the change in dollars demanded when the interest rate rises by one percentage point. Why does money demand depend negatively on the interest rate? Since the interest rate is the return on the alternative asset (bonds), and it can be interpreted as the opportunity cost of holding money. Alternatively, the interest rate can be understood as the cost of borrowing. Someone who wants more money on hand must pay interest, i, to obtain it. Either way, the interest rate is the cost of holding money. The higher the cost, the less money actors will hold.

Notice, we assume that in the money market, the central bank is the supplier and all other actors – firms, households, the government – make up the demand side. We do not care about money market interactions internal to the demand side because what we are interested in is the central bank's role in determining the total amount of money in circulation. Money transferred from firm k to firm j was in circulation before and remains in circulation afterward, only now held by firm j instead of firm k. By contrast, money in the central bank's vaults is officially out of circulation; it enters circulation when the central bank uses it to pay for assets in the domestic market or the foreign exchange market.

Returning, now, to our mathematical analysis, we substitute equations (14.4) and (14.5) into equation (14.3) and solve for the interest rate:

$$i = -\left(\frac{1}{h}\right)\left(\frac{\overline{M}}{P}\right) + \left(\frac{k}{h}\right)Y \quad <LM\ \text{curve}> \qquad (14.6)$$

Again we have a linear relationship between Y and i, this time representing the equilibrium between money and bonds in the financial market. This line is called the *LM* **curve**, which abbreviates "*L*iquidity preference equals *M*oney supply." **Liquidity** is money's ready availability for transactions, and liquidity preference is an older term for money demand. The higher the level of economic activity, as indicated by income Y, the greater the need for liquidity, and the more actors must expect to pay (given a fixed amount of money circulating), in the form of interest, i, to hold money. Thus for the *LM* curve, i is positively dependent on Y.

We have two equations, (14.2) and (14.6), with the same two unknowns. We can substitute the latter into the former and then solve for Y to obtain an updated version of equation (13.20) giving the equilibrium income:

$$Y_0 = \underbrace{\left(\frac{1}{1 - c + m + \frac{bk}{h}}\right)}_{\equiv \hat{\alpha}}\left[\overline{A} + \overline{X} - \overline{IM} + (n + v)\overline{q} - \left(\frac{b}{h}\right)\left(\frac{\overline{M}}{P}\right)\right] \qquad (14.7)$$

Notice that equilibrium income now depends on the level of autonomous spending, the real exchange rate, and the money stock (in real terms). The equilibrium interest rate, i_0, can be found using equation (14.7) to substitute for equation (14.6). Notice also that the new

14.2 POLICY OPTIONS FOR AFFECTING OUTPUT

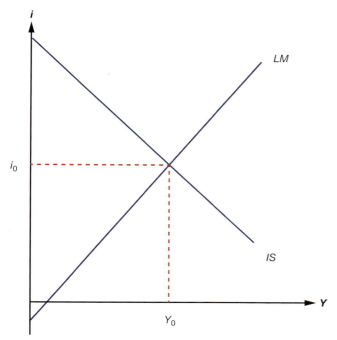

Figure 14.3 The IS and LM Curves This diagram shows the combination of interest rate and income, which deliver equilibrium in the real side of the economy (*IS* curve) and the combination of interest rate and income which deliver equilibrium in the financial side of the economy. The intersection of the two curves is the only point where both sides of the economy are in equilibrium.

multiplier, $\hat{\alpha}$, is made smaller than the old one, $\bar{\alpha}$, by the addition of the bk/h term in the denominator. This will be discussed further in the next section.

Graphically, Y_0 is the income at the point of intersection in a Keynesian Cross where the aggregate demand function has been modified by replacing $\bar{I}$ with $I = \bar{I} + \left(\frac{b}{h}\right)\left(\frac{\bar{M}}{\bar{P}}\right) - \left(\frac{bk}{h}\right)Y$ on the basis of equations (14.1) and (14.6). But the Keynesian Cross does not display the interest rate. If we plot equations (14.2) and (14.6) with Y on the horizontal axis and i on the vertical, we obtain a visual depiction of the *IS*–*LM* model, as it is called; see Figure 14.3.

Equilibrium income and interest rates are determined by the intersection of the two curves. Note the following characteristics of these curves:

- The position of the *IS* curve depends on $\bar{A}, \bar{X}, \overline{IM},$ and $\bar{q}$, which together determine the intercept on the Y-axis. Increases in $\bar{A}, \bar{X},$ and $\bar{q}$ shift the *IS* curve to the right (outward), while an increase in $\overline{IM}$ shifts the curve to the left (inward).

- The position of the *LM* curve depends on the real money stock, $\bar{M}/\bar{P}$, which determines the intercept on the i-axis. An increase in $\bar{M}$ shifts the *LM* curve down – or, what amounts to the same thing, to the right.

The intersection point (Y_0, i_0) is where the economy and all its submarkets are in equilibrium.

14.2 POLICY OPTIONS FOR AFFECTING OUTPUT

It is easiest to explain the intuition for the *IS*–*LM* model by showing how policy works in model. First, we will consider fiscal policy (as discussed in Chapter 13); second, monetary policy; and, finally, exchange rate policy.

Fiscal Policy

An increase in government spending increases autonomous spending (remember that $\bar{G}$ is part of $\bar{A}$); initially, aggregate demand rises by $\Delta G = \Delta A$. To meet the aggregate demand, more goods have to be produced, and production requires that the factors of production have to be paid. With the resulting income, households have higher disposable income, a portion of which they consume. In the absence of effects due to investment and the demand for money, the multiplier effect described in Chapter 13 will kick in: each real dollar's worth of increase in government spending yields a series of spending increases $\Delta G + (c - m)\Delta G + (c - m)^2 \Delta G \ldots$ In Figure 14.4, the government spending increase shows up as a rightward shift of the *IS* curve (black arrow) by a distance $\bar{\alpha}\Delta G$, so that, if interest rates were to stay constant, income would rise to Y'_0.

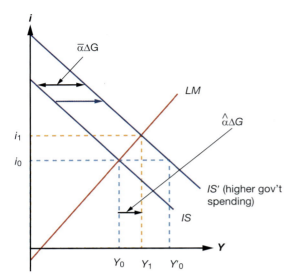

Figure 14.4 The Response to a Government Spending Increase This diagram shows that an increase in government spending shifts up (and out) the IS curve, resulting in an increase in income and interest rates.

What happens, now, if we incorporate the effects from investment and the demand for money, as reflected in the interest rate? Recall that money demand depends on income. As GDP and income rise (due to the above mechanism), the quantity of money demanded rises. However, the central bank is assumed to hold the money supply constant. If, initially, the quantity of money demanded equaled the quantity of money supplied (i.e., the economy was on the LM curve), then without a change in the interest rate, the quantity of money demanded will exceed the quantity of money supplied. The interest rate must rise to keep the quantity of money demanded in equilibrium with the (fixed) quantity of money supplied.

Due to the higher interest rate, income does not rise to Y'_0 (which would have been the case using the model in Chapter 13) but only to Y_1. Equivalently, the increase in output $\hat{a}\Delta G$ is smaller than what would have been implied by the simple Keynesian multiplier, $\bar{a}\Delta G$.

The increase in output is less in this model because of **crowding out**. Higher government spending leads to higher output, which leads to more transactions, which leads to higher demand for money. This, given a constant money supply, results in a higher interest rate. The higher interest rate depresses investment spending, thereby offsetting in part the increase in output. What has happened is that economy-boosting government spending has partly crowded out spending by firms. Output still increases, but not as much as it does without the crowding out effect.

Monetary Policy

Now we turn to monetary policy, which in this model means changes in the money supply. In the real world, many central banks target a particular interest rate and make whatever adjustments necessary to the money supply to drive the interest rate to that point. This monetary policy is often described as focusing on the interest rate the central bank controls. An increase in the money supply, holding everything else constant, is the same as a decrease in that interest rate. If $\overline{M}$ is increased while $\overline{P}$ remains constant, then $\overline{M}/\overline{P}$ rises, and the LM curve shifts to the right, as shown by the black arrow in Figure 14.5.

When the money supply increases, at the original income levels and interest rates there is an excess quantity of money. This excess quantity of money implies an excess demand for bonds. The resulting rise in the price of bonds is the same as a decline in the interest rate, i.e., a decline in the return on bonds. To see this, consider a coupon bond that pays $10 per year (the coupon payment). At a market price of $100, the current yield, or interest rate, is 10%. If the price were to

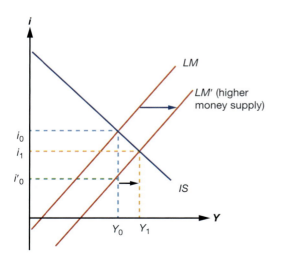

Figure 14.5 The Response to a Money Supply Increase This diagram shows that an increase in the money supply shifts down (and out) the LM curve, resulting in an increase in output and decrease in interest rates.

14.2 POLICY OPTIONS FOR AFFECTING OUTPUT

rise to $110, the current yield would drop to 9.1%. Holding income constant, the interest rate would fall to i'_0. That, however, is not the end of the story. The lower interest rate results in a higher level of investment spending (recall Figure 14.2), which means a higher level of aggregate demand and hence output (which in turn induces some additional money demand). Interest rates end up at i_1, and income at Y_1.

To sum up, expanding the money supply drives down interest rates and hence spurs investment, which increases income. This makes expansionary monetary policy part of the toolkit for any central bank seeking to keep GDP from slipping downward. The US Federal Reserve, which is formally charged with keeping the unemployment under control, is a case in point.

Exchange Rate Policy

Finally, consider the impact of an exchange rate policy. An increase in the real exchange rate that makes the domestically produced goods more affordable than their foreign counterparts increases net exports (more exports, fewer imports), which results in an increase in aggregate demand. This has the same overall effect as government spending, namely a shift in the *IS* curve in Figure 14.6 it the right (black arrow), resulting in an increase in output. Once again, however, the effect is partly offset by diminished investment due to the higher interest rate.

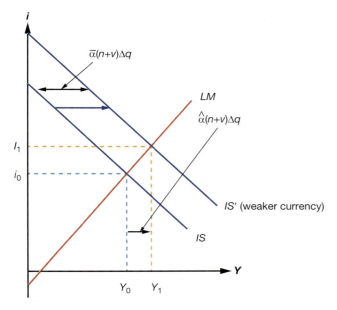

Figure 14.6 The Response to a Devaluation This diagram shows that a devaluation (increase in the exchange rate) shifts up (and out) the *IS* curve, resulting in an increase in output and interest rate.

The Relative Magnitudes of Policy Effects

We can relate the magnitude of the change in the economy's output, Y, to changes in the policy variables. Take equation (14.7), and break it up into the constituent changes (i.e., take a total differential):

$$\Delta Y = \widehat{\alpha} \left[\Delta A + \Delta X - \Delta IM + (n+v)\Delta q + \left(\frac{b}{h}\right)\Delta\left(\frac{M}{P}\right) \right] \tag{14.8}$$

Then the change in income, or GDP, can be attributed to a combination of changes in the amount of autonomous spending, changes in the money supply, or changes in the real exchange rate.

To determine the impact of changes from just one of those factors, one sets all the other changes to zero. For government spending *only*, after re-arranging, one obtains the following:

$$\frac{\Delta Y}{\Delta G} = \widehat{\alpha} \geq 0$$

For a change in the real money supply *only*, the impact on income is:

$$\frac{\Delta Y}{\Delta(M/P)} = \widehat{\alpha}\left(\frac{b}{h}\right) \geq 0$$

The final policy tool in our model is **devaluation/revaluation** of the real exchange rate. For a change in this rate *only*, the impact on income is:

$$\frac{\Delta Y}{\Delta q} = \widehat{\alpha}(n + v) \geq 0$$

If the exchange rate rises (devalues or depreciates), then exports increase and imports decrease, leading to a boost in income, which is magnified by way of the usual multiplier process.

14.3 INTRODUCING AN EXTERNAL BALANCE CONDITION

Thus far, we have not incorporated any restrictions on how exchange rates or financial flows might be affected by the country's interaction with the rest of the world. In order to account for that interaction, we need to include some sort of equilibrium condition that reflects the addition of the rest of the world as, in effect, another sector in our model of the economy.

This new condition is based on the balance of payments identity, which was described in Chapter 11. Recall that by this identity, the current account, the financial account, and official reserves transactions must sum to 0:

$$CA + FA + ORT \equiv 0 \tag{14.9}$$

This means that if there is a deficit on the current account, one of two things must be true. Either the financial account is in surplus, $FA > 0$, meaning that foreigners are lending domestic actors enough to finance the deficit, or else foreign exchange reserves are declining, $ORT > 0$, because the central bank is exchanging domestic currency for foreign currency to facilitate foreign imports.

Our equilibrium condition related to the balance of payments is that official reserves transactions are zero. On the assumption that the current account can be approximated by the trade balance, we use $TB + FA$ to represent the balance of payments and require that this equal zero:

$$TB + FA = 0 \tag{14.10}$$

That is, our definition of external equilibrium is a condition where foreign exchange reserves are neither increasing nor decreasing. Since it is sustainable, this is a reasonable condition. In concrete terms, this means that, if the country is running a trade deficit, importing more than it exports, then the rest of the world must be willing to lend enough to finance that deficit. If exports are purchased by foreigners with foreign currency, and imports are purchased with foreign currency held by the home country, then foreigners must be willing to lend enough foreign currency to make up the difference.

We have already described the behavior of the trade balance in Chapter 13. However, we have yet to say anything about what the financial account depends on. As usual, we use a linear function with an autonomous constant term and a linear term:

$$FA = \overline{FA} + \varkappa(i - \bar{i}^*) \tag{14.11}$$

The parameter $\varkappa$ is the sensitivity of financial flows to the interest differential. That is, $\varkappa$ describes the extent to which a higher domestic interest rate, i, compared to the interest rate in the foreign country, $\bar{i}^*$, promotes foreign purchases of domestic debt instruments – in our model, domestic bonds.

The higher the interest rate differential, $i - \bar{i}^*$, the more financial capital flows into the home country, holding all else constant. This is simply a reflection of the fact that a higher return on domestic financial assets makes those assets attractive to foreign purchasers. So, for instance, a foreign firm that could earn interest $\bar{i}^*$ on bonds issued by its own government or higher interest i by purchasing a US government bond will tend to prefer the latter. The bond purchase constitutes a loan to United States and thus an inflow of resources.

Substituting the expression for the trade balance (exports $\overline{X}$ minus imports $\overline{IM}$) and the just-developed expression for the financial account into equation (14.10), we can then *re-arrange* to solve for the interest rate and thereby obtain the **BP = 0 curve**:

$$i = -\left(\frac{1}{\varkappa}\right)\left[(\overline{X} - \overline{IM} + \overline{FA}) + (n+v)q\right] + \bar{i}^* + \left(\frac{m}{\varkappa}\right)Y \quad <BP = 0 \text{ curve}> \quad (14.12)$$

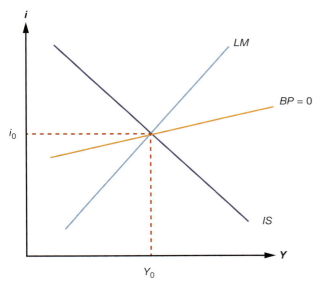

Figure 14.7 The IS–LM–BP = 0 Diagram This diagram adds the BP = 0 curve, an external equilibrium condition that private capital inflows match the trade deficit, to the IS–LM curves. The only point where the real side, financial side, and external sector are in equilibrium is where all three curves intersect.

The overbar over i^* indicates that the foreign interest rate is treated as given (or exogenous). Notice that the slope of this curve is positive $(m/\varkappa)$, and that anything that changes the autonomous components of exports, imports, and financial flows $(\overline{X}, \overline{IM}, \text{and } \overline{FA})$ will shift the curve. So, too, will changes in q.

The $BP = 0$ curve is the combination of all points for which the trade balance and financial flows are such that the balance of payments equals 0, so that official foreign exchange reserves do not change. The slope of the $BP = 0$ curve is positive because higher income is associated with higher imports and a lower trade balance; to maintain $TB + FA = 0$, then, financial inflows must be higher. This occurs when the interest rate is higher, holding foreign interest rates constant.

The *IS* and *LM* and $BP = 0$ curves are all shown in Figure 14.7. The figure pictures an economy in equilibrium both internally and externally, at interest rate i_0 and income level Y_0. This model combining the *IS–LM* model and an external condition related to the balance of payments is called the *IS–LM–BP* model. It is also called the **Mundell–Fleming model.**

The advent of this model reflects the confluence of new ideas of the workings of the aggregate economy, and new developments in the real world. Marcus Fleming was an economist, who worked most of his career at the International Monetary Fund (IMF), a multilateral institution charged with monitoring the exchange rate systems that member countries operated.

Robert Mundell was an academic economist who also worked at the IMF for two years just before the publication of his paper. As a Canadian, Mundell had a natural interest in how differently economies behaved under differing exchange rate regimes, since Canada was one of the rare countries that had switched between fixed and floating exchange rate systems, going on the float in 1950, and returning to a fix against the dollar in 1962.

Both economists had to contend with the new phenomenon of increasingly large cross-border capital flows. The model that the two economists developed, largely independently, deal with these challenges. The key difference lies in how they treated the nature of capital flow. Fleming's approach is largely consistent with the economy described in Figure 14.7. Mundell's paper examined the case where the $BP = 0$ curve is flat because financial capital is unimpeded, i.e., $\varkappa = \infty$.

The key insight that Mundell and Fleming both identified was that monetary policy was relatively less effective in a financially open economy under fixed exchange rates, as opposed to a closed economy, while a fiscal policy was more effective. The reverse is true for countries operating under flexible exchange rate regimes.

14.4 POLICY OPTIONS UNDER FIXED EXCHANGE RATES

We now examine the implications of the model when policymakers fix the exchange rate. In the fixed exchange rate situation, q does not change unless the government devalues or revalues the currency. That commitment to keeping the exchange rate fixed constrains monetary policy, but not fiscal policy.

Fiscal Policy

To denote the fact that the real exchange rate is controlled by the central bank, and is changed exogenously, we put a bar over q, hence $\bar{q}$.

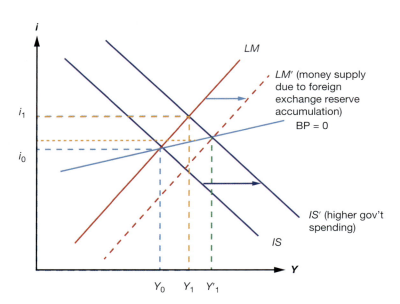

Figure 14.8 The Response to a Government Spending Increase under Fixed Exchange Rates This diagram shows that an increase in government spending shifts out the IS curve, resulting in an increase in output and interest rates, when capital mobility is relatively high, here shown as a $BP = 0$ curve flatter than LM curve. Under fixed exchange rates, the higher interest rate spurs financial inflows that increase the money supply resulting in a shift out of the LM curve. Output again increases.

Shifts in the IS and LM curves occur for the same reasons as before. Consider what happens if government spending increases, as shown in Figure 14.8. The IS curve shifts outward (denoted by the blue arrow).

In this case, the equilibrium income and interest rate rise. Notice that the new equilibrium interest rate, i_1, is higher than that consistent with external equilibrium (i.e., $BP = 0$). As a consequence, the balance of payments is in surplus, so $ORT < 0$, and foreign exchange reserves are increasing.

What happens next depends critically on the actions of the central bank. The increase in foreign exchange reserves implies an increase in currency or bank reserves (i.e., money), unless some offsetting action is undertaken. Any such offsetting action is termed **sterilization**. In the absence of sterilizing intervention, the LM curve will shift rightward to the new LM (light blue arrows), setting income at level Y'_1. However, if the central bank sterilizes the inflow, then the LM curve remains at its original position, with income at Y_1.

14.4 POLICY OPTIONS UNDER FIXED EXCHANGE RATES

To show why a net financial inflow causes an *LM* shift in the absence of sterilization, we have to digress in order to examine the workings of the central bank. A central bank purchases domestic assets (such as government bonds) and foreign exchange, and pays by issuing currency and crediting private banks with bank reserves. The central bank balance sheet, in Table 14.1, reflects the cumulative effect of these operations:

Table 14.1 Central Bank Balance Sheet

Assets	Liabilities
Domestic assets (DA)	Currency (CU)
Foreign exchange reserves (FXRes)	Bank reserves (Res)

The sum of central bank liabilities (**currency** and **bank reserves**) is termed the **money base**. This is technically different from the money supply, which determines the position of the *LM* curve, but, for our purposes, we will just assume that when the money base increases, the money supply increases. The money supply consists of currency and checking deposits; the former is a liability of the central bank, while the latter is a liability of the private banking system. If banks are forced to hold a minimum amount of bank reserves as a share of total checking deposits (say 10%, so $100 deposits requires $10 bank reserves), then there will be a fixed relationship between money supply and money base. (This assumes that the private banks do not hold any reserves above the required minimum.)

The central bank typically increases or decreases the money supply by conducting **open market operations**. For instance, in Section 14.2, the central bank would increase the money supply by buying **domestic assets**, such as government bonds (*DA* in Table 14.1) from the private banks, paying for them with currency.

Suppose, now, that there is a financial inflow that more than offsets a trade deficit. This will cause foreign exchange reserves (*FXRes*) to rise. Notice that when *FXRes* rises on the asset side of the balance sheet, then the money base also rises. For instance, if the *FXRes* rises by the equivalent of 1 billion Chinese yuan, then the effect on the central bank balance sheet will be as shown in Table 14.2. The resulting increase in the money supply leads to the outward shift in the *LM* curve shown in Figure 14.8.

Table 14.2 Change in Central Bank Balance Sheet Due to Unsterilized Balance of Payments Surplus

Assets	Liabilities
	+1 CNY (CU)
+1 CNY (FXRes)	

What happens in the case of sterilization, by contrast, is that the central bank keeps the money supply constant by selling *DA* in exchange for currency. The process of exactly offsetting the increase in *FXRes* with a decrease in *DA* is termed a "sterilization of reserve accumulation." This is illustrated in Table 14.3. The net change in the money base is 0. So then, if the inflow is sterilized, then the *LM* curve does not shift outward in Figure 14.8.

Table 14.3 Change in Central Bank Balance Sheet Due to Sterilized Balance of Payments Surplus

Assets	Liabilities
−1 CNY (DA)	+1 CNY
	−1 CNY (CU)
+1 CNY (FXRes)	

In Figure 14.8, the $BP = 0$ curve is drawn flatter than the LM curve; this flat $BP = 0$ curve arises because $\varkappa$ is large relative to m. This situation is often characterized as a case of high **capital mobility**: financial flows respond strongly to small interest rate changes in interest rate differentials – and therefore to small changes in the domestic interest rate, given that the foreign interest rate is assumed to be fixed.

Nothing, however, guarantees that the $BP = 0$ line, with slope $m/\varkappa$, will be flatter than the LM curve, with slope k/h. One can imagine that international investors might be reluctant to place their financial capital in, say, a small, developing country unless the capital will earn a very high rate of return. Under those conditions, financial flows will not be very sensitive to interest differentials, making $\varkappa$ small. Then the slope of the $BP = 0$ curve will be steep, perhaps steeper than that of the LM curve.

Under those conditions, the effect of a fiscal expansion will be as depicted in Figure 14.9. The IS curve shifts outward (the gray arrow), and output and the interest rate rise as before. Now, however, the equilibrium interest rate is *lower* than that required for external equilibrium. Hence, $BP < 0$, $ORT > 0$, and foreign exchange reserves decline. If the central bank does not sterilize, the foreign reserves' decline and the LM curve will shift inward until external equilibrium is restored at income

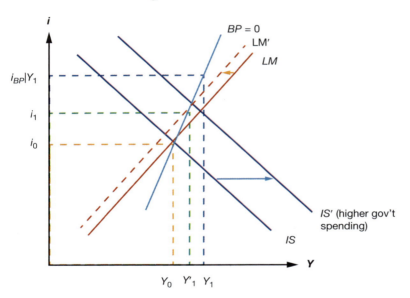

Figure 14.9 The Response to a Government Spending Increase under Fixed Exchange Rates with Low Capital Mobility This diagram shows the effect of an increase in government spending which shifts out the IS curve. Under low capital mobility, shown as a $BP = 0$ curve steeper than the LM curve, the interest rate rises, but less than necessary for balance of payments equilibrium, resulting in a loss of reserves and shrinkage of the money supply, shifting in the LM inward to LM'.

Y_0. If the central bank does sterilize, then the LM remains where it was, with income at Y_1. Of course, this must come to an end when foreign exchange reserves are depleted.

Monetary Policy under Fixed Exchange Rates

Now we consider monetary policy, by examining the case of high capital mobility in Figure 14.10. (The low mobility scenario yields the same result.) An expansion of the money supply shifts the LM curve shifts outward, driving the interest rate down to i_1.

In this case, the resulting equilibrium interest rate i_1 is less than what is required for external equilibrium. $(i_{BP=0} | Y_1)$. As a consequence, there is a balance of payments deficit, $ORT > 0$, and

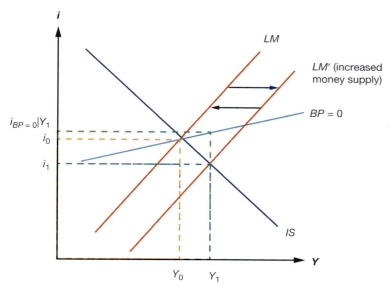

Figure 14.10 The Response to a Money Supply Increase under Fixed Exchange Rates with High Capital Mobility This diagram shows what happens when the money supply is expanded, and capital mobility is high. The *LM* curve shifts out, and the interest rate drops below that consistent with external balance, reserves decline and money supply shrinks, pulling the *LM* curve back to where it started.

foreign exchange reserves are run down. In the absence of offsetting sterilization by the central bank, the money supply shrinks, and the *LM* curve shifts back (black arrows). This process stops only when the interest rate is back at i_0 – in other words, when the monetary policy is undone. This happens because monetary policy is subordinated to the pegging of the exchange rate.

If the central bank were instead to shrink the money supply, shifting the *LM* curve inward, then the reverse process would occur. The resulting higher interest rate would draw in financial flows in amounts exceeding what is needed to maintain foreign exchange reserve levels. The increase in foreign exchange reserves would result in a corresponding increase in the amount of domestic currency circulating, thereby increasing the money supply. That process undoes the initial monetary policy.

The fact that monetary policy is undone by the response of capital flows is a demonstration of the loss of a country's **monetary autonomy** when it enters into a fixed exchange rate system. Since the loss of foreign exchange reserves is faster when capital mobility is high, then the higher the degree of capital mobility, the greater the loss in autonomy. (This applies when countries use market forces to set the equilibrium exchange rate at the official pegged rate. Sometimes countries also use **capital controls** and other exchange restrictions to set the rate at the official rate, as in the case of China.)

As noted above, this process can be delayed by sterilization. Again, however, sterilization of can continue only as long as the central bank possesses foreign exchange reserves. When reserves are exhausted, sterilization is no longer feasible, and the money supply will once again be out of the central bank's control. Sterilization of capital inflows does not face the constraint of foreign exchange reserves; in principle, reserves could increase without bounds. However, in order to maintain the money base and to keep the money supply constant, the central bank has to sell domestic assets as the stock of foreign exchange increases. Here it is the exhaustion of the stock of domestic assets the central bank holds that puts an end to sterilization. At that point, the money supply increases.

The greater the degree of capital mobility, the less the scope for monetary autonomy. At the limit, when capital mobility is infinite ($\varkappa = \infty$), under fixed exchange rates there is no monetary autonomy whatsoever. Under this condition, policymakers must choose either a fixed exchange rate with no monetary autonomy or monetary autonomy and a freely floating exchange rate. This choice is part of the International Trilemma discussed at further length in Section 15.4.

Responding to Balance of Payments Deficits: Devaluation vs. the Interest Rate Defense

In our model, the government exerts control over the economy through three levers: fiscal policy, monetary policy, and the value of the currency. By changing the value of the currency –

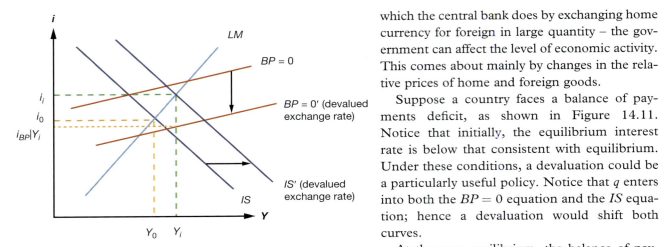

Figure 14.11 A Balance of Payments Deficit and Devaluation This diagram shows the economy at an initial point of balance of payments deficit. The devaluation shifts down the $BP = 0$ curve and out the IS curve. In the new equilibrium, the balance of payments is in surplus.

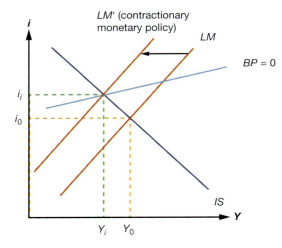

Figure 14.12 The Interest Rate Defense under Fixed Exchange Rates This diagram shows the economy initially with a balance of payments deficit. Reducing the money supply results in an increase in interest rates that brings enough capital inflows to produce a balance of payments equilibrium.

which the central bank does by exchanging home currency for foreign in large quantity – the government can affect the level of economic activity. This comes about mainly by changes in the relative prices of home and foreign goods.

Suppose a country faces a balance of payments deficit, as shown in Figure 14.11. Notice that initially, the equilibrium interest rate is below that consistent with equilibrium. Under these conditions, a devaluation could be a particularly useful policy. Notice that q enters into both the $BP = 0$ equation and the IS equation; hence a devaluation would shift both curves.

At the new equilibrium, the balance of payments is in surplus, since interest rate i_1 is greater than rate $i_{BP|Y1}$. The balance of payments problem has been remedied, and in fact foreign exchange reserves will now accumulate.

The balance of payments surplus will be undone over time, however, if the central bank does not sterilize the reserve accumulation. As foreign exchange reserves rise, the money base increases, shifting the LM curve outward. Eventually, the interest rate will fall to the level consistent with external balance, and reserve accumulation ceases.

Now, let us return to the question raised at the beginning of the chapter. Why would raising the interest rate – what is called an **interest rate defense** – remedy a balance of payments deficit? We start with the same conditions as in Figure 14.11, but now the central bank raises the interest rate by tightening monetary policy so that the LM curve shifts inward (black arrow), as in Figure 14.12.

The resulting equilibrium is sustainable in terms of the balance of payments, but, as depicted in Figure 14.12, would result in a lower level of income. Hence, the interest rate defense brings with it serious costs.

Rarely do central banks use just one of the tools available to them. In 2014, Russia used the interest rate defense and subsequently allowed the currency to weaken. The interest rate defense worked at the cost of weakening the economy. As financial capital outflows increased, the currency weakened despite the interest rate defense, and eventually, by mid-2015, the central bank relented, allowing the currency to weaken in value.

14.4 POLICY OPTIONS UNDER FIXED EXCHANGE RATES

APPLICATION   China's Surpluses and Reserve Accumulation

One of the best illustrations of the impact of a fixed exchange rate is China. Beginning in 2002, China began running significant current account surpluses (Figure 14.13). These surpluses arose from a variety of factors, including China's joining the World Trade Organization, which could be interpreted as an exogenous increase in net exports.

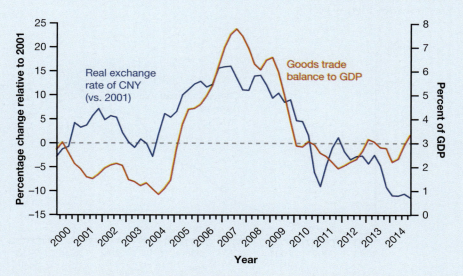

Figure 14.13 Exchange Rate Undervaluation and the Accumulation of Reserves This figure shows the percentage change in the Chinese real exchange rate relative to 2001 (blue, left scale, up is a Chinese currency depreciation), and four-quarter moving average of the percent share of Chinese goods trade balance to GDP (red, right scale).

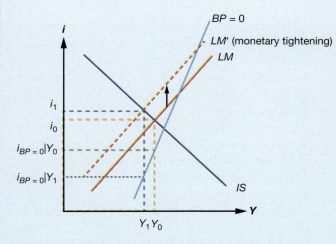

Figure 14.14 Monetary Tightening When the Balance of Payments Is in Surplus This diagram interprets the Chinese monetary policy over the period 2004–2005.

In addition, rapid productivity growth can be interpreted as a depreciation in the real exchange rate. In the $IS - LM - BP = 0$ model, each of these effects result in an outward shift in the IS curve and a downward shift in the $BP = 0$ curve. The resulting equilibrium is illustrated in Figure 14.14. Notice that the equilibrium interest rate i_0 exceeds that necessary for external equilibrium, $i_{BP|Y0}$.

Over the next two years, China's current account surplus increased, resulting in accelerating reserve accumulation. Notice that in order to prevent the LM shifting outward (which would have increased GDP and reduced the current account), the central bank had to sterilize the reserve accumulation. Instead of selling Chinese government bonds (reducing DA on the central bank balance sheet), the People's Bank of China

(PBoC) relied mostly on forcing the banking sector to hold more bank reserves. This served to reduce the money supply relative to what it otherwise would have been.

In 2004, the PBoC tried to offset the expansionary effect of a weak currency by tightening money policy (black arrow). This shifted the *LM* curve upward, raising the interest rate, and widening the gap between the equilibrium interest rate i_1 and the interest rate consistent with external balance, $i_{BP|Y_1}$. In other words, government policy exacerbated reserve accumulation. Chinese foreign exchange reserves surged starting in 2004, as shown in Figure 14.15.

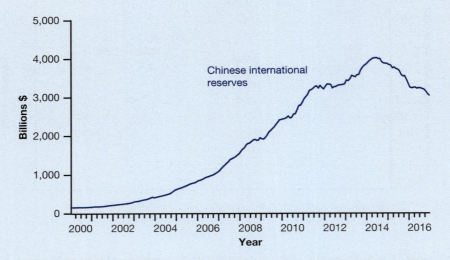

Figure 14.15 China's International Reserves This figure shows China's international reserves, excluding gold, in millions of USD.
Source: IMF, International Financial Statistics.

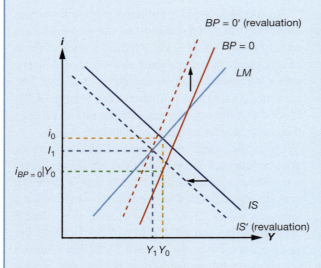

Figure 14.16 Revaluation when the Balance of Payments Is in Surplus This diagram shows an alternative exchange rate policy incorporating revaluation that China could have undertaken in 2005–2008.

A much more reasonable approach would have been to revalue the Chinese yuan. This would have shifted the *IS* curve inward (achieving the goal of reducing GDP) and shifted the $BP = 0$ curve upward (see the black arrows). These effects are on display in Figure 14.16.

A currency revaluation could have accomplished the dual aims of cooling off the economy and reducing the current account surplus and pace of reserve accumulation. This is essentially the policy China finally undertook, under pressure from the international community, when China went off its de facto peg against the US dollar in July 2005. By June 2015, after years of yuan appreciation, Chinese foreign exchange reserves peaked, at *over $4 trillion*.

Since that time, China's financial outflows have increased, so that, when combined with foreign exchange intervention, China's reserves had declined by nearly a trillion dollars by early 2017, and has stayed at roughly those levels until mid-2022.

CONCLUSION

This chapter developed a model of the economy that incorporates a role for money and interest rates. Monetary policy affects output by changing interest rates, thereby affecting any interest-sensitive components of aggregate demand. In the model developed, the interest-sensitive component is investment. Fiscal policy retains influence, albeit diminished, by virtue of the crowding out effect: when output rises with an increase in government spending, the rising demand for money induces an elevated interest rate that reduces investment and output somewhat. This framework is called the *IS–LM* model.

External equilibrium is defined as stability of foreign exchange reserves. This occurs when a trade deficit is financed by financial capital inflows, or a trade surplus finances financial capital outflows. Combining this external balance condition with the *IS–LM* model results in the Mundell–Fleming model.

When the real exchange rate is fixed by the central bank, then monetary policy is not autonomous in the long term. Monetary policy has to accommodate fiscal policy and is therefore unable to undertake independent measures. If changes in foreign exchange reserves are offset, or sterilized, monetary policy can independently affect output over a limited time frame. That ability ends when the central bank's relevant reserves, of either foreign currency or domestic bonds, run out.

In the next chapter, we examine the alternate scenario, where the exchange rate is allowed to move freely. Then the balance of payments is always in equilibrium, so that official reserves transactions are essentially held at 0. In that case, monetary policy will have greater scope for independent action, and fiscal policy correspondingly less.

SUMMARY

1. A model that distinguishes between the economy's real and financial sides is developed. The real side is linked to the financial side by way of investment sensitivity to interest rates.
2. Fiscal policy is less powerful in the new model than in the simple Keynesian one, because higher income induces higher interest rates, which depress investment.
3. Monetary policy works by changing interest rates, thereby affecting investment and total aggregate demand.
4. In an economy on a fixed exchange rate, the central bank is committed to buying and selling foreign exchange to peg the currency at a certain value.
5. Both monetary and fiscal policy are effective in affecting output, but monetary policy only remains effective so long as foreign exchange changes are sterilized.
6. The degree of capital mobility is important in determining the effectiveness of either fiscal or monetary policy.

KEY CONCEPTS

Bank reserves, page 315
Bonds, page 305
$BP = 0$ curve, page 313
Capital mobility, page 316
Currency, page 315
Crowding out, page 310
Devaluation, page 312

Domestic assets, page 315
Interest rate defense, page 318
IS curve, page 307
Liquidity, page 308
LM curve, page 308
Monetary autonomy, page 317
Money, page 307

Money base, page 315
Money demand, page 308
Money supply, page 307
Mundell–Fleming model, page 313

Open market operations, page 315
Revaluation, page 312
Sterilization, page 314

REVIEW QUESTIONS

1. Equilibrium in which market is represented by the *IS* curve?
2. Which markets are in equilibrium when on the *LM* curve?
3. What are the key differences between money and bonds?
4. Are corporate bonds included in the model?
5. How is the money supply increased or decreased by the central bank?
6. How does the central bank "peg" the exchange rate? (*Hint*: Refer to Chapter 12.)
7. If a country has a trade deficit and foreigners are not willing to lend enough to finance that deficit, what must happen to foreign exchange reserves? Assume net income and net transfers are zero.
8. Will a devaluation typically reduce a trade deficit?
9. What are the implications of tightening of monetary policy for interest rates and the economy?

EXERCISES

1. In the *IS–LM* model, is it true that the interest rate is determined solely in the financial sector?
2. Assume one does not have to consider the external balance condition. What is the size of the government spending multiplier, compared to that in Chapter 13, if investment spending does not depend on the interest rate? Is it larger or smaller than in Chapter 13?
3. Monetary policy works by changing the money supply so as to affect the interest rate. How can the central bank change the money supply?
4. Consider fiscal policy in an economy described by the following equations:

    (1) $Y = AD$

    (2) $AD = C + I + G + X - IM$

    (3) $C = \overline{C} + c(Y - T)$

    (4) $T = \overline{T}$

    (5) $I = \overline{I} - bi$

    (6) $G = \overline{G}$

    (7) $X = \overline{X} + vq$

    (8) $IM = \overline{IM} + mY - nq$

EXERCISES

(9) $\dfrac{M^d}{P} = \dfrac{M^s}{P}$

(10) $\dfrac{M^s}{P} = \dfrac{\overline{M}}{\overline{P}}$

(11) $\dfrac{M^d}{P} = kY - hi$

For now, ignore the external balance condition.

a. Solve for the *IS* curve, with *Y* on the left-hand side.
b. Solve for the *LM* curve, with *i* on the left-hand side.
c. Graph the *IS* and *LM* curves on a single graph. Show the vertical intercepts, the slopes, and the intersection.
d. Solve for equilibrium income. Show your work.
e. Calculate the change in income resulting from a given increase in government spending, ΔG.
f. Show graphically what happens when government spending is increased. Clearly indicate the distance of the curve shifts, and the amount of the income change.
g. Is the effect of government spending on income greater or less in this model, as compared to the simple Keynesian model? Explain why the difference occurs, in words.
h. Answer part (g) again, assuming the interest sensitivity of money demand to be infinite.
i. Answer part (g) again, if the interest sensitivity of investment were infinite.

5. Consider the same economy described in Exercise 4.
   a. Calculate the change in income for a given change in money supply, $\Delta(M/P)$. Assume that the price level *P* is fixed at 1.
   b. Show graphically what happens when the real money stock is increased. Clearly indicate the distance of the curve shifts and the amount of the income change.
   c. Suppose that the interest sensitivity of investment is extremely high. Show graphically the effect upon output and interest rates that result from an increase of the real money stock. Clearly indicate the size of the change in income.
   d. Suppose that the interest sensitivity of money demand is extremely high. Show graphically the effect upon output and interest rates that result from an increase of the real money stock. Clearly indicate the size of the change in income.

6. Suppose the economy is described by the following set of equations, as in the Mundell–Fleming model.

   1. $Y = \overline{\alpha}\left[\overline{A} + \overline{X} - \overline{IM} + (n+v)\overline{q} - bi\right]$ <*IS* curve>

   1'. $i = \dfrac{\overline{A} + \overline{X} - \overline{IM} + (n+v)\overline{q}}{b} - \left(\dfrac{1 - c(1-t) + m}{b}\right)Y$ <*IS* curve>

   2. $i = -\left(\dfrac{1}{h}\right)\left(\dfrac{\overline{M}}{\overline{P}}\right) + \left(\dfrac{k}{h}\right)Y$ <*LM* curve>

3. $$i = -\left(\frac{1}{\varkappa}\right)\left[(\overline{X} - \overline{IM} + \overline{FA}) + (n+v)\overline{q}\right] + \overline{i^*} + \left(\frac{m}{\varkappa}\right)Y \qquad <BP = 0 \text{ curve}>$$

   a. Draw a graph of initial equilibrium, where the goods and money markets are in equilibrium, as is the balance of payments. Assume that $m/\varkappa < k/h$.
   b. Show what happens if government spending is increased, both immediately, and over time, assuming no sterilization.
   c. At the new equilibrium, what is true about (i) the level of output; (ii) the level of investment; (iii) the real exchange rate; and (iv) the trade balance?
   d. Redraw the graph in part (a), and show the impact of a monetary contraction, both immediately and over time. Assume that over time, financial flows are sterilized.
   e. Explain why the process you lay out in part d. occurs.
   f. Answer part (d) if financial flows are not sterilized.
   g. Does your answer to part (d) change if $m/\varkappa > k/h$?
7. Consider the same economy described in Exercise 6, with $m/\varkappa < k/h$.
   a. Assume the economy begins in equilibrium. Show what happens in the short term if the foreign interest rate rises exogenously.
   b. Assume the central bank sterilizes inflows/outflows. Is the balance of payments in surplus, deficit, or equal to 0?
   c. Suppose the central bank wishes to re-establish balance of payments equilibrium. What policies can it implement in order to achieve that goal?
8. In the same economy examined in Exercise 7, show the impact in the short term of a revaluation of the currency. What happens to output, the interest rate, and the balance of payments?
9. Suppose a country is running a balance of payments deficit. What are the policy options for remedying the deficit?

RECOMMENDED RESOURCES

James M. Boughton, "On the Origins of the Fleming–Mundell Model," *IMF Staff Papers* 50(1) (2003): 1–9.

CHAPTER 15

Floating Exchange Rates and the International Trilemma

LEARNING OBJECTIVES

In this chapter, we learn about:
- how floating exchange rates adjust to restore external equilibrium
- how, with floating rates, fiscal and monetary policy affect output and exchange and interest rates
- how floating rates make fiscal policy less effective but monetary policy more effective
- how the effectiveness of fiscal and monetary policies depends on the exchange rate regime when there is perfect mobility of capital
- how a liquidity trap will prevent expansionary monetary policy from increasing output
- why an economy cannot simultaneously achieve stability, monetary independence, and financial integration

INTRODUCTION

In late 2017, the US economy was nearing full employment. Unemployment was at a 40-year low of 4.2%, yet President Trump and the Republican-controlled Congress embarked upon a policy of tax cuts. The Federal Reserve, seeking to avoid overheating the economy, tightened monetary policy, raising interest rates. In other words, the two policies were working in opposite directions. The dollar rose in value, making US exports more expensive to foreigners, making imports cheaper to Americans, and thus worsening the trade deficit. How and why these events played out motivates the development of the model in this chapter.

In contrast to the model presented in Chapter 14, the central bank in this new model is no longer committed to exchanging home currency for foreign currency at a designated exchange rate. Rather, the central bank eschews foreign exchange intervention, and thus gains monetary policy autonomy. Foreign exchange reserves no longer change in response to changes in interest rates and trade flows. Instead, the exchange rate freely adjusts in response to market forces, so as to keep foreign exchange reserves constant. Because of this switch in which variable is free to move and which is not, the model's predictions differ substantially from those obtained in Chapter 14.

This episode was a replay – in smaller scale – of events in the 1980s. Then, fiscal and monetary policies collided, giving rise to much larger dollar appreciation, trade deficit deterioration, and the hammering of the manufacturing sector, so much so that manufacturing employment fell even as overall employment rose. The reverberations of those events, now 40 years ago, continue, giving rise to the term "Rust Belt" to describe that region of the US that was de-industrialized.

We first show how monetary and fiscal policy work under floating exchange rates. Next, the relative effectiveness of the policies under floating and fixed exchange rates are contrasted. After showing some empirical estimates of these policy effects in the two different regimes, we examine how monetary and fiscal policies can sometimes work at cross purposes. Finally, the implications of perfect capital mobility are described, which sets the stage for the discussion of the International Trilemma: countries can choose only two of three objectives fully at any given time: exchange rate flexibility, monetary autonomy, and financial openness.

15.1 FISCAL AND MONETARY POLICY UNDER FLOATING EXCHANGE RATES

We retain the IS, LM, and $BP = 0$ schedules as described in the previous chapter, but with one critical difference: the real exchange rate q is now an endogenous variable instead of an exogenous one. That is, the rate is now allowed to float instead of being fixed by policy.

Here are the three key equations from the last chapter, with q's new status marked by the removal of the overbar:

$$Y = \overline{\alpha}\left[\overline{A} + \overline{X} - \overline{IM} + (n+v)q - bi\right] \qquad <IS \text{ curve}> \qquad (15.1)$$

$$i = -\left(\frac{1}{h}\right)\left(\frac{\overline{M}}{\overline{P}}\right) + \left(\frac{k}{h}\right)Y \qquad <LM \text{ curve}> \qquad (15.2)$$

$$i = -\left(\frac{1}{\varkappa}\right)\left[(\overline{X} - \overline{IM} + \overline{FA}) + (n+v)q\right] + \overline{i^*} + \left(\frac{m}{\varkappa}\right)Y \qquad <BP = 0 \text{ curve}> \qquad (15.3)$$

In the fixed exchange rate case, q is treated as a constant; it changes only when the central bank decides to devalue or revalue the currency. With a floating exchange rate, q is free to move in response to other forces. When the equilibrium interest rate is above (or below) that consistent with external equilibrium, the currency appreciates (or depreciates) so as to maintain the $BP = 0$ condition. When the economy is at external equilibrium, as shown in Figure 15.1, there is no tendency for q to change.

Figure 15.1 looks identical to Figure 14.7. The differences become apparent when we examine the implications, first, of fiscal policy and second of monetary policy.

Fiscal Policy

Consider what happens when the government increases its spending. With increased $\overline{A}$, the IS curve shifts out, as in Figure 15.2 (light blue arrow). Output initially rises to Y_1, and interest rates to i_1. However, now the equilibrium interest rate is greater than that consistent with external equilibrium; it attracts inflows of foreign financial capital beyond those necessary to offset the trade balance. In the fixed exchange rate system, this would mean increases in official reserves. However, under the floating exchange rate system, the home currency appreciates, i.e., q falls.

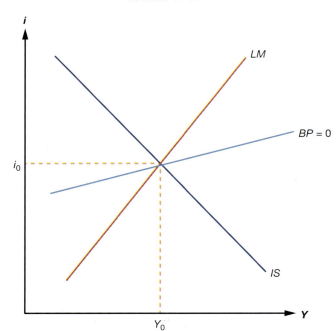

Figure 15.1 IS–LM–BP = 0 Diagram This diagram depicts equilibrium in the IS–LM–BP = 0 model, under floating exchange rates.

15.1 FISCAL AND MONETARY POLICY UNDER FLOATING EXCHANGE RATES

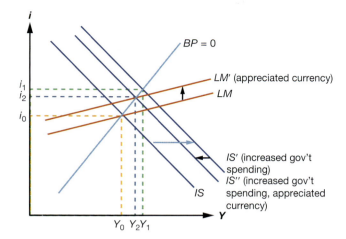

Figure 15.2 The Response to a Government Spending Increase under Floating Exchange Rates This diagram shows the effect of an increase in government spending, which shifts out the IS curve, under high capital mobility. The rise in interest rates spurs a capital inflow that appreciates the currency. The currency appreciation shifts up the $BP = 0$ curve, and inward the IS curve.

As q falls, this affects two curves: by equation (15.1), a fall in q shifts in the IS curve, and by equation (15.3), a fall in q shifts up the $BP = 0$ curve. The two shifts are depicted in Figure 15.2 (black arrows). Equilibrium income falls back to Y_2 and interest rates retreat to i_2, although both of these values are still higher than the initial values, Y_0 and i_0.

Why do the IS and $BP = 0$ shifts occur? As q falls (appreciates), exports ($X = \overline{X} + vq$) fall and imports ($IM = \overline{IM} + mY - nq$) increase. That means a decline in aggregate demand and an inward shift of the IS schedule. Meanwhile, as exports decrease and imports increase, with an appreciated currency, financial inflows must be higher for any given income level in order for external balance to hold. The only thing that attracts financial inflows is a higher interest rate, or, in other words, an upward-shifted $BP = 0$ curve.

In the end, in an open economy, some of the fiscal expansion is offset by reduced net exports. Another way to think about this phenomenon is that there is now an additional channel for crowding out – two components of aggregate demand that are sensitive to interest rates: investment spending and net exports. Net exports are not explicitly interest sensitive, but they do depend upon the exchange rate. To the extent the exchange rate in turn depends upon interest rates, net exports are in effect interest sensitive, after all.

Monetary Policy

Now we consider what happens with a monetary expansion. Here we examine only the high capital mobility case, where (recall from Chapter 14) the slope $m/\varkappa$ of the $BP = 0$ curve is shallow. The qualitative results are the same for a steeper $BP = 0$ curve.

In Figure 15.3, the monetary expansion shifts out the LM curve (light blue arrow). The resulting equilibrium interest rate i_1 is less than that required for external equilibrium. As a consequence, financial inflows decline, there is an incipient balance of payments deficit, and the exchange rate depreciates. The depreciated exchange rate results in increased net exports, so the interest rate required for external equilibrium falls (the $BP = 0$ curve shifts downward). The increase in net exports also means an increase in domestic aggregate demand, so

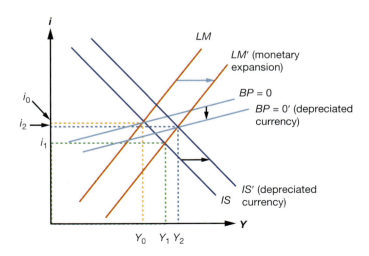

Figure 15.3 The Response to a Money Supply Increase under Floating Exchange Rates This diagram shows the effect of an increase in money supply under high capital mobility, which shifts out the LM curve, resulting in a lower interest rate that depreciates the currency. The currency depreciation shifts out the IS curve and down the $BP = 0$ curve.

the IS curve shifts out. The economy settles into equilibrium at income level Y_2 and interest rate i_2.

Notice that monetary policy is relatively powerful. The increase in the money supply decreases the interest rate and hence spurs capital investment, thereby increasing output. The lower interest rates also puts negative pressure on the balance of payments and, under a free float, this manifests itself in a depreciation of the home currency. This shifts down the $BP = 0$ curve (blue arrow). The depreciation spurs exports and discourages imports, so the expansionary monetary policy "crowds in" net exports, as well as investment.

This result highlights the fact that in an open economy under a floating exchange rate regime, monetary policy is generally more powerful than in the case of a closed economy. That is because monetary policy can now exert its influence through two channels – the investment channel and the net exports channel. The greater the degree of financial capital mobility, the more this is true.

In a fully floating exchange rate regime, market conditions determine the currency's value. However, as we just saw, this does not mean that the central bank (and the government) cannot influence that value. In particular, the central bank can, by affecting the interest rate, affect the market conditions that underlie the exchange rate's level.

Interest Rate Shocks

We have been examining the effects of domestic policies. However, the model is also quite useful for examining how events in the rest of the world can affect exchange rates and income at home. In mid-2014, for instance, expectations of a US interest rate rise relative to the euro area rate led to a depreciation of the euro against the US dollar.

If we model this event from the euro area perspective, the increase in the US interest rate is a rise in $\bar{i}^*$ in equation (15.3). There, a rise in $\bar{i}^*$ contributes one-for-one to a rise in the interest rate, i, which equilibrates the balance of payments. Thus, if the foreign (US) interest rate rises (exogenously) by a 1 percentage point, the $BP = 0$ curve will shift up one percentage point. The

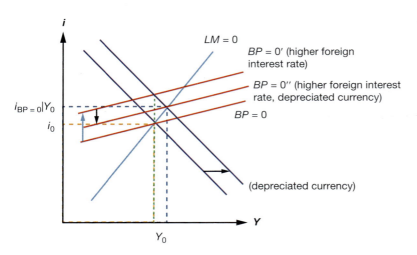

Figure 15.4 **The Effect of an Increase in the Foreign Interest Rate** This diagram illustrates the effect of an increase in the US interest rate on the home economy $BP = 0$ curve, which shifts up. With the home interest rate lower than that required for balance of payments equilibrium, the currency depreciates shifting out the IS curve and the $BP = 0$ curve (partway) down.

outcome in the high capital mobility case is depicted in Figure 15.4.

As the foreign interest rate rises (light blue arrow), the euro area interest rate is now below the interest rate consistent with external balance at income Y_0, namely $i_{BP=0}|Y_0$. The euro thus depreciates to q, shifting down the $BP = 0$ curve and shifting out the IS curve (black arrows). In the end, the euro area interest rate rises to i_1 in response to the foreign interest rate increase, although not one-for-one.

To stabilize the exchange rate, the monetary authority (in this case the European Central Bank) could raise euro area interest rates. In Figure 15.4, this would entail a shift backwards of the LM curve. In other words, the authority could maintain the exchange rate at a given level, at the cost of losing control over output. In this case, the economy would undergo a recession. Since the euro area was already experiencing slow growth in 2014, the ECB did not tighten monetary policy. This episode illustrates the tradeoffs that policymakers make. While it might be desirable to stabilize the currency's value, that benefit has to be weighed against the benefits of maintaining the current level of output.

15.2 SUMMARIZING EFFECTS UNDER FIXED AND FLOATING EXCHANGE RATES

In the last chapter and this one, our examination of the effects of different policies has generated a large number of outcomes, depending on the exchange rate regime, degree of capital mobility, and whether the central bank sterilizes financial capital flows. Table 15.1 summarizes these results, assuming relatively high capital mobility.

There is no entry for floating under real exchange rate, because under a floating regime, the exchange rate is an endogenous variable, rather than one set by policy.

Empirical Estimates of Policy Effects

Theory provides insights into the effectiveness of fiscal, monetary, and exchange rate policies in open economies. Under fixed exchange rates, fiscal policy should be relatively effective but monetary policy relatively ineffective (particularly in the longer term). The reverse is true under floating exchange rates: fiscal policy should be less effective, but monetary policy more effective, holding all else constant.

How well do these predictions hold up in the real world? Ethan Ilzetzki, Enrique Mendoza, and Carlos Végh (2013) used data on a number of national economies to infer how output, the current account, and the real exchange rate would respond to a hypothetical sudden increase (shock) in government spending, equal to 1% of GDP. They also considered the response of the central bank's policy interest rate.

Figure 15.5 shows the response of each variable over 20 quarters, with fixed exchange rate regimes on the left and floating rate regimes on the right. The red lines indicate the estimated

Table 15.1 The Impact of Policies and Foreign Developments

	Exchange rate regime	Income	Interest rate	Real exchange rate	Trade balance	Foreign exchange reserves
Government spending	Fixed (w/sterilization)	Increase	Increase	No change	Decrease	Increase
	Fixed	*Increase*	Increase	No change	Decrease	Increase
	Floating	Increase	Increase	Appreciation	Decrease	No change
Real money supply	Fixed (w/sterilization)	Increase	Decrease	No change	Decrease	Decrease
	Fixed	No change	No change	No change	No change	Decrease
	Floating	*Increase*	Decrease	Depreciation	Increase	No change
Real exchange rate[1]	Fixed (w/sterilization)	Increase	Increase	Devaluation	Increase	Increase
	Fixed	Increase	Increase	Devaluation	Increase	Increase
Foreign interest rate	Fixed (w/sterilization)	No change	No change	No change	No change	Decrease
	Fixed	Decrease	Increase	No change	Increase	Decrease
	Floating	Increase	Increase	Depreciation	Depreciation	No change

Note: Responses of each variable in the column to a change in the indicated variable in the left column, under fixed exchange rate regime with sterilization, without sterilization, and free floating. Entries in bold italics indicate relatively large changes.

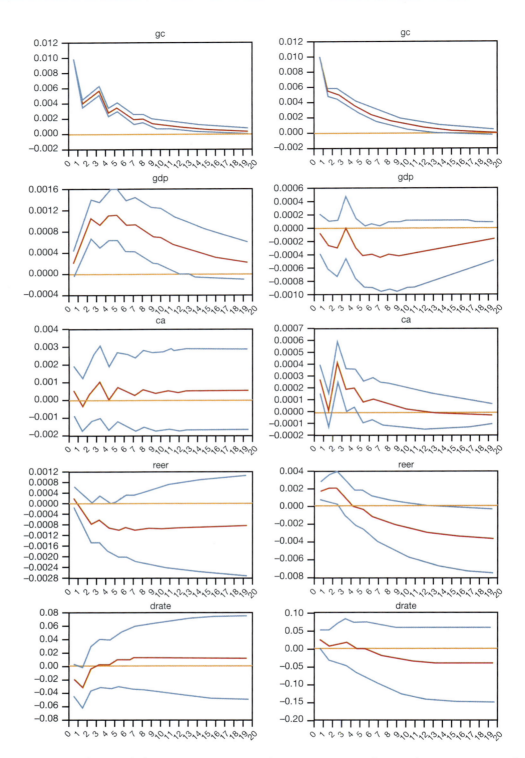

Figure 15.5 The Empirical Response to an Increase in Government Spending Impulse responses to a 1% shock to government consumption in episodes of fixed exchange rates (left panels) and flexible exchange rates (right panels). Impulse response from top to bottom: government consumption (i.e., spending on goods and services); gross domestic product; current account as a percentage of GDP; the real effective exchange rate (defined so that a rise is a currency appreciation); policy interest rate of the central bank. The time dimension is quarterly. Light blue lines represent 90% confidence intervals based on Monte Carlo simulations.

Source: Used with permission of Elsevier, Ethan Ilzetzki, Enrique G. Mendoza, Carlos A. Végh, "How Big (Small?) are Fiscal Multipliers?," Journal of Monetary Economics, 60, 2, 2013.

effects, while the light blue lines mark the 90% confidence intervals for these estimates. A response is statistically significant when both red lines lie on the same side of the zero line.

Fixed exchange rate regimes. With fixed exchange rates, GDP increases, with the peak effect coming about a year after the government spending shock. Over time, the impact tails off toward 0 (which matches up with theory that will be outlined in Chapter 16). Within three years of the government spending increase, the impact on GDP is not statistically significant.

The current account and the real exchange rate responses deviate from 0 only by a statistically insignificant amount. The policy rate is the rate set by the central bank, rather than the market rate discussed in the model. In the estimates, the policy rate deviates by an economically and statistically insignificant amount. To the extent it moves, it falls (i.e., monetary policy is accommodative).

Floating exchange rate regimes. With floating rates, GDP does not respond in a statistically significant manner. The fact that the response under floating is less than under fixed is consistent with the Mundell–Fleming model. The real exchange rate initially appreciates, and then reverts back to 0 within a year. The policy rate rises slightly in response to the fiscal policy.

The current account, which approximately equals the trade balance, responds somewhat counter-intuitively. Instead of declining, as it should under flexible rates, it rises (erratically) in the middle of the first and second quarter after the government spending occurs. Why this result is obtained is a hard question to answer, partly because the predictions are clear if everything else is held constant. In reality, the degree of openness to international trade, the degree of capital mobility, and the degree of capital openness all vary. This anomalous result might arise because developing countries, which account for a large number of floating exchange rate regimes, exhibit this behavior. For those countries, a government spending increase results in an increase in the current account, something that is not predicted by any particular theory.

The data from the real world confirm the key conclusion that fiscal policy is less effective under flexible rates than under fixed.

APPLICATION   Monetary and Fiscal Policy at Cross Purposes

In 2017, US President Donald Trump and the Republican controlled Congress passed the Tax Cuts and Jobs Act, a measure that reduced Federal tax revenues by about $1.7 trillion over a decade.

This was an expansionary fiscal policy implemented at a time when output was near full employment levels. With the Fed seeking to stabilize output at around full employment levels, it raised interest rates by shifting the *LM* curve.

In Figure 15.8, this appears as an inward shift of the LM curve (black arrow), so that the interest rate rises to i_1. Assuming high capital mobility, this combination of fiscal and monetary policy leads to a large appreciation of the currency, which leads to shifts of the $BP = 0$ and *IS* curves (black arrows).

Figure 15.6 The Tax Cuts and Job Act President Trump Speaks on the Passage of the GOP Tax Plan at the White House in 2017.
Source: Chip Somodevilla/Getty Images.

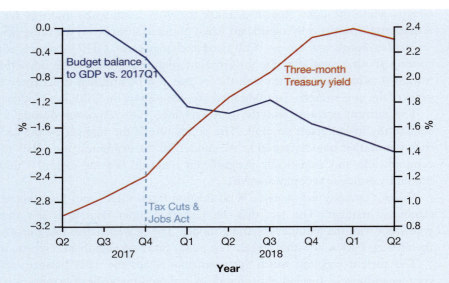

Figure 15.7 Budget Deficits and Interest Rates This figure shows the percentage point change in the budget balance to GDP since the first quarter of 2017 (blue), and three month Treasury yield in percentage points (red). Source: BEA, 2022Q2 third release.

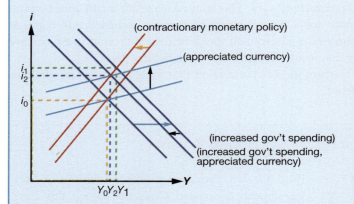

Figure 15.8 Colliding Policies This diagram shows the effect of increasing government spending and reducing the money supply, under high capital mobility. The higher government spending shifts out the IS curve, and tighter monetary policy shifts up the LM curve. The higher interest rate causes a currency appreciation that shifts up the BP=0 curve while shifting in the IS curve.

The economy settles at income level Y_2 and interest rate i_2. The final income level exceeds the starting level, Y_0, but not by as much as would have been the case if monetary policy had been less contractionary. This collision of expansionary fiscal policy and contractionary monetary policy is like stepping on the gas and brake pedals at the same time.

The model also implies that the interest rate increase from i_0 to i_2 should appreciate the dollar. That is exactly what happened, as Figure 15.9 illustrates.

While the dollar had been depreciating before the Tax Cuts and Jobs Act, the collision of expansionary fiscal and contractionary monetary policy led to a reversal of trend, and appreciation of roughly 5%.

Net exports – excluding petroleum which is not very sensitive to the exchange rate – deteriorated by about half a percentage point over the next year.

The simultaneous onset of deterioration in the budget and trade balances is sometimes termed a Twin Deficits phenomenon. In this case, the magnitudes were fairly small. In contrast, in the 1980s, the collision of expansionary fiscal policy (tax cuts, increased defense spending) under President Reagan, and contractionary monetary policy under Fed Chairman Paul Volcker, led to what became known as *the* Twin Deficits. The appreciation of the dollar – by about 40% – made US exports relatively uncompetitive in markets overseas, while it made imported goods cheaper for US consumers and firms. By 1987, net exports

15.2 SUMMARIZING EFFECTS UNDER FIXED AND FLOATING EXCHANGE RATES   333

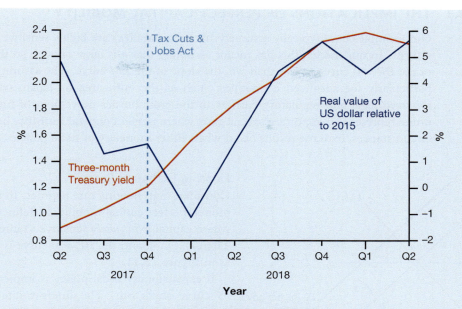

Figure 15.9 A Rising Interest Rate and Exchange Rate Appreciation This figure shows the three month Treasury yield, in percentage points (red, left scale) and the percent change in the US real exchange rate from 2015 (blue, right scale).
Source: Federal Reserve Board.

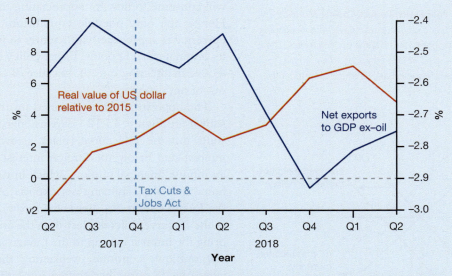

Figure 15.10 The Exchange Rate and Net Exports This figure shows the change in real value of the US dollar from 2015, in percent (red, left scale), and net exports as a percent of GDP (blue, right scale).
Source: Federal Reserve Board, and BEA.

fell by about 2.5 percentage points of GDP, to a record (at the time) −3%. The industrial cities of the Great Lakes region, from New York to Illinois, suffered deeply, earning that stretch of geography an unwelcome new nickname: the Rust Belt.

15.3 THE IMPLICATIONS OF PERFECT CAPITAL MOBILITY

Our examples have typically assumed that financial flows are highly sensitive to differentials in returns. In our model, this has meant assuming that $\varkappa$ is large enough so that $m/\varkappa$, the slope of the $BP = 0$ curve, is less than k/h, the slope of the LM curve. The assumption makes sense particularly for advanced economies, such as the euro area or Japan, which have largely removed legal and regulatory barriers to the cross-border movement of funds. These economies represent an important special case, where **perfect capital mobility** holds. Under those circumstances, extreme results occur when either monetary or fiscal policies are implemented.

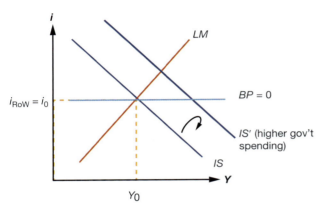

Figure 15.11 Fiscal Policy with Perfect Capital Mobility This diagram shows the effect of an increase in government spending under perfect capital mobility, and floating exchange rates. The *IS* curve shifts out, and capital inflows appreciate the currency, so that net exports decline pulling the *IS* back to where it started from.

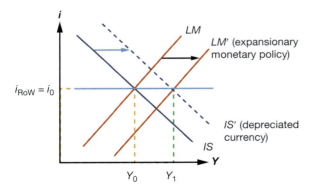

Figure 15.12 Monetary Policy under Perfect Capital Mobility This diagram shows the effect of increasing the money supply under perfect capital mobility, and flexible exchange rates. The increase in money supply shifts out the *LM* curve, driving down the interest rate, which then causes a capital outflow that depreciates the currency, shifting out the *IS* curve.

Floating Exchange Rates

Consider, first, floating rate regimes. In the context of the model, perfect capital mobility is defined as the situation where capital is *infinitely* sensitive to interest differentials. Then $m/\varkappa = 0$, and the $BP = 0$ curve is a horizontal line, as in Figure 15.11.

If expansionary fiscal policy is implemented, then the *IS* curve shifts out. The interest rate rises above the foreign interest rate, inducing an infinitely large financial inflow that causes the home currency to appreciate, pulling the *IS* curve back in. As long as the interest rate is above the other currencies, infinite amounts of capital will continue to flow in, appreciating the home currency. Hence, the only possible equilibrium is one where the currency is appreciated sufficiently to pull the *IS* back to its original starting point. Fiscal policy is completely ineffective in affecting output, because of complete crowding out of net exports.

The opposite result is obtained for monetary policy, as shown in Figure 15.12. Expansionary monetary policy shifts out the LM curve (black arrow), resulting in an interest rate below the foreign interest rate. This causes an infinite financial outflow, which in turn depreciates the home currency, spurring net exports. As a consequence, the *IS* curve shifts out (light blue arrow). However, as long as the *IS* curve shifts out less than the amount necessary to bring the interest rate up to the foreign interest rate, financial outflows continue, weakening the currency. Only when the *IS* curve has shifted out sufficiently to set the home interest rate equal to the foreign rate does the process end. Then output will have increased substantially, from Y_0 to Y_1. Thus, with perfect capital mobility, monetary policy is perfectly effective.

Fixed Exchange Rates

Interestingly, these results are in turn exactly reversed if the economy is under a *fixed* exchange rate regime.

Then fiscal policy is completely effective (because interest changes would induce infinite financial inflows or outflows that cannot be sterilized, and hence change the money base until the original interest rate is restored). Monetary policy is completely ineffective, because any move that shifts the LM curve induces an interest rate change. This triggers either infinite financial inflows or infinite outflows, which undo the original money base change.

Is there an example of a completely fixed exchange rate regime, combined with completely open financial accounts, by which to assess whether an independent monetary policy is possible in such circumstances? The euro area countries, which have given up their own currencies, constitute an extreme example. A less extreme case, where the country retains its own currency, is Denmark, which from approximately 1988 onward has had no cross-border capital controls. As shown in Figure 15.13, when the exchange rate is not pegged, the Danish interest rate can deviate from the German. When Denmark effectively pegs in 1987, first to the German mark and then the euro, the interest differential shrinks. When the peg becomes credible in 1997, the interest differential becomes essentially constant at 0.

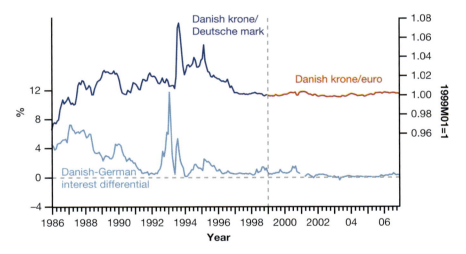

Figure 15.13 Denmark under Fixed Rates This figure shows the Danish money market interest rate minus German money market interest rate, in percent (light blue, left scale), and the Danish kroner per German mark (blue), and Danish kroner per euro (red) exchange rates, both set to January 1999 = 1 (right scale). Vertical dashed line at 1999M01 represents inception of the euro.
Source: IMF, International Financial Statistics, and Federal Reserve System.

Notice the interest differential is not exactly zero to begin with; that is because at the beginning, there is some expected probability of devaluation of the krone. Remember, the expected depreciation is what the interest differential should equal under uncovered interest parity (when financial capital is perfectly mobile).

15.4 THE INTERNATIONAL TRILEMMA

The **International Trilemma**, first coined by Obstfeld and Taylor (1997), is the hypothesis that a country may simultaneously pursue any two, but not all three, of these goals, i.e.

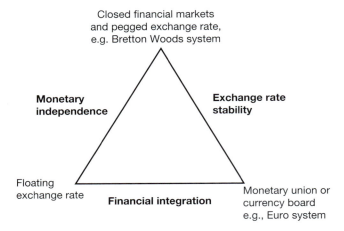

Figure 15.14 The International Trilemma This diagram illustrates that it is only possible to fully achieve two of the three objectives simultaneously.

monetary independence, exchange rate stability, and financial integration. This conclusion leaps out from our discussion of perfect capital mobility in the previous section. The trilemma is illustrated in Figure 15.14, where at each vertex of the triangle two goals are realized but the third is out of reach. Because the three goals are not all simultaneously attainable, they are sometimes called the Impossible Trinity.

Monetary independence means that the monetary authorities of an economy are, as it were, masters of their own fate. An economy with a high degree of monetary independence can be stabilized through a monetary policy without being at the mercy of other economies' macroeconomic management. Hence, monetary independence can in principle allow individual countries to stabilize output in the face of developments in the rest of the world economy.

Exchange rate stability – at the extreme, keeping the nominal value of a currency fixed against a specific foreign currency – is a means of providing a nominal anchor. One of the potential benefits of such an anchor is enhanced price stability. In addition, during times of an economic stress, a pegged exchange rate can enhance policy makers' credibility and soothe investor anxieties. However, high levels of exchange rate fixity deprive the economy of the use of the exchange rate as a shock absorber.

Financial integration with foreign markets allows more efficient resource allocation, mitigates information asymmetry, and enhances and/or supplements domestic savings. However, it subjects the economy to the whims of volatile cross-border financial flows. "Sudden stops" – dramatic reversals of financial flows – have led to boom–bust cycles in numerous smaller economies, particularly over the three decades starting in in 1994 with the Mexican peso crisis. This point is discussed at further length in Chapter 18.

Throughout history, various international financial arrangements have pursued different two-out-of-three combinations of policy goals. The **Bretton Woods system**, which prevailed in the post-World War II period, sacrificed capital mobility for monetary autonomy and exchange rate stability; it is shown at the top of the triangle in Figure 15.14. The characterization of the Bretton Woods system as being one of pure fixed exchange rates is not completely correct.

John Maynard Keynes (discussed in Chapter 12), who along with American statesman Harry White, help plan the Bretton Woods institutions, declared:

> In general I remain in favour of independent national systems with fluctuating exchange rates" . . . [but] . . . "there need be no reason why the exchange rate should in practice be constantly fluctuating.

The exchange rates were adjustable, when economic conditions warranted changes in the value of foreign currency.

Until a couple of decades ago, developing countries similarly pursued monetary independence and exchange rate stability, but largely kept their financial markets closed to foreign investors (see the case of China, recounted in Chapter 14).

The euro system is built upon the fixed exchange rate arrangement and free capital mobility, but member countries give up monetary autonomy; hence, this system is placed at the lower right vertex. The freely floating exchange rate regime (lower left) best characterizes the United States, as well as the euro area as a whole, to the extent that policymakers in these economies do not systematically intervene in foreign exchange markets to manage their currencies.

Empirical Evidence of the Trilemma

Does the trilemma apply in the real world? To answer that question, Joshua Aizenman, Menzie Chinn, and Hiro Ito (2010) constructed operationalized measures of the degree to which each goal in the Impossible Trinity is reached.

Monetary independence is gauged by the correlation of interest rates with those in a major country. If a country's interest rate moves in perfect tandem, percentage point for each percentage point, with the rate in, say, the United States, then the degree of monetary independence is zero. If, at the other extreme, there is 0 correlation, then there is full monetary independence, value 1.

Exchange rate stability is the inverse of exchange rate volatility. Suppose the standard deviation of month-to-month changes in the exchange rate against a reference currency (such as the US dollar) is zero; then the exchange rate is fully stable.

Finally, capital mobility is measured using an index based on the legal restrictions on cross-border transactions, as reported by each country to the International Monetary Fund. Chinn and Ito (2006) calculate an index of financial openness that takes on a value of 1 if there are no restrictions, and a value of 0 if there are very tight restrictions.

Applying these variable measures to a large set of countries, for data covering the period 1970–2010, Aizenman, Chinn, and Ito (2013) found that countries do face a trilemma. As one of the three goals is favored, one of the two other goals has to be sacrificed – and sometimes both. The evolution of the three indices, averaged over the countries studied, is shown in Figure 15.15.

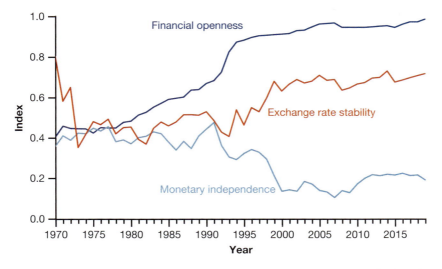

Figure 15.15 Measuring the Trilemma This diagram shows the average value of indexes for monetary independence (light blue), exchange rate stability (red), and financial openness (blue) for all industrial countries.

The patterns in the data demonstrate that since the breakdown of the Bretton Woods system in 1971, industrialized countries have loosened the constraints on the free flow of financial capital and stabilized exchange rates, while abdicating monetary autonomy. Some of the movement that occurred in 2000 is due to the advent of the **Economic and Monetary Union** (EMU), popularly known as the creation of the euro. EMU entailed the surrender of independent currencies, and hence the abandonment of independent monetary policies.

In sum, the theoretical framework laid out in Chapter 14 and this chapter are verified in the real world. When exchange rates are fixed and capital mobility is high, as in the case of Denmark, then monetary autonomy is limited. However, as in the case of China (as discussed in Chapter 14), when impediments to financial flows are high, countries can retain both rigid exchange rates and an independent monetary policy.

15.5 ANOTHER LIMIT TO MONETARY POLICY EFFECTIVENESS

Even in circumstances where the exchange rate is not fixed, it may still happen that monetary policy is perfectly ineffective. For most of the post-World War II era, monetary policy has been able to spur output, including net exports, by dropping the interest rate, thereby boosting investment. However, as the twenty-first century got under way, central banks seeking to stimulate economic growth began to encounter the **zero lower bound**, where bonds no longer pay any interest at all. As Figure 15.16 shows, Japan was the first to run up against this limit, around 2000. In 2008, as the world fell into recession, the US, the UK, and the euro area followed suit.

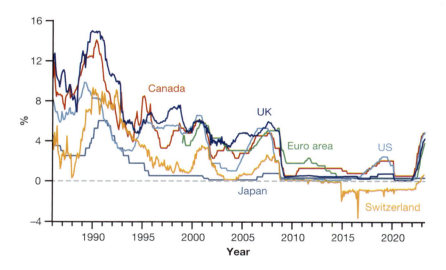

Figure 15.16 The Zero Lower Bound This figure illustrates overnight interbank interest rates in US (light blue), Canada (red), euro area (green), Japan (teal), United Kingdom (blue), and Switzerland (tan).
Source: IMF, OECD.

When bonds pay no interest, actors holding money have no incentive to buy bonds; they would be giving up liquidity and getting nothing in return. Consequently, the monetary authorities are deprived of a means of affecting investment and exchange rates. This situation is termed a **liquidity trap**, because it represents conditions under which ordinary monetary policy ceases to be an effective tool for stimulating income growth. Getting out of the trap requires extraordinary measures, which penalize holders of money by imposing negative interest rates.

To represent this situation using our model, we must modify the *IS* and *LM* curves to reflect that fact that it is very difficult to move interest rates below 0%. At $i = 0$, the two curves must flatten out as shown in Figure 15.17. For the sake of illustration, we initially

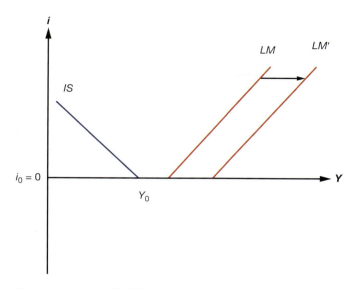

Figure 15.17 In the Liquidity Trap This diagram shows the IS and LM curves in a situation where the curves intersect at zero interest rates. An increase in the money supply then fails to decrease the interest rate. This situation is called a "liquidity trap."

ignore the $BP = 0$ schedule. The money supply is sufficiently large so that the IS curve intersects the LM curve on the flat portion, at Y_0. Under those conditions, an increase in the money supply (black arrow) does not have any effect on the interest rate; it remains at 0.

In order to examine how the presence of a liquidity trap affects the effectiveness of monetary policy in an open economy, we now re-introduce the $BP = 0$ schedule, as shown in Figure 15.18.

Notice that the equilibrium interest rate is above the rate that equilibrates the balance of payments. As a consequence, the currency appreciates, shifting up the $BP = 0$ schedule, and shifting in the IS curve. Output falls to Y_1.

Interestingly, not only is monetary policy ineffective in boosting output. Over time, the adjustment process leads to a reduction of output. For this reason, the presence of a liquidity trap poses an especially difficult obstacle to stimulating the economy in the face of an economic contraction.

This challenge arises because of the placement of the $BP = 0$ schedule. The $BP = 0$ schedule could be placed higher; in that case, the equilibrium interest rate would be below that necessary for external balance. The currency would depreciate, shifting the IS curve out and the $BP = 0$ curve down. Then equilibrium would be re-established by the adjustment process.

Which situation is more likely to prevail? As shown in Figure 15.16, interest rates of advanced countries were fairly low, if not effectively zero, from 2008 to 2018. During this period, monetary policy working through the short-term interest rate was ineffective, exactly because the situation illustrated in Figure 15.18 prevailed.

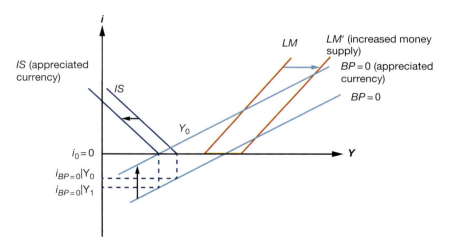

Figure 15.18 The Liquidity Trap in an Open Economy This diagram shows that if zero interest rates is above the interest rate that provides balance of payments equilibrium, the currency appreciates, further driving output down despite expansionary monetary policy.

Notice that expansionary *fiscal* policy could be effective in raising output. Appreciation of the currency, arising from the higher interest rate, would tend to offset some of the expansion, but overall, output would increase.

THEORY   Negative Interest Rates

How can interest rates become negative? That surely seems counter-intuitive, since it means that individuals and firms have to pay a fee to deposit their savings in a private bank. Here, we explain how interest rates can become negative. In order to do so, we need to explain the linkage between the money base – what the central bank controls – and the money supply.

As discussed in Chapter 12, the central bank only *directly* controls what is called the money base, the sum of currency and bank reserves. Bank reserves are the funds that private banks own but are on reserve with the central bank. For every dollar deposited in a private bank, by regulation a certain portion cannot be loaned out, but must rather be kept on reserve. Private banks can also hold reserves in excess of the required amount.

Now consider how the central bank typically controls the interest rate. It sets a deposit interest rate that the central bank pays to banks on excess reserves held overnight in the banks' accounts with the central bank, and a lending rate at which banks could borrow overnight from the central bank. The deposit rate sets a lower bound on the interest rate at which banks lend to each other – why would one bank lend to another at 2.5% if the first bank could instead earn 3% by depositing the money with the central bank? The borrowing rate likewise sets a ceiling – why would a bank borrow from another bank at 5.5% if the central bank will lend any desired amount at 5%? This will keep the interest rate between these two rates, in what is called "the corridor system." The central bank can buy or sell government securities to affect the amount of reserves in the system, thereby determining the actual interest rate within the corridor.

Now suppose that instead of a positive deposit rate, the central bank sets a negative rate. Individual banks will try to avoid the cost now associated with central bank deposits. If Bank A, facing the prospect of being charged 0.1% annually sees a three-month government security paying, say, 0.2%, that bank will want to purchase the security on the open market, thereby replacing a 0.1% loss with a 0.2% gain. But Bank B, which sold the security to Bank A, will realize that with the money it received, it would be better off getting the 0.2% return than paying 0.1%, so it will also be buying any short-term securities that yield 0.2% in the hope of not getting stuck paying a fee on deposits. In the end, some bank somewhere will be left, at the end of the day, paying the 0.1% fee. Either that, or with all those banks trying to purchase

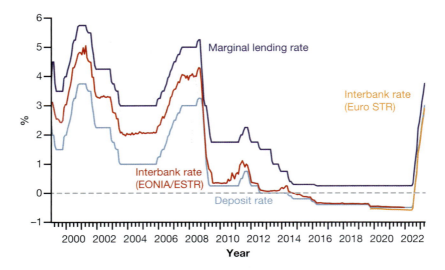

Figure 15.19 The Corridor System This figure shows the ECB's corridor system and negative interest rates.

short-term government securities, the price of short-term government securities will get bid up, until the return on those securities is also negative.

The European Central Bank (ECB) has implemented a negative interest rate policy since June 2014, with only a return to positive rates in 2022. Figure 15.19 gives a graphical depiction of the operation of the corridor system; the marginal lending facility rate is the equivalent of the discount rate, EONIA, replaced with a more comprehensive measure called ESTR in January 2022, is the overnight interest rate banks charge each other.

There is a limit, however, to how far below zero interest rates can be driven. At some point, the penalty rate charged on deposits at the central bank will induce private banks to lend out the funds, instead of holding them as excess reserves. To date, no major central bank has set interest rates below −1% on a sustained basis.

CONCLUSION

When an economy operates under a floating exchange rate regime, the central bank commits to allowing market conditions to fully determine the value of the currency. Implied is that the central bank's stock of foreign exchange reserves should be constant, while the exchange rate adjusts in response to changes in exogenous variables, such as government spending, the money supply, and foreign income and interest rates.

Compared to fixed exchange rates, flexible exchange rates leave fiscal policy with less influence on output, because there are now two channels of crowding out: higher interest rates, which reduce investment, and by appreciating the currency, which also reduce net exports. Conversely, with flexible rates monetary policy gains in effectiveness. This occurs because expansionary monetary policy, by changing the interest rate, now affects two components of aggregate demand: investment and net exports.

As the degree of capital mobility increases, the polarity in effectiveness between fiscal and monetary policy becomes more and more pronounced. At the limit, when capital mobility is perfect so that the smallest of interest differentials triggers infinite flows of capital, with flexible exchange rates, fiscal policy becomes completely ineffective and monetary policy perfectly effective.

The International Trilemma is a consequence of the Mundell–Fleming model. If financial integration is complete, then a country can pursue monetary autonomy by allowing exchange rates to float, or it can pursue fixed rates while giving up monetary independence. However, by giving up financial integration, a country could pursue fixed exchange rates and monetary independence at the same time. What is not possible is simultaneously achieving all three goals – exchange rate stability, monetary autonomy, and financial integration.

SUMMARY POINTS

1. In a flexible exchange rate regime, the exchange rate adjusts so that changes in foreign exchange reserves are zero.
2. Under a flexible exchange rate regime, when financial capital mobility is relatively high, fiscal policy is relatively less effective and monetary policy more effective, as compared to a fixed rate regime.
3. When a country faces higher foreign interest rates, a higher rate of expected currency depreciation, or an exogenously lower amount of financial inflows, the exchange rate will tend to depreciate, in the absence of a tightening monetary policy.
4. If monetary policy is tightened in response to a balance of payments deficit, the economy will tend to contract.

5. Under full capital mobility, with a fixed exchange rate regime, monetary policy is completely ineffective and fiscal policy completely effective. With a flexible rate regime, the reverse becomes true.
6. By the International Trilemma, an economy cannot simultaneously achieve financial openness, exchange rate stability, and monetary policy autonomy. At best two out of three of those goals can be realized.
7. When the economy is in a liquidity trap, monetary policy will be completely ineffective in increasing output.

KEY CONCEPTS

Bretton Woods system, page 336
Economic and Monetary Union, page 338
Exchange rate stability, page 336
Financial integration, page 336

International Trilemma, page 335
Liquidity trap, page 338
Monetary independence, page 336
Perfect capital mobility, page 334
Zero lower bound, page 338

REVIEW QUESTIONS

1. Under a pure floating exchange rate regime, official reserves transactions are always zero, so that the economy is always on the $BP = 0$ schedule. What variable, or variables, adjusts in order to ensure that this condition holds?
2. Under a pure floating exchange rate regime, is overall economy-wide equilibrium always characterized by all three curves intersecting at the same point (in contrast to what is true in a fixed rate regime)? Why or why not?
3. Under a pure floating exchange rate regime, and relatively high financial capital mobility, will fiscal policy be less or more effective in affecting output? Compare two economies identical except for one is completely closed (no exports or imports, and no borrowing and lending from the rest of the world).
4. Under a floating rate regime, is the central bank able to affect the exchange rate, despite the fact that it is committed to not intervening in the foreign currency market?
5. Is it possible to conduct an independent monetary policy if the exchange rate is fixed, but the degree of capital mobility is zero?
6. Suppose capital mobility is infinite. Can a country simultaneously pursue a fixed exchange rate regime and an independent monetary policy?

EXERCISES

1. Suppose the economy is described by the following set of equations, as in the Mundell–Fleming model.

   (1) $\quad Y = \bar{\alpha}\left[\bar{A} + \bar{X} - \overline{IM} + (n+v)\bar{q} - bi\right] \qquad <IS\text{ curve}>$

   (1') $\quad i = \frac{\bar{A} + \bar{X} - \overline{IM} + (n+v)\bar{q}}{b} - \left(\frac{1-c+m}{b}\right)Y \qquad <IS\text{ curve}>$

EXERCISES

(2) $\quad i = -\left(\frac{1}{h}\right)\left(\frac{\overline{M}}{\overline{P}}\right) + \left(\frac{k}{h}\right)Y \qquad\qquad <\text{LM curve}>$

(3) $\quad i = -\left(\frac{1}{\varkappa}\right)\left[(\overline{X} - \overline{IM} + \overline{FA}) + (n+v)\overline{q}\right] + \overline{i^*} + \left(\frac{m}{\varkappa}\right)Y \quad <BP = 0 \text{ curve}>$

    a. Draw a graph of initial equilibrium, where the goods and money markets are in equilibrium, as is the balance of payments. Assume that $m/\varkappa < k/h$.
    b. Show what happens if government spending is decreased, both immediately and over time. You might wish to break the answer up into two steps.
    c. At the new equilibrium, what is true about (i) the level of output; (ii) the level of investment; (iii) the real exchange rate; and (iv) the trade balance?

2. Consider the economy discussed in Exercise 1.
    a. Draw a graph of initial equilibrium, where the goods and money markets are in equilibrium, as is the balance of payments. Show the impact of a monetary contraction, both immediately and over time.
    b. Explain why the process you lay out in part a occurs.
    c. Does your answer to part b change if $m/\varkappa > k/h$?

3. Consider the same economy described in Exercise 1.
    a. Assume the economy begins in equilibrium. Show what happens in the short term if the foreign interest rate falls exogenously. What happens to output, the interest rate, and the exchange rate?
    b. Suppose the central bank wishes to maintain output at pre-shock levels. What policies can it implement to achieve that goal?

4. Consider the same economy described in Exercise 1.
    a. Assume the government wishes to reduce the trade deficit by imposing tariffs to decrease the amount of autonomous imports, $\overline{IM}$. Graphically show the impact on output and interest rates.
    b. Does the trade balance improve by the amount that autonomous imports decrease?

5. Consider a closed version of the economy in Exercise 1. Exports and imports are both zero, and no financial capital flows cross the border.
    a. Suppose the economy is in a liquidity trap. Show the impact of a decrease in government spending. Is fiscal policy effective in changing output?
    b. Suppose the economy is in a liquidity trap. Show the impact of a decrease in the money supply, if the resulting interest rate is positive. Is monetary policy effective in changing output?

6. Consider the economy described in Section 15.5, with the equilibrium interest rate below the interest rate consistent with balance of payments equilibrium.
    a. Illustrate the initial equilibrium.
    b. Show how the economy adjusts over time.

7. Consider the Mundell–Fleming model, with infinite capital mobility. Show each of the following, using a diagram:
    a. The impact of contractionary fiscal policy under fixed exchange rates.
    b. The impact of contractionary monetary policy under floating exchange rates.
    c. The impact of contractionary fiscal policy under floating exchange rates.
    d. The impact of contractionary monetary policy under fixed exchange rates.

RECOMMENDED RESOURCES

Joshua Aizenman, Menzie David Chinn, and Hiro Ito, "The "Impossible Trinity" Hypothesis in an Era of Global Imbalances: Measurement and Testing," *Review of International Economics* 21(3) (2013): 447–458.

Michael W. Klein and Jay C. Shambaugh, "Rounding the Corners of the Policy Trilemma: Sources of Monetary Policy Autonomy," *American Economic Journal: Macroeconomics* 7(4) (2015): 33–66.

CHAPTER 16

Income, Money, and the Price Level in an Open Economy

LEARNING OBJECTIVES

In this chapter, we learn about:
- how the price level adjusts over time
- how monetary and fiscal policies affect output over different time horizons
- how expected inflation can affect actual inflation
- how shocks to the price of production inputs can affect output and the price level
- how the economy adjusts when the exchange rate is fixed

INTRODUCTION

In June of 2016, voters in the United Kingdom narrowly approved a referendum on leaving the European Union (EU), a common market wherein labor, capital, and goods and services are free to move between countries without impediment. The vote in favor of Britain's exit – or "Brexit" – set in motion a process by which the country would leave the EU within two years.

Brexit meant that the desirability of building new factories in the UK, or buying companies based there, diminished; post-Brexit, goods produced in the UK would no longer be exported to members of the European Union tariff-free, nor would banks based in London be able to operate freely anywhere in the EU.

As a result demand for British assets diminished, leading to a precipitous drop in the value of the British pound, by nearly 8.5%, as investors started taking their savings out of the UK, and new capital flows to the country diminished (Figure 16.1). A weaker pound in turn resulted in an increase in the prices paid for imported foreign goods, i.e., goods and services produced outside of the UK, including those from the rest of the European Union. These events are shown in Figure 16.2.

Figure 16.1 Future Prospects and Exchange Rates As economic prospects for the UK dimmed with the Brexit decision, financial capital flowed out of the country, weakening the pound against the euro...and other currencies.
Source: Marian Kamensky/www.CartoonStock.com.

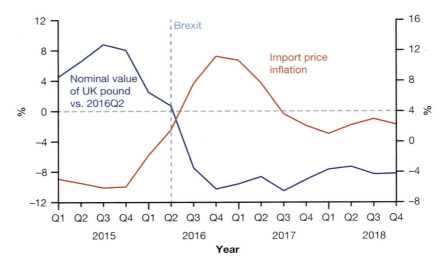

Figure 16.2 Depreciation and Import Prices This figure shows the UK nominal trade weighted value of the pound (blue, left scale), where down is a depreciation, and UK manufactured goods import price inflation, in percent (red, right scale).
Source: Bank for International Settlements, and OECD.

In July alone, monthly import prices for manufactured goods rose by 6%. Since imported goods and services account for some portion of goods that firms use as production inputs (think of imported oil, or semi-conductor chips that go into British-made electronics), as the pound weakened, the general price level also rose. This correlation is shown in Figure 16.3. Consumer price inflation rose, and, as time progressed, GDP growth increasingly lagged other economies, particularly those of the euro area and the United States.

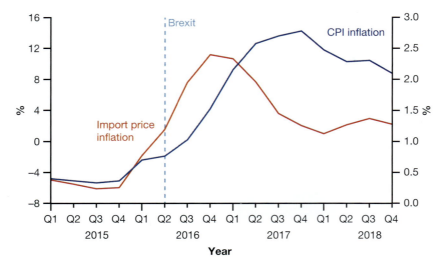

Figure 16.3 Import Prices and Consumer Price Inflation This figure shows UK manufactured goods import price inflation, percent year on year (red), and UK consumer price inflation, year on year (blue).
Source: OECD, ONS.

In essence, the Brexit referendum led to a weakening of the balance of payments, a drop in the value of the currency, a rise in inflation, and a stagnation in growth (despite the stimulative monetary policy). The immediate 10% depreciation led to a 1.7% increase in the inflation rate in the year following the referendum (Breinlich et al., 2017). In order to explain how these developments advanced, we need a model that incorporates the supply – as well as the demand – side of the economy, one that allows the price level to change over time.

In this chapter, we relax the assumption that the price level is fixed. Once we allow the price level to change over time, we model the response of the price level to aggregate demand (determined by the interaction of *IS*, *LM*, and $BP = 0$) relative to the normal productive capacity of the economy, what is termed aggregate supply. The impact of expected inflation is incorporated. Finally, we analyze the response of the economy to shocks emanating from input costs, such as oil or imported goods.

16.1 ALLOWING THE PRICE LEVEL TO CHANGE

In preceding chapters, we have held the price level fixed, so we could focus on the behavior of the economy in the short run. However, the assumption of a fixed price level is less tenable if we want to examine the economy's behavior over a longer time span. In the United States, the price level has generally risen from one year to the next. Figure 16.4 shows the US's **inflation rate** over seven decades, as measured by the annual percentage change in the consumer price index. The rate has moved up and down, but mostly it has remained modestly positive – greater than zero, but below 5%.

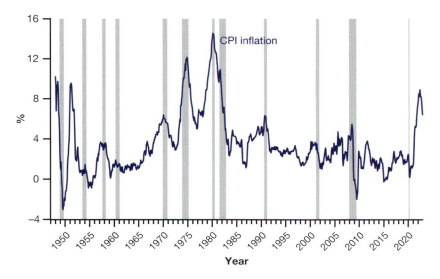

Figure 16.4 The Inflation Rate This figure shows the annual US CPI inflation rate. Recession dates shaded gray. Source: BLS.

In this chapter, we develop a framework in which the price level can adjust over time in a way that is, to some extent predictable, consistent with what is observed in the real world. Our challenge is to uncover the forces that cause the price level to move, and to understand how changes in the price level feed back into the variables we have examined earlier, such as aggregate demand, the trade balance, and the exchange rate.

The core premise of our revised model will be that the price level changes in response to the amount of "slack" in the economy. When output is below a normal level of output, the price level tends to fall, as firms lower prices in order to spur sales. If, on the other hand, output is above the normal level, then the price level will rise as firms respond to high sales by raising prices. However, in both cases this response of prices to the **output gap**, the difference between output and the normal baseline, occurs with a delay. That is, prices are "**sticky**."

In this framework, fiscal and monetary policies can raise or lower output in the short run. Over time, however, any such effects on output are negated by changes in the price level, so that output gradually returns to a level consistent with full employment. That change in price level means inflation or deflation over some time period. Policy aimed at lower output, i.e., negative growth, with deflation as the eventual result, is increasingly rare. But policy moves to rein in unhealthily rapid economic growth are common, precisely because growth that is too rapid leads to high inflation.

Although the extent of economic slack is the key variable, it is not the only determinant of inflation. We will also consider the effect of the *expectations* economic actors have regarding future inflation, because firms' pricing decisions are based partly on their assessment of what is happening with prices in general; that will impact their production costs, their competitors' pricing, and so on. Finally, we will consider the effects of external shocks, such as the price of the inputs into the production process; these include, most importantly, the price of petroleum, as well as imported inputs that might be denominated in foreign currency.

Our modification of the *IS*, *LM*, and $BP = 0$ model will relax the assumption that the price level is held fixed. This results in a negative relationship between aggregate demand and the price level. We will then show how the price level responds to the output gap, when actors' expectations are for zero inflation. We will put the two pieces together in order to examine the short- and long-run implications of fiscal and monetary policies. Next, we will allow firms and households to anticipate inflationary pressures. Specifically, we will assume that firms and households expect inflation to equal the inflation observed in the prior period. Finally, we will examine how the model behaves when the prices of inputs into the production process, such as oil, vary exogenously.

16.2 THE DEMAND AND SUPPLY SIDES

Our modification of the *IS*, *LM*, and $BP = 0$ model will produce an improved representation of the economy's demand side, whereas the response of the price level to the output gap is a supply-side phenomenon. We start with the demand side.

The Demand Side

The demand side of the model is based on the *IS*, *LM*, and $BP = 0$ equations used in the previous chapters, where for simplicity, we assume the exchange rate is floating. The difference we now introduce is that we allow the price level, *P*, to vary. Because it is now an endogenous variable, we remove the overbar. As *P* varies, so does the real money stock, $\overline{M}/P$, thereby implying a different level of aggregate demand for different price levels, as shown in Figure 16.5.

At price level P_B, the *LM* curve intersects the *IS* curve at interest rate i_B and income level Y_B. Consider what would happen if the price level was higher than P_B, at P_A, then the real money stock would be smaller, resulting in an inward shift of the *LM* curve. Given the level of

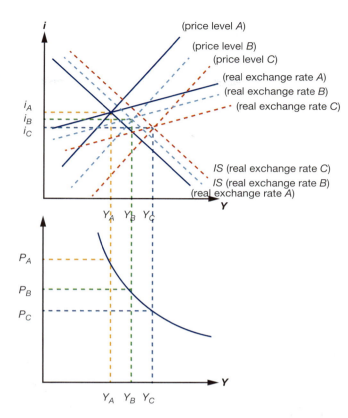

Figure 16.5 The Aggregate Demand Curve This diagram shows the combinations of price level and income for which aggregate demand equals income.

autonomous spending and real exchange rate q_B, the interest rate would be greater than that consistent with external equilibrium, resulting in financial capital inflow. This inflow causes the real exchange rate to appreciate (q falls). This crowds out net exports, so the IS curve shifts in until $I = i_A$, which is true at income level Y_A.

Now consider what would happen if the price level were lower than P_B, at P_C. Then the real money stock would be larger, resulting in an outward shift of the LM curve. If the IS curve were to stay fixed, the resulting interest rate would be less than the foreign interest rate, resulting in a financial outflow. The real exchange rate would depreciate, increasing net exports, and shifting the IS curve out to a point where the external balance was restored, at income level Y_C.

Notice the negative relationship between the price level and the level of aggregate demand. The logic is that if the money supply is held constant, a higher price level results in a higher interest rate, causing the currency to appreciate, crowding out net exports, and, hence, decreasing aggregate demand. In contrast, a lower price level induces a lower interest rate and hence a weaker currency, crowding in net exports and resulting in a higher level of output. In addition, investment is also lower with higher interest rates, and higher with lower interest rates. This means that the negative relationship between the price level and aggregate demand would hold even under fixed exchange rates.

The aggregate demand curve is drawn for given levels of autonomous spending. Anything that increases autonomous demand, such as tax cuts or added government spending, would shift the aggregate demand curve outward. The aggregate demand curve is also drawn for given levels of the nominal money stock, $\overline{M}$, so increases in that variable would also shift out the aggregate demand curve.

We now turn to developing the supply side of the economy, which shows how *producers* in the economy adjust prices and output.

The Supply Side

The supply side of the model is predicated on a simple relationship: when output is above the natural rate of output – i.e., when the output gap is positive – prices will rise over time. The natural output rate is sometimes called **full employment output**, meaning not the output of an economy where literally every worker is employed, but rather the output of an economy where unemployment is as low as it realistically, i.e. sustainably, can be. Most economists today equate an unemployment rate of about 5% or 6% with "full" employment, at least as far as the US is concerned. The output rate is also sometimes called **potential GDP**, again meaning not the highest possible GDP but the highest level that can be realistically sustained for an extended period of time. Thus, output can exceed potential GDP for short stretches.

The response of prices to the output gap is not instantaneous. When output (which equals aggregate demand) exceeds the natural rate, firms first raise production. They do not immediately increase the prices they charge; rather, they only do so after a delayed period. Conversely, when output is below potential, then firms will eventually make adjustments by decreasing prices. This relationship between the output gap and the inflation rate is called the **Phillips curve**, after the British economist A.W. Phillips who uncovered it during the 1950s Using subscripts t and $t-1$ to distinguish an arbitrary period from the one just prior, we write:

$$\frac{P_t - P_{t-1}}{P_{t-1}} \equiv \pi_t = f\left(\frac{Y_{t-1} - Y^{FE}}{Y^{FE}}\right) \tag{16.1}$$

P is the price level, and the percentage change per period in the price level is the inflation rate, π. (Here "percentage change" just means that the difference $P_t - P_{t-1}$ is divided by the starting value, P_{t-1}. The result need not actually be expressed as a percentage, which is why no multiplication by 100 is shown.) On the right, the quotient in the parentheses is the output gap expressed as a ratio: the difference between output and full employment output, divided by full employment output. The rate at which prices are raised in the *current* period is proportional to the gap between output and potential in the *previous* period; the f parameter is the proportionality constant, which gives the sensitivity of inflation to the gap.

In other contexts, the Phillips curve is sometimes expressed as a relationship between inflation and the unemployment rate – when the unemployment rate (u) is high, then inflation tends to be low. This alternative definition of the Phillips curve follows if unemployment is higher than the full employment level (u^{FE}) when output is below the full employment level of output, and vice versa. All one has to do is reverse the sign in the relationship, so $\pi_t = -f\varphi(u - u^{FE})$.

The aggregate demand equation discussed in the previous section involves the price level at a given time. In equation (16.1), we only have an expression for inflation. To get the Phillips curve into a form we can combine with the aggregate demand curve, we need to re-express the equation in terms of the price level. We then obtain equation (16.2):

$$P_t = P_{t-1} + P_{t-1} \times f\left(\frac{Y_{t-1} - Y^{FE}}{Y^{FE}}\right) \tag{16.2}$$

This is one expression for **aggregate supply** (AS) in the short run, a relationship indicating how much firms, on average, price goods and services as a function of output for the last period. Formally, the current price level is equal to the last period's level if the last period's output equaled potential GDP (the value of which defines the position of the long run AS curve, AS^{LR}). The current price level will be higher than the last period's if last period's output exceeded potential output; that is, firms will raise their prices. This process is shown in Figure 16.6. If output is higher than full employment output in period 1, $Y_1 > Y^{FE}$, then the price level will rise to P_2 in period 2, as all firms adjust their prices upward. If in period 1 output had been below Y^{FE}, then the reverse would have occurred, and the price level line would have shifted downward in period 2.

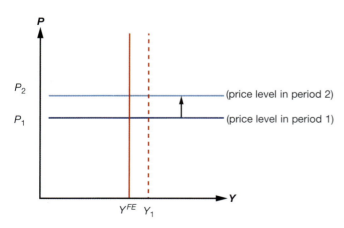

Figure 16.6 Price Level Adjustment over Time This diagram shows the impact of price adjustment, and how it relates to full employment output.

16.3 PUTTING THE DEMAND AND SUPPLY SIDES TOGETHER

Now we can bring the aggregate demand and aggregate supply sides of the economy together, into an **AD–AS model**, in order to solve for the equilibrium output and price level. Along the aggregate demand curve, aggregate demand depends on the price level; at the same time, the aggregate supply curve determines the price level as a function of the output level (relative to potential output) from the prior period.

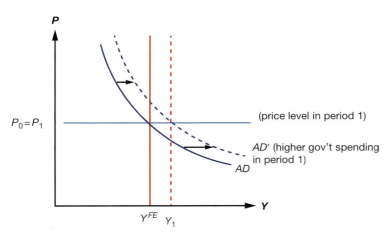

Figure 16.7 The Short Run Response to a Government Spending Increase This figure shows how an increase in government spending shifts out the AD curve, resulting in higher output, but no price increase, in the short run.

Fiscal Policy

To see how the system finds its equilibrium point, suppose in Figure 16.7 that $Y = Y^{FE}$ in period 0. Assuming there were no subsequent changes in taxes or government spending, and no changes in the money supply or the exchange rate, the economy would be in equilibrium from the start. But now consider an expansionary fiscal policy, so that autonomous spending rises in period 1. The AD curves shift outward (black arrows). In the background, the IS curve shifts out, and the $BP = 0$ curve shifts upward as the higher interest rate leads to an appreciation of the currency. Output increases to Y_1 as firms respond to higher demand solely by increasing production. As yet, however, there are no price increases; prices in period 1 are the same as in period 0.

Thus far, the story is identical to the one from Section 15.2. The advantage of the AD–AS model is that it allows us to pursue the story further. In period 2, the price level rises relative to that in period 1, since output in period 1 exceeds potential output. Using equation (16.2),

$$P_2 = P_1 + P_1 \times f\left(\frac{Y_1 - Y^{FE}}{Y^{FE}}\right) \tag{16.3}$$

As the price level rises from P_1 to P_2 (Figure 16.8, arrow), movement along the aggregate demand curve represents the fact that in the background, the LM curve is shifting inward, pushing up the interest rate, appreciating the currency and depressing investment (shifting in the IS curve). Output falls from Y_1 to Y_2.

Output Y_2 is still above the full employment level, so the upward pressure on the price level persists. In period 3, the price level will rise again, but by a smaller increment, so output continues to fall. The price level keeps on rising over successive periods, as long as output exceeds potential output; see the black arrow in Figure 16.9. Only when the price level has risen enough to crowd out enough investment and net exports so that output equals potential output will the process end. At that point, the price level equals P_{Final}.

In the long run, output is back where it began, the price level is higher, and the real exchange rate is stronger. The composition of output is also different than before the expansionary fiscal policy. With the interest rate higher, but output at the same pre-fiscal expansion level, net exports and investment must be lower than they were to begin with.

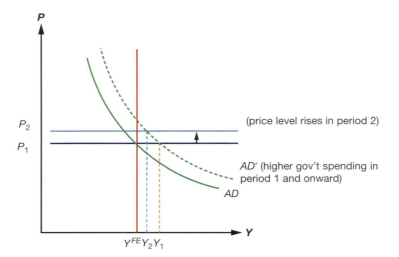

Figure 16.8 The Response over Time to a Government Spending Increase This figure shows price adjustment in response to expansionary fiscal policy.

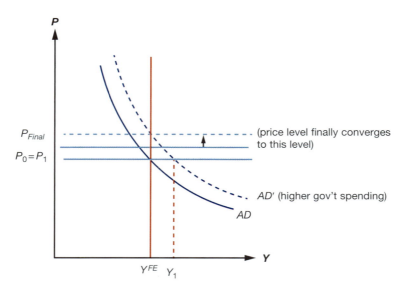

Figure 16.9 The Long Run Response to a Government Spending Increase This diagram shows the adjustment process of the price level over the long run in response to a one-time increase in government spending.

Hence, fiscal policy has an impact on output in the short run, but not the long run. That part of the story could not be told in the fixed price model recounted in Chapters 13 through 15.

Monetary Policy

The short- and long-run effects of monetary policy play out in a broadly similar fashion, as shown in Figure 16.10, but with some differences in the details. Again, let the economy start out in equilibrium, with $Y = Y^{FE}$. An expansionary monetary policy shifts out the AD curve (white arrow). The price level stays the same in period 1, so $P_1 = P_0$. In the background, the LM curve shifts out, the interest rate falls, and the currency depreciates, so the IS shifts out and the $BP = 0$ curve shifts down. With output in excess of full employment levels, the price

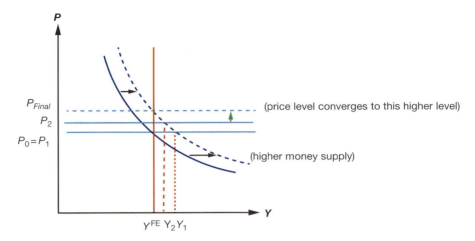

Figure 16.10 The Response to a Money Supply Increase This diagram shows the effect of an increase of money supply in the short run and over the long run as the price level rises.

level will rise. As the price level rises (light blue arrow), the real money stock shrinks, shifting the *LM* curve back, so interest rates rise. The output level falls to Y_2.

Only when the price level has risen sufficiently far so as to set output back at potential output does the process end. As the price level rises to P_{Final} (black arrow), the LM shifts back to its original position. The real exchange rate appreciates back to the starting level, the $BP = 0$ shifts upward to its original position, and the *IS* curve shifts inward towards its original position. In the long run, all the real magnitudes revert to their original values. The only difference is that the nominal magnitude, the price level, is now higher than it was originally. In Chapters 14 and 15, we made a distinction about the relative efficacy of monetary and fiscal policy under fixed versus flexible exchange rate regimes, in the short run. In the long run, by contrast, neither policy is effective in raising output.

In the long run, money neutrality holds – that is, all the real magnitudes, such as real GDP, are unchanged, while nominal magnitudes, such as the price level are changed. If the money supply was increased by 10%, then the price level would have increased by 10% in the long run. The nominal exchange rate is also weaker by 10%. Thus the model indicates that an expansionary monetary policy weakens the nominal exchange rate in both the short run (as in Chapter 15) and the long run.

16.4 ADDING IN EXPECTATIONS OF INFLATION

In this section, we first discuss how to incorporate the expectations of workers, consumers, and firms into the Phillips curve. We then trace out how the path of output and prices differs when inflation expectations are adaptive – that is depend on past actual inflation – versus when inflation expectations are always zero.

An Expectations-Augmented Phillips Curve

Up to this point, our treatment of inflation has had firms raising prices solely as a function of the lagged output gap. For instance, if $f = 0.5$, then an output gap of 2% implies that firms will raise prices by 1% (= 0.5 × 2%). However, if firm owners all *expect* 4% inflation, then raising prices by only 1% would mean that the expected real price of the goods the firms sell will fall by 3% (= 1% – 4%). Clearly a better description of real-world price setting incorporates a role for what firms expect the general price level to be. This can be written into a more comprehensive version of the Phillips curve, called the *expectations-augmented* Phillips curve:

$$\pi_t = \pi_t^e + f\left(\frac{Y_{t-1} - Y^{FE}}{Y^{FE}}\right) \tag{16.4}$$

π_t^e is the inflation expected in period t, based on the information the market provides in period $t - 1$. Now the output gap is the basis for an adjustment to expected inflation, in order to obtain actual inflation.

The problem with equation (16.4) as a modeling tool is that the market's expectations of inflation are unobservable. In order to make the model usable, we need an observable proxy for π_t^e. A plausible assumption is $\pi_t^e = \pi_{t-1}$, which is to say that expected inflation in period t is just the actually realized inflation rate in period $t - 1$. Using this assumption, we obtain the expectations-augmented Phillips curve with **adaptive expectations** of inflation:

$$\pi_t = \pi_{t-1} + f\left(\frac{Y_{t-1} - Y^{FE}}{Y^{FE}}\right) \tag{16.5}$$

To see how the price level evolves in this new setup, we revise the price level equation, equation (16.2), to take into account expected inflation – here equal to lagged inflation. Replacing equation (16.1) with equation (16.5), and again solving for P_t, we obtain

$$P_t = P_{t-1} \times \left[1 + \pi_{t-1} + f\left(\frac{Y_{t-1} - Y^{FE}}{Y^{FE}}\right)\right] \tag{16.6}$$

Now consider what happens when inflation initially equals zero, but then there is an increase in output. When output rises to Y_1 in period 1, the price level stays constant. Only in period 2 does the price level rise (since $Y_1 > Y^{FE}$):

$$P_2 = P_1 \times \pi_1 + P_1 \times f\left(\frac{Y_1 - Y^{FE}}{Y^{FE}}\right) \tag{16.7}$$

Since inflation in period 1 was zero, the expected inflation in period 2 is also zero, and the rise to P_2 is the same here as it was in Section 16.4.

In period 3, prices rise again, but notice that since $P_2 > P_1$, $\pi_2 > 0$:

$$P_3 = P_2 \times \pi_2 + P_2 \times f\left(\frac{Y_2 - Y^{FE}}{Y^{FE}}\right) \tag{16.8}$$

From here on, the successive values of the price level diverge from those in the model with no expectation of inflation. The exact trajectory of the price level depends on the size of the parameter f, as well as on the slope of the aggregate demand curve. But as long as expected inflation equals lagged inflation, the price level will initially overshoot the long-run value, before eventually settling at P_{Final}, which is the same value as it would be in the case where inflationary expectations did not matter, as in Figure 16.10. Similarly, Y will overshoot and oscillate but converge, over the long run, to its final value, Y^{FE}. The bottom line is that eventually, output and the price level return to where they would have gone if $\pi_t^e = 0$, which effectively is the model of Section 16.4.

The Dynamics of Output and the Price Level

Figures 16.11 and 16.12 show the evolution of the price level and output, respectively, in response to a hypothetical 5.6% increase in the money supply in 2001. Each figure compares the base case where expectations of inflation are zero with the case where expected inflation

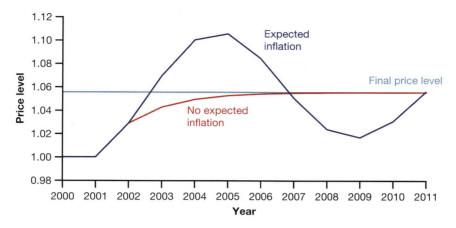

Figure 16.11 The Evolution of the Price Level This figure shows the impact on the price level of expansionary monetary policy in year 01 assuming no expected inflation (red) and expected inflation (blue).

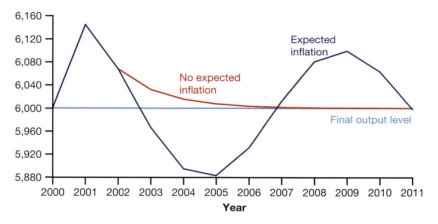

Figure 16.12 The Evolution of the Output Gap This figure shows the impact on output of expansionary monetary policy in year 01 assuming no expected inflation (red) and expected inflation (blue).

equals lagged inflation. The figures show just one full oscillation cycle; oscillations continue in later periods but get progressively smaller. In Figure 16.11, because the money supply has increased by 5.6%, the price level that started at 1.00 converges to a new value, 1.056, that is 5.6% higher. In Figure 16.12, output converges back to its starting value, 6,000, which represents potential GDP.

A final note: it might be tempting to think that the economy could be coaxed into permanent higher-than-potential output if policymakers were to accept permanently higher inflation – say, 20% annually. However, one of the characteristics of the expectations-augmented Phillips curve is that if policymakers try to maintain output at a level higher than the stable equilibrium that potential output represents, inflation will accelerate upward. That is, it will not stay at 20% but instead rise to 25%, then 30%, and so forth, which is to say, there is no long run trade-off to be had between output and inflation.

There are other ways in which inflationary expectations can behave. If firms and households believe that the long-term inflation rate will not deviate far from a rate targeted by the monetary authority, then inflation expectations are described as **anchored**. If inflation expectations are completely anchored, perhaps because the central bank's commitment to a fixed target inflation rate is credible, then monetary and fiscal policies will not result in an acceleration or deceleration in inflation. Rather, the outcome is much like in the case of the simple Phillips curve (equation (16.1)), where expected inflation does not play a role. In the medium term, there is no overshooting in response to a one shot stimulus.

16.5 SUPPLY SHOCKS

In this section, we first discuss how to incorporate the role of intermediate inputs into the Phillips curve. We then trace out how the path of output and prices differs when there is a shock to the cost of those inputs. Finally, we discuss the effects of a policy response to such shocks.

What is a Supply Shock?

The preceding analyses focused on changes in aggregate demand that spurred changes in output and inflation. Sometimes, however, a **supply shock** – such as a change in the price of the production inputs – is what sets events in motion. One important input is oil, used in both production and transportation. Another possible source of a shock on the supply side is a big drop in the value of the currency, or the imposition of tariffs, which makes all imported goods more expensive. If lots of imported goods are used in the production process, firms will tend to pass those higher costs along to buyers in the form of higher prices.

To account for shocks on the supply side, we must again modify the Phillips curve:

$$\pi_t = \pi_{t-1} + f\left(\frac{Y_{t-1} - Y^{FE}}{Y^{FE}}\right) + \delta z_t \tag{16.9}$$

The $\delta \times z$ term represents the shock effect. The variable z represents the percentage change in input prices, while δ is a parameter that measures the sensitivity of overall inflation to that one-time input price increase. For instance, if δ is 0.2, then a one-time 10% increase in input prices bumps the inflation rate up by 2 percentage points for the affected period.

Again we revise the price level equation:

$$P_t = P_{t-1} \times \left[1 + \pi_{t-1} + f\left(\frac{Y_{t-1} - Y^{FE}}{Y^{FE}}\right) + (\delta \times z_t)\right] \tag{16.10}$$

The Dynamics of a Supply Shock

To see the effect of this revision, suppose once more that the economy starts out in equilibrium, with zero inflation and $Y = Y^{FE}$, and now posit that in period 1 there is a one-time increase in the price of inputs, $z_1 > 0$. (Then $z_t = 0$ for all later periods.) As Figure 16.13 shows, in period 1 the overall price level rises to P_1 (tan arrow) and output falls to Y_1. Since inflation in period 1 was greater than zero, inflation expected period 2 is greater than zero. With the lagged output gap negative in period 2, due to the production slowdown that the higher price level induces in period 1, the price level falls (blue arrow), assuming the f parameter is sufficiently large. Then output rises in period 2 relative to that in period 1, but remains lower than output in period 0.

In the background, what is happening is that the real money stock is eroded by the higher price level in period 1. Interest rates rise, decreasing investment and net exports, the latter by way of an appreciated currency. Working through the multiplier, output falls and

16.5 SUPPLY SHOCKS

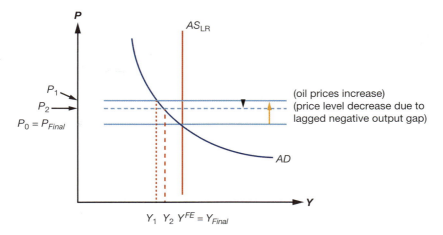

Figure 16.13 An Oil Price Shock This diagram shows the effect of an oil price shock in period 1, with an expectations augmented Phillips curve, and no offsetting policy. The price line shifts up. Over time, as output falls below full employment level, the price level falls.

unemployment rises. In period 2, the negative output gap pulls down the price level (unless f is relatively small, in which case the decline might occur in a later period).

Eventually, output will return to the full employment level, and the price level will return to the initial level. However, there will be overshooting on the way to a steady state equilibrium. The overshooting occurs when lagged inflation enters in as expected inflation, as in equation (16.10). If expected inflation is always zero, then output will converge to full employment and the price level to the original level, without overshooting.

Offsetting the Contractionary Impact of the Supply Shock

In order to cushion the decline of output and bring it to a soft landing at Y_{Final}, the central bank could increase the money supply. This would result in an outward shift in the AD and a rise of the price level to P_1 (blue arrows in Figure 16.14).

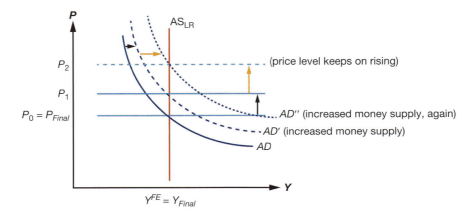

Figure 16.14 Expansionary Monetary Policy during an Oil Price Shock This diagram shows the upward shift in the price line in period 1 as actual inflation in period 0 feeds into expected inflation in period 1, and the shift of the AD curve outward if the central bank seeks to offset the negative impact on output by increasing the money supply.

If the monetary expansion succeeds in making Y_1 equal to Y_{Final}, then the inflation in period 2 will equal the lagged inflation in period 1; hence, the AS curve will again shift and the price level will rise (tan arrows) despite the fact that input prices are no longer rising. In other words, the expansionary monetary policy has validated the price shock, building in inflation. In order to keep output at its potential, the government will have to increase the money supply again (tan arrow).

The bottom line is that if policymakers want to maintain output in the face of a supply shock such as an oil price increase, then entrenched inflation is likely to be the result – at least assuming expected inflation is set equal to the previous period's inflation rate. However, if policymakers wanted to stop the supply shock from spilling over into a general price increase, they could implement contractionary fiscal and monetary policies, and use high unemployment to stifle the upward movement in the price level.

Whether it is desirable to allow continuous inflation or to try to eliminate inflation by enduring a period of low output depends on the costs of inflation versus that of underemployment of resources, including labor, as well as the amount of output that has to be sacrificed as the percentage point decrease in inflation. Notice that input prices need not only be interpreted as energy prices. They could also be the prices of imported goods used in the production process – in which case when the exchange rate exogenously depreciates, the input prices will tend to rise. The episode described at the beginning of the chapter is exactly one such instance of a cost-induced inflationary bout, spurred by higher import prices.

APPLICATION   Understanding the Inflation of 2021–2022 in the US

During the 1970s, US inflation rose at the same time that output was stagnant. The combination of the two phenomena was dubbed **stagflation**, and for some economists it proved perplexing. The simple Phillips curve described in Section 16.3 would have had a difficult time accommodating the correlation illustrated in Figure 16.15. Notice that through most of the 1960s, the output gap and inflation are positively correlated, as predicted by a simple Phillips curve. By 1974, however, and again in 1979, output is falling even as inflation is rising.

What could explain why the two series diverged in the 1970s? The root cause is the changing price of oil, shown in Figure 16.16 for the same time period. Before the 1970s, the price of oil was pretty constant. Then prices tripled in 1974, and more than doubled again in 1979.

However, rising oil prices are not in themselves sufficient to explain the acceleration of inflation in the face of a negative output gap. For that, expected inflation has to be included, as well. The price shock in 1974 pushed the price level up and output down, as shown in Figure 16.15. Monetary and fiscal policy were partially accommodative, so that inflation was allowed to rise. Because the accommodation was only partial, output fell below potential, and yet the accommodation, even if only partial, allowed inflation to be built into expected inflation. This led to an upward trend in inflation, so that when the next oil price shock struck in 1979, inflation was already at a higher level.

The model also predicts that wringing inflation out of the system requires a prolonged period of high unemployment and low output. This is exactly what happened in the early 1980s, when the Federal Reserve Chairman Paul Volcker implemented a tight monetary

16.5 SUPPLY SHOCKS

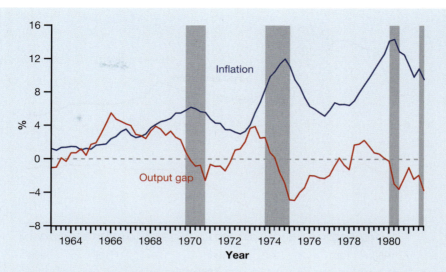

Figure 16.15 Inflation and the Output Gap This figure shows the annual CPI inflation rate in percent (blue) and output gap in percentage points of GDP (red).
Source: BLS and Congressional Budget Office.

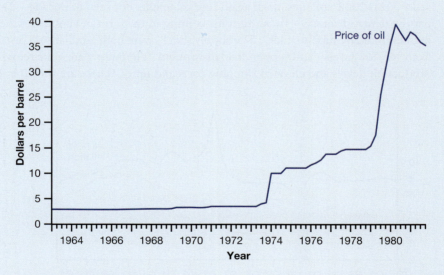

Figure 16.16 Oil Prices This figure shows the price of oil (West Texas Intermediate) in dollars per barrel.
Source: EIA.

policy that pushed the Fed funds rate, which effectively is "the" interest rate for the economy, to new highs. See Figure 16.17.

The Fed funds rate does not look particularly high, even in 1981. But considering the drop in inflation, the real (or "inflation-adjusted") interest rate was extremely high. In short, the expectations-augmented Phillips curve incorporating supply shocks provides a good explanation of the relationship between output and inflation in the US in the 1970s and early 1980s.

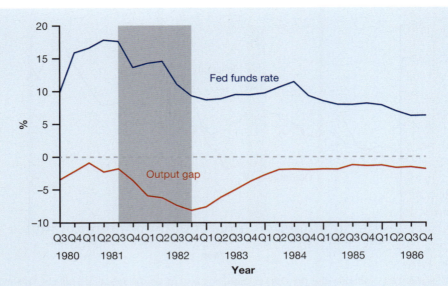

Figure 16.17 The Fed Funds Rate and Output Gap Fed funds rate (blue) and output gap (red).

In 2021–2022, inflation once again rose to heights not seen in decades. This was driven in part by demand shocks – fiscal stimulus coming in the form of various rescue packages – but perhaps more by supply shocks. The supply shocks were both familiar – oil price increases albeit from very low levels – and supply chain disruptions. The latter were quite remarkable, including production delays and elevated shipping costs and times. These are shown in Figure 16.18.

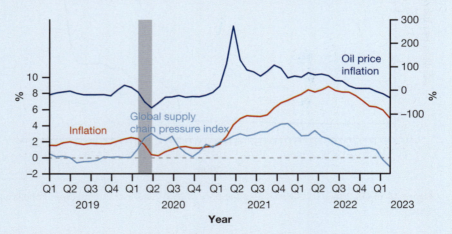

Figure 16.18 Inflation and Supply Chain Disruptions CPI inflation (red, left scale), Global Supply Chain Pressure Index (light blue, left scale), and year-on-year change in oil prices (blue, right scale). Recession dates shaded gray. *Source: BLS, EIA, NY Fed, NBER.*

The rapid disinflation that occurred in 2023, as supply chain pressures eased but unemployment remained low, reinforces the primacy of supply factors in this episode.

In other words, the inflation bout of 2021–2022 is in some ways not mysterious in terms of why it occurred. It was surprising insofar as the drastic oil price increase was not anticipated, nor was the persistence of supply chain disruptions.

IN PRACTICE The Declining Impact of Oil Prices on Inflation and Output

The experience of the 1970s, with their dramatic and until then unprecedented increases in oil prices and inflation, established among macroeconomists a view of the world that dominated the field for decades. Conventional wisdom through the 1990s held that increases in oil prices would necessarily result in higher inflation rates – both directly, because the cost of gasoline and heating oil factored into the consumer price index, and indirectly, as the elevated cost of living percolating through the economy in pushing up production costs and wages.

During the early 2000s, the price of oil once again rose. This time, however, inflation did not rise as quickly as before. In Figure 16.19, showing annual CPI inflation and the annual percentage growth rate of oil prices, the blue line's responses to dramatic movements of the red line are much more muted starting around 1984 than before.

During the period 1984–2017, the associated addition in inflation was only 0.022 points. Since concurrent events could obscure the true impact, it is necessary to parse out the causal effect of oil shocks. Blanchard and Riggi (2013) determined the effect of an oil price shock in the 1984–2009 period to be about one third of what it was in the earlier period.

Why was this association weaker in the latter period than the former? Several hypotheses have been advanced:

1. The intensity with which the US economy relies on energy, particularly oil, has declined.
2. Reduced labor bargaining power means that higher costs of living do not lead as easily to higher wage demands.

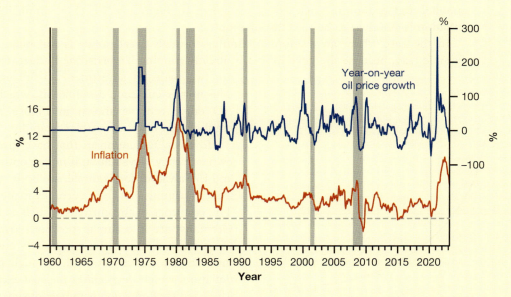

Figure 16.19 Inflation and Oil Price Growth This figure shows the annual CPI inflation rate in percentage (red, left scale) and year-on-year percentage change in oil prices (blue, right scale). Recession dates are shaded gray.

Between 1960 and 1983, each additional 1% increase in oil price inflation was associated with an additional 0.086 percentage points of inflation.

3. Greater central bank credibility means that the markets have more confidence in announced inflation targets.

> The first hypothesis can be rejected, because the decline in inflation has occurred in many advanced economies, whereas the decline in reliance on energy is highly variable. Energy intensity of production has declined in the United States but remains high in many other developed nations.
>
> Blanchard and Riggi (2013) found merit in both of the latter two hypotheses. In their structural model, they concludedthat more flexible wages and greater central bank credibility could both plausibly explain the recent lower inflation sensitivity to oil prices.
>
> The same observations apply to downward pressures on inflation. Declines in oil prices, such as the abrupt, dramatic drop in 1986, should have decreased inflation. And it did, but already to a lesser extent than might have been expected just a few years earlier. By 2014, a deep dip in the price of oil price resulted in only a relatively small decrease in inflation.

16.6 ADJUSTMENT UNDER FIXED EXCHANGE RATES

We have discussed, at length, the implications of the relationship between prices and aggregate demand under flexible exchange rates. It turns out that as long as capital mobility is less than perfect, the same basic results hold for fixed exchange rates, as well. Increases in autonomous spending lead to increased output, which, if it exceeds full employment output, results in rising price levels.

However, instead of the real exchange rate appreciating, it may depreciate as the rising price level combines with a fixed nominal rate. Particularly illuminating is the case where the exchange rate is credibly fixed against another country's currency, financial capital is perfectly mobile, and economic slack exists, as shown in Figure 16.20. (For simplicity, expected inflation is assumed to be zero throughout.)

In the case where an economic stimulus through fiscal policy is for some reason not feasible (say, because the government is already running a worrisome budget deficit), there are two paths to adjustment to full employment. The first is currency devaluation, which shifts the AD curve out, as shown in Figure 16.21. Full employment output is restored rapidly.

However, for countries that have given up their own currency, devaluation is not an option. Panama and El Salvador, for example, are both "fully dollarized," meaning that their currency is the US dollar. The countries of the euro area, such as France and Germany, are in a similar position, insofar as they use a currency issued by a monetary authority that they do not directly control. In such cases, price deflation, which depreciates the real exchange rate, is needed for home goods to become competitive on the world market. This process, sometimes known as **internal devaluation,** is shown in Figure 16.22.

Initially, output is substantially below potential GDP. As that slack pushes the price level downward, to P_1 (black arrow) in period 1, the real exchange rate depreciates, making exports more competitive and imports more expensive. The trade

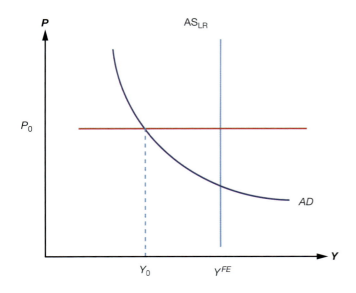

Figure 16.20 Aggregate Demand and Supply under Fixed Rates
Output below full employment under fixed exchange rates This figure shows output when aggregate demand depends on the real exchange rate.

CONCLUSION

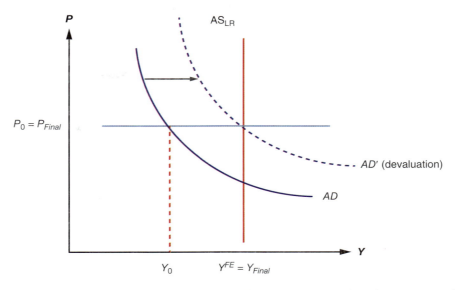

Figure 16.21 Adjustment by Exchange Rate Devaluation This diagram shows how a currency devaluation can shift the aggregate demand curve out and restore full employment levels of output quickly.

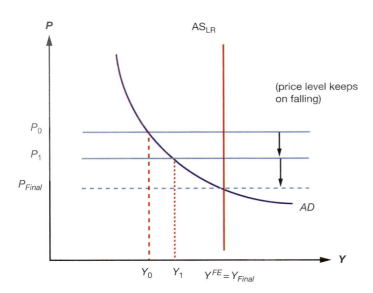

Figure 16.22 Adjustment by Internal Devaluation This diagram shows how price adjustment by letting low output and high unemployment push down the price level can take time.

balance improves, so output rises to Y_1. In period 2, with the output still below potential, the process repeats and the price level again falls. Output rises, but still falls short of potential. Over time, the price level continues to fall (the sequence of black arrows), until it finally reaches P_{Final}, and full employment output is attained.

While both approaches in the end achieve full employment output, devaluation is likely to attain the end goal more rapidly. The more inflexible, or rigid, prices are (that is, the smaller the f parameter in the Phillips curve), the more prolonged the adjustment process under internal devaluation, and hence the period of elevated unemployment

As we will see in Chapter 20, in the examination of the euro area crisis, the combination of a single currency for all euro zone members with a slow rate of adjustment resulted in a extended and painful adjustment period.

CONCLUSION

Monetary and fiscal policies can affect output in the short run when the price level is fixed. Over time, however, the price level adjusts so as to push output toward full employment levels. If output is pushed above potential GDP, then the price level tends to rise, eroding the real money stock, pushing up interest rates, and crowding out investment and net exports. If output is below potential GDP, then the reverse happens, with the price level tending to fall, expanding the real money stock, pushing down the interest rate, and crowding out investment and net exports. Because of this self-adjusting mechanism, monetary and fiscal policies have only a transitory effect on output.

If expectations of inflation are adaptive, then attempts to keep output consistently above potential GDP will result in ever-accelerating inflation. Similarly, maintaining output consistently below potential GDP will cause ever-decelerating inflation (eventually negative inflation). Even temporary, but persistent, attempts to keep output above potential can lead to bouts of inflation.

When inflation expectations are anchored, so that lagged inflation does not impact expected inflation, then these bouts of actual inflation will tend to be moderated. In the period of the last two decades, inflation expectations in advanced economies such as the United States have tended to be fairly consistent, exhibiting little movement.

Shocks to material input prices can also cause movements in output and the price level. These shocks will have a bigger impact the larger the share of material inputs into the production process, and the less anchored inflation expectations are.

When a small country on a fixed exchange rate experiences economic slack, and fiscal policy is not available as a policy option, there are two approaches to restoring full employment. The first is to devalue the currency. If this option is not available because the country does not use its own currency, then internal devaluation – adjustment of the real exchange rate by way of price level deflation – is the only remaining route. Depending on the degree of price flexibility, this can be a long and economically painful process.

SUMMARY

1. In the short run, the price level is fixed, so that firms respond to changes in demand by adjusting output.
2. Firms also respond to changes in demand by adjusting prices, but only with a lag. (Prices are sticky.)
3. The Phillips curve summarizes the relationship between inflation on the one hand and expected inflation, the lagged output gap, and supply shocks on the other hand.
4. If expected inflation equals lagged inflation – a form of adaptive expectations – then output and the price level will oscillate in the short run. In the long run, output will converge to full employment output, and the price level will converge to a steady limiting value, as well.
5. Under adaptive expectations, supply shocks in the form of increased oil prices or imported input prices can spark a simultaneous increase in inflation and decrease in output, a phenomenon termed stagflation.
6. If inflation expectations are credibly set by the central bank, then oil price shocks will have a muted effect.
7. A small open economy under fixed exchange rates can adjust toward full employment by fiscal policy, currency devaluation. or internal devaluation (price level deflation). If fiscal policy is constrained, and no independent currency circulates in the economy, then internal devaluation is the only adjustment path.

KEY CONCEPTS

AD–AS model, page 351
Adaptive inflation expectations, page 354
Aggregate supply, page 350
Anchored inflation expectations, page 355
Full employment output, page 349
Inflation rate, page 347

Internal devaluation, page 362
Output gap, page 348
Phillips curve, page 350
Potential GDP, page 349
Stagflation, page 358
Sticky prices, page 348
Supply shock, page 356

REVIEW QUESTIONS

1. When an aggregate demand shock (government spending increase, money supply decrease, consumer confidence increase) occurs, is the immediate response of firms to alter production schedules or change prices?
2. Do firms respond quickly to changes in the cost of production, such as an increase in wage costs or input costs?
3. When the output gap is positive ($Y > Y^{FE}$), is there a relatively low level of unemployment?
4. Should firms take into account the inflation they expect when setting the prices of the goods and services they produce?
5. What determines in the real world the *expected* rate of inflation?
6. If inflation has been positive for a long time, what do you expect would be a good approximation for the expected inflation rate?
7. Suppose the output gap is negative, the exchange rate is fixed, and for some reason you cannot devalue your currency. How can full employment output be achieved?

EXERCISES

1. Consider an aggregate demand equation:

$$Y = 2000 + 10 \times \left(\frac{M}{P}\right)$$

   where $M = 100$.
   a. Draw the aggregate demand curve, using 0.5, 1, 1.5, and 2 as values for the price level.
   b. Suppose $Y^{FE} = 3{,}000$. Add this to the graph you drew for part a.
   c. Suppose the Phillips curve is given by

   $$P_t = P_{t-1} + 0.1\left(\frac{Y_{t-1} - Y^{FE}}{Y^{FE}}\right)$$

   and your answer to part a pertains to period 1. Show what the situation looks like in period 1. What is the price level?
   d. Suppose that the constant in the aggregate demand curve increases to 2,500 in period 2; show what happens in period 2 to output and to the price level.
   e. What happens in period 3 to the price level? To output? Show your calculations.
   f. Show graphically what happens in the long run.

2. Consider the aggregate demand–aggregate supply framework in initial short-run and long-run equilibrium. Suppose lump-sum taxes are increased. You can assume for simplicity that expected inflation is always zero.
    a. Show what happens in an *IS–LM* and *AD–AS* graph in the period where the tax increase occurs.
    b. Show what happens over time to output, the price level, the real exchange rate, and the interest rate.
3. Consider the aggregate demand–aggregate supply framework in initial short-run and long-run equilibrium. Suppose lump-sum taxes are increased. Assume that expected inflation equals last period's inflation, and for simplicity, assume that initial inflation is zero.
    a. Show what happens in an *IS–LM* and *AD–AS* graph in the period where the tax increase occurs.
    b. Show what happens over time to output, the price level, the real exchange rate, and the interest rate.
4. Consider an *AD–AS* model where the parameter f is infinite. You can assume for simplicity that expected inflation is always zero.
    a. Show graphically what the *AD–AS* model looks like in initial equilibrium.
    b. Consider an increase in the money supply of 10%. Show graphically what happens to output.
    c. Given what happens to output, can you say quantitatively what happens to the price level?
5. Consider an *AD–AS* model. Show what happens if $\overline{FA}$, the inflow of foreign financial capital, exogenously declines, so that the real exchange rate depreciates. You can assume inflation expectations are always zero.
    a. Show graphically what happens in the *AD–AS* graph.
    b. Suppose that policy authorities did not want the price level to rise. What policies could they implement?
6. Consider an *AD–AS* model. Show what happens if $\overline{Z}$ exogenously decreases. You can interpret this as due to a decrease in commodity prices. You can assume inflation expectations are always zero.
    a. Show graphically what happens in the *AD–AS* graph.
    b. Suppose that policy authorities did not want the price level to rise. What policies could they implement?
7. Consider a small, open economy on a fixed exchange rate with a larger country, experiencing an economic downturn so that the output gap is negative. Consider the relative merits of currency devaluation versus internal devaluation, first if prices are very flexible and then if prices are perfectly inflexible.

RECOMMENDED RESOURCES

Olivier Blanchard and Ben Bernanke, "What Caused the US Pandemic-Era Inflation?" NBER Working Paper w31417 (2023).

Kristin J. Forbes, "Inflation Dynamics: Dead, Dormant, or Determined Abroad?" *Brookings Papers on Economic Activity* 2 (2019): 257–338.

Phillips, Alban W. "The Relation between Unemployment and the Rate of Change of Money Wage Rates in the United Kingdom, 1861–1957," *Economica* 25(100) (1958): 283–299.

CHAPTER 17

The Determinants of the Exchange Rate

LEARNING OBJECTIVES

In this chapter, we learn about:
- the exchange rate being an asset price
- how monetary factors affect the nominal exchange rate when prices are flexible
- how expectations of future fundamentals can affect the exchange rate today
- how exchange rates behave when prices are not free to move in the short run
- how productivity differentials affect the real exchange rate
- why higher income countries have stronger inflation-adjusted currencies

INTRODUCTION

In 2014, Fabrice Brégier, then chief operating officer of Airbus, called for the European Central Bank to intervene as the strength of the euro was "crazy." He wanted them to push it down against the dollar by 10% from an "excessive" $1.35 to between $1.20 and $1.25. We learned in Chapter 14 how a strong currency makes it harder for domestic manufacturers to export goods, so we can understand why a European executive trying to sell commercial airplanes might worry that a strong euro was making his job harder. And it is a fact that in 2014, Airbus was registering disappointing sales compared to its rival across the Atlantic, Boeing. But why would it be "crazy" for the euro to be worth $1.35, and yet normal and acceptable for the euro to be worth 10% less than that? And how did Fabrice Brégier expect the European Central Bank to adjust the euro's value, when the euro is under a floating, rather than a fixed, exchange rate regime?

In Chapter 12, we described the exchange rate as the price of foreign currency, determined in the foreign exchange market. Characterizing the exchange rate as just a relative price of currencies determined by supply and demand factors was a powerful insight, but only abstract factors – such as increased demand for home goods or decreased supply of foreign assets – were tapped as determinants. We did not explain in detail how those supply and demand factors were related to observable macroeconomic variables. That is the task this chapter takes on.

One of the key challenges for identifying the factors that determine exchange rates is the fact that the exchange rate seems to move a lot more than the variables one might think are important for exchange rate movements. Figure 17.1 depicts the month-to-month percentage changes in the exchange rate for the most commonly traded currency pair in the world, dollars and euros. Also plotted are the changes in the ratio of the money supply to national income in the US as compared to the euro area, and the difference between the US and euro area interest rates. Clearly the exchange rate is more volatile than the latter two economic variables.

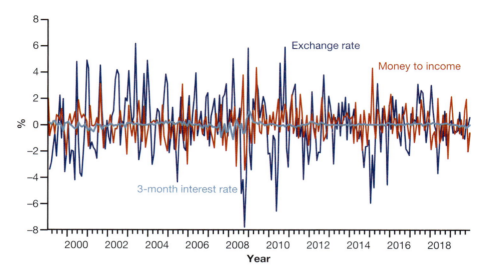

Figure 17.1 Volatility of the Exchange Rate and Its Determinants This graph shows the month-to-month percentage changes in the US dollar/euro exchange rate, the money–income ratio between the US and the eurozone, and differences in the respective three-month interest rates. Money is measured as M2, income proxied by industrial production.

Here is something else that is interesting about Figure 17.1. Chapter 15 explained how a rising interest rate should stimulate foreign demand for dollar-denominated financial instruments and thereby boost the value of the dollar. And yet in the figure, sometimes the red and blue lines move in the same direction. When they move up together, the interest rate difference tilts in favor of the US, but the value of the dollar falls. When they move down together, the rate difference tilts against the US, and yet the dollar gains in value. The correlation between the interest rate differential and the movement of the dollar is just −0.04, not anywhere near statistically significant.

This seemingly idiosyncratic behavior of the currency suggests how difficult it would be for the European Central Bank (ECB) to determine how to help Airbus – and other euro area firms – by weakening the currency. Would it want to raise or drop the interest rate?

To explain these puzzles, we begin by outlining a model where the supply of, and demand for, monies of different countries determines the exchange rate. To simplify the model, we first examine the determinants of exchange rates when prices are perfectly flexible. A case study of Zimbabwe's experience demonstrates the predictions of this model. To make the model applicable to countries with less extreme conditions, we examine the implications when the price level is sticky, more in line with the assumptions in Chapter 16. This modification allows one to explain the seemingly fickle nature of exchange rates as well as the fact that a higher real interest rate leads to a strengthening of currency values. Finally, we examine the determinants for inflation adjusted exchange rates over the longer term.

17.1 THE MONETARY APPROACH WITH FLEXIBLE PRICES

In this section, we first link the exchange rate to current factors affecting money demand and supply. We then show, by virtue of uncovered interest parity, that expectations about the future monetary fundamentals affect the present exchange rate.

The Exchange Rate as a Function of Contemporaneous Factors

The **monetary approach** to exchange rate determination relies on interactions between money demand and money supply. We denote the spot exchange rate as S, measured in home currency units per foreign currency unit. For concreteness, let us take the foreign country to be the euro; then from the American perspective, S is the number of US dollars required to purchase a single euro. This means that when S rises, the dollar is weakening against the euro.

First, to impose some constraints that reflect how our various macroeconomic variables are related to one another, we now assume that the price of a steel beam, either in the US or the euro area, is equal when both prices are expressed in dollars (or both prices are expressed in euros). In other words, the **Law of One Price** applies. In fact, we will require that in the US and the euro area, all goods – not just steel beams, but also cars, loaves of bread, and so on – are priced the same, and that goods are consumed in the same proportions in the two respective economics. This means that at any given time t, the price in dollars of a representative bundle of US goods equals the price in dollars, converted from euros using the current exchange rate, of an identical euro area bundle:

$$P_t = S_t \times P_t^* \tag{17.1}$$

This condition is called **purchasing power parity** (PPP). To illustrate the concept, consider a Big Mac sold in Chicago versus one sold in Berlin. They are composed of the same ingredients in the same proportions ("two all-beef patties, special sauce, lettuce, cheese ..." and so on, in the words of a 1970s ad jingle). According to purchasing power parity, the dollar price of a US Big Mac should equal the euro price of a euro-area Big Mac, multiplied by the exchange rate in dollars per euro. In July 2013, the euro-area Big Mac cost 3.62 euros, so at the then-current exchange rate of 1.286 dollars/euro, a euro-area Big Mac cost \$4.66. By comparison, a US Big Mac cost \$4.56 – a difference of only about 2%.

For what we will be doing, it turns out to be easier to use the natural log of the variables, denoted by lowercase letters: the natural log of S is denoted by s, and the log of the price level is denoted p. Equation (17.1) can be rearranged and re-written in log terms as:

$$s_t = p_t - p_t^* \tag{17.2}$$

Next, we relate the real demand for money to income and interest rates. We will assume that money demand looks like this:

$$(m_t - p_t)^d = \varphi y_t - \lambda i_t \tag{17.3}$$

The d superscript indicates demand; m is the money stock, p is the price level, and y is income – all in natural logs – and i is the interest rate, in percentage points. While equation (17.3) looks different from the money demand equation used in Chapters 14 and 15, in terms of intuition it is the same: when income rises by 1%, then the demand for money (after adjusting for the price level) rises by φ%; when the interest rate rises by 1 percentage point, the demand for real money drops by λ%. For simplicity, we will assume (as in the previous chapters) that the money supply is set exogenously by the central bank and that money supply equals money demand, and that all home conditions apply identically to the foreign country. This results in the following expression for the (log) exchange rate:

$$s_t = (m_t - m_t^*) - \varphi(y_t - y_t^*) + \lambda(i_t - i_t^*) \tag{17.4}$$

The exchange rate, remember, is the relative price of currencies, which in turn depends upon the *relative* demand versus supply for money *between* countries. From the US perspective, when more dollars are printed (m rises), then the exchange rate depreciates (s rises). When US income rises, the demand for money (US dollars) rises, and this drives down, or appreciates, the exchange rate. Finally, the higher the US interest rate, the weaker the exchange rate (s is higher), as higher interest rates reduce money demand – and the exchange rate depends on the balance between money supply and money demand.

Now, assume that individuals' reallocations of funds over assets denominated in different currencies move interest rates until no one expects to receive a higher rate of return saving in one country versus another. This condition, called uncovered interest parity, was discussed in Section 12.4:

$$i_t - i_t^* = \Delta s_{t+1}^e \equiv s_{t+1}^e - s_t \tag{17.5}$$

On the left, i_t and i_t^* are, respectively, the domestic and foreign interest rates at time t. On the right, s_{t+1}^e is what people at time t *expect* the (log) exchange rate to be at time $t + 1$, while s_t is the *actual* exchange rate at time t. The equation says that the interest differential between the two countries, expressed in percentage terms, equals the expected relative depreciation of the home currency, in percentage terms. Notice $\log(X/Z)$ is the same as $\log(X) - \log(Z)$, or, in the notation where lowercase letters denote logged terms, $x - z$. The term $x - z$ is a percentage difference. When one replaces x and z with s_{t+1} and s_t, respectively, then one has a percentage growth rate, or rate of change in percentage terms.

To illustrate: suppose Home is the United States and Foreign is the euro area, the US interest rate on a one-year bond is 4% while the counterpart euro area interest rate is 3%, and the expected depreciation of the dollar relative to the euro is 2% annually. Then a US bond buyer has two options: either (1) earn 4% by holding the US bonds for a year, or (2) convert dollars to euros, earn 3% by holding euro area bonds for a year, and then earn another 2% after converting back to dollars. Assuming the buyer is not worried about uncertainty, the second option, with 5% total earnings, is the best, and in fact it makes sense to borrow in the US and save the borrowed money in the euro area.

Once investors figure this out (it will not take long), enough capital will flow from the US to the euro area so that either euro area interest rates will fall, or US interest rates will rise, or the expected dollar depreciation will decline. We do not know which will occur, but suppose it is the second of those possibilities. Then we might end up with a US interest rate on a one-year bond of 5%, and if the euro area rate stays at 3%, and the expected dollar depreciation remains at 2%, then equation (17.5) is satisfied and there is no profit-making strategy available.

Substituting equation (17.5) into equation (17.4) yields:

$$s_t = (m_t - m_t^*) - \varphi(y_t - y_t^*) + \lambda(s_{t+1}^e - s_t) \tag{17.6}$$

The last term tells us that the more the exchange rate is expected to depreciate in the future, the weaker the currency is today.

17.1 THE MONETARY APPROACH WITH FLEXIBLE PRICES

Contrast the results of this model with the predictions of the Mundell–Fleming model discussed in Chapter 15. In that approach, higher relative income results in a *weaker* currency, and a higher relative interest rate induces a *stronger* currency. Both of these predictions are opposite of those obtained in this monetary model.

The difference in predictions about how the interest rate affects the exchange rate stems from the assumption that prices are free to adjust without any friction. In a Mundell–Fleming model, a higher interest rate causes a financial capital inflow, with the resulting demand for home currency appreciating the currency. In the monetary approach, a higher interest rate causes a lower money demand, relative to money supply, and hence a weaker currency.

The Effect in the Present of Expectations about the Future

One of the most important insights to be gained from the monetary approach is that the future matters. This point is obscured in equation (17.4), where the exchange rate in *this* period depends on the money supply, income, and interest rates in *this* period. However, expectations about the future are actually present in that expression, as the present-time interest differential depends on what is expected to happen to the exchange rate over time, as shown in equation (17.6), and hence depends on what is expected to happen to the fundamentals in the future.

The present exchange rate s_t appears on both sides of equation (17.6). By solving for s_t, we can make the dependence of s_t on expectations fully explicit:

$$s_t = \left(\frac{1}{1+\lambda}\right)[(m_t - m_t^*) - \phi(y_t - y_t^*)] + \left(\frac{\lambda}{1+\lambda}\right)s_{t+1}^e \tag{17.7}$$

The present exchange rate depends on the present **monetary fundamentals** – money and income – but also on expectations about the next period: the more valuable one expects the currency to be tomorrow, the more valuable it will be today.

Notice, now, what the preceding implies about s_{t+1}^e, the expected exchange rate in period $t+1$: it in turn depends on the expected monetary fundamentals in period $t+1$ and the expected exchange rate in period $t+2$. This analysis can be repeated indefinitely far into the future. Representing the expected monetary fundamentals in period $t+i$ as $\widehat{M}_{t+i}^e \equiv (m_{t+i}^e - m_{t+i}^{e*}) - \phi(y_{t+i}^e - y_{t+i}^{e*})$, we write:

$$s_t = \left(\frac{1}{1+\lambda}\right)\left[\widehat{M}_t + \left(\frac{\lambda}{1+\lambda}\right)\widehat{M}_{t+1}^e + \left(\frac{\lambda}{1+\lambda}\right)^2\widehat{M}_{t+2}^e + \left(\frac{\lambda}{1+\lambda}\right)^3\widehat{M}_{t+3}^e \ldots\right] \tag{17.8}$$

The exchange rate in the present period depends on *all* the expected future values of the monetary fundamentals. Notice, though, that the expected fundamentals in period $t+20$ have a much smaller impact than those in period $t+1$. In other words, our estimate of the monetary fundamentals 20 years from now matters a lot less for today's exchange rate than our estimate of the monetary fundamentals tomorrow.

The interpretation of the exchange rate as the present "discounted value" of current and future fundamentals helps explain why the exchange rate can move even if nothing substantial changes today. If people simply alter their *views* about what is going to happen in the future, then that will have an effect. We also see why seemingly negligible changes in today's observed fundamentals can induce big contemporaneous changes in the exchange rate. It is all (or mostly) in the expectations of the future.

Suppose, by way of illustration, that credible rumors suddenly begin to circulate about the central bank's plans to expand the money supply more rapidly in the near future. This will cause the exchange rate to devalue today, instantaneously. The bigger the sensitivity of money to the interest rate (λ), the bigger the jump. The disproportionate movement in the exchange rate is called the **magnification effect**.

APPLICATION   Hyperinflation in Zimbabwe

In the late 1990s, the government of Zimbabwe began running large budget deficits, as expenditures from its involvement in the Second Congo War collided with the collapse in tax revenues due to a shrinking economy. An intensification of the land redistribution program in the late 1990s led to a severe drop in agricultural output, as well as general economic activity, resulting in a severe drop in government revenues. Since the government was not able to borrow from international markets and domestically, the central bank purchased government debt, effectively printing money. This can be shown by referring back to the definition of the government's budget constraint. The budget deficit (BuD) is the excess of government spending over tax revenues:

$$BuD \equiv G - T \tag{17.9}$$

The budget deficit must be financed, by selling government bonds to either the private market or the central bank. Expressed in nominal terms:

$$P \times BuD = \Delta B + \Delta B_{CB} = \Delta B + \Delta MB \tag{17.10}$$

where B is government bonds held by the private sector, and B_{CB} is the bonds held by the central bank – in this case the Reserve Bank of Zimbabwe (RBZ). The RBZ purchased the bonds with money base MB, described in Chapter 14 as the sum of currency and bank reserves. In the case of Zimbabwe, few domestic and foreign lenders were willing to purchase bonds from the government, given fears that the government would be unwilling to honor the debt. As a consequence, the budget deficit was completely financed by "printing money." The change in the money supply, ΔM, is a multiple of the change in the money base.

The deficits were so large that vast amounts of money had to be printed. Hyperinflation – inflation in excess of 50% – was the result, with prices rising at an annualized rate of nearly 80 billion percent by the end of 2008 (Hanke and Kwok, 2009).

Far before inflation reached these levels, prices were no longer sticky. It is easy to see why: when the prices of goods rise minute by minute, shopkeepers and workers will adjust what they charge very quickly.

Figure 17.2 Zimbabwean Dollars The Zimbabwean currency was printed in very large denominations during the hyperinflation of the 2000s.
Source: Steve Allen/Photodisc/Getty Images.

This is a case where the flexible price monetary model applies, so that equation (17.4) defines the exchange rate. At such high inflation rates, the interest rate is equal to inflation; in addition, the foreign country – in this case the US – can be ignored without too much concern. We then obtain:

$$s_t = (m_t) - \varphi(y_t) + \lambda(\pi_t) \tag{17.4'}$$

For simplicity, assume $\varphi = 1$. Depicted in Figure 17.3 below are the exchange rate $(m-y)$ and price level, all normalized to 2000 values equal to 1. Because all the variables move so drastically, the series are graphed on a log scale. Notice that by purchasing power parity, the exchange rate s should move in a same way as the price level, p. The model implies that the series move together, more or less proportionately, and they do.

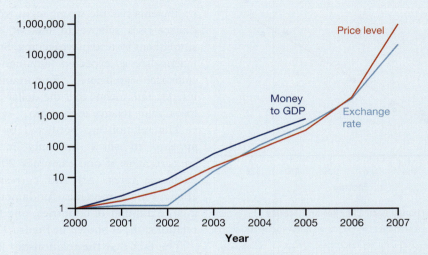

Figure 17.3 The Price Level, Exchange Rate, and Money Stock This graph shows the ratio of money to real GDP (blue line), the price level (red line) and exchange rate in Zimbabwe dollars to US dollar (light blue line), all normalized to a value of 1 in 2,000, and on a log scale. Money is proxied by currency.

The exchange rate series depicted in the figure is the official, rather than actual market, exchange rate, so the pace of depreciation is understated. However, given the rapid pace of devaluations, movements in the official series give some indication of changes in the market (or parallel) rate. The point is that the pace of monetary fundamentals growth is proportional both to the rate at which the price level rises and to the rate of exchange rate depreciation.

By 2008, the rate of inflation and currency depreciation were so rapid that the South African rand, the US dollar, the pound, and the euro substituted for the Zimbabwe dollar in most transactions. As part of an emergency plan to stabilize the economy, the government consented to the use of foreign currency in transactions in February of 2009, and in April, the US dollar was adopted for transactions by the Zimbabwe government. Other currencies, such as the rand, were allowed to circulate as well; the point is that monetary policy was taken out of the hands of the Reserve Bank of Zimbabwe, and hyper-inflation and currency depreciation ceased to be an issue.

17.2 HOW WELL DOES THE FLEXIBLE PRICE MONETARY MODEL WORK IN NORMAL TIMES?

The current model provides insights into the determinants of exchange rates between currencies of advanced economies. However, this does not automatically mean that in the real world, our input variables affect the exchange rate in the way the model predicts. For instance, one can use a statistical technique called linear regression to estimate the relationship between the exchange rate, money stocks, incomes, and interest rates implied by equation (17.4), for the dollar/euro exchange rate over the 1999Q1–2006Q4 period. Linear regression yields the following equation:

$$s = -0.59m - 0.63m^* - 1.70y + 3.70y^* - 2.31(i - i^*) \tag{17.11}$$

Notice that compared to equation (17.4), one of the coefficients has the wrong sign: when the supply of dollars rises relative to that of euros, the dollar strengthens instead of weakening. Still, the other coefficients are as expected (although not always with statistical significance). Importantly, a higher US interest rate means that the dollar gains, rather than loses, value relative to the euro.

The relationship predicted by equation (17.4) appears to show up only in the long run. In particular, if one examines 20-year changes in exchange rates (Δs) and corresponding 20-year changes in the monetary fundamentals ($\Delta \widehat{M}$) across a large number of countries, one finds the positive relationship, as shown in Figure 17.4.

The fact that the relationship holds in the long run, but not in the short run, suggests what might be wrong with the flexible-price monetary model: in the short run, prices might not be perfectly flexible.

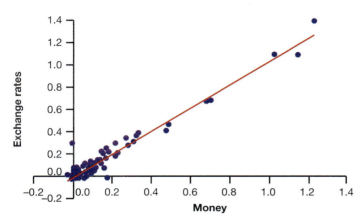

Figure 17.4 Long-Term Exchange Rate Changes and Money This graph shows twenty-year average growth rates in exchange rates and in monetary fundamentals over the 1984–2004, for 94 countries.
Source: Cerra and Saxena (2010).
Used with permission of International Monetary Fund, from Valerie Cerra, Sweta Chaman Saxena, "The Monetary Model Strikes Back: Evidence from the World," Journal of International Economics, 81(2), 2010, 184-196.

Identifying the Problem: Prices Are Not Perfectly Flexible

A key building block of the model is PPP, which assumes that prices are equalized in common currency terms on an ongoing basis. However, in everyday observations we do not see firms adjusting prices minute by minute, or even necessarily month by month. So there is no obvious reason to believe that purchasing power parity actually holds, except perhaps *on average*.

The assumption of purchasing power parity is easy to test. If it does hold, then the exchange rate should follow closely the relative price level. Figure 17.5 displays two series, the US dollar/euro exchange rate and the price level in the US relative to that in the euro area, in log terms. (Price levels are measured using consumer price indexes, using baskets of goods that are not identical between US and the euro area but function more or less as if they were).

The figure highlights the fact that the two series do not move together, as they should if PPP held continuously. Rather, large and persistent deviations from PPP are evident. At the same time, one can see that the exchange rate does not seem to wander completely away from the relative price level over time, so there is some role for purchasing power parity.

17.3 EXCHANGE RATES AND STICKY PRICES

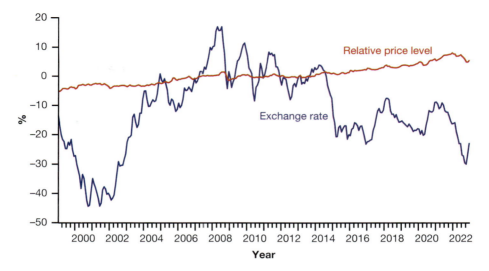

Figure 17.5 The Exchange Rate and Relative Price Levels This graph shows the US dollar/euro exchange (blue), and US euro area relative price level (red), difference from 2010, %.

Why does purchasing power parity fail to hold in the short term? One reason is the existence of transaction and transportation costs. Prices will tend toward parity if it is easy to buy in one place and sell in another. But if buying and selling involves auxiliary costs (government fees, for instance, or expenses associated with complying with regulations), or if the transportation of the goods is costly, then there is no reason for prices to be driven to equality. The same is true for tariffs and quotas that restrict international trade. These factors explain why there might be gaps in prices.

Those factors do not, however, explain why the price gaps vary over time. For that we need another explanation. We might speculate that the money demand equation is not stable over time. Or maybe the central bank adjusts the money supply in response to other factors. Here, however, we will seek to explain the failure of purchasing power parity *and* the variability in price gaps by supposing that prices are not, after all, fully free to move period by period.

If firms or households do not adjust prices instantaneously as market conditions change, gaps between prices in one country and another country can open up. However, it does not make sense to argue that prices are fixed forever. A more realistic view is that prices are fixed today, but over time can move; in other words, prices are sticky but not stuck. Everyday experience suggests that sticky prices are prevalent, an impression confirmed by statistical analyses. For instance, empirical studies indicate that for the United States, the typical length of time the price of a consumer good stays unchanged is about eight months. "Typical" in this case means "median," and pertains to a sample analyzed over the 1998–2005 period.

17.3 EXCHANGE RATES AND STICKY PRICES

One of the key assumptions of the model with flexible prices is that nominal interest rates vary primarily because of changes in the expected inflation rate. One way to test the validity of this assumption is to examine how actual one-year interest rates and expected one-year inflation

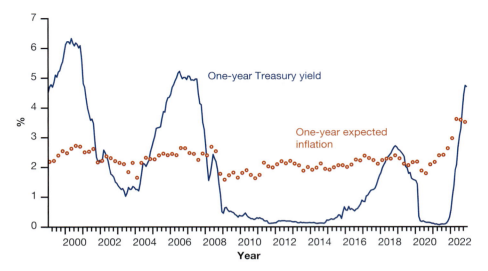

Figure 17.6 Interest Rates and Expected Inflation This graph shows yields on one-year US Treasury bonds (blue), and expected inflation from surveys (red circles).

rates evolve over time. Figure 17.5 plots data for the United States. The interest rate is represented by the yield on one-year US Treasuries. Expected inflation was determined by surveys of professional forecasters in the financial industry.

If prices were perfectly flexible, and the only shocks were monetary in nature, then the blue and red series should parallel each other closely. The fact that at best the curves display similar trends over a three-decade time span, with no similarity of behavior on a smaller time scale, suggests that the flexible price assumption is a poor one. Hence, it is not surprising that the flexible price monetary model fails so badly in predicting exchange rates.

We will now develop a more realistic model that drops the assumption of perfectly flexible prices, replacing it with an assumption of sticky prices in the short run. The result is a model where the exchange rate overshoots its long-run value in response to monetary shocks; this is sometimes called an **overshooting model** of the exchange rate.

A More Realistic Model

Let us assume that equation (17.5) holds *in the long run*. Since in the long run, a difference in interest rates reflects a difference in inflation rates, we can replace $i_t - i_t^*$ with $\pi_t - \pi_t^*$. Then with tildes ($\tilde{\ }$) denoting the long term, equation (17.4) becomes:

$$\tilde{s}_t = (\tilde{m}_t - \tilde{m}_t^*) - \phi(\tilde{y}_t - \tilde{y}_t^*) + \lambda(\tilde{\pi}_t - \tilde{\pi}_t^*) \tag{17.12}$$

To get an expression for the *short*-run exchange rate, we assume that exchange rates revert back towards the long-run value at a rate proportional to the short-run deviation from the long run. This phenomenon is called overshooting. We must also factor in the difference in inflation rates, because the greater the difference, the faster one currency is in losing value against the other, with everything else held constant. These considerations suggest the following description of the evolution of the exchange rate:

$$\Delta s_{t+1} \equiv s_{t+1} - s_t = -\theta(s_t - \tilde{s}_t) + (\tilde{\pi}_t - \tilde{\pi}_t^*) \tag{17.13}$$

17.3 EXCHANGE RATES AND STICKY PRICES

When the exchange rate is weaker than its long-run value ($s_t > \tilde{s}_t$), the exchange rate will go down, i.e., appreciate; and when the exchange rate is stronger than its long-run value, it will depreciate. The parameter θ is the **rate of reversion**. If $\theta = 0.5$, for example, then a 10% undervaluation induces a 5% exchange rate appreciation in the subsequent period, holding everything else constant.

We now make two assumptions: (1) that people's *expectations* about exchange rates match equation (17.13), and (2) that each of the fundamental variables (money, income, inflation rate) follows a **random walk**, meaning that the present value of variable X is always the best estimate of X's long-run average value. Then, as detailed in the Appendix to this chapter, we can use equations (17.12) and (17.13) to obtain an equation for the exchange rate that is applicable in the short term:

$$s_t = (m_t - m_t^*) - \varphi(y_t - y_t^*) - \left(\frac{1}{\theta}\right)(i_t - i_t^*) + \left(\lambda + \frac{1}{\theta}\right)(\pi_t - \pi_t^*) \tag{17.14}$$

Since the nominal interest rate minus inflation equals the real interest rate, $r_t \equiv i_t - \pi_t$, we could also write equation (17.14) as:

$$s_t = (m_t - m_t^*) - \varphi(y_t - y_t^*) - \left(\frac{1}{\theta}\right)(r_t - r_t^*) + \lambda(\pi_t - \pi_t^*) \tag{17.15}$$

As in the previous model, the current exchange rate depends positively on current money stocks and inflation rates, and negatively on income levels and interest rates. The key difference – that a higher nominal interest rate (holding inflation constant) means a stronger currency – is driven by the fact that interest rates and inflation rates now do not move in tandem. A common error in using this model is to reason as follows: higher real interest rates in the US induce an inflow of foreign capital. This causes a greater demand for US dollars, thereby appreciating the currency. This interpretation cannot literally be correct since, in this model, the current account and the financial account are both zero. Recall also that uncovered interest parity always holds, so investors are always indifferent between holding US versus foreign assets. Since the real interest rate shows up in equation (17.15), this model is sometimes called the **real interest differential** model. It is also called the Dornbusch–Frankel model.

It is easiest to explain the workings of the model using an example. Assume for simplicity that the foreign country's variables are held fixed. Then Figure 17.7 shows the evolution of log money (m), log price level (p), the interest rate (i), and the log exchange rate (s) over time, when the money supply increases abruptly by 50% at time T.

To understand how the graphs are generated, consider first the sticky-price case, represented by the red lines. When the money supply increases, then *with prices fixed*, real money balances increase by 50%. That in turn means that domestic interest rates fall, while foreign rates stay constant. If the exchange rate immediately depreciated to its long run value, i.e., 50% higher, then future expected depreciation would be 0, and uncovered interest parity could not hold. Hence, it must be that the exchange rate depreciates *above* the long-run value of the exchange rate, such that in the long run it is expected to *appreciate* over the long run so as to satisfy uncovered interest parity.

Now let us compare what happens if we repeat the experiment but prices are perfectly flexible (the blue lines). When the money supply increases, the price level immediately rises by 50%, as well, so that real money balances remain unchanged. Moreover, since prices are perfectly flexible, purchasing power parity holds, and the exchange rate depreciates by exactly

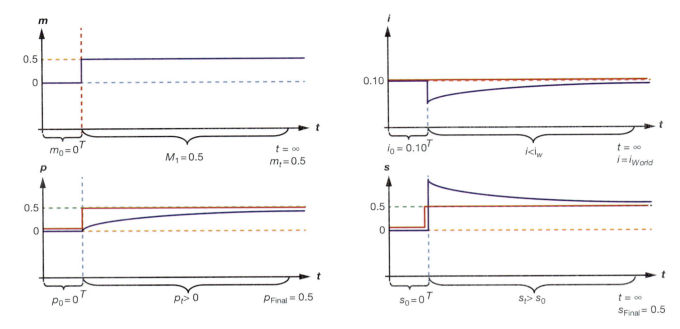

Figure 17.7 The Response of the Exchange Rate, Price Level and Interest Rate to a Money Shock These figures show the evolution of money (m), price level (p), interest rate (i), and exchange rate (s), all in logs except for the interest rate. The blue line denotes the paths for a sticky price model, and the red line denotes the path for the flexible price model.

50%. Note that an immediate jump in the exchange rate to its long-run value is entirely consistent with uncovered interest parity, since the domestic interest rate equals the foreign one.

One way to think of the contrasting results is that when prices are perfectly flexible, a shock to the system – in this case a monetary shock – results in proportionate movements in the related nominal variables. When one of the variables is not free to move – such as the price level – then the other variables have to do a disproportionate share of the adjustment. In this case, the real interest rate moves, and the exchange rate overshoots its long-run value.

17.4 EMPIRICAL EVIDENCE FOR THE STICKY PRICE MODEL

Numerous studies have attempted to evaluate the usefulness of the monetary model of the exchange rate. The translation from theory to empirical work is difficult, in part because the specification requires that the long-run values of money and income, which we do not observe, be included in the regression equation. To the extent that the actually observed money and output variables deviate from the long run, the model should not do particularly well.

In fact, in the short run, for month-to-month fluctuations in the exchange rate, the monetary model does not fit the data very well. In the long run, the model works somewhat better. Alquist and Chinn (2008) examined quarterly data for the United States, Canada, Japan, the UK, and the euro area from 1975 to 2005. Narrow money (M1) was used for the money variable, with the exception of the UK, where M4 is used; and inflation was calculated using consumer price indices.

The model is estimated using a statistical procedure that isolates the long-run relationship between the variables.

Table 17.1 DOLS estimates of the monetary model

	EUR	GBP	CAD	JPY
Money	−0.154	−0.224	0.029	0.422
	(0.263)	(0.192)	(0.058)	(0.395)
Output	−1.035	−2.696^n	−2.938^{nnn}	1.604
	(0.899)	(1.567)	(0.512)	(1.181)
Interest rates	−1.602	−0.351	−2.558^n	−7.713
	(1.495)	(1.441)	(1.419)	(2.393)
Inflation	9.942^{nn}	1.314	3.523^{nnn}	3.080
	(4.317)	(1.314)	(1.181)	(6.000)
Adj. R-sq.	0.56	0.20	0.59	0.59
Sample	81Q4-05Q4	75Q4-05Q4	75Q2-05Q4	80Q4-05Q2
T	95	119	121	99

Note: Point estimates from DOLS(2,2). Newey-West HAC standard errors in parentheses. ^{n}; ^{nn}; ^{nnn} Indicate statistical significance at the 10%, 5%, 1% level.

IN PRACTICE   Can We Predict Exchange Rates?

There is ample evidence that movements in exchange rates can be statistically explained by movements in money supplies, incomes, and interest and inflation rates. However, it is an open question whether there is a way to forecast exchange rates in the future at economically meaningful horizons, like a quarter or a year.

Over 40 years ago, two economists, Richard Meese and Kenneth Rogoff (1983), demonstrated that even when one assumed knowledge about the actually realized values of the theoretically important variables, it was extremely difficult to predict the future movement of the exchange rate. In fact, it seemed that the best prediction (the one that minimized the variance of the prediction errors) was provided by the assumption that the exchange rate followed a random walk – meaning the best predictor of the future exchange rate was today's exchange rate.

There is actually good reason to think that if one *did not* know anything about money supplies, incomes, and any other macroeconomic variables tomorrow, the best guess of tomorrow's exchange rate would be today's. That is because the current value of the exchange rate incorporates current best-estimate expectations about all future fundamentals, so that there is no future movement still remaining to be inferred from the currently available data, aside from a relatively small interest differential component.

However, it should be the case that, if one knew the money supply, income, interest, and inflation rates a year from now, and had a reliable knowledge of the parameters linking these variables and the exchange rate, then the exchange rate *could* be predicted.

Meese and Rogoff showed that neither the flexible price nor the sticky price monetary model, nor a model augmenting the sticky price model with cumulated trade balances, out-predicted a no-change forecast. Why did they obtain this finding? One explanation is that, in general, the parameters of the models are very imprecisely estimated.

Subsequent studies failed to robustly overturn this finding, at least at horizons of up to a year. Mark (1995) and Chinn and Meese (1995) found some evidence that at horizons of up to four years, these types of models could out-predict a random walk. In the most recent comprehensive analysis, extending up to 2015, researchers found that some models, such as interest rate parity and purchasing power parity, do well relative to a random walk at horizons of a year to five years (Cheung et al., 2019). In the end, the fundamentals do seem to matter, but it is difficult to tease out the effects except at long horizons. At short horizons, other factors seem to dominate.

For all exchange rates of the dollar against the other currencies, interest and inflation rates point in the right direction – that is, higher interest rates appreciate the dollar, while higher inflation rates depreciate the dollar. Higher relative income also tends to appreciate the currency. On the other hand, money stocks do not seem to have a robust impact on the exchange rate. This might be due to the fact that the money demand equations are, contrary to the assumptions in the model, not very stable.

17.5 REAL MODELS OF THE REAL EXCHANGE RATE

As explained in Chapter 12, the real exchange rate is the inflation-adjusted rate of exchange. The previous model focuses on how monetary factors influence the value of a currency in nominal terms. In the long run exchange rates primarily track with how much money has been printed in one country relative to another, as in the dollar/euro exchange rate. However, particularly for some exchange rates involving economies of drastically different levels of income, real factors seem to take on a larger role. That requires we dispense with purchasing power parity, even in the long run.

This point is easiest to see when examining the real exchange rate. Using the notation from earlier, define the real exchange rate as:

$$\log(q_t) \equiv s_t - p_t + p_t^* \tag{17.16}$$

Again, the real exchange rate is the inflation-adjusted exchange rate. Alternatively, it's the rate at which one would give up bundles of home goods for a unit bundle of the foreign goods.

Purchasing power parity (as expressed in equation (17.2)) implies that the real exchange rate is a constant, namely 1 (the log of which is zero). Figure 17.8 displays the (log) real exchange rate of the Japanese yen against the US dollar.

While Japan today is at roughly the same per capita income level as the United States, back in 1960 this was not the case. From then up to about 1990, the dollar/yen exchange rate – rather than reverting to a constant average value – trended upward. That means that over several decades, the yen was gaining greater and greater strength against the US dollar. How could this occur? Purchasing power parity is assumed to hold when people can arbitrage goods across borders, thereby forcing the equalization of prices of individual goods. However, not everything is traded. Services, in particular, have long been considered nontradable. (Haircuts are hard to export.)

Suppose, then, that the (log) price level is a weighted average of prices of **nontradable goods** (including services) and **tradable goods**.

17.5 REAL MODELS OF THE REAL EXCHANGE RATE

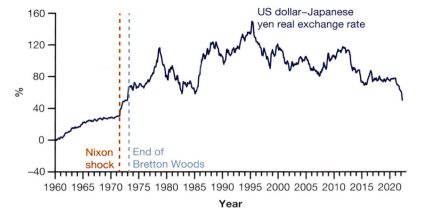

Figure 17.8 The Real Exchange Rate This graph shows the difference from January 1960 for the real US dollar/Japanese yen exchange rate, calculated using CPIs. An upward movement denotes a real appreciation of the Japanese currency.

$$p_t = \alpha p_t^N + (1-\alpha) p_t^T \tag{17.17}$$

where the N and T superscripts denote nontraded and traded goods, respectively. Assume the foreign country has the same structure. Making the appropriate substitutions into equation (17.16), rearranging, and using $\widehat{p}$ to denote $p^N - p^T$, the (log) relative price of nontradable goods in terms of tradable ones, we obtain:

$$\log(q_t) = \log(q_t^T) - \alpha(\widehat{p}_t - \widehat{p}_t^*), \text{ where } \log(q_t^T) = s_t - p_t^T + p_t^{T*} \tag{17.18}$$

So the real exchange rate can differ from zero if it is nonzero for tradable goods, or if the relative price of nontradable goods versus tradable goods differs across countries. In order to focus on the long-term determinants of the trend in the real exchange rate, let us assume that $\log(q^T)$ is zero. That is equivalent to stating that purchasing power parity holds for the goods that are tradable.

The consequence of letting purchasing power parity pin down the tradable goods' prices is to make the real exchange rate depend negatively on the relative price of nontradable goods, in the home country compared to the foreign one. For instance, the faster the relative price of nontradable goods in South Korea rises, the faster the Korean won appreciates in real terms.

These effects should show up in cases where relative prices change a lot; one instance of this would be the East Asian countries during the period of rapid growth in that region, up through the 1990s. Figure 17.9 shows the change in real rates plotted against the

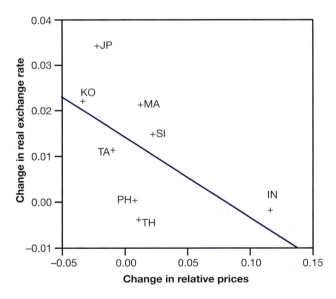

Figure 17.9 The Real Exchange Rate and the Relative Price of Nontradables This graph shows the average growth rate in the real exchange rate against the US dollar versus the average annual change in the relative price of nontradable to traded goods, 1972–1992. *Source: Used with permission of John Wiley & Sons, from "The Usual Suspects? Productivity and Demand Shocks and Asia–Pacific Real Exchange Rates," Menzie D. Chinn,* Review of International Economics, 8(1), © 2002; *permission conveyed through Copyright Clearance Center, Inc.*

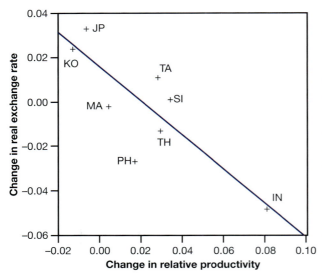

Figure 17.10 The Real Exchange Rate and Relative Productivity
This graph shows the average growth rate in the real exchange rate against the US dollar versus the average annual change in the relative productivity of traded to nontraded goods, 1972–1992. Source: Used with permission of John Wiley & Sons, from "The Usual Suspects? Productivity and Demand Shocks and Asia–Pacific Real Exchange Rates," Menzie D. Chinn, Review of International Economics, 8(1), © 2002; permission conveyed through Copyright Clearance Center, Inc.

change in relative prices over the 1972–1992 period. We expect a negative relationship, the way the variables are defined.

One reason the relative price of nontradable goods might move is productivity. Consider the relative price of haircuts and mobile phones: rapid productivity growth in mobile phone production means that haircuts become relatively more expensive (at least in terms of mobile phones). Moreover, since mobile phones are traded internationally, the price of mobile phones is tied down. Hence, over time, the more rapid the productivity growth in the (traded) mobile phone sector, the faster the rise in the price of haircuts, and the faster the rise in the total price level. That means that the higher tradable-good productivity, the lower the real exchange rate (i.e., the stronger the currency is in real terms).

Figure 17.10 presents this relationship for the same East Asian countries, with the change in real exchange rates plotted against the change in relative productivity ratios. Again, we expect to see a negative relationship, given the definitions of the variables.

The negative relationship is consistent with the view that faster productivity growth in the manufacturing sector of East Asian countries (roughly, the tradable goods sector) as compared to that in the United States has been a key driver in the appreciation of those currencies against the US dollar. This phenomenon, relating productivity trends to real exchange rates, is known as the **Balassa–Samuelson effect**.

The fact that higher income countries (with higher productivity in the tradable sectors) have stronger currencies is one of the most robust findings in the literature.

IN PRACTICE Tales from the Big Mac

In our earlier discussion of purchasing power parity, we compared the dollar price of a US Big Mac to the dollar price of a euro-area Big Mac; the difference was only about 2%. However, it turns out that, in general, price differences are much wider. Figure 17.11 is a scatterplot of the (log) relative dollar price of the country's Big Mac (compared to an American Big Mac) against the relative per capita income. The United States is at (0, 0), since everything is compared to the US. If all Big Macs were equally priced across countries, then all the observations would lie along the horizontal straight line at 0.

Contrary to the predictions of purchasing power parity, not only is there substantial dispersion in the relative prices of Big Macs across countries, there also seems to be a pattern in the deviations from purchasing power parity. The higher per capita income is, relative to the US, the higher the price of a Big Mac. A regression using the 2020 data (the red line) indicates that for each percentage point increase in relative income, Big Mac prices go by about 0.15 percentage point. This is a manifestation of what Samuelson (1994) termed the **Penn Effect**, after the University of Pennsylvania economists who

CONCLUSION

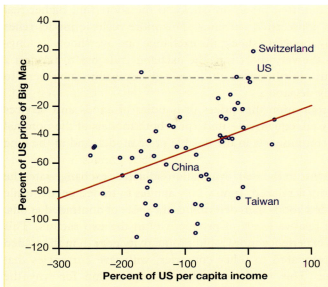

Figure 17.11 Big Mac Parity This graph shows the July 2020% of dollar price of a Big Mac in indicated country relative to that in the United States versus% of in per capita income relative to the United States (in PPP terms). The red line is a regression fit.

developed the dataset in which the price–income relationship was first detected. The same pattern shows up if one broadens the scope of observation to several years (although the coefficient is typically larger up to 0.25). In other words, the pattern is not a fluke.

Why is it that arbitrage does not drive Big Mac prices together? And why do Big Mac prices rise with income?

There are several answers to the first question. One is the factor discussed in Section 17.3, namely sticky prices: firms do not adjust prices instantaneously. Another is that Big Macs, being highly perishable, are not tradable internationally, and so arbitrage pressure on prices is limited. (At the same time, some of the *components* of a Big Mac – flour, beef, tomatoes – are traded.)

Neither of these explanations addresses the second question: why does the long-term relationship between relative Big Mac prices and relative per capita income hold? Here, it matters that labor costs account for a relatively large share of the costs of production. Labor is essentially not traded across borders. Furthermore, wage rates in high income countries are higher than those prevailing in low-income countries. So when next you travel to either South Asia or to Northern Europe, do not be surprised if the price of a Big Mac, converted into dollars by the exchange rate, differs from the dollar price you remember from your experience in the United States

One of the practical implications of this pattern is that it provides a concrete definition of undervaluation or overvaluation, i.e., **misalignment**. For instance, China, which has long been criticized for manipulating its currency to keep it undervalued, looks very guilty indeed – according to the PPP criterion, to the tune of something like 70%. But taking into account the Penn Effect, the undervaluation in 2013 was less than 20%.

CONCLUSION

The nominal exchange rate is the relative price of currencies, so it is natural to think of the determinants as being the relative supplies and demands for money. The insight that the exchange rate is an asset price is useful, because it highlights the fact that expectations about the future will determine the price today. Partly because expectations fluctuate more than the underlying variables, exchange rates are more variable than the fundamentals (money, income).

In the flexible price monetary model, increases in the home money supply lead to depreciation of the home currency, while increases in income (which increases the demand for money) lead to appreciation. Higher interest rates are associated with a weaker currency. This is because under flexible prices, a higher interest rate is associated with a higher inflation rate, i.e., a depreciation of the currency against a bundle of real goods.

Under the more realistic assumption that prices are sticky in the short run, higher real interest rates are associated with an appreciated currency. This more realistic model relies upon the idea that, in response to any monetary shock, the exchange rate overshoots its long-run value. Since prices are fixed in the very short run, the exchange rate has to take on a greater share of the role of adjustment,. Furthermore, this means the exchange rate reverts to the long-run value in response to any deviation.

Purchasing power parity – the proposition that prices of bundles of goods and services denominated in a common currency are equalized – underpins both models of the nominal exchange rate. Prices are equalized continuously in the flexible price model, and in the long run in the sticky price model.

In explaining longer-term movements in the real, or inflation-adjusted, exchange rate, the assumption of purchasing power parity is relaxed. It now only applies to traded goods, while the relative price of nontraded to traded goods then determines the price of nontraded goods. That relative price is driven by the relative levels of productivity in the two sectors. This means that over time, countries that experience more rapid productivity growth in the traded sector than the nontraded, when compared to other countries, will have currencies that appreciate in real terms over time. This model provides an explanation for why the Japanese yen appreciated rapidly over the post–World War II period, up to 1990.

SUMMARY

1. Purchasing power parity is a condition wherein price levels expressed in a common currency are equalized.
2. Changes in expectations about the future values of the fundamentals will affect the exchange rate today, even when the fundamentals do not change today.
3. In a monetary model of exchange rates, increases in money supply depreciate the currency, while higher income (which increases demand for money) appreciates the currency.
4. When prices are perfectly flexible, higher interest rates are due to higher expected inflation rates; hence, higher interest rates depreciate the currency.
5. When prices are sticky, a higher real interest differential appreciates the currency.
6. In the long run, purchasing power parity may not hold, if some goods are nontraded.
7. One determinant of the relative price of nontraded to traded goods prices is the productivity differential between the nontraded and traded sectors.
8. The Balassa–Samuelson effect is result of higher traded sector productivity resulting in stronger currencies.
9. The Penn Effect is the long-term positive association between currency strength and per capita income.

KEY CONCEPTS

Balassa–Samuelson effect, page 382
Law of One Price, page 369
magnification effect, page 372
misalignment, page 383
monetary approach, page 369
monetary fundamentals, page 371
nontradable good, page 380

overshooting model, page 376
Penn Effect, page 382
purchasing power parity, page 369
random walk, page 377
rate of reversion, page 377
real interest differential, page 377
tradable good, page 380

REVIEW QUESTIONS

1. If purchasing power parity always holds, and the foreign price level suddenly rises by 2%, while the home price level stays constant, what must happen to the exchange rate?
2. In the monetary model, demand for money relative to the supply of money in the home country relative to the foreign determines the exchange rate. True or false?
3. The implication that a high interest rate – relative to that in the foreign country – results in a weaker currency is due to the approach of treating the exchange rate as a function of stocks of money in the two countries. True or false?
4. The expected pace at which the monetary fundamentals grow relative to the foreign country only determines the pace at which the currency depreciates. True or false?
5. If prices are sticky, then will purchasing power parity hold at all times? If not, when?
6. Does purchasing power parity hold in the long run for all countries?
7. Are all goods tradable?
8. If hair-cutting technology starts improving faster than manufacturing technology (all relative to the foreign country), what will happen to the real exchange rate?

EXERCISES

1. Consider the flexible price monetary model.
   a. Using equation (17.7), show what happens if overnight the markets re-set their expectations of the dollar/euro exchange rate one year from now to be higher by 10%? What do you expect to happen to the dollar/euro exchange rate today, assuming nothing else changes? Assume $\lambda = 5$.
   b. Using equation (17.8), show what happens if overnight the expected monetary fundamentals for $t + 3$ are increased by 10% (and nothing else changes)? What happens to the exchange rate overnight? Assume $\lambda = 5$.
2. In the flexible price monetary model of exchange rates, where the semi-elasticity of money demand is 5, consider the following events.
   a. If the money supply increases by 5% today, and in all future periods stays 5% higher than it was expected to be, what happens *quantitatively* to the nominal exchange rate and nominal interest rate today, and into the future?
   b. Suppose the fundamentals are initially expected to grow by 0% per annum. Suppose the expected growth rate increases to 5%. Show graphically what happens to the exchange rate, if anything, the instant the expected growth rate changes.
3. In the sticky price monetary model of exchange rates,
   a. Explain what happens if the monetary authority in US decreases the money supply by 5%? In your answer, indicate the time paths of M, P, M/P, $r - r^*$, s. Use graphs.
   b. Suppose θ is effectively infinite. Redo part a.
4. Suppose South Korean productivity growth in manufacturing exceeds that in services by 10%, but US productivity in manufacturing and services are growing equally fast. Further suppose the share of nontraded goods (services here) is 60%. How fast should the Korean real exchange rate appreciate against the US dollar, on average?
5. Using the "Trade, exchange rates, budget balances and interest rates" Table in the *Economist*, http://www.economist.com/, answer the following questions. (Be sure to specify which issue you use.)

a. Given the inflation rates over the past year, what should have been the rate of change in the US dollar/euro exchange rate, if relative purchasing power parity (in growth rates) held?
b. Interpret the most recent *Economist* poll of the expected inflation rate for the current year as the expected change from December last year to December this year. What is the expected change in the US dollar/euro over that period if relative PPP holds?
6. Download the latest available data from https://github.com/TheEconomist/big-mac-data. It contains data on Big Mac prices. Column D is the price in local currency, column E is the exchange rate expressed as local currency per USD, and column F is the local currency price expressed in USD. Column H is per capita GDP in US dollar terms (assume this is a good proxy for per capita GDP in PPP terms)
   a. Calculate the percentage misalignment (in log terms) for China, Venezuela, Switzerland, Argentina, using purchasing power parity, taking the US as benchmark.
   b. Calculate the percentage misalignment (in log terms) for China, Venezuela, Switzerland, Argentina, using the Penn Effect, taking the US as benchmark. In order to estimate this, run a regression:

$$p_i = \alpha + \beta y_i + u_i$$

where p_i is the log of the dollar price of a Big Mac in country i divided the dollar price of a Big Mac in the US, and y_i is the log of country i per capita income divided by US per capita income. The misalignments are then the residuals from the regression.

RECOMMENDED RESOURCES

Yin-Wong Cheung, Menzie Chinn, and Eiji Fujii, "Pitfalls in Measuring Exchange Rate Misalignment: The Yuan and Other Currencies," *Open Economies Review* 20(2) (2009): 183–206.

Jeffrey A. Frankel, "On the Mark: A Theory of Floating Exchange Rates based on Real Interest Differentials," *American Economic Review* 69(4) (1979): 610–622.

David C. Parsley and Shang-Jin Wei, "A Prism into the PPP Puzzles: The Micro-Foundations of Big Mac Real Exchange Rates," *The Economic Journal* 117(523) (2007): 1336–1356.

Paul Samuelson, "Theoretical Notes on Trade Problems," *Review of Economics and Statistics* 46 (1964): 145–154.

Robert Summers and Alan Heston, "The Penn World Table (Mark 5): an expanded set of international comparisons, 1950–1988," *The Quarterly Journal of Economics* 106(2) (1991): 327–368.

APPENDIX 17.A

Derivation of the Sticky Price Monetary Model

To obtain equation (17.14), we assume that the flexible-price monetary model holds in the long run:

$$\tilde{s}_t = (\tilde{m}_t - \tilde{m}_t^*) - \phi(\tilde{y}_t - \tilde{y}_t^*) + \lambda(\tilde{\pi}_t - \tilde{\pi}_t^*) \tag{17.12}$$

We also assume the overshoot description of the short-term evolution of the exchange rate:

$$\Delta s_{t+1} \equiv s_{t+1} - s_t = -\theta(s_t - \tilde{s}_t) + (\tilde{\pi}_t - \tilde{\pi}_t^*) \tag{17.13}$$

If, further, we assume rational expectations, so that people's beliefs about future exchange rates conform to equation (17.11), then we can replace s_{t+1} with s_{t+1}^e:

$$s_{t+1}^e - s_t \equiv -\theta(s_t - \tilde{s}_t) + (\tilde{\pi}_t - \tilde{\pi}_t^*) \tag{17.A1}$$

We use the uncovered interest parity condition, $i_t - i_t^* = s_{t+1}^e - s_t$, to substitute on the left-hand side:

$$i_t - i_t^* = -\theta(s_t - \tilde{s}_t) + (\tilde{\pi}_t - \tilde{\pi}_t^*) \tag{17.A2}$$

Solving for the exchange rate,

$$s_t = \tilde{s}_t - \left(\frac{1}{\theta}\right)\left[(i_t - \tilde{\pi}_t) - (i_t^* - \tilde{\pi}_t^*)\right] \tag{17.A3}$$

Substituting the right side of equation (17.10) in for $\tilde{s}_t$,

$$s_t = (\tilde{m}_t - \tilde{m}_t^*) - \phi(\tilde{y}_t - \tilde{y}_t^*) + \lambda(\tilde{\pi}_t - \tilde{\pi}_t^*) - \left(\frac{1}{\theta}\right)\left[(i_t - \tilde{\pi}_t) - (i_t^* - \tilde{\pi}_t^*)\right] \tag{17.A4}$$

We can eliminate the tildes if we assume random-walk behavior for m, y, and π, so that their present actual values are the best estimates of their long-term average values. Thus,

$$s_t = (m_t - m_t^*) - \phi(y_t - y_t^*) + \lambda(\pi_t - \pi_t^*) - \left(\frac{1}{\theta}\right)\left[(i_t - \pi_t) - (i_t^* - \pi_t^*)\right] \tag{17.A5}$$

Combining like terms gives the desired result:

$$s_t = (m_t - m_t^*) - \phi(y_t - y_t^*) - \left(\frac{1}{\theta}\right)(i_t - i_t^*) + \left(\lambda + \frac{1}{\theta}\right)(\pi_t - \pi_t^*) \tag{17.14}$$

CHAPTER 18

Emerging Market Crises: The Boom–Bust Cycle

LEARNING OBJECTIVES

In this chapter, we learn about:
- what a currency crisis is
- how policies and events in large industrial countries affect emerging markets
- how emerging market policymakers can respond to external conditions
- whether restrictions on inflows and outflows of capital work to insulate emerging markets
- why devaluations can sometimes fail to solve the crisis

INTRODUCTION

After decades of roaring growth, the "East Asian Miracle" – as touted in a 1993 book published by the World Bank – seemed to be in full swing. Yet a mere four years later, the region was engulfed in chaos. What became known as the Asian Financial Crisis unfolded in July 1997. As foreign exchange reserves were depleted, the Bank of Thailand was forced to let the Thai baht float freely. The currency immediately depreciated by 21%. By January 1998, the baht was 54% weaker against the dollar than it had been six months earlier. The turmoil was not restricted to Thailand; Singapore, Malaysia, Indonesia, and the Philippines also experienced stresses on their balance of payments as capital flows reversed course, with net flowing out rather than in. In November 1997, the Bank of Korea floated its currency after years of keeping its currency, the won, tightly managed against the dollar. By January 1998, the won had fallen in value by 39%. Figure 18.1 tells the story graphically.

The drop in the currency values of these two countries coincided with a sharp drop in economic growth, as shown in Figure 18.2. A few months later, the Thai economy's year-on-year growth had collapsed to –15% before starting to bounce back, while Korea's economy bottomed out at an almost as dismal –9%. How did two countries apparently enjoying healthy growth suddenly descend into deep distress, their economies not just stagnating but, for a brief time, actually shrinking? And what role did the collapse in currency values play?

At the root of these questions lies the phenomenon of **currency crises**, in which central banks lose the ability to maintain their controlled exchange rate regimes. To understand how one central bank's policy challenges can become a huge headache for multiple national economies, it is useful to have a little background on how the international financial system has evolved. The defining characteristic of the last half-century, from a macroeconomic

INTRODUCTION

Figure 18.1 Currency Crashes This figure shows how the Thai baht plunged in value in July of 1997, and the Korean won lost value at a pace that accelerated in November 1997. Dashed lines indicate the end of pegged exchange rate regimes for each of the Thai and Korean currencies.

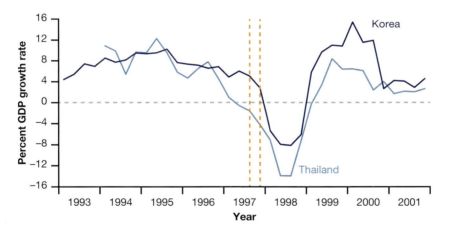

Figure 18.2 Financial Crises and Growth This figure shows the annual growth rate of GDP for Thailand (light blue) and Korea (blue).

perspective, is the increasing integration of the global economy. Ever-greater shares of economic activity are engaged in international trade in goods and services. Households devote ever-larger proportions of their spending to imported goods, while firms use more and more on imported components in their manufactured products.

The most remarkable transformation, however, is in finance. Borrowing and lending now take place with unprecedented ease. Households can borrow and lend more freely to smooth their consumption out over time. Firms with ready access to international financial markets can more easily borrow for investment. All of this means that cross-border holdings of assets and liabilities have increased dramatically.

These trends have been playing out all around the globe, but they have been especially pronounced in emerging markets and developing economies. And it is here that the worrisome implications of these developments have become most apparent: openness to international trade, and particularly financial trade, tends to amplify economic boom–bust cycles.

In this chapter, we first document the ebbs and flows of financial flows to the emerging markets and developing countries, and how they induce boom–bust cycles. The policy challenges of – and potential responses to – those inflows are then examined. Currency or "balance of payments" of crises occur when policy is unable prevent the exhaustion of foreign exchange reserves due to net outflows. The last section describes the financial crises wherein mismatches in assets and liabilities take on a dominant role.

18.1 CAPITAL SURGES AND REVERSALS

In Chapters 14 and 15, we examined situations in which financial capital mobility took on a range of values. Since a chief characteristic of the modern international economy is the ease with which financial capital moves between countries, an appropriate modeling of that economy will take capital mobility to be, if not perfect, then at least very nearly so.

As capital flows have increased over the past few decades, they have also tended to reverse direction with surprising frequency and suddenness. That is, capital might flow into a country, or set of countries, for several years but then abruptly start flowing out – or vice versa. Figure 18.3 illustrates a series of such reversals over a span of a little more than three decades, for emerging and developing nations.

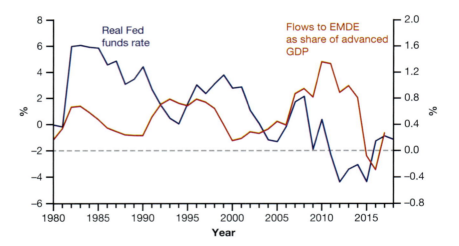

Figure 18.3 Capital Surges and Reversals This figure shows net financial flows to emerging and developing countries (two year average) as a share of advanced country GDP (red), and the US Fed funds interest rates minus current annual inflation rate (blue).
Source: For flows, Hannan (2018), GDP, IMF, World Economic Outlook, October 2018; for interest rates, Federal Reserve Board, Wu and Xia (2016), for annual inflation, BLS.

Notice that capital flows to emerging markets and developing countries follow a cyclical pattern: 1981 is followed by a trough in 1984, then comes a long boom that peaks in 1995, then a trough around the turn of the century, and then a boom peaking in 2007. There is a final boom in 2010. The relationship between capital flows and interest rate differentials is (roughly) inverse: the inflows tend to rise when real returns in advanced economies drop.

(Here the ten-year US interest rate, adjusted for inflation, stands in for other advanced-nation interest rates.)

What are the real-world implications of these financial flows? Financial capital provides resources for consumption and investment, so it is not surprising that output booms during periods of net inflows, as shown in Figure 18.4. It is also true that when net financial flows dry up, growth often drops. Hence, capital flows appear akin to a two-edged sword, promising greater growth but also threatening economic stability.

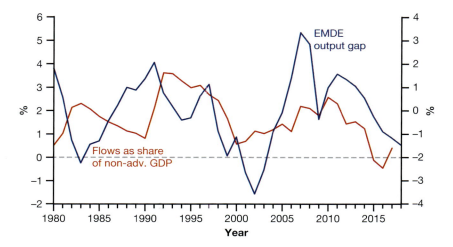

Figure 18.4 Capital Inflows and Economic Booms This figure shows net financial flows to emerging and developing countries as a percent of emerging and developing country GDP (red), and the output gap in emerging and developing countries as a percent of GDP (blue).
Source: For flows, Hannan (2018), GDP, IMF, World Economic Outlook, *October 2018.*

In order to examine the challenges facing economies integrated into the global financial system, we follow the evolution of a boom–bust cycle. First we discuss boom times, called *capital flow bonanzas* by Reinhart and Reinhart (1998). Then we turn to the busts. Calvo (1998) popularized the label *sudden stop*, first coined by Dornbusch et al. (1995) for events in which financial capital inflows cease and even reverse. The boom–bust cycle was aptly described by the title of a book about Argentina's economy in the 1990s and 2000s: *And the Money Kept Rolling In (and Out)*, referencing a song title from the musical *Evita*, set in Argentina.

18.2 MANAGING BOOMS

Capital flow surges to emerging markets and developing countries occur with some regularity. Why do these surges occur? Most economists would agree that it is a combination of **push factors** from the advanced economies – such as low interest rates – and **pull factors** – such as policy reform – in the developing countries. The big question concerns the relative importance of these sets of factors; here there is much less agreement.

Regardless of the exact origins of inflow surges, they pose a challenge to policymakers in emerging markets because they force difficult choices, even when conditions appear to be favorable. To see exactly what the choices are, consider a country on a fixed exchange rate, with high capital mobility, confronted by a sudden drop in rest-of-world interest rates, as in

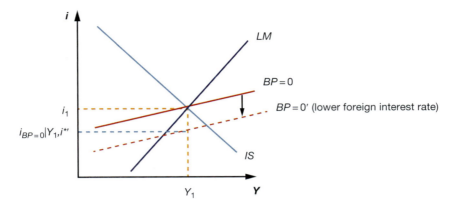

Figure 18.5 Global Financial Loosening and Small Open Economies This diagram shows how a decline in the rest-of-world interest rates shows up as a drop in the $BP = 0$ line.

Figure 18.5. To begin with, the economy is in internal and external equilibrium, with interest rate i_1 and income level Y_1. The drop in i^* shifts the $BP = 0$ schedule downward, as indicated by the black arrow. The current domestic interest rate, i_1, is then greater than that required for external balance; hence, $BP > 0$.

Policymakers have four options for responding to this situation: (1) allow the inflows to swell foreign exchange reserves, so the LM schedule shifts out; (2) sterilize the inflows; (3) revalue the currency, shifting the $BP = 0$ curve back up; or (4) impose capital controls.

Option 1: Accumulate Foreign Exchange Reserves

Option 1 is selected by default if the central bank takes no action, either by choice or because it lacks the means to do anything else. As shown in Figure 18.6, the increase in foreign exchange reserves, purchased with domestic currency, drives the domestic money supply up, thereby shifting out the LM curve (blue arrow) and lowering the interest rate. This process continues until the interest rate is low enough to restore external equilibrium. (A variant of this option is for the monetary authority to increase the money supply immediately, so as to restore external equilibrium without delay.)

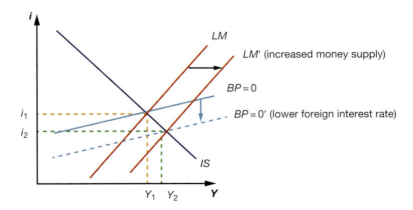

Figure 18.6 A Monetary Response to Capital Inflows This figure shows how the central bank's increase of money supply in response to a drop in the rest-of-world interest rate can restore balance of payments equilibrium.

Since output increases from Y_1 to Y_2, this response to the drop in rest-of-world interest rates may seem like a welcome development, not something to worry about. However, if Y_1 already represented full-employment output, then the increase in the money supply has caused the economy to overheat: output at Y_2 is unsustainable, and now the economy is primed for a crash in which the output will drop to less than Y_1. Under those conditions, policymakers will want an alternative to the default option.

Option 2: Sterilize the Inflows

If the authorities sterilize the increase in foreign exchange reserves, then the LM schedule remains in its original position, and the economy remains at i_1 and Y_1. Recall from Chapter 14 that sterilization requires, in this case, that the central bank reduces its holdings of domestic assets, such as government bonds, by selling them in open market operations. For every foreign currency unit's worth of increase in foreign exchange reserves, the central bank must sell a foreign currency unit equivalent's worth of government bonds. This process can continue only so long as the central bank has government bonds to sell. If the assets of the central bank come to consist solely of foreign exchange reserves, sterilization drops off the central bank's menu of options.

The advantage of option 2 is that foreign reserves are accumulated. Sufficiently large reserves will help when the international financial environment is less benign, and net capital inflows turn negative or the current account deteriorates. Building up a big war-chest of reserves is a form of **self-insurance**, which can deter a **run** on the central bank, where investors attempt to withdraw foreign currency before it becomes much more expensive to do so (which occurs when a currency is devalued). In this context, a run on the central bank is called a speculative attack. As discussed below in Section 18.3, the mere speculation, not actual realization, of a possible devaluation impels the withdrawal of funds.

Option 3: Revalue the Currency

A third option for monetary authorities is to revalue the currency (or to allow a currency appreciation, if the currency is on a managed float), as illustrated in Figure 18.7. With the revaluation comes a fall in the real exchange rate, from q to q', so that the $BP = 0$ curve shifts part-way back up (black arrow) *and* the IS curve shifts in (blue arrow). In this outcome, the interest rate and income level end up lower than they where when they started. For an economy that was originally at full employment output, the lower final income level is a drawback of this option.

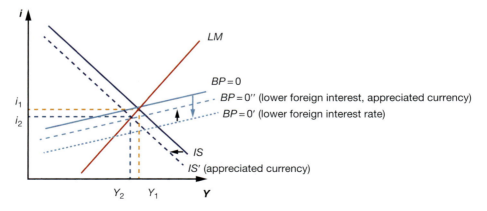

Figure 18.7 A Revaluation in Response to Capital Inflows This shows how a currency revaluation in response to a drop in the rest-of-world interest rate can restore balance of payments equilibrium.

Option 4: Capital Controls

Finally, if a government is concerned about unhealthy financial inflows, it can impose capital controls, i.e., restrictions on cross-border financial flows. The controls can take the form of blocks on certain types of financial transactions, or of explicit or implicit taxes on inflows. Such measures have the effect of decreasing $\varkappa$ in the $BP = 0$ equation. Since the slope of the $BP = 0$ curve is $m/\varkappa$, a reduction in $\varkappa$ rotates the curve counter-clockwise, as shown in Figure 18.8.

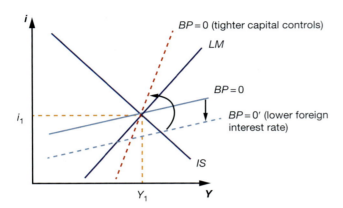

Figure 18.8 Tightening Capital Controls in Response to a Capital Inflows This diagram shows the effect of tightening capital controls in response to a drop in the rest-of-world interest rate.

Ideally, the capital controls will be calibrated so as to restore internal and external equilibrium at the original interest rate and income levels. In reality, there is no guarantee that this will happen. The $BP = 0$ curve will certainly rotate counter-clockwise, but there is no means of ensuring that it will end up in the ideal position.

How Well Do Capital Controls Work?

In theory, capital controls can be quite effective at restoring internal and external equilibrium,. However, if the returns to saving in the home country are sufficiently high, individuals will work hard to circumvent those controls. How effective are capital controls in practice?

When the government is sufficiently determined, the answer is "very." North Korea is one government that manages to control financial capital inflows and outflows so stringently that essentially no private funds get in or out. Of course, that country is remarkable along many dimensions, and it is doubtful that it provides an instructive model for other nations.

To judge the effectiveness of capital controls in a way relevant for most countries, one has to define "effective." If effective controls are ones that make cross-border financial transactions *more difficult*, so that return rates are not equalized, then controls probably do work. Japan provides an example. Prior to liberalization of the financial account (what was then called the capital account), a substantial interest rate differential existed between yen-denominated securities traded on shore, in Japan, and off shore, in the UK. As shown in Figure 18.9, once the controls were lifted in mid-1979, the differential shrank to zero.

However, we might instead define effective controls as ones that actually deter financial inflows or outflows, rather than just giving rise to a cross-border interest differential. Controls that insulate an economy in this way create greater latitude for an independent monetary policy.

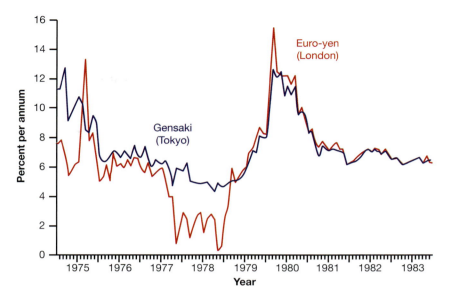

Figure 18.9 The Covered Interest Differential This diagram shows the onshore and offshore interest rates on the yen. *Source: Economic Report of the President, Transmitted to the Congress, February 1984, Together With the Annual Report of the Council of Economic Advisers (Government Printing Office).*

When the bar is thus set higher, the question of effectiveness becomes more complicated, because now we need to ask exactly what kind of controls we are talking about. Some controls apply to the economy overall, others merely to specific sectors. Some limiting measures apply to all types of financial capital flows, others only to specific types (equity vs. debt vs. direct investment). Some controls are long-term, while others are only temporary. Some measures take the form of explicit controls (e.g., cross-border bank loans cannot exceed some limit amount), while others take the form of implicit taxes (e.g., some proportion of an inflow has to be placed on deposit with the central bank, where it earns zero interest).

The general consensus among researchers is that capital controls, particularly comprehensive, durable ones, can somewhat insulate an economy, as demonstrated by weakened interest rate linkages. Figure 18.10 shows the sensitivity of a given interest rate change to the interest change in the country to whose currency the home currency is pegged, or managed against. The higher the bar, the greater the sensitivity. The bars are differentiated by combinations of exchange rate regime and financial openness (i.e., absence of capital controls).

As the figure shows, the co-movement (i.e., linkage) of interest rate changes is highest when the financial account is open and the exchange rate regime is rigidly pegged. As the country's financial account becomes more closed, or the exchange rate regime becomes less rigid, the extent of co-movement declines. That, at least, is the state of things with all-embracing, long-term controls. It is much more difficult, studies suggest, for temporary and selective capital controls to insulate the economy from capital flows, and to block interest rate linkages. As for the role of the currency management regime, Klein and Shambaugh (2015) document how capital partial controls do not seem to break the linkages between the interest rates in two countries when one country's currency is pegged to the other's.

There are yet other ways to define the effectiveness of controls, besides providing some room for greater exchange rate and monetary autonomy. Perhaps capital controls alter the

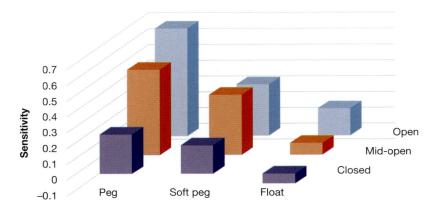

Figure 18.10 The Local Interest Rate Sensitivity to Interest Rates in the Reference Country Each bar indicates the sensitivity of the change in home country interest rate to the change in interest rate in the base country. Peg, soft peg, and float refer to exchange rate regime; open, mid-open, closed refer to financial openness according to the Chinn-Ito index.
Source: Klein and Shambaugh (2015).

composition of financial capital inflows, so that "less-fickle" capital flows in. There is a widespread presumption that longer-term capital, such as foreign direct investment, is less likely to leave the country abruptly. Qureshi et al. (2011) found that the combined effect of capital controls and macroprudential measures – domestic regulations such as loan-to-value restrictions aimed at stabilizing the entire financial system – is to tilt the composition of external liabilities away from debt, and to other forms of borrowing.

On the evidence, then, certain kinds of capital controls can insulate an economy from the rest of the world, but policymakers' ability to carefully calibrate changes in capital controls, in order to hit exactly the right degree of insulation during a specific time interval, is probably limited. That does not mean that capital controls are not useful. Countries might wish to insulate their economies from international financial markets for extended periods, or to alter the composition or duration of external liabilities.

18.3 UNDERSTANDING HOW BUSTS HAPPEN

Crises can occur for a variety of reasons, but the following two dominate. One is that foreign interest rates rise, drawing away capital. Then the i^* term rises in the $BP = 0$ equation:

$$i = -\left(\frac{1}{\varkappa}\right)\left[(\overline{X} - \overline{IM} + \overline{FA}) + (n+v)q\right] + \bar{i}^* + \left(\frac{m}{\varkappa}\right)Y \quad <BP = 0 \text{ curve}> \tag{18.1}$$

Notice that if the foreign interest rate goes up, the BP=0 curve moves up percentage point for percentage point.

Another possible cause of a crisis is that, because of fears that the government will not be able to pay its debt, the interest rate required to attract sufficient financial capital rises. In this case, the financial account equation from Chapter 14 is written with an additional term, ρ, representing the premium necessary to induce investors to hold the country's government bonds:

$$FA = \overline{FA} + \varkappa(i - \rho - \bar{i}^*) \tag{18.2}$$

18.3 UNDERSTANDING HOW BUSTS HAPPEN

This in turn modifies the $BP = 0$ curve equation:

$$i = -\left(\frac{1}{\varkappa}\right)\left[(\overline{X} - \overline{IM} + \overline{FA}) + (n+v)q\right] + \rho + \bar{i}^* + \left(\frac{m}{\varkappa}\right)Y \quad <BP = 0 \text{ curve}> \quad (18.3)$$

If investors feel the government may default (i.e., not pay interest on the bonds, or not pay back the loans), then ρ increases, which shifts up the $BP = 0$ curve. So whether capital is lured away by rising foreign interest rates or driven away by fears of home-government insolvency, either way the $BP = 0$ schedule rises.

A Rise in Foreign Interest Rates

We now consider both cases in more detail, starting with the first, shown in Figure 18.11.

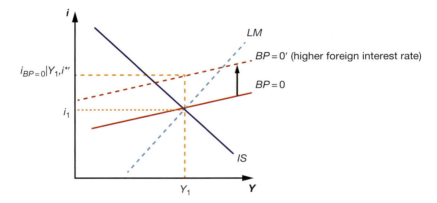

Figure 18.11 Global Monetary Tightening and the Small Open Economy This diagram shows how an increase in the rest-of-world interest rate shifts up the $BP = 0$ curve, resulting in a balance of payments deficit.

The crisis is easiest to conceptualize for a country on a fixed exchange rate regime. When the $BP = 0$ schedule shifts upward from a point of initial internal and external equilibrium, the balance of payments goes into deficit, and foreign exchange reserves begin falling. This situation can be accommodated as long as the central bank can sterilize capital outflows by purchasing net domestic assets, such as government bonds, *and* as long as foreign reserves are positive. Eventually, however, reserves are exhausted, so that the exchange rate peg is unsustainable; then a crisis occurs, and the country is forced to float the currency.

The fixed exchange rate assumption is just an approximation. As long as a country manages the exchange rate so that it is not freely floating, and is held at a stronger rate than what would occur in the absence of central bank intervention, the previous analysis holds. As Figure 18.1 shows, Thailand and Korea did not maintain hard, fixed, pegged exchange rates against the US dollar, and yet they were subject to balance of payments pressures that eventually led to currency crises.

In the real world, an exchange rate peg will likely collapse well before the last unit of foreign exchange is exhausted. That is because as foreign exchange participants recognize the eventual collapse of the peg, international investors (or the "speculators" in this case) will try to withdraw their funds earlier, before the currency collapses, in order to avoid capital losses. This constitutes a run on the central bank, analogous to a run on a private bank. The central bank, recognizing the realities of speculator behavior, bows to the inevitable even before the exhaustion of reserves. This interpretation, developed by Paul Krugman (1979), is often characterized as a "first-generation" model of currency crises. In the Krugman model of speculative crises, the central bank is committed to monetize the government's debt and defend the exchange rate peg. The central bank cannot simultaneously accomplish both objectives at all times. At certain junctures, the two become inconsistent; a crisis is then inevitable.

In contrast, *third*-generation crisis models focus on the revelation of additional government liabilities – so-called contingent liabilities – that dim the prospects of the government successfully servicing its debt, so that ρ rises. Events then play out as above: speculators begin a run on the central bank, trying to withdraw their foreign currency before the inevitable devaluation. The difference from the first-generation models is that the government need not actually be running explicit deficits in order to get into trouble. The fact that the government is undertaking policies that *might* bankrupt it, depending on how the future unfolds, is sufficient. For example, the public may suddenly perceive that the government will have to bail out the private banks, and as a result might have to default on its own debts. Fears of that kind of outcome can drive a run on the central bank, just as in the first-generation model. This is one interpretation of the Thai crisis of 1997.

Why are currency crises costly? One big reason is the disruptive nature of a cutoff of imports. Typically, countries that encounter balance of payments difficulties are running trade deficits and therefore drawing down foreign exchange reserves. When the reserves are exhausted, imports can no longer exceed exports. Since it is hard to increase exports overnight, a sharp reduction in imports results.

In principle, the currency devaluation should improve the external situation, as discussed in Chapter 14: a weaker currency encourages exports and discourages imports, thereby improving the trade balance, and hence aggregate demand. The logic is sound – but the crisis hits quickly, whereas the adjustments take time. In the crisis depicted in Figure 18.12, we are assuming that, in the very short run, the responsiveness $(n + v)$ of net exports to the real exchange rate is essentially zero. When combined with an initial trade deficit these crisis-hit countries are always running trade deficits. This results in the trade balance worsening, reducing output through the traditional multiplier process. This is represented as an inward shift of the IS curve. Another channel could come from the supply side. The reduction in imports crimps production, since many goods use imported inputs in the production process. Without oil imports, for example, some countries' economies would grind to a halt.

Loss of Confidence in Government Solvency

The second mechanism by which a crisis may arise is through a loss of confidence in a government's ability to meet its obligations. When this occurs, the expectation of depreciation typically rises, so that investors' expected returns decline. If expected depreciation reaches a point where investors do not believe the government can honor its foreign currency denominated debt (almost all governments borrow abroad in foreign currency debt), then lenders might refuse to lend at any interest rate. This extreme situation has been characterized as a **sudden stop**, depicted in Figure 18.12.

Often, these crises are triggered by an exogenous shock. An increase in the foreign interest rate is one such event (shown as an upward shift of the $BP = 0$ curve). When investors completely lose confidence in the government paying back its debts denominated in foreign currency, the $BP = 0$ curve rotates counter-clockwise to a vertical position, representing the

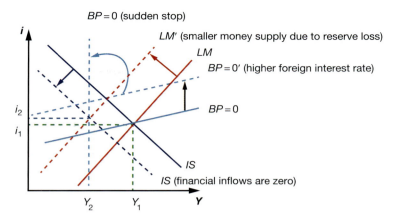

Figure 18.12 A "Sudden Stop" This diagram shows what happens when financial inflows are no longer sensitive to interest rate differentials, rotating the $BP = 0$ curve counterclockwise. The cessation of inflows can be addressed by reducing the money supply and/or shifting in the IS curve as borrowing is curtailed.

fact that the lenders are completely insensitive to interest rates (light blue curved arrow). The IS curve shifts far inward (blue arrow) so that the financial account is zero, i.e., no lending from abroad occurs; and the LM curve is shifted up as the monetary authorities shrink the money supply, in order to avoid excessive currency depreciation.

Notice the vertical slope of the $BP = 0$ schedule means that FA equals $\overline{FA}$, autonomous net inflow. In other words, there is a fixed amount of lending, which in this example is zero. The trade balance has to be zero, and income and output must adjust to achieve this constraint. As the IS curve shifts in, output falls from Y_1 to Y_2. The LM curve is shifted upward in order to stem the decline in the real exchange rate, but in the absence of such a monetary policy move, the IS curve would have to shift even further in, to meet the constraint of no financial inflows.

Figure 18.12 also illustrates the role of the IMF. In a full-blown financial crisis, the economy can operate at a point to the right of the $BP = 0$ curve (i.e., $BP < 0$) for a time if the IMF provides a temporary loan of foreign exchange reserves. The loan can also reduce the likelihood of government debt default, thereby reducing ρ. The existence of an IMF loan program might also heighten confidence sufficiently so that $\kappa > 0$, thereby rotating the $BP = 0$ curve clockwise.

In principle, it is possible to forestall a full-blown crisis. The prospect of a sudden stop looms because the monetary policy is, in some sense, overly loose. Pre-emptively tightening monetary policy and shifting back the LM curve, as in Figure 18.13, would restore external equilibrium. As the LM curve shifts back, the interest rate rises sufficiently to draw in enough financial capital so that foreign exchange reserves are not depleted.

If this policy works so well, why is it not implemented routinely? Because it comes at a cost:

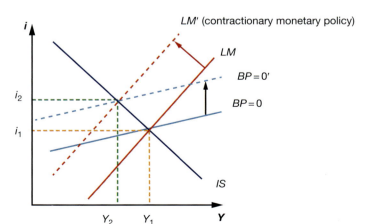

Figure 18.13 The Interest Rate Defense This diagram shows how reducing the money supply can restore the balance-of-payments equilibrium arising from an increase in the rest-of-the-world interest rate.

output declines from Y_1 to Y_2. In other words, the economy slides into a recession. In principle, increasing government spending or reducing taxes could shift out the IS curve to meet the LM curve halfway, so to speak, raising interest rates to restore the balance of payments equilibrium while maintaining output at Y_1. However, concerns about the government's ability to service its debt will be exacerbated by the likelihood of larger budget deficits; hence, when the $BP = 0$ schedule rises because of an increase in ρ, this option is unlikely to be pursued, as it would tend to further shift up the $BP = 0$ schedule.

The other real-world problem with the policy combination shown in Figure 18.13 is a potential lack of confidence in government resolve: international creditors may not believe in the government's commitment to maintaining high interest rates, even at the cost of a recession. Fears that the government will not persevere can lead to a heightened probability of devaluation, and a further upward shift of the $BP = 0$ curve. That could in turn precipitate the very eventuality the heightened interest rates were aimed at avoiding. However, if the speculators had believed in the government's commitment to the defense of the currency, then the policy might have been successful. The fact that either outcome was plausible is the hallmark of what have come to be known as "second-generation models" of currency crises (Obstfeld, 1995, 1996).

18.4 WHY IS DEVALUATION CONTRACTIONARY?

One policy option for avoiding a balance of payments crisis is currency devaluation – at least in principle. A devaluation would, it seems, reverse the upward shift in the $BP = 0$ curve in Figure 18.13 and could, if implemented with sufficient lead time, restore external equilibrium. In Figure 18.14, the devaluation shifts down the $BP = 0$ curve and shifts out the IS curve (black arrows). Over time, then, income rises to Y_3, and interest rates to i_3.

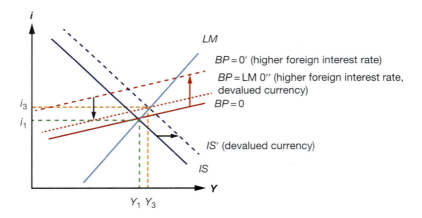

Figure 18.14 Devaluation under Balance of Payments Deficit This diagram shows how a devaluation can restore balance of payments equilibrium in the wake of a balance of payments deficit induced by higher rest-of-world interest rate.

However, while the increase in income is an attractive outcome, there are at least three reasons why in the middle of a crisis, devaluations are unlikely to prove expansionary and in fact are more likely to have a contractionary effect: (1) low trade elasticities in the short term, (2) currency mismatch in balance sheets, and (3) the inflationary impact on the price level.

Low trade elasticities, meaning near-zero n and v, were already mentioned in Section 18.4. In the immediate to short run, prices of imports and exports all rise, so if there is a trade deficit to begin with, the nominal value of the trade deficit is likely to increase. It is only over time – time that the country might not have – that the trade balance improves sufficiently to shift the $BP = 0$ schedule up. In the short term, the fact that the quantity response of exports and imports are zero or small in the beginning combined with a trade deficit means that the initial impact on aggregate demand might be negative. In that case, the IS shifts in and output declines.

The second channel by which devaluation exerts a contractionary effect relates to the composition of a country's balance sheet – specifically the currency composition of assets versus liabilities. If countries always borrowed and lent in their home currencies, then the balance sheet would not be such a big concern. However, items are denominated differently on the asset and liability sides of the balance sheet, and a depreciation can have a negative effect.

Most less-developed countries firms and governments borrow in foreign currency; thus, their liabilities are in currencies such as US dollars or euros. Their assets might be in dollars, as well (for instance, foreign exchange reserves). But many of the assets – for instance factories – are denominated in the domestic currency. When that currency is devalued, the value of debt from the perspective of the local firm or household goes up. If the value of the liabilities goes up enough, firms are rendered bankrupt. The government's debt (in terms of the taxing capacity of the government, which is in domestic currency) goes up as well, casting doubt on the government's ability to make good on its debt. This **balance sheet channel** is discussed at further length in Section 18.5.

The third channel for the contractionary effect of devaluation is by way of prices. A devaluation raises the prices of both imported and exported goods. Less-developed countries tend to be very open to international trade, with a high share of consumption and production reliant on imports. Higher import prices feed into the overall price level, just like a supply shock. This reduces the real money supply, pushing up the interest rate and hence crowding out investment.

To see this process in play, consider Figure 18.15, which shows the aggregate demand–aggregate supply graph developed in Chapter 17. Assume that the initial income level Y_0 is equal to potential (i.e., full employment) GDP, Y^{FE}. A higher price level means that in the short term, the price level shifts up. The higher price level shrinks the real money supply, inducing a higher interest rate. The higher rate results in a stronger currency and reduced output, at Y_1. Then the AD curve shifts in, because it is assumed that the trade balance is initially in deficit and trade elasticities are low in the short run, so that the trade deficit initially worsens. Thus, overall output falls from Y_0 to Y_2 as the price level rises, and the economy falls into recession. This phenomenon is sometimes called **contractionary devaluation**.

Eventually, the AD curve will shift back towards its initial position, as import and export flows respond positively to the exchange rate depreciation. Even

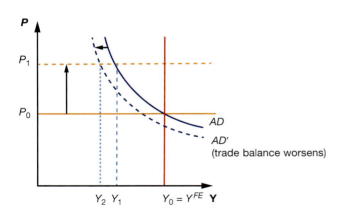

Figure 18.15 Contractionary Devaluation This diagram shows how devaluation and the resulting inflation can result in a contraction of the economy.

when that occurs, however, output will remain lower than full employment, in the absence of further adjustment in the price level. Over time, with a negative output gap, the price level will fall back down, restoring output to full employment, at Y^{FE}. However, this process is likely to be quite prolonged, as it requires downward adjustment in nominal wages and prices.

For the government, there is a temptation to mitigate the negative impact of the devaluation and price increase using a combination of expansionary monetary and fiscal policies. That outcome would result in higher output without the prolonged process of eroding the price level by running a slack economy. The key shortcoming of this policy is that it entrenches inflation, particularly if inflationary expectations are adaptive – for instance, if this period's inflation rate equals last period's inflation rate.

18.5 COMPLICATIONS: BALANCE SHEET EFFECTS

The preceding explanations for balance of payments crises rely upon the behavior of flows – flows of goods and services, and of financial capital. However, another source of instability has been introduced by the increasingly integrated nature of global financial markets. Because of increased cross-border holdings of assets and liabilities, the net international investment position – the difference between assets and liabilities – does not convey fully the exposure of a country to changes in the international environment.

Such increasing cross-border exposure is shown for two countries, Thailand and Korea, in Figures 18.16 and 18.17 below. To factor out economic growth, both asset and liability series are normalized by GDP. Notice that before the crises in 1997, both assets and liabilities were increasing, while the *net* position – assets minus liabilities – looked stable, particularly in Korea.

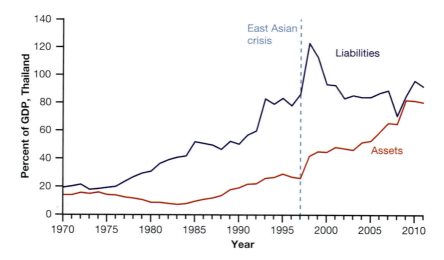

Figure 18.16 Thai Assets and Liabilities This figure shows Thai cross-border assets and liabilities as a percent of GDP. Source: Lane and Milesi-Ferretti (2018) and World Bank World Development Indicators.

The compositions of the gross positions are key: if the composition of assets differs substantially from that of liabilities, that is when changes in the economic environment that affect assets and liabilities differently can have considerable effects on the state of the economy.

18.5 COMPLICATIONS: BALANCE SHEET EFFECTS

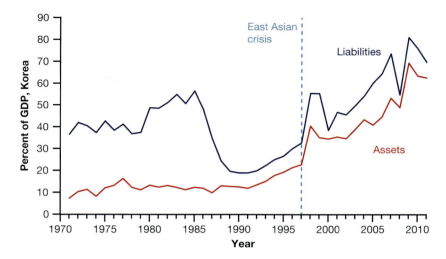

Figure 18.17 Korean Assets and Liabilities This diagram shows Korean cross-border assets and liabilities as a percent of GDP.
Source: Lane and Milesi-Ferretti (2018) and World Bank World Development Indicators.

Composition can differ along several dimensions: terms of maturity, capital structure, and currency of denomination. If a country has borrowed extensively in the short term but is a net lender in the long term, this constitutes a **maturity mismatch**. Should foreign lending sources decide not to roll over short-term debt, the mismatch in assets and liabilities can, in essence, cause a run on the country to occur. A **capital structure mismatch** occurs if, say, the liabilities are in the form of debt while assets are in equity. If economic conditions deteriorate, the country may be forced to default on its debt.

Currency mismatch has been perhaps the most serious and longstanding challenge. Suppose liabilities are mostly denominated in foreign currency, while assets are in domestic currency. Then a depreciation of the currency might not yield a net positive impact on the economy, as implied by the standard model covered in Chapters 14 and 15. Rather, the depreciation will tend to shrink the economy by increasing the value of the liabilities (defined in terms of domestic currency) while leaving the value of assets unchanged.

If the mismatch applies to the government, then the government's net liabilities increase. If it applies to the private sector, then firms and households will see their net liabilities increase, perhaps forcing some into insolvency. Firm closures reduce aggregate supply. Even if firms do not go bankrupt, their reduced net worth makes them poorer credit risks (at least from the banks' perspective), thereby reducing the firms' ability to borrow in order to invest in plant and equipment. This effect further depresses the economy.

Table 18.1 identifies the vulnerabilities that different types of balance sheet mismatch can create for the government, the private financial sector (banks), the private nonfinancial sector (firms and households), and the economy overall. The lesson of the table is that trouble, in the form of mismatches, can show up almost anywhere in the economy, and in many forms.

Many of the financial crises of the last few decades were characterized by currency mismatches, in government debt (Mexico, Brazil, Turkey, Argentina, and Russia), and/or in the banking sector (Korea, Thailand, Indonesia, Turkey, Russia, and Brazil), and/or in the nonfinancial corporate sector (Korea, Thailand, Indonesia, Turkey, Argentina, and Brazil). Notice how, in Figures 18.16 and 18.17, the level of liabilities increases sharply in the wake of

Table 18.1 How Balance Sheet Risks Apply to Different Sectors

Risk sector	Maturity mismatch	Currency mismatch	Capital structure mismatch	Solvency (liabilities v. assets)
Government	Government's short-term hard currency debt (domestic and external) v. government's liquid assets (reserves)* Short-term domestic currency denominated government debts v. liquid domestic currency assets of the government *not all central bank reserves are available for government debt service; some may be pledged to back currency, lent to banks, etc	Government's debt denominated in foreign currency (domestic and external) v. government's hard currency assets (reserves)	N/A	Liabilities of government and central bank v. their assets. Assets include discounted value of future primary surpluses (including seignorage revenue) and the financial assets of the government and central bank, including privatizable state owned enterprises Liabilities may include implicit liabilities from pension plans as well as contingent liabilities stemming from government guarantees
Banks	Short-term hard currency debts (domestic and external) v. banks' liquid hard currency assets (and ability to borrow from central bank) Short-term domestic currency debts (often deposits) v. liquid assets	Difference between foreign currency assets (loans) v. foreign currency liabilities (deposits/interbank lines)	Deposits to capital ratio (closely related to capital to assets ratio)	Bank liabilities v. bank assets and capital
Firms	Short-term debts v. firms' liquid assets	Debts denominated in foreign currency (domestic and external) v. hard currency generating assets.	Debt to equity ratio	Firms liabilities v. present value of firms' assets

Households	Short-term debt v. liquid household assets	Difference between foreign currency assets (deposits) v. foreign currency liabilities (often mortgages)	N/A	Liabilities v. future earnings (on wages and assets)
Country as a whole	Short-term external debt (residual maturity) v. liquid hard currency reserves of government and private sector* *foreign exchange reserves of the central bank/government plus liquid foreign currency reserves of banks and firms	Net hard currency denominated external debt *External debt denominated in hard currency minus external assets denominated in hard currency	Net external debt stock (external debt minus external assets) relative to net stock of FDI. *Flow analogue: heavy current dependence on debt rather than FDI to finance current account deficit	Stock of external debt relative to both external financial assets held by residents and the discounted value of future trade surpluses, (resources for future external debt service)* *A more complex analysis would need to include remittance of profits on FDI as well. While such remittances are variable, they are another claim on the external earnings of the country as a whole

Note: Debts between residents should appear on the sectoral balance sheet. Debts between non-residents, particularly if the debts are denominated in a foreign currency, can be a source of financial difficulty. For example, if the banking system borrows foreign exchange from the household sector and lends foreign exchange to firms, this should appear as a foreign currency asset on the household balance sheet and an equal foreign currency liability on the balance sheet of firms.

Source: Allen, Mark, Christoph Rosenberg, Christian Keller, Brad Setser, and Nouriel Roubini, 2002, "A Balance Sheet Approach to Financial Crisis," IMF Working Paper No. 02/210.

the currency crises. That pattern is a natural outcome of the sharp exchange rate devaluations shown in Figure 18.1.

How do these currency mismatches arise? One big contributing factor appears to be the presence of pegged or highly managed exchange rate regimes. Figure 18.1 highlights the relative stability of the Thai and Korean rates prior to their respective crises. These fixed exchange rate regimes reduced the uncertainty associated with foreign currency denominated debt, and thus encouraged the accumulation of debt in foreign currency. In some cases, the real appreciation associated with the pegs provided additional impetus for accumulation.

Mismatches in the private sector can have spillover effects on the government sector. If, for instance, the government has to bail out the banking system, then private firm insolvency due to currency mismatch can be transferred to the public sector. The fact that private sector liabilities sometimes become public sector liabilities, thereby triggering a deeper crisis, is one manifestation of the phenomenon of contingent liabilities, which as previously mentioned underpins the third-generation models of currency crises. In the midst of a crisis, the government cannot credibly commit to not bailing out key players in the economy, such as the banking system. These liabilities depend upon the state of the economy (say an economic downturn, or a currency devaluation); hence they're called contingent liabilities.

The policy implications are relatively straightforward. Mainly, currency mismatches in debt, either by the public sector or the private, should be avoided. Unfortunately, achieving this objective is difficult, because governments are often unable to borrow on international markets in their own currency. This condition has been termed **"original sin"** by Eichengreen, Hausmann and Panizza (2007).

Balance sheet effects introduce a new set of tradeoffs during crises. Consider the case where a country has both a currency mismatch on public sector debts – borrowing in a foreign currency, such as dollars, while collecting tax revenues in the local currency – and a maturity mismatch on private sector debts, namely short-term borrowing and long-term lending. An interest rate defense of the currency will mitigate a deterioration in the government's position while exacerbating interest rate risk (short-term interest rates will typically rise relative to long term). This tension in policy effects is layered on top of the obviously counterproductive effect higher interest rates have on aggregate demand. Hence, the presence of balance sheet mismatches greatly complicates the problems of managing a currency crisis.

THEORY   Can We Predict Emerging Market Crises?

Given that currency crises in emerging markets are so costly, should we seek to avoid them? To avoid crises, at a minimum we need a means of telling when a crisis is imminent – a sort of **early warning system**. However, despite the large body of literature, what such a system might look like remains elusive.

The first problem is defining exactly what a crisis is. As shown in Section 18.3, when the crisis arrives, the pressure can be manifested in a depletion of reserves, an increase in the interest rate, a devaluation of the currency, or a combination of all three. The typical approach is to take a weighted average of all three of these variables as measured, and when the index composed of these measures exceeds the average amount sufficiently, that is defined as a crisis.

The empirical determinants of currency crises have been identified as currency overvaluation, a lending boom, a large stock of short-term debt relative to foreign exchange reserves, a large current account deficit (as a share of GDP), and slow economic growth. All of these turn out to be statistically significant determinants of crises, and can be linked to the theoretical determinants examined before.

First, when the currency is overvalued, the interest rate has to be higher, holding everything else constant, in order to sustain enough financial capital inflows to maintain the balance of payments (a lower q means a higher $BP = 0$ curve).

A lending boom usually leads to a lending bust, which means the government is likely to incur additional debt financing a bank bailout. If short-term debt is large, or reserves small, then the likelihood of the government's being unable to service debt in foreign currency is higher, and foreign investors are more likely to leave. If a current account deficit is large, then the country needs to attract larger net capital inflows; in other words.

Finally, when economic growth is slow, policymakers' ability to credibly commit to a high interest rate defense – which would likely tip the economy into recession – is reduced. Of these factors, the most important – in terms of raising the probability of a crisis when the variables rise to crisis levels – are exchange rate overvaluation and credit booms.

Using a statistical model incorporating these variables, and estimated over the entire sample, Bussiere and Mulder (1999) correctly predict 66% of the crises, which sounds like a pretty good record. However, 58% of the alarms failed to be a crisis. That is using the following rule – if the probability of a crisis is predicted at greater than 20%, then a crisis warning is sounded. If the threshold was lowered to 15%, the proportion of correctly predicted crises would rise, but at the cost of a higher proportion of false alarms.

More importantly, it is one thing to find significant correlations in a sample but quite another, and more difficult, to *predict* a crisis in the future, based on the data you have today. Bussiere and Fratzscher (2006) use a model based upon these determinants and estimated on data up to the end of 1996 to predict the crises that took place in 1997. The model predicts crises in Colombia, Czech Republic, the Philippines, Poland, and Russia. Of these, only the Czech Republic and the Philippines suffered crises over the next year. However, the model fails to predict the crises that did occur in Indonesia, Korea, Malaysia, Singapore, and Thailand (although the model comes close for the last country).

This outcome demonstrates that in general, it is easy to find factors associated with currency crises, but difficult to use that information to identify when and where the crises will occur in the future.

APPLICATION   The Mexican Peso Crisis

The year 1994 was an eventful, both in and out of Mexico. Canada and the United States had signed an agreement to establish a free trade area in the form of Nafta, solidifying measures that promised a new era of pro-market reforms. In Mexico, the presidential campaign was underway; the Institutional Revolutionary Party (PRI) under President Carlos Salinas de Gortari had primed the pump, increasing government spending. The economy was booming. And yet, several events were to cut short this new era.

First, in 1994, the Federal Reserve began to raise interest rates after years maintaining a loose monetary policy, as shown in Figure 18.18.

Rising foreign interest rates meant a reduction of financial capital flows to Mexico (foreign direct investment actually increased during the year, due to Nafta implementation); this trend was problematic given the trade deficit Mexico was running, approximately 7% in 1994.

With high capital mobility, Mexican authorities faced an unenviable choice between letting the Mexican peso depreciate to facilitate adjustment, or maintain the exchange rate by depleting foreign exchange reserves. (The Mexicans did not maintain a hard peg, but rather a crawling peg with a floor and ceiling.) This difficult choice was accentuated by a "one-two punch" of the Zapatista insurrection in the Chiapas region, beginning in January, and the assassination of the PRI's hand-picked presidential candidate, Luis Donaldo Colosio, in March.

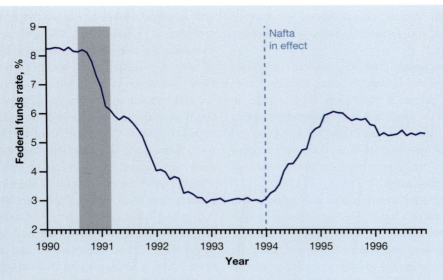

Figure 18.18 US Monetary Policy This diagram shows the Federal funds rate, % (blue). Recession dates are shaded gray.

The central bank allowed a small depreciation in March, and then ran down reserves particularly November. Only in December did Banco do Mexico relent and allow the peso to depreciate, as shown in Figure 18.19.

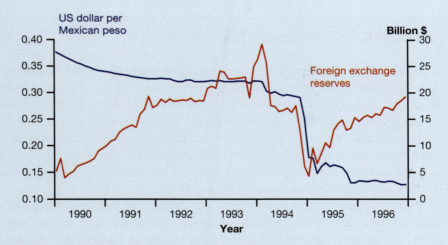

Figure 18.19 Mexico's Exchange Rate and Foreign Exchange Reserves This diagram shows the US dollar/Mexican peso exchange rate, where a decline is a depreciation of the peso (blue), and Mexican foreign exchange reserves ex.-gold, in billions of US$ (red).

Mexico's challenges were further accentuated by the authority's decision to allow the issuance of a special type of debt instrument, called Tesobonos, which included government bonds denominated in US dollars instead of pesos. Borrowing in Tesobonos meant that the risk associated with devaluation was eliminated, insofar as foreign investors were concerned.

However, when the peso depreciated in December, this immediately resulted in a massive increase in the government's real debt liability. Hence, even as the devaluation improved the trade balance via the expenditure switching effect, financial capital flowed out because of the uncertainty the government could make good on its dollar denominated debt, much of which was set to mature in January 1995. The central bank raised interest rates to stem outflow, but this was not sufficient to overcome these concerns.

Only the commitment by the US of its own funds, combined with IMF and Bank for International Settlements financing, totaling nearly $50 billion, was sufficient to reassure international investors. Thereafter, the foreign exchange reserves recovered.

Michal Camdessus, the IMF's managing director at the time, called the Mexican peso crisis of "the first financial crisis of the 21st century." As he characterized it, the crisis was the first taking place in a highly globalized world of massive capital flows. This manifested itself in the primary importance of expectations, and the outsized effect of currency mismatches in the country's balance sheet. Such novel outcomes would lead at least one prominent observer to characterize the episode as "petty crime and cruel punishment" (Calvo and Mendoza, 1996).

The lessons that the penalties inflicted by the international investor community could be seemingly disproportionate would only be partly learned before the 1997 East Asian crises, recounted at the beginning of the chapter.

CONCLUSION

The fortunes of any given emerging market country are dependent upon events both at home, and abroad, particularly in the large advanced economies. Developments in the US and other financial centers – particularly changes in monetary policy – drive capital flows to and from the emerging markets. Low interest rates in the advanced economies tend to induce net flows to emerging markets. Tightening of monetary policy causes the reverse to occur.

The foregoing does not exclude the possibility that domestic policies have some role in a given crisis. If during times of a benign international conditions – low interest rates, strong global growth – policymakers run an excessively expansionary fiscal policy that expands government debt or overvalue the exchange rate causing a large trade deficit, the return of a more hostile environment could result in a balance of payments crisis.

Whether a crisis occurs depends on a number of factors: if the authorities try to keep the exchange rate too strong, whether the risk is associated with the country's foreign debt, or international investors view the central bank's commitment to the peg as questionable – and sometimes none of the policy responses lead to particularly desirable outcomes.

SUMMARY

1. Developments in the large advanced economies, particularly changes in monetary policy, partly drive capital flows to and from the emerging markets.
2. Low interest rates in the advanced economies tend to induce net flows to emerging markets, which force those countries to respond.
3. Emerging market economy policymakers can respond by loosening monetary policy, revaluing the exchange rate, or by implementing capital controls to limit inflows.

4. When capital flows reverse, policymakers have various options, including higher interest rates, currency devaluation, and capital controls to limit outflows.
5. If measures to stem the capital outflow are not effective, the country might suffer a currency crisis. A speculative attack might occur even before foreign exchange reserves are depleted, as investors seek to withdraw their funds before incurring losses.
6. When capital flows completely cease, and cannot be restarted even by very high interest rates, this is termed a sudden stop.
7. The standard remedy of devaluation might make conditions worse in the short run when trade elasticities are very low, so that the trade deficit deteriorates rather than improves.
8. Balance sheet effects are important when cross-border liabilities (such as debt) are denominated in a foreign currency. In such cases, a devaluation can worsen the country's situation by making indebted institutions insolvent.

KEY CONCEPTS

Balance sheet channel, page 401
Capital structure mismatch, page 403
Contractionary devaluation, page 401
Currency crisis, page 388
Currency mismatch, page 403
Early warning system, page 406
Maturity mismatch, page 403

Original sin, page 406
Pull factors, page 391
Push factors, page 391
Run, page 393
Self-insurance, page 393
Sudden stop, page 398

REVIEW QUESTIONS

1. What are push factors? What are pull factors?
2. What is a capital flow bonanza?
3. What is a sudden stop?
4. What is self-insurance, and what are the costs involved with it?
5. How do first-, second-, and third-generation crises models differ?
6. Why are devaluations sometimes contractionary?
7. What is the balance sheet channel for devaluation?
8. How can a currency mismatch in the asset and liability sides of the balance sheet worsen a crisis?

EXERCISES

1. Consider a small open economy with a fixed exchange rate, and imperfect capital mobility in initial equilibrium. Suppose the financial capital account behaves as follows:

$$FA = \overline{FA} + \varkappa(i - i^* - \Delta s^e_{+1})$$

Suppose also, then, that the IS curve is conventionally defined.
   a. To begin with, everyone believes the peg is perfectly credible, so expected depreciation is zero. Then, with an election of a new government, people believe that there is a 50–50 chance of a 20% depreciation. Interpret the impact on the economy using an $IS - LM - BP = 0$ graph; assume the central bank sterilizes.

b. Should the government devalue the currency or raise interest rates? Explain your answer using $IS - LM - BP = 0$ graphs.
c. How does your answer to part b change if raising the interest rate decreases the market's expectation of depreciation to zero?

2. Consider a small open economy with a fixed exchange rate, and imperfect capital mobility in initial equilibrium. Suppose the financial capital account behaves as follows:

$$FA = \overline{FA} + \varkappa\left(i - i^* - \rho - \Delta s^e_{+1}\right)$$

Suppose also, then, that the IS curve is conventionally defined.

a. To begin with everyone believes the peg is perfectly credible, and there is no risk, so expected depreciation and the risk premium are both zero. However, the risk premium ρ on home country debt rises from zero due to perceived higher likelihood of default. Interpret the impact on the economy using an $IS - LM - BP = 0$ graph; assume the central bank sterilizes.
b. Should the government devalue the currency or raise interest rates? Explain your answer using $IS - LM - BP = 0$ graphs.
c. How does your answer to part b change if raising the interest rate increases the market's expectation of debt default?

3. Consider a small open economy with a fixed exchange rate, and imperfect capital mobility, but a balance of payments deficit. Suppose the financial capital account behaves as follows:

$$FA = \overline{FA} + \varkappa\left(i - i^* - \rho - \Delta s^e_{+1}\right)$$

Suppose also that investment depends on firm balance sheets. Assume a large portion of firm debt is denominated in foreign currency, while assets are denominated in home currency, so there is a currency mismatch.

a. To begin with everyone believes the peg is perfectly credible, so expected depreciation is zero and remains zero. What happens if the currency is devalued?
b. To begin with everyone believes the peg is perfectly credible, so expected depreciation is zero and remains zero. What happens if the currency is devalued, and ρ increases from zero because worries of default rises with the devaluation?
c. Given your answer to part b, discuss whether an interest rate defense would be preferable to an exchange rate devaluation.

4. Consider the aggregate demand–aggregate supply model of an open economy under floating exchange rates.

a. Show what happens if the currency is devalued, assuming imported goods prices constitute part of the general price level, and prices are sticky.
b. Assume inflationary expectations are adaptive. Should expansionary fiscal policy be pursued? Why or why not?

RECOMMENDED RESOURCES

Guillermo A. Calvo, "Explaining Sudden Stops, Growth Collapse and BOP Crises: The Case of Distortionary Output Taxes," NBER Working Paper No. 9864 (2003).

Roberto Chang and Andres Velasco, "A Model of Currency Crises in Emerging Markets," *Quarterly Journal of Economics* 116 (2001): 489–517.

Giancarlo Corsetti, Paolo Pesenti, and Nouriel Roubini, "Paper Tigers?: A Model of the Asian Crisis," *European Economic Review*, 43(7) (1999): 1211–1236.

Michael P. Dooley, "A Model of Crises in Emerging Markets," *The Economic Journal*, 110 (460) (2000): 256–272.

Paul Krugman, "A Model of Balance-of-Payments Crises," *Journal of Money, Credit, and Banking* 11 (1979): 311–325.

Maurice Obstfeld, "Models of Currency Crises with Self-Fulfilling Features," *European Economic Review* 40(3) (1996): 1037–1047.

Maurice Obstfeld, *The Logic of Currency Crises* (Berlin, Heidelberg: Springer, 1995).

CHAPTER 19

The Global Financial Crisis

LEARNING OBJECTIVES

In this chapter, we learn about:
- how a boom–bust cycle developed in the US
- how the housing collapse led to a financial crisis in the US
- how financial systems interact with the economy to produce a feedback loop
- what are the channels by which the downturn crossed borders
- how governments responded using fiscal and monetary policies

INTRODUCTION

In September 2008, the oldest investment bank on Wall Street, Lehman Brothers, declared bankruptcy. Immediately, the world's financial system seized up. Hundreds of billions of dollars' worth of financial assets were frozen in place, the value of securities made uncertain, and the solvency of seemingly rock-solid financial institutions called into question. By the end of 2008, the United States' economy was in freefall, shrinking at an annualized rate of 8%. Growth rates in other major industrialized economies also plummeted as well. The recession was so deep, and the recovery so labored that it took more than a decade for output to return to full employment levels. Figure 19.1 illustrates the situation rather dramatically.

Growth in emerging markets and less developed countries also fell, though less drastically and with somewhat of a lag. For the world overall, the period of negative growth lasted only three quarters, but the long-term effect was essentially the same as the one shown in Figure 19.1: output was put on a seemingly permanent lower growth path.

The precise origin of this series of events is difficult to identify, because the global crisis of 2008 was such an all-encompassing and wide-ranging phenomenon. It is clear, however, that the episode started in the US, where fiscal, monetary, and regulatory policy created a combustible situation. We start the analysis by explaining why the crisis originated in the United States. In the next section, the propagation of the crisis to the rest of the world is described. We then turn to outlining how the policy response helped stabilize the world economy.

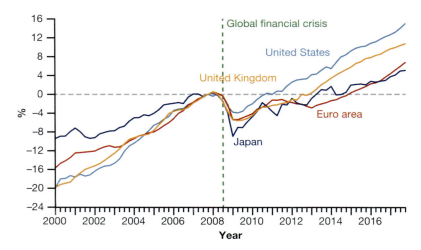

Figure 19.1 Diverging Recoveries from the Great Recession This figure shows the difference from 2007Q4 in real GDP for US (light blue), eurozone (red), UK (tan) and Japan (blue). Vertical line at Lehman Brothers bankruptcy.

19.1 WHY DID THE GLOBAL CRISIS START IN AMERICA?

The global financial crisis of 2008 began as a crisis in the US financial sector a year earlier. The stage was set by the excessive degree of **leverage** in the global financial system. When a firm borrows money to buy a capital asset, the leverage of the transaction is the ratio of the amount borrowed to the value of the asset purchased. This concept can be extended to firms and even to entire economies by comparing total debt to total assets.

A highly leveraged position, where debt greatly exceeds present asset value, can make sense if the leveraged firm expects to earn a large future return from its asset or assets. Thus, in any enterprise, the greater the amount of leverage, the more the owners of the firm benefit from asset price appreciation, because this is a form of return. But if assets do not appreciate as expected, or if an appraised value turns out to be inflated, a highly leveraged position can quickly threaten the firm's stability. This is true whether the firm is a manufacturer or a retailer – or a financial institution, such as an investment bank.

Overleveraging came about because of a confluence of tax cuts and low interest rates in the early 2000s, and by under-regulation of the financial industry.

Interest Rates and Tax Policy

In the wake of the dot-com bust of 2001, when many high-tech companies founded in the 1990s ran out of capital and closed up shop, the Fed dropped the Fed Funds rate quickly and kept it low for an extended period, in order to keep the US economy from relapsing into recession. By the end of 2002, the Fed's benchmark interest rate was approaching 1%, at a time when inflation was between 2% and 3% per year. Interest rates were kept at this extremely low level through 2004 and only went above 2% in early 2005.

The Fed's policy of extended monetary ease led to a prolonged period of negative real interest rates that contributed to a dramatic increase in household borrowing. Easy financing, combined with tax cuts pushed through Congress in 2001 and 2003, led to a surge in housing prices (Figure 19.2). Rising house prices meant that the likelihood of mortgage default was perceived as being low, because the borrowing homeowners quickly built up equity wealth as their homes gained in value. This development further reinforced the ease of lending. This

19.1 WHY DID THE GLOBAL CRISIS START IN AMERICA?

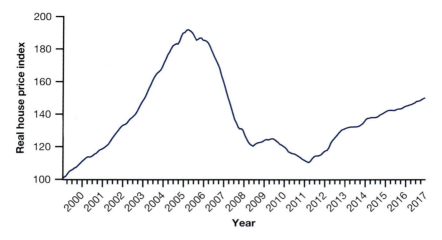

Figure 19.2 The Housing Boom and Bust This figure shows real house prices in ten US cities, deflated by CPI. January 2001 = 100.
Source: Standard & Poors Case–Shiller Index, and BLS.

feedback loop moved house prices far beyond previous historical highs – a classic bubble that was bound to deflate eventually.

Under-regulation and Financial Innovation

During the 2000s, financial engineering – the creation of complex derivatives ultimately based on income streams generated by mortgages, credit cards, and auto loans – developed. Of these, **mortgage-backed securities (MBSs)** experienced the most rapid growth. These securities were further securitized into what were called **collateralized debt obligations**.

These bonds were unlike traditional ones, in two senses. First, the interest payments were funded not by firm revenues based on sales, but income streams from other bonds. Second, there was no real track record for these securities, especially during times of stress. Consequently, the credit ratings on these derivatives (i.e., how likely default was) were based, not on historical performance, but complicated statistical models. These attributes led to an under-estimate of the amount of risk banks took on when they held these securities.

The understatement of risk meant that banks could borrow more, and hold less shareholder capital, for a given amount of asset holdings than was safe. In other words, the banks could acquire more leverage, which boosted returns to the shareholders, at the cost of a higher likelihood of bankruptcy in difficult times. Investment banks – financial firms that borrowed on short-term capital markets instead of from depositors – were subject to different, less-stringent, rules than deposit taking banks. Consequently, they were even more leveraged on the eve of the financial crisis. This is why the first banks to fail were investment banks – Bear Stearns and Lehman Brothers. This phenomenon is illustrated in the following Theory box.

THEORY Leverage, Liquidity, and Financial Crisis

Leverage is the ratio of borrowed money to a firm's own money; a highly leveraged firm has a great deal of debt compared to its equity (the value of its capital). For banks, leverage is the company's business: financial institutions do have their own capital, but the money they lend comes from money they borrow. That is, banks intermediate, channeling money from people from whom they borrow (savers) to people to whom they lend (debtors). The more a financial institution borrows, the more it can lend.

For a given amount borrowed and lent, the more the lending rate exceeds the borrowing rate, the greater the banks' return to equity. From the perspective of the owners, a financial institution would like to have none of its own money at risk at all. However, financial institutions, particularly commercial banks and savings banks, are required by regulatory authorities to hold a certain minimum of capital relative to assets, to limit the risk that unavoidably accompanies the greater earnings associated with higher degrees of leverage.

Risk arises on both the asset and the liability sides of the leverage ledger. On the asset side, assets such as mortgage loans or assets backed by mortgage loans, can go bad, i.e., the debtor may turn out to unable to repay the loan. If the resulting losses exceeds the lending bank's capital, it will be forced to go bankrupt. Hence, the more highly leveraged a financial institution is, the more exposed it is to problems if some of the assets sour.

To see the dangers imposed by high leverage, consider two banks: one with low leverage (and a high ratio of capital to assets) and one with high leverage (and a low capital–assets ratio). A $9 million loss leaves the low-leverage bank (ratio 1–10, left side of Figure 19.1) still solvent, because capital remains in positive territory.

Table 19.1 A Low-Leverage Bank, before and after the Writeoff of $9M in Bad Loans

Commercial Bank (Before)			
Assets		Liabilities	
Reserves	$10M	Deposits	$90M
Loans (Mortgages, CRE) T-Bills Other bonds (GSEs)	$90M	Bank Capital (or "equity")	$10M

Commercial Bank (After)			
Assets		Liabilities	
Reserves	$10M	Deposits	$90M
Loans (Mortgages, CRE) T-Bills Other bonds (GSEs)	$81M	Bank Capital (or "equity")	$01M

However, the high-leverage bank (ratio 1 to 20, Table 19.2) is not so fortunate. A $9 million loss wipes out bank capital – the bank is **insolvent**. Since the loss exceeds the capital, the rest of the loss is incurred by the depositors. The more highly leveraged the firm is – the more it owes to others – the more exposed it is to the risk of this kind of outcome.

Table 19.2 A High-Leverage Bank, before and after a $9M Bad-Loan Writeoff

Commercial Bank (Before)			
Assets		Liabilities	
Reserves	$10M	Deposits	$95M
Loans (Mortgages, CRE) T-Bills Other bonds (GSEs)	$90M	Bank Capital (or "equity")	$5M

Commercial Bank (After)			
Assets		Liabilities	
Reserves	$10M	Deposits	$91M
Loans (Mortgages, CRE) T-Bills Other bonds (GSEs)	$81M	Bank Capital (or "equity")	$0M

The reason why banks, if unregulated, tend toward high leverage is shown by comparing the **return on equity** (ROE):

$$\text{ROE} = \frac{\text{Income on Assets} - \text{Payments on Liabilities}}{\text{Bank Capital}} \quad (19.1)$$

Suppose the two banks each earn 5% interest on loans (their assets) and pay 2% on deposits (their liabilities). The low-leverage bank's ROE is $((0.05 \times 90) - (0.02 \times 90))/10 = 2.7/10 = 0.27$ (27%), while the high-leverage bank's ROE is $((0.05 \times 90) - (0.02 \times 95))/5 = (4.5 - 1.9)/5 = 2.6/5 = 0.52$ (52%). Clearly, the profitability is much greater with high leverage, providing a tremendous incentive to minimize capital. Unhindered by regulation – as was the case for pre-2008 investment banks and hedge funds – the financial system will tend toward low capital ratios, and hence toward high fragility.

Moving from the asset side of the balance sheet to the liability side, problems can arise if depositors fearing a bank failure begin withdrawing their money. If withdrawals snowball into a bank run, the bank will indeed fail – precisely because depositors feared it might. In most advanced economies, deposit insurance provided by the government reduces the likelihood that depositors will panic in this way. However, if commercial paper holders and other short-term lenders to the bank become anxious and refuse to roll over loans, the financial institution may simply run out of money and be unable to honor its commitments. That outcome is called a **liquidity crisis**.

While solvency and liquidity problems can be thought of as independent concepts, in practice they are difficult to disentangle. For instance, in the 2008 financial crisis, some financial institutions encountered difficulties borrowing because of concerns over solvency.

The elevated leverage of the global financial system was centered in the US, particularly in the under-regulated **shadow banking sector** – investment banks, hedge funds, and special entities that repackaged home mortgages into securities – and the housing sector. Excessive leveraging was not restricted to the US, however. Because of a misappraisal of the riskiness of assets, banks in all the developed countries were over-leveraged, and susceptible to a downturn.

The Feedback Loop

As the housing market boomed, a self-reinforcing circle was established. With housing prices rising, mortgages were easily paid or refinanced. This led to banks lending even more readily to the housing market, further pushing up house prices. This dynamic pushed house prices to record heights, peaking in 2006.

As housing prices fell, mortgage defaults rose, uncovering the riskiness of new financial instruments. The Fed's process of raising interest rates further diminished the availability of funds for home loans. The newfound reluctance to lend further depressed demand for homes and thus accelerated the decline in home values.

As home prices in some cases fell below the value of mortgages, increasing numbers of homeowners now found it advantageous to default. As the derivatives backed by mortgages on bank balances sheets lost value, the solvency of financial firms went further and further in doubt, dousing the willingness of financial institutions to lend.

The shadow financial system was critical to the unfolding of the crisis. Essentially, the development of an unregulated financial sector circumvented the system of banking regulation developed in the wake of the Great Depression. This made the financial system vulnerable to traditional bank panics. The absence of regulatory oversight (particularly in allowing high leverage), in the presence of too many institutions "too big to fail" – that is, too important to the economy for the government to *let* them fail – meant the buildup of implicit financial liability on the part of the government.

Financial innovation and lack of regulation also played a role in allowing for the buildup of such governmental "contingent liabilities" in the form of institutions "too interconnected to fail." The insurance company AIG was a prime example. AIG's financial products division was heavily involved in the trading of **credit default swaps**, essentially contracts that reimbursed the holder of an asset declared in default. The insolvency of AIG would have caused a cascade of firm defaults that would have threatened the entire financial system.

The return to earth of sky-high house prices meant a dramatic loss in value of securities backed by home values, which in turn struck at the solvency of financial institutions, mainly in the United States, but also around the rest of the world. The debt crisis of 2008 would have occurred in the absence of credit default swaps and other exotic financial instruments. But these factors greatly magnified the impact of the debt crisis and significantly complicated the policy response to the ensuing events.

19.2 THE CRISIS GOES GLOBAL

Lehman Brothers' September 2008 declaration of bankruptcy sparked an evaporation of trust in the solvency of other financial institutions, not just in the United States but around the world. Remember, the now toxic mortgage backed derivatives had been sold around the world, so they ended up on balance sheets in European banks. With would-be lenders now worried about loans not being repaid, lending dried up. In general, such lenders' anxiety shows up in the form of a spread between an interest rate on risky loans and a risk-free interest rate. An often-used risky rate is the London Inter-Bank Offered Rate, or **Libor**, which was the average rate at which private banks in London offered to lend to each other. The US Treasury yield is a convenient risk-free rate, since the US government is unlikely to default on its debts. The difference between the two rates, called the **TED spread** named for the two three-month rates being compared: T-bills and EuroDollars, measures the amount of fear on the part of lenders. Figure 19.3 shows the evolution of this spread from 2006 through 2009.

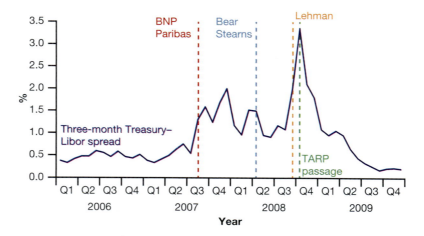

Figure 19.3 The TED Spread This graph shows the Treasury–three-month Libor spread, %.

Notice that the amount of perceived risk was quite low – historically unnaturally low, in fact – until it climbed dramatically in 2006. Risk jumped sharply in 2007, and then waxed and waned until the full-fledged crisis hit in September 2008. But the late-2008 spike in the TED spread probably understates, if anything, the amount of perceived risk in the financial system at that point. Libor was an indicative rate – that is it was a nonbinding statement of the interest rate major banks in London say they would be willing to lend at; at the height of the crisis it is unlikely they actually made any loans at all at these rates. In other words, the true spread was probably infinite.

As lending collapsed, so did economic activity. In the fourth quarter of 2008, after the financial crisis, GDPs in leading industrialized nations declined dramatically, as shown in Figure 19.2. US real GDP plunged at an annualized rate of over 8%, while that in the eurozone fell by a slightly smaller 7%. Japan's GDP plummeted by over 12.5%.

19.2 THE CRISIS GOES GLOBAL

The GDP drop was synchronized to a remarkable degree among the major advanced economies. What linkages pulled the advanced economies together, causing their synchronized crisis response? The first linkage was finance, the second was trade.

Financial Linkages

Economies around the world were bound together by banks and other financial institutions – hedge funds, investment banks, mutual funds — that borrowed and lent to each other across borders. When Lehman Brothers declared bankruptcy, that borrowing and lending ceased. Figure 19.4 illustrates how lending peaked in late 2008/early 2009.

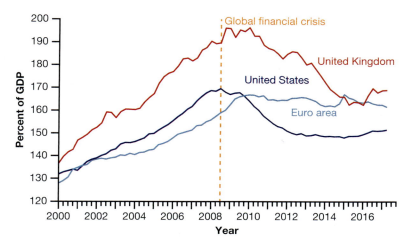

Figure 19.4 The Lending Boom This figure shows total credit to the private nonfinancial sector as a percentage point of GDP share for US (blue), Eurozone (light blue), UK (red).
Source: Bank for International Settlements.

The extent to which institutions were unable to access capital markets depended on several factors. In part, it depended upon the institutions' holdings of mortgage backed securities and collateralized debt obligations. As the value of those securities plummeted the solvency of banks came into question. But institutions' inability to borrow also depended upon the fact that many institutions had excessively relied upon short-term borrowing. When the short-term loans become difficult to roll over into new loans, the institutions' cash flow problems made them less attractive to potential longer-term lenders. This is explained in more detail in the Theory box.

Linkage through Trade

Heading into the crisis, economies were also linked through trade. As shown in Figure 19.7, world exports dropped much more precipitously than world GDP: while world GDP fell by 3% relative to peak, world exports fell by 24%. The sharp decline in trade can be attributed to several factors. The first is the contraction in income when the crisis hit, which led to a commensurate decline in consumption, part of which is imports. A second reason is that trade credit – lending specific to facilitating trade – became more difficult to obtain. But perhaps the most important reason is that a large portion of trade is in durable goods, and durable goods are particularly sensitive to movements in income – more so than food or clothing.

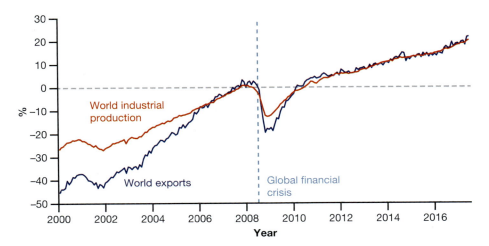

Figure 19.5 Production and Trade in the Great Recession This figure shows the difference from December 2007, for real exports (blue) and real industrial production (red). Vertical line at Lehman Brothers bankruptcy.
Source: Netherlands Bureau of Economic and Policy Analysis.

A drop in trade propagates a worldwide contraction in output by way of reducing aggregate demand. So, for instance, a decline in US imports is also a decline in the rest of the world's exports. But this means a drop in aggregate demand for the rest of the world, which then reduces their imports, which are in turn US exports, and so the income decline compounds. Thus, trade flows are both a cause and an effect of the global recession. The cycle begins with exogenous events: a decline in autonomous consumption and in autonomous investment. The consumption declines as perceived wealth, in the form of home values and securities based on them, erodes. Investment collapses because banks cease to lend.

As shown in the two-country Keynesian model in Chapter 13, the multiplier for a change in autonomous spending is larger with feedback effects than without them. For instance, if the marginal propensity to consume is 0.8 and the marginal propensity to import is 0.3, then the multiplier is nearly 3, whereas the multiplier would be 2 in the case where all the import effects leaked out completely. (The calculation assumes zero interest rate effects, which is consistent with being at the zero lower bound, as was the case in 2008–2009.) Hence, trade both propagates a contractionary impulse across borders and magnifies the contractionary impact on the source country.

19.3 THE POLICY RESPONSE

How did policymakers respond to this crisis? First, they responded directly against the sources of the financial aspects of the crisis. Central banks, first and foremost the Federal Reserve under Chairman Ben Bernanke, made sure that private banks and other financial institutions could borrow easily. In other words, the Fed became the lender of last resort to a much wider swath of the financial system than before. It also allowed central banks to access dollars for lending by engaging in "swaps" with certain central banks – the ECB, the Bank of England, the Bank of Japan, and the Swiss National Bank, among others – thereby allowing those banks to act as lenders of last resort for banks under their jurisdiction. This mitigated the liquidity problem.

If the private financial institutions were insolvent, all the central bank lending could not solve that problem. As long as there was a lack of trust between institutions, lending would be frozen. Governments around the world bailed out the private banks – essentially becoming part owners of banks. In the United States, this measure was implemented under the Troubled Asset Recovery Program, or "TARP." This gave confidence to market participants that the banks would be made solvent by the Federal government.

These two measures calmed the financial markets, and kept the financial plumbing working, at the potential cost to the US taxpayer. Similar measures in other countries placed corresponding burdens on their taxpayers.

As for dealing with the macroeconomic conditions, fiscal policymakers engaged in expansionary policies – cutting taxes and increasing spending. In the United States, one of the key measures was the American Recovery and Reinvestment Act, or "ARRA." This legislation, passed early in 2009, involved roughly $800 billion in additional deficits. While a large amount in absolute terms, it only amount to 5% of 2009 GDP. Moreover, the spending was spread out over several years. Nonetheless, as shown in Chapter 13, governments around the world coordinated an increase in spending in order to offset as much as possible the propagation of contractionary trade effects. At least this was true in 2008 to 2009.

Monetary policy also became accommodative to expansionary fiscal policy, so much so that short-term interest rates (like the Fed funds rate in the US) were dropped to zero – what became known as the **zero interest rate policy**, "ZIRP." In principal, the central banks would have like to reduce interest rates enough to spur the economy back to full employment, but this would have required negative interest rates. Since it is hard to get nominal interest rates to be negative, the Fed tried to push other interest rates – on mortgage backed securities and on long term Treasury bonds – lower by buying those securities. In what became known as **quantitative easing**, the Fed bought these securities, hoping to push up their prices thereby lowering their interest rates. Higher mortgage backed securities prices would make it easier for banks to make mortgage loans that could then be sold off. More lending could support the housing market which had collapsed. Lower long-term Treasury yields would pass through to lower corporate bond yields and other interest rates, hopefully spurring broader economic activity.

These policies served to stimulate recovery around the world. However, the impaired financial system, combined with a certain hesitancy to maintain strongly expansionary fiscal policy into 2010 onward, led to a lackluster recovery.

CONCLUSIONS

The global financial crisis highlights the importance of excessive leverage (i.e., overborrowing), feedback loops, and international linkages. Deregulation and financial innovation, combined with an asset price boom, led to a collapse that threatened the international financial system. The ensuing global recession occurred because of trade linkages, as well as the fact that the toxic assets held by financial institutions around the globe lost value precipitously.

Because the financial crisis and recession was global in nature, the response was global, at least in part. Those responses included both textbook expansionary fiscal and monetary policies, but also innovative policies, such as quantitative easing. That being said, US policymakers took the lead in policy stimulus, partly by virtue of the US's greater ability to borrow, and the central importance of the Federal Reserve.

SUMMARY POINTS

1. The global financial crisis of 2008 occurred because financial institutions had become overleveraged.
2. The overleveraging resulted in a financial system susceptible to losses in asset values arising from the downturn in housing prices.
3. Doubts about the solvency of the financial system led to a freeze in lending, which in turn resulted in an economic downturn.
4. The downturn was propagated across borders due to the fact that mortgage-backed securities and other derivatives based on upon real estate assets were held by banks around the world.
5. As banks assets lost value, perceived risk rose,
6. Downturns in each country were transmitted to other countries by reduced export demand.

KEY CONCEPTS

Collateralized debt obligation, page 415
Credit default swap, page 417
Feedback loop, page 415
Insolvent, page 416
Leverage, page 414
Libor, page 418
Liquidity crisis, page 417

Mortgage-backed security, page 415
Quantitative easing, page 421
Return on equity, page 416
Shadow banking sector, page 417
TED spread, page 418
Zero interest rate policy, page 421

REVIEW QUESTIONS

1. Was the decline in housing investment (e.g., construction of houses) a major contributor to the financial crisis?
2. What are mortgage backed securities, and how do they differ from conventional corporate bonds?
3. What happens if the assets a bank owns – loans, securities – lose so much value, so that bank capital goes to zero?
4. Government regulations required banks hold a certain amount of capital for each dollar of assets; the riskier the assets, the more capital the bank owners have to hold. Why would a bank owner want to hold the minimum amount of bank capital?

EXERCISES

1. Consider Table 19.1 for a high capital commercial bank.
   a. What is the capital to asset ratio to begin with, assuming the weight on loans and securities is one?
   b. Suppose the capital to asset ratio that is required by law is 9 to 1 (each dollar of assets has to be backed up by one dollar of capital). Is this bank in compliance?
   c. Suppose the capital to asset ratio is changed to 8 to 1. What does the bank have to do in order to stay in compliance?
   d. What is the return on equity before and after the new regulation?
   e. Would the owners of the bank likely oppose or support the new regulation?
2. A financial crisis reduces desired spending on the part of firms and households.

a. Show the impact of the financial crisis on output in an *IS–LM* framework.
b. Show how fiscal policy can offset the negative impact of this outcome.
c. Suppose the shift in the IS curve reduces interest rates to zero. Can conventional monetary policy effectively offset the decrease in aggregate demand?

RECOMMENDED RESOURCES

Menzie Chinn and Jeffry Frieden, *Lost Decades: The Making of America's Debt Crisis and the Long Recovery* (New York: W.W. Norton, 2011).

Council of Economic Advisers, *Economic Report of the President* (Washington, DC: US Government Printing Office, 2009).

CHAPTER 20

The Eurozone Crisis

LEARNING OBJECTIVES

In this chapter, we learn about:
- what an economic and monetary union is, and how it relates to the eurozone
- why monetary policy is unable to respond adequately
- why the eurozone was hit by a sovereign debt crisis
- how the debt crisis caused a eurozone-wide recession
- how sovereign debt crises and banking crises are linked
- whether the eurozone problems have been solved

INTRODUCTION

In this chapter, we discuss the causes of the eurozone crisis, by first recounting the lead up to monetary union. In the subsequent section, the economic arguments for and against are explained. Next, we detail the onset of the crisis in banking, government debt, and growth, and the implications of the immediate policy response. The final section explains how the recovery to date has been incomplete.

20.1 LEAD-UP TO THE EURO

The creation of the euro – formally the completion of Europe's **Economic and Monetary Union** (EMU) – is the latest step in a long process of politically motivated economic integration. In the wake of World War II, leaders of the main European countries sought to bind the economies of the former antagonists in interdependence. First they established the European Coal and Steel Council, which harmonized trade in these critical commodities. This led to the 1957 creation of the European Economic Community, which, in principle, established a "common market" wherein goods were free to move across borders. This was quite an accomplishment, given that these countries had been at war a few years earlier.

After the breakdown of the fixed exchange rate system of Bretton Woods in 1971, Europeans sought to minimize the variability of intra-Europe exchange rates. Central banks committed to intervening – by buying and selling foreign exchange – to achieve that aim. There was some modest success, especially after the 1979 establishment of the European Monetary System, which linked other European Union (EU) member currencies to each other. After 1985, the system included most EU members and some non-members.

In 1992, EU members agreed to a program of economic and monetary union, the culmination of which would be the creation of a common currency called the euro, managed by the **European Central Bank** (ECB). The plan envisioned a multi-stage process toward this single currency. First, there would be a period of tight management by central banks so that currency values did not vary more than 3% from target, or "par," values. Finally, the currency values would, under the careful management of individual central banks, converge toward the final conversion rates, established by common agreement. Along the way, the authorities would have to bring inflation down to a sufficiently low level so that the rates did not diverge substantially. In addition, the agreement required that, as a share of GDP, national budget deficits should not exceed 3%, and government debt should not exceed 60%.

Despite most countries' failure to abide by these conditions, most notably during the European Monetary System crises of 1992 and 1993, and despite the UK's dropping out of the plan completely, the euro came into being on January 1, 1999. The physical currency was rolled out in 2001.

A decade after the beginning of the global crisis, the aggregate GDP of the countries comprising the eurozone has come nowhere near regaining its earlier level, and in fact the countries that share the euro as common currency have repeatedly teetered on the edge of financial crisis or economic downturn. The reasons for this state of affairs seem complex, but in the end, the explanation for why the eurozone fell into, and remains in, crisis are quite straightforward. The eurozone crisis is the result of at least two key weaknesses in the original project of European monetary integration: first, the common currency and its monetary policy were applied to a set of economies very different from one another; and, second, investors interpreted the creation of the union as an implicit guarantee of member countries' government debt.

20.2 ECONOMIC MOTIVATIONS FOR AND CHALLENGES OF MONETARY UNION

In this section, we first recount the challenges of forming a monetary union. We then discuss how the particular structure of the monetary union induced a reduction in perceived risk that spurred excessive borrowing.

Challenges of a Common Currency

Having many currencies is bothersome and costly. Trade involving two currencies incurs conversion costs. Moreover, exchange rates can be quite volatile. When one is thinking about long-term projects that involve investing across borders, this volatility brings with it a risk that impedes the flow of goods and capital across borders. Currency unification therefore encourages trade and financial integration. In the context of the EU's quest for economic integration, a **currency union** appeared to be a logical step.

However, a flexible exchange rate allows economies to adjust to changes in economic conditions, as shown in Chapter 15. The exchange rate thus serves as a sort of macroeconomic **shock absorber**. For instance, if demand for US cars decreases, a weakening of the dollar, which makes US cars cheaper for foreigners, can help offset the negative impact on the economy. Fixing one's exchange rate to a certain value or, at the extreme, giving up one's currency, eliminates that shock absorber. A transnational currency requires a nation's government to give up one of the most powerful tools of macroeconomic policy.

When do the benefits of a unified currency outweigh the costs? The answer depends on many factors. But in broad terms, a unified currency makes sense when one of two things is the case: (1) all users of the currency tend to be subject to the same economic influences, so that when shocks hit, they are **symmetric shocks,** or (2) the users of the currency have shock absorbers besides flexible exchange rates.

One important shock absorber is **fiscal union** in the form of a revenue stream, managed by a central authority, that responds to asymmetric shocks by compensating hard-hit economies with automatic transfers from better-performing economies. Within the US fiscal union, for example, if, say, the state of Wisconsin experiences an economic downturn, then federally funded net transfers (unemployment insurance, reduced tax payments) increase, partially offsetting the negative impact. A second shock absorber is labor mobility, which within the United States is fairly high. When economic conditions deteriorate in Wisconsin, out-migration to the rest of the country increases, while in-migration decreases. Unemployment is less volatile with this "escape valve."

The fundamental problem with the eurozone was neither of the above conditions applied: shocks were not sufficiently symmetric, and there was neither a fiscal union nor sufficient labor mobility to absorb asymmetric shocks. In the lingo of economists, the original group of 11 nations – Austria, Belgium, Finland, France, Germany, Ireland, Italy, Luxembourg, the Netherlands, Portugal, and Spain – did not constitute an **optimal currency area.**

The argument that the eurozone countries did not constitute an optimal currency area was well known – given the criteria laid out by Mundell (1961), McKinnon (1963), and Kenen (1969) – prior to Economic and Monetary Union. Tamim Bayoumi and Barry Eichengreen (1993, 1994) measured the extent to which the shocks hitting the eurozone economies were different; they established that only a few economies could be construed to fit the requirements of symmetric shocks (the Northern European countries, within the eventual eurozone). This point is shown in Table 20.1, which shows the correlation of aggregate supply shocks. Aggregate supply shocks are identified as shocks that have a permanent effect on output and the price level. Such shocks include, for instance, changes in the level of technology. The shocks are estimated over the 1960–1988 period. The correlation was relatively high for the geographically contiguous countries of Northern and Central Europe (the red triangle), normally above 0.3 and often quite a bit higher. In sharp contrast, the correlations of shocks between, say, Germany on the one hand and Italy, Ireland, and Finland on the other were all well below 0.3 – not to mention the *negative* correlation between Germany and Norway. When monetary policy was too tight for Germany, it is likely to be too loose for Norway, and vice versa.

The proponents of EMU were not unaware of these concerns. However, currency union seemed desirable to many as a way of encouraging further integration within Europe; if it had a (perhaps temporary) price, that price might be worth paying. Moreover, groups in the EU strongly favored economic and monetary union because it promised to provide them with powerful benefits – firms and industries with major cross-border economic interests particularly stood to gain. For them, whatever problems economic and monetary union might cause for the EU as a whole were counter balanced by the positive impact on them.

European Union policymakers therefore sought to make individual economies more flexible and increase cross-country mobility of labor by way of harmonizing regulations and reducing inter-country barriers. Increasing trade integration (which would tend to be one result of reducing exchange rate volatility) would also make the effects of asymmetric shocks less pronounced. But while trade integration increased dramatically in the wake of EMU,

Table 20.1 Correlation of Aggregate Supply Shocks

Correlations of supply disturbances across Western Europe

	Ger	Fra	Net	Bel	Den	Aus	Swi	Ita	UK	Spa	Por	Ire	Swe	Nor	Fin
Germany	1														
France	0.52	1													
Netherlands	0.54	0.36	1												
Belgium	0.62	0.4	0.56	1											
Denmark	0.68	0.54	0.56	0.37	1										
Austria	0.41	0.28	0.38	0.47	0.49	1									
Switzerland	0.38	0.25	0.58	0.47	0.36	0.39	1								
Italy	0.21	0.28	0.39	0.00	0.15	0.06	−0.04	1							
United Kingdom	0.12	0.12	0.13	0.12	−0.05	−0.25	0.16	0.28	1						
Spain	0.33	0.21	0.17	0.23	0.22	0.25	0.07	0.2	0.01	1					
Portugal	0.21	0.33	0.11	0.40	−0.04	−0.03	0.13	0.22	0.27	0.51	1				
Ireland	0.00	−0.21	0.11	−0.02	−0.32	0.08	0.08	0.14	0.05	−0.15	0.01	1			
Sweden	0.31	0.30	0.43	0.06	0.35	0.01	0.44	0.46	0.41	0.20	0.39	0.10	1		
Norway	−0.27	−0.11	−0.39	−0.26	−0.37	−0.21	−0.18	0.01	0.27	−0.09	0.26	0.08	0.10	1	
Finland	0.22	0.12	−0.25	0.06	0.3	0.11	0.06	−0.32	−0.04	0.07	−0.13	−0.23	−0.10	−0.08	1

Source: Bayoumi, Tamim A., and Eichengreen, Barry J. 1994. *One Money or Many?: Analyzing the Prospects for Monetary Unification in Various Parts of the World* (Vol. 76). Princeton: International Finance Section, Department of Economics, Princeton University.

labor mobility did not increase sufficiently. While professionals can move without too much difficulty, lower-skilled workers faced considerable impediments to relocation. In addition, cultural and linguistic ties seem to exert a substantial pull, keeping cross-border labor flows small, as compared to US levels.

The other problem was the absence of fiscal integration. So long as taxation and government spending decisions were left to the individual sovereign states, there was no mechanism for transfers that would naturally tend to shift financial stress from struggling economies to those in better shape. This brings us to the second problem, namely investors' assumption that when EU member nations got into trouble, case-by-case bailouts would take the place of automatic transfers.

Disappearance of Risk

Investors interpreted the creation of the union as an implicit guarantee of member countries' government debt. It seemed clear that if a serious financial crisis erupted in one eurozone member country, the risks of contagion to the rest of the zone and of a negative effect on the euro would force other countries to bail out the member in crisis. Investors embraced this interpretation even though no such formal guarantees were made. These implicit guarantees were problematic because they pushed interest rates lower, which, in turn, gave governments, businesses, and households incentive to borrow more than they would have, had they properly understood the risks.

In other words, risk was underpriced due to the perception of an implicit guarantee. The result was that Southern Europe experienced unnaturally low interest rates, borrowed more than was sustainable, and suffered from the resulting over-borrowing. And, in certain countries, this problem of over-borrowing is compounded by a long-term problem of public spending on pensions and health care that has exceeded levels supportable by the rate of economic growth.

In the eurozone, investors' belief that a bailout would be forthcoming if a member state got into trouble considerably loosened European borrowing constraints. This is shown in Figure 20.1; the implicit guarantees associated with economic and monetary union drove interest rates down toward German levels – even for the countries, such as Greece, that arguably had poorer fiscal prospects – and encouraged more borrowing, a situation that fed upon itself in a self-reinforcing loop.

The credit boom hid the risk problem for the better part of a decade. In this sense, the apparent "disappearance of risk" in the eurozone paralleled a similar phenomenon in the US. In the eurozone, the underpricing of risk resulted in excess borrowing by households, firms, and governments, and in commensurate capital flows from Northern European countries to Southern European countries. In the US, the private sector borrowed excessively, pulling in record capital inflows – manifesting in record current account deficits.

20.3 THE EURO SOVEREIGN DEBT CRISIS AND ADJUSTMENT DEFERRED

When the global recession of 2008–2009 struck, most eurozone governments went further into deficit, as social welfare and unemployment benefit payments increased and tax revenues collapsed. In some cases, the problem, which the recession aggravated, was a structural deficit associated with overgenerous social spending and insufficient tax collection. This description applied most profoundly to Greece. However, the characterization of excess public spending does not pertain to all the problem eurozone countries.

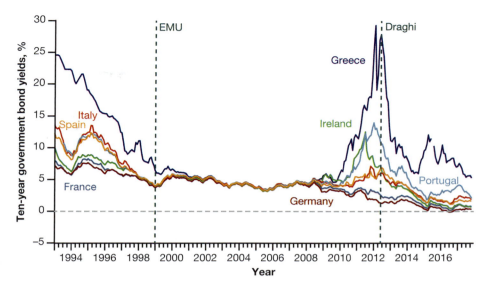

Figure 20.1 Government Bond Yields in the Euro Area This diagram shows the interest rates on ten-year bonds issued by the governments of the euro area. Long dashed line at inception of Economic and Monetary Union. Short dashed line at beginning of term of Mario Draghi as European Central Bank chair. Greece enters EMU in 2001.

Ireland, for instance, was a paragon of fiscal rectitude, at least on paper. During a boom in financial and housing markets, the Irish government ran budget surpluses. When the financial crisis hit, however, the government implemented a complete bank deposit guarantee and subsequently bailed out major banks, resulting in massive increases in the government's debt. Similarly, Spain was running a budget surplus until the collapse of its own housing market.

The phenomenon of hidden government liabilities suddenly showing up at the onset of a crisis is not new. In fact, the East Asian crises of the 1990s brought to the fore the concept of "contingent liabilities." A government can appear to be in an enviable fiscal situation, when in fact the government is on the hook for massive debts, because it cannot allow a banking system to become insolvent.

This point highlights the linkage of the banking system debt problem with the sovereign debt problem, when portions of the banking system are insolvent. In the case of the United States, the federal government had the resources to bail out the financial system without seriously endangering its ability to borrow. In the eurozone, because some countries' governments already had high debt loads, the additional borrowing associated with bank bailouts would only make the sovereign debt problem worse. Once the downturn struck, eurozone governments had the option of allowing natural adjustment processes to play out, eventually leading to recovery of full employment output. Why did they not simply do this? The answer is that it takes an extended period of time for wages and prices to adjust the relative price level, whereas an exchange rate devaluation gets the job done much faster.

To see this, recall the aggregate demand equation, equation (14.2), and now assume perfect capital mobility, so that $i = i^*$:

$$Y = \bar{\alpha}\left[\overline{A} + \overline{EX} - \overline{IM} + (n+v)q - b\vec{i}^*\right] \quad <IS \text{ curve}> \tag{20.1}$$

Now, set the nominal exchange rate, S, to be constant, and assume the foreign price level to be constant, as well:

$$Y = \bar{\alpha}\left[\bar{A} + \overline{EX} - \overline{IM} + (n+v)\left(\frac{\overline{S} \times \overline{P}^*}{P}\right) - bi^*\right] \quad <AD \text{ curve}> \quad (20.2)$$

Notice that there is a negative relationship between the price level and output. However, the reason why a higher price level is associated with a lower level of aggregate demand is different from the one described in Section 16.3; instead of a higher price level eroding the real money stock for a given nominal money stock, the higher price level results in an appreciation of the real exchange rate, given a fixed nominal exchange rate.

The way to think about the eurozone is that, with the nominal exchange rate between eurozone countries irrevocably fixed at 1, a lower P is associated with a higher q, i.e., the country's production is more competitive against other countries within the currency area.

This adjustment process in the wake of a contractionary shock is shown in Figure 20.2. The contractionary shock is shown as an inward shift of the AD curve in period 2 (the red arrow). Immediately, output declines from Y_1 to Y_2.

In period 3, the price level declines because of the slack in the economy in period 2. The lower price level induces an increase in exports and a decrease in imports as the real exchange rate depreciates (q rises). The higher level of net exports means higher aggregate demand, resulting in an increase in output to Y_3. This process continues as long as the output gap is negative. In the end, the price level declines to P_{Final}, while the output returns to its starting point: $Y_1 = Y_{\text{Final}} = Y^{FE}$.

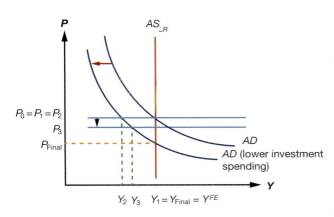

Figure 20.2 Internal Devaluation This diagram shows how the adjustment of the price level restores full employment.

The problem is that the process of driving down prices – i.e., internal devaluation – by way of high unemployment can be very protracted. If there are additional negative shocks to aggregate demand – such as contractionary fiscal policy – that can prolong the process even further. Certainly, this is a much slower process than what could be achieved by an exchange rate devaluation, as examined in Chapter 14.

Figure 20.3 depicts the labor cost of production in each country, after adjustment for productivity (called **unit labor costs**), relative to the other members of the eurozone. The higher the country's relative unit labor cost, the more costly the goods produced in that country. Unit labor costs decline, exports rise and imports decline.

Notice that with the onset of the crisis, relative unit labor costs dropped, with varying degrees of rapidity. They began falling earliest in Ireland, mostly because of the large shock to the Irish financial system, which was large relative to the size of the Irish economy. Labor costs also fell in Spain, as the massive housing bubble collapsed. But in the country that triggered the crisis, wage adjustment was slow to come: Greek relative unit labor costs only started declining in 2011. The problem was that even with relative labor costs coming down, they were not coming down fast enough to spur aggregate demand.

In the wake of the 2008 crisis, government debt ballooned, albeit for different reasons, in each country. In the GIIPS countries – Greece, Ireland, Italy, Portugal, Spain – all overburdened by debt as the crisis developed, tax revenues fell, while expenditures for social safety net programs increased. In Ireland, and to a lesser extent Spain, bank bailouts accounted for

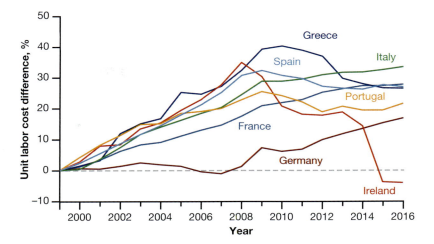

Figure 20.3 Labor Costs in the Euro Area This diagram shows the relative unit labor costs for Germany (dark red), France (blue) and the so-called GIIPS countries, percent difference from 1999.
Source: European Commission.

a big share of the debt accumulation. As worries about the ability to service government debt increased, interest rates spiked, particularly in Greece, Ireland, and Portugal. Higher interest rates meant even faster accumulation of government debt, reinforcing anxieties about debt repayment, and pushing debt yields to even higher levels.

The dynamics of debt accumulation at work can be described by an equation:

$$\underbrace{\frac{B_t}{Y_t} - \frac{B_{t-1}}{Y_{t-1}}}_{\text{change in debt ratio}} = (r - g) \underbrace{\frac{B_{t-1}}{Y_{t-1}}}_{\text{initial debt ratio}} + \underbrace{\frac{G_t - T_t}{Y_t}}_{\text{primary deficit ratio}} \tag{20.3}$$

B is the stock of government debt, r is the real interest rate, g is the growth rate of real GDP, G is government spending (excluding interest payments), and T is tax revenue.

This equation states that the *change* in the government debt–GDP ratio (on the left-hand side) depends on the gap between the real interest rate and the real GDP growth rate $(r - g)$, the initial government debt–GDP ratio, and the current ratio of the primary budget deficit (the difference between government spending and tax revenue) to GDP. The higher last year's debt load or this year's budget deficit, the more likely the debt ratio is to rise. And the higher the interest rate, or the lower the growth rate, the faster the accumulation of debt.

Armed with equation (20.3), one can examine the implications of the various policy measures implemented over the past six years. First, attempts to reduce government interest rates by embarking upon tight fiscal policy (i.e., increases in tax rates and reductions in government spending), a policy, sometimes called **austerity**, proved counterproductive. Rather than instilling confidence that resulted in a decline in borrowing costs, these policies only pushed the economies deeper into recession, driving up budget deficits and driving down Y (in the denominator of each term), thereby increasing the debt–GDP ratio and further exacerbating concerns about the ability of GIIPS governments to repay their debt. Such concerns fed upon themselves, elevating interest costs yet more.

Lower, or even negative, growth rates drove up unemployment rates, as shown in Figure 20.4. Even when GDP growth resumed, unemployment rates remained stubbornly high.

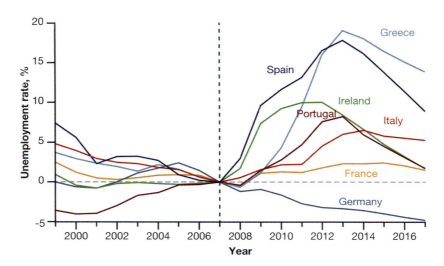

Figure 20.4 Changes in the Unemployment Rates in the Euro Area This figure shows differences in unemployment rates compared to 2007 levels, in percentage points.
Source: IMF, World Economic Outlook database.

The eurozone crisis – although in remission – continues to this day; a temporary reprieve has been granted by the drastic reduction of borrowing costs for the GIIPS, starting in mid-2012. Expansionary monetary policy, executed by the ECB, is to be credited. At that time, a new ECB chair, Mario Draghi, committed to additional measures to prevent bond yields from rising. This action stabilized debt dynamics. However, since growth remained stagnant, debt levels remained high, as shown in Figure 20.5. The euro debt crisis is hardly solved.

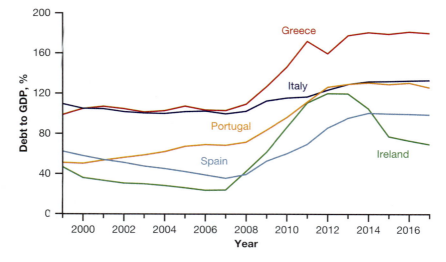

Figure 20.5 Government Debt Ratios Gross government debt to GDP ratio, in percentage points of GDP.
Source: IMF, World Economic Outlook database.

20.4 THE INCOMPLETE RECOVERY

By 2015, the eurozone economies have largely recovered to pre-global financial crisis levels. However, on the eve of the pandemic, growth was not robust, and remained vulnerable to another shock.

Several problems confront the eurozone. First, there has been little progress on overcoming the impediments to the eurozone constituting an optimal currency zone. There is little evidence that labor mobility has been substantially enhanced. And the possibility of greater scope for countercyclical fiscal transfers has, if anything, been reduced by the greater debt loads. This point was highlighted by the more restrained fiscal policy undertaken during the pandemic, in which eurozone governments undertook much smaller measures to support their economies.

In July 2020, the European Union announced a willingness to engage in large scale issuance of public debt, on the order of 750 billion euros. If that were to happen, individual states would be less likely to exacerbate downturns by forced spending cuts when tax revenues declined. However, bonds in that amount were never issued, as the EU member governments could not come to an agreement on the revenue source (such as a new carbon border adjustment tax, a tax on digital platforms like Google and Microsoft, or on multinational corporations).

Second, the development of a banking union to handle a future eurozone-wide crisis has only begun, with some supervisory components in place by 2015. The banking union remains incomplete as it lacks a common deposit insurance scheme. The prior crisis entailed bank bailouts by individual countries; the elevated public debt levels limit the scope for a repeat.

If reforms did not take place, a complete or partial breakup of the eurozone might eventually occur. In recent years, the increasing debt load in, particularly, Italy has led to a worsening of debt dynamics there, much the same as occurred during the earlier Euro crisis. However, in 2022, the scope for the ECB to cap Italian government bond yields, and the prospects for a political solution to enhancing growth, both seemed darker than before. This is shown in the Italian spread – the extra interest rate that must be paid in order to borrow – relative to the perceived safe asset of German government bonds.

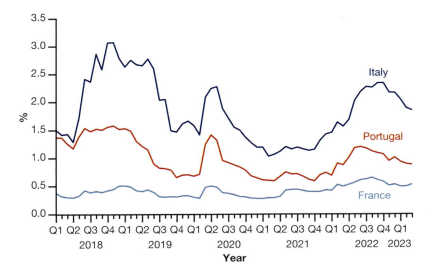

Figure 20.6 Government Bond Spreads This figure shows the spread between the ten-year interest rate for Italy (blue), for Portugal (red), and for France (light blue) versus the ten year interest rate for Germany, in percentages.

As of August 2022, the Italian government had to borrow at a higher interest rate, by 2.24 percentage points, than the German government for a period of ten years. That spread represents the risk investors associate with Italian debt, and that a higher interest rate leads to a faster accumulation of debt.

While a breakup would allow for adjustments of exchange rates in a way that would lead to a faster recovery in Italy and other problem economies, the resulting chaos and economic uncertainty associated from litigating all the trillions of euros worth of contracts could far outweigh those benefits. This option has so much downside risk that it has not been contemplated thus far, even as challenges to the monetary union become ever more daunting.

CONCLUSIONS

In the eurozone crisis, the seeming disappearance of risk, along with an overly loose monetary policy in the GIIPS countries – a policy associated with Economic and Monetary Union – led to overborrowing and an asset boom, and then collapse. The response to the bust was hampered by the fact that the currency union prevented adjustment by way of nominal devaluation. That point highlights the importance of exchange rate adjustment as a key buffer for economies. Foregoing that means that economic stability is going to be extremely dependent on relatively flexible prices and wages, well-functioning financial systems, or both.

A reprieve was afforded by the global recovery up to 2019, and the ECB's commitment to keep government bond yields relatively low, thereby short-circuiting the tendency toward a worsening downturn and debt crisis. That reprieve was temporary, and the fundamental problems in the union remain.

SUMMARY POINTS

1. The eurozone is a currency union of countries that share a common currency – the euro.
2. Since there is only one currency, the monetary policy is shared by all the countries of the union, even though different policies might be appropriate to different countries, particularly if the countries differ in their characteristics.
3. This means that no single monetary policy fits all; policy was too loose for some and too tight for others.
4. The creation of the currency union reduced the perceived risk of sovereign default, resulting in lower yields and overborrowing.
5. Banking crises interacted with sovereign debt crises and recession to result in downturn in the eurozone countries of Greece, Ireland, Italy, Portugal, and Spain.
6. Since fiscal policy was constrained, adjustment could only occur by real exchange rate depreciation. However, the currency union prevented devaluation so real depreciation could only occur by price deflation, which required elevated unemployment that led to larger deficits and faster debt accumulation.
7. A looser monetary policy in 2012 helped break the debt spiral.
8. The eurozone remains susceptible to another downturn and debt crisis.

KEY CONCEPTS

Austerity, page 431
Currency union, page 425

Economic and Monetary Union, page 424

European Central Bank, page 425
Fiscal union, page 426
Optimal currency area, page 426
Shock absorber, page 425
Symmetric shocks, page 426
Unit labor cost, page 430

REVIEW QUESTIONS

1. What is a monetary union?
2. How does a monetary union differ from having countries peg their exchange rates to each other?
3. If shocks are symmetric, is a monetary union feasible?
4. Is the United States a monetary union?
5. Is the Eurozone a fiscal union?
6. If there is only one currency in a monetary union, how do individual countries adjust to changes in demand for their products so as to achieve full employment?
7. If real interest rates are higher than the growth rate of real GDP, will the level of debt to GDP rise or fall?
8. How did the ECB end the euro crisis of 2010–12?

EXERCISES

1. Using an aggregate demand-aggregate supply graph, show an economy on a fixed exchange rate with output initially below full employment levels.
    a. Show how fiscal policy can restore full employment.
    b. Suppose fiscal policy cannot be conducted because the government is unable to borrow further (assume the government budget is initially in balance). Can the government use monetary policy to restore full employment *and* keep the exchange rate at its current level?
    c. If devaluation is ruled out, will the economy adjust automatically to restore full employment? If so, show how.
    d. Why might a policymaker wish to use exchange rate policy rather than automatic adjustment?
    e. If prices are very sticky, would that make devaluation a more or less appealing choice.
2. Consider equation (20.3).
    a. Can the debt–GDP ratio decline if $r - g > 0$? How?
    b. If one decreases the primary deficit a lot, and the growth rate of GDP is unchanged, would that reduce the rate at which debt accumulates?
    c. Is it plausible that a decrease in the primary deficit (say, by increasing taxes or decreasing government spending) would not affect the growth rate of GDP, assuming the model in Chapter 13 holds?

RECOMMENDED RESOURCES

Menzie Chinn and Jeffry Frieden, *Lost Decades: The Making of America's Debt Crisis and the Long Recovery* (New York: W.W. Norton, 2011).

Jay Shambaugh, "The Three Crises of the Euro," *Brookings Papers on Economic Activity* (Spring, 2012).

REFERENCES

Aizenman, Joshua, Menzie D. Chinn, and Hiro Ito (2010). "The Emerging Global Financial Architecture: Tracing and Evaluating New Patterns of the Trilemma Configuration," *Journal of International Money and Finance* 29: 615–641.

Aizenman, Joshua, Menzie D. Chinn, and Hiro Ito (2013). "The 'Impossible Trinity' Hypothesis in an Era of Global Imbalances: Measurement and Testing,"*Review of International Economics* 21(3): 447–458.

Allen, Mark, Christoph Rosenberg, Christian Keller, Brad Setser, and Nouriel Roubini (2002). "A Balance Sheet Approach to Financial Crisis," IMF Working Paper No. 02/210.

Alquist, Ron and Menzie Chinn (2008). "Conventional and Unconventional Approaches to Exchange Rate Modeling and Assessment," *International Journal of Finance and Economics* 13: 2–13.

Amiti, Mary, Stephen J. Redding, and David E. Weinstein (2019). "The Impact of the 2018 Tariffs on Prices and Welfare," *Journal of Economic Perspectives* 33(4): 187–210.

Arkolakis, Costas, Arnaud Costinot, and Andrés Rodríguez-Clare (2012). "New Trade Models, Same Old Gains?" *American Economic Review* 102(1): 94–130.

Autor, David H., David Dorn, and Gordon H. Hanso (2013). "The China Syndrome: Local Labor Market Effects of Import Competition in the United States," *American Economic Review* 103(6): 2121–2168.

Baldwin, Robert E. (1969). "The Case against Infant-Industry Tariff Protection," *Journal of Political Economy* 77(3): 295–305.

Baldwin, Robert E. (2008).*The Development and Testing of Heckscher–Ohlin Trade Models A Review*, Cambridge, MA: MIT Press.

Bartelme, Dominick, Arnaud Costinot, Dave Donaldson, and Andres Rodriguez-Clare (2021). "The Textbook Case for Industrial Policy: Theory Meets Data," Working Paper.

Barwick, Panle Jia, Myrto Kalouptsidi, and Nahim Zahur (2021). "Industrial Policy Implementation: Empirical Evidence from China's Shipbuilding Industry," *Review of International Economics*.

Bayoumi, Tamim A. and Barry J. Eichengreen (1993). "Shocking Aspects of European Monetary Integration," in Francisco Torres and Francesco Giavazzi (eds.), *Adjustment and Growth in the European Monetary Union*, Cambridge, UK: Cambridge University Press, 193–235.

Bayoumi, Tamim A. and Barry J. Eichengreen (1994). "One Money or Many?: Analyzing the Prospects for Monetary Unification in Various Parts of the World," *Princeton Studies in International Finance* 76.

Beaulieu, Eugene (2002). "The Stolper–Samuelson Theorem Faces Congress," *Review of International Economics* 10(2): 337–354.

Bernard, Andrew B., Jensen, J. Bradford, and Schott, Peter K. (2009). "Importers, Exporters and Multinationals: A Portrait of Firms in the U.S. that Trade Goods," in T. Dunne, J. B. Jensen, and M. J. Roberts (eds.), *Producer Dynamics: New Evidence from Micro Data*, Chicago, IL: University of Chicago Press, 513–552.

Bernhofen, Daniel M. and John C. Brown (2005). "An Empirical Assessment of the Comparative Advantage Gains from Trade: Evidence from Japan," *American Economic Review* 95(1): 208–225.

Bhagwati, Jagdish (2008). *Termites in the Trading System: How Preferential Agreements Undermine Free Trade*, New York: Oxford University Press.

Blanchard, O.J. and Riggi, M. (2013). "Why Are the 2000s so Different from the 1970s? A Structural Interpretation of Changes in the

Macroeconomic Effects of Oil Prices," *Journal of the European Economic Association* 11(5): 1032–1052.

Blonigen, Bruce A. (2011). "Revisiting the Evidence on Trade Policy Preferences," *Journal of International Economics* 85: 129–135.

Blonigen, Bruce A., Benjamin H. Liebman, Justin R. Pierce, and Wesley W. Wilson (2013). "Are All Trade Protection Policies Created Equal? Empirical Evidence for Nonequivalent Market Power Effects of Tariffs and Quotas," *Journal of International Economics* 89: 369–378.

Bourguignon, François (2016). "Inequality and Globalization: How the Rich Get Richer as the Poor Catch Up," *Foreign Affairs* 95(1): 11–15.

Branstetter, Lee G., Guangwei Li, and Mengjia Ren (2022). "Picking Winners? Government Subsidies and Firm Productivity in China," NBER Working Paper No. 30699.

Breinlich, Holger, Elsa Leromain, Dennis Novy, and Thomas Sampson (2017). "The Brexit Vote, Inflation and UK Living Standards," Centre for Economic Performance Brexit Analysis No. 11.

Broda, Christian and David E. Weinstein (2006). "Globalization and the Gains from Variety," *Quarterly Journal of Economics* 121(2): 541–585.

Burda, Michael C. and Mark Weder (2017). "The Economics of German Unification after Twenty-five Years: Lessons for Korea," SFB 649 Discussion Paper, No. 2017-009, Humboldt University of Berlin.

Bussiere, Matthieu and Marcel Fratzscher (2006). "Towards a New Early Warning System of Financial Crises," *Journal of International Money and Finance* 25(6): 953–973.

Bussiere, Matthieu and Christian Mulder (1999). "External Vulnerability in Emerging Market Economies: How High Liquidity Can Offset Weak Fundamentals and the Effects of Contagion," IMF Working Paper no. WP/99/88.

Caliendo, Lorenzo and Fernando Parro (2015). "Estimates of the Trade and Welfare Effects of NAFTA," *Review of Economic Studies* 82(1): 1–44.

Calvo, Guillermo A. (1998). "Capital Flows and Capital-Market Crises: The Simple Economics of Sudden Stops." *Journal of Applied Economics* 1(1): 35–54.

Calvo, Guillermo A. and Enrique G. Mendoza (1996). "Petty Crime and Cruel Punishment: Lessons from the Mexican Debacle," *The American Economic Review* 86(2): 170–175.

Card, David (1990). "The Impact of the Mariel Boatlift on the Miami Labor Market," *Industrial and Labor Relations Review* 43(2): 245–257.

Caselli, Francesco and James Feyrer, (2007). "The Marginal Product of Capital," *Quarterly Journal of Economics* 122(2): 535–568.

Cerra, Valerie and Sweta Chaman Saxena (2010). "The Monetary Model Strikes Back: Evidence from the World," *Journal of International Economics* 81(2): 184–196.

Cheung, Yin-Wong, Menzie D. Chinn, Antonio Garcia Pascual, and Yi Zhang (2019). "Exchange Rate Prediction Redux: New Models, New Data, New Currencies," *Journal of International Money and Finance* 95: 332–362.

Chinn, Menzie and Jeffrey A. Frankel (2007). "Will the Euro Eventually Surpass the Dollar as Leading International Reserve Currency?" *G7 Current Account Imbalances: Sustainability and Adjustment*, Chicago, IL: University of Chicago Press, 283–338.

Chinn, Menzie and Hiro Ito (2006). "What Matters for Financial Development? Capital Controls, Institutions and Interactions," *Journal of Development Economics* 61(1): 163–192.

Chinn, Menzie D. and Richard A. Meese (1995). "Banking on Currency Forecasts: How Predictable Is Change in Money?" *Journal of International Economics* 38(1–2): 161–178.

Clemens, Michael A. (2011). "Economics and Emigration: Trillion-Dollar Bills on the Sidewalk?" *Journal of Economic Perspectives* 25(3): 83–106.

Clemens, Michael A., Ethan G. Lewis, and Hannah M. Postel (2018). "Immigration Restrictions as Active Labor Market Policy: Evidence from the Mexican Bracero Exclusion," *American Economic Review*, 108(6): 1468–1487.

Costinot, Arnaud and Andres Rodriguez-Clare (2014). "Trade Theory with Numbers: Quantifying the Consequences of

Globalization," in Gita Gopinath, Elhanan Helpman, and Kenneth Rogoff (eds.), *Handbook of International Economics*, Amsterdam: Elsevier.

Council of Economic Advisers (1984). *Economic Report of the President*, US GPO.

Coughlin, Cletus C. (2010). "Measuring International Trade Policy: A Primer on Trade Restrictiveness Indices," *Review, Federal Reserve Bank of St. Louis* 92: 381–394.

Davis, Donald R. and David E. Weinstein (2001). "An Account of Global Factor Trade," *American Economic Review* 91(5): 1423–1453.

DiPippo, Gerard, Ilaria Mazzocco, Scott Kennedy, and Matthew P. Goodman (2022). *Red Ink: Estimating Chinese Industrial Policy Spending in Comparative Perspective*, Washington, DC: Center for Strategic and International Studies. Available at: www.csis.org/analysis/red-ink-estimating-chinese-industrial-policy-spending-comparative-perspective.

Dixit, Avinash and Gene Grossman (2005). "The Limits of Free Trade," *Journal of Economic Perspectives* 19(3): 241–244.

Dornbusch, Rudiger, Ilan Goldfajn, and Rodrigo O. Valdés (1995). "Currency Crises and Collapses," *Brookings Papers on Economic Activity*, 2: 219–293.

Edwards, Sebastian and Daniel Leiderman (2002). "The Political Economy of Unilateral Trade Liberalization: The Case of Chile," in Jagdish Bhagwati (ed.), *Going Alone: The Case for Relaxed Reciprocity in Freeing Trade*, Cambridge, MA: MIT Press.

Eichengreen, Barry, Ricardo Hausmann, and Ugo Panizza (2007). "Currency Mismatches, Debt Intolerance, and the Original Sin: Why They Are Not the Same and Why It Matters," in Sebastian Edwards (ed.), *Capital Controls and Capital Flows in Emerging Economies: Policies, Practices and Consequences*, Chicago, IL: University of Chicago Press.

Estevadeordal, Antoni and Alan M. Taylor (2013). "Is the Washington Consensus Dead? Growth, Openness, and the Great Liberalization, 1970s–2000s," *Review of Economics and Statistics* 95(5): 1669–1690.

Etkes, Haggay and Assaf Zimring (2015). "When Trade Stops: Lessons from the Gaza Blockade 2007–2010," *Journal of International Economics* 95: 16–27.

Fajgelbaum, Pablo D, Pinelopi K. Goldberg, Patrick J. Kennedy, and Amit K. Khandelwal (2020). "The Return of Protectionism," *Quarterly Journal of Economics* 135: 1–55.

Feenstra, Robert C. (1988). "Quality Change Under Trade Restraints in Japanese Autos," *Quarterly Journal of Economics* 103(1): 131–146.

Feenstra, Robert C. (2010). "Measuring the Gains from Trade under Monopolistic Competition," *Canadian Journal of Economics* 43(1): 1–28.

Feenstra, Robert C. (2018). "Alternative Sources of the Gains from International Trade: Variety, Creative Destruction, and Markups," *Journal of Economic Perspectives* 32(2): 25–46.

Fernandez, Raquel and Dani Rodrik (1991). "Resistance to Reform: Status Quo Bias in the Presence of Individual-Specific Uncertainty," *American Economic Review* 81(5): 1146–1155.

Feyrer, James (2019). "Trade and Income – Exploiting Time Series in Geography," *American Economic Journal: Applied Economics* 11(4): 1–35.

Flaaen, Aaron, Ali Hortaçsu, and Felix Tintelnot (2020): "The Production Relocation and Price Effects of US Trade Policy: The Case of Washing Machines," *American Economic Review* 110(7): 2103–2127.

Frankel, Jeffrey A. and David Romer (1999). "Does Trade Cause Growth?" *American Economic Review* 89(3): 379–399.

Freund, Caroline and Martha Denisse Pierola (2012). "Export Surges," *Journal of Development Economics* 97(2): 387–395.

Friedberg, Rachel M. and Jennifer Hunt (1995). "The Impact of Immigrants on Host Country Wages, Employment and Growth," *Journal of Economic Perspectives* 9(2): 23–44.

Gandal, Neil, Gordon Hanson, and Matthew Slaughter (2004). "Technology, Trade, and Adjustment to Immigraiton to Israel," *European Economic Review* 48(2): 403–428.

Goldberg, Pinelopi Koujianou, Amit Kumar Khandelwal, Nina Pavcnik, and Petia Topalova (2010). "Imported Intermediate

REFERENCES

Inputs and Domestic Productivity Growth: Evidence from India," *Quarterly Journal of Economics* 125(4): 1727–1767.

Hakobyan, Shushanik and John McLaren (2016). "Looking for Local Labor Market Effects of NAFTA," *Review of Economics and Statistics* 98(4): 728–741.

Hanke, Steve H. and Alex K.F. Kwok (2009). "On the Measurement of Zimbabwe's Hyperinflation," *Cato Journal* 29: 353.

Hannan, Swarnali Ahmed (2018). "Revisiting the Determinants of Capital Flows to Emerging Markets – A Survey of the Evolving Literature," IMF Working Paper No. 18/214, International Monetary Fund, Washington, DC.

Harrison, Ann and Andrés Rodríguez-Clare (2010). "Trade, Foreign Investment, and Industrial Policy for Developing Countries," in Dani Rodrik and Mark Rosenzweig (eds.), *Handbook of Development Economics*, vol 5: 4039–4214.

Hufbauer, Gary Clyde and Sean Lowry (2012). "US Tire Tariffs: Saving Few Jobs at High Cost," Policy Briefs PB12–9, Peterson Institute for International Economics.

Hunt, Jennifer (1992). "The Impact of the 1962 Repatriates from Algeria on the French Labor Market," *Industrial and Labor Relations Review* 45(3): 556–572.

Ilzetzki, Ethan, Enrique G. Mendoza, and Carlos A. Végh (2013). "How Big (Small?) Are Fiscal Multipliers?" *Journal of Monetary Economics* 60(2): 239–254.

Irwin, Douglas A. (1991). "Mercantilism as Strategic Trade Policy: The Anglo-Dutch Rivalry for the East India Trade," *Journal of Political Economy* 99(6): 1296–1314.

Irwin, Douglas A. (2003). "The Optimal Tax on Antebellum Cotton Exports," *Journal of International Economics* 60: 275–291.

Irwin, Douglas A. (2017). *Clashing over Commerce: A History of US Trade Policy*, Chicago, IL: University of Chicago Press.

Irwin, Douglas A. (2020). *Free Trade Under Fire*, 5th edition, Princeton, NJ: Princeton University Press.

Johnson, Harry G. (1970) "A New View of the Infant Industry Argument," in I. A. McDougall and Richard H. Snape (eds.), *Studies in International Economics*, Amsterdam: North-Holland.

Kee, Hiau Looi, Alessandro Nicita, and Marcelo Olarreaga (2008). "Import Demand Elasticities and Trade Distortions," *The Review of Economics and Statistics* 90(4): 666–682.

Kee, Hiau Looi, Alessandro Nicita, and Marcelo Olarreaga (2009). "Estimating Trade Restrictiveness Indices," *Economic Journal* 119(534): 172–199.

Kenen, Peter (1969). "The Theory of Optimum Currency Areas: An Eclectic View" in R. Mundell and A. Swoboda (eds.), *Monetary Problems of the International Economy*, Chicago, IL: University of Chicago Press, 41–60.

Kenen, Peter (1983). "The Role of the Dollar as an International Currency," Occasional Paper No. 13. New York: Group of Thirty.

Kitano, Taiju and Hiroshi Ohashi (2009). "Did US Safeguard Resuscitate Harley Davidson in the 1980s?," *Journal of International Economics* 79: 186–197.

Klein, Michael W. and Jay C. Shambaugh (2015). "Rounding the corners of the policy trilemma: sources of monetary policy autonomy," *American Economic Journal: Macroeconomics* 7(4): 33–66.

Krueger, Anne O. (1974). "The Political Economy of the Rent-Seeking Society," *American Economic Review* 64(3): 291–303.

Krugman, Paul (1979). "A Model of Balance-of-Payments Crises," *Journal of Money, Credit, and Banking* 11: 311–325.

Krugman, Paul (1990). *The Age of Diminished Expectations: U.S. Economic Policy in the 1990s*. Cambridge, MA: MIT Press.

Krugman, Paul (1993). "The Uncomfortable Truth about NAFTA: It's Foreign Policy, Stupid," *Foreign Affairs* 72(5): 13–19.

Krugman, Paul (1994a). "Competitiveness: A Dangerous Obsession," *Foreign Affairs* 73(2): 28–44.

Krugman, Paul (1994b). "Does Third World Growth Hurt First World Prosperity?" *Harvard Business Review*, July–August.

Krugman, Paul (2007). "The Trouble with Trade," *New York Times*, December 28.

Available at: www.nytimes.com/2007/12/28/opinion/28krugman.html.

Krugman, Paul (2008). "Trade and Wages, Reconsidered," *Brookings Papers on Economic Activity*, 103–137.

Lane, Philip R. and Gian Maria Milesi-Ferretti (2018). "The External Wealth of Nations Revisited: International Financial Integration in the Aftermath of the Global Financial Crisis," *IMF Economic Review* 66: 189–222.

Lerner, Abba P. (1936). "The Symmetry between Import and Export Taxes," *Economica* 3(11): 306–613.

Lewis, William (2004). *The Power of Productivity: Wealth, Poverty, and the Threat to Global Stability*, Chicago, IL: University of Chicago Press.

Magee, Stephen P. (1980). Three Simple Tests of the Stolper Samuelson Theorem," in Peter Oppenheimer (ed.), *Issues in International Economics*, Stocksfield: Oriel Press.

Mayda, Anna Maria and Dani Rodrik (2005). "Why Are Some People (and Countries) More Protectionist Than Others?" *European Economic Review* 49(6): 1393–1430.

McKinnon, Ronald I. (1963). "Optimum Currency Areas," *The American Economic Review*, 717–725.

Meese, Richard A. and Kenneth Rogoff (1983). "Empirical Exchange Rate Models of the Seventies: Do They Fit Out of Sample?" *Journal of International Economics* 14(1–2): 3–24.

Melitz, Marc J. and Daniel Trefler (2012). "Gains from Trade When Firms Matter," *Journal of Economic Perspectives* 26(2): 91–118.

Milbank, Dana (1994). "British Customs Officials Consider Mr. Spock Dolls to Be Illegal Aliens," *Wall Street Journal*, August 2, p. B1.

Mill, John Stuart (1848, 1909). *Principles of Political Economy*. London: Longmans.

Mohammad, Sharif and John Whalley (1984). "Rent Seeking in India: Its Costs and Policy Significance," *Kyklos* 37: 387–413.

Mundell, Robert A. (1961). "A Theory of Optimum Currency Areas," *The American Economic Review* 51(4): 657–665.

Obstfeld, Maurice (1995). *The Logic of Currency Crises*, Berlin: Springer.

Obstfeld, Maurice (1996). "Models of Currency Crises with Self-Fulfilling Features," *European Economic Review* 40(3): 1037–1047.

Obstfeld, Maurice and Alan M. Taylor (1997). "The Great Depression as a Watershed: International Capital Mobility in the Long Run," NBER Working Papers No. 5960 (March).

Pavcnik, Nina (2002). "Trade Liberalization, Exit, and Productivity Improvements: Evidence from Chilean Plants," *The Review of Economic Studies* 69(1): 245–276.

Perkins, Dwight (2013). *East Asian Development: Foundations and Strategies*. Cambridge, MA: Harvard University Press.

Price, Debbie M. (2017). "In Appalachia's Foothills, a Leaner Textile Industry Rises," *Undark Magazine*. https://undark.org/2017/02/24/catawba-county-fabric-textile-industry.

Qureshi, Mahvash S., Jonathan D. Ostry, Atish R. Ghosh, and Marcos Chamon (2011). "Managing Capital Inflows: The Role of Capital Controls and Prudential Policies," NBER Working Paper No. 17363.

Radelet, Steven (2016). *The Great Surge: The Ascent of the Developing World*, New York: Simon & Schuster.

Radford, R.A. (1945). "The Economic Organisation of a P.O.W. Camp," *Economica* 12(48): 189–201.

Reich, Robert B. (1991). "Dumpsters: The End of an Unfair Trading Practice," *New Republic*, June 10, 9–10.

Reinhart, Carmen M. and Vincent. R. Reinhart (1998). "Capital Flow Bonanzas: An Encompassing View of the Past and Present," NBER Working Paper No. 14321.

Romalis, John (2004). "Factor Proportions and the Structure of Commodity Trade," *American Economic Review* 94(1): 67–97.

Samuelson, Paul A. (1994). "Facets of Balassa–Samuelson Thirty Years Later," *Review of International Economics* 2(3): 201–226.

Samuelson, Paul A. (2004). "Where Ricardo and Mill Rebut and Confirm Arguments of Mainstream Economists Supporting Globalization," *Journal of Economic Perspectives* 18(3): 135–146.

Scheck, Justin (2008). "Mackerel Economics in Prison Leads to Appreciation for Oily Fillets: Packs of Fish Catch On as Currency, Former Inmates Say; Officials Carp," *Wall Street*

REFERENCES

Journal, October 2, www.wsj.com/articles/SB122290720439096481

Schmitz Jr., James A. (2005). "What Determines Productivity? Lessons from the Dramatic Recovery of the US and Canadian Iron Ore Industries Following Their Early 1980s Crisis," *Journal of Political Economy* 113(3): 582–625.

Smith, James L. (2009). "World Oil: Market or Mayhem?" *Journal of Economic Perspectives* 23(3): 145–164.

Stolper, Wolfgang F. and Paul A. Samuelson (1941). "Protection and Real Wages," *The Review of Economic Studies* 9(1): 58–73.

Topalova, Petia and Amit Khandelwal (2011). "Trade Liberalization and Firm Productivity: The Case of India," *Review of Economics and Statistics* 93(3): 995–1009.

Trefler, Daniel (1993). "International Factor Price Differences: Leontief Was Right!" *Journal of Political Economy* 101(6): 961–987.

Trefler, Daniel (2004). "The Long and Short of the Canada–US Free Trade Agreement," *American Economic Review* 94(4): 870–895.

United Nations Conference on Trade and Development (2003). *Trade and Development Report 2003: Capital Accumulation, Growth, and Structural Change,* New York: UNCTAD.

Wacziarg, Romain and Karen Horn Welch (2008). "Trade Liberalization and Growth: New Evidence," *The World Bank Economic Review* 22(2): 187–231.

Westphal, Larry E. (1990). "Industrial Policy in an Export Propelled Economy: Lessons from South Korea's Experience," *Journal of Economic Perspectives* 4(3): 41–59.

Wu, Jing Cynthia and Fan Dora Xia (2016). "Measuring the Macroeconomic Impact of Monetary Policy at the Zero Lower Bound," *Journal of Money, Credit and Banking* 48(2–3): 253–291.

INDEX

Locators in *italics* refer to figures, however these are not separately indexed when figures are interspersed in principal text discussion.

absolute advantage 51
  vs. comparative advantage 51, 53–55, 57–58
  international factor mobility 107, 111
  Production Possibility Frontier 53–55
accounting
  balance of payments records 241–245
  double-entry accounting 242
  external balance condition 312–314
  financial account and the net international investment position 249–251
  financial and capital account 245–249
  measuring the economy 235–238, 251–252
  saving, investment and the current account 238–241
  see also balance of payments; the current account balance
AD–AS model 351–353
ad valorem taxes 150, 156–157
adaptive expectations 353–354
aggregate demand (AD) 281
  AD–AS model 351–353
  contractionary devaluation 401
  eurozone crisis 429–430
  fiscal policy 304–310
  price level 348–349
  real exchange rate 311
aggregate supply (AS) 350
  AD–AS model 351–353
  contractionary devaluation 401
aggregate supply shocks 426
Airbus 195–203, 367
aircraft market 193–203
American Recovery and Reinvestment Act (ARRA) 421
anchored inflation expectations 355–356
Annual Report on Exchange Arrangements and Exchange Restrictions (AREAER) 262–266

antidumping duties 205–228
appreciation 261
  Balassa–Samuelson effect 382
  flexible prices model 383–384
  foreign exchange market 171
  increase in government spending *327*, 331–332, 334
  leverage 414
  liquidity trap 339
  sticky price model 380, 384
  see also exchange rates
Argentina
  boom–bust cycle 390–391
  exchange rate regime 273–274
  export taxes 166–167
  spread of technologies 105
Asian Financial Crisis 388
assets
  exchange rates and currency trading 259–270
  financial account 238, 245
  net factor income 238
  net international investment position 249–251
austerity 431
Australia
  terms of trade 38
  trade restrictiveness index (TRI) 172–173
autarky 12–16
  absolute and comparative advantage 53–55
  autarky equilibrium and trade 126–131
  comparative advantage 55
  competitive equilibrium under 17–19, *17*
  export taxes 167
  maximizing consumer utility 17
  Pareto improvement 43–44
  as self-sufficiency 12
  static versus dynamic gains from trade 40–42
  trade with the rest of the world 19–23
  utility possibility frontier 44
  world relative prices 58–59

automobile industry
  market-size effects 129
  monopolistic competition 127, 128
  product variety 133–135
  tariff engineering 152
  in the US 123–124
autonomous spending 282, 283–287
  see also government spending
average cost (AC), monopolistic competition 123–126, 146–147, 148
average revenue (AR), monopolistic competition 123–126

balance of payments
  as account of international transactions 241–245
  China 250–251
  the current account balance 242–245
  emerging market crises 402–409, 403–404
  following Brexit 345–347
  overall balance of payments 247
  responding to deficits 317–319
balance of payments identity 241–242, 312–314
balance sheet channel 401
balanced budget multiplier 284–287
balanced trade 35–36
Balassa–Samuelson effect 382
Baldwin, Robert 178–192
banking
  capital controls 268
  China's current account surpluses 319–320
  currency trading 259–270
  eurozone crisis 424–425, 433–434
  financial sector modeling 304–309
  global financial crisis (2008) 413, 420–421
  global financial linkages 419
  leverage and liquidity 414, 415–417
  monetary policy autonomy 325–326

INDEX

money base 315
negative interest rates 340–341
run on the bank 393
shadow banking sector 417
bankruptcy
   Harley-Davidson motorbikes 227–228
   Lehman Brothers and the 2008 crisis 413, 418, 419
beer industry 129
beggar-thy-neighbor policy 183, 195, 219
Berlin Wall, reunification of Germany 118–119
Big Mac pricing example 382–383
bilateral exchange rate 270, 272
bilateral trade agreements 215, 216–219
blue-collar workers
   impact of price change 81
   income distribution 79–80, 87–88, 90–95
   international factor mobility 113–114
   labor mobility 113–114
   mobile factors model 83–87, 88, 90–95, 114–116
   Pareto improvement 45, 88
   production function 73–76
   Rust Belt 45, 325–326, 332–333
   specific factors model 74, 75, 82–83, 90–95
   US job losses 218, 325–326
Boeing 195–203, 367
bonds
   collateralized debt obligations 415
   exchange risk premium 269–270
   hyperinflation in Zimbabwe 372–373
   IS–LM model 305–306
   modeling the financial sector 304–309
   monetary policy effectiveness 310–311, 338–341
   sterilization 393
   understanding how busts happen 396–400
booms
   boom–bust cycle 390–391
   how to manage 391–396
   see also emerging market crises
BP = 0 curve
   capital mobility 316
   capital mobility – perfect 334
   China's current account surplus 319–320
   devaluation 400–402

fiscal policy 327
managing booms 391–392, 394
monetary policy 327–328
price level 348–350
the trade balance 304–313
understanding how busts happen 396–400
Bretton Woods system 336, 337–338
Brexit 345–347
Britain see United Kingdom
the budget constraint (consumers) 15–16, 20–21
busts
   understanding how busts happen 396–400
   see also emerging market crises; recessions

Canada
   autarky equilibrium and trade 130–131
   productivity gains from foreign competition 140–144
   shakeout effect 131–132
capital
   international factor mobility 99–113
   Production Possibility Frontier 12–14
   in the specific factors model 74–82
the capital account 238
   balance of payments 241–245
   statistical discrepancy 248–249
   of the US 245–249
capital controls 268, 317, 394–396
capital flow bonanzas 390–391
   managing booms 391–396
capital mobility
   eurozone crisis 429–430
   fiscal policy 316
   monetary policy 316–317
   perfect capital mobility 334–335
   summarizing policy effects 329–333
   surges and reversals 390–391
capital structure mismatch 403–404
Card, David 116
Central American Free Trade Agreement (CAFTA) 208–209
central bank liabilities 315
central banks
   currency crises 388–389
   European Central Bank (ECB) 341, 367, 424–425
   global financial crisis (2008) 420–421

Chile
   productivity gains from foreign competition 141
   trade policy 171
China
   absolute and comparative advantage 51–55
   balance of payments 250–251
   communism under Mao 28, 47, 207
   comparative advantage and the gains from trade 55–58
   distribution of income 80–82
   economic growth 62–63
   exchange rate regime 262–266, 319–320
   impact of the "China Shock" on imports 95
   industrial policies 198–200
   infant industry protection 192–203
   the multi-good Ricardo model 64–69
   opening up of the economy 28, 207
   opportunity cost 52–53
   Production Possibility Frontier 53–55
   relationship to world trade 27–28
   wages and productivity 59–63
Clemens, Michael 99–103, 117
closed economy 235–237
   monetary policy 328
   Mundell–Fleming model 313–314
clothing sector
   the budget constraint 15–16
   competitive equilibrium 17–19
   consumption and trade 20–21
   gains from trade 11–12
   import tariffs 151–152
   indifference curves 14–15
   maximizing consumer utility 17
   the multi-good Ricardo model 64–69
   Nike shoes 67–69
   production and trade 20
collateralized debt obligations 415
common currency 425
   see also Euro area, formally known as Economic and Monetary Union (EMU)
communism
   Maoist China 28, 47, 207
   reunification of Germany 118–119
comparative advantage 51–52
   vs. absolute advantage 51, 53–55, 57–58

comparative advantage (cont.)
  gains from trade 55–58
  international factor mobility 107, 111
  the multi-good Ricardo model 64–69
  opportunity cost 52–53
  Production Possibility Frontier 53–55
  wages and productivity 59–63
compensation
  Pareto improvement 43–44
  utility possibility frontier under autarky 44
  utility possibility frontier with trade 44–46
competition
  between countries 63
  exporting firms 136–139
  import-competing firms 139–140
  market-size effects 128–129
  productivity gains from foreign competition 140–144
  see also monopolistic competition
competitive equilibrium
  under autarky 17–19, 17
  autarky and trade 19–23
Concorde case study 193–203
cone of diversification 115–116
consumer preferences
  benefits of market integration 132
  the budget constraint 15–16
  product variety 133–135
  utility function 14–15
consumer price index (CPI)
  oil prices 358–362
  real exchange rate 272
  real wage 37
consumer surplus 27–28
  export subsidies 164, 165–166
  export taxes 166, 167
  import quotas 160
  import tariffs 152–154, 191
  infant industry protection 191
  OPEC welfare 181–182
  trade agreements 217–218
consumer utility
  maximizing 17
  variety gains from trade 133–135
consumption
  deadweight losses 154
  gains from trade 21–23, 55–58
  marginal propensity to consume 282
  measuring the economy 237
  mobile factors model 85–87
  Pareto improvement 43–44
  specific factors model 77, 82
  and trade 20–21
  trade policy 169–170
  utility possibility frontier 44–46
consumption function 282
consumption taxes
  comparison to import tariff 185–186, 188
  equivalency of trade policy and domestic policies 154–155
  and export subsidies 166
contingent liabilities see government liabilities
contractionary devaluation 400–402, 430
contractionary shocks 430
copper market, Zambia 38
Corn Laws 73–83, 213
countervailing duties 220–221, 225–226
covered interest parity (CIP) 268
CPI see consumer price index
credit default swaps 417
credit ratings 415
crises see emerging market crises; recessions
crowding out 310
currencies
  dollars as international currency 257–259
  economic motivations and challenges of forming the European currency union 425–428
  IS–LM model 305–309
  revaluation 393–394
  stability of currency value 304–305
  variability in value 8, 270
  see also exchange rates
currency crises 388–389
  see also emerging market crises
currency devaluation see devaluation
currency mismatch 403–406
currency trading
  balance of payments deficits 317–319
  dollars as international currency 257–259
  and exchange rates 259–270
  supply and demand 259–261
currency union 425
  see also Euro area, formally known as Economic and Monetary Union (EMU)
the current account balance
  of China 250–251, 319–320
  in deficit 249–251
  eurozone deficits 428
  external balance condition 312–314
  measuring the economy 238–241
  subcategories 242–245
  of the US 242–245
customs unions 215–216

Davis, Donald 90
deadweight losses
  arguments for trade intervention 179
  consumption 154
  import demand 149–156
  production 153–154
  tariffs for revenue 185–186
  trade policy 172–173
debt forgiveness 248
deindustrialization 45, 325–326, 332–333
demand
  competition between countries 63
  of foreign currencies 259–261
  Keynesian cross model 280–284
  monopolistic competition 123–126
  spillover effects of fiscal policy 293–297
  tariffs and quotas 161–163
demand curve
  exporting firms 133–138
  import tariffs 155–156
  monopolistic competition 126, 128–132
  optimal tariff 181–203
  partial equilibrium 23–27
  producer and consumer surplus 27
  terms of trade 58–59
demand side
  AD–AS model 351–353
  aggregate demand 281
  money market 308
  price level 348–350
democracies
  evolution of US trade policy 209–213
  policymaking in 207–209
denominated stocks 255
depreciation 260, 269–270
  currency mismatch 403–406
  following Brexit 345–347
  Mexican Peso crisis 407–409
  monetary policy 328
  see also exchange rates
devaluation
  to achieve full employment 362–363
  contractionary 400–402, 430

full employment 362–363
  increase in GDP 290
  internal 362
  Mexican Peso crisis 408–409
  real exchange rate 292–293, 312
  responding to balance of payments deficits 317–319
  understanding how busts happen 398
  why is devaluation contractionary? 400–402
developed countries
  capital mobility 103–104
  exporting firms 136
  global financial crisis (2008) 413, 417, 418–419
  interest rate parity 268
  trade policy 172–177
  trade restrictiveness index 172–173
developing countries
  Asian Financial Crisis 388
  capital mobility 103–104
  exporting firms 136
  foreign assets 401
  global financial crisis (2008) 413, 419–420
  trade policy 172–177, 401
  trade restrictiveness index 172–173
  see also emerging market crises
differentiated products 124–125
  see also product variety
discriminatory tariff reduction 216–219
distribution of income *see* income distribution
distribution of trade
  Pareto improvement 43–44
  utility possibility frontier under autarky 44
  utility possibility frontier with trade 44–46
dollar exchange rate 272–274
dollars in international currency trading 257–259
domestic assets 315
domestic consumption
  pattern of trade 85–87
  small country assumption 18–19
  and trade 20–21
domestic production
  pattern of trade 85–87
  small country assumption 18–19
  and trade 20–21
Dornbusch–Frankel model 377–378
double-entry accounting 242

dumping
  antidumping duties 205–228
  countervailing duties 225–226
  predatory pricing 223
  price discrimination 223–224
  trade law on 223–225
duopoly 195
dynamic gains from trade 39–42, 46–47

early warning systems 406
  see also the future
East Asian Miracle 192–193, 388
Economic and Monetary Union (EMU) 337–338
economic downturn (2008) *see* global financial crisis (2008)
economic integration
  economic motivations and challenges of forming a monetary union 425–428
  firm effects 131–132, 136–139
  globalization 3–4
  international trade 7–8
  lead-up to the Euro 424–425
  monopolistic competition 130–131
  reunification of Germany 118–119
economic unions 216
  see also Euro area
economic welfare *see* welfare
economies of scale
  industrial policies 198–200
  market-size effects 128–129
  monopolistic competition 128–132, 146–148
  product variety 124–125
the economy
  balance of payments 241–245
  financial account and the net international investment position 249–251
  financial and capital account 245–249
  measuring 235–238, 251–252
  relationship between government budget and trade balances 287–288
  saving, investment and the current account balance 238–241
  see also emerging market crises; global financial crisis (2008); recessions
education levels *see* blue-collar workers; white-collar workers
effective exchange rate index 270
effective rate of protection 156–157

Egypt
  Suez Canal 40–41
  trade intermediaries 22
elasticity of demand
  arguments for trade intervention 180–181
  import tariffs 155–156
  oil prices 184–185
elasticity of exports/imports 293
elasticity of substitution 134–135
electronics market 65
emerging market crises 388–390
  balance sheet effects 402–409
  capital surges and reversals 390–391
  managing booms 391–396
  Mexican Peso crisis 407–409
  understanding how busts happen 396–400
  why is devaluation contractionary? 400–402
  see also recessions
employment
  impact of trade on 35
  international mobility 100–103
  regional mobility 100
  tariffs to increase 186
  US 2017 tax cuts 325–326
  see also blue-collar workers; full employment; labor; wages; white-collar workers
endogenous variables 282
equilibrium exchange rate 259–261, 317
equilibrium output
  AD–AS model 351–353
  Keynesian cross model 280–284
  see also general equilibrium; partial equilibrium
equilibrium price
  comparative advantage 55–58
  competitive equilibrium 17–23, 17
  number of firms 147–148
escape clauses 226–229
Euro area, formally known as Economic and Monetary Union (EMU)
  economic motivations and challenges of forming a monetary union 425–428
  impact of the 2008 global financial crisis on the eurozone 295–297, 428–433
  interest rate shocks 328–329
  lead-up to the Euro 424–425
European Central Bank (ECB) 341, 367, 424–425
European Economic Community (EEC) 215–216, 424

European Union (EU)
  Airbus subsidies 195–203
  Brexit 345–347
  intra-Europe exchange rates (prior to common currency) 424–425
  public debt 433
eurozone crisis 428–433
  incomplete recovery 433–434
exchange rate, determinants of 367–368
  monetary approach with flexible prices 369–374
  monetary approach with flexible prices – model accuracy 374–375
  real models of the real exchange rate 380–383
  sticky price model – evidence for 378–380
  sticky prices 375–378
exchange rate pegs
  capital controls 395–396
  rise in foreign interest rates 397–398
  supply and demand 261
  see also fixed exchange rate regimes
exchange rate policy 171, 311
  see also fixed exchange rate regimes; floating exchange rate regimes
exchange rate stability
  advantages and tradeoffs 304–305, 336
  definition 337
  International Trilemma 335–338
exchange rates 255–256
  currency supply and demand 259–261
  and currency trading 259–270
  eurozone crisis 429–430
  external balance condition 312–314
  hybrid floating and fixed regimes 262–266
  real value of a single currency 272–274
  relationship to interest rates 266–270
  trade interconnectedness 8
  value of a single currency 270
  see also fixed exchange rate regimes; floating exchange rate regimes; real exchange rate
exchange risk premium 269–270
exogenous variables 281–282
expectations-augmented Phillips curve 353–354

expenditure approach, measuring the economy 236, 237
expenditure reduction 290–293
expenditure switching 290–293
export subsidies
  countervailing duties 225–226
  the large country case 194–195
  strategic trade policy 193–203
  trade policy analysis 163–167
export supply
  arguments for trade intervention 180–181
  partial equilibrium 25
  value of world exports 5–6
export taxes 166–167
  arguments for trade intervention 179
  arguments for trade intervention – terms of trade 179–185
  in general equilibrium 170–172
  Lerner Symmetry Theorem 170, 171–172
  optimal tariff 181–203
  prohibitive 167
  rare earth minerals market 178
exports
  absolute and comparative advantage 51
  balanced trade 35–36
  comparative advantage 55–58
  dominated by a single commodity 37–38
  exchange rates 292–293
  exporting firms 136–139
  measuring the economy 237
  mercantilist view 34–35
  mobile factors model 83–84
  spillover effects of fiscal policy 293–297
  terms of trade 36–39
external economies of scale 198–200
externalities, use of tariffs to correct 186–188

factor intensity 85
factor price equalization 116
factors of production
  empirical evidence on trade and factor endowments 88–90
  empirical evidence on trade and income 90–95
  models overview 95–96
  Production Possibility Frontier 12–14, 74–77
  quantity of goods 12–14

  and trade 73–74, 88–90
  see also international factor mobility; mobile factors model; specific factors model
fair-trade laws 205–223
Fed funds rate 358–359
feedback loops 414–415, 417–418
Feyrer, James 23
final goods and services 236
finance
  globalization of 3–4
  growth of international finance 7–9
  see also financial markets
the financial account 238
  external balance condition 312–314
  net international investment position 249–251
  total financial account 238, 249–251
  of the US 245–249
financial integration, International Trilemma 335–338
  see also economic integration
financial markets
  currency supply and demand 259–261
  currency trading 259–270
  dollars as international currency 258–259
  global financial crisis (2008) 413, 415, 420–421
  global financial linkages 419
  IS–LM model 304–309
firms
  infant industry protection 189–203
  in international trade 135–142
  market-size effects 128–129
  monopolistic competition 125–127
  shakeout effect 131–132
first–best policy 185
first mover advantage 196
fiscal policy
  at cross purposes with monetary policy 331–333
  global financial crisis (2008) 421, 430
  IS–LM model 304–310, 314–316, 326–327
  policymaking 304–310
  price level 351–352
  spillover effects 293–297
  see also government spending
fiscal union 426
  see also Euro area, formally known as Economic and Monetary Union (EMU)

INDEX

fixed exchange rate regimes 261–262
  China's current account surpluses 319–320
  the end of the fixed exchange rate system 8–9
  external balance condition 312–314
  hybrid floating and fixed regimes 262–266
  perfect capital mobility 334–335
  policy options 314–320
  price level 362–363
  stability of currency value 304–305
  summarizing policy effects 329–333
  understanding how busts happen 397
Fleming, Marcus 313
flexible price monetary model 369–374
  accuracy of 374–375, 379–380
  appreciation and depreciation 383–384
  compared to sticky prices 375–378
  long run 374, 386–387
floating exchange rate regimes
  definition 260, 261
  fiscal policy 326–327
  hybrid floating and fixed regimes 262–266
  interest rate shocks 328–329
  monetary policy 327–328
  perfect capital mobility 334
  summarizing policy effects 329–333
food sector
  the budget constraint 15–16
  competitive equilibrium 17–19
  consumption and trade 20–21
  free trade and the Corn Laws 73–83, 213
  gains from trade 11–12
  indifference curves 14–15
  maximizing consumer utility 17
  production and trade 20
  US sugar policy 149–150, 156–157, 159, 205–211
foreign assets
  currency devaluation 401
  financial account 245
  net international investment position 249–251
foreign direct investment (FDI) 245
foreign exchange prices 257–258
  see also exchange rates

foreign exchange reserves (FXRes) 242, 247–248, 315, 392–393
forward exchange rate 260, 268
France
  Algerian immigration 118
  Concorde case study 193–203
  unit labor cost 430
Frankel, Jeffrey 23, 259, 377
free trade
  arguments for and against trade intervention 179, 185–189
  compared to import tariffs scenario 162, 164, 170
  democratic policymaking 207–209
  gains from 22, 108
  infant industry protection as exception 189–190
  mobile factors model 94–95, 111
  productivity effects 140–144
  public opinion and democratic policymaking 207–209
  in the real world 150
  small and large countries 182–203
  specific factors model 73–83
free trade agreements (FTAs)
  Central American (CAFTA) 208–209
  definition 215
  North American (NAFTA) 46–47, 207, 215, 218–219
  types of 215–216
full employment
  currency devaluation 362–363
  fiscal and monetary policy 331–333
  supply side 349–350
the future
  exchange rate expectations 371–372
  inflation expectations 348, 353–356
  predicting emerging market crises 406–407
  predicting exchange rates 379–380

gains from trade 11–12, 21–23
  autarky economy trading with the rest of the world 19–23
  comparative advantage 55–58
  does everyone benefit? 43–47
  empirical evidence on trade and income 23
  mercantilist view 34–35
  static versus dynamic gains 39–42, 46–47

terms of trade 36–39
variety gains from trade for consumers 133–135
game theory 196
Gaza Strip, Israeli blockade 41–42
General Agreement on Tariffs and Trade (GATT) 219–221
  fair-trade laws 205–223
  as multilateral agreement 215
  Uruguay Round 221
general equilibrium
  export taxes 170–172
  import tariffs 167–172
  as microeconomic analysis 24
Germany
  exchange risk premium 269–270
  reunification of 118–119
  spread of technologies 105
  unit labor cost 430
global financial crisis (2008)
  the crisis goes global 418–420
  eurozone crisis 428–433
  impact on GDP 413, 418–419
  origins in the US 414–418
  policy response 420–421
  spillover and spillback effects 295–297
  US stimulus plan 279–280
globalization 3–4
  financial linkages 419
  global nature of 2008 crisis 418–420
  growth of international finance 7–9
  and inequality 93
  thinking about trade 4–7
goods/services
  demand as a function of income 281–282
  exchange rates 255–256
  measuring the economy 236
  real exchange rate 272, 380–382
government debt, eurozone crisis 430–431
government goods, measuring the economy 237
government intervention *see* trade intervention, arguments for
government liabilities
  currency mismatch 403–406
  emerging market crises 398–400
  eurozone crisis 428, 429, 430–431
  eurozone crisis – incomplete recovery 433–434
  global financial crisis (2008) 417
  hidden 429
  solvency 398–400, 403–404

government policymaking *see* policymaking
government spending
  accounting practices 240–241
  affect on income 284–287
  exogenous variables 281–282
  fiscal policy 293–297, 304–310, 326–327
  global financial crisis (2008) 279–280, 431
  relationship between government budget and trade balances 287–288
Great Depression (1930s) 219
  see also global financial crisis (2008)
Greece, eurozone crisis 428
gross domestic product (GDP)
  China' relationship to trade 28
  definition 237
  eurozone crisis 430
  financial flows 391
  global financial crisis (2008) 413, 418–419
  impact of government spending and taxation 284–287
  international trade 5–6
  measuring the economy 236–237, 239
  potential GDP 349–350
  relationship between government budget and trade balances 287–288
  reunification of Germany 118–119
  static versus dynamic gains from trade 42
  technology and labor 13
  trade policy 171
Gross National Income (GNI) 236
Gross National Product (GNP)
  the closed economy 237
  measuring the economy 239
  the open economy 237

Harley-Davidson motorbikes 227–228
Heckscher–Ohlin theorem 83–84, 87–88, 90
historical context
  China in world trade 27–28
  evolution of US trade policy 209–213
  mercantilism 34–35
  multilateral trade agreements 219–222
  static versus dynamic gains from trade 40–42
  unilateral tariff reductions 213

house prices, global financial crisis (2008) 414–415, 417–418
Hunt, Jennifer 118
hyperinflation 372–373

immigration
  economic and cultural issues 99–100
  empirical evidence on immigration and wages 116–118
  gains from international labor mobility 100–103
import demand
  arguments for trade intervention 180–181
  partial equilibrium 24
import quotas
  non-equivalence of tariffs and quotas 161–163
  trade policy analysis 159–163
import tariffs
  arguments for trade intervention 179
  under Donald Trump's presidency 157–177
  evolution of US trade policy 209–213
  general equilibrium 167–172
  infant industry protection 189–203
  Lerner Symmetry Theorem 170, 171–172
  non-equivalence of tariffs and quotas 161–163
  partial equilibrium 150–177
  tariff engineering 152
  tariffs for revenue 185–186
  terms of trade 183–184
  unilateral tariff reductions 213
  welfare effects 155–156, 216–219
imports
  absolute and comparative advantage 51
  balanced trade 35–36
  comparative advantage 55–58
  determinants of the patterns of trade 51
  diversified array of goods 37–38
  and efficiency 50–72
  exchange rates 292–293
  impact of the "China Shock" 95
  import-competing firms 139–140
  marginal propensity to import 282
  measuring the economy 237
  mercantilist view 34–35
  the multi-good Ricardo model 64–69

specific factors model 73–83
spillover effects of fiscal policy 293–297
sugar policy 149–150, 156–157
terms of trade 36–39
the income approach, measuring the economy 237
income (consumers)
  effects of labor mobility 99–103
  evidence on trade and income distribution 90–95
  financial sector modeling 304–309
  fixed-rate regimes 314–316
  impact of government spending and taxation 284–287
  Keynesian cross model 280–284
  mobile factors model 87–88
  Penn Effect 382–383
  real wage 37
  specific factors model 77–83
income distribution
  between capital-owners, blue- and white-collar workers 79–80, 87–88, 90–95
  mobile factors model 87–88, 90–95
  specific factors model 77–83, 90–95
income (national)
  empirical evidence on trade and income 23
  gains from trade 21–23
  static versus dynamic gains from trade 42
  trade policy 149–169
  see also gross domestic product (GDP)
income sensitivity of money demand 308
India
  balance of payments crisis 213
  diffusion of technology 106
  economic growth 62–63
  gains from trade 135
  rent seeking 173–177
indifference curves 14–15
  maximizing consumer utility 17
  product variety 133
  role of trade 34
  variety gains from trade for consumers 133–135
industrial policy 198–200
inequality
  and globalization 93
  in wages 90–92
  see also income distribution
infant industry protection 189–203

INDEX

inflation
  allowing the price level to change 347–348
  expectations and the price level 348, 353–356
  hyperinflation in Zimbabwe 372–373
  oil prices 358–362
insolvency
  currency mismatch 403–406
  eurozone crisis 429
  global financial crisis (2008) 420–421
  high-leverage banks 416
  interconnectedness 417
inter-industry trade 124
interest rate defense 304–318
interest rate parity 268
interest rate shocks 328–329
interest rates
  fiscal policy 304–310
  International Trilemma 337–338
  IS–LM model 305–309
  monetary policy 304, 310–311
  negative rates 340–341
  relationship to exchange rates 266–270
  responding to balance of payments deficits 317–319
  tax policy 414–415
  understanding how busts happen 396–400, 407–409
interest sensitivity of money demand 308
intermediaries *see* trade intermediaries
internal devaluation 362
international currency, the dollar as 257–259
  see also exchange rates
international factor mobility
  empirical evidence on immigration and wages 116–118
  gains from international capital and technology mobility 103–106
  gains from international labor mobility 100–103
  immigration 99–100
  mobile factors model 114–116
  reunification of Germany 118–119
  Ricardo model 100–111
  specific factors model 111–114
international finance 7–9
International Monetary Fund (IMF)
  the end of the fixed exchange rate system 8–9

exchange rate regimes 262–266
  Mexican Peso crisis 409
international shipping 6–7
international trade
  China' relationship to 27–28
  competition between countries 63
  controversies and unease about 5–7
  emerging market crises 402–409
  firms in 135–142
  interconnectedness and finance 7–8
  mercantilism 34–35
  role in the global financial crisis (2008) 419–420
  terms of trade 36–39
  trade barriers 6
  transport costs 6–7
  utility possibility frontier 44–46
International Trade Commission (ITC) 224–226
  escape clauses 226
International Trilemma 335–338
  empirical evidence 337–338
intervention *see* trade intervention, arguments for
intra-industry trade 124
  monopolistic competition 125–127
  product differentiation and economies of scale 124–125
investment
  IS–LM model 305–309
  measuring the economy 237, 238–241
  net international investment position 249–251
  relationship between government budget and trade balances 288
Ireland
  current account 245
  eurozone crisis 428–431
  unit labor cost 430
iron ore industry 140–144
IS curve 307
IS–LM–BP model *see* Mundell–Fleming model
IS–LM model 305–309
  balance of payments deficits 317–319
  exchange rate policy 311
  fiscal policy 304–310, 314–316, 326–327
  interest rate shocks 328–329
  monetary policy 310–311, 316–317, 327–328
  policy options under fixed exchange rates 314–320

price level 348–350, 352–353
  relative magnitudes of policy effects 311–312
Israel
  blockade of the Gaza Strip 41–42
  immigration of Soviet Jews 118
  trade intermediaries 22

J-curve (trade balance) 293
Japan
  absolute and comparative advantage 57–58
  exchange risk premium 269–270
  historic economic isolation 40
  real exchange rate 380–383
  spread of technologies 105

Keynesian cross model 280–284
Knight, Phil 67–69
Korea
  Asian Financial Crisis 388
  cross-border exposure 402
  floating exchange rate 397
Krugman, Paul
  competition between countries 63
  currency crises 398
  wages and productivity 61–62
  wages and trade 90–91, 92

labor
  absolute and comparative advantage 51–52, 57–58
  "China Shock" 95
  comparative advantage and the gains from trade 55–58
  eurozone crisis 430
  evidence on trade and income distribution 90–95
  international factor mobility 93–95, 100–103, 113–114
  mobile factors model 85–87, 93–95
  opportunity cost 52–53
  Production Possibility Frontier 12–14, 53–55
  productivity gains from foreign competition 140–144
  Ricardo model 64–69, 100–111
  specific factors model 74–77, 93–95
  unit labor cost 64–65, 430
  wages and productivity 59–63
  see also employment; wages
land, as factor of production 12–14, 74
Law of One Price 369
legal context *see* trade laws
Lehman Brothers bank 413, 418

INDEX

Lerner Symmetry Theorem 170, 171–172
leverage 414
  global financial crisis (2008) 415–417
Lewis, Ethan 117
Libor (London Inter-Bank Offered Rate) *418*, 418
liquidity 308
  global financial crisis (2008) 415–417, 420–421
  liquidity crisis 416–417
  liquidity trap 338–339
  see also IS–LM model
logrolling 211
long run
  exchange rates and sticky prices 376–380
  flexible price monetary model 374, 386–387
  import tariffs and export taxes 184–185
  monetary policy 353
  price level 351–352, 353
  real exchange rate 380–383
long term portfolio investment 245–247
lump-sum taxes 282, 286

macroeconomics 7–9
Magee, Stephen P. 94–95
magnification effect 372
manufactured goods
  blue-collar vs. white-collar workers 45
  Brexit 346–347
  in China and India 62–63
  evolution of US trade policy 209–213
  exchange rates 255–256
  export taxes 179–180
  exporting firms 136–139
  infant industry protection 192–193
  trade restrictiveness index (TRI) 172–173
  US job losses 218, 325–326
marginal costs (MC)
  exporting firms 137–144
  monopolistic competition 147–148
  tariffs and quotas 162–177
marginal products of labor 101–103
marginal propensity to consume 282, 420
marginal propensity to import 282, 294, 420

marginal rate of substitution (MRS) 15
  under autarky 17–20
  indifference curves 17
marginal rate of transformation (MRT) 13
  under autarky 17–20
  indifference curves 17
marginal revenue (MR)
  exporting firms 133–137
  monopolistic competition 123–126, 147–148
marginal value product of capital 77–80, 82, 113–114
market-size effects 128–129
  monopolistic competition 148
Marshall–Lerner–Robinson condition 293
maturity mismatch 403–404
measuring the economy 235–238, 251–252
  balance of payments 241–245
  financial account and the net international investment position 249–251
  financial and capital account 245–249
  relationship between government budget and trade balances 287–288
  saving, investment and the current account balance 238–241
median voter theorem 207–208
Meese, Richard 379–380
mercantilism
  historical context 34–35
  as strategic trade policy 198–203
Mexico
  absolute and comparative advantage 107
  labor mobility 108–110
  Peso crisis 407–409
  technology mobility 99–108
microeconomics, partial and general equilibrium 23–28
Mill, John Stuart 111, 189–190
misalignment, currency value 383
mobile factors model 83–87
  evidence on trade and factor endowments 88–90
  evidence on trade and income distribution 90–95
  income distribution in 87–88
  international factor mobility 114–116
  policymaking 208
mobile factors of production 74

monetary autonomy 317, 335–338
monetary policy
  at cross purposes with fiscal policy 331–333
  global financial crisis (2008) 421
  IS–LM model 310–311, 316–317, 327–328
  limits to effectiveness 317, 338–341
  Mundell–Fleming model 313–314
  price level 352–356
  US 2017 tax cuts 325–326
money 304–309
money base 315
money demand 308
  exchange rate linked to 369–374
  fiscal policy 304–310
  income sensitivity 308
  interest sensitivity 308
money supply 307–317
  exchange rate linked to 369–374
  flexible prices model 383–384
  monetary policy 310–311, 316–317, 328
  price level 353
monopolistic competition 124–128
  in algebraic terms 146–148
  dumping and antidumping duties 223–225
  economies of scale 128–132, 146–148
  market-size effects 128–129
  and trade 128–132
monopsony power 183–184
mortgage backed securities (MBSs) 415, 418–420, 421
most-favored nation (MFN) 219–221
multilateral trade agreements 215, 219–222
multipliers
  equilibrium income level 283
  government spending 285, 302–303, 309
Mundell–Fleming model 313–314
Mundell, Robert 313

national income accounting 235–237
National Saving Identity 240
national security
  government spending on 188–189
  restricting imports 205–222, 227–228
negative externalities 186–187
negative interest rates 340–341

INDEX

net exports 288, 290
  see also trade balance
net factor income 237, 238
net international investment
  position (NIIP) 249–251
net unilateral transfers 237
Nigeria, infant industry protection
  178–193
Nike shoes 67–69
no-arbitrage condition 267
nominal rate of protection 156–157
non-discriminatory tariff reduction
  216–219
nontradable goods 380–382
North American Free Trade
  Agreement (NAFTA)
  a "bad deal"? 218–219
  as Pareto improvement 46–47
  policymaking 207
  rules of origin 215

Obama, Barack
  global financial crisis (2008)
    279–280
  import tariffs 158–159
official reserves transactions *247*
  balance of payments identity
    241–242
  external balance condition
    312–314
  overall balance of payments 247
  total financial account 238
  in the US *247*, 247
oil prices
  arguments for trade intervention
    178–203
  gains from trade 38
  inflation in the US 358–362
open economy
  measuring the economy 237–238
  monetary policy 328
  Mundell–Fleming model
    313–314
open economy macroeconomics 7–9
open market operations 315
opportunity cost
  comparative advantage 52–53
  IS–LM model 306
  world prices 21–22
optimal currency area 426
  see also Euro area, formally known
    as Economic and Monetary
    Union (EMU)
optimal tariff 181–203
Organization of Petroleum
  Exporting Countries (OPEC)
  absolute and comparative
    advantage 57–58

arguments for trade intervention
  178–203
export subsidy scenario 194–195
gains from trade 38
"original sin" 406
output
  AD–AS model 351–353
  demand side 348–349
  expectations-augmented Phillips
    curve 353–354
  externalities 186–188
  fiscal policy 304–310, 314–316,
    331–333
  as a function of capital 74–77
  Keynesian cross model 280–284
  marginal revenue 133–137
  monetary policy 338–341
  oil prices 358–362
  price level 347–348, 354–356
  production possibility frontiers
    12–14
  quotas and tariffs 162–163
  spillover and spillback effects
    295–297
  supply side 349–350
output gap 348, 358–360
over the counter, currency trading
  257
overall balance of payments 247
overshooting model 376

Pareto improvement 43–44
  dynamic gains from trade
    46–47
  mobile factors model 88
  specific factors model 81
  utility possibility frontier 44–46
partial equilibrium 23–28
  exchange rates 292–293
  import tariffs 150–177
  as microeconomic analysis 24
Penn Effect 382–383
perfect capital mobility 334, 336,
  429–430
perfect competition
  cost of production 64–65
  demand curve 126
  Stolper–Samuelson theorem 88
peso exchange rate 273–274
Phillips curve 350
  inflation expectations 353–354
  supply shocks 356–362
policymaking
  exchange rate policy 311
  exchange rate regimes 262–266
  expenditure reduction or
    switching 290–293
  fiscal policy 293–297, 304–310

fixed exchange rate regimes
  314–320
global financial crisis (2008)
  420–421
monetary policy 310–311
trade politics 206–209
  see also trade policy analysis
polluter pays 187
portfolio investment 245–247
Portugal, eurozone crisis 430–431,
  433
positive externalities 187
positive-sum game 5
Postel, Hannah 117
potential GDP 349–350
PPF *see* production possibility
  frontier
PPP *see* purchasing power parity
predatory pricing 223
predictions *see* the future
preferential tariff reduction 216–219
price
  comparative advantage 51–52,
    55–58
  distribution of income 80–82
  export subsidies and taxes
    163–167
  import tariffs 151–152
  market integration 132
  monopolistic competition 126
  producer and consumer surplus
    27–28
  product variety 133–135
  Russia's invasion of Ukraine 33–34
  single commodity exports 37–38
  see also relative price
price discrimination 223–224
price level
  AD–AS model 351–353
  adjustment under fixed exchange
    rates 362–363
  allowing the price level to change
    347–348
  demand and supply sides
    348–350
  following Brexit 345–347
  inflation expectations 348,
    353–356
  supply shocks 356–362
primary income, the current
  account 243
private financial account 238,
  241–242, *247*
producer surplus 27–28
  export subsidies *164*, 165–166
  export taxes *166*, 167
  import quotas 160
  import tariffs 152–154, 191

product variety
  differentiated products and economies of scale 124–125
  market-size effects 128–129
  variety gains from trade for consumers 133–135
production
  absolute and comparative advantage 53–55
  comparative advantage and the gains from trade 55–58
  deadweight losses 153–154
  measuring the economy 237
  mercantilist view 34–35
  mobile factors model 85–87
  social costs 187–188
  specific factors model 74–77
  trade policy 149–169
  see also factors of production
production possibility frontier (PPF) 12–14, 13
  absolute and comparative advantage 53–55
  under autarky 20
  the budget constraint 15–16
  factors of production 12–14, 74–77
  full employment 35
  indifference curves 14–15
  international factor mobility 99–110
  role of trade 20–23, 34
  trade policy 149–169
productivity
  absolute and comparative advantage 51–52
  competition between countries 63
  effects of labor mobility 99–103
  foreign competition 140–144
  the multi-good Ricardo model 64–69
  opportunity cost 52–53
  Production Possibility Frontier 53–55
  real exchange rate 382
  in the specific factors model 82
  and wages 59–63, 65–66
prohibitive export tax 167
prohibitive tariffs 151
protectionism
  under Donald Trump's presidency 157–177
  infant industries 189–203
  logrolling 211
  on national security grounds 227–228
  second-best arguments 185–189
  Smoot–Hawley Tariff (1930) 212
  see also import tariffs; trade intervention, arguments for
pull factors 391–396
purchasing power parity 367–371
  Big Mac pricing example 369, 382–383
  misalignment 383
  real exchange rate 380
  testing the assumption 374–375
push factors 391–396

Quantitative Easing (QE) 421
quantity of goods 12–14
  see also production
quota rent 160–163, 173
quotas see import quotas

random walk 377
rare earth minerals market 178
rate of return
  capital mobility 99–113
  IS–LM model 306, 316
  the relationship between exchange rates and interest rates 266–270
  specific factors model 78, 79–80
rate of reversion 377
raw materials
  export taxes 179–180
  rare earth minerals market 178
  terms of trade 37–38
  use of export taxes 184–185
real exchange rate 270–272, 288–293
  aggregate demand 311
  current account surpluses 319–320
  economies in recession 362–363
  fiscal policy 314–316
  real models of 380–383
  relative magnitudes of policy effects 311–312
real interest differential model 377–378
real wage 37
  in the mobile factors model 87–88
  in the specific factors model 80, 81
  wage distribution 91
recessions
  boom-bust cycle 390–391
  price level and exchange rates 362–363
  understanding how busts happen 396–400
  see also emerging market crises; global financial crisis (2008); Great Depression (1930s)

Reciprocal Trade Agreements Act (RTAA) 213, 219
reciprocity 214–215
redistribution see compensation
regional trade agreements
  definition 215
  welfare effects 216–219
relative price
  under autarky 19–20
  the budget constraint 16
  comparative advantage and the gains from trade 55–58
  elasticity of substitution 134–135
  Heckscher–Ohlin theorem 83–84, 87–88
  labor mobility 108–110
  producer and consumer surplus 27
  terms of trade 36–39, 58–59
  world compared to autarky relative prices 34
relative price line 16, 39
relative productivity of labor 50–53, 60–61
remittances 238, 245
rent seeking 160, 173–177
rental price of capital
  impact of a change in productivity 82
  impact of price change 73–81
  income distribution 79–80
  specific factors model 78, 79
reserve currency 258
resource allocation 82, 151–152, 336
return on equity (ROE) 416
revaluation
  China's current account surpluses 319–320
  managing booms 393–394
  real exchange rate 312
Ricardo, David
  determinants of the patterns of trade 51
  imports and efficiency 50–72
  international factor mobility 100–111
  mobile factors model 83–87
  the multi-good Ricardo model 64–69
  specific factors model 73–83
risk
  eurozone common currency 428
  exchange risk premium 269–270
  the relationship between exchange rates and interest rates 266–270
Rogoff, Kenneth 379–380

INDEX

Romalis, John 90
Romer, David 23
rules of origin 215
run on the bank 393
Russian currency fluctuations 304
Rust Belt 45, 325–326, 332–333

safeguard clauses 226–229
Samuelson, Paul 108
saving
   financial integration 336
   IS–LM model 305–309
   measuring the economy 238–241
   National Saving Identity 240
second-best arguments for protection 185–189
secondary income, the current account 243
self-insurance 393
self-sufficiency 12, 34
   see also autarky
shadow banking sector 417
shakeout effect 131–132
shipbuilding industry 200
shock absorber 336, 425–426
shocks, economic 288, 328–329
   see also recessions
short run
   attaining equilibrium 280–284
   exchange rates and sticky prices 376–380
   flexible price monetary model 374
   import tariffs and export taxes 184–185
   monetary policy 353
   price level 353
short term financial capital flows 245–247
Silicon Valley 199
skilled workers see white-collar workers
small country assumption 18–19
   export subsidies 164
   export taxes 179–185
   import tariffs 151–152
   mobile factors model 115
   production possibility frontier 149–169
   world prices 18–19, 115, 156–157
Smith, Adam 4–5, 22, 34–35
   determinants of the patterns of trade 51
   infant industry protection 189–190
   wages and productivity 61–62
Smoot–Hawley Tariff (1930) 212
solvency, government 398–400, 403–404

South Korea
   infant industry protection 192–203
   opening up of the economy 207
specific factors model 74–77
   evidence on trade and factor endowments 88–90
   evidence on trade and income distribution 90–95
   impact of changes in specific factors 82–83
   income distribution 77–83
   international factor mobility 111–114
spot exchange rate 260
stagflation 358–360
start-ups see infant industry protection
static gains from trade 39–42
status-quo bias, policymaking 207–209
steel industry
   infant industry protection in Korea 192–203
   infant industry protection in Nigeria 178–193
   trade laws 205–228
   US 2018 steel tariffs 158–177, 205–222, 227–228
sterilization
   feasibility and constraints 317
   as fiscal policy 314–315
   impact of policies and foreign developments 329
   inflows 393
   of reserve accumulation 315–316
sticky prices 348, 375–378
   evidence for 378–380
Stolper–Samuelson theorem 87–88, 92
subsidies see export subsidies
substitution, elasticity of 134–135
sudden stop 398–400
Suez Canal 40–41
sugar policy, US 149–150, 156–157, 159, 205–211
supply
   of foreign currencies 259–261
   tariffs and quotas 161–163
supply curve
   import-competing firms 139–140
   infant industry protection 190–191, 193–203
   partial equilibrium 23–27
   producer and consumer surplus 27
   terms of trade 58–59
supply shocks 356–362

supply side
   AD–AS model 351–353
   price level 348–350
   production output 281
   symmetric shocks 425–426

tariff engineering 152
tariffs see import tariffs
taxation
   ad valorem 150, 156–157
   affect on income 284–287
   and interest rates 414–415
   lump-sum taxes 282, 286
   non-economic objectives 188–189
   relationship between government budget and trade balances 287–288
   tariffs for revenue 185–186
   US 2017 tax cuts 325–326, 331–333
   see also export taxes; import tariffs
technology
   evidence on trade and income distribution 92–93
   factor endowments 90
   international factor mobility 99–108
   mobility in the Ricardo model 100–111
   Production Possibility Frontier 12–14
   specific factors model 74–77
   static versus dynamic gains from trade 39–42
TED spread (T-bills and EuroDollars) 418
terms of trade 36–39
   argument for export taxes 179–185
   determinants of 58–59
textile industry
   import tariffs 151–152
   the multi-good Ricardo model 64–69
   Nike shoes 67–69
   productivity gains from foreign competition 141–144
Thailand
   Asian Financial Crisis 388
   cross-border exposure 402
   floating exchange rate 397
total financial account 238, 249–251
toy industry 159–160
tradable goods 380–382
trade
   autarky 12–16
   autarky, competitive equilibrium under 17–19

trade (cont.)
    autarky, trade with the rest of the world 19–23
    balance 35–36
    determinants of the patterns of 51
    empirical evidence on trade and income 23, 90–95
    and factor endowments 73–74, 88–90
    logic of 4–5, 22
    and monopolistic competition 128–132
    in partial equilibrium 23–28
    specialization and exchange 5
    see also gains from trade; international trade
trade agreements
    arguments in favor of 213–215
    General Agreement on Tariffs and Trade (GATT) 219–221
    multilateral 219–222
    North American Free Trade Agreement (NAFTA) 46–47, 207, 215, 218–219
    Reciprocal Trade Agreements Act (RTAA) 213, 219
    types of 215–216
    welfare effects 216–219
    withdrawal of US from Trans-Pacific Partnership 205–206
trade balance 245
    balance sheet effects 315, 401
    currency devaluation 398
    and the current account 245, 248–254, 312–313, 331
    exchange rates 290–293
    and government budgets 287–288
    Marshall–Lerner–Robinson condition 293
    NAFTA as a "bad deal" for the US? 218–219
    "Twin Deficits" 240–241, 332–333
trade barriers 6
    empirical evidence 172–177
    historical context 7–8, 219–222
    impact of trade agreements 205–206, 213, 219
    and productivity 135
    winners and losers 93–94, 149–150, 158–159, 209
    see also export taxes; trade tariffs
trade creation 216–217
trade deficits
    balance sheet effects 315, 401
    currency crises 398, 401, 407
    in different sectors 245, 325–326
    exchange rates 290–293

and government budgets 287–288
NAFTA as a "bad deal" for the US? 218–219
relationship between government budget and trade balances 287–288
responding to 317–319
see also balance of payments
trade distribution *see* distribution of trade
trade diversion 216–217
trade intermediaries 22
trade intervention, arguments for 178–179
    export subsidies and strategic trade policy 193–203
    infant industry protection 189–203
    second-best arguments for protection 185–189
    terms of trade argument for export taxes 179–185
trade laws 205–223
    dumping and antidumping duties 223–225
    escape clauses 226–229
    evolution of US trade policy 209–213
    subsidies and countervailing duties 225–226
trade policy analysis 149–150
    empirical evidence on trade barriers 172–177
    equivalency 154–155
    evolution of US trade policy 209–213
    export subsidies and taxes 163–167, 193–203
    import quotas 159–163
    import tariffs in general equilibrium 167–172
    import tariffs in partial equilibrium 150–177
trade politics 206–209
    evolution of US trade policy 209–213
    government and policymaking 206–209
    trade agreements 213–215
    unilateral tariff reductions 213
trade restrictiveness index (TRI) 172–173
trade tariffs *see* import tariffs
trade weighted exchange rate index 270
Trans-Pacific Partnership (TPP), withdrawal of US from 205–206

transactions costs 267, 374–375
transport costs
    international trade 6–7
    purchasing power parity 374–375
transshipment 215
trilemma *see* International Trilemma
Troubled Asset Recovery Program (TARP) 421
Trump, Donald
    NAFTA as a "bad deal"? 218–219
    protectionism 157–177
    tariffs on steel 158–177, 205–222, 227–228
    withdrawal of US from Trans-Pacific Partnership 205–206
"Twin Deficits" 240–241, 332–333
two-country model 100–111, 293–296, 302–303

uncovered interest parity (UIP) 267, 269–270
unemployment
    eurozone crisis 426, 431–433
    fiscal policy 430
    fiscal union 426
    impact of trade on 35
    labor mobility 100
    Phillips curve 349–350
unilateral tariff reductions 213, 216
unit iso-cost line 85, 88
unit labor cost 64–65, 430
unit-value isoquants 84–85, 114–115
United Kingdom
    Brexit 345–347
    Concorde case study 193–203
    free trade and the Corn Laws 73–83
United States
    absolute and comparative advantage 51–55, 57–58, 107
    autarky equilibrium and trade 130–131
    comparative advantage and the gains from trade 55–58
    distribution of income 80–82
    impact of the "China Shock" 95
    impact of the global financial crisis (2008) 413, 417
    labor mobility 108–110
    the multi-good Ricardo model 64–69
    NAFTA as a "bad deal"? 218–219
    opportunity cost 52–53
    Production Possibility Frontier 53–55

INDEX

productivity gains from foreign competition 140–144
shakeout effect 131–132
static versus dynamic gains from trade 40
technology mobility 99–108
trade policy 149–150
wages and productivity 59–63
withdrawal of US from Trans-Pacific Partnership 205–206
Uruguay Round 221
utility function
  gains from trade 21–23
  indifference curves 14–15
  maximizing consumer utility 17
  product variety 133–135
utility possibility frontier
  under autarky 44
  static versus dynamic gains 46–47
  with trade 44–46

value added 237
voluntary export restraint (VER) 160–161

wages
  in China and India 62–63
  effects of labor mobility 99–111, 113–114
  empirical evidence on immigration and wages 116–118
  evidence on trade and income distribution 90–95
  Nike shoes 67–69
  and productivity 59–63, 65–66
  real wage 37
  in the specific factors model 80–82
  see also income (consumers)
washing machine industry 205–228
Weinstein, David 90
welfare
  arguments for trade intervention 181–182
  export taxes 167, 182–183
  impact of government spending and taxation 284–287
  import quotas 160
  import tariffs 155–156, 216–219
wheat market, Russia's invasion of Ukraine 33–34
white-collar workers
  immigration effects 118
  impact of price change 81
  income distribution 79–80, 87–88, 90–95
  international factor mobility 113–114
  labor mobility 113–114
  mobile factors model 83–87, 88, 90–95, 114–116

Pareto improvement 45, 83
production function 73–76
specific factors model 74, 75, 82–83, 90–95
within-market effect 129–130
World Bank 8–9
world exports, value of 5–6
world prices
  gains from trade 37–38, 39
  infant industry protection *178–190*, 193–203
  opportunity cost 21–22
  small country assumption 18–19, 115, 156–157
  terms of trade 58–59
World Trade Organization (WTO)
  Airbus subsidies 197
  consensus and disputes 222
  establishment of 221–222
  national security grounds 227–228

xenophobia 99
  see also immigration

Zambia, copper market 38
zero interest rate policy (ZIRP) 421
zero lower bound 338–341
zero-sum game 5, 37
Zimbabwe, hyperinflation in 372–373